PROCESS AND EVENT

ALEXANDER BARD

JAN SÖDERQVIST

PROCESS AND EVENT

Translated by John Wright

Process and event

Futurica Media
Stora Nygatan 7
111 27 Stockholm
Sweden

Cover: Per Gustafsson
Interior: RPform

ISBN: 978-91-7965-341-5

Contents

1
Everything is history and time is a god with four faces

Everything is history. In the beginning there was above all *a beginning*. History is everything that exists and that has existed in a single long edited series. That which exists, exists in time. Nothing that exists, exists outside time. To be outside time is to not exist at all. Anything of that nature is impossible to even imagine. Why? Well, because what we call existence consists of two physical quantities that require an anchoring in precisely time: either objects that we fixate and apprehend as encapsulated in a kind of being, that is connected to the time axis, or dynamic phenomena whose development and constant change we observe along the time axis as an indispensable reference. Thus the history of philosophy becomes a single long dialogue between on the one hand being and on the other hand becoming *vis-à-vis* this indispensable time axis. Which really is precisely indispensable. We tend to think of space as the enormous receptacle of everything, as some sort of storage container where being and the Universe spin in eternal trajectories, but time is the receptacle, or arena, in which space itself takes place, and where nothing is static, save the mathematical models that physicists and philosophers construct to cast a spell on all the alarming instability.

So what then is time? We apprehend it as extremely real in our everyday lives; our lives play out as a series of moments lined up along a time axis, one after the other. But since Man for long has imagined that there is a higher reality than the empirical, a transcendent dimension of being in the style of Plato's world of ideas, one has within a main current of both philosophy and physics long chosen to regard time as an illusion. The really true, one argues within these schools, must be an eternal truth, or it simply is not true. Consider the laws of nature! – someone surely will object. For they must be eternally valid, you sort of get that from the name. They must in some mysterious way precede the nature that is subservient to them. But laws can of course be rewritten and abolished when they for sundry reasons have lost relevance and validity, and what we call laws of nature should rather be viewed as deep-rooted habits – with roots in nothing but a highly arbitrary and particularly local extreme state – which nature merely follows as long as a particular set of conditions are at hand.

This in no way means that the laws of nature are eternal or timeless, merely that they can be observed here and now, and that they probably will exert a considerable influence in the near future, since the conditions in question do not change just like that. But at some point they will change, everything that exists in time changes, and as soon as we start speaking about some kind of laws or some kind of mathematical construction that so to speak precedes and dictates the reality that actually is real, we have entered the realm of the fairytales. We imagine that our ideas about nature are discovered instead of created by ourselves. Then we believe that the truth about the world is to be found not in the world but outside the world. Outside dark caves and beyond reprehensible societies. Which makes everything much more difficult and compels us to start cheating. Since we of course do not actually have – and by definition cannot have – any access to the timeless world, we will, as American physicist Lee Smolin points out, sooner or later start making things up. Which is what both physics and philosophy largely have devoted themselves to. One has made things up. For instance that time is an illusion.

Isaac Newton's breakthrough and influence over all conceivable sciences is of course connected with the fact that his model of the Universe was timeless – an eternally hovering equilibrium underpinned by eternal laws. This equilibrium became the Holy Grail that researchers in every field sought. The whole business was made simple if you, just as Newton himself, were deeply religious. For him absolute space quite simply was a theological postulate, something that was preordained by God. Everything that remained genuinely incomprehensible about absolute space – for instance that one never could observe or study anything other than phenomena in a relative space in a reality that Newton and all others were forced to be content with – one could calmly hand over to God to take care of, to the extent that he felt like it. Naturally, creation was perfect and thus eternally immutable. Therefore change – and time – must be illusory and nothing to attach any importance to. Hereby the conception that mathematical models underpin and therefore also are primary *vis-à-vis* the material cosmos and physical nature themselves, is confirmed. And mathematics is by definition unalterable, it lies outside time. However in reality change continues incessantly. There, one moment is incessantly followed by another. There, time is real. The solution to the problem is to insist that change merely is illusory, since it only entails that already known facts are arranged in new constellations: the same thing but with a somewhat modified appearance.

He who, on the face of it, definitively weeded out time from the physical equation was Albert Einstein with his two theories of relativity. According to Einstein, time becomes one of several dimensions of space, and this newly-discovered reality of spacetime manifests itself in a so-called *block universe* where the entire cosmic history is real at once – that is: past, present and future are all equally real and there is no meaningful distinction to be made between the one and the other (and the third). Everything is the same thing in a single solid great block where the present has no special privileges whatsoever. Despite all apparent processes of change that are observable, the Universe is fundamentally static – a block of compact spacetime. However this entire approach ignores what is called *directionality*: the development toward increasingly complex systems. And this is where we reconnect with Lee Smolin: Complexity is improbable and demands an explanation. It cannot arise unless there is a gradual development in many small steps, since a single giant leap from the simple to the complex presupposes magic, and then of course we might as well stop doing both physics and philosophy. Our universe has a history and this history unfolds in a time that is anything but illusory, a time that is most real and the very prerequisite for the necessary sequence of minor displacements and changes. Complexity cannot even be imagined in a static universe. And if there is no time, then nor is there an open future to speculate around or try to influence.

There are early insights into this being the case – thought systems where time is divine. The Zoroastrian *zaotars* in ancient Persia created, for instance, a secret process religion of their own called *Zurvanism*, that the priests resolutely kept for themselves behind closed doors. Within this teaching, which was transferred orally rather than in writing between generations, one worshiped the god *Zurvan*, which was the name of the sole authentic god who concealed itself beneath all the other gods, who merely functioned as useful fictions, as a sort of hand puppets in a theatrical piece for a crowd with no deeper insights. The zaotars were simply compelled to sweeten the truth for the masses. This Zurvan is neither more nor less than time itself – a time without space or any other substance, a sort of sexless monster with no beginning and no end, a demon that manipulates existence completely at its own discretion, without sparing a single thought for the conceited humans and their well-being.

No religion could very well call for a more brutal grounding in reality amid a clergy than this Zurvanism, which thus becomes the total antithesis to the escapism that otherwise is popular among the masses. Zurvanism eventually migrates to India, where it is transformed into *Brahmanism,* the Indian priesthood religion within which one worships the breath of existence as the only god behind all other illusory gods. To the Persian zaotars, the symbol for existence's constant mutability along the relentless time axis is fire; to the Indian yogis, it is breathing. Nothing in these images is fixed, everything is in motion and constant change. Existence is in a state of *panchronism*. Everything is within time. Nothing is outside time. The eternal, the perfect, and the infinite are phenomena that only can be found in the world of fables.

Martin Heidegger is probably the closest we come to a (reasonably) contemporary Zurvanite. Heidegger forcefully rejects – as did Hegel a century earlier – all attempts to transcend time and history. We call this stance *absolute historicism*. By this is not meant that one can rule out the presence of extraordinary events that fundamentally change history – quite the contrary! These events only assume more weight and greater importance. In his classic work *Being and Time* Heidegger argues that nothing ever can escape or posit itself outside time; but that inside history anything can happen. Here there is contingency and not necessity. It is further, argues Heidegger, temporality and not spatiality that gives a thing its specific *being vis-à-vis* its evident becoming. Thereby an exciting, alternative thread in the history of philosophy appears, stretching from Zoroaster and Heraclitus – the earliest process philosophers during antiquity, both with roots in Persian culture – up to German thinkers such as Hegel, Nietzsche and Heidegger. From this perspective space does not have the same original status as time. It is possible to imagine time without space, but it is not possible to imagine space without time. And this is exactly how the natural sciences also function. Einstein's mistake was to presume time as the fourth dimension *vis-à-vis* space in Einsteinian spacetime, when he could have placed the three dimensions of space on top of time as the foundation instead. But then Einstein was only concerned with a single dimension of time. Today we are experimenting with four – two of them ontic and two ontological. Einsteinian spacetime quite simply only corresponds to one of the four necessary time dimensions. These four dimensions must in turn be studied as a series of different synergist dialectics in the aggregate metaphysics that we call *transcendental emergentism*.

In the opening chapter of our book *Syntheism – Creating God in the Internet Age* we write that everything is religion. And then we add that this applies in particular to the convictions that imagine themselves to be something completely other than religion, rather these are to be viewed as particularly treacherous precisely because they lack self-awareness. It can, for instance, be a case of sundry sorts of political ideologies to which one recruits new disciples. So when we now say that everything is history, it does not constitute a contradiction, but that we add a complementing dimension to this basically existentialist reasoning. Everything is religion *and* history at once. Another popular name for this all-encompassing religious history and historical religion is God. History is thereby, on closer inspection, a *chronotheology*, a journey through time from, to, or in parallel with, the divine. And the perspective is gradually displaced with time. As long as one could bring oneself to regard the stories in the Old Testament as valid, a total history comprising 6,000 years was a near-infinite period of time. But with today's Internet-driven view of history, and with the new cosmological knowledge that now is common property, the more than 200,000 years that we humans, *Homo sapiens sapiens*, have existed are just a tiny drop in the enormous ocean of history. History as a god has expanded, just like the Universe, and continues to do so, just like the Universe.

There is a connection between conceptions of time and the only radically new, original ideas that we can discern in the history of ideas. The original *nomadology* in the orally memorizing nomadic tribe viewed everything as the eternal recurrence of the same, without exception. Which is logical considering the nomads' cyclical existence, built on the changing of the seasons. Zoroaster then adds *eventology* – the idea that a unique event, a new idea, or a new mode of architecture, can lead history in a completely new direction and achieve enduring change. That insight is of course built upon the dramatic effects of information accumulation during the Bronze Age, with the first empires and nations as a result. It is not possible to build an empire unless you have an established court language so that orders from the power center can be communicated undistorted to the periphery of the realm. And with a written court language information accumulation suddenly takes a gigantic leap, which automatically brings a completely new complexity to the societal structure and a new historical turn.

It becomes decisive to be close to the court and speak its specific tongue to have any power and influence to literally speak of in the feudalist society. Eventology arrives with the birth of civilization and Zoroaster is thereby the first *civilizationist* in history. The world of the son need no longer be identical to the world of the father, it can even aspire to be regarded as an improvement. Zoroaster does *de facto* found the entire philosophical discipline – the ancient Persian term *mazdayasna* means "love of wisdom", a concept which is translated to the Greek *philosophia* circa 1,200 years after its first documented use – which since then cannot be regarded as anything other than *a series of footnotes to Zoroaster.* Sure, nomadology is with hindsight history's rule, but eventology is history's exception that both confirms and dialectically completes the rule. Rather Zoroaster's idea is the only radically new idea during the entire written history of ideas, and all other ideas worthy of the label stem from his ingenious insight and the ensuing *dialectics of process and event.* The existentialist *dialectics of mortido and libido* and the metaphysical *dialectics of oscillation and negation* are merely developed variants of the same basic dialectics of the permanently nomadic and the temporarily settled.

From this insight during the Bronze Age, it takes all the way up until the early 19th century before a genuinely new and pioneering idea is developed and introduced within philosophy. It is then that Hegel in Prussia completes the dialectical method by adding *the negation of the negation* which precedes both the process and the event – a sort of philosophy's equivalent to the epochal event within mathematics when the zero was presented to the world (in Mesopotamia). Thereby we join Hegel when he describes his new order as *the absolute*, or to describe the matter even more Hegelian: when he completes the ultimate revolt against all previous revolts. *The real* precedes *the imaginary* and *the symbolic*. And out of the negation springs *the negation of the negation* that drives a constantly mutable existence onward. Man patches up his various phallic fantasies in the seismological landscape that is called existence. But there and only there existentialist freedom can be found. For until these fantasies are established only *the contingent chaos* prevails (sexually personified as the hypersexual virgin), while thereafter the eternalisation of the fantasies is nothing but *the law-bound necessity* (sexually personified as the asexual matriarch). The phallic freedom can only be manifested in the actual and mutually admiring collaboration between the imaginary *will-to-transcendence* and the symbolic *will-to-intelligence* behind *the barred absolute*. We call this necessary creation *the two-headed phallus*.

In the book *Less Than Nothing* (2012), Slovenian philosopher Slavoj Žižek builds his variant of *dialectical materialism* on what he sees as a basic incompleteness in Hegelian metaphysics. Please note, however, that there is no need for any basic incompleteness as long as we can abandon the Platonist and Kantian axiom that there can only exist one single time dimension. If we instead may be as bold as to presume at least two time dimensions, we will right there have created a seismological relation between eternalist hypertime (the negation) and mobilist spacetime (the oscillation). The time axes will inexorably grind against each other. This entails that everything atop the underlying *subphysics* in such a physical universe must oscillate. If for no other reason than a total fixation requiring far too much energy. And if everything oscillates, there is really no need for incompleteness in order to set things in dialectical motion. There is nothing that is fixated in itself, quite simply because there is no absolute space and no stable point of reference to relate to. Everything is in motion in relation to everything else, even within itself. The *implicata-as-virtuality* can, but need not be, some form of preceding variant of the coming *explicata-as-actuality* albeit minus some kind of anal, mysterious ingredient. Rather, it is a case of various virtual membranes that have not yet collided with each other – within subphysics such a hypertemporal state is called *subsistence* rather than *existence* – so that our relationalist universe can be manifested as an actual nature.

We thus replace Žižek's dialectical materialism with *transcendental emergentism* which uses *the dialectics of eternalism and mobilism* (see for instance our book *The Global Empire*) as a starting point for a *radical relationalism*. Matter is not incomplete, matter is mobile in itself. And matter is not even fundamental, since there is a hypertime that precedes and operates beneath the spacetime where Žižek and other *monochronists* get stuck with their beloved matter. Hypertime is namely not bound to a mass that requires space, and is therefore not material in a classical sense, as British physicist Roger Penrose remarks in his book *Cycles of Time* (2010). In the book *Einstein's Unfinished Revolution* (2019) Penrose's American colleague Lee Smolin launches the excellent concept *temporal relationalism* for a worldview that places time before space. Space is, according to Smolin, nothing other than the description of the historical network of relations between events. For instance, a phenomenon like *quantum entanglement* cannot be explained in any other way. Smolin explicitly argues that quantum entanglement is a remnant from the point in history when only time and no space existed. A subphysics before and beneath physics. A remnant that lingers on in our universe as a reminder that existence is fundamentally temporal and as such aspatial.

Without himself using the concept, Smolin has thus formulated a time that *temporally precedes spacetime* without need for space and this is of course *hypertime* which we add to the discourse of temporal relationalism. Hypertime is thus fundamental, while spacetime is emergent and contingent *vis-à-vis* hypertime. And quantum entanglement must be understood as a hypertemporal phenomenon. It is true that entropy and information constantly grow in an expanding universe, and that the expansion in itself consists of entropy and information. However, the expansion of entropy and information is a byproduct of time, it is not time in itself. Neither in the spacetime where the expansion occurs, nor in the hypertime where the expansion no longer matters, since hypertime in itself lacks mass and thereby also lacks space. Physicists can then sit and tinker with time back and forth and discuss its reversibility. But what is unique about hypertime is precisely that it is so radically irreversible. The fact is that it is precisely time's irreversibility – what we in popular parlance call *the arrow of time* which only points forward – which is its most hypertemporal rather than spatiotemporal quality. Or as physicist Martina Cortez expresses the matter; the asymmetrical and the irreversible in time is exactly what proves that it is more fundamental in existence than space which *de facto* can be bent to and fro in a kind of reversible eternity. *The big time* precedes *the big space*, as Tibetan monk Tarthang Tulku describes the matter in his exposition of Vajrayāna Buddhism's cosmology.

The reason for the natural sciences finding it so hard to embrace these thoughts and put them into practice is, as Smolin observes, that the natural sciences constantly get stuck in what Einstein condescendingly terms *constitutive theories* instead of first building relevant underlying *principal theories*. The metaphysical emergence vector theory that we are devoting ourselves to here is such a principal theory, the various natural and cultural sciences that then develop within the emergence vectors in question are however merely constitutive theories. In the actual context we express this as hypertime being *subphysical* and not physical, it has a kind of passive *subsistence* rather than some kind of active *existence*, as Danish philosopher Alexander Wrede Elung points out. Above all, hypertime is continuous rather than discrete, it cannot be reduced to delimited ones and zeroes and can therefore not be measured by clocks – since hypertime lacks mass, and clocks can only exist inside a universe consisting of spacetime-bound, gravitation-generating, quantitative mass – to the despair of many 21st century Platonist computationalists. The Universe is not a computer. Rather, subphysics consists of an implicate, virtual, continuous and passive subsistence brooding in hypertime, pending its being able to give rise to an explicate, actual, discrete and active existence once spacetime arrives. Only then do, literally, the relations and the diversity that characterize our universe explode. Negation morphs into oscillation. As a temporal relationalism with spacetime as a byproduct.

The rest is a question of – and only a question of – relations interwoven in countless other relations, which expresses itself as increasingly tight and increasingly complex domains developed after various dramatic *emergences* (so-called *emergence vectors*) where our own universe's *big bang* (or rather *big bounce* if we take hypertime seriously) is the most well-known example. This does not least apply to the relation between hypertime and spacetime in itself, whose *seismology* replaces Žižek's mysterious completeness minus one as metaphysical foundation. The contingent before the necessary is not triggered by some kind of mysterious imbalance in the contingent. The contingent is contingent for real, *there is no balance there.* It is rather this constant quest for balance that time and time again throughout history leads thoughts astray. When Hegel writes that necessity only arises afterward, he means precisely this. The relation must arise in order for the world to be enriched with *relata,* and only relata can provide the illusion of even the least temporary balance between the plethora of oscillations in existence. A balance that the eternalist subject is extremely eager to interpret as sustainable and enduringly fixed objects drenched in imaginary and symbolic meaning. Which usually works fairly well, up until the next existential earthquake. But first there are always relations and only later follow relata, as British philosopher Alfred North Whitehead establishes.

Or to express the matter in the spirit of Hegel and Heidegger: First there must be a *project*, it is only in the active engagement with one another that a *subject* and an *object* can arise.

Before Einsteinian spacetime arises and physics is born, there are already lots of virtual fields or membranes. This is called *subphysical membranics*. The virtual fields do not behave as fields within classical spacetime. They are first of all both infinitely small and infinitely large, since they need not take space in the usual sense into consideration. And they exist only ontically, but not actually, since they need not take space-bound time in the usual sense into consideration either. It is rather when these virtual membranes collide with each other that the first relations are generated and it is with these relations that processes arise as actualities. This is what we call *radical relationalism*. The virtual fields are metaphysically spectacular since they are precisely virtual rather than actual, but they must still be regarded as ontic rather than merely ontological. What is important is to understand that the virtual membranes are not ontic on their own, but that they receive their onticity precisely through being in motion *vis-à-vis* collisions with, and thus establish relations with, other virtual fields. We express this as the virtual membranes being *fields of virtualities* and belonging to *the implicate order* in existence, while the radical relations that arise when the virtual fields interact with each other are called *fields of potentialities,* which belong to *the explicate order* in existence. We can quite simply regard the implicate order as a kind of nature's own subconsciousness, while the explicate order is a sort of nature's consciousness, where only the latter is possible for us to observe and measure in any meaningful sense. And it is of course possible to study the difference between consciousness and subconsciousness in the same way, as an explicate and an implicate order respectively, that meet in the emergent moment that Canadian cognitive scientist John Vervaeke calls *relevance realization*.

The moment we accept the possibility that there may be several different dimensions of time, we also have to consider the possibility that there are several different gods; or perhaps rather several different religions. We have, to start with, the two ontic time dimensions *global hypertime* and *local spacetime*, where global hypertime belongs to the implicate order, while local spacetime belongs to the explicate order in the natural sciences, where the explicate order for instance can arise via a *negative dialectics*, that is: there is suddenly something missing in the implicate order that enables the actualization of the explicate order. The transition from subphysics to physics entails for instance a shrinking and not an expansion of the basic prerequisites. A related narratological example from the biblical world is how God was so perfect as *The One* that God was forced to split in two and become man and woman as a human and thus be actualized. The abstract implicate order is in this case Man, and the concrete explicate order is the man and the woman as incompatible but still inseparable entities. And then we have hardly even begun to study how the majority of humans gladly would have stayed and subsisted as an inseparable unity with the maternal body's *mamilla* their entire lives to avoid having to exist as independent creatures of their own.

In the book *The Field – The Quest for The Secret Force of The Universe* (2008) British philosopher J M E McTaggart sets out the distinction between an A series of time and a B series of time, where the A series is time as continuous duration and becoming, while the B series is time as discrete time and being. McTaggart's A series makes the present the only real time, while the past and the future lack substance. But his B series makes all points in time equivalent, it eternalizes time itself as a kind of timeless being. Naturally this is the case of two necessary time dimensions, hypertime as the time of the entire Universe even before it had arisen, and spacetime as a dimension bound to the expanding space to harbor the Universe's information, energy and matter. We need and there really are two dimensions of time: global or continuous hypertime versus local or discrete spacetime. Global time precedes *the big bounce* and is independent of space and its content. Local time arises in conjunction with the big bounce and is through and through dependent on space and its content. To this we add the two ontological time dimensions *vis-à-vis* which Man and his tribal psyche orient themselves, namely *phallic linear time* which is manifested philosophically in eventology and *matrichal cyclical time* which is manifested philosophically in nomadology. Where phallic linear time refers to the explicate order and matrichal cyclical time refers to the implicate order for civilization in its entirety.

Thus the global, the matrichal and the virtual belong together, and the study of this *emergence vector* we call *the cosmic nomadology*. The local, the phallic and the actual also belong together, and we call the study of this emergence vector *the cosmic eventology*. We thus write a philosophy about world history as a story of processes and events. The interaction between process and event is the fundamental pattern for this project and – we maintain – for precisely everything else. Thus it very much becomes a story of values. The cosmic nomadology sees everything as a recurrence of the same. Thereby everything that happens is bound to cause and effect without exception. There is quite simply nothing to learn from history since everything is repeated all the same and nothing changes, therefore nothing can improve (or deteriorate) either. Therefore, according to cosmic nomadology, there are no valid reasons to build a library full of accumulated, relevant information to promote a development that may be seen as generally favorable to humanity. Instead every activity in existence is based on a pagan *karma*. There is no forgiveness and thus not any hope of being accorded a second chance in life either. This is the core of what we call *the religion of nature* (and please note how history and religion constantly are interwoven – everything is religion; and history). Meanwhile nomadology can of course not be revised until it is confronted with the cosmic eventology, which starts from the idea that a single, unexpected event can upend the playing board and provoke the emergence of completely new rules for how the development occurs in the future.

Suddenly a completely different, previously inconceivable, future becomes possible. And now information accumulation becomes immensely valuable. History contains learning that is useful for those who want to comprehend and equip themselves for – and perhaps even change and control – a development that no longer is completely predictable. Both successful and unsuccessful experiments are useful; the latter signify which chosen paths are fruitless, which is extremely important to know. Thereby *forgiveness* becomes a foundation in all eventological worldviews. If you fail, get up and try again. One mistake is not the end of the world, you have (hopefully) learnt something from it, which improves your prospects of succeeding at your next attempt. Further, the recording of experiences becomes important. And communication. Write and let others read, share your experiences just as you benefit from others' to avoid repeating their mistakes. By and by we jointly filter out the blind alleys of development. We build a culture, and thus atop the religion of nature we establish *the religion of culture*. What then remains is *the syntheist revolution* – a transition from *the nomadological religion based on magic* to *the eventological religion based on technology*. When architects and engineers have the opportunity to unimpededly experiment in a phallic spirit, a state that British-American engineer E M Burlingame calls *the endless game*. Yesterday's magic is transformed into tomorrow's technology. This ideal state of the information age is what we refer to as *netocratic protopianism*.

After the arrival of eventology in the history of ideas it becomes impossible to regard the nomadological conception of history as anything other than a defense of a hypertime that finds itself over, under and beyond linear spacetime itself. It is this division that enables us to conceive of an emergence vector before physics that we call *hypertemporal subphysics*, while physics as an emergence vector only is introduced with the genesis and expansion of Einsteinian spacetime, a hot topic which is discussed in an all-encompassing theory construction within physics and cosmology called *loop quantum gravity*. Thereby all similarities between hypertime (and if one wishes, an associated hyperspace) on the one hand, and classical spacetime on the other, disappears. Nomadology and eventology are reduced to two equivalent but incompatible metanarratives about the future. Absolute historicism is thus the Hegelian idea of the coexistence of these two metanarratives in an interconnected world where the stories are used for radically different purposes. We land with eventology as our *yang* and nomadology as our *yin* in a dance where their continued coexistence is guaranteed through their unambiguous incompatibility, the metaphysical state which Lee Smolin, a pioneer of loop quantum gravity, calls temporal relationalism.

The crux of the matter is that hypertime always precedes hyperspace in a way that does not occur within classical spacetime, which has dramatic consequences for temporal relationalism. When quantum physics was revealed to the natural sciences, it was discovered that two particles could behave synchronously with frightening precision even if they were located several light years apart. This phenomenon is called *quantum entanglement* where thus the very entanglement only operates in time, clearly independent of space. Thus there is no ongoing transmission of information between the particles. A phenomenon such as a quantum entanglement can appear in wildly differing places simultaneously, but never have a symmetrical identity at different points in time. Thus it is space that fundamentally is an explicate phenomenon, while time is both an implicate phenomenon (as global hypertime) and an explicate one (as local spacetime). It is important to note that it is only hypertime that moves via subphysics from a universe to another at a big bounce, and that thereby has both ontic and ontological qualities. Even information transmission between universes can occur without any space of significance, via a phenomenon that American philosopher Alex Ebert calls *compression*. Time always precedes space, above all in an implicate sense. Space only arises when the mass in a universe needs a space. And secondary spacetime only arises when space is forced to interact with primary hypertime. The history that follows within this universe is then a kind of dialectical squeaking between hypertime and spacetime, with phenomena such as quantum entanglement as proof and reminder of a brutal subphysical reality beneath classical physics.

Existence is monist and not dualist. Not because it must be so, but because it happens to be so. Thus nor is there any *moralator* or objective evaluator who can determine that one emergence vector is more important than another – it is merely the Gnostic yearning for objective value hierarchies (with the Gnostic himself on top) that generates the dualist illusion of a separation between creator and creation – wherefore monism must be neutral in terms of valuation in order to be credible. This has pervasive consequences for civilization's history about itself. According to the eventological principle that time precedes space in metaphysics, it must be when and not where an event occurs that determines the event's significance for history. And this valuation can and should constantly be reevaluated dialectically, as both Zoroaster and Hegel point out. The chronology controls the topography and not the other way around. This also means that *absolute historicism* gets the upper hand *vis-à-vis neutral monism* in our narratology. Only time can be absolute. History is fundamentally chronocentric and not topocentric. And ironically all this has to do with the cyclical nature of hypertime.

Or as we write in *Digital Libido – Sex, Power and Violence in the Network Society:* everything begins and ends with mortido and its matrichal circularity. Libido and its phallic linearity never becomes anything other than a temporary protest and a vain wish to escape the existential, eternal recurrence of the same, not least on a cosmological level. We are born and we die, and the same thing applies to the Universe itself. What is produced in between can never be more than a transient protest before death ultimately afflicts both us and everything else. On a metaphysical level it eventually becomes impossible to oppose the Indian *Jains* and their eons of hypertemporal cycles. Whereafter the Persian Zoroastrians complete what Man can achieve with his phallic fantasies of an eventological history and existence in protest against Jainism's matrichal superloop. History in between them is *the history of processes and events.* The history of processes we call *nomadology* and the history of events we call *eventology.* The Greeks of antiquity make a distinction between the two time gods *Chronos* and *Kairos.* It is Chronos who has the nomadological qualities and Kairos who has the eventological and never the twain shall meet. While the Greeks, in line with the Persians, pay tribute to *the kairotic event* as their existentialist ideal.

History consists of two implicate time dimensions and two explicate time dimensions that together comprise everything else. Together they form *the chronotheological quadrant* which naturally matches *the syntheological quadrant* that we present in *Syntheism – Creating God in the Internet Age.* The implicate time dimensions are natural and profane, while the explicate time dimensions are cultural and sacred. The implicate time dimensions we call hypertime and spacetime. Hypertime is the ontic and virtual time. Syntheologically it is called *Atheos.* Spacetime is the ontic and actual time. Syntheologically it is called *Pantheos.* Hypertime is mortidinal while spacetime is libidinal. The explicate time dimensions we call cyclical time and linear time. Cyclical time is the ontological and nomadological time, that is to say ploytheist being in all its rich variety. Syntheologically it is called *Entheos.* Linear time is the ontological and eventological time, that is to say the monotheist future with its completion of history. Syntheologically it is called *Syntheos.* Cyclical time is mortidinal and linear time is libidinal. Hypertime generates subphysics as the first emergence vector. Spacetime generates physics as the second emergence vector. Cyclical time generates the nomadological metanarrative and linear time generates the eventological metanarrative. Together they lay the ground for the metaphysics of processes and events. The dynamics required to comprehend these stories are the year and life as *the dialectics of cosmos and chaos*, that is to say the dialectics of eternalism and mobilism.

The natural sciences have always wrestled with the problem of existence's innermost essence and *determinism* versus *indeterminism*. The question does not become easier by processes being able to behave locally deterministically but still result in globally indeterminist outcomes, as well as being able to behave locally indeterministically but result in seemingly globally determinist outcomes. And then the question is whether it is the process in detail or the process in its entirety that shall decide if we are facing the one or the other. Upon closer examination of processes within subphysics and physics, it turns out that determinism often appears reasonable when processes are studied afterward, but that indeterminism becomes the only logically sustainable possibility when processes are taken into account in advance. This entails that the problem of the dichotomy determinism versus indeterminism is fundamentally erroneously conceived. We must rather regard it as yet another pseudo-problem that constitutes a remnant from the old traditional fairytales of dualist creator-gods, who precede the creation, and the like.

Existence is instead characterized both as entirety and in detail by *transdeterminism*, a concept that we have developed in a series of podcasts with our colleague Alexander Wrede Elung. And once we develop transdeterminism we discover that the erroneous thinking that prevented its development is intimately connected with fantasies about infinite magnitudes and infinite tininesses. Any such infinities and infinitesimals are however neither found in nature nor as precise numbers within mathematics, as German mathematician Georg Cantor shows in the early 20th century when he names the outermost numbers *transfinities* instead – there is no infinite number in itself, the only things that can be formalized are infinities in relation to other infinities, hence the concept transfinities. Rather, we had better speak of *enormities* that have expanded and *enormitesimals* that have shrunk to the extent they have been able to do so far during the history of thc Universe. Spacetime contains neither infinities nor infinitesimals. However, spacetime contains enormities and enormitesimals that are free to expand, but also solely can expand, along the time axis. And with these tools we can only measure either discretions or continuities – and then just locally and not globally – however not both simultaneously.

Thus *the principle of universal oscillation* in a relationalist and transdeterminist universe reads: Since the relation between the exact circle and the exact discrete number is inexact, this means that everything that is real in existence is inexact as soon as it relates to anything else. Eternalism can only precede mobilism in the hypothetical world of a mathematician. In the emergent reality it is on the contrary mobilism that precedes eternalism, since the mobilist *relation* always precedes the eternalist *relata*. The objects may be fixed and dead, but the phenomena move and live. Everything oscillates. The zero vibrates, the one vibrates, the circle vibrates – as soon as they leave the culture and find themselves in nature. The oscillation in the actualized phenomenon cannot be measured at the same time as the phenomenon is being fixed as an object (which in the natural sciences is called *Heisenberg's uncertainty principle*). The dialectics of eternalism and mobilism is thus also *the dialectics of discretion and continuity*. And consequently there must also ultimately be two separate time dimensions, a fixed local time (spacetime) for the discretion, and an oscillating global time (hypertime) for the continuity.

We can only experience and measure classical spacetime. But we see the consequences of hypertime within classical spacetime in retrospect. We express this theologically as though we are torn between a constantly present god (physics) and another god who only makes his presence felt through his equally constant absence (subphysics). This neither means that existence is minutely controlled in advance, that is to say as a clock that is wound up by a divine creator hand and keeps on ticking as it must (determinism). Nor does it mean that every event conceals an unpredictable randomness (indeterminism). Rather, existence in its *enormous but not infinite complexity* behaves transdeterministically when processes are scrutinized, and when the actual processes interact with other processes in a multitude of different directions. The contingency thus has no need for chance in order to be contingent. It merely needs the causal freedom, and causal freedom contingency receives from hypertime since the future does not exist yet, which specifically within spacetime is expressed as the future's level of complexity not yet having been attained. Thus we can also see transdeterminism as a necessary condition for *relationalism* as a principle for all known emergence vectors in our neutrally monist universe. Above all for the development of a *systemic perspectivism* for which we strive to include all emergence vectors as a metaphysical whole.

This brings us to the distinction in part between ontics and ontology, in part between virtualities, potentialities and actual events. After Immanuel Kant's philosophical revolution in the 18th century the noumenal environment is converted to ontics and the phenomenal experience to ontology. The only snag is that once we accept that existence consists of processes and events and their underpinnings, we also accept that existence fundamentally consists of emergences and their vectors rather than of physics and matter. Physics and its materiality is but one emergence vector among others. This entails that we must accept a subphysics as a basis for physics and with that we also accept fields of virtualities, and it is only when these membranes collide with each other and establish relations between each other that existence is actualized and Einsteinian spacetime becomes a necessity. This means that we accept virtual fields as ontic realities without them actually having been potentialized yet. Actuality is fundamentally composed of processes and relations, and we call this process-philosophical ontology *radical relationalism*. The virtual and ontic world exists along the hypertime axis and in principle requires no space. But when the virtual and ontic fields collide with each other, Einsteinian spacetime arises and the result is an actualized world that emerges as a physical world out of subphysics. The materiality is actualized.

Everything is history and history is everything. There is nothing outside history. The present is merely history's most recent manifestation. The future is a blank page that thus does not yet have existence. Existence is neither characterized by determinism nor indeterminism, but is instead subordinate to transdeterminism. Certain things cannot be predicted at all. Other things can be predicted with frightening accuracy, but never with completeness. Thus we stand open to the future. What happens, happens without our own influence as a result of infinitely complicated processes beyond our control. And the fact that we live in a transdeterminist universe means that the metaphysical struggle between emergentism and reductionism is settled. Existence is fundamentally emergent and not fundamentally reduced in any direction. Emergences happen, vectors form, and laws and rules arise and apply locally within the actual emergence vectors but nowhere else in the Universe. If spacetime arises only after the (re)birth of the Universe, this means not only that there are at least two time dimensions, but also that subphysics precedes physics as the most fundamental building block of our transdeterminist universe. Furthermore, it is no big secret that chemistry, biology, biological intelligence and technological intelligence follow as emergence vectors after subphysics and physics. When we say that existence is fundamentally emergent, we mean precisely this: existence is emergent and not physical. Which may sound counterintuitive, but even so this follows by necessity from the prerequisites we have discussed.

Reincarnation as the eternal recurrence of the same must sooner or later give rise to the fantasy of an exit, a total and final breakdown for cyclical time – this breakdown is called *ekpyrosis* in Greek. But behind every ekpyrosis the world is still born anew, which most aptly can be likened to a spiritual big bounce, which we in retrospect can define eventologically as *the ekpyrotic event*. Cyclical time, often mythically symbolized by the self-eating snake *Ouroborus*, is according to this analysis infinite and thus in a real sense timeless behind the clearly delimiting spacetime. This concept is called *zurvan akarana* in the Old Persian language Avestan – or *sarvanum akarnum* in the Indian twin language Sanskrit – that is to say, the primordial origin of everything else. Please note that *zurvan akarana* is neither a subject nor an object, nor is it even dependent on a place or even on space in general. Instead it is a case of a primordial time that precedes everything else in existence and from which everything else stems. We are now speaking of time as an attribute and not as a dimension. A universe where nothing ever is erased. At least not before this universe collapses, loses most of its information, and is replaced by a new one out of the remnants from its predecessor.

It is out of this eschatology of one world's demise and another world's birth within nomadology that we find the germ of what later in history will be expressed as eventological thinking. If worlds can die and be reborn within eschatology, decisive events must also be able to arise during the development of the linear time that changes history once and for all. It is of course this emergent event that propels the birth of eventology. Absolute historicism is thus *eventology par excellence*, which in Hegelese can be expressed as *the history about historicism itself* being the pure eventology – while *Jainism* in India is an excellent example of a consistently applied cosmic nomadology, a religion without gods but with eons of constantly repeated cyclical time. A religion claiming that God is constantly available to us, or that we are constantly available to God, is thus a religion underpinned by a foundation of untruth. The hypergod behind God is forever inaccessible to us and we to him. Between us and the hypergod *the principle of explanatory closure* strikes with full force. Which makes God himself inaccessible to most behind what we call *the barred absolute*.

In the information society – with its dramatic dissolution of space and the insight of acute planetary limitations – the ancient Greek time gods Chronos and Kairos are pretty much converted into two demons. Nationalism begets the nation as an event. Imperialism begets the empire as an event. But beneath everything hovers capitalism as the global phallic force without events or limits (see *The Global Empire*), followed by the abstract dream of *communism* via *attentionalism* as the recurrence of the original nomadic tribe, *the sociont*. However since the space within which the demons expose themselves is finite, these demons have in concert invoked a crisis from two directions simultaneously. The fantasies of an immortal philosopher-king who expands his perfect territory in an infinite space has reached the end of the road. Mortality, imperfection and finitude have caught up with Man. There is nothing else to do but to endure the brutal crash landing that is inflicted on the Platonist roller coaster, to return to an ever deeper history of humanity, to thus find a new stronghold, a new *root-of-the-phallus*, to be able to build a new and more robust phallic vision for informationalism. The old demons must be tamed and submitted to the new *protopias* we aim for. And the path leading there goes via the Protopia which rises from history as though it really was there all along, which is called religion, and which for our paradigm bears the name *syntheism* and which we explore thoroughly in a book fittingly called *Syntheism – Creating God in the Internet Age*.

No matter how strong libido is, mortido is still invariably stronger. The will to life is always trumped by the death drive. The snag here is that Man generally only is conscious of his libido but not of his mortido. It is solely in conjunction with extremely powerful experiences that we call *ecstasy* or *trauma* that mortido steps out of the shadows and commandeers Man's conceptual world. Ecstasy creates this effect through enticing Man with immortality; trauma through enticing Man with life's immediate termination. We call these experiences decisive events, both with regard to a dividual human life and with regard to the history of an entire society. The doctrine of how these events control our lives is called eventology and it is, of course, driven in the reverse by *the dialectics of libido and mortido*, which we deal with in our book *Digital Libido – Sex, Power and Violence in the Network Society*.

In the same way that mortido governs our very earliest impulses in life, it is mortido that also returns and takes charge at the moment of death, which expresses itself in the acceptance of our personal mortality. What eventology underlines – with the greatest conceivable clarity – is that mortality always is preferable to immortality and what Man can strive for never can be anything deeper than survival and life extension, not immortality in itself. This is because libido, the will to life, merely is conceivable against the backdrop of a conception of life's finitude, of the definitive termination of every history, which of course entails that another story can commence. Life only receives color and meaning through being presumed at some point to reach an ending, the thought of an eternity ultimately becomes unbearable. This means that history also only receives color and meaning through being presumed to reach its ending at some point. Which entails that society only receives color and meaning if it at some point is presumed to reach its ending. Which means that humanity only receives color and meaning if it at some point is presumed to reach its ending. This is what spacetime teaches us as spatiotemporal creatures, namely that all that *exists* rather than just *subsists*, also has an ending.

It is only thanks to the four different time dimensions that we can comprehend this fully. Hypertime is – and is only – the metahistorical container within which the other time dimensions are played out. Spacetime is the arena within which Man, technology and their mutually developed relations are played out. Hypertime reminds Man of the virtual infinity within which all actual finitudes, such as himself, his humanity and his technologies, *de facto* exist. Spacetime reminds Man of the actual finitude that makes him finite. This means that hypertime (*Chronos*) is mortidinal in nature while spacetime (*Kairos*) in essence is libidinal. And correspondingly, among the ontological time dimensions, nomadology and its eternal recurrence of the same corresponds to *the matrichal mortido* as the origin and objective of everything human. At the same time as eventology builds *the phallic libido* as a kind of temporary and – even from the start, literally speaking – doomed protest against mortido's indomitable power.

This means that what all the world's engineers and other civilizationally tamed warriors and hunters really are devoting themselves to during all of civilization, are two separate construction projects. Consciously the engineers build the Saoshyant or the Messiah machine that is to save humanity from the apocalypse. But subconsciously the engineers ultimately simultaneously build the god who is to succeed and take over after humanity when humanity itself has perished. The syntheist project is thus the ultimate expression of *womb envy*. This is ironically manifested with the most nomadological construction project of all throughout history, namely *The Silk Road*, which bound together East and West across the entire enormous Eurasian landmass. The trade routes are of such dignity and achieve the interconnecting function. In history we find three different types: the land route, the sea route, and what we may add as the air route – to which we include both the modern air transportation that has made the entire planet (in principle) physically accessible within 24 hours, and the satellite communication that has made the entire planet potentially accessible in a second.

The deepest subconscious motivator of eventology is that the man himself shall bring forth the son that executes and replaces him without the influence of the matriarchy (*the patricide*). This is the fundamental fantasy that propels the enormous mortidinal engine behind the phallic libido. We plan and we construct, just as Man always has done, to make ourselves immortal. But we do not only do this on our own behalf when we are confronted with our mortality, but we also do this for civilization in its entirety, just over a much greater time span. And it is basically this and only this that is the primordial source of sexual desire. The expression "I feel that I'm alive" can only be understood as an expression of an intense feeling of immediate mortality. Man can sit and divide his narratives between *logos* and *mythos* to his heart's desire, but in the existential conflict between the gods and the authentic priests, he has no access to any other narrative than *the pathical dialectics of libido and mortido*.

In that conflict mortido must ultimately triumph, and as a consolation prize libido is awarded a hope of transcendence after the inevitable death, that is: the dying libido is replaced by a new libido *ad infinitum*, physiological or technological matters not one bit, at least not between engineers. We should always contemplate the somewhat shameful fact that it is precisely when we leave this fundamental Zurvanite understanding of our existential conditions – particularly during the axial age and enlightenment epochs we naively and uncritically have praised – that we humans create all the world's evil; a misery and a confusion that only entails complicated detours for ourselves. For it is then and only then that the necessary authentically phallic chieftains and priests are replaced by smug but impotent boy-pharaohs and pillar-saints. The Zoroastrian *mobeds* constantly warn us of what the Gnostics can bring about. They saw already back in the Sassanid empire of ancient Persia how the Gnostics through their mendacious separation between body and mind soon started to fantasize about the mind having a freedom that only machines but not humans could be assigned.

This means that the necessary re-write of the entire history of ideas that informationalism requires of us, must begin with a humble manifesto. We realize that we are all born to be *the slaves of Zurvan* and we accept this as a logical and existential necessity. The dialectics of libido and mortido teaches us that we are all going to die, that there is a single cohesive history for humanity, a history that is not determinist but that we all participate in creating. Further, we learn that this history has a mortidinal objective, and that this objective is our own extinction. Which conveniently is an objective that we as humanity cannot fail at. Thus Man need not focus on that objective; rather, we can comfortably place it far away in a distant future and call that objective God. Instead Man can devote his energy to worrying about what he should do with the time during the time, that is: *How do we handle the pathic power that we call libido?*

All this requires a new and deepened understanding of time in itself as a phenomenon. It is interestingly enough probably a voyage – as Lee Smolin observes in the book *Time Reborn* (2013) – that hardly even has begun, since all the boy-pharaohs and pillar-saints of the past three millennia have preferred to dwell on infantile phantasms such as eternity and immortality, rather than on pragmatically tangible engineering matters such as time and space. This ironically means that we must commence the necessary re-write of philosophy's and theology's history with one massive *back to go*. We must start over. The simple fact is that if we are to carry out informationalism's *exodology*, we must not only have a sense of where we are going – that is to say which libidinal objective we set for our own age before the barred absolute, while this protects us against our collective mortido – we must first of all know where we are and how we got here. And to do this we must delve deeper into history than we have ever done before. Thanks, dear Syntheos, for there being machines to aid us in this too. Welcome to the brave new world of data anthropology.

Paradigm shift shock is the chaos that awaits when a new information-technological paradigm breaks through. It takes time for the constant Man to adapt to the variable Technology. The first millennium after permanent settlement was established was for instance the bloodiest period in human history, since the participants in question still lacked a metanarrative about connectedness that could serve as a foundation for a long-term, strategic collaboration. Everyone simply helped themselves to anything they could as soon as the opportunity presented itself. One reasoned short-sightedly and selfishly. No actor invested in any form of future. It was not until organized religion arrived and built joint temples on the shamanic borderland between the river valleys – from which it preached the new grand narrative of the shared root-of-the-phallus – that fairly long periods of peace could be maintained, and trade and growth could flourish. And there is no reason to believe that the present paradigm shift from industrialism to informationalism, and from capitalism to attentionalism (see *The Netocrats*), will be the least bit easier than previous ones.

Particularly since our entire world is shifting paradigms simultaneously this time. While no one seems to understand what is underway while it is underway, since the dominant actors are strapped into their old political, industrial and academic models that have become completely irrelevant. They are acting in a new world while they are thinking in an old one.

It is time to not only go back to history, but also to re-write history as though it had a new Hegelian necessity about it. And this new necessity to which the root-of-the-phallus points is *the informationalist paradigm*, with its shift from a religion based on magic – via pathetic attempts to no religion at all – to a religion based on technology. Everything is history and since it concerns a paradigm shift, the new paradigm can only be understood if it receives its own new history. We once again visit history to understand ourselves, but this time we do so with social-technological and data-anthropological glasses. If religion has stopped being magical and instead has become technological, the phallic hope will no longer be based on a faith, but actually on what Hegel calls *absolute knowledge*. The old Zoroastrian dream that the truth (*asha*) one day shall defeat the lie (*druj*) in a battle of near-cosmic proportions comes true, when the free and open algorithm plays its hand. Welcome to the information society and the development of its necessary stories about itself.

2
Logos, mythos and pathos – The narratological triad

The original nomadic tribe, or the *sociont* – that is to say the tribe from which we all stem, the *geneplex* that was formed evolutionarily over the tens of thousands of years as *Homo sapiens* spread across the world and with extremely streamlined models adapted to survival in a host of different climate zones and natural landscapes – has three narratological arenas with a dialectical and therefore constantly mobile relationship to one another. Since ancient Greece we call these arenas the battlefield or *logos*, the campfire or *mythos*, and the ritual site or *pathos*. The battlefield as logos is the phallic meeting place between the father and the son, the campfire as mythos is the matrichal meeting place between the woman and the child, while the ritual site as pathos is the sexual meeting place between the man and the woman. Each of these three narratological arenas is connected to its respective archetypes and set of rules in the cultural conceptual world that is the context in which the sociont's collective existence is embedded. This is reflected within classical culture's ideas of *enculturation* in the form of the Latin *trivium*, where logos corresponds to *grammar*, mythos to *dialectics*, and pathos to *rhetoric*. Evolution has shaped the sociont in such as way that it naturally prioritizes between grammar, dialectics and rhetoric, depending on what it apprehends as narratologically favorable for survival under the prevailing circumstances.

In the 19th century G W F Hegel reformulates the three metanarratives as *logic* or *the doctrine for being* as a representative of logos, *the spirit* or *the doctrine for the concept* as a representative of mythos, and *nature* or *the doctrine for the essence* as a representative of pathos. Friedrich Nietzsche returns to the narratological triad in *Thus Spoke Zarathustra* in the form of *the camel* for logos, *the child* for mythos, and *the lion* for pathos. Following Hegel and Nietzsche in the 20th century, French psychoanalyst Jacques Lacan develops their images of the three arenas. He divides the three metanarratives according to the following: *the intellect* or *the symbolic order* corresponds to logos, *the soul* or *the imaginary order* corresponds to mythos, and *the body* or *the real order* corresponds to pathos. According to Lacan, Man constantly strives in vain to set up stable symbolic and imaginary orders to establish an overview and be able to navigate through existence – the trivial concerns of everyday life constantly hide in a kind of pseudo-dialectics of the symbolic and the imaginary – but unfortunately he is constantly thrown back to the real order and the equally tangible and untamable body. This is of course due to the fact that nothing is more secured in the real order than the robustly coded genetic inheritance from the sociontological primordial tribe itself, the loftiest tribal ideal for Man that Islamic renaissance philosopher Ibn Khaldun – clearly inspired by Zoroastrianism's comprehensive social ideal *hambandagi* – investigates under the concept *asabiyya*.

Every time Man attempts to escape from his biological nature – a practice he for some peculiar reason constantly tries to impose on himself and his environment in the form of all manner of metaphysical and ideological pretensions – he is sooner or later brutally forced back into his own and humanity's universal geneplex. Lacan is uncompromising on this point. Man is not just a historical creature, as Hegel maintains, but he is a historical creature tied to a code developed by evolution, and this code is drenched in *asabiyya*. Man constantly repeats the sociont in everything he thinks, says and does. Darwinian evolution does not move any faster than that. Individualism is and and will remain a fantasy among a small band of philosophical autists in the Western world with delusions of grandeur, simply because they were the ones who happened to read too many printing press products on their own. They underestimate the force of *asabiyya* or *hambandagi* enormously. Or as American anthropologist Marvin Harris lays down cultural materialism in *The Rise of Anthropological Theory* (1968): At the bottom there is always *the infrastructure* (pathos), on top of this *the social structure* (logos) is then formed, and last of all the entire cake is glazed with and held together by *the superstructure* (mythos). This entire structuralism is forcefully coded in the human geneplex and is then repeated under new, temporary labels within every new paradigm.

If we translate these concepts into narratological terms that are relevant to 21st century discourse, we find that the contemporary equivalent of logos is science, that the equivalent of mythos is (the medial) theater, and that which fills the function of pathos is religion in any of the many guises in which it appears today ("Everything is religion"). Conducting and writing about science we call *logopoeia* in Greek, writing drama we call *mythopoeia*, and expounding on religion we call *pathopoeia*. Thereby logos is also the sociont's necessary history, mythos is the sociont's evident presence, and pathos is the sociont's potential future. We arrive at a metanarrative that entails that we leave the battlefields behind us, we gather around the campfire and dream of ecstatic rituals, before it is time to fight the next necessary battle to complete and repeat the narratological cycle. If we want to clarify the process with the aid of an educational simplification, we can claim that the left cerebral hemisphere is logos, while the right hemisphere is pathos; together they desperately (and in vain) attempt to unify in the form of mythos. The fact is that it is perfectly possible to refer to life itself as a literally electrical interplay between *information* (logos) and *chemistry* (pathos) which only temporarily can be merged as a constantly elusive *subjectivity* (mythos).

Or to express the matter in a Freudian manner (and thus also sexually), inspired by the narratological triad we realize that there also is a need for a *dialectics of consciousness*; a meeting place must arise between *consciousness* (logos) and *the unconscious* (pathos), and this meeting place we call *the subconscious* (mythos). French psychiatrist Jean-Michel Oughourlian takes this triadic thinking to a head when he in *The Mimetic Brain* (2013) claims that Man actually is endowed with three completely different brains: *the rational brain* corresponding to logos, *the mimetic brain* corresponding to mythos, and *the emotional brain* corresponding to pathos. Where the, according to Oughourlian himself, repeatedly most underrated and misunderstood of the three brains – the mimetic brain – consequently gives the book its title. Why does Man's brain devote such an enormous amount of time and energy to *mimetics* – women even more so than men – if not because Man is a deeply social creature, a herd animal for which *asabiyya* or *hambandagi* takes precedence over everything else? Mimetics is quite simply Man's method to maintain the illusion that everything in existence is interconnected. Which in turn, according to Oughourlian, explains why mental disease always starts with an acute crisis in the mimetic brain, a breakdown in the relation between the actual subject and the sociont, a tragedy we refer to as *social phobia*, and which indeed is followed by a breakdown between the two cerebral hemispheres in themselves, *psychotic depression*, or as Oughourlian calls this state: *the tsunami of the three brains*.

What Nietzsche then does in the 19th century is to split the phallus and define logos as *the Apollonian* (light, civilization, reason) after the Greek god Apollo, and pathos as *the Dionysian* (darkness, nature, ecstasy) after the Greek god Dionysus. As with everything else with Nietzsche, one then must split even these two phalluses in two halves and pit them against each other. One of the poles in these two dichotomies then becomes the active, actionary or authentic; while the other pole is constituted by the passive, reactionary or superficial. In this type theory the actionary in the Apollonian also becomes *the Messianic*, while the reactionary in the Apollonian appears as *the tyrannical*. If we then instead turn to the Dionysian phallus, the actionary becomes *the Saturnalian*, while the reactionary in the Dionysian concurrently becomes *the apocalyptic*. Russian demagogue Alexandr Dugin even suggests that we for Nietzsche's own sake must save him from a total return to the pagan through dividing his Dionysian pathos between a Dionysian swarm with constructive overtones and a Cybelian lynch mob with destructive overtones (called Cybelian after the Greek goddess Cybele who fell in love with her castrated grandson Attis, and therefore restlessly treks around the world with an army of eunuchs, as a kind of woke zombies of antiquity). The Dionysian swarm harbors *the hyperject* which *de facto* has the potential to develop into the Messianic. While the Cybelian mob instead cultivates the *anoject* which gladly develops into the tyrannical. This is the difference between Nietzsche's aristocratic ideal and pagan anarchy. Or if you will, the difference between Nietzsche himself and a certain Adolf Hitler.

Which of these qualities makes a breakthrough and dominates, hinges on whether the Apollonian or the Dionysian respectively is predominantly driven by what Nietzsche calls *the master mentality* (Zoroastrianism's *asha*) or what he calls *the slave mentality* (Zoroastrianism's *druj*). Please note how Nietzsche for the sake of consistency places the Messianic in the Apollonian and the Saturnalian in the Dionysian within eventological ethics. This is the territory of heroes. At the same time as Nietzsche does not pass moral judgment on, but rather dismisses the tyrannical and the apocalyptic as the forces' own, internalized enemies – which he in turn bases on the inevitable outcome of every kind of cultivation of the cyclical *ressentiment*, the constant yearning back to the self-eating primordial snake *Ouroboros*, after eventology has made its entrance in history and the Nietzschean *Übermensch* thus has become possible to imagine. The actual, necessary development cannot very well lead to anything but resentment and self-contempt, since the tyrant and the Cybelian lynch mob in all their banal mediocrity are measured against the hyperjective *Übermensch* (in Nietzsche concretely personified by the founder of Zoroastrianism, namely Zoroaster himself).

This is where the qualitative discrepancies within the Nietzschean conception of will-to-power enter the equation. *Pathos* forges ahead into the future as will-to-transcendence. *Logos* fills out the history of the past as the will-to-intelligence. *Mythos* is in principle the frenetic attempt of two cerebral hemispheres to create a common story both backward and forward, to be performed at the campfire in the present; the great cohesive story about Man himself. We call the doctrine of these social dynamics and their directions and expressions *exodology*. So if nomadology is the doctrine of how the genes or the *geneplex* move across the physical landscape, eventology is the doctrine of how the memes or the *memeplex* move across the mental landscape. Exodology, then, is the doctrine of how eventology finally sets nomadology itself in motion, how the memes ultimately gain power over and control the genes. It is this adultification of humanity that we call the shift from religion-as-magic in the form of *theology* over to religion-as-technology in the form of *syntheology*. American philosopher Forrest Landry describes this historical shift in his book *An Immanent Metaphysics* (2009) as a kind of enlightenment of the Internet Age built on the insight that *transcendence* (Landry's correspondence to the imaginary order), *omniscience* (the symbolic order) and *immanence* (the real order) recur dialectically during the Internet Age as transcendent *vision*, omniscient *strategy*, and real *culture* as a historical realization of Man's very deepest insight into his own being. Man's existentialist choice being consciousness in itself.

What propels this entire process is the constant tension that makes logos and pathos fundamentally incompatible, their vain attempts to still unify as a sustainable mythos. Or as the mythologies preach since time immemorial: The masculine is the attempt to unite logos and pathos as mythos – the Nietzschean project *par excellence* – while the feminine is a mythos that does not succeed in separating logos from pathos but forever remains stuck in the mythical sphere. Or to use the Hegelian method applied to the relations: Pathos is *the negation*, logos is *the abstraction*, and mythos is *the concretion* in narratological dialectics. Or to use Landry's method: The brutal, historical insight into Man's choice as his own being entails that the syntheist revolution is realized. It occurs when vision and strategy step out of culture as imaginary transcendence, and symbolic omniscience is born directly out of real immanence. The Machine realizes symbolic omniscience to perfection, but leaves imaginary transcendence wholly to Man himself to handle through making tribally conscious choices.

Hegel formulates the narratological dialectics when he interconnects pathos with *nature*, logos with *comprehension*, and mythos with *reason* in conjunction with the subject writing itself into history. But Hegel does not settle for this, but further presumes that all these three metanarratives have the capacity to describe each other from their own special perspectives and with their own specific terminology. This is called *panlogism* and is the basis for the Hegelian idea that his dialectical method attains the narratological *absolute*. We can thus perfectly well complement Hegelian panlogism with our own *panmythism* (everything is myths) and *panpathism* (everything is forces). Because there are no predetermined metaphysical reservations in the Hegelian absolute for any such border-defying narratives. The subject and the object are thus not at all forever separated in Hegel, as they are in Immanuel Kant, but merely tell different stories about each other, stories that are entirely possible to unify should one take the path via narratology. It is true that there are, in accordance with this viewpoint, no metalaws nor any metalanguages, but there is a *metanarrative*, and this is what Hegel refers to as *the absolute*. The subject *realizes* in Hegel that it both shapes language and to no less degree allows itself to be shaped by language (there is nothing outside our history about ourselves), a phenomenon within linguistics which since the 1920s is called *the Sapir-Whorf Hypothesis*, after the Hegelian authors Edward Sapir and Benjamin Lee Whorf.

The unbridgeable opposition between the subject and the object in Kant dissolves dialectically by adding a third component in the form of *the Hegelian project*. And in true biblical spirit we then call this project the exodus from the old to the new. It is this exodus that makes all the difference. It even has an associated priestly *exodology*, analogous to Hegel's own variant, which of course was the realization of the Napoleonic nation-state. As for the narratives along the time-line, we would thus be wise to apply logos concerning *the past*, mythos concerning *the present*, and pathos concerning *the future*. All else leads thoughts astray: It is when humanity reverses this chain that we get stuck in alternative worldviews built on delusions of secret signs that must be interpreted, magic numbers that form patterns, conspiratorial networks that operate covertly, and all manner of other superstitions. Mythos is the story where the predecessor logos and the dissolver pathos are united. Mythos is thus the temporary dialectical solution to the conflict between pathos and logos, not the other way around. Unsurprisingly Nietzsche's despised losers, the Rousseauian mob, always get stuck in the mythical rewriting instead of facing the brutal inclusion in one's own history. The tyrannical and the apocalyptic come to life and receive nourishment from the ressentiment, which in turn is damaged by and recoils from *amor fati*, the love of fate. Without the phallic grounding in reality the tyrannical and the apocalyptic can never develop into anything other than a bloody, lacerating catastrophe, what we refer to as *the Cybelian lynch mob*.

The truth thus appears in three different guises and comes to Man via three different parallaxes. Each of these metanarratives operates within its own vectors, follows its own laws and rules, within what philosopher Peter Sloterdijk calls *spheres*. We thus have *the logical sphere*, *the mythical sphere* and *the pathical sphere*. There are no other paths for those who want to attain the truth than to go into these spheres and then gain an understanding of what conditions prevail and how the narratological dialectics works. Cognitive scientist John Vervaeke calls this aggregated and balanced composite image that one receives by placing the three spheres on top of each other *ratio*. If we follow this train of thought, this means that we lack a complete basis for decision-making, a *rationality*, unless we have access to this complete image with components from all three spheres. In the same way that we previously have reasoned ourselves around the existentialist ideal *truth-as-an-act* (see *Syntheism – Creating God in the Internet Age*), Vervaeke returns to the rationalist ideal *truth-as-allegiance-to-a-focus*. Passive intelligence, then, will not suffice, active transcendence is also required. The fuel that actually activates the logical will-to-intelligence is actually the pathical activity in will-to-transcendence. Thereby the *radical relationalism* we advocate merges with Vervaeke's idea of *radical rationalism*.

During every historical paradigm these three narratological spheres recur in shifting guises that are colored by the prevailing cultural conditions. We receive a logical, a mythical and a pathical arena. The logical arena is historically led by the priest or his acting substitute, the mythical sphere is led by the matriarch or her replacement, and the pathical arena is led by the chieftain or his equivalent. The costumes vary but the functions remain essentially intact. This means that the sociont at its deepest is a *triocracy* as it is governed by a classic power triad. In contrast to, for instance, the often more mobile but invariably less flexible and above all invariably less intelligent dictatorship, which is a *monocracy*. This long-term sustainable power sharing pattern recurs with full power in the trinities of the monotheist religions. Zoroastrianism separates the phallus between Ahura, which stands for preservation, and Mazda, which stands for creativity. Together they form *Ahura Mazda*, the divine phallus. The third pole – which holds the other two responsible for their obligations, that is: *the matriarch* within nomadology – is in eventological

Zoroastrianism transformed into *spenta mainyu*, or the spirit that seeks strength, expansion and creativity. The spirit is transformed into the very communication between Ahura and Mazda, which keeps the entire construction intact.

This means that eventology can start working from the conception that one should be able to break the original eternal recurrence of the same – within mythology often presented in the form of the primordial snake *Ouroboros* that devours itself from behind. And the one who succeeds in breaking the constantly grinding circularity, the one who draws his sword and delivers the lethal cut to Ouroboros, is the hero who personifies the specific event that actually changes the course of history and leads the development in a completely new direction. This means that history now can be liberated and at last become an authentic history in a Hegelian sense. And it is of course this eventological trinity that Christianity opportunistically mimics in the form of *The Father* for Ahura, *The Son* for Mazda and *The Holy Spirit* literally as *spenta mainyu*. Unsurprisingly, it is within the Zoroastrian and Christian popular religions that the holy mother returns from the sociont's nomadological patterns and gets to replace the holy spirit that never really became anchored among the masses. Solely thanks to this casting the divine family becomes complete.

The sociontological leadership overall is characterized by a chain of hierarchical *parentiality* where the ancestors lead the patriarchs and the matriarchs, where the patriarchs and matriarchs lead the adults, and where finally the adults lead the children. The domain where children are not allowed in, where the adults play lesser gods, we call *the pathical narrative*; and the domain where not even the adults of the sociont are allowed to be located, where priests play higher gods, we call *the barred absolute*. In both cases – as regards both children and laymen in these two examples – an entry is possible only if the child or the adult first has left *mythos* and stepped into *logos*. This explains why we call the personal development during the dividual's lifetime *the voyage toward phallus*, away from mamilla. This first entails a voyage from *mythos* to *logos* and then, when the dividual is mature enough for the next phase, the possible final voyage from *logos* to *pathos*, from science into art, to there fully express the sociontological variant of the ideal that Michel Foucault calls *life as a work of art.*

The distinction between *logos* and *pathos* in Eastern philosophy corresponds to the distinction between *sutra* and *tantra*, where *sutra* is taught in the form of logic and mimicry, while *tantra* is taught in the form of pathics and *the crazy wisdom* that exists beyond the rational. This means that out of these three metanarratives, it is *pathos* that is the deepest story and the hardest to comprehend, the story that is not evident but merely reveals itself at the very moments when the children are shut out and the adults in advance have to prepare to even understand what is happening. This is because it is pathos that is the engine that provides energy to the entire narratological process. Pathos is the story of Man's showdown both with himself and with nature. Pathos dwells in the collective subconscious and its expressions, which the authentic religion handles, are called *sexuality*, *violence*, *art*, and *the sacred*. It is thus *the pathical energy in the present*, not the logical or the mythical, which Hegel in the early 19th century captures in the concept *Zeitgeist*. That religion would have a pathical rather than a logical or mythical origin was a thought that vanished at some point between the Renaissance and the Enlightenment in Europe. The Enlightenment divided all knowledge between logos (the natural sciences) and mythos (the humanities), while one left pathos to the world of medicine, within which one soon rebuilt the pathical narrative to a whole repertoire of various mental illnesses, or so-called *pathologies*.

Such was the state of affairs until the perspective was adjusted with the revolution within anthropology that took place in the early 20th century. Not until Rudolf Otto in 1917 publishes his masterpiece *Das Heilige*, are all conceptions of religion's logical (via theology) or mythical origins (via mythology) discarded. It is rather in *the shamanic experience* of the force and unpredictability of nature that religion has its robustly pathical origin. Otto calls these experiences a *tremendum* that is followed by a *fascinans*. The pathical religion develops a dialectics between on the one hand nature and its demands for submission, and on the other hand culture and its demands on the taming of the forces of nature. Otto's Romanian disciple Mircea Eliade describes this process as the believer first going through a *hierophany*, being transformed into a *homo religiosus*, only to thereafter be confronted with a sacred cosmos (phallus) in contrast to a profane chaos (matrix). Culture is manifested here through people building their temple with the opening toward the skies, as the original trading venue between the humans and the gods. Where the shamans are turned into priests, who have an oligopoly on the communication with the gods behind *the barred absolute*. The fact is that Otto later inspires his countryman Carl Schmitt to discern the same shift from logos and mythos over to pathos as the origin of secular ideologies in *political theology*. Everything really is religion, not least politics.

Pathos comes in four steps: First as *potential pathos*, then as *actual pathos*, thereafter as *directed pathos*, and finally as *transcendental pathos*. Syntheologically these four states of course correspond to Atheos for potential pathos, Pantheos for actual pathos, Entheos for directed pathos, and finally Syntheos for transcendental pathos. From this perspective *syntheology* appears as the necessary fourth category in the history of metaphysics, made possible by the arrival of eventology, whereafter history of course no longer must be one single eternally repeated recurrence of the same. Every sexual, athletic or artistic showdown goes through all these four stages. And in the final transcendental stage Man memorizes himself in opposition to physiological nature and technological culture as a unique, human creature. At the same time the many historical guises we call *pillar-saints* have fought to prioritize logos over pathos. From Plato to Kant there is this ongoing protest against Zoroaster's and Hegel's confessions of the pathical narrative as the deepest. The clearest text for this endeavor is Plato's *Republic* which constitutes an exemplary manual for the Ptolemaic dictatorship in Egypt. Thus Plato becomes the Egyptian Greek in opposition to Heraclitus, as the Persian Greek. It is Plato who remains in the sutric and refuses to accept the tantric, and who solves his dilemma through positing a moral dualism where *logos* and *pathos* are separated with the purpose of elevating logos and suffocating pathos.

Thereby the problematic idea of *rationalism* as the only answer to every human problem is born. Of course, rationalism's own passive-aggressive pathos is the concealed, underlying propelling force which therefore becomes rationalism's eternally blind spot. The two-headed phallus is thus a necessary fundamental prerequisite for epistemology as well. The difference between *sutra* and *tantra* in the three Silk Road religions – Persian Zoroastrianism, Indian Buddhism, and Chinese Taoism – can be viewed as equal to the difference between being adult and being enlightened. Up until the point when one becomes an adult, one is devoted to mimicking the chieftain's phallus. But as for the priest's phallus, on the other hand, it is only available behind the barred absolute, that is: not available at all, and it is thus not possible to imitate for anyone, but can only serve as inspiration to everyone's own isolated path onward to *the Enlightenment*, in Western discourse best exemplified precisely as the Nietzschean *Übermensch*. The voyage from logos toward pathos is thus not equivalent to any form of banal ascension toward some kind of heaven or some other form of reward for demonstrated cleverness or goodness, but instead conversely the uncompromising voyage down toward the glowing *root-of-the-phallus*, an existentialist choice that is made by those who choose *tantra* over *sutra* as the ultimate *truth-as-an-act* (see *Syntheism – Creating God in the Internet Age*). And it is only the priest who, in this manner, may and can live in the deepest existential state which syntheologically is called *the infinite now*, where no spiritual truth is inaccessible or incomprehensible anymore.

Nomadology is the doctrine of humanity as a mobile tribe in a constantly alterable world. All meaning in Man's life emanates from within the sociont, which means that nomadology is the story of all meaning creation. The two patriarchs lead the nomadological movement and the lone matriarch is its living terminus (behind her there is only chaos and death). Behind the matriarch walks the primordial mother. In front of the patriarchs walks the primordial father. The patriarchy is the outer circuit of the sociont. The matriarchy is the inner circuit of the sociont. The androgynous caste walks between the tribal circuits and the shamanic caste walks between the various socionts in themselves. Nomadology is a polytheist religion – indeed, it is even an oligotheist religion and literally so. There is not just the specific worship of the chieftain, the priest and the matriarch, which then is replicated in all other religions, but it is *de facto* a case of three different parallel religions under a joint umbrella which we call nomadology.

Nomadology's purest and most uncompromising expression in contemporary religiosity is *Jainism*, an Indian doctrine about limitless eons of constant recurrences of the same, where phallus is reduced to the naked guru's literally naked penis without any phallic effect on the Universe. Unsurprisingly, it is Jainism that wins most of the rationalist battles when the metaphysical claims of the various religions ultimately are logically compared. The shift within subphysics during the 2010s from *the Big Bang* to *the Big Bounce* as the universal starting point, confirms that nomadology ultimately incorporates and absorbs even eventology within its metaphysics. It is always the *matriarch* and *mortido* – the death drive – that wins in the end. This is also the case within the world of the natural sciences. What happens during the course of history is that we get separate phallic, matrichal and mystical religions. And religions that at least attempt to get two of the three religions to interact. The phallic religion is called *logos*, the matrichal religion is called *mythos* and the mystical religion, the religion behind religion itself, the gods' own religion, is called *pathos*. The phallic and matrichal iconologies are for the masses. The mystical religion is only for the clergy's own internal use.

A simple indication of this is that what culture generally tries to keep from the children – for instance sex, violence, art and money – belongs to pathos. The pathical narrative is the story that evokes the strongest emotions, as if taken straight out of brutal reality. Everything conceivable from pornography via bank account statements to therapy couches belong to the pathical narrative. The most adult, the most private, the most sensitive, the most repressed – this is the pathical. Pathos is thus the driving force, it is the electricity within the sociont. Logos is then the attempt to steer pathos in the desired direction, even if that ambition constantly fails when a seemingly curbed pathos returns with full force in the form of *Saturnalism*. Cosmos is thrust into chaos at the end of each cycle of the eternal recurrence of the same. Saturnalism entails that chaos devours cosmos, God is killed by the marine monster – as Mircea Eliade describes the process – but God can thus be reborn and cosmos be resurrected out of chaos in the form of a *cosmogony*. It is hardly a coincidence that Christianity chose to place the birth of Christ on the exact date that others in the vicinity had thus far celebrated in part the Roman Saturnalia, in part the Persian Saoshyant's birth as the war god Mithras.

Mythos is the story of the gravity and significance of pathos and logos for the rest of the sociont. This means that pathos is the primary narrative, logos is the secondary, and mythos the tertiary. Together they constitute nomadology, quite simply because everything is nomadology. Within this primordial religion it is the matriarch via mythos who represents *nature*, it is the chieftain via pathos who represents *culture*, and it is the priest via logos who represents *religion* in itself. This sacred triad of power recurs right through all of history as the most stable of all social structures. Both when the sociont is on the move as well as when it has settled somewhere. A clear example of this is the Jewish myth of *the Exodus from Egypt,* where the three siblings Moses, Aron and Miriam get to assume precisely these roles. Moses is the priest and Aaron is the chieftain, while Miriam is the matriarch who holds the other two responsible for what they have promised the sociont, while she right at the back of the long procession urges on the laggards and tries to encourage as many of them as possible to continue the arduous trek. Behind her – and behind them – there is constantly the chaos of the primordial mother, from which the sociont's cosmos admittedly is sprung, but who nevertheless constitutes a constant threat of swallowing and destroying her environment.

Those who search will find this sacred triad of power in many places, for instance in the American Constitution where the executive power corresponds to the chieftain, the legislative power corresponds to the clergy, and the judicial power corresponds to the matriarch. Further, one can easily note that the balance between logos, mythos and pathos is shifted over time, for instance when written language appears roughly at the same time in four different places in the world – in China, the Indus Valley, Mesopotamia and Egypt. Under the new conditions for the exercise of power that quickly are established, logos rapidly becomes dominant by virtue of legislation, issuing of orders and bookkeeping. This shift in balance becomes all the more marked by the fact that written language is excellently suited for the mathematics that requests an exact system for eternalizing notation. Mathematics explodes and expands the moment it can be written down and conveyed in writing, this prepares the ground for an escalating civilization process that quickly generates growth and surplus. Thanks to written law Man is domesticated further, which also is a necessity when he is incorporated in ever greater and more heterogeneous structures. The written characters formalize language and regulate existence for those who are part of constantly expanding systems. The size of the systems by necessity entails that the sociont's natural trust must be replaced by relations that are regulated by laws and agreements. Strangers have to be able to interact and simultaneously be able to feel secure. Narrowly delimited village life is gradually replaced by an increasingly intense togetherness with strangers inside the walls of the new, expanded cities.

Unsurprisingly, there are soon self-appointed pillar-saints in the midst of the town squares, preaching the logical mindset as the solution to everything. The rationalist fantasy makes its entrance in history. What cannot be captured within logos, soon breaks loose and expresses itself via *mythos*. During the Axial Age, from the 9th century BC and onward, drama explodes as an art form and cultures from Greece in the West to China in the East compete to be able to build sizable public theaters. In the same manner as *the religious ritual* had done previously during the Bronze Age, *the theatrical ritual* succeeds in capturing the deepest and most complex aspects of Man. But as periods of peace become longer and generate increasing growth and accumulated wealth, drama is degraded to pure entertainment and logos can once again conquer an increasingly large share of the attention. And thus pathos, this in truth both animalistic and divine power within Man, largely disappears from the public arena and is expelled to the outermost margins of society, where it expresses itself as the uninhibited expression of drives: sex, violence and shamanism as far from the spotlights of the main stage as possible.

It is important to understand the revolutionizing consequences of this gradual adjustment when it comes to the balancing of the narratological dialectics. The early religious texts that are written down during the Bronze Age are still imbued with pathos and do not hesitate to express themselves with the aid of mythos rather than logos to attain the real depths and develop their full expressive power. But what happens during the Axial Age is that boy-pharaohs and pillar-saints step forward and impress the masses with their written-language-driven fixation with logos. Soon enough they bash people over the head with both bibles and law books and other logical texts. If the ritual earlier had been the place where the neurotic and psychotic extremes of the human psyche had been possible to handle, the power of the phallic gaze is now shifted from the priests to the twisted worldviews of boy-pharaohs and pillar-saints. The conscious castration of the priests is thereby gradually replaced by the boy-pharaohs and the pillar-saints and their uninhibited dreams of perfection, infinity and immortality.

Aside from logos, mythos and pathos, the ancient Greeks also use three other approaches for narratology, but not for the metanarratives in themselves but rather rhetorically about where, when and how the different narratives should be used. These three concepts are *kairos*, *topos* and *ethos*. *Kairos* concerns when the narrative shall be told, *topos* concerns where the narrative shall be told, and *ethos* concerns how and why the narrative in question shall be told. Moreover, the three metanarratives are connected to various forms of love, attraction and dedication. Logos is connected to brotherly love or *philia*, mythos is connected to divine love or *agape*, and pathos is connected to sexual attraction or *eros*. At the same time as none of these three loves attain the highest ideal that philosopher Baruch Spinoza presents in the 17th century and calls *amor Dei intellectualis*. In the greater metanarrative it is naturally only behind the barred absolute that *amor Dei intellectualis* can be experienced in any meaningful way whatsoever – and then as the bridge between the other three human passions.

American psychoanalyst Joan Copjec describes *phallus* as the name of the nomadological totality *vis-à-vis* the exception, while *matrix* is mentioned as the name of the nomadological totality *vis-à-vis* the void. Syntheologically this means that the sociont meets in the midst of existence as Pantheos. But matrix symbolizes Pantheos *vis-à-vis* Atheos and phallus symbolizes Pantheos *vis-à-vis* Entheos. Thus there is also a nomadological direction to the sociont's movement; it moves from matrix toward phallus without either leaving matrix or succeeding in reaching phallus. And it is not just the sociont as a whole that moves in this manner through the horizontal nomadology, but also the dividual within the sociont who moves in this manner over the course of life through the vertical nomadology. This has cosmological consequences. The dialectics of process and event is namely nothing other than the cosmological pulse that causes mortido to set libido in motion. Or to express the matter in Hegelese: Matrix is the negation, the sociont and/or the dividual is the abstraction, while phallus is the concretion that never can be attained and which thereby keeps nomadology in continued, constant motion.

At the same time there is a relation here – sometimes with near-cosmological ambitions – between on the one hand phallus and on the other hand mamilla, most clearly illustrated within Islam with the unabashed construction of the mosque (mamilla) between the minarets (phalluses). In their mutual relationship to each other the minaret symbolizes *phallic abundance* as its attribute, and the mosque symbolizes *matrichal generosity* as its attribute. It is the minaret that urges military or priestly order, while it is the mosque that constitutes the gathering place for the temporary restoration of *the ummah* or the congregation. Ironically this process is of course a kind of sexless mimicry of the original nomadological ritual site where the priest calls for order and structure while the matriarch takes charge of the ritual's hierarchies and prioritisations. Within nomadology the situation is sexually charged and the libidinal energy in the worship that takes place is directed toward future territorial conquests. This can be compared with the Muslim prayer call and the call to the service, which are sexless, desexualized and directed toward nothing less than a prophetic burial site, that acts the role of *axis mundi*, that is: the centre of the Universe, the mortidinal Mecca.

The purpose of nomadology is to tame existence. The playing children shall be tamed, socialized, and thus become adult. The adults and their sexuality shall also be tamed so that they and their behaviors serve the sociont. The women shall be tamed so that they enter the prescribed role which includes giving birth to and raising the children. And the men, not least, shall be tamed so that they accept protecting and supporting the family's women. The priests shall be tamed so that they agree to refrain from all personal ambitions beyond death, to instead devote themselves wholeheartedly to appeasing the gods and leading the next generation toward new objectives. Everything, absolutely everything, revolves around the sociont and what is best for the sociont. Thus nomadology is a totalitarian religion, and thereby also the religion that all totalitarian ideologies later allude to and use for their own purposes. It is only later in history – in conjunction with the construction of greater social units, what we call *the sociont-plus* – that phenomena such as diversity and criminality come into play. Thus there is a horizontal and a vertical nomadology. Horizontal nomadology describes the sociont's movement and direction, while vertical nomadology is concerned with the dividual's personal voyage through life. When one attains an objective and then identifies a new one during the course of the voyage, we call the transition that occurs *transcendence*. It is not possible to attain an ultimate objective, since the sociont continues to move after and beyond the dividual's death. The dividual itself does however attain its own objective precisely through death and the transcendence it entails to hand over the sociont to a new generation through *the heritage*. And around this transition, replete with meaning, there have always been sacred rites.

Please note how the sociont constantly is in motion. It can only allow itself to be stationary very temporarily and provisionally. The sociont practices a *dialectics of libido and mortido* (see *Digital Libido: Sex, Power and Violence in the Network Society*) where libido sets the sociont in motion while mortido enjoys the temporary breaks during the voyage that the tribe considers one can afford. But there is never any permanent abode, the sociont never settles for good. That is: it never does so until it actually does precisely this, but then again it then ceases being a nomadic tribe. This means that the modernist existentialists – such as for instance Martin Heidegger, with his tribute to Man's *Heimat* – commit a cognitive error when they get stuck in Man's search for a robust anchoring in a specific geographical location. On the contrary, the existential foundation exists within the sociont itself, which in essence is nomadological motion and not letting oneself be fixed. Decadence and disintegration appears when the sociont stops and ceases to dream of new expeditions to new territories. The death of exodology is synonymous with the death of libido. Everything halts, and when everything halts it dies.

This does not mean that the permanent address is lacking within nomadology, but here it is a question of *axis mundi*, a fixed address situated at some fixed point which in turn is situated along a route that the sociont constantly returns to. This fixed address is only accessible for temporary visits, and then only by the priests. However, the fixed address is never allowed to be used for permanent settlement. Rudolf Otto and Mircea Eliade provide a detailed account for the anthropological differences between on the one hand the sacral space and the profane space, and on the other hand sacral time and profane time. It is only at especially vulnerable times that it is permitted to visit *axis mundi*, and it is only at these points in time that a sacral event can arise. Unsurprisingly, these select, sacred places at inland ports and trade oases recur later in history as the sites where one builds the first temples. And the temples in turn become the institutions where one practices the rituals and proclaims the narratives that unite the socionts and keep them together by giving them joint histories, directions and objectives.

Nomadology is built on two different histories, two different dimensions of history as such. In part, we first have *horizontal history,* which is the religious story about the present sociont and its members, how one makes a historical voyage from birth to death. Horizontal history is concrete and physical. But in part, behind, above and under horizontal history, we also have *vertical history*, which is the religious story of the primordial fathers that walk ahead (the inspiration) and the primordial mothers that walk behind (the aspiration). Vertical history is abstract and transcendental. Man interacts with and is an active co-creator in horizontal history. But he is subject to and worships vertical history, since it determines his conditions, while it lies wholly outside his control. Horizontal history is the voyage from matrix (birth) back to matrix (death), where phallus manifests itself during the course of the voyage as the libido that rises in a kind of powerless, temporary protest against the permanent mortido that vanquishes everything. Vertical history is however the story of phallus itself, how it rises from *the root-of-the-phallus* (the origin of the phallus, or the sociont's deepest biological history) to *the-apex-of-the-phallus* (the direction of the phallus, or the sociont's loftiest vision). Horizontal history teaches Man that even the desirable and feared phallus is subject to fate as the *ultimicity* of the entire existence. At the same time as vertical history entices Man to submit to the phallic power to thereby be able to transcend to the next phase in his own and the sociont's development.

When horizontal history transcends the generations, it gives rise to the matrichal and cyclical religion and its fixation with the eternal recurrence of the same, as *the reincarnation of the sociont itself* as history's deepest expression. Precisely this is the core of nomadology. When vertical history transcends the generations, it gives rise to the phallic and civilizationist religion and its fixation with the heritage that passes between the various generations, where every generation is expected to strive for the higher, the better, the more refined in comparison to what the previous generation succeeded in attaining. Precisely this is the core of eventology. If the heritage is not handed over in time – regardless of in which state it happens to be – it then triggers *patricide*, the murder of the father, which simply means that the younger generation kills the older generation because the older generation for one reason or another has failed to hand over the heritage in time, failed at the sociont's *regeneration*. Or quite simply just has failed to be a generation of able parents and mentors in general, that is: the parent generation has decayed into *degeneration*. Which explains why matrichal religions such as Buddhism and Christianity are obsessed with the end of horizontal history, since they build their worldview on an exit from reincarnation and thus on a fundamental conception of the end of history, while phallic religions such as Zoroastrianism and Judaism conversely are obsessed with the constant continuity of vertical history, since they build their worldview on a conception of the heritage's and thus also of history's constant continuation.

The matrichal religions seek enlightenment or salvation as a possibility to finally evade the cyclical; the phallic religions, however, defend *the barred absolute* as the protopian engine that propels the building of the next civilization. The matrichal religions attain their purpose through invoking, and as far as possible realizing the opportunity of creating a direct relation between the divine and the believer; the phallic religions dispute that something of that nature even could be possible in theory and thus keep the transcendental process going from the one generation to the next. Instead, the phallic religions rather see every attempt to overthrow the spiritual hierarchy of existence as the most dangerous and most mendacious of all conceivable projects. This causes the priests to develop their own third religion – which is carried out behind the barred absolute, and outside both heritage and reproduction – to be the foundation for all phallic religions. Behind the most sacred room in the temple there is always an utmost sacred room, which is exclusively reserved for the priests themselves. There the priests meet gods and ancestors, there one conducts the rituals that are necessary in order to appease these, in the best interests of the entire patriarchy. And religion is always, as William James puts it, Man's constant attempt to adapt himself and his behavior to a menacingly invisible order.

Vertical nomadology operates in a movement that starts from the child to the adult and then further to the clergy and finally to the divinity. *The archetype* is in this context the character who walks ahead, who invents new technologies and breaks new ground. *The erchtype* is the character that mimics the archetype in order to thus produce an optimal outcome for the sociont. Within mythos there is only the archetype and the erchtype within the various generations. However, within logos the possibility for the erchtype to not only imitate the archetype, but also to break with it and create the new and developing itself, is liberated. This means that as long as the narrative remains within mythos, nomadology is the only possible story. However at the very moment that the historiography also comprises logos, eventology becomes a real possibility. This is first expressed in the provision of the erchtype's genealogical chart, a background in the form of a single long series of fathers and sons, to thus confer legitimacy on the erchtype to achieve the creative break with the mimicked and the learnt, in order to instead create the genuinely new and thus oneself assume the role as archetype. Creativity is catapulted out of this eventological break with the traditional and inherited.

This in turn explains the difference between the patriarchal religion (the monotheist eventology) and the matriarchal spirituality (the polytheist iconology). Eventology is the pathical narrative that oscillates between the two poles of *ecstasy* and *trauma*. Therefore pathos is the basis for the monotheism or eventology of the priests, while mythos is the basis for the polytheism or iconology of the masses. Out of pathos logos then emerges as the formalized religion that organizes the relation between eventology and nomadology. This is the religion called *the law*. This means that the priests represent a tantric religion of pathos behind the barred absolute, something which is converted into a sutric religion by logos before the barred absolute. The brutal pathical reality behind the barred absolute is converted into the organized logical law before the barred absolute. This state of affairs explains why the priest in the Silk Road religions is associated with *will-to-intelligence manifested as logos*, practiced as *sutra,* while the chieftain is associated with *will-to-transcendence manifested as pathos*, practiced as *tantra*.

Nomadology is built on a blend of sociontology and the Jungian archetypes – the basic, original patterns within the dividual and the tribal subconscious. Individualism arises only much later in history and then only in individualist cultures that have killed off God and severed the connection to the sociont as the fundamental existential building block. Here the twisted *shaman envy* enters the picture; that is to say when the dividual does not settle for the voyage from child to adult, but moreover strives to transcend beyond adult life to the freedom and responsibility of the shamans. When this endeavor approaches its unavoidable failure, the result is modern Man's *hypernarcissism*, his inability to handle both the shamanic function's freedom and responsibility. The result is a twisted, monotonous narrative that revolves around one's own empty ego, which in no way is the authentic story of the sociont's origin and destination that the priests recount.

It is here that the three concepts will-to-power, will-to-intelligence and will-to-transcendence enter the stage. The will-to-power exists everywhere in all of nature. The will-to-intelligence is the matrichal form of the will-to-power (Taoism's *yin*), the will-to-transcendence is the phallic form of the will-to-power (Taoism' *yang*). Architecture and materials represent being (Zoroastrianism's *ahura*), energy and objectives represent becoming (Zoroastrianism's *mazda*). Here the ultimate objective, *the phallic vision*, gives the phallic value to everything else which is located in an earlier phase of the causal chain. The energy jump starts the will-to-power, but this is either locked in as a repetitive loop in the form of a will-to-intelligence (Taoism's *yin*), or it is set free in the form of a will-to-transcendence (Taoism's *yang*). The dialectics between these is nomadology in its full potency. It is only in the territory that the will-to-transcendence has successfully conquered that the will-to-intelligence can establish itself. The Zoroastrian name for this state is *frashokereti*, and here we refer to it as *protopianism*.

Please note how nomadology requires that phallus is split in the same way as the child's separation from the mother requires matrix to split, which expresses itself in the *mamilla*, which becomes the mother's and the child's new meeting place after the birth, whereafter they are two separated dividuals. The splitting of phallus is therefore not a separation of the man and the woman in themselves, but the separation of on the one hand the man, and on the other hand the difference between the man and the woman. It is thus precisely the androgynous state where neither the man nor the woman dominates that is *the-shadow-of-the-phallus*, where the will-to-intelligence and strategy dominates over the will-to-transcendence and vision. This is the priest's domicile in the social theater. Therefore nomadology is driven by three rather than two characters, namely the chieftain, the matriarch and the priest. And it is the priest who personifies the difference between the man and the woman. Because it is the priest who holds together precisely that which sexual attraction and its conditional *ambivalence* pulls apart. In the same way that the matriarch holds the two patriarchs responsible for what they should deliver to her and the inner circuit of the sociont.

The man thus constantly oscillates between logos and pathos in his search for mythos, without ever being able to find any mythical resting place. Jacques Lacan calls this state *the whole with the disturbing exception*. While the woman constantly is in mythos, but is wrestling with handling logos and pathos as disturbances in her mental frequencies. Mythos is the complete story of the sociont within the sociont itself. However the contextual order (logos) and chaos (pathos) both disturb the coziness inside the world of the social theater. Lacan calls this state *the whole disturbed by the missing signifier*. This entails that freedom for the man is to temporarily be in a mythos with minimal influence from logos or pathos. Sexual intercourse becomes a dear visit inside the inner circuit where the man himself does not belong. At the same time as freedom for the woman is to be allowed to remain in her natural mythos without being disturbed by neither logos nor pathos. Sexual intercourse becomes an exciting visit to the outer circuit where the woman herself does not belong. The woman is constantly in the present while the man always seeks a present that never arrives, since he either is stuck in the logos of the past with its discretions (the root-of-the-phallus) or in the pathos of the future with its continuities (phallus in itself), wherefore the union never can become anything other than *the myth of the present*, what Lacan calls *the barred subject*.

This means that if the man considers himself to have attained mythos without the woman, this ends with utopian tyranny, and that if the woman insists on remaining within mythos without having to take the separation between logos and pathos into consideration, this ends with dystopian Cybelianism. The man and the woman thus find themselves in a dialectical deadlock between each other and it is this very locking that generates sexual attraction. The dream of redemption lies forever concealed within the other sex, unattainable and therefore forever attracting. To dare remain in this dialectical deadlock and use its productivity, without trying to transcend the actual dialectics, is exactly what the tantric imperative *to not cum* is all about. At the same time as the androgynous caste masters the border between the inner and outer circuits without being quite at home in either one of them. While the shamanic caste moves effortlessly across the entire intertribal map, but without being able to experience anything other than sex being just sex, almost as if sex was about chewing gum. The sex for the shamanoids is always at home in the tantric realm.

Nations and corporations devote themselves to *research* with the purpose of attaining *progress* when they make their investments in the future. Research is the root-of-the-phallus and progress is phallus in itself. The stronger and more stable the root-of-the-phallus, the greater the possibility that phallus hits its mark in the future. This is the first division that Man must learn to handle before divisions such as *hunting versus war* and *man versus woman* reach the agenda. And this is of course just another way to express the biblical appeal that one must build one's house on a foundation of rock and not on loose sand. Please note the dialectics here between three, rather than two poles. Logos is *consciousness*, pathos is *unconsciousness*, and mythos is the impossible yet necessary attempt to unify the other two poles as *the subconscious*. Research is the root-of-the-phallus, which is logos; progress is phallus in itself, which is pathos; the vibrating present where both these forces meet can therefore only be shaped as a mythos about the actual sociont, for instance as the *flag* of a nation or the *brand* of a corporation. It is in the mythical and only in the mythical that the subject can assume a form, accumulate its *imaginary power*, and this applies equally for *the tribal subject* as for *the dividual subject* within the sociont in question.

We can observe how four different drives detach themselves from the human drive system instead of just the two that classical psychoanalysis deals with (see *Digital Libido – Sex, Power and Violence in the Network Society*). The classical pair of opposites *drive* and *desire* must be complemented by an *instinct* that precedes drive and desire and a *transcendence* that follows after the other three. *Animalistic drive* or instinct is the combination of logos and the subconscious. *Mechanical drive* or pure drive in itself is the combination of pathos and the subconscious. *Human drive* or desire is logos and consciousness, and *divine drive* or transcendence is pathos and consciousness. None of these drives can express itself consciously or subconsciously without interacting with each other to create a temporary mythos. And it is this mythos that is subjectivity in itself, both within the single dividual and for the sociont as a whole. As it is fundamentally barred from itself, according to Lacan, it can only experience itself *subconsciously*, as a strictly mythical narrative.

This means that Man mimics – an awful lot and all the time. Sociologist and historian of religion René Girard investigates Man as a mimicking creature with his *mimetic theory*. The child mimics the adult, the adult mimics the priest, the priest mimics God, and God mimics the child. But above all we mimic each other horizontally. These activities continue, without any disturbances to speak of, until resources become scarce, or until a perception that the resources threaten to become scarce takes hold in the general perception. Then mimicry is turned into rivalry. Society brims with rivalry, a rivalry that gradually intensifies as inside a pressure cooker that eventually threatens to explode. The higher the temperature rises in the pressure cooker, the more powerful the explosion. The most extreme of all social explosions of this kind is war. But in order for a civil war not to break out within the sociont, it falls to the priest within nomadology to tame these forces so that the explosion is delayed and weakened as much as possible. It is thus because of the priests taming these forces and thus domesticating the sociont, that the sociont can begin to mimic the taming so that it not only tames itself but also the surrounding *nature* to be able to transform it into *culture*. Civilization is this taming of flows in the form of water, wind, sun, energy, blood and electricity. Civilization thus also concerns territories and their borders, spheres and their membranes, irrigations, impoundments and ejaculations. Both inside and outside Man, inside and outside the sociont, inside and outside the world. The civilization process delimits and distinguishes, takes note of and regulates traffic between, inside and outside.

Death is life's completion and thus also the potential deification of the dividual. The dead have absolute authority. Only the dead, but never the living, can serve as lesser gods. The primordial patriarch is the patriarch of the patriarchs. The primordial matriarch is the matriarch of the matriarchs. Envy toward the authority of the dead is the foundation for the boy-pharaohs' hubris and the engine behind history's many pyramid construction projects. The dead cannot worship the dead, thus the living have the task of worshipping these dead – this is the core of religion, the voyeurism of the living in combination with the exhibitionism of the dead, so that the dead in a mirrored manner can become the voyeurs of the living in everyday life as *the lesser gods*. So where and when does the playing field for Man's fantasy change and above all shrink? A clear departure occurs through the *desexualisation* that is imposed upon Man when he becomes settled. The outer circuit within the sociont is pushed into the inner circuit. Logos, mythos and pathos are blended together in a kind of sociological pressure cooker. Sex, violence and shamanic rituals are stigmatized. Art loses its pathical strength and is infantilized. The phallic, worshipping gaze is shifted from the primordial fathers, the chieftain and the priest, to the primordial mother, the matriarch and the child. And with this shift logos disappears for lack of pathos and is replaced by a universal mythos that speaks of eternal peace and eternal happiness, wishful dreaming based on the infantile fantasy of the eternal child with a soul divorced from the increasingly adult and increasingly sexual body.

Gnosticism arrives in history as the infantile fantasy of being able to go directly from child to God without having to pass through sexuality and adult life. We call this state *the Peter Pan syndrome* in a contemporary context. The dream of eternity and infinity is never dreamed by an adult man, but by a boy who refuses to grow up and who therefore wishes for a life without the adult body with its inherent forces and responsibility. The original release occurs through the priests carrying out ritual sacrifices to appease the gods. And they teach the sociont how and where one can relieve the pressure to avoid an explosion. The priests are looking for their own son, the Messiah. Christianity's illusion is that the nomadological cycle can be halted. Christianity's illusory hope is thus that just one single sacrifice at one single occasion can redeem all societies throughout history and then somehow the entire problem is solved. What a nasty surprise it must be that even the priest must be sacrificed, naturally, which means that both the Messiah (the son) and the priest (the father) unconditionally must die. The rain-god is sacrificed as a virgin before his mother, and the sun-god disappears in the process since he now lacks both a heritage and a future.

This is what Nietzsche sees clearly when he maintains that Christianity had both atheism and nihilism built into its own doctrine right from the very start. Christ on the cross merely becomes the mimicry of how the Egyptian priests sacrificed their boy-pharaoh Tutankhamen to end the Atenist autocracy 1,300 BC and reintroduced Egyptian polytheism. At the same time as they allowed the Atenists to evade persecution by letting them emigrate to be able to develop their own monotheist religion as Judaism (see Sigmund

Freud's *Moses and Monotheism*). And thereby we also get an explanation for the core of anti-Semitism, since the Jew gets to take the blame in popular religion as he who killed the Messiah – as though some other tribe had infringed on the sociont's territory and killed the sociont's next king – at the same time as Christianity's inner core consists of a clergy that hates that the father still makes himself known via the Jewish rabbis who are their rivals. Christianity solves this by claiming that through Christ's sacrificial death on the cross, the believer has liberated himself from the Jewish Law and replaced it with an eternal energy machine called Grace, as though the reward for killing the father is that the judge at the end of life has disappeared. This entails that the Christian nation is taught to hate the Jewish rabbis, while the Christian priests can renounce the violence in their own society – through the separation of a heavenly church from an earthly state – so that they as priests shall feel superior to their kings, cultivate their new status as self-aggrandizing, pacifist eunuchs, and realize Plato's and Saint Augustine's fantasies of finally being allowed to be and remain Peter Pan.

Christianity is thus built on a failed patricide of Judaism in the same way that Islam is built on a failed patricide of Zoroastrianism. In Islam the murdered *mobed* survives in the form of the locally interpretative *mullah*, who stands above the text as *Shia*, while the illusory belief that the Zoroastrian mobed is murdered, and that the boy can wage war any way he wishes without the priest's intervention, is called *Sunni*. If Christianity is *the pillar-saint's religion par excellence*, then Islam is *the boy-pharaoh's religion par excellence*. The adult, the genuine, the sophisticated and the brutally natural in the predecessors is thrown out and replaced with the childish, the mimicking, the easily seduced and the spectacularly supernatural. This is civilization's recurring curse: How easily the dialectics of logos, mythos and pathos is sacrificed to be replaced with a more popular vulgarized copycat. And here the unifying *abject* comes into play. An abjectification is a projection on an alien intruder with the purpose of unifying the sociont. It matters not whether the abjectification is motivated or completely arbitrary, the function is the same. The abject is turned into *the scapegoat* and through the sacrifice of the scapegoat the pressure inside the sociont is released and the sociont can unify temporarily before the pressure increases anew and the need for another abjectification rises.

Nomadology, whose universal symbol is the self-eating primordial snake *Ouroboros*, was always doomed to be caught in this eternal loop. Only through the phallus worship of the approaching eventology can humanity start to dream of an end to the constantly returning hell of the lynch mobs. The world is heading for a new order, a new *nomos*, that finally can function because of history's insights into the resilience of social systems. And above all thanks to a great amount of new and innovative technology. This means that *communism*, as the last history of Man, comes with the problem that nomadology in itself always was communist. So when communism later in history is to be re-established as a collectivist fantasy via socialism, this fails completely. The explanation lies in that the Atenist dictatorship is the worst possible way to restore nomadology, and that nomadology never can function within a greater entity than the sociont itself. Thus communism ironically can only be re-established as a temporary tribal plurarchy, that is: as a kind of *digital gated community*. But neither the city, nor the nation, nor the empire can ever be communist. The global empire belongs to the Machine and only to the Machine. Man must instead laboriously return to the one thing he ever has been comfortable with, the sociont itself, that is to say *the tribal singularity*. Anything else is nothing but misanthropic fantasies with no connection to reality whatsoever.

3
Tribopoiesis – Everything begins and ends with The Sociont

The ground moves beneath our feet; existence and our society now changes so rapidly that even those who try to stay away and hide eventually are compelled to step out into a world which in essential respects is completely new. The three major megatrends that more than anything else shape the shift to informationalism are *digitalization*, *nodalization* and *globalization*. This entire complex, cohesive process is a result of the interactive revolution (see *The Global Empire*). In important aspects this process entails a return to age-old patterns, albeit – needles to say – in a powerfully updated version. Digitalization reawakens the sociobiologically preprogrammed *sociont* within Man and leads, on the collective level, to what we call *psychological tribalism*. The ensuing nodalization reawakens a passion for the common language and the common history, which in turn constitute the prerequisites for an old-school *sociological nationalism*. This development occurs simultaneously and in parallel with the technological revolution – which is completely indifferent to every type of national border – blasting off in the direction of a rapidly stepped-up globalization. World society got what we must regard as a global constitution with the breakthrough of informationalism as early as in the 1980s in the form of *the Internet*

Protocol, and the entire phenomenon that we refer to as *technological imperialism*.

One could also view this from a different angle: The information society is characterized by a *technoimperialism* at the global level, by a *socionationalism* at the regional level, and by a *psychotribalism* at the local level. And the class structure of the emerging society is quickly shaped according to a corresponding pattern: we can discern a structure with the global netocracy and its *anywheres* atop (see David Goodhart's influential book *The Road to Somewhere*), the regional consumtariat in the middle, and the local consumtariat and its *somewheres* at the bottom. While technology pushes for increased globalization, large population groups – primarily the old upper class and the new underclass – understandably react with vociferous demands for intensified isolation and a tougher drawing of boundaries. This is a recurring and wholly logical phenomenon in revolutionary times which is called *impansionism* and in summary it means that every group identifies its interests and makes an effort to promote these with all available means. At the same time as we further ahead see a netocratic elite emerge that need not care about physical geography at all; in the horizon we witness a paradigmatic exodus consisting of *everywheres*.

The study of the human original tribe, *the sociont*, a phase of civilization that lasted for at least 60,000 years – and during which almost all our species-distinguishing genes were shaped – is called *sociontology*. If the Planck length, named after German physicist Max Planck, is used as the smallest meaningful unit of length within the natural sciences, the same goes for *Dunbar's number*, named after British sociologist Roger Dunbar, within sociontology. This Dunbar's number is usually estimated at 150 – it simply estimates how many people with whom one single person can maintain lasting social relationships – although it actually displays a remarkable flexibility in the interval between 100 and 250. And this plasticity is needed for us to be able to explain the differences in terms of the need and capacity to handle strangers within the tribe's inner circuit, its outer circuit, and within the shamanic caste. Within sociontology, social units that comprise a number of people corresponding to Dunbar's number are customarily called *clans*. Several clans then join to form *tribes*, which makes sociontology a theory and study of *tribalism*. The original sociont balances between clan and tribe in size, depending on needs and purposes. It is a question of the number of fellow humans in the social arena that we have the mental equipment to handle in a functional way. Which means that it also is a question of our ability for collective interplay, which in turn means that the individualism that eventually emerges in the wake of humanism should be regarded as nothing but the sociont's neurotic perversion. Rather it is when we humans have no other social archetype to fall back on to structure our collective interaction, it is the sociont and only the sociont that has any relevance whatsoever.

Sociontology's development as a computer science entails a radical reckoning with liberalism's *individualism* and socialism's *collectivism*, both of which collapse under pressure from the increasingly expanding digital subcultures. It is rather the case that neither the individual nor the collective has any anchoring whatsoever in the sociobiology that was formed during the sociont's extended existence. Quite the contrary. The sociont shaped Man to a fundamentally tribal creature, where the dividual person and the group in question are the same sort of dividuals, albeit that they appear in different guises and also at different stages of emergence. Thus human existence is most deeply viewed dividualist and tribalist. There really is no further need for the individuals or collectives that the capitalist epoch required and therefore also conjured up from fantasy as part of its ambitious ideology production. What we instead observe is how society goes through an enormous *retribalization* during informationalism. The strongest membrane can once again be found around the sociont itself, what Arabian renaissance philosopher Ibn Khaldun calls *asabiyya*, the internal loyalty within the sociont that defeats all other values. Ibn Khaldun even claims that *asabiyya* generates an even stronger loyalty among the priests within the sociont, not just *vis-à-vis* the sociont itself, but also as the recurring ambition to keep the deepest secret under the lock and the key that is called *the barred absolute*. This insight explains why even a crass realist such as Niccolò Machiavelli in renaissance Italy, inspired by Khaldun, despite everything prefers the republic to the despot, quite simply because the republic's socioemotional ties are stronger. A system that prioritizes the privileges of old elites above authentic innovation quickly moves toward its demise – this is only natural.

There has long been a tendency among European thinkers such as Slavoj Žižek and Alain Badiou to get mired in the individualist paradigm that arises with humanism, a paradigm where the subject lives in the emptiness that arises after the subject has killed God and instead longs for a party or a political movement to come and fill the void, which never happens. We call this strained predicament *liberal castration*. However there are other ways of orienting oneself in a landscape without God. In his mammoth trilogy *Spheres*, philosopher Peter Sloterdijk builds a spatial rather than a temporal metaphysics, based on the isolated units that Man uses to make existence comprehensible. Sloterdijk converts Man's phenomenological fixations from bubbles via globes to fluffy foam. The fundamental nomadology, the story of Man as a creature in constant motion, greatly concerns these spheres, their relations to each other, and above all how these must be set in motion to remain alive.

So how do the immune systems of the spheres work; how do they protect themselves and how do they grow strong, in part when they are stationary, in part when they accelerate anew and move through the topography that is at hand? How do the spheres react when an external phallus cracks the codes with which they protect themselves against the surrounding world and penetrates through the enclosing membrane? And how does this very reaction determine which of all the spheres dominate exactly which paradigm and under which circumstances this can occur? What, for instance, causes the powerful historical swings between on the one hand the sphere of the individual and on the other hand the sphere of the collective? The study of the nature of these spheres and their development is called *membranics,* while the study of the shifting life conditions of these spheres is called *paradigmatics.* Or to give Sloterdijk, a sincere Kantian if ever there was one, the sort of Hegelian constructive criticism his stylish *sphereology* deserves: What is interesting in an age obsessed with network dynamics and relationalism is not the spheres in themselves, but the relations within and between them. This is why Hegelian membranics with its studies of the general boundary rules within and between the spheres is so much more interesting than a Kantian sphereology. While time indefatigably grinds on outside and between the spheres, which means that when time collides with the spheres, each of these receives their own paradigmatics, without any other laws than contingence itself prevailing between the paradigmatically controlled spheres.

The single sphere that by far is of greatest importance to Man is his own sociont. And the sociont has its own *archetypology* which is developed during a process that goes under the designation *tribal mapping* (see *Digital Libido – Sex, Power and Violence in the Network Society*). The inner circuit is the matriarchy. The outer circuit is the patriarchy. *The androgynous caste* constitutes the sociont's internal intermediaries, a personification of the membranics of the sexes. *The shamanic caste* however lives in the borderland or gray zone between the various tribes, where the belonging to any of them is never one hundred percent. The shamanic caste thus functions as the sociont's external intermediaries, a personification of the sociont's own membranics. We speak of these odd relatives within the sociont as *the shamanoid archetypes.* There is always an *intra muros*, a world inside the walls, that is characterized by intratribalism. However the shamanoid minority moves unconcernedly on both sides of the walls, which thus are permeable to these exceptional people that are difficult to place and who since birth live in an intertribalist world – for them the walls are only furnished with diplomatic membranes. And since the shamanoids have received the tribe's assignment to manage *the horizontal diplomacy vis-à-vis* the other socionts, they might just as well enjoy a monopoly on *the vertical diplomacy* with the gods and the spirit world too. Strangers are after all just strangers.

Thus it is best to allow all sensitive and potentially violent goings-on to occur outside the walls. We call these external border areas *the shamanic colonies,* and it is there and nowhere else that Man has taken the decisive civilizational steps that it entails to erect temples and set up trading posts. It is perfectly possible to apply this figure of thought to modern history; an illuminating example is historian Thaddeus Russell's important book *A Renegade History of The United States*, where the author convincingly revises American history in its entirety from the perspective of the shamanoids. A more solid *exodological* platform for an America heading into the Internet Age is hard to imagine. Here once again it is inculcated that the shamanoid characters really are *outcasts* in the literal sense of the word; whenever the surrounding world appears menacing and hostile, pattern interpretation and explanation is requested, the shamanic caste is called in to interpret the intentions of gods, demons and strangers alike *vis-à-vis* the sociont. But when the intratribal tensions grow in strength and the lynch mobs are stomping down streets or raging in media channels, then it is the blood of the shamanoids one is after, then these outcasts are the ones who are sacrificed as witches and sorcerers at the heretics' stake. Suddenly all the external contacts, just recently exemplarily beneficial, appear basically suspect and turn these notorious outcasts into perfect scapegoats. The one who has sold his own soul to the Devil and has become an *informer* can hardly believe that there are any innocent worshippers left. We express this apocalyptic state as the anojective drenching the hyperjective in the crowd.

Life within the sociont does of course largely hinge on people's ability to find their way around the archetypal categories to thereby enable themselves to become the *erchtype* that mimics the corresponding archetype. Philosopher and anthropologist René Girard terms this extensive imitation that arises within the sociont *mimesis*. And this *mimesis* is without a doubt fundamental both for the human drive system and for the entire social theater that arises around it. Man is a mimetic herd animal. Testimony to this is the persistent search for *the lesser gods* – that is: the erchtypal mimicking of these icons and idols, a conduct that is connected to an intense yearning for the merciful attention and confirmation from these – with numbing emphasis. It is not even possible to make the conventional division into masters and slaves without first taking the constant mimicry into consideration. Humans imitate each other absolutely all the time, and with good reason: functional behaviors work, and to deviate from the crowd is frightening and can lead to sundry forms of ejection and isolation. Only he who, in this context, can be labeled heroic can create something novel, and if so, it only occurs as an exception. To create something new is fraught with risk and moreover difficult. The slave therefore does nothing but imitate his environment, which is what makes him precisely a slave. And he moreover does so without caring or understanding why. To unreflectively repeat is what appears natural and anything else would therefore be unthinkable. The slave is stuck in this forced repetition; the direct mimicking thus becomes a kind of curse of one's short-term memory. It lacks both history and future, intelligence and transcendence, which is what the hero strives for and attains in his blessed moments. This is also why mimicking eventually becomes a mimicking of desire in itself, what Girard calls *mimetic desire*. And when mimetic desire is stepped up, there is but one exit remaining: the Cybelian lynch mob and its liberating sacrifice of the more or less arbitrarily chosen scapegoat.

It is important in this context to understand that all human societies at many different levels – clans, tribes, nations and empires

– fundamentally are constructed as antagonisms between the inner life of the sociont and its shamanoid *outcasts*. This is the cohesive force, and Girard demonstrates in his work how the process consists of a regularly recurring *abjectification* of the shamanic caste in the outskirts of society. The internal dynamics in society, both within the inner and outer circuits, is created through mimicry and rivalry. But the mimicry and rivalry in turn create enormous and hard-to-manage tensions over time, tensions that ultimately must be channeled and find an outlet through some suitable victim being selected, that this victim is ripped out of the anonymous mass and appointed scapegoat, to then be slaughtered ritually. After this ritual slaughter the victim is transformed and incorporated with the lesser gods that are iconologically available for the herd members' own worship. No victims then work as well as, or are closer at hand than, the shamanoids who happen to find themselves within the sociont's borders. Thus the abjectification of the shamanic caste serves no less than three different purposes simultaneously. First it separates the shamanoids and keeps these at a considerable distance from both the emotionally driven intrigues of the inner circuit and the methodical strategies of the outer circuit. Secondly the abjectification generates a reassuringly strong cohesion and identity within the entire sociont, whose extension and borders become clear only when it defines itself *vis-à-vis* what lies outside and cannot quite be trusted. And thirdly it offers a liberating outlet for the growing pressure that arises within the sociont through mimicry and rivalry, wherefore society – if only temporarily – can heave a sigh of relief and recreate the illusion of stability and social normalcy. Albeit soon enough it is time to repeat the same process anew.

During the European Enlightenment in the 17th and 18th centuries, individualism and collectivism turned out to be the pair of opposites whose antagonism could develop the energy that supported capitalism. However this was, and is, a purely intellectual construction; Man is neither individualist nor collectivist. At least not more than he is fundamentally neurotic or psychotic – the two extreme states that Man tries to balance *vis-à-vis* each other to reach a measure of constructive and creative equilibrium. Both liberalism and socialism thus are built on ideologically colored wishful thinking. Man is fundamentally tribal. His world consists of a safe, intratribal sphere that is built around an *axis mundi*, the axis that unites phallic heaven and matrichal earth. Life within the sociont constantly wrestles with issues of independence, cohesion and hierarchy. In the book *The Righteous Mind* (2012), American psychologist Jonathan Haidt divides these three categories into six subcategories. *Care* (and its opposite harm) corresponds to intimate independence. *Freedom* (and its opposite oppression) corresponds to distanced independence. *Justice* (and its opposite cheating) corresponds to intimate cohesion. *Loyalty* (and its opposite betrayal) corresponds to distanced cohesion. *Authority* (and its opposite subversion) corresponds to intimate hierarchy. While *Sacredness* (and its opposite humiliation) corresponds to distanced hierarchy. But this relatively idyllic world exists in relation to a challenging and often threatening, external, intertribal world.

The six subcategories work because they presume a unifying threat outside the membrane. Inside the membrane the subject flourishes, outside the membrane the abject threatens. Within *intratribalism* Man is safe and secure, within *intertribalism* Man is constantly challenged and threatened (see *Digital Libido – Sex, Power and Violence in the Network Society*). This means that the intellectual challenge that constituted a real threat to the capitalist paradigm was not as widely assumed *the death of God* – which on the contrary constituted a prerequisite for and cornerstone of the entire project – but instead *the death of The World*. The solid, cohesive world had been under attack since the Axial Age, with its torrent of self-absorbed gurus and self-help teachers who constantly oppose an understanding of the world as a whole and instead fill all the gaps that emerge with their own narcissistic delusions. Ever since the printing press had its breakthrough in the form of newspapers, books and pamphlets, the pressure against this entire cohesive conceptual world had been overwhelming. Individualism was realized in North America after the Europeans had been ejected and independence had been declared. Cartesian individualism thus became the cohesive American state religion. If Christianity once largely was an imitation of Judaism, in the same way that Judaism can be said to have been an imitation of Zoroastrianism, then American individualism developed into one big imitation of Christianity and its ideals. Unsurprisingly all the three American religious movements that have arisen since – Jehovah's Witnesses, the Mormons and Scientology – are nothing else but hysterical pathologies that profit from Christianity's built-in self-contradictions.

Comparing with the theologically extremely more sophisticated *Silk Road Triad* that arose along the trade routes in Eurasia, we simply refer to these three exclusively American religions as *the Disney World Triad,* and the entire short but intense American history of ideas can be read into these three bizarre iconologies. So how do these new religions handle the American landscape that they just have conquered through extensive genocide and wars of extermination? Well, Jehovah's Witnesses constitute the fundamentalist, fully logical interpretation of Christianity's many shortcomings, that is: as *text.* Unsurprisingly, Jehovah's Witnesses get stuck geographically right in the city where the colonists disembark, New York. The Mormons are then the fundamentalist, mythical interpretation of Christianity's shortcomings, that is: as *land.* Therefore the Mormons geographically seek out the most isolated part of the American Midwest to build an American Israel in the area around Salt Lake in Utah. The Disney World Triad is then rounded off with Scientology, as the fundamentalist pathical interpretation of Christianity's shortcomings, that is: as *media.* From now on religion is exclusively about the unabashedly, laceratingly commercialized postmodern market forces' completion of the Christian project. Naturally the Scientologists promise prefabricated paradises that lie on empty, frozen, inhospitable planets and moons far out in space, perfectly in line with the U S Space Program, which confers honor on the relatively young nation and entails an apparent and eager imitation of how Columbus once conquered America. Therefore the space program is allowed to cost astronomical sums, while the genocides on the continent itself are silenced and the entire process of conquest is systematically euphemized in the most vulgar fashion imaginable.

As for Scientology it is now no longer even a question of appeasing an autocratic God and milking him for resources to ensure good harvests or prosperity increases in general. No, now the ambition is instead to tame religion as such in order *to milk religion in itself for its resources*. Without the least excuse or further ado. It is therefore perhaps not surprising to anyone that Scientology picks up considerable pace precisely among Hollywood movie stars in California, where one awaits salvation from outer space and where *those who pay the most* constitute *the chosen ones*, a status that continually is confirmed through maximal medial exposure. Scientology is quite simply Cartesian individualism as a cornerstone in the capitalist religion in a surreally caricatured version. The practitioners no longer even pretend to have any genuine relations with each other, or with the Universe, unless these relations first are formulated in financial terms. First there is gobbling (*das Freßen*), as Bertolt Brecht poetically wrote, and only thereafter come morals. So what is it that America ultimately perfects if not Christianity's dream of *the transparent society*, where *the barred absolute* has been eliminated for good? All curtains and barriers are removed, there is no longer anything that blocks the believer's direct connection with God! America is the laboratory where European capitalism has succeeded in developing the most vulgar nonsense imaginable into pseudospiritual ecstasy. The religions within the Disney World Triad are rather touchingly illustrative textbook examples of *vulgar eventology* as theological concept.

But whatever one thinks of the spiritual ambition, at least one cannot deny the medial creativity, nor the ideological stringency, that expresses itself in some quarters of the United States. It is the Indians and the Americans who on their respective home turfs and continents are the main standard bearers of iconology during informationalism, and make it useful as the people's own religion. In precisely this respect the eventological capitals Persepolis, Jerusalem and Rome do not have much to offer against the nomadological capitals Bollywood and Hollywood (which also receive a measure of fire support from Nigerian Nollywood). At least not when it comes to peddling as many knick-knacks with connection to the lesser gods as possible. Jehovah's Witnesses are the neurotics, the Mormons are the psychotics, and the Scientologists are the perverts in the United States' religious madhouse. But it is undeniable that all three religions hold onto the heritage from Cartesian Gnosticism with an admirably powerful grip. The problem is just that informationalist attentionalism finds no fertile ground in this religious madhouse, wherefore yet another exodus is to be expected. This time it is about leaving what long was the shimmering paradise at the horizon for all migrants: postcapitalist United States. When vertical thinking's cult of innovation is replaced by horizontal thinking's decoration worship, phallus is castrated even in America and progress simply moves somewhere else, as it must. It is toward the phallic heaven and not toward the matrichal earth that we must direct our spiritual energy if we want innovation to pick up pace anew.

In a series of books, Korean-German philosopher Byung-Chul Han thoroughly analyzes how Cartesian individualism during late capitalism is developed into an out-and-out, isolationist *hypernarcissism*. This no longer even concerns a creature having been made invisible at the bottom of the societal hierarchy à la the Italian Giorgio Agamben's concept *Homo sacer*, but instead a liberated, atomized and efficiency-optimized *Homo liber* obsessed with *autoexploitation*. We have, as French philosopher Bernhard Stiegler observes, gone from the *biopolitics* of the disciplinary society to the *psychopolitics* of the achievement society. And we have, as Moroccan sociologist Eva

Illouz so unerringly expresses the prevailing condition, landed in the midst of *emotional capitalism*. Nowhere is Byung-Chul Han's *Homo liber* more prominent than in the Californian obsession with *flow* and *healing* to optimize the quantitatively measurable in life and a vapid conception of good health before a true quality of life and depth of thought. American cyberneticist Curtis Yarvin even advocates an American dictatorship built solely on a state-directed optimization of the health of the populace as the solution to all of the network society's strenuous internal conflicts. Could the emptiness of Gnosticism possibly become any more obvious than this?

It is clear that the development upward and forward ever since the Bronze Age has been technological, while the development within religion only has plunged deeper and deeper down into a massive vulgar popular culture. Man's imitation of technology itself has created the illusion of a religious and spiritual development, when the only thing that has happened is that religion *de facto* has been vulgarized in its quest to make itself popular, and that it has lost every shred of sophistication. If religion once was about the long and difficult path to wisdom, it has with the aid of the increasingly quick and cheap media instead been turned into an easily sold packet of *quick fixes* and *shortcuts*. This is proven by the journey from sophisticated Zoroastrianism in ancient Persia to vulgar-commercial Scientology in the postmodern United States. The difference could not be more glaring. Once a career used to be based on a lifetime of learning, while it is now expected to occur through a moment of magical transformation. Religion about the object has fortunately gone from magic to technology, but this has been carried out at the cost of the religious subject having sped in the opposite direction, from a technology one must deserve through hard work to false promises of easily attained salvation. A development that was launched back in the days of the Manichaean shift from Judaism to Christianity and with the Mazdakian shift from Zoroastrianism to Islam in the Middle East of late antiquity.

A major problem confronting this drastic vulgarization of religion is that the world is monist – not dualist. Everything is dependent upon and interconnected with everything else. This is not a metaphysical assumption, but an observable fact. What exists, exists, and what does not exist, does not exist. There is no in between, and if there were, there would of course be an in between, which would bring us back to strict monism. Our planet is fully conquered, there are no white spots left on the map, at least none of real interest, and outside the planet there is nothing of value to add. Thus humanity approaches a kind of existential claustrophobia, which afflicts us since the horizon has come so close to us. *What you see is what you get.* The infinite world furnished with infinite resources turns out to be an illusion. The world is finite, the boundaries cannot be manipulated. Which at the same time makes the world coherent and internally interconnected. This makes planet Earth a global empire requiring a structured and advanced collaboration between strangers in different places for the empire to even survive, since it faces various threats of devastation. That is: the planet itself will of course survive, it is we humans who along with most animal species risk being wiped out when or if our living conditions become too poor. This being the case is not conditioned by humans having striven or voted for the global empire, but is merely in accordance with technology's own agenda. It is quite simply what is in the cards.

Then the question is: who has best succeeded in handling the conflict between the coherence of The World and the psychological fragmentation of Man? What actually made the original sociont function, when both the capitalism and communism that are built around the false pair of opposites the individual and the collective have failed so spectacularly in handling humanity's basic survival issues? The problem is not primarily, as Sigmund Freud claims, that Man is discontent in culture because it alienates him from his Dionysian drive system, but rather, and at least to a greater extent, that religion has decayed so much that it no longer serves as a compass for those who wish to orient themselves through an increasingly unfathomable existence. There quite simply is no functioning instrument left with which Man can tame himself and the rest of nature to create a culture that gets the job done. We are discontent to no use at all.

Thus it is the lack of *authentic religion*, and not some excess production of culture in the form of a civilizational straitjacket, which is humanity's great dilemma when entering informationalism. It is not sufficient, as does Michel Foucault, to advocate that life should be lived as an individual work of art. In an interactive age where Man's dominant state is an aesthetic pathos, life must rather be lived as if *the sociont sees itself as a tribal work of art.* We call this spontaneous expression *tribopoiesis,* and its pathos *protopianism*. Individualism versus collectivism was never more than the false dichotomy of the capitalist paradigm. The individual and the collective are actually completely dependent on each other as concepts, two sides of the same capitalist coin, and none of them – and certainly no artificial antagonism either – reflects Man and his prerequisites. What does reflect Man, however, is the concept tribopoiesis and the idea of the tribal singularity as Man's origin and only reasonable identity. We were never either individuals or a collective, we were always tribal and only tribal creatures. And everything we need, as single dividuals, is an archetypology that tells us where on the tribal map each of us belong. What we need is a proper and complete *archetypography.*

Freud himself would reasonably agree that a *socioanalysis* is necessary before we can devote ourselves to any meaningful form of *psychoanalysis*. Before we can reform the subject and its struggle in part with itself, in part with its surrounding world, we first must comprehend the surrounding world itself as though it were a world ready to face the psyche. Karl Marx invented the concept *symptomatology* ahead of Freud and his successor Jacques Lacan. But it is Freud and Lacan (and between them the German-Jewish Frankfurt School, which builds on and further develops both Marx and Freud) who from the 1930s and onward excel precisely as symptomatologists. The search for pioneering events within eventology and the search for pathological traumas within traumatology merge in the search for comprehensive and extensive patterns in society as social symptomatology. Psychoanalysis is thereby converted to socioanalysis. And this is where the 21st century Hegelian renaissance comes in. G W F Hegel himself, the predecessor of the Marxist symptomatologist and the Freudian socioanalyst, is the gestalt that personifies the Hegelian *Zeitgeist* of informationalism.

Hegel views the insight into the altered state of affairs as a platform for *the event*, that is: as the foundation on which the trustee of *der Zeitgeist* steps forward and leads the exodus toward the new paradigm or the promised land (both of them work equally well). When Hegel describes Napoleon as he who embodies the *Zeitgeist* in his own age, he finds it hard to rein in his enthusiasm. This is the priest's worship of the chieftain in its most pristine form. It is then Marx with his symptomatology and Freud with his socioanalysis who attempt to repeat the Hegelian turn. Marx does this by searching for early signs of the beloved *proletariat* as a kind of postcapitalist Hebrews who are to leave the factories in odious Egypt, while Freud does it through searching for early signs that the enlightened *analysand* shall rise up from the therapy couch. And it is, interestingly enough, the extrovert Marx who becomes the utopian and the (comparatively) reserved Freud who becomes the dystopian of the twain. The Frankfurt School can, in the crack between the two of them, not really settle as anything else but *critical theory* without any possible intellectual exit, other than through a renaissance for Hegelian dialectics. It is in the encounter between the dialectical deadlock between Marxist utopianism (collectivism) and Freudian dystopianism (individualism) on the one hand, and the digital age's energetic arrival on the other hand, that the Messianic hope of *netocratic protopianism* forges ahead. And this Hegelian concretion is wholly based upon the return of the sociont in the history of ideas.

A prerequisite for this necessary reconnection with Hegel is an even more comprehensive and profound reconnection with Zoroaster. This entails that it becomes necessary to revise the Western self-image by returning to – and settling the account with the entire tenacious myth of – the so fervently cherished period that Karl Jaspers has labeled *the Axial Age*. It is true that the Eurasian landmass entered a new era, colored by new forms of communication (software) in interplay with new metals (hardware) around 800 BC, and it is true that this new era was characterized by unusually long periods of peace, robust economic surpluses, and a dramatic population increase, and that this applies from Europe and North Africa in the West to China and Japan in the East. Naturally a result of this was also extensive production of both art and ideas, which overall entailed a veritable golden age for a flourishing, expansive culture. The quantitative increase is remarkable and indisputable; it is however by no means clarified that this culture also would be qualitatively superior to earlier periods in history. The major theories for how empires and nations shall be conducted had already been developed and practiced in Asia and the Middle East. So that this culture also would be qualitatively superior to earlier periods in history is extremely doubtful. Rather, the Axial Age merely contributed with increasingly self-absorbed navel-gazing and decadence, and hampered the priestly work of creating peace, trade and prosperity.

Balance is always desirable. Just as an overview and afterthought, strategy and purposefulness. One-sidedness, extremism and wishful thinking are, on the other hand, detrimental. Which is only natural. But in a situation where society has everything to gain by stimulating the outer circuit to contribute maximally to the progress of the entire sociont, the intellectual arena has been captured by a bizarre set of Gnostic and unworldly theories that mindlessly identify with the woman, the child and above all the narcissistic pillar-saint. Matrichal myths such as pacifism, vegetarianism and reincarnation have gradually become all the rage. The alpha males can supposedly to some extent still mate – it is only possible to violate biology to a certain extent – but otherwise one would rather put them in the doghouse than use them for what they are really good at: expanding a society's resources and defending it against external threats. The inner circuit despises the outer circuit and speaks of "toxic masculinity" instead of devoting much thought to future deliveries of protection and provision. This really does not bode well. What is important to understand is that Buddhism, Taoism, Christianity and Platonism all are products of the Axial Age. In varying degrees – and for better or worse – they place the woman, the child and the pillar-saint at the center of things. The problem is that the authentic phallus is lacking in all such models, wherefore it all tends to develop into a Gnosticism that becomes entrenched in the presexual or the asexual. It is about a figure of thought that aggressively opposes phallus itself, which in turn leads to ideologies that consistently are driven by *the Peter Pan syndrome*, the eagerness to acquire all the advantages of the adult phallus, without having to affirm the phallic energy and ambition.

Buddhism rejects the libido and desire itself; it creates ideology out of contempt and denial. One strives to abandon nomadological circularity, which only the self-glorifying pillar-saint can manage, wherefore the pillar-saint's virtues are highlighted and praised. The idealization of the extinguished libido made mortido so strong that Buddhism irremediably was split into two different branches: the Hinayana Buddhists' obstinate embrace of the Buddha's refusal to compromise as regards the extinguished desire, which leads to an indifference at Man's actual suffering in existence, compelled an exodus to Mahayana Buddhism, which enabled one to accept and even welcome warmth and compassion within religion. Thereby one could at least complement the ascetic pillar-saint with a nurturing mother figure. Christianity follows precisely the same track by explicitly rejecting sexuality and anything at all that is associated with the corporeal, which expresses itself in a constant willingness to try to sweep sexuality's enormous power under the rug by paying tribute to the savior who dies on the cross precisely for the sake of our sins, and who himself is the eternal virgin and the only scapegoat that ever will be needed. It is in no way a coincidence that a sorry multitude of the saints that the Catholic Church initially produces are more or less psychotic young women with severe eating disorders as they are imbued with a glowing hatred of their own bodies.

Taoism makes the same phallus-dodging maneuver by describing existence as a constant dance between phallus and matrix, but without concerning itself with the bothersome discordant exception that sexuality constitutes and that the priest personifies by being he who separates phallus and matrix. Sexuality is of course no idyllic picnic and the idea of a harmonious paradise existence during earthly life is a prime example of existential illusion being manufactured. The dialectics between logos and mythos is constantly disturbed by a third narrative in the form of *pathos*, which of course makes its presence felt precisely when *yang* and *yin* seem to interact optimally. Platonism refuses to recognize the split phallus at all and instead separates reason from the body with the purpose of placing the former above the latter, which naturally makes all the world's Gnostic pillar-saints cheer and spurs them on to compete to death in asceticism. This entire figure of thought is basically hostile to life. A society really has no reason to celebrate that the asexual pillar-saint is allowed to believe himself to be a more elevated creature than all the warriors and hunters that have protected and provided for the sociont over the course of history, and who therefore also have taken center stage over millennia of nomadological rituals.

It is only a society that has attained significant material prosperity and that has had the luxury of avoiding war over a longer period of time that even can indulge in playing with this sort of infantile fantasies, which of course always idealize the immature boy on the pillar, an actor who intoxicates himself on his own vainglory but who cannot manage either the chieftain's or the priest's ungrateful toil in the outer circuit's patriarchy. It is thus a case of a psychosocial luxury disease that no society can afford when survival is at stake, a kind of occupational therapy for inadequately stimulated chatterboxes without burdensome knowledge in either history or psychology. Or religion! It is, moreover, always time to be vigilant whenever pacifism and vegetarianism are trending on the opinion stock market. This does of course not entail that violence and war are bad habits that are about to be eradicated, but it means that violence and war are eliminated from religion and placed far below religion as if it were a case of some sort of waste products from toxic masculinity. In fact, war is of course, as Carl von Clausewitz observes, "merely a continuation of politics by other means". And indeed: eventually they sit there, the fancy pillar-saints, spread out across deserts and in the wilderness, warring with each other via armies of ideological *know-it-alls*. In this way Gnosticism acquires its most powerful expression when the Mazdakites, whom the monist Zoroastrians frenetically fight within the confines of the Persian Sassanid Empire, return in Arabic form under an Islamic banner in the early 7th century.

For what is Islam if not a bunch of pillar-saints spread out across deserts and mountainous regions who whack soldiers on the head with decrees and proceed to bait them against each other in a single long *jihad* without any end in sight? Where the only remaining difference between Sunni Islam and Shia Islam is that Sunni Islam demands that the soldiers shall read the Quran and submit to the scripture in the same way that the pillar-saint does, while Shia Islam demands the the soldiers shall submit to the pillar-saint's own private interpretation of the Quran – a variant of the same conflict (that is no less bloody) as that between Catholicism and Protestantism. It has been fortunate for the rest of the world that it is fundamentally impossible for Islam to unite under one single pillar-saint. Allah can never be anything other than vague in his leadership under such conditions. The illiterate Muhammad may be his only prophet and mouthpiece, but the pillar-saints are many and in deep disagreement. Admittedly Islam, in contrast to Christianity, does not sweep the violence and sex under the rug with dogmatic brooms; Islam does of course have a totalitarian ambition whose aim is to color every fiber in society and control both politics and markets as well as private life in minute detail. But since Islam proclaims an aggressively Gnostic view of violence and sex, Islamic culture becomes strongest and most vital exactly when the religion's total grip on culture and society is weakened. When the Quran embraces all of society with an iron fist, all oxygen quickly disappears; the level of enculturation drops and there is a general dumbing down of discussions.

The four important religions from the Middle East must be understood in the following way: Since Zoroastrianism worships the military phallus, Islam can never be anything other than *the imitation of the worshipping of the military phallus.* And since Judaism worships the priestly phallus, Christianity can never be anything other than *the imitation of the worshipping of the priestly phallus.* Thus it appears wholly reasonable that Islam is founded by and constantly refers back to a military by the name of Muhammad, while Christianity is founded by and constantly refers back to a priest by the name of Peter. This becomes possible through the Gnostic maneuver to blow up the door to the barred absolute and reshape the barred religions of the militaries and the priests to more easily digestible messages tailored to the masses.

It is precisely this maneuver that must be reversed for eventological religion to deserve a new historical opportunity. What is needed is a new worldview: that we understand *the West* as the territory west of the Gobi Desert and the Hindu Kush where the hope of the phallic event was developed – Europe is merely a recent phenomenon propelled by printing presses and gunboats in the northwestern corner of the Western world – a development which radically breaks with the nomadology that was dominant in the East. And from this perspective, the Persian-Jewish renaissance is completely decisive. Zoroastrianism and Judaism were after all built as religions for *the adults of God*, while Christianity and Islam attract *the children of God* with free access to God, who in this context is reduced to one big *mamilla*. At the same time as the East's obsession with *samsara* – the only thing that exists is the eternal recurrence of the same – only can end with the yearning for *mahamudra* – the return to matrix, the fusion of all divisions in history, and thus the annihilation of everything – where death and only death is the single and closing event. Because if phallus never arrives, culture is invariably turned inward against itself and its own demise.

What happens during the transition from the Bronze Age to the Iron Age is that the old social ties within the sociont are torn apart. Sedentary life has now established such a high degree of social complexity that old nomadological structures such as clans and tribes do not suffice to keep a territorially and population-wise constantly expanding society together. The new eventological narratives speak of greater social units, and dreams of empires and nations are stirred to life. This is very clear from the Bronze Age's two best-known narratives, imperialist Zoroastrianism and nationalist Judaism. However this expansion also entails that *the shamanic caste* is pushed out and away and ends up at an increasing distance from the center of society. The shamanoids leave the densely populated river valleys and seek out desolate mountainous areas where they soon establish what the ancient Persians call *castag* – a phenomenon explored in detail by Panamanian anthropologist Pablo Vazquez – that is: monasteries, orders and other institutions for precursors to later monks and nuns. The shamanoids also seek distance from the densely populated river valleys to secluded oases, distant port cities and other more or less insignificant places along the new, expanding trade routes, both on land and at sea, where they soon operate the local inns, public baths, night clubs and brothels.

Seeking out the shaman in the forest for spiritual or sexual adventures, or seeking out the shaman in the forest for therapeutic contacts with the gods in heaven and the underworld, or ritual contacts with the strangers from the terrifying and partly unfamiliar surrounding world, now acquires completely new meanings. But it is still a tribal map with the same women from the inner circuit, the same men from the outer circuit, and the same *outcasts* from the shamanic caste. The only difference is that the map has grown considerably, in step with the sociont having expanded from clans and tribes to empires and nations. And thus the separation between on the one hand the two main circuits that harbor the majority of the population and, on the other hand, the shamanic caste outside and the minority that can be found there, becomes dramatically magnified. The walls' smooth permeability is lost. The monasteries in the mountains, the oases in the deserts, and the trading cities at the river mouths take over the sociocultural role that the cult sites and trading posts outside the walls, administered by the shamanic caste, had served during the sociont's heyday.

That this is the case is evident for Zoroaster when he around 1700 BC in his text *Gathas* formulates Zoroastrian eventology as a pervasive reformation of the nomadology of the Indo-Iranian tribes. Zoroaster is uncompromising in his criticism of the shamanoids, when they as early as the Bronze Age venture so far away from the sociont that they lose the sense of their vital role within the same, as the sociont's cohesive outsiders, as the particular within the universal that *de facto* makes the universal identity possible. This explains why Zoroastrianism to this day does not recognize any monk or nun orders outside society's internal order. But when the Iron Age commences, the boundaries are widened to such a large extent that a panoply of doctrines of worlds outside the world arise. The Eurasian landmass enters an era of increasingly longer periods of peace and burgeoning prosperity. Around the corner awaits the Axial Age. Soon societies from China in the East to Rome in the West are filled with one new philosophy after the other. Intellectual life enters a completely new phase. And what unites these actually incompatible doctrines is the new, suddenly arisen interest in precisely the shaman's separation from the sociont and all the new existentialist fantasies that gain nourishment from this.

If there is anyone that deserves to be called an *individual*, if it actually had been possible to imagine such a character, it is *the shaman*. The shamans do of course *de facto* live in the outskirts of the tightly cohesive sociont, they are excluded from many social contexts, so view them from the outside, perhaps not always without a certain yearning. But it is only if the sociont is afflicted with loosening and dissolution tendencies and the social extremes are emphasized as exemplary, that it is possible to peddle individualism as some sort of universal religion. And precisely this happens in Europe, where reading and writing proficiency starts to take effect broadly and create pervasive societal changes during the 17th century. As the answer to all the questions that arise in the field of tension between Descartes' atomism, Spinoza's pantheism and Leibniz's relativism, the Kantian subject, which quickly sets a precedent and acquires influence, is launched. It is no coincidence or the result of some abstract academic wars of words – this subject is precisely what the new nation-states with their institutions and military machines request. Soldiers and citizens alike must be able to read and write in order to absorb the orders issued and the propaganda that drives and regulates the entire machinery. Authorities and bureaucracies dictate existing regulations in writing. The entire social inheritance from Napoleon is based on the single individual that personally can be held responsible for his or her actions. As an immediate collectivist reaction, there ensues the unrealistic fantasy that wafted through Europe like a cursed ghost: *communism*.

In this equally fictive and pointless dichotomy between individual and collective much of the political discussion became mired, while the really interesting issue in this context – the dialectics of subject and substance – garnered no attention whatsoever and slowly dropped beneath the horizon. But what is at issue is how the ego arises and defines itself *vis-à-vis* the world as part of the world, where the ego, as Johann Gottlieb Fichte points out, is limited while the world is unlimited. We call this *the eternalist subject*. Please observe that the subject apprehends itself as stable and immutable, while the surrounding world appears chaotic and mutable. The neurotic illusion that both subject and world can be eternal and immutable results in unmanageable delusions of grandeur. The psychotic illusion that the subject in no way takes root in, nor can establish a meaningful relation with a chaotic and mutable world, is the other side of the same coin. The psychosis thus creates a worldview where the subconscious devours consciousness and the ego experience disappears in a chaotic collapse of unsorted impressions without a mutual hierarchy. From this follows – naturally – that the eternalist subject by no means is tasked to experience the world as it actually is, without culling and structuring, arranging and prioritizing, so that the world opens up and becomes navigable. It is no truth producer, but merely a hypothesis machine that continually corrects itself when needed.

The eternalist subject invents and processes problems, creates and solves riddles, by building value hierarchies. Subjectivity thus arises in conjunction with the trade-off between various alternatives in a choice situation. And subjectivity as such makes itself known and allows itself to be experienced when a problem must be put aside and be saved for future processing, quite simply because the perception apparatus and the attached interpretation must be oriented toward something else, a more important and/or more acute problem that has surfaced. The classical question of the possible existence of a *free will* is thus incorrectly posed and uninteresting (see *The Body Machines*) – free in relation to what? And who or which agency would exercise this possible freedom now that the individual and the ego have proven to be fictions? The interesting question one could pose instead is whether free choice, without any speculations about who or what, if so, it is that chooses the one or the other, exists. Does even the choice option, that is the foundational prerequisite for the eternalist subject, exist? Here we can glimpse the distinction between Zoroastrian ethics and Abrahamic moralism. Will is of course nothing other than a question of access to libidinal energy. So is there a libidinal will at all that has access to several options, and where the chosen option (or the postponement of the same) entails a possibility of renewed and updated self-identification?

It is absolutely vital here to understand how self-awareness arises. Self-awareness is in itself a consequence of shortcomings and limitations, or it would not have arisen at all. Thinking is the activation of the failure to intuitively understand and interact with the surrounding world. No one understands or investigates this better than Hegel, who builds his theory of the subject as a constant failure on a constantly ongoing antagonism, which in turn drives all of the arisen subject's dialectical reasoning. Here Hegel sides with Zoroastrianism and Protestantism in contrast to Taoism and Catholicism. There is no logical or mythical order and structure in this process that instead is clearly pathical, disharmonious and unbalanced. Instability is right from the start built into the Hegelian synthesis, and it is then released in the form of internal antagonisms. And it is precisely this which, according to Hegel, makes *the subject the strongest expression of the substance*. Just as his predecessors David Hume and Immanuel Kant, Hegel attacks the Cartesian subject that has been the norm since the mid-17th century. However they handle the issue in different ways and come to different conclusions. Hume settles for a stable subject that tries to relate to a mobile world, Kant, on his part, gets stuck with a mobile subject that is encapsulated in a fixed world (which in theory it would be able to experience directly if it were not for the subject's own limitations), while only Hegel succeeds in handling constant movement at all levels of the complex. No person and no thing is fixed. Both substance and subject are relations that consist of other relations where relata only constitute temporarily surfacing byproducts connected to the ongoing processes. The pathical subject pulsates and vibrates ambivalently behind both logos and mythos.

Hegel's argument *vis-à-vis* Kant is that the latter demystifies the subject in a way that nevertheless is fundamentally mystifying. Kant works with a psychology for the soul, a cosmology for the world, and a theology for God. Psychology for the soul is a Kantian pathos. Cosmology for the world is a Kantian logos. And theology about God is a Kantian mythos. All these three quantities are foregone conclusions in an unclear manner, according to Kant. Hegel's revolt against Kant is a battle for *a narratological liberation*. The Hegelian subject is namely liberated from all forms of preordained psychologies, cosmologies and theologies; it has to settle for its own internal dialectics. This speculative *pandialecticism* is *the Hegelian absolute*. All metanarratives – logos, mythos and pathos – are fundamentally dialectical, according to Hegel. It is not even possible to speak of a psychology, cosmology or even a theology as something other than dialectical phenomena in Hegel, and definitely not as any preordained eternalizations, as in Kant. Thanks to Hegelian pandialecticism, which affirms and handles movement in all of being's dimensions, it becomes possible to take the path of thinking toward *radical relationalism*.

In Zoroastrian terms we would express this as though the *ameretat* our generation longs for already lies inherent in our worldview and lies ready to pathically explode as the next generation's *haurvatat*. Where what is important is that the subject is *pathical* and neither logical nor mythical. The dividual identity sprouts from the sociont and its history as the barred absolute. In front of this barred absolute, dividuality is awakened as the embodiment of an actual archetype in the form of *the mimicking erchtype*. The subject's primary function is to entwine *the great trauma* in the form of an abandonment of mamilla with *the great event* in the form of the yearning for phallus. Mamilla is the barred absolute from the past, phallus is the barred absolute in the future. The path backward is however barred forever. The subject can therefore only hope to become the agent who carries out his *truth-as-an-act* by submitting to phallus. This irrefutable demand for submission is the strength of phallus as *the concrete absolute*.

However monotheist phallus worship does not suffice. The sociont does not merely need a vision and a direction, but moreover a strategy, and a strategy one can only build on knowledge. Or to use a more solemn word: wisdom. Therefore religion's origin is every bit as much an issue of *mana* as an issue of *phallus*. Romanian anthropologist Mircea Eliade traces the *mana* to the theological shift from the ancestors to the gods. At the same moment that the ancestors, in the capacity of the symbolic vessels for and intermediaries of the transmitted wisdom within the sociont, are depersonified and universalized – that is: when it no longer matters who within the sociont is offspring to which primordial father or primordial mother, when the entire tribe has been accorded the same common primordial father and primordial mother – the ancestors are converted into the lesser gods. It is this conversion that is called *metaphysical reification,* and it can only be applied to the already dead (there is always something vulgar and dubious about statues and other memorials of people who are still alive). The function is the *mana*, a kind of impersonal but constantly present force that humanity must struggle with in all situations. It is thus on top of this *mana* that the priest names the gods to concretize what sacrifices the gods require from the faithful.

For the masculine subject, this displacement and radical self-identification occurs through *the subject submitting to culture as logos.* For the feminine subject, the same process occurs through *the subject submitting to nature as mythos.* This means that *the law* is introduced to organize the outer circuit, while the inner circuit is free to act precisely as it wishes, since it still only can act within the confines of the consequences of the law being upheld in the outer circuit. This explains why all the world's prisons are full of heterosexual men and a few lesbians, but not of heterosexual women or homosexual men. *The law* is thus the name of the phallic religion that makes it possible to expand the sizes of clans and tribes further toward city states, nations and entire empires. And no religion carries this out more naturally than Judaism, with its unique union between the nation and religion under the same roof. Antisemitism is not just like any racism, antisemitism is deep down *nation envy.*

The balance between logos, mythos and pathos is maintained

through the narrative constantly reiterating the importance of Zoroastrian ethics through *the phallic principle of tribal contribution*. The question of what the tribe can do for you is the child's question, while the question of what you can do for the tribe is the adult's question. Every time someone demands a freedom or a right without conveying something of value in return, we are in practice seeing a little child who vociferously tries to cry its way to even more breast milk. And this, of course, we would rather not have to see grown-up people do, just like this applies to subservient beggars and infuriated demonstrators alike, both of whom give rise to virtually the same unease. A proud adult who takes responsibility for themselves and their own, who finds joy in contributing to the common good, is however beautiful, not least in their own eyes.

From The Frankfurt School to Betty Friedan in *The Feminine Mystique*: the totalitarian Platonism of the Western left is underpinned by a total ignorance of, or an equally total disinterest in Man's pathical tribalism. One instead chooses to focus on a logical conflict between individual and collective that then is attacked via Platonist theories of *false consciousness*. Please note that the demand that is directed from the subservient beggar or the infuriated demonstrator always is a demand without discernible direction or final destination. There is no point where the demand is satisfied and where the beggar or the demonstrator is done demanding, has taken their responsibility as an adult and fully-fledged member of the community by starting to do their part for the common good. These are mouths that never become satiated. The revenue from begging and the benefits one, if applicable, has succeeded in hassling one's way to receiving, are usually spent in the form of immediate consumption rather than as investments in a future where the little child's dependence on an offering mamilla would be but a memory.

The childishly demanding position is not conceived as a transitory phase. The extended paper cup outside the supermarket entrance and the indignant list of demands from the allegedly aggrieved group will never disappear. It is a question of compensation for supposed injustices in the past and certainly no help for self-help. The stern and demand-ridden gaze of the self-pitying child will never be tempered. It is no passing phase but a permanent scenario. What we are witnessing here is the development of *the permanent dependence on mamilla*, a dependence that is seen as a given by all the narcissists who by pure principle refrain from growing up and taking their own responsibility. In the postcapitalist society even the slaves are no longer working. The workers have, in Jean Baudrillard's words, been turned into *work mannequins*. Not because there necessarily is a lack of tasks, but because these for various reasons can be claimed to be humiliating to carry out. Hence all these reproachful gazes and angry accusations, all these hungry mouths in all these rich societies, mouths that never can be satiated, demands that never are met.

Whenever it is possible to score political points on claimed injustices, the rulers get out their tax tables and start to outline changes that are aimed at leveling. This is a principle that tends to dominate in systems where politicians primarily strive to become re-elected and only thereafter may consider achieving something of value. The money one pulls in from working people as if by magic becomes common funds and the state coffers become one big mamilla squirting out breast milk to all who ask for it, and even to many others for the sake of re-electability. One for instance doles out child allowance to everyone, as if the idea that parents themselves should support their children were completely absurd. In such a society matrichal magic knocks out phallic technology, mythos is decoupled from logos, ideas of cause and effect are denied and ridiculed. The entrepreneurs become fewer in step with bureaucrats increasing their numbers, and the struggle for provision increasingly turns into a struggle for privileges. One distributes a shrinking pie instead of primarily ensuring that the overall pie is growing. When the phallic principle of tribal contribution is weakened, society loses momentum and prosperity-creating dynamics. Increasing numbers consider themselves belonging to so-called weak groups to be propped up by a dwindling few. With increased poverty comes increasing anarchy: different factions that demand benefits from each other.

Furthermore the phallic principle of tribal contribution applies equally for social groups relative to larger entities as it applies to the single dividual. We can view two popular subcultures from late capitalism that appear to survive and develop even in the Internet Age, namely *feminism* and *androgynism*. Both these movements arose during late capitalism as matrichal reactions to the catastrophes that contributed to ending the golden age of the phalluses, with concrete phallic failures such as Hitler and Stalin and abstract phallic threats such as the atomic bomb and environmental pollution. Feminism further harvested public opinion success when it proudly emphasized women's shouldering responsibility for half of society and demanded matching remuneration from the state and the market for this contribution. Androgynism also succeeded when it proudly emphasized the androgynous caste's contribution to society as a mediating vessel between the male-dominated outer circuit and the female-dominated inner circuit in society. The androgynous person does of course not become an adult by developing from a boy to a man, or from a girl to a woman, but attains their adulthood through blending a cocktail of both the man and the woman. It is precisely in the role as the one who moves across boundaries that the androgynous person discovers their adulthood, precisely through personifying the phallic principle of tribal contribution as the sociont's own internal *go-between*.

Thus far all this is excellent. A society that is not constantly questioned stagnates, and sustainable ideas can withstand criticism. The problem is that both feminism and androgynism developed diverse sects and cults marked by infantile internarcissism. The principle of tribal contribution that generates pride and strength was eventually replaced by *the eternal accusation* that can only generate bitterness and greed. When Western feminism and androgynism in practice had finished triumphing and should have closed down their activism in the form of a becoming matricide – or perhaps better yet should have migrated to other more needy parts of the world – the movements were instead usurped by state-financed funeral wailers who constantly hunt increasingly absurd renderings of alleged crimes to keep alive the eternal production of accusations that never can be compensated for. And as long as there is no demand for a stated final destination from these movements, they will gladly milk the phallus via the state apparatus for a constantly snowballing compensation for old, increasingly fabricated injustices. If there is a system to exploit, it will be exploited. That is: until a Messianic project arrives that reinstates the sociont and its integrity. For the phallic principle of tribal contribution will return with full power the moment society is presented with a complete and authentic archetypology for humanity. We are working on it.

4
Eventological monotheism versus nomadological iconology

The phallic and priestly eventology is monotheist and/or oligotheist; it focuses on the higher and inaccessible gods. In syntheist terms it can be expressed as though eventology strives toward *Pantheos*. The matrichal and popular nomadology is, however, polytheist and iconological; it focuses on the lesser and accessible gods. And if we apply the syntheist perspective on that handling, we say that nomadology strives toward *Entheos*. *Nomadology is the universal and horizontal exodology*. In ancient Greece the nomadological timeline is called *chronos*. *Eventology is the exceptional and vertical exodology*, and the ancient Greeks call the eventological timeline *kairos*. Hence we refer to the sacral event as *the kairotic moment*. The timeline that we call *chronos* generates the mobilist history of nature, while *kairos* generates the eternalist history of culture. The moment that both these dimensions establish contact, when eventology meets nomadology – which means that the nomadic movement in itself is transformed into an actual event – there arises an *exodology*: the history of the transition between two different paradigms, how both old territories and old ideologies are abandoned for the civilizational conquest of the new. If we once again apply a syntheist view of the process, we see how exodology eventually must strive toward *Syntheos* (see further

Syntheism – Creating God in the Internet Age), the greatest exodus of all for mankind.

These two metanarratives complement and balance each other; none of them is functional without the other. In a globalized world, eventological monotheism without a counterweight is developed into *dictatorship*. And in the same globalized world, nomadological iconology without a counterweight is developed into *anarchy*. A stable civilization must rest on a more or less stable balance between the two metanarratives – eventology's *yang* or *Shiva* against nomadology's *yin* or *Shakti*. Hegel regards the nomadological worldview as the philosophical generator that drives what he calls *reflective thinking*, which is personified by the priest, while the eventological worldview is the generator that drives *speculative thinking*, which in turn is personified by the chieftain. With the merger of these metanarratives, Zoroastrianism's two-headed phallus *Ahura Mazda* is enfolded in Western thinking, where it fills a vital function. The concept is actually so vital that it generously compensates for the fact that it eventually becomes the nail in the coffin of Hegel's greatly beloved Christianity.

In order to handle the difference between reflective and speculative thinking, two different kinds of historiography are required. Nomadology's *the eternal recurrence of the same* must be complemented by a unique eventological historiography that starts from *the root-of-the-phallus*. The Old Testament's endless chants about who had which son that became the father of which son that became the father of which son, and so on, is an illustrative example one only can imagine on painstakingly accounted for roots-of-the-phallus. Another example is Hegel's distinction between the necessity in the past as the root-of-the-phallus that must encounter the brutal contingency of the future, as precisely *phallus in itself*, which has the strongest possible attachment to history. A third example is the sociobiological heritage in the form of the human genome that is passed on from generation to generation, what we call Man's *archetypology*. He who then following Hegel formulates nomadology in the form of the myth of the eternal recurrence of the same is of course Nietzsche.

The very concept of nomadology is invented around the mid-20th century by philosopher and Nietzsche disciple Gilles Deleuze, but the concept as such gets its main meaning from anthropologist Mircea Eliade's contemporary theories of *the Arcadian ontology*. Nomadology constantly oscillates, and the reason is that it has so many archetypal icons by which to orient itself. It is thus about the original doctrine of the original tribe, *the sociont*, and its foundation, structure and direction. It is through the science of psychology that we ever since the sociont's heyday comprehend the nomadological mindset and its horizontality. The nomadological transfer of knowledge occurs via *the principle of absolute mimesis without exception*, which is cherished by the inner circuit. Precisely everything is zealous imitation. The consequence of this cult of mimicry will of course, as everyone realizes, be that nomadology as such does not endorse innovation. There is quite simply no room for any radical history-altering event. Instead history must constantly be retold as an eternal cycle of repetition. Imitation and repetition is the exemplary and desirable; occasional deviations from the expected can only be regrettable accidents or capricious input from gods and/or spirits that absolutely should not be imitated. The sociont stands and falls by *the tradition* that everyone and everything must pay tribute and submit to.

Over the course of history – over the course of everything – there is *Genetrix* (or *Magna Mater*, as she is called by classic psychoanalysts such as Carl Jung and Erich Neumann) in a state of spectacular loneliness. Genetrix is thus the name of the completely unadulterated mortido that is entirely driven by the matrichal ability to redeliver the world, but that completely lacks the phallic urge to alter it (see *Digital Libido – Sex, Power and Violence in the Network Society*). Genetrix is the name of the inverted sexuality, birth and death in one and the same conceptual nutshell, without any lived life in between – what Neumann refers to as *ouroboric incest* – a phenomenon that does not know its own time limit, that turns toward itself as a *centroversion*, and that therefore suffocates the possibilities of sexuality to develop into a living dialectics. To the extent that Genetrix is allowed to operate undisturbed, *the phallic intrusion* into the child's life is inhibited, which means the phallic train toward adulthood leaves the platform, while the child, that is doped-up on safety concerns, attaches itself by suction to mamilla and refuses to yield. *The sexual negation,* which is necessary in order to lay the ground for an adult sexuality, does not occur. Which is the recurring tragedy that unfolds every time that mortido suffocates libido over the course of history (see *Digital Libido – Sex, Power and Violence in the Network Society*). What remains is a kind of constantly grinding nomadological machinery that only acts reactively to ensure survival, but which is incapable of actively engaging to achieve change and development. The many archetypes that are required to shape the adult archetypology, and ultimately also be perfected as the living iconology, die from lack of oxygen under the pressure from Genetrix and her mortido as *The One.*

The Hegelian negation (the original and underlying mortido) is no longer followed by *the negation of the negation* (the dialectical and overarching libido). Or as Neumann sums it up in his classic work *The Origins and History of Consciousness* from 1949: Ouroboric incest leads to *adolescent incest* and thereafter to the sacrificing of phallus itself. The son dies in his mother's arms as *the Cybelian act par excellence*. Nomadology thus has its clearly defined function, but it also has its clearly defined limitations. Without a counterweight it cannot produce anything other than its own castration, this since nomadology gets its energy from a constantly grinding machine of repetition – life after life after life without any authenticity, what Siddhartha Gautama, the founder of Buddhism, simply defines as the *suffering* of existence. Eventology instead operates according to the principle of the temporary increase of the engine's combustion, that is: if and when extra energy is available. We understand the eventological mind and its *verticality* via the art of *socioanalysis;* we observe how the transition from nomadology to eventology enables a transition from an exclusive (and excluding) horizontality to a state where the vertical gains entrance into the horizontal. It is in this manner that we must view the transition from paganism to Christianity, a paradigm shift that Nietzsche wrestles with while he fails at separating the Dionysian forces in the exodological field.

Nietzsche struggles with an aristocratic ideal in the form of the *Übermensch* as a historical event – this is essentially the same shamanoid character that author Ernst Jünger later calls *the anarch* – while he himself constantly reverts to a nomadological thought pattern without really taking hold in the history of eventology. For Nietzsche fails to separate *Ahura* from *Mazda* (the concept of the two-headed phallus within Zoroastrianism) within his own overarching concept of *will-to-power*, this since the Übermensch must manifest two different wills without autonomy. Therefore he does not understand, in contrast to Zoroaster and Hegel, the difference between a nomadological worldview with only will-to-intelligence, where history therefore must be circular, on the one hand, and on the other hand an eventological worldview, that contains both will-to-intelligence and will-to-transcendence, and which therefore must be understood as the path which leads out of the nomadologically circular and that encompasses a genuinely exodological event.

Nietzsche quite simply lacks the tools of Zoroastrianism and Judaism that have been lost in Christianity and Islam – in their successful simplification of the existential conditions – namely the tantric tools that hide behind *the barred absolute*. Nietzsche does not succeed in thinking death as an *anti-event* before he thinks life as an event, he does not succeed in thinking *negatology* before he thinks eventology, to use Canadian philosopher Cadell Last's vocabulary. Nietzsche is still too Christian to understand that mortido drives libido and not the other way around. He never thinks *the Cybelian mob* as the collective subconsciousness and *the Dionysian swarm* as the thin libidinal surface atop, even if he clearly sees the Apollonian order as the collective consciousness atop the latter, as civilization itself. We are frankly concerned here with a system error that is built into Christian theology which Nietzsche inherits. The Übermensch is by definition an anarchic recluse, drenched in *infinite freedom*, who has no idea of where he is going or how his superhuman gifts (technology) best are used.

The point here is that the difference between monotheism and polytheism is not a matter of the number of gods to whom a believer must devote his worship, but instead of how many directions that are actual simultaneously and therefore also possible to follow. Eventological monotheism contains a conception of the vertical and linear movement upward, while nomadological iconology contains a conception of the horizontal and circular movement forward. This explains why the monotheists turn toward a single spot when they are practicing their submission, the spot where the sacred event has taken place (*the root-of-the-phallus as an event*) or shall take place (*the phallus in itself as an event*). The polytheists, on their part, quite simply turn toward the effigy of a single lesser god that they for the moment happen to worship for one reason or another. It thus means that the difference between eventological monotheism and nomadological iconology is not a question of quantity as regards the number of gods, but a question of quality. What eventology adds to the process is the phallic focus that is directed away from mamilla, toward – and by all means past – phallus itself. The phallic focus entails that all energy is channeled in a single direction toward a single god. It is this single god that the monotheist aims to mimic, not other people that in turn imitate lesser gods.

The dramatic transition from nomadology to eventology – the only ideological revolution of genuine and really transformative significance in human history – occurs in conjunction with the Zoroastrian reformation in Central Asia around 1700 BC, an event that later had Christianity, among others, as an eventological grandchild. Certainly, the same impressive religious reformation can be found in other cultures that contemplate and manifest the new conditions of sedentary life, for example within *Tengrism* among the Mongols and *Waaqeffanna* among the Oromo people in Ethiopia, both monotheist cults around the phallic god in heaven. However Zoroaster is not only a religious reformer but also history's first authoring philosopher. Without the Zoroastrian reformation it is impossible to conceive of a Judaism, Christianity or Islam. But neither of a Confucianism, Taoism, Buddhism or Brahmanism during the Axial Age in the East. And above all no Hegel or Nietzsche. Where thus *authentic eventology* (Zoroastrianism and Judaism) dares to think death as the absolute negativity, while *false eventology* (Christianity and Islam) terrifyingly conceals death behind grotesque, infantile fantasies of eternal life.

Thanks to eventology Man can travel inside his head every bit as well as with his body in the physical world. What previously merely was genetics now receives a superstructure in the form of *memetics* (see any of the three books in *The Futurica Trilogy*). The eventological transfer of knowledge and wisdom now occurs via the outer circuit's *principle of mimesis with the phallic exception*. Everything is imitation except *authentic innovation as an event*. In one fell swoop, this enables teachable people to imitate the creative gods that create worlds. In every respect it pays better to complement *nomadology's horizontal mimesis* with *eventology's vertical mimesis*. Phallus can now stage its exodus toward the divine via technology, and the radical difference lies in this exodus now having a single direction: forward, upward, away. Those who follow phallus no longer risk getting lost in winding circles from which there is no exit. The Zoroastrian concept *khvarenah* captures the aura or charisma that distinguishes the perfect project. The encounter between the deep historical anchoring in the root-of-the-phallus (the reflection) and the flashes from the phallic hammer (the speculation) generates the *khvarenah* that makes everything else pale, and which true believers follow as soon as it appears on the horizon. Thus the fact that the *khvarenah* only appears at one single occasion explains the arrival and success of monotheism.

This does not mean that history as such will go through some qualitative change. The transition from the two-dimensional view of history, which only is compatible with horizontal nomadology, to the three-dimensional view of history that is built on and presumes the dialectics of horizontal nomadology and vertical eventology, should be regarded as an admittedly transformative shift in perspectives but not as the introduction to a new historical era. This *pharmakon* of a construction from the history of ideas brings both possibilities and risks. In books such as *Straw Dogs* and *Black Mass* from the early 2000s, philosopher John Gray aims sharp criticism against all attempts to describe history as some kind of refinement process, even if this thinking merely concerns the social context wherein Man finds himself and no longer experiments with any delusions of a gradually increasing refinement of human nature. Ideas of this sort Gray subsumes within the concept *meliorism* (from the Italian verb *migliorare,* which means precisely to improve, refine). It is quite reasonable, as does Gray, to blame the European Enlightenment and its underlying Christianity, which in turn is a hybrid between Judaism and Platonism, for these meliorist ideals. Any of those are however nowhere to be found among the Zoroastrians, who with their worldview as only *processes and events* do not acknowledge the presence of any Platonist forms, and who consequently neither take an interest in any form of superreality that is considered more real than, and preceding, actual reality. The event is rather just what it is.

What Zoroaster does is rather to present an alternative to nomadological iconology, and that alternative is eventological monotheism. Events *can* occur and events *can* change history forever. Thanks to the new information accumulation outside Man's own memorizing head. And they further tend to be technological in nature and not ideological, that is: they are conditioned by a dominating media technology of the moment that elevates certain talents and abilities at the expense of others, for no other reason than precisely because some talents simply happen to be aligned with the prevailing media climate, rather than them being products of some ideological ambitions or considerations. This insight and this recognition is *in itself* – in the most profound Hegelian sense – the greatest event of them all, a true transformation in spirit. We relate to the world afresh. Where existence previously only consisted of horizontal processes there is now a complementing dimension of vertical events. As a result one can see the history of philosophy as a long series of footnotes to Zoroaster, where *the thought* (personified by the priest) constantly submits to *the act* (personified by the chieftain), instead of the reverse scenario which one tends to think wishfully about within meliorism.

This radically changes the relation to the divine. Instead of begging the lesser gods for assistance through existence in blatant favor of one's own interests, what Zoroaster calls *dev yasna* in ancient Persian, Zoroaster stipulates a direct and personal relation with the divine, via the wise thought he calls *Mazdayasna*. Which is both more rewarding and more demanding. And this is precisely where the decisive division between monotheism and polytheism arises. Zoroaster's point is thus not a question of how many gods that appear in the sacred scriptures, but what is central is the relation itself between Man and the divine. *Dev yasna* is an indirect relation by proxy which results in personal responsibility vanishing. Icons are merely images that one can accept with one's eyes without building any deepened relation to. The childishly light-hearted polytheism can be likened to leafing through colorful weeklies or scrolling through an Instagram feed brimming with vacation and food images. You are not really living your life yourself, it is someone else who lives life for you. It is someone other than you who acquires the decisive, pervasive insights; It is someone else who carries out the radical actions that alter existence – it is not you. Someone else does all this in your place, you are only carrying out simple imitations while living an indirect life.

The multidimensional figure of thought in Zoroastrianism opens up for the phallic exodus from primitivism to civilization, something that now becomes both conceivable and possible. And when monotheism with its strong and sole phallic direction makes an earnest breakthrough, the ideological exodology called Zoroastrianism will soon be followed by the geographical exodology called Judaism. In essence exodologies are exactly this: Man's ultimate attempt to identify and realize the divine within himself. Zoroaster's own religion, *Mazdayasna,* requires knowledge of the practitioner and only those who actually possess the deep and extensive knowledge can approach the divine. Where this act, to take responsibility for one's own destiny – which generates history's first and still most consistent existentialism, namely the Zoroastrian religion and its love of the mind and wisdom – manifested in an act, affects and changes history forever. *Eventology* is born. Love of the icon, *dev yasna* or iconology, lives on as an acceptable popular religion and is developed later in history to the worshipping of saints and martyrs. But for the intellectual elite, who are serious about optimizing their life opportunities, it is instead *Mazdayasna*, love of wisdom, what the Greeks a thousand years later start calling *philosophia*, that matters.

There are two directions to choose between: either, for those who advocate *vertical mimesis,* upward toward a fixed phallic point, and thus this religion must be a *monotheism*. Or else, for those who find *horizontal mimesis* more comfortable and less demanding, one is free to imitate everything and everyone in a flat world. A religion built on this pattern of thought consequently becomes a polytheism or an *iconology*. What is said here does not entail that monotheism and polytheism are each other's opposites, only that they constitute different directions with regard to the focus for Man's desire to constantly imitate. So what this concerns is whether we only dare to imitate each other, or if we in view of civilization's development actually summon the courage to imitate God himself. The iconological imitation can surely generate intelligence, but nothing over and above intelligence, while the theological imitation moreover can generate the transcendence that makes us godlike through both wanting and being able to create new worlds. What this entails, becomes evident for anyone with the least insight: the high-octane debate on theism versus atheism that has been raging in Western discourse, is built on completely erroneous conceptions and misses the whole point of theology. The questions are incorrectly posed. Theology does not deal with the question of whether God exists or not, but rather devotes itself to whom or what has God's function, and that thus *becomes God*, and what consequences follow from this. For what is the typical atheist if not an isolated little god who does not wish to posit any other or greater god beside themselves? This despite the lamentable fact that these people themselves cannot even figure out whether they are to submit to nomadological moralism or eventological ethics.

It is thus only eventology that can cultivate the fantasy of *the permanent fixation for a creative purpose*. Only eventology can regard a game as a job; only an eventology can develop into *netocratic protopianism*. Within nomadology the permanent fixation is nothing other than precisely the eternal sitting still. Which therefore tends to be filled with intrigue and gossip – rather than with visions and strategies – in copious amounts. This explains why European enlightenment men such as Jean-Jacques Rousseau with his *The Great Mother* and Marquis de Sade with his *Mother Nature* are more known for oceans of intrigue and gossip during their scandal-ridden lives than for any phallic visions for the sake of humanity. They are driven by Cybelian rather than Dionysian fantasies. All the while nomadology clings to the radical monism which claims that everything in existence is dependent upon and influences everything else, while eventology struggles to maintain monism, despite the fact that it tends to crumble into a dualism whenever process and event by mistake are apprehended as two different substances, when they actually are just two different attributes of one and the same substance. This error in thought is a recurring phenomenon that we refer to as *the Gnostic delusion*.

This business of maintaining monism within eventology has been a contentious issue within philosophy and theology ever since the emergence of written language. It is also the core of the criticism that Baruch Spinoza aims at René Descartes' dualism during the Enlightenment – a criticism that anti-Cartesian eventologists such as Hegel and Nietzsche take most seriously when they, in the 19th century, build their considerably more mobile but equally monist worldviews in Spinoza's wake. To this we must add *the phallic exception*, which underpins the concept – *the sovereign* – that German philosopher Carl Schmitt develops in the early 20th century. The sovereign is simply the leader in political theology that displays such exceptional qualities, such a strong *khvarenah*, that he (or she) can lead the collective by virtue of the paradigmatic exception that dissolves all other laws. *The exceptional* thinks past and overrules *the general* through mustering an intense passion, according to Schmitt. Ultimately power is a question of the pathos of the exceptional defeating the logos of the general. It will be the chieftain with his exceptional will-to-transcendence, and not the priest with his general will-to-intelligence, who *de facto* leads the people with Messianic overtones in extraordinary times. But it naturally happens with the acceptance and pronounced support of the priest in a spirit of mutual admiration. Schmitt is of course himself such a priest in search of a sovereign to submit to.

Fantasy, innovation and creation *ex nihilo* can only be imagined within the shamanic caste in the fringes of the sociont. Inside the sociont's membrane one is only comfortable with what one recognizes from before, wherefore all events appear in the form of repetition and imitation, one mimics what has already been thought, said and done by others. Here it is not possible to speak of any eventological *actions,* only of nomadological *reactions,* this since one devotes oneself to reproduction after well known role-models, the sociont retells its own history of itself for itself. Consequently it is thus psychoanalysts such as Sigmund Freud and Carl Jung, and not clinically active psychologists, who put their patients, or rather analysands, on the divans of therapy salons to get them to focus on the ideas and obsessions that they try to liberate themselves from, to thus liberate undelivered creativity. With eventology specific *momenta* that radically change history once and for all, become conceivable and thus also possible. The body can now be complemented by technology, a civilization can start to grow and evolve. Later we can by all means start to be discontent in it, as Freud could remark, but that is another story (see *Digital Libido – Sex, Power and Violence in the Network Society*).

Eventology – the doctrine of the history-altering event – focuses on the history people create together, but basically takes technology as its point of departure. Because technology represents change proper, Man as a biological creature hardly changes at all. This in turn means that eventology comprises two epochal exodologies. The first, Zoroastrian exodology, speaks of the exodus from the genetic mutation that resulted in the species Man and his cyclical, horizontal life during nomadism via the memetic event and the development that followed upon this, something that first is observed and formulated by Zoroaster in Bronze Age Persia. The other, syntheist exodology, speaks of the exodus from the purely human via the mechanical progress to an existence that is qualitatively new thanks to technology. This concerns the transition it entails when the priestly *will-to-intelligence as logos* shifts from Man to Machine and only the royal *will-to-transcendence as pathos* remains to explore and express in Man himself. From this moment history is no longer just a drama where Man's two cerebral hemispheres, *logos* and *pathos*, strive to unite around a human *mythos*. The dimension that is added is a quest for The Machine's *logos* and Man's *pathos* to unite around a biotechnological mythos called *Syntheos* or *symbiotic transcendence*.

When Hegel distinguishes between the substance and the subject, he just repeats the distinction that Zoroaster makes as early as 3,500 years before between *Ahura* (being or the substance) and *Mazda* (mind or the subject). Thereby the dialectics of process and event encompasses both a universal dimension with Ahura as *substance-as-process* and a particular dimension with Mazda as *subject-as-event*. Zoroaster and Hegel are thus in complete agreement that religion must be described as a *Mazdayasna*, or the subject's worship of its own capacity as subject within the substance, instead of a grindingly empty *Ahurayasna* where, for instance, both the Buddha and Spinoza get stuck with nomadologies lacking decisive and defining events. While Kant is stuck somewhere in between as a hopelessly autistic agnostic. In retrospect we can in Zoroaster's and Hegel's spirit define *the sociontological subject* that during the course of history is developed as a series of paradigmatic events, namely as *the nationalist subject*, *the imperialist subject*, and last but not least *the cosmopolitanist subject*, where the last mentioned was always prepared and cultivated among the shamanoids themselves in the form of the phallic *Saoshyant*, particular precisely in his universality.

Eventology produces *the law* proper, the written-down legal framework that transcends the nomadological sociont and makes it possible to first build empires and later also nations – a process that is intimately entwined with the incremental breakthrough of written language (see *The Netocrats*). The nomadological habit as implicate order is transformed to the eventological law as explicate order. Please note that it is impossible to build greater social units than the clan and the tribe without access to the law. The cohesive social corset would not suffice, disloyalty and betrayal within the larger groups would not be possible to control, criminality would run rampant to the extent that the larger structures would collapse. With the genesis of the law the shaman is transformed to a priest, dons the robe supplied by the church and proclaims the law in connection with all the new temples that are built in the borderland between the socionts and that gradually become the hubs around which the first cities, in some sort of reasonable sense, arise. The largest temples with the greatest potential for exercise of power, provided with the clearest and most comprehensive law books, are built in the mountains that surround the plains that lie between the great rivers in Eurasia. We call the historiography that deals with this process *the genealogy of the ziggurats.* The cosmic mountain is, according to Mircea Eliade, the phallus between the rivers that unites the various river cultures under one and the same primordial father. One simply builds a religious corporation. Babylon is, for instance, regarded as the door to the gods and the covenant between heaven and earth. Babylon thus becomes the city as an event in itself.

The phallic and eventological worship of the law itself becomes most powerful within Judaism, which therefore also forms the perfect breeding ground for developing the first *nationalism.* The Jewish clergy are even a separate tribe within the nation, the Levites, who similarly to the shamanic caste must live furthest out on the tribal map, which explains why *outcasts* is the most common designation for the shamanoid personalities in American English. The Levites lack a territory of their own within the nation, and they consequently have priestly and thus also judicial claims on the entire territory. Unsurprisingly, Judaism in its capacity as *the judicial nation* is the most priestly of all the world religions. No Jew ever opposes the global rabbi, and thus neither the local matriarch.

The man in eventology becomes *the particular* in search of the universal, while the woman becomes *the universal* in search of the particular. The tension between these two poles endures despite, or rather precisely because there never arises any equilibrium between them. Philosopher and psychoanalyst Slavoj Žižek expresses this state of affairs in a Hegelian manner when he writes that phallus symbolizes *the exceptional*, while matrix symbolizes *the incomplete.* Matrix can be ubiquitous since it never is completed anyway. Phallus is *the extimate object*, at once intensely present and totally absent, that is: *the libidinal subject par excellence.* Matrix is the world in lack of phallus, and therefore always open and incomplete. Phallus can be ubiquitous since it never becomes consumed by matrix. Universality is thus always a universality without completion, a *work in progress*, a constantly ongoing project. Particularity in this context is always the libidinal and temporary deviation from universality, which enables universality, in a Hegelian sense, to even be possible. Matrix is apprehended as a membranic phenomenon, while phallus is apprehended as *the extramembranic project par excellence*. In light of this, our life becomes the impossible voyage from mamilla to phallus with the purpose of bypassing phallus and finally return to matrix and the eternal peace that awaits us there.

This paradox, this inaccessibility in the midst of an ocean of accessibility, is what makes all other accessibilities even possible, and it is called *the barred absolute*. The direct effect of the barred absolute is a constant reminder for Man of his own inadequacy and his own shortcomings. To live is to handle one's own inadequacy, to want to be whole, to constantly fail. Subjectivity in itself is precisely the experience of the subject's incompleteness. The heterosexual romantic relationship stages the barred absolute between man and woman, and it is the inaccessibility in the midst of this relationship that generates sexual attraction, a vain quest to reach all the way and calm the desire. One's own identity is enhanced and fortified in the presence of the other, this is what creates the allure, not the mere fact that the opposite sex is accessible. Keeping an attraction alive is not the easiest thing, which only too many can attest to – it is ultimately a question of one's own sexual identity continually being strengthened and not weakened over time. The man seeks the intimacy in the mamilla of the woman: the woman seeks the passion from the phallus of the man – and both seek in vain. Since none of them find what they seek, the search must constantly be repeated, again and again.

Homosexuality functions in the same way in as much as it mimics heterosexuality, with the difference that it shifts the mirroring in the other to one's own sex. Phallus and matrix respectively literally become present through their absence. Sexuality is androgynized. All this is possible since heterosexuality in itself is one long series of mimicry where every generation mimics the preceding one, which in turn has mimicked the preceding one, and so on *ad infinitum*, a series that loses itself in a haze where one can finally only imagine that the standards have been set by gods that one has been able to imitate. Since this obsessive mimicking is one-sided – one only mimics one's own role and the action that is scripted – it does not matter one bit whether there is any correspondence on the other side. Rather the greater the difference between the conceptions of what is going on, the stronger and more sturdy the attraction will be. It is the impossibility of the project that makes possible what, despite everything, is possible. The result of the mimicry is never the intended or sought-after. The man in vain seeks the sustainable intimacy, just as the woman in vain seeks the sustainable passion. But to live is to constantly seek an impossible completeness, to follow desire to the objective that looms on the horizon. Thus the mimicry must start all over again and continue, the process must be endlessly repeated.

The man seeks a union between logos and pathos in a mythos that never arrives. He remains divided. The woman lives in a mythos that she never succeeds in dividing between logos and pathos. She remains tied down. The man sees it as his role in the world of ideas to spread ideas around him as if they were sperms, as far and wide as humanly possible, while the woman sees it as natural to safeguard her ideas and protect them against undue intruders, as if they were brittle, rare and therefore precious eggs. The former approach is markedly eventological, while the latter is equally markedly nomadological. And never the twain shall meet! Which may be frustrating, while at the same time this happens to be a prerequisite for a continuous flow of energy. A religion can remain alive and kicking if it is allowed to remain open and accepting of impulses such as the muscular *dialectics of process and event.*

This does not mean that it is impossible to attain closure. Spinoza addresses that issue theologically through thinking his way past the barred absolute within Judaism and launching the concept *amor Dei intellectualis* as a response to classical antiquity's thoughts of three different kinds of love: *agape*, *eros* and *philia*. What Spinoza realizes is that it indeed is possible to circumvent the barred absolute but that, if so, it occurs at the expense of the passions that are connected with divine love, erotic love and brotherly love. *Amor Dei intellectualis* is God's dispassionate love for one's own intellect, and for Spinoza it appears the highest and deepest form of love that even is conceivable, which demolishes the classic hierarchy in which the three human loves are subsumed. There is a striking similarity here between Spinoza's insight and the internal Zurvanite religion of the Zoroastrian mobeds which we find in the Persian empires. Zurvan is of course time, which is the superordinate god to which all other gods relate as subordinates, completely indifferent to the humans of which Zurvan takes no notice whatsoever, which means that humans are completely left to their own devices.

These two phenomena, *amor Dei intellectualis* as a concept and Zurvanism as a movement, can only exist within the confines of eventological monotheism. Spinoza's ideas are simply incompatible with the nomadological iconologies. This also explains why chronotheist Zurvanism is and must be a strictly priestly monotheism. The other half of the patriarchy instead engages in a phallic iconology with gods as heroes. Within Zoroastrianism this phallic iconology is called *Mithraism*, and it is successfully exported both to the Roman empire in the West and to the Chinese and Indian empires in the East. This in turn explains why it is the sun-god that represents authentic monotheism, while the rain-god only appears as a complementing divinity of lower rank, or as a property of the sun-god. Zoroastrianism solves that issue with a monotheism with a two-headed phallus, *Ahura* and *Mazda*. Judaism solves it with a syncretization of various older religions by uniting the Egyptian sun-god *Adonai* and the Canaanite volcano-god *Yahweh*. Christianity for its part solves this issue through making the sun-god the father, the rain-god the son, and the matriarch the holy spirit within the Christian trinity. In Christian iconology the abstract concept of the holy spirit is then replaced by the concrete concept of God's sacred mother, the Virgin Mary, which facilitates the practical exercise of religion. Christ himself, who of course is something of a main character in this passion drama, becomes both *mythos* in the form of the child in the sacred mother's arms, and *logos* in the form of the rain-god abandoned by the sun-god, sacrificed and tormented on the cross over several days.

Judaism borrows the imperial division of Zoroastrianism for its own monotheism. *The Zadokites*, (named after Zadok, the first high priest in the Jewish temple) also called *the Sadducees*, apply a strict monist religion with existential freedom, ethical but amoral, without supernatural phenomena, and without any conceptions at all about some sort of life after death. Naturally such rigor and lack of illusions must lead to that they, much like the Zurvanites in Persia, constitute an internal religion for the priests themselves and a kind of spiritual upper class within Jewish society; what distinguishes them is the ability to handle the truth about existence behind the barred absolute. Pitted against the Zadokites are the *Pharisees,* who represent the people's and the army's Judaism with a tolerance for all possible kinds of supernatural phenomena, with conceptions of a doomsday and a life after death, and with a simple morality where good is pitted against evil. The Zadokites are cosmopolitans and known for introducing Hellenistic culture, that is: they constitute the interconnecting link between the Persians and the Greeks, to the Jewish culture. While the Pharisees, on the other hand, are isolationist and strict nationalist and will not tolerate any kind of Hellenism among the Jews. They protect their religion from alien contamination, as if it were a fragile egg.

Please note that it was the Zadokites and not the Pharisees who saw to it that Christ was executed. A Gnostic with a universal megalomania, who intended to rise up against both the Greeks and the Romans – Christ was raised by the Gnostic and dualist sect *the Essenites,* who by virtue of their ascetic lifestyle in the desert considered themselves spiritually superior to both the Zadokites and the Pharisees – was really no preacher that the Zadokites were the least bit interested in supporting or even tolerating. According to their cosmopolitanist attitude, Palestine's role as a nation within the Roman Empire was optimal and therefore nothing to make a fuss about. It was of course just as precious as the Jewish nation's previous role as a model nation within the Persian Empire during the construction of the second temple. Rather, the Zurvanite and Zadokite clergies united in the defense of cosmopolitanist monism against various Manichaean and Mazdakite Gnostics. They were quite simply prophetic in their comprehension of all these narcissistic pillar-saints and their supporting forces, they realized what a curse to humanity the Gnostics constituted. That is to say basically the same struggle between *anywheres* and *somewheres* that journalist David Goodhart sees us repeating during informationalism.

The sociont's inner circuit is the matriarchy. The matriarchy is polytheist and iconological, and thus constitutes what one might call *the left* of political theology. The outer circuit is the patriarchy, which is monotheist and eventological, which makes the patriarchy *the right* of political theology. The androgynous caste are the sociont's intermediaries. The shamanic caste populates the borderland between the tribes. Eventology is the sociont's memetic memory and corresponds to Taoism's *yang*, while nomadology is the sociont's genetic memory and corresponds to Taoism's *yin*. We see the same power triad recurring in all the religious and political myths that underpin stable societal formations. See for example the exodus from Egypt, which was led by three siblings: the priest Moses, the chieftain Aaron and the matriarch Miriam. Later in history we see the same structure underpinning the American Constitution with *the president* as the imaginary or pathical power as the chieftain, *congress* as the symbolic or logical power as the priest, and *the supreme court* as the real or mythical power as the matriarch.

Dialectics is always a game of three: in part the one, in part the other, and finally their incompatibility and the result of the process that this sparks. Sexual dialectics follows this pattern as well. The man allows himself to be duped by the male sexual delusion, which is manifested in that he seeks *sex-and-intimacy* in the woman. The woman on her part is dazzled by the female sexual delusion, which manifests itself in that she seeks *sex-and-passion* in the man. These illusory equations naturally do not add up, which of course is the whole point; the opposite and contradictory ambitions, constantly frustrating, are what drive sexual dialectics and the entire erotic desire machinery. To once again go out into the world and then return with the prosperity that is the fruits of the phallic achievements, the man requests sex-and-intimacy as healing and upload. For the woman sex-and-passion, aside from it literally being a download in the form of the mating, is moreover a way to ensure herself of the loyalty that guarantees that the phallic surplus is delivered to the matrichal base station where the download has taken place.

It is only within ritual settings – with the blessings of priests and matriarchs as guarantees that the entire economy of dependences is respected – that it is possible to loosen up this structure so that both the man and the woman without inhibition can enjoy sex-as-just-sex-and-nothing-else-but-sex. This can only happen in the tantric world behind the barred absolute, but not in the sutric world where the couple in question have their conjugal bedroom. It is a constantly repeated mistake to confuse sexuality with intimacy. Libido is cool and distanced, mortido is a warm engine that constantly is turned on. The problem with libido is that it constantly is tempted by the grass that looks greener on the other side, and as soon as libido shifts its attention elsewhere the attraction is quickly snuffed out in the ongoing relationship. Female sexuality reflects male sexuality. The woman on the one hand wants the man to penetrate into the inner circuit and conquer her, but on the other hand she absolutely does not want him to become a couch potato and settle down at home. No, back into the world he shall go and conquer it anew, to then bring his war booty to their common home where the woman eagerly awaits with the enthusiastically welcoming priest at her side.

The original sociont has no problem managing coagulating accumulations around the unifying object. The totem pole as phallus or mamilla maintains its function intact regardless of secondary corrosions. That is however dramatically changed when Man, thanks to written language and permanent settlements, starts to build larger and increasingly more complex social systems. The temporary ritual site is transformed into a permanent temple. The Mesopotamian *ziggurat* is built as an *axis mundi,* a link between heaven and earth, the vital connection between the spheres that the Babylonians call *duranki*. What is most important inside the ziggurat is an *imago mundi*, an image of the world as phallic order, as a *nomos*, instead of the world as a matrichal chaos; an image that is created directly on top of the temple's very cornerstone, that is: the temple's own root-of-the-phallus. Around this temple coagulate all manner of activities such as trade and various intrigues that include both friend and foe, family members and strangers. Soon enough a fortress is built around the temple, a bulwark that creates an inside and an outside of an arena where the social theater unfolds. The walls of the fortress are regarded as a membrane, and at the gates of the fortress membrane sentries are posted to check who is let in and what is pushed out. The sphere that now arises inside this permeable membrane is called *the city,* and out of this concept of the city the concept of citizenship is gradually developed, just as the passports and other documents that are connected to this judicial fiction that gradually attains an increasing importance.

As the urbanization process becomes increasingly complicated and information-heavy, this requires an increased intelligence. The growing need for intelligence begets a bureaucracy that produces laws, rules and document registration, et cetera, to protect the city both from external threats and internal dissolution, at the same time as it works, if possible, toward expanding the city's territorial claims. Thereby arises *a sphere of transcendence* inside *a membrane of intelligence* which is of course what constitutes civilization itself. But inside this outer system marked by *strategies* there also arise inner courts that are governed by *intrigue*. The outer circuit and the inner circuit from the nomadological sociont recur in an urbanized form. War, hunting, trade and strategies dominate the outside of the sphere. Peace, construction, enculturation and intrigue dominate the inside of the sphere.

From this fundamental architecture, development may take off in a variety of directions. One might imagine that the city considers itself able to manage the activities on its own, as its own sociont and establish itself as a city-state. One alternative is that the city assesses the prevailing power relations differently, and therefore creates alliances with other cities with similar language and culture in the surroundings, which eventually results in a nation. Yet another alternative is that the city expands further, forms a nation that conquers distant territories through colonization and thus builds an empire. The question of which of these alternatives is realized chiefly depends upon how far the sphere's transcendence dares to think itself, and how far the membrane's intelligence then stretches. And this in turn is only about information management, making and implementing functional and efficient laws, and not least bringing about a powerful technological progress.

The problem is however that every kind of permanent settlement leads to the social chase for status, and so the obsessive comparisons between both groups and dividual citizens explode. When inequality is sufficiently pronounced, it is apprehended as inherently natural, but the archetypal differences within the nomadic sociont that were recognized and unproblematic, acquire a completely different meaning in the fixed settlement where one becomes increasingly obsessed with comparing one outcome with another. Where one earlier balanced privileges with duties, one now focuses increasingly on the distribution of reward. Gradually the law receives another function, what previously had been an institutionalized care for the entire sociont's well-being as an organism is gradually changed to an instrument for the redistribution of wealth between different groups and dividual citizens.

This is a system that constantly works under great pressure from different interest groups, who attempt to manipulate it and create various loopholes as best they can. The holistic perspective is constantly subject to erosion from beneath, wherefore all empires and nations in history have the fall already written into their upward trajectory. The ascent is connected with the leveling distribution of resources to begin with being perceived as fair, which creates cohesion and energy. The law expands and society with it. The fall is connected with the same system and the fact that it has to devote an increasing amount of its energy to concealing that it actively encourages corruption, something that different groups, as well as single actors, resort to in order to manipulate the distribution to their own advantage. The mechanisms gradually become increasingly clumsy and counterproductive. Eventually it appears quite reasonable to generally demand and avail oneself of advantages from the system, without ever contributing in any way whatsoever.

Eventology is built on the phallic dialectics of the chieftain's pathos in the form of *will-to-transcendence* and the priest's logos in the form of *will-to-intelligence,* a process that is kept intact by a unifying mythos that speaks of the common primordial father as *The One* within eventological monotheism. This means that Zoroaster's eventological revolution in Bronze Age Persia – on the whole the most transformative and most pervasive revolution in the history of ideas – liberates phallus, which now can worship itself without matrix. This happens through the mutual admiration and respect that arises between the chieftain's will-to-transcendence and the priest's will-to-intelligence, something that appears as its own independent loop with the chieftain as Taoism's *yang* and the priest as Taoism's *yin*. In this manner eventology breaks with the Chinese and Indian obsessions with *the eternal recurrence of the same*. It is thus neither in China nor in India, but in Persia that linear time is invented and starts to function as a contrast to circular time. The underlying, circular time is degraded by the Persians to a lower iconological category. This occurs at the same time as circular time continues to dominate in Asia through Taoism in China and Buddhism in India.

It is in the Middle East, and only there, that eventology is developed. It arises, as mentioned before, first within Zoroastrianism as a parallel world alongside iconology, later within the Abrahamic religions with their stubborn attempts to disengage eventology from nomadology altogether, a project that was spurred on by *the Gnostic delusion* among the boy-pharaohs and pillar-saints that ensured themselves of considerable influence, a conception of pathos and logos respectively being able to operate completely disengaged from each other. This explains why the Gnostic delusion in the Middle East expresses itself in the form of the Gnostic religions – first Manichaeism and Mazdakism, thereafter in various simplified and popularized variants such as Christianity and Islam – doctrines that share the obsession of liberating the good and innocent soul from the evil and corrupt body. In China and India the Gnostic delusion expresses itself as the self-satisfied longing to step out of the circular time that is apprehended as reigning supreme overall. That is: one cultivates a feverish yearning for extinction (*moksha*), a revocation of the cursed reincarnation and of a life that entails nothing but painstaking endeavors and suffering. Unsurprisingly this movement is initiated during the Axial Age by an actor who began his path as a boy-pharaoh and ended up as a pillar-saint: Siddhartha Gautama. It is only under very special conditions that such a gentleman can appear exemplary.

The Zoroastrians furiously reject all attempts to convert their monism into a metaphysical dualism. In his classic text *Gathas*, Zoroaster himself firmly rejects all self-glorifying religious teachers who claim to stand outside and therefore also above civil society. A boy-pharaoh wants to govern the world in splendid isolation, as a chieftain without a priest by his side, and he therefore celebrates the body at the expense of the soul. The pillar-saint, on his part, wants to govern the world alone, as a priest without a chieftain at his side, and he therefore celebrates the soul at the expense of the body. Soon enough these fabricated conflicts are reduced to stereotypical battles between good and evil, where the boy-pharaoh's and the pillar-saint's respective favorite sides automatically get to represent good while the adversary becomes evil. Thereby existence is reduced to a Gnostic struggle between good and evil, almost as in a children's book, while society furiously speeds right into the apocalypse. Zoroaster therefore insists that existence is monist, that everything is dependent on everything else, and that visionary leadership must be built on well-considered collaboration and not on competition between the chieftain's will-to-transcendence and the priest's will-to-intelligence. God is by necessity both *Ahura* and *Mazda* at once. The role of religion is admittedly to first separate the soul from the body, but not in order to make them each other's ideological opposites but to thereafter reunite them in a new and innovative way.

We have on the one hand a sun year, on the other hand a moon year. These are not equally long, the difference between them is just over eleven days, which has caused problems for producers of calendars through the ages. After an *intercalative* process that is called *embolism*, the difference of eleven actual days is recalculated to five symbolic days (six days during a leap year), which are called the *epagomenal* (from a Greek word which means "added") days. These additional days in the calendar revolve around an object that is called *the epagomene,* and since phallus is the extramembranic epagomene, the sun year is transformed into the phallic, libidinal year that is connected to culture and daylight and that has the epagomene as a cohesive symbol, while the moon year becomes the matrichal, mortidinal year that is connected to nature and nocturnal darkness as the eternal recurrence of the same. The moon thereafter represents the eternal recurrence of the same without exception, a process with no event, while the sun year represents the eternal recurrence of the same with an exception, the *epagomene*, that is: as a process that leads to an altering event. Every religion is then largely characterized by how one chooses to handle these epagomenal days outside the regular cycle. Should one celebrate them, should one quite simply apply repression, or should one just plainly deny their existence?

The epagomene is an object that constantly reminds humanity that its phantasmic self-image does not hold together. Thus people either celebrate the epagomene with enthusiasm, for example in the form of the *Saturnalia* among the Romans or the *Nowruz* among the Persians, which most of all is a recurring strategy within successful imperial religions. An alternative solution is to repress the epagomene, which is what happens for instance in connection with Christianity's worship of the newborn savior. One does the same within Islam, where one steadily denies the sun year altogether, to instead hold onto the moon year, which is the ultimate cultural expression of a spasmodic clinging to mamilla and a refusal to leave mamilla for phallus. If we observe the tantric religions along the Silk Road, we see that *sutra* is the knowledge of all the other days of the year, while *tantra* is the knowledge of how the epagomenal surplus must be handled. If you choose to avoid tantra, the epagomenal forces in the form of sex and violence will haunt you and everything you do. These will afflict you with full force when you least wish so, something that lies completely outside your control. These are exactly the forces of nature within Man himself that religion is tasked with taming and handling.

This means that the authentic celebration of the new year – something that Christianity as well as Buddhism and Islam avoid, or for unclear reasons lack – is the tantric celebration of the epagomene as the eternal recurrence of the same with its wholly decisive difference, its excess, its surplus, its enabling of innovations affecting history forever. Moreover it is a fact that the rarer such an event is, the more information it contains. The amount of information thus objectively viewed determines an event's or a field's eventological value. This means that if one takes the epagomene seriously, one digs deep during a *Saturnalia* or a *Nowruz* that one celebrates precisely during the epagomenal days of the calendar. Above all this is the time of the year when the domesticated sexuality and the subdued violent behavior gets a controlled outlet and emerges into full daylight during a limited period. It is here and now that the new and the deviating are possible at all. Within the outer circuit this is expressed as the son having the possibility of developing his own personality, his own epagomenal expression, divorced from the father's. And with this, eventology becomes possible as a separate ideology, divorced from nomadology. Suddenly the idea of history being linear and irrevocable takes hold in the collective consciousness, in contrast to the deeply anchored, tribal conviction that time must be circular and that everything must be set in a constantly eternal rebirth. As *reincarnation*.

Reincarnation as the eternal recurrence of the same drives the fantasy of an exit, a kind of total and final breakdown for circular time, and this breakdown is called *ekpyrosis* in Greek. But behind every ekpyrosis the world is still reborn anew, as a kind of spiritual *big bounce*, which we in retrospect can define eventologically as *the ekpyrotic event*. Circular time within this analysis appears infinite and timeless behind the clearly limiting spacetime and is called *zurvan-akarana* in Persian. It is out of this eschatology that speaks of a world's demise and another world's birth within nomadology that we find the seed to what later in history shall manifest itself as eventological thinking. If worlds can die and be reborn as occurs within eschatology, events must also be able to occur along the linear time axis that alter history forever. It is, naturally, this conviction that lays the ground for *eventology*.

It is worth noting in this context that sutra and tantra run in parallel straight through both the original nomadology and the eventology that arises and joins later on. However, the barred absolute, which separates tantra from sutra, acquires completely different and largely complementing places along the time axis, that is: complementing to the extent one is capable of using both these perspectives simultaneously. Where tantra is continuous, sutra is discrete. Nomadology places the barred absolute at sexuality's temporal boundary, it materializes only after sexual reproduction has fully played its role. Eventology, on the other hand, places the barred absolute at sexuality's spatial boundary, it materializes only after the priest through a voluntary decision has chosen to refrain from taking part in the sexual rivalry, chosen to observe it from a distance and thereby has placed himself outside the entire ritual dance of mimicry and theatrical rivalry that characterizes phallic sexual energy. Thus it is the sexual exclusion that generates wisdom and power in the two judges that these processes generate, that is: the sacred alliance between *the nomadological matriarch* and *the eventological priest* that keeps the sociont stable.

Thus the public religion has created the terms that enable the original attentionalism. For who are this matriarch and this priest together, if not the *primordial audience* that can be found behind the barred absolute and before which people perform the entire social theater in the arena that exists in front of the barred absolute? No other attention is as sought-after. The matriarch with the matrichal gaze becomes the primordial mother who becomes the goddess. The priest with the phallic gaze becomes the primordial father who becomes the god. Together they bless and guarantee the social structure that they symbolize in the form of the most distinguished audience conceivable, concealed behind the barred absolute. They can be compared with the king and queen of later times that spread luster and glamour over the theatrical performance which they honor through attending in their special, royal box to which no one else has access.

Consequently the nomadological ambition for sutra will be to mimic and repeat what already is at hand with the greatest possible precision, while the eventological ambition for tantra will be to resemble the gods and goddesses that hide behind the barred absolute, to conduct an active search for genuine innovation. Sutra is craft and tradition built on imitation of selected paragons. Tantra is experiments and innovation built on a development of, and not seldom a break with the same tradition, where especially talented provocateurs are at the vanguard. Sutra is mythos in the form of the synthesis of logos and pathos. Tantra is the new pathos that ensues after the break-up from the old mythos. Sutra is the doctrine of the eternal recurrence of the same. Tantra is the doctrine of the existing possibility that a minimal deviation can lead to a genuine innovation that leads history onto a new trajectory, which propels it upward and forward.

Tolerance and diversity can – for better or worse – only arise in a society that harbors at least two different religions for different classes within one and the same intratribal hierarchy. Authentic monotheism is a phallic priestly religion, while authentic polytheism is a matrichal popular religion. Fundamentalism arises only when a group of Gnostics mimic the priests without any insight into the existing *root-of-the-phallus* and therefore undermine the hierarchy in itself. This leads to a society collapsing under the pressure from the false monotheism that preaches the god as a child and/or the child as a god in a world without nomadological hierarchies. The Gnostics seek immediate enlightenment and wisdom through effortless chatter. They incite a culture revolution. Youths reject or even literally beat their parents to death and the sociont crumbles. And the same thought recurs as the fundamentalist demand for an absolute dualism. The most devastating invective within Muslim culture is, for instance, *dahri* or *dahriyoon*, which precisely describes a human or a credo that refuses to accept that the creator and the creation are fundamentally separate. A faith in a world that creates and develops itself is the greatest blasphemy of all, according to Islamic dualism. Consequently *dahriyoon* is an invective that many monist Zoroastrians in the Middle East have had hurled at them from adamantly dualist Muslims.

What is central here is not whether monist existence in itself is material or spiritual, what is central is instead that monist existence consists of a single substance that assumes innumerable varieties of expressions. And to avoid a regression down to the Universe's first and smallest component before any big bang, a particle that comprises everything else that the Universe later expands into, one must distinguish between essential and non-essential expressions for the only substance. The most essential expressions are the emergences or singularities that generate their own vectors and establish their own ground rules, admittedly still interactively dependent upon, but still in significant respects detached from other and preceding emergence vectors. These emergence vectors thus constitute a kind of nature's own eternalizations on which the next level of mobilism can unfold, in accordance with the ground rules that we traditionally refer to as laws of nature and that with time become increasingly fixed. The emergence vector in the Universe that is closest at hand is physics. What precedes the Universe, potentially and historically, is another emergence vector that we call subphysics. Other parallel universes can exist independently of and in parallel with our universe – or dependent upon it through a shared subphysics – as their own emergence vectors. Starting from physics follow chemistry, biology, consciousness and culture; our universe in time produces a host of new emergence vectors. We thus defeat *reductionism* with *emergentism*. And the emergence vector theory in itself is the ontological *meta-emergence* within which all other ontic emergences are contained. We call this metaphysical system *transcendental emergentism*.

Transcendental emergentism is applicable within all spheres that Man perceives. So too in the information-technological paradigms that humanity goes through. The paradigms are in themselves a kind of historical emergence vector, where special laws and rules apply inside the membranes that the different information technologies constitute. Man is born adapted to the tribalism that is interconnected with the genesis of spoken language, which in turn is connected precisely with the species human, Homo sapiens sapiens. But for Man to be able to adapt and submit to a more complex and multifaceted social paradigm, a greater and more comprehensive narrative is required. When written language arises more or less at the same time in four different places, the dream also arises of a cohesive empire, by Zoroaster in Persia and by Akhnaten in Egypt. Now eventological monotheism appears as a religion dictated from above, as an assemblage consisting of the chieftain's and priest's two different mystery religions. Thus there arises an incessant conflict with the already established and underlying nomadological iconology that would plunge a complex social structure down into pure anarchy, if it were not for eventological monotheism acting as a balancing counterweight.

In order for a complex societal machinery to be able to function, there simply has to be a radical centrality. And only eventology can deliver this. Out of this empire – a conglomerate of different tribes – the idea of the culturally cohesive nation is born, an idea that we associate with Moses and the Jewish nation that gathered around their monotheism, which was borrowed from Egyptian Atenism and which also borrowed strong features from Zoroastrian Persia. But not as an imperial religion, but now as a national religion. The Hebrew alphabet and written language made this possible. While the imperial religions could only be spread and exercised via the court languages. The Jewish nation as a concept is completed many millennia later by Hegel in the early 19th century with the idea of the Germanic nation-state. Therefore the path to a functioning empire theory for the 21st century goes via a resumed reading of Hegel. Later in the same century his disciples Marx and Nietzsche launched their respective ideals in the form of *the proletarian* and *the Übermensch*. The project that remains to be realized is a union of both these dated ideals toward *the netocrat* of informationalism. Only when that project is brought to a successful conclusion, can the global empire become a reality.

5
The two-headed phallus and the dialectics of will-to-transcendence and will-to-intelligence

We always work on the basis of two time dimensions. On the one hand we have the priestly duration and subphysics, on the other hand we have the royal time and physics. Eventology is the dynamic interplay between them. Or if we start from Roman philosopher Seneca's idea that religion is what people believe to be true, what the wise know is false, and what the leaders find useful, nomadology is what people believe to be true, while eventology is what the priests and chieftains must agree on, after every paradigm shift, as the theoretical and practical implication respectively of the common worldview. Within the Zoroastrian tradition the priestly duration and subphysics has its own religion in the form of *Zurvanism*, and the same is true for the royal time and physics, whose religion is *Mithraism*. The starting point in the former case is our instinctive unwillingness to determine our own date of death in advance. The necessary submission occurs when Zurvan intervenes and kills the priest, as the formal opposite of when Mithras defeats and kills the bull. Zoroastrianism is then the aggregate nomadology that harbors both these phallic religions and arranges an encounter with the third, matrichal religion, which goes under the name of *communism* and which makes use of a polytheist *iconology*. The imperialist religion is only complete as three religions under one and the same umbrella, as three different metanarratives under one *narratology*.

Each of these different power centers within nomadology also has its own shadow. Every center, every religious story, does by virtue of this shadow represent its own expression of violence within the pathical narrative. *Open aggression*, which is represented by the chieftain, we call *violence of the first order. Virtual aggression,* which is represented by the priest, we call *violence of the second order.* And *passive aggression,* which is represented by the matriarch, we call *violence of the third order.* Together, layered on top of each other, these three different levels of violence constitute the basis for the exercise of power in any given society. In modern society it is the military that exercises violence of the first order, while it is the police that exercises violence of the second order. The judicial system – as a paradigmatic substitute for the original, pagan lynch mob – then exercises violence of the third order. In each of the three cases, just as is naturally the case for the aggregate, sanctioned exercise of violence, the state claims a monopoly on violence. This is how the state safeguards power over a society. At the same time it is the libidinal aggressiveness at the dividual citizen level that underpins necessary creativity. The chieftain is, for instance, ultimately a warrior who is, or at least is expected to be, prepared to sacrifice his own life (Zoroastrianism's *haurvatat*) for the sociont's survival (Zoroastrianism's *ameretat*). A situation where this comes to a head contains enormous amounts of open aggression. The chieftain as a warrior therefore personifies *nomadology at war.*

However the war comes and goes, and is periodically replaced by a more or less sustainable peace during which a society can build prosperity and prepare for an uncertain future. Then the chieftain's archetype is transformed from the warrior to the hunter, which thereby is the ideal for *nomadology at peace*. When Man later leaves nomadic life for permanent settlement, open aggression is reshaped, which means that the chieftain's archetype for *eventology at war* is transformed to the military as the ideal, while the chieftain's archetype for *eventology at peace* is transformed to the engineer as the ideal. What then happens when humanity gets used to permanent settlement, is that the same open aggression receives a new function and meaning in a new context; gradually the chieftain's archetype for *eventology at war* is transformed to the military as the ideal and for *eventology at peace* to the engineer as the ideal. Consequently the chieftain of the open aggression is eventually appointed king of the nation and emperor of the empire. It is the hero of open aggression who possesses the decisive leadership quality that sociologist Max Weber calls *charisma*.

The world consists namely of spheres – as German philosopher Peter Sloterdijk describes existence in his ambitious trilogy *Spheres* – and these spheres are delimited by *membranes*. Within and between the spheres there is an intense traffic of flows that are slowed down, controlled and channeled onward in accordance with the system's regulatory framework of membrane sentries. These memory functions of these membrane sentries are what underpin what we call *intelligence*, and we call the study of these functions *membranics*. Nourishment must be added and excrement must be displaced, so what is nourishment and what is excrement for the sphere in question? And how is such knowledge programmed or built up by evolution over time? When this vigorous intelligence then is accumulated to a certain critical level, *will-to-transcendence* is activated. This phenomenon, will-to-transcendence, must thereafter be channeled. Further, it is necessary to tame and nurture it, to cultivate will-to-transcendence until it is developed to some sort of territorial or ideological vector. Throughout history this has occurred in the form of various phallic projects, for instance hunting, war, trade and technological innovation. Will-to-transcendence, which is called *eros* among the ancient Greeks and *ahura* among the ancient Persians, is expressed as the pathical *truth-as-an-act*. It is summed up on the drawing board as *the vision*. In his classical treatise *The Art of War* Chinese military strategist Sun Tzu expresses this will-to-transcendence as the formal leadership for an army. Will-to-intelligence, what is called *thumos* among the ancient Greeks and *mazda* among the ancient Persians, is expressed as the logical *truth-as-a-fact*. It is summed up on the drawing board as *the strategy*. Sun Tzu quite simply sums up will-to-intelligence as the real leadership for an army. The relation between these two wills to power receives an elegant twist at the very event. Truth-as-an-act generates *the implicate self*, the subject that leads history up to the event. Truth-as-a-fact generates *the explicate ego*, the subject that ties history together and creates narratological continuity after the event.

According to an accepted and deeply rooted view in a Western discourse that prefers to gaze into its own Western navel, it is Greek philosopher Parmenides who first of all splits *The One* and distinguishes between being on the one hand, and thought on the other hand. Which is to distort history substantially. It is a delusion to think that it could be as simple as a diffusely defined Eastern discourse continuing to entertain a nomadological worldview, while an equally diffusely defined Western discourse would develop a new eventological worldview after Parmenides had arrived at his unique and revolutionary insight. What anyone who is broad-minded and unprejudiced instead can observe, is that this break-up occurs much earlier, in conjunction with the cultural settlement between the Persians and the Indians. It is Persian reformer Zoroaster who tidies up among the concepts and loosens the ties between the different phallic components in the Indo-Iranian triad – *trika* in Sanskrit – which was comprised of *iccha* for desire, *jnana* for knowledge and *kriya* for the act. The eventological remark Zoroaster makes is that desire in itself is an act in the form of a will-to-transcendence, in the same way as knowledge in itself is an act in the form of a will-to-intelligence. Thereby the concept of *kriya* is depleted of all real meaning and no longer fills any function within *trika*. Fundamentally everything in a Zoroastrian or Nietzschean worldview is permeated by a single will to activity – quite simply a will to power – what Zoroaster calls *asha vahishta*, which can be translated as *libido* in Latin.

With this maneuver, and the void that arises within *trika*, there is space for Zoroaster to develop a third position which causes the triad to stand strong. And this third position is death as the defining event that separates the perfect life, or *haurvatat,* from the life that transcends life itself, or *ameretat.* This most ultimate of all events Zoroaster terms *chinavat.* With this concept existence for the first time in history becomes mortal, and with this concept Man is removed from the eternal recurrence of the same, or *reincarnation.* When Siddhartha Gautama later develops *nirvana* as the desirable ideal within his persistently nomadological Buddhism, this is, in other words, nothing more nor less than an individualization of the tribal event that *chinavat* already is within eventological Zoroastrianism. The wheel is thereby invented once again, but is used in a different way. It is admittedly true that precisely you are extinguished at the moment of death, but the sociont, or *anjuman,* survives you. The Zoroastrian point is that it is your death that, *vis-à-vis* the *anjuman,* affords life both a purpose, a meaning, as well as hope. Death is quite simply *the event par excellence* in Zoroastrian eventology, the hub around which the entire existence revolves. An idea that is only fully developed in Western philosophy with Hegel and Nietzsche in 19th century Germany. Which is precisely what we mean when we say that narratology, with its logos and pathos, replaces the old mythos of reincarnation with the new mythos of the event.

What Buddhism can offer is one long struggle, replete with denial and deprivation, only to ultimately attain the extinction of the dividual subject as the most anti-climatic non-event conceivable, a quest whose only transcendental endpoint is that the Buddha himself, like a shaman who is long lost in the wilderness, finally must return to the sociont to proclaim his unique wisdom of denial and deprivation, since everything else would transform the entire project into one big pretentious ego-trip. In this manner Buddhism also receives a community. Zoroastrianism's cherished *anjuman* becomes Buddhism's cherished *sangha*. The difference is that the *anjuman* harbors an eventological culture built on a dialectics of negation and oscillation, while the *sangha* harbors a nomadological culture built solely on negation. It is perhaps not surprising that these two religions were able to live in peace as spiritual neighbours along the Asian trade routes and cross-fertilize each other. Tibetan Buddhism under the heading *vajrayana* is a perfect hybrid.

Zoroaster's reversal of the relation between the two wills has dramatic consequences. He places the *yang* and och *yin* of Taoism and the *Shiva* and *Shakti* of Hinduism furthest back in the theological sequence – where the sexual dichotomy reasonably belongs – subordinate to the sociont's overarching interests and not culled from the interests of the anjuman. This means that the prerequisites for the Hindu dance that is carried out by the god *Shiva* as consciousness and the goddess *Shakti* as energy, are not at hand. Instead it will be within Shiva himself that the first dichotomy arises, when the divine consciousness is split and becomes the two-headed phallus. Consciousness can only be manifested as the collaboration between priestly wisdom and royal energy. This lays the ground for the necessary phallic dichotomies, in part between intelligence and transcendence, in part – and later – between war and hunting. This in turn entails that female primordial power is manifested by the matriarch who organizes the sexual ritual, and not by the virgin who has been trained by the matriarch to become the chieftain's energetic mistress. Nomadological reincarnation is of course no longer included in the equation. Archetypology is subordinated to the event rather than to the process.

The matriarch is thus the mother who once bestowed life, who controls reproduction and who ultimately returns as the mortidinal mother who reclaims life. The matriarch is the judge, *chinavat*, and it is only after having obtained her approval that Shiva can have his Shakti as a reward for having killed the dragon. And precisely this is the whole point, since there neither exists a *chinavat*, a *haurvatat*, or even an ecstatic *ameretat* without the matriarch who in the guise of the mortidinal mother reclaims what in any case always had been on loan, since this of course actually is hers and the sociont's property. Thus *chinavat,* as well as the ensuing *polgazar* – becomes the ritual celebration of the memory of the dead person – exactly the events where an aged generation dies and makes room for a new, younger generation to which it passes the torch. This means that the actual power ultimately lies not with the two-headed phallus, but with fate itself, with the matriarch who constitutes the final institution before which war, hunting, and eventually life in its entirety is tried.

Then the question is: Who has the ultimate power over the ritual which marks that Shiva, in the capacity of the figure – phallus – that unites the king and the priest, finally will get to meet the energy-bestowing, virginal Shakti, as the matrix, if not *Zurvan*, the sexless primordial god, who of course *de facto* is time itself? It is hard to even conceive of anything more matrichal than this Zoroastrianism's genuinely fundamental construction. It is thus no coincidence that the massively erudite Nietzsche chooses the historical Zoroaster – the beginning and end of morality, according to Nietzsche himself in *Ecce Homo* – as the main character in his masterpiece *Thus Spoke Zarathustra.* He does this by accompanying the truth-seeking Zarathustra with *the camel* as logos, *the lion* as pathos, and *the child* as mythos. The camel personifies priestly will-to-intelligence, the lion personifies royal will-to-transcendence, while the child personifies matrichal *will-to-reproduction*. Please note that there never exists any possibility whatsoever of narratological release via logos or pathos but only via mythos. It is only via the child's innocent mimicry (*ameretat*) of the preceding generation's behavior (*haurvatat*) that a new narratology becomes possible.

This is because the child always tells its story as an attempt to copy the preceding story, what Nietzsche calls *the eternal recurrence of the same*, but with a minimal, decisive deviation. And it is thanks to this deviation, enabled by the impossibility of exact repetition – via for instance a new medial expression, as Marshall McLuhan remarks – that the event, according to Nietzsche, becomes possible in contrast to the otherwise monumental process. Hegel agrees as he also maintains that neither *logic* nor *emotion* can generate the releasing narratology, it can only be conveyed by *the spirit*, which produces a temporary release before the entire dialectics is repeated. In his constantly rewritten lifework *Science of Logic*, Hegel expresses this as the subject being a necessary surface *vis-à-vis* the substance that is a contingent depth, and then gives the relation between them the name *the throne of God*. The necessary surface is logos, the contingent depth is pathos, together they form the Hegelian two-headed phallus, and then rule the world from this throne of God, as history's own mythos. Where Hegel's (in)famous a*bsolute knowledge* is the insight that this always is and always has been the case, and that this paradoxical relation (see *The Global Empire*) never reaches any end. The narratology eventually becomes conscious of itself as narratology in itself, and this is the absolute knowledge.

The historical Zoroaster gives the two-headed phallus the name *Ahura Mazda* (or *Mazda Ahura,* depending on preference), where *Ahura* represents "being" and *Mazda* represents "mind" within *The One*. Process and event – the only meta-ideas worthy of the name – are united in one and the same theology. Ahura is the reification of the material world or *getig*. Mazda is the reification of the mental world or *menog*. Following this move Zoroaster creates the first philosophical religion without any supernatural elements whatsoever, by consciously choosing a ranking where Mazda precedes Ahura. He chooses what the anthropologist Erich Neumann calls *the higher phallus* or Mazda before *the lower phallus* or Ahura. There and then dialectics is born with the separation and merging of *getig* and *menog* as a continuous process, a becoming in being, in a joint world.

Mazdayasna means precisely "love of wisdom", the concept that the Greeks a millennium later translate to *philosophia*. Parmenides was thus not the first. The Greeks' greatest invention was rather the development of the matrichal *drama* as will-to-reproduction *vis-à-vis* the Persians' two-headed phallus.

This is a conscious choice for the Persians, a transcendental *truth-as-an-act* in itself. Man designates logos or the higher phallus as primary *vis-à-vis* pathos or the lower phallus. This constitutes the very definition of culture's victory over nature, even if culture naturally is directly connected with and dependent on nature (the Zoroastrian symbol for the cultural connection with history is called *barsom*). The Persians could also have chosen to follow the path of least resistance and just continued favoring nomadology at the expense of eventology; they could have continued being *ahurayasna* instead of *mazdayasna*, they could have made a permanent self-image that focused on the love of being rather than on the love of wisdom. They could have continued to dedicate their prayers to the Universe in itself, instead of developing the libidinal activity within this universe. But then no change would ever have occurred, something of that nature would not even have been conceivable, all of humanity would have remained in the nomadological primordial religion over an obscurely long period, and the project called civilization would have been postponed for a highly indeterminate future. The lower phallus would also in the future be the sole and one-headed phallus. *Shiva* as well as *Shakti* would remain as miserably lonely. But most important by far is that society now is led by the two-headed phallus. The alternative would be nomadological demise, at the same time as eventology is and remains an impossibility. Or as British general Charles Gordon so unerringly expresses the matter in his memoirs from the late 19th century: "The society that separates its scholars from its warriors will have its thinking done by cowards and its fighting done by fools".

Interestingly, Hinduism retained the nomadological orientation by continuing to preach reincarnation and the recurring separation of the rain-god Shiva from the sun-god Vishnu. Which can be compared with Italian Renaissance philosopher Niccolò Machiavelli's insightful recommendation for all the world's princes to always keep a naysaying *devil's advocate* at hand, armed with complete freedom *vis-à-vis* the prince's court with all its conflicts and intrigues. Shiva and Vishnu shall not just be kept separate – they are subjects to a myriad of their own archetypal cults within the colorful Hindu caste system – moreover they shall finally be united anew, but now as separate institutions. This is an expression of the principle of *the two-headed phallus par excellence.* It is not about avoiding the god or the prince becoming angry, it is about avoiding the god or the prince becoming stupid. Which is much worse, of course. At the same time as Zoroastrianism during the Axial Age developed via Gnostic mimicry into Christianity and Islam, Hinduism developed during the Axial Age via Gnostic mimicry into Buddhism and Jainism, the ingratiating and therefore popular religions of the pillar-saints, which in their orthodox forms tended to implode. This is the same Gnostic mistake that later is repeated within the political ideologies that propagate either just liberalism, or also just socialism, during industrialism.

Without the two-headed phallus *the barred absolute* disappears, and thereby the difference between the sacred and the profane also disappears. In such a society the priest is at best replaced by the Machine, which mass produces intelligence, but without any ability whatsoever to produce transcendence. What remains then is but a caustic soup of cynical nihilism. But what else could be expected? Intelligence without transcendence can of course never be anything over and above the mimicking craft. American philosopher Forrest Landry takes this necessity to a head in his work *Immanent Metaphysics.* His argument is brilliant in all its simplicity: Complexity cannot *per se* be handled with even more complexity. Believing such a thing is rather to repeat a mistake that constantly recurs throughout history.

Rather complexity is what will-to-intelligence handles on its own. Thus an ingenious simplicity, a decisive principle, *a decisive existential choice* rather than an expression of any free will, must break through the intelligence as a radical will-to-transcendence to thus enable the decentralized diversity that is necessary for humanity's and civilization's survival. Landry achieves this splitting of phallus through starting from matrix as a cultural rather than a natural phenomenon. The real hides in the culture that Landry calls *immanence*. The symbolic hides in the strategy that Landry calls *omniscience*. And the imaginary hides in the vision that Landry calls *transcendence*. Where no matter how much strategy, nothing can ever function unless there first is a single clear, cohesive vision that runs the entire process – the philosophical Messianic project *par excellence*. Landry even uses mathematical formulae to prove this in his work.

The exodological ground rule is that the pathical narrative must lead the logical narrative and not the other way around. Similarly, authentic art always requires a will-to-transcendence that is built on a foundation of optimal intelligence. Or to express the matter in a Zoroastrian manner: there is no Zoroaster without a Vishtaspa. Or to put it in Jewish terms: there is no Moses without an Aaron. The art that aims higher and deeper than something purely decorative, must take an eventological worldview as its point of departure and a conception of genuine change, transformation. Thereby the *museification* of late capitalist society should be regarded as a nostalgic retreat to the nomadological stage and thus also as a portent of *the death of Art*. The projectivity of Art is to constantly strive for and constantly fail in externalizing the unwieldy oscillation of existence, but not to museify the already fixed approximations. In authentic eventology the two heads of the phallus meet in mutual admiration behind the barred absolute. There and only there can Parmenides' cherished *The One* be found. Pathos and logos are united into mythos. If it is will-to-intelligence that freezes the world in order to be able to tame and comprehend it, it is will-to-transcendence that then sets the world in motion anew, in order to thus be able to widen it and conquer a piece of new territory.

Will-to-intelligence is called *the-root-of-the-phallus*, will-to-transcendence is called *the phallus*. These two wills meet and collaborate during war and during hunting. The pathical activism during war and hunting is synonymous with will-to-transcendence. The logical activism during war and hunting is synonymous with will-to-intelligence. The body and the mind interact with each other; the mind is also body – what else could it be? Another way of saying this is that biology and psychology interact intensely and intimately and ultimately are different aspects of the same thing. The purpose of all these processes is to produce optimal protection (war) and optimal provision (hunting). We call these phallic battlefields and trading posts *the outer circuit*. The outer circuit then generates *phallic membranics,* behind which the inner circuit arises. Here the objective and significance of transcendence, which constitutes the outer circuit's future beyond one's own death, is placed. The woman with the child, who survives the man; the man's heritage, protected and controlled by the matriarch, the inner circuit's undisputed leader. The borderland between the outer and inner circuits is called *sexuality*, an area that religion regulates through *the sexual ritual* as the reward that is granted after successful hunting, war and reproduction, about which the matriarch always has the final word. How could it be otherwise? The sociont's welfare stands and falls with protection and resources being delivered to her. Without that delivery, all dreams perish of any heritage whatsoever that can be passed on after a man's long life. This is the core of religion.

The warriors of the outer circuit (the Indian caste system's *kshatriya*) conquer and defend a territory on behalf of the entire inner circuit as *protection*. We call this *will-to-expansion,* something that at a later stage in history generates *urban industrialism*. The hunters of the outer circuit (the Indian caste system's *vaishya*) take down their prey and deliver this to the inner circuit as *provision*. We call this *will-to-accumulation*, something that later in history generates *rural agriculture*. When permanent settlement is established, society's warriors are tamed and re-schooled to the engineers that lead society's artisans and create civilization's infrastructure. As part of the same process society's hunters are tamed and re-schooled to the instructors that supervise society's agricultural laborers. None of this occurs without friction. The envy that arises toward what is perceived as undue privileges, results in a by-product by way of an attack on phallus as such in the form of ideologies critical of civilization, such as pacifism (directed against the warrior) and vegetarianism (directed against the hunter).

The problem is that every time anti-phallic ideologies of this kind take root throughout history, the outer circuit is drastically weakened. Under these new prerequisites the inner circuit can at an initial stage cash in a higher status and exercise greater influence, only to then discover that it is without protection against external attacks and that it is afflicted with an alarming resource shortage as a consequence of the outer circuit's sudden weakness. *The utopian project* sports a splendid, self-aggrandizing rhetoric but leaves the inner circuit without a necessary, protective membrane. The anarchic state that then arises is *the apocalypse,* a prelude that signals the onset of an empire's or a paradigm's collapse. The recently cheering inner circuit suddenly realizes that it is exposed to the uninhibited ravages of alien powers. During the apocalypse the primary line of defense is destroyed first, in the form of chieftains and priests. Thereafter the secondary line of defense is destroyed, consisting of warriors and hunters. What then remains is the third line of defense – ordinary men and women, defenseless against the rage of the gods, the forces of nature, and the hostile powers. The entire pathical energy is transformed from violence to a sexuality that rapidly is brutalized (see *Digital Libido – Sex, Power and Violence in the Network Society*).

For lack of battlefields and trading posts, libido's entire phallic energy is channeled through the sexual expression, which then is the only outlet that remains. It is above all this that characterizes the apocalyptic state: the phallic causality chain is broken. The first two stations – the battlefield and the trading post – are wiped out and sexuality, which has been moved furthest ahead, now becomes the objective and meaning of everything. A consequence of this is that the non-sexually mature children are sexualized, which is because the children no longer can/may spend their childish years of growing-up slowly learning to create an adult stance to mind and body, nor to war and hunting. Instead they are directly forced, wholly unprepared, into the complicated dichotomy between phallus and matrix. The shamanic activities that adults also carefully avoid taking part in without due preparation, suddenly become available to all, including the very young. Sex and drugs become hobbies that occupy children that are so small that they have attained neither the biological nor the psychological maturity that is necessary in order to be able to handle such forces. Which perhaps they may never be able to do. If phallus is abjectified and rejected, this is exactly what one can and should expect. Precisely everything falls prey to nihilistic hedonism. Which is the kiss of death for civilization's own libido, which in turn opens the door to a sphere entirely ruled by mortido. This is precisely how Friedrich Nietzsche imagines what he calls *the death of God*. In the attentionalist network society with its obsession with exhibitionism and voyeurism, we straightforwardly call this phenomenon *the absence of the phallic gaze* (see *Digital Libido – Sex, Power and Violence in the Network Society*).

Before the barred absolute the perspectives are rapidly diminished from the divine to the human (all too human). For lack of the rejected testosterone, what once was strategy slackens to instead appear as *intrigue*, and intrigue is driven by the banal *truth-as-gossip*. The ability for systematization that was favored before the apocalypse is now completely superseded, requested by no one, and replaced by a constant demand for empathy. Everyone feels sorry for themselves and insist on sympathy from the surrounding world. Everyone suffers from mental illness and wants attention both for this and for having the courage to publicly admit how they are suffering. The formal ambition is to break what is called "a culture of silence", which leads to no one being silent any longer, which in turn means that no one is listening since everyone is screaming at each other. One has to be empathetic with oneself, to the extent this is possible. What used to be visions for a future disappears with the phallic energy; what remains is pure survival and the marking of the same in the form of fashions, labels and various other banal status markers. This condition without phallic presence, drained of the substance of authentic truth, is what we call *decorationism* (exhaustively treated in *Digital Libido – Sex, Power and Violence in the Network Society*). And decorationism explodes precisely during the pre-apocalyptic state, when the *Saoshyant* is lacking the most.

The apparently paradoxical but fully logical consequence is that war, hunting and not least sex become the subject of general contempt. One loses all discernment and cannot separate the potentially destructive but in regulated forms nonetheless functioning sexuality, on the one hand, and the lamentable abuse on the other, rather one is mistaken for the other and soon enough they are treated as one and the same thing. Apparently this even becomes a position on which one can build an entire academic career. In the void that arises then, various expressions of decadence thrive, such as pacifism, vegetarianism and asexuality (which naturally is nothing other than an expression of a desperate denial). Such a state can only prevail over a limited period, namely until the pathos returns with full force in the form of *the real* and thus corrects people's sense of reality and reminds us that there actually is both an inner and an outer reality to relate to. Imaginary as well as symbolic fantasies will only take us thus far, sooner or later the proper work of relating to reality has to be undertaken anyway.

The two-headed phallus is built on *the dialectics of eternalism and mobilism* (see *The Global Empire*). But before we in this way split

Nietzsche's will-to-power into in part will-to-intelligence, and in part will-to-transcendence, it is necessary to first in the same manner expose his predecessor Kant's phenomenology. Because we do have a problem with Kantian phenomenology: it cannot be used as a universal model that applies for all relations between subject and object, where the subject always creates a phenomenon that starts from the relation to a noumenon that by definition is inaccessible. Several philosophers attack Kant precisely for this *correlationism* – for instance French syntheologist Quentin Meillassoux, who advocates a speculative realism in his work *Après La Finitude* from 2006. But it is hardly correlationism as such that is the problem here. What is problematic, however, is the lack of imagination that is expressed in the repeated quest to, at any cost, cling to Kantian phenomenology, as though it were universally valid for all subject/object-relations. Kant successfully negates the passive monism in Spinoza, but as with Taoism he eventually settles for a kind of mortidinal correlationism that does not harbor any explanation for the energy that monism actually develops.

So what then propels the relation between subject and object? And if indeed there is a drive beneath that relation, why would it, in that case, allow itself to be confined to Kant's metaphysical prison where everything is preordained? In that case it would not be of much value. And as so often, it is within sexuality we are shown how much the accepted dialectics underestimates the power in the dynamics that are at stake. When it comes to sexuality, and above all our Freudian relations to the three different sex organs, *matrix*, *mamilla* and *phallus* (see *Digital Libido – Sex, Power and Violence in the Network Society*), it is precisely the relation to these organs that is the noumenal and not the phenomenal. This means we must replace a Kantian phenomenology with an interactive *phenomenoumenology* in order to be able to detach ourselves from Kant and move on to Hegel, which is the same as detaching ourselves from passive dualism in order to transition to active monism, which entails a considerable leap in Western thinking. Consequently it is the matrix out of which we are born – and which a large part of us constantly longs back to – which is the noumenon, not the phenomenon; in the same way as it is the mamilla – that feeds us and which we suck with heart and soul from birth until *the phallic intrusion* – which is the noumenon and not the phenomenon, just as the phallus that robs us of the mamilla's illusorily promising security – only to eject us into a chaotic and contingent world through which we make our arduous journey toward adult maturity – which also is the noumenon and not the phenomenon. Kantian dualism is a dead end and the instinctual archetypology leads us out of it, since it does not provide us with any guidance regarding life's most intense moments.

A phenomenological reduction of these quantities to simply three banal sex organs is something that occurs later in life and which therefore is secondary in the phenomenology that thereby becomes inverted. This means that Kantian correlationism as such admittedly is correct, but if the very correlation shall be possible to take seriously we must reformulate the complex in the form of a relationalist phenomenoumenology. Here the logical phenomenology is the engine that powers the priestly will-to-intelligence, while the pathical *noumenology* is the engine that powers the royal will-to-transcendence. Together both these figures of thought constitute the foundations for an understanding of the world that lies beyond the Kantian reactionary worldview and that is aligned with the Zoroastrian actionary worldview. *The logical truth-as-a-fact* can be complemented with *the pathical truth-as-an-act* the very moment Kantian correlationism is completed by being transformed into an interactive phenomenoumenology.

If the phenomenal is a direct experience, and if the noumenal is an indirect and so to speak editorially processed experience, they are still only the explicate and implicate versions respectively of one and the same phenomenoumenological relation. The correlation must be operational and cannot be substantial, since it is only through the very operation that the unit in question receives its relationalist substance. This is exactly what Hegel emphatically maintains when he criticizes both Spinoza and Schelling for solely relying on *Verstand* (Hegel's expression for logos) but not, however, on *Vernunft* (Hegel's expression for pathos). It is thus the lack of *pathos* in both Spinoza and Schelling that causes the necessary shift from logos via pathos to mythos not to take place, nor being able to take place within the confines of their philosophical systems. They never succeed in scaling or circumventing the Platonist wall that Kant has built around his autistic worldview. Spinoza and Schelling simply do not understand the enormous power of sexuality. This is a mystery that is overlooked in silence. Instead these gentlemen stroll happy-go-luckily through life in a kind of romantic haze, hand-in-hand with the mother figure that never leaves their side. They rather absentmindedly and in a distanced manner observe various objects around them, objects that they are far too afraid of to engage with for real. A perverse stance is admittedly the best suited for the philosopher. But it is, *nota bene*, a stance that he or she has attained after having been engaged in sexuality and fully has understood the enormous power of the libido – definitely not by fearfully choosing to view the world through the presexual eyes of an inhibited teenager.

It is thus Hegel who launches *the two-headed phallus* in Western philosophy. This is the concept that Hegel calls *the divided One*. Will-to-intelligence is *the Hegelian subject* as *Verstand*, as logos, but will-to-transcendence is *the Hegelian project* as *Vernunft,* as pathos. Elsewhere the religious mythologies constantly return, before Christianity's division between on the one hand the father, and on the other hand the son, to the two twins that are born out of the original matrix. This is all about the phallic dialectics of the visionary chieftain with his *project* and the strategic priest with his *system* within the patriarchy. The project is carried out while affected systems are upheld. It is about the pathical myths of *the dragon* and *the tower*, with the dragon as a symbol of sexuality and the tower as a symbol of religion. The dragon must be defeated for the tower to be erected, and the tower is then adorned by the door to the barred absolute. Will-to-power rules within all of nature. It drives forth the twins' very existence. But will-to-power is split between will-to-transcendence and will-to-intelligence within culture. The chieftain and the priest together personify will-to-power, which the patriarchy have made sure to tame through the conversion from nature to culture. The chieftain personifies *the explicate phallus* through his physical presence, while the priest personifies *the implicate phallus* through his virtual potentiality.

Martin Heidegger identifies these two perspectives as *the ready-to-hand* and *the present-at-hand* in the object, and these stand in a dialectical relation to each other. Will-to-transcendence is to apply the present-at-hand to the ready-to-hand, precisely as the chieftain does in and through his activities. It is this application that is called *vision*. Will-to-intelligence is conversely to apply the ready-to-hand to the present-at-hand precisely as the priest does in his activities. It is this application that is called strategy. Will-to-transcendence is the eventological form of will-to-power (Taoism's *yang* and Zoroastrianism's *ahura*) that is exercised by the phallic chieftain; will-to-intelligence is the nomadological form of will-to-power (Taoism's *yin* and Zoroastrianism's *mazda*) that is exercised by the pseudo-androgynous priest. Will-to-transcendence is driven by libido as a protest against mortido – for libido is precisely the will that stubbornly attempts to transcend life itself, as a kind of life's overwhelming surplus. Mortido, however, expresses itself as will-to-intelligence through binding itself in a nomadological manner to life's circularity. But mortido's collection and processing of data would never occur if will-to-transcendence did not inspire and lead mortido in the Taoist tango they are dancing together. Or if we use the Hegelian conceptual apparatus: Libido is best described as a single isolated point called *the subject* in an ocean of mortido called *the substance*. It is thus the subject that is the event and the substance that is the process in Hegel, and the subject is always transcendental in the sense that it attempts to defeat and conquer the substance to avoid being drowned by it. This is will-to-power in its deepest and most dialectical form.

The priest represents the sun-god and being, and is called *Majestes*, while the chieftain represents the rain-god and becoming, and is called *Tremendum*. Majestes impresses through the accumulated knowledge, Tremendum impresses through the optimized capacity to act. Together Majestes as *logos* and Tremendum as *pathos* form the optimized will-to-power, whose *mythos* is called *Imperium*. The priest then has an advantage over the chieftain, which is that the priest can handle the hormonal shrinkage of the priestly strategy to *the matrichal intrigue*. No corresponding shrinkage of the royal vision exists. The vision is either libidinal and functioning, or else it is mortidinal, which leads to its collapse. However, the strategy can readily shrink to an intrigue – in principle this is the difference between injecting either testosterone or estrogen into the process – just as well as the intrigue can be widened to a strategy. Exactly this art of scaling is the central task of the priestly archetype. Classic stories by authors such as Shakespeare and Dostoevsky are largely built on those dynamics, and pronounced priestly figures such as Machiavelli and Richelieu have masterfully developed their ability to manipulate with the aid of these differences for the purpose of running a sophisticated power play. It is the priest and no one else who smoothly moves from the military battlefield to the royal court, and back again, by virtue of his shamanoid talent for crossing boundaries.

This has dramatic consequences for the large majority of men who are sociobiologically subordinate to the chieftain. They comprehend the vertical hierarchy which is a prerequisite for giving orders, and they comprehend the horizontal exercise of power that is a prerequisite for successfully executed teamwork. What they however do not understand at all is the feminine hierarchization that enables a diagonal contact and giving orders between different levels in the social rank, that is: from a given higher position without either a formal or informal responsibility for the lower position obliquely beneath. This is the blind spot for a large majority of men, quite simply because it is pointless during both war and hunting since unambiguousness and clarity is then of the greatest importance. However this is a hierarchy that exists in every nightclub queue and at the door to every VIP lounge in the world, and it is handled nonchalantly as a matter of course more or less solely by women with elevated status and by members of the boundary-crossing shamanic and androgynous castes. The condescending authoritarian gaze obliquely downward from above is, thus, the heterosexual man's blind spot in the urban, digital society, something that is exploited maximally by women *vis-à-vis* both men and other women in the form of various modern variants of classic *shit testing*: different kinds of gambits to put the other to the test through crassly assessing the reaction. It is the attention and sensitivity to all these minor, symbolic details that makes the outer circuit strongly dependent on the priest and his powerfully carried out will-to-intelligence. There is no *phallus* to access for the man or for anyone at all unless there is first a robustly anchored *root-of-the phallus*.

Please note that the sociont collapses the moment the priestly will-to-intelligence stands alone without the royal will-to-transcendence, and vice versa. The dynamics between the two of them are necessary for the sociont's survival and development. When for instance Iranian philosopher Reza Negarestani convincingly argues for a *philosophy that advocates intelligence* rather than a *philosophy that advocates mind* in light of Man's historic encounter with the Machine, he overlooks that intelligence without transcendence is lost in a kind of eternal Platonist sterile loop. His Swedish colleague Nick Bostrom makes the same Platonist error in his book *Superintelligence.* They arrive where they arrive because intelligence in itself neither has any will nor any movement. It is not heading anywhere at all. We are left powerless with a root-of-the-phallus without phallus, a logos without pathos, an engine without fuel, a kind of Kantian power without any

Hegelian movement, or for that matter any Nietzschean will. What we really need, to a greater extent than ever, is will-to-transcendence, this because history should not throw itself – and us – out and down into the abyss of crippling nihilism. What originally was the nomadological will to get up in the morning and journey on toward greener pastures on the horizon, is transformed during the development of civilization to the eventological will to move on to new, more creative and innovative platforms to henceforth operate from these. It is this force that is called *pathos,* and it is this symbol that is called *phallus.* Without these we are lost in an ocean of possibilities that cannot be valued or compared with each other.

The eventological knowledge transfer occurs via *the principle of mimesis with the phallic exception*, which is generally contained within the outer circuit. Everything is mimicry except *authentic novelty as an event.* The phallic exception recurs behind a concept that philosopher Carl Schmitt in the early 20th century terms *the sovereign.* Thus the sovereign is simply the leader in political theology who is so exceptional that he can lead by virtue of the exception that dissolves other laws. *The exceptional* thinks past and runs over *the general* with intense passion, according to Schmitt. Ultimately power is a question of *pathos* as the exceptional defeating *logos* as the general. It is the chieftain with his exceptional will-to-transcendence, and not the priest with his general will-to-intelligence, who achieves the phallic leadership that extraordinary times require. The priest personifies the library, the chieftain personifies the body mass and blood circulation. Together they represent the dynamic societal body. The priest is driven by a sense of *reality* and provides *legitimacy* to phallus as a representative of and expert on history. Will-to-intelligence starts from the-root-of-the-phallus and collates the profound history of the sociont in particular and humanity in general. The chieftain is driven by a sense of *life* and provides *justification* to phallus as a representative of and expert on the future. Will-to-transcendence starts from the utopian ideal and collates the long-term strategy for the sociont in particular and humanity in general. Will-to-intelligence is *the father* from history and will-to-transcendence is *the son* from the future; both meet in the present as *the holy spirit* and deliver the priestly vision, as the eventological architecture, and the royal vision, as the nomadological engineering science, to the matriarch, so that the sociont can be divinized in the form of the sacred family.

Please note that *forgiveness* as an ethical principle only occurs in eventological religions. Since nomadological religions only preach the eternal recurrence of the same, the act as such also recurs and can therefore only result in a pagan *karma*. You are sentenced for your actions, and punishment is meted out as in *Dante's Inferno*, forever. This explains why pagan lynch mobs constantly exact eternal punishment and endless compensation (for themselves) for alleged injustices. Eventology is of course revolutionary inasmuch as it enables a future that is more or less radically different from the past. Thus eventology permits one making mistakes as long as one learns something from these mistakes, so that the next time one carries out an act, one has modified one's course of action and hopes for a more favorable outcome. And should it once again become evident that one has made a mistake, it is important that it is another mistake and not the same, and then one has to return to the drawing board yet again. This is absolutely central to the transition from *nomadological moralism* to *eventological ethics*. One mistake is anything but an unreasonable consequence of new circumstances, not a sign of stupidity, which is why one simply just gets up and tries anew. This means that the nomadological fixation with *the act* is replaced by the eventological fixation with *the intention*. Thus the prerequisites disappear for every conception of *karma*, and also, as Zoroaster understands at an early stage, all need for reincarnation and resurrection from the dead as exits from the pagan, closed loop. After Zoroaster it is but the odd boy-pharaoh and pillar-saint who invokes nomadological moralism as a principle, in the form of shaming and accusing people of sin in order to compel them to submit to their infantile doctrines. The construction of civilization as such continues unabated, but with ethics proper and without banal moralism.

What the civilization process ultimately is about is how to continually transform what was yesterday's magic into tomorrow's technology. The creating god with his magic has to give way to the created god that comes with technology. What is fundamental is then precisely the principle of the great forgiveness – you make an attempt, and you make a new one, again and again, and as long as you make new attempts and learn from the mistakes you are doing the right thing. Which of course also applies to the development of religion itself (there are no religions, there is just religion as such, and religion must like everything else be paradigmatically adjusted and reformed). This is *phallic forgiveness*, one of eventology's most essential and most valuable contributions to humanity. And this forgiveness is both imperial and infinite when it arises from the priest's will-to-intelligence, since it then is the priest's forgiveness of the chieftain's incessant shortcomings. Which does not prevent that phallic forgiveness at the same time is national and finite when it arises out of the chieftain's will-to-transcendence, since it then becomes the chieftain's forgiveness of the priest's incessant shortcomings.

This is how one builds something enduring, and it is these theories and this activism of forgiveness that nationalists and imperialists alike devote so much effort to with the purpose of, in similarity with the alchemists, sifting out the exceptional gold that trumps the general, which customarily otherwise settles for clans, tribes and regional subcultures. Carl Schmitt is clear on the world being monist and not dualist, which means that *there cannot be any division between religion and politics.* Religion is political in the same way that politics is religious. All of this is included in the same memeplex. Schmitt uses the concept of political theology, and therein includes all of Man's thoughts and activities. This view is what we emphasize when we say that "everything is religion" (see *Syntheism – Creating God in the Internet Age*). Nonetheless, the history of ideas is one big graveyard filled with misdirected and false dualism, where the most striking example of all is the Western division between church and state, which arises in the 5th century AD. The explanation is a repeatedly unsuccessful mimicry of the first and inevitable duality, namely the organizational division between the chieftain on the one hand and the priest on the other, the construction that we call *the two-headed phallus*.

While the Zoroastrian Persians developed the two-headed phallus as the principle for the exercise of power, the Egyptians tried to dream themselves past the necessary division between an embodiment of in part body, in part mind in the Persian landscape of four twin rivers, of not just one but two Mesopotamias. Instead the Egyptians extended the monist autocracy in their *Monopotamia*, a project that was realized by the Atenists under the pharaoh Akhnaten in the 14th century BC. The result was pure hell. One placed all energy and all resources in Atenist Egypt on the pharaoh's own worship of the sun disc, while the subjects were ordered to worship their pharaoh as the only one with legitimacy to worship this worship-worthy sun disc. All other activities in Egyptian society ground to a halt. Neither defense nor food production functioned any longer. The connections with Nazi gas chambers and the Chinese culture revolution are evident. This is the authentic dictatorship under the false phallus, while of course phallic authenticity requires a two-headed phallus, a condition that quite simply is ignored. It is precisely through this stubborn avoidance of the phallus' necessary power-sharing that history fills up with boy-pharaohs and pillar-saints, figures that act predecessors to the pathetic individualists of late capitalism, narcissists and eventually autists, locked into their pompous, atomist fantasies of their own awesomeness.

The reasonable response to this Messiah complex pandemic is of course a resounding renaissance for the Nietzschean reading of Zoroaster and Heraclitus: "There is nothing less than two". Syntheistically we express this as though the only unit that is just one is the Universe itself, and its name is *Pantheos*. The concealed predecessor to the Universe, the empty virtuality without actuality, is called *Atheos* and it is Atheos who rules out that anything other than Pantheos can be less than two in number. Instead the inner god inside Pantheos, that is to say *Entheos*, is the god of multiplicity. And the first instance of Entheos is the two-headed phallus, where the one phallic head is the priest, who is anchored in Pantheos in the form of will-to-intelligence, while the other phallic head is the chieftain who is anchored in Syntheos in the form of will-to-transcendence. Entheos is thus the name of the place where the priest and the chieftain meet. The sociont and its history is the entire eventological movement that stretches from Atheos to Pantheos, and via Entheos further to Syntheos (see *Syntheism – Creating God in the Internet Age*).

If the woman lives on in the nomadological realm and furthermore represents biological reproduction, the man lives in the eventological realm and represents technological development. The woman bears the child, which is human nature, while the man builds the god which is human culture. This means that without the two-headed phallus humanity soon loses its way. Instead of complementing logical dualities, boy-pharaohs and pillar-saints start dividing existence into moral dualisms. When the sun is pitted against the rain, it is the rain that must be sacrificed, otherwise it is no longer possible for the hedonist boy-pharaoh to be eternalized in the sunlight. When the soul is pitted against the body, it is the body that must be sacrificed, otherwise the ascetic pillar-saint cannot pride himself with having liberated himself from the desires of the flesh. But these antagonisms are not genuine but just as falsely constructed as they are destructive. The combination of power and infantility requires that the fantasy about the child-god and/or god-child is maintained. And this is possible only if one ignores – or rather annihilates – the link between the child and the god, that is: the adult world in all its brutal monism.

Heidegger is fully aware of what order is at hand when he claims that *logos* must start from *pathos* in order to become the Nietzschean will-to-power. This also applies to the philosopher himself, since *philosophy is the translation of pathos to logos*, if we transfer Heidegger's priorities to our own vocabulary. But when Heidegger regards violence (that is *pathos*) as a necessary engine of living thought (that is *logos*), which is reasonable, Heidegger makes the mistake to try to read the nuances into the concept logos as a Greek logos à la Heraclitus, which he praises as commendably civilizational, and pits this against a Jewish logos à la the Gospel of John, which he rejects as primitive. It is actually within Heidegger's own protestant Christianity that logos and pathos are mixed up and become impossible to separate. They appear here either as submission *vis-à-vis* a logos without pathos within *Protestantism,* or else as submission *vis-à-vis* a pathos without logos within *fascism*. Unsurprisingly Heidegger joins the German Nazi Party, and thus willingly submits to an Adolf Hitler who of course is the boy-pharaoh *par excellence*, while it is protestant priests, for instance Dietrich Bonhoeffer, who actually sacrifice their own lives in protest against Hitler and the Nazi mass murders.

The dynamics between logos and pathos is complex – they act as two different components in a future *mythos*, something that both the Persians and the Jews as well as the pre-Socratic Greeks were fully aware of, before Plato began promoting the pillar-saint's delusory dream of a logos that precedes and is primary *vis-à-vis* pathos, that is: a mathematical universe of ideas of which our reality only is an imperfect copy. Out of this delusion follow Plato's political ideas of the philosopher as dictator. Without the phallic dialectics this is of course where the patriarchy must arrive, with the philosopher-king realized as Adolf Hitler. The priest may not become the chieftain and the chieftain may not become the priest. *Mazda* and *Ahura* must always be kept separate to be able to complement each other and keep each other in check. Or to view it from a different angle: the quality of the information that is conveyed upward in a hierarchy, and thereby also the quality of the basis for the decision-making that is at hand, drops dramatically when it is a dictator to whom one reports. A dictator lacks legitimacy and rather goes about strengthening his own position than the quality of decision-making in other respects. Bearers of bad news tend not to be so long-lived. The information flow is developed toward *convergence* and away from *divergence.*

In the world of bodies, it is will-to-transcendence that is the substance, while will-to-intelligence is the subjectivity, this is the case since it is subjectivity that rides the body mass as its substance. The first subject is always *the priest*, who stands alone in the wilderness and observes the world and the sociont at a distance. This is abundantly clear when Zoroaster in the capacity of priest and founder of religion is superordinate to the chieftain Vishtaspa within Zoroastrianism. This is also clear when Moses as priest and legislator is superordinate to Aaron as chieftain and warlord within Judaism. However, in the sensual world, these roles shift with will-to-intelligence as substance and will-to-transcendence as subjectivity, this since it is subjectivity that rides the sensual fantasy as its substance. In both these situations will-as-substance is much more powerful and comprehensive than subjectivity. The subject in this context, is only the less important rider who is located atop the enormous beast that is called will-to-power. Not infrequently, the explosive will-to-power dislodges the subject who sits anything but firmly in the saddle. Psychoanalyst Jacques Lacan calls this event *the intrusion of the real.* Libido is a force of nature, literally, which the subject in vain strives to harness.

In Lacan's own works it is Hegel who represents the priestly office as *knowledge* in the form of will-to-intelligence (truth-as-a-fact), while Marx represents the royal office as *truth* in the form of will-to-transcendence (truth-as-an-act). Lacan thus handles the pressure from the real with the aid of a symbolic order à la Hegel and an imaginary order à la Marx. The real remains seemingly tamed like a slumbering volcano until the next eruption no longer can be avoided. One can thus say that Lacan confirms Zoroaster's prophecy that the history of philosophy ultimately only can be understood as a love affair between these two phallic poles. What Lacan contributes is that the matrichal – or chaos – causally always precedes the phallic – or order. First there is the chaos goddess in the form of the real, blowing up Man's dreamy fantasies. Only thereafter can the priest with the aid of knowledge restore the symbolic order (Hegel) including anointing the chieftain, while the chieftain with the aid of truth can recreate the imaginary order (Marx). The priest and the chieftain at the apex of the Mithraic hierarchy must time after time slay the libidinal bull with joint efforts. The priest with the knowledge-based strategy and the chieftain with the truth-based vision. Where the matrix at hand moves from the old to the new paradigm, or from the old to the new territory.

The phallic dialectics of will-to-transcendence and will-to-intelligence is one axis in a diagram where the phenomenological dialectics of eternalism and mobilism constitutes the other axis. These wills must be seen in relation to the general drive system that Man is subject to. In the book *Digital Libido – Sex, Power and Violence in the Network Society* we give an account of four such drives. The first of these is *instinct*, which Man shares with animals and which we therefore also call *animalistic drive*. Instinct operates through direct contact with and within the body and in accordance with pre-learned or biologically programmed patterns. Thereafter comes pure *drive* in itself, which appears fixed and machine-like for Man and which therefore also is called *mechanical drive*. When Man seeks security and safety in the familiar, and stubbornly returns to the same repetitive compulsive behavior, it is pure drive that affects our senses and our decision-making. But also direct, insistent needs with an origin in the body such as hunger, thirst, weariness and sexual excitement belong to the domains of drive.

After pure drive there is *desire*, which is driven by language and by illusion, according to which what is named actually corresponds to what the drive system seeks; desire is therefore also called *human drive*. Since desire really only strives to remain active, its obscure objective constantly shifts and never allows itself to be conquered. That is: desire is doomed to always be disappointed even with its most successful conquests – the object never corresponds to the unreasonably lofty expectations – wherefore the search always must start anew, again and again, and continue forever. Eventually, when what is hopeless in the project becomes painfully evident, the drive arrives that tempts Man beyond life itself, a new phase in the quest for the new and higher, *transcendence*, or as it is also called: *sacral drive*. If desire is a byproduct of language and thinking, transcendence instead is a byproduct of culture and Man's interaction with his fellow humans, within and beyond the local sociont.

The libidinal will-to-transcendence and will-to-intelligence also have their mortidinal equivalents. Will-to-transcendence corresponds to the mortidinal *will-to-extinction*. Will-to-intelligence corresponds to the mortidinal *will-to-arrogance*. At the same time will-to-power in itself has a truly mortidinal engine that keeps the machinery running. It is, as Slavoj Žižek observes – with respect to Hegel's concept of *the night of the world* as the subject's foundation – the subject itself that is exactly the catastrophe that it deep down fears and that it does everything possible to try to avoid becoming. Will-to-transcendence and will-to-intelligence thus operate as a thin film atop a powerful mortidinal engine, which becomes obvious when these wills are threatened by corruption or manipulation from the surrounding world. This becomes particularly clear when we define these wills through *the phallic gaze*, which they by definition themselves comprise. The chieftain's phallic gaze is horizontal and internal. The priest's phallic gaze is vertical and external. This creates the internal dynamics where people see the chieftain, where the chieftain sees the priest, where the priest sees the people, and where the people's role is personified by the matriarch, who completes the nomadological power triad. Which is then connected to people mimicking the matriarch's gaze, in order to identify their desires with hers.

What is interesting is how the domestication of Man's animal nature in three steps under a priestly subjectivity that Zoroaster advocates, has such striking similarities with *the ethics of psychoanalysis* that Lacan constructs in the 20th century. Zoroaster begins with identifying a subjectivity in the imaginary that he calls *humata*. He then continues by identifying a subjectivity in the symbolic that he calls *hukhta*. And he completes the loop by identifying a subjectivity in the factual, mimicking activity that he calls *huvarshta*. You are *humata*, you are *hukhta* and you are *huvarshta*, and you cannot escape anywhere else – you are even in a Hegelian sense the conflict between the three steps, since your subjectivity identifies with all three steps at once as a loop – but you are forced to wholly and fully identify yourself with these experiences and activities. It is then and only then that you deserve to be called an *ashavan*, a retainer of truth. Then and only then do you deserve through your *navjote* to be a member of your *anjuman* – a state for which the correct contemplation, *tushna maiti*, is excellent support. Unsurprisingly these three ethical steps recur in tantric Buddhism, Zoroastrianism's sister religion. Within Dzogchen Buddhism *humata* corresponds to *dharmakaya*, *hukhta* corresponds to *sambhogakaya*, and *huvarshta* corresponds to *nirmanakaya*. It is then only logical that neither Zoroastrianism nor Buddhism contain any laws or moral rules that one must obey within the congregation – Zoroastrianism's *anjuman* or Buddhism's *sangha* – since an insight into what the connection between *humata*, *hukhta* and *huvarshta* actually means is all that is needed in order for one to be able to create a complete ethics. It is fully possible for *the local ashavan* to serve *the global Saoshyant* with a clean conscience, when or if he arrives.

The imaginary and the symbolic recur as a kind of Hegelian fantasies in Lacan, where the third step is *the real* that casts aside and crumbles these fantasies, as a much-needed break in the production of fantasies and symbols, something that throws Man back to the starting point of the loop called subjectivity. Fantasies are thereafter built anew, they comprise to a certain extent the insights that followed after the real's intrusion into the previous activity. But what then is *the real*? Well, it is absolutely not reality as such in any pre-Kantian sense, but the real must rather be understood as a radically effective reminder that there actually is an external reality beyond the representations on the whole, a reality that does not allow itself to be controlled by the dividual's or the sociont's increasingly self-absorbed fantasies about their own significance. This means that the real by no means needs to come from an external source, rather it is even more effective and more tumultuous if it is an internal phenomenon that the subject completely lacks control of. And Sigmund Freud had of course already solved that issue for Lacan. The subject is, as we know, not master in its own house and only controls part of its own activity. All that remains, the entire dark, unexplored continent that the subject has no insight into, is *the real par excellence*. The proper Freudian name for this phenomenon is *the subconscious*.

So how does Zoroaster's *huvarshta* relate to Lacan's *the real* and Freud's *the subconscious* if all three still refer to one and the same existentialist ethics? Here Belgian philosopher and mathematician Thomas Hamelryck is of great interest, since he tends to connect anthropologist René Girard's idea of universal mimicry and rivalry with both Buddhist tantra and Lacanian psychoanalysis. For Zoroaster *huvarshta* first and foremost is an act, the ultimate truth-as-an-act which it is possible to uncompromisingly identify oneself with (see *Syntheism – Creating God in the Internet Age*). You become what you do, the act tells the truth. And what you do further determines how you in the next step reflect on, or rather fantasize about the world, if we return to Lacan. Thus far Zoroaster and Lacan are in complete agreement.

However history does not end there. Girard argues that since Man's behavior to 99 per cent is about the mimicking of superordinate authorities and nothing else, identity can only be generated tribally and precisely through repeated mimicking. However, Girard admits that the mimicry is concealed to Man as precisely mimicry. Man experiences, as Zoroaster observes, his actions as original and thereby identity-generating. Which makes subjectivity one big existentialist hoax, since truth-as-an-act ultimately just is *mimicking-as-an-act*. And this is most clearly seen in that the dividual not just mimics the behaviors of others, but also fantasizes of the other's desire and then mimics the other's desire. This generates an intense rivalry over the same object of desire within the sociont, which leads to enormous tensions that sooner or later must have an outlet. And this outlet is the search for the *abject*, the arbitrarily selected scapegoat, whose elimination recreates the illusion of unity and collaboration within the sociont. At least until the entire process must be repeated again, which occurs time after time.

The problem here is that it is impossible for us to see this chain of events in ourselves. The difference between the original act and the act of mimicking is every human's blind spot. And it is this blind spot that, according to Hamelryck, is subjectivity in its purest form, precisely because it is the difference between the hoax called *consciousness* and the brutal and inconvenient truth about our non-existence as terrified and unimaginative automatoms in a herd that we are totally dependent on, even for the most simple needs that are connected with our survival, called *subconsciousness*. Only the god can carry out the genuinely original act, and only the priest can seem to be doing the same in the capacity of he who mimics the god himself, a god that fortunately is concealed to the rest of us behind the barred absolute. For all that the rest of us do is to mimic our leaders and role models, from the moment we are born until we die. Zoroaster's ethical imperative thereby becomes even stronger and more relevant: You are and can only be your actions, and your highly temporary fantasies of these actions' significance for history. The name for this ethical principle is the untranslatable *huvarshta*.

6
Boy-pharaohs, pillar-saints and the Gnostic delusion

As Eurasian civilization reaches a period, relatively speaking characterized by peace and growing prosperity, called *the Axial Age* – a concept which philosopher Karl Jaspers launches in the book *The Origin and Goal of History* (1949) – that is: from around 900 BC and onward, there is suddenly an abundance of philosophers, artists and founders of religion who have tired of waiting for the heavens to achieve a miracle, and instead seek and proclaim the fastest shortcuts to rewards of every conceivable kind. For those who listen, the distance shrinks drastically from the little boy filled with dreams, via priests and respected elders, parents and other adults, to God. Both *logos* and *pathos* cannot remain intact if we are to regard *mythos* as the deepest truth about existence and our conceptions of it.

Which brings us close to an ideal that hard-to-handle Enlightenment philosopher Jean-Jacques Rousseau formulates around the middle of the 18th century. The thought is as follows: nature is good and civilization is one big process of decay whereby Man and his existence are corrupted. Ever since the dawn of time – possibly with the one exception of the Christian savior's birth in the manger in the stables, meaning *the boy-pharaoh par excellence* has arrived – everything has just gone downhill. Which in turn means that the pristine and ignorant virgin by definition is preferable to any enlightened and (possibly) cynical life experience. What is practical here is that the person who is best suited to escort this beautiful and innocent mindset naturally must be just as touchingly innocent himself. And who might then be better suited for this, than the self-appointed *pillar-saint* who bears the name Jean-Jacques Rousseau?

Rousseau simply appears as the perfect adversary of the barred absolute and as the most eloquent propagandist for *innate wisdom* as an ideology. So why not simplify things by elevating the virginal child to an omnipotent decision-maker? Why not institutionalize a constantly ongoing cultural revolution while you're at it? And why not rewrite the history about the most elevated god, who henceforth acts as the virginal child? The problem is that this daring maneuver requires a revolutionary change of society's entire self-comprehension, given that one suddenly and forcefully separates religion from sexuality – two disciplines that during the nomadological period most definitely were one and the same thing. The small child may, as Sigmund Freud argues, be enveloped in sexuality, but this is nothing that it believes itself to master or know anything about. Gods do not have the least idea what virginity is; it is but a toy among countless others for them. The only common denominator that unites the child and the god is then the narcissism that excludes adult men and women who take social responsibility.

A society that excludes or marginalizes the adults, or even worse propels a collective infantilization, is a society colored by a comprehensive *internarcissism* (see *Syntheism – Creating God in the Internet Age*). The boy-pharaoh dreams of the uncompromising phallus without limitation. The pillar-saint on his part dreams of the uncompromising consciousness without limitation. The boy-pharaoh starts as the body that hates its soul. The pillar-saint starts in the opposite way as the soul that hates its body. But since it is the pillar-saint who just like the priest writes the narrative, Gnosticism always boils down to an idea of the perfect spirit that must liberate itself from the imperfect body, which is connected to the low drives and all manner of moral filth. That is: as a narrative which the boy-pharaoh mimics and quite simply steals from the pillar-saint in the form of a personification of the only remaining god as a human. But above all the boy-pharaoh and the pillar-saint cultivate envy toward, rather than admiration of, another man's body and/or soul. And in this hatred and contempt *vis-à-vis the other* within themselves, both of them are rapidly infantilized. The humor, that previously was seen as sacred within religion, is replaced by the programmatic *humorlessness* typical for dictatorships and their dogmatisms.

Prophets and tricksters are murdered before they have the opportunity to speak, and nor is truth the great transition's first victim, but it is free speech, which is abolished long before the question of what is true or not can even be posed. What is decisive is what is suitable. And with the disappearance of free speech *the barred absolute* too ceases to exist. Dictatorship and dogmatism want complete insight into, and thereby also control of the barred absolute, which therefore no longer can continue being barred and which therefore no longer can continue existing in any meaningful form. Truth in itself goes from being a *processuality* – truth must not only constantly be redefined via mutable paradigmatics, but that which truth deals with also constantly changes, since everything in existence is and remains impermanent processes – to being presumed *a fixation for all eternity* (naturally established by the Gnostic himself in accordance with his timeless and unrivaled *gnosis*). For the same reason humor – transparency's superior ideal – is rejected by Axial Age ideologues, who consequently celebrate anyone who, in the name of stability, exercises total control, while at the same time attacking and discrediting anyone who uses irony and exposes the public lie.

In this manner, as early as during the Axial Age, the attacks on the extremely functional *Silk Road triad* in the East (Persian *Zoroastrianism*, Indian *Buddhism* and Chinese *Taoism*) begins, although the triad handles the dialectics of nomadology and eventology with outstanding success. Instead the foundation is laid out for its radical opposite, which we can refer to as *the Disney World triad* – that is: the Jehovah's Witnesses, Mormonism and Scientology – which grows particularly popular in North America in the late 20th century, as it realizes the total commercialization and individualization of religion as a narcissistic sacrificial cult, without even a simulated connection to a genuine search for the objective and procedural truth about existence.

Hidden within this development lies what Swedish-American philosopher Benedict Beckeld refers to as *oikophobia*, the exoticization of the alien and near-unattainable ideal, ill-concealed beneath the contempt toward one's own home and/or one's own tribe. Oikophobia is thus a destructive luxury that humanity repeatedly is afflicted by when prosperity reaches the level where the sociont drags around boy-pharaohs and pillar-saints that it lacks enough sense to rid itself of. Like the grand old Zoroastrian high priest and master strategist Kartir icily remarks in the Sassanid Empire in the 3rd century AD: The culture that does not get rid of its self-appointed boy-pharaohs and pillar-saints will soon be dragged down into hell by these death worshippers, full of hatred toward their own sociont but prepared to give their all for another world that does not exist. Kartir's prophetic warning (then directed toward Persian Gnostics like Mani, and later Mazdak) greatly concerns the oikophobia of our age, the anti-phallic cultivation of a hatred toward one's own culture as the ultimate expression of decadence.

It makes perfect sense to speak of Gnosticism as a curse within political ideology. History demonstrates several examples of false phalluses, where Hitler and Stalin in this context appear as the 20th century's *boy-pharaohs par excellence.* Whenever reality departs from one's wishful thinking, it is reality that either must be remedied or repressed. What is primary is always to safeguard the dictator's narcissistic little ego that stumbles around in its own pathological darkness. This is the Gnostic delusion, which constantly haunts humanity and causes one catastrophe after another. The roots are to be sought within the Christianity and Islam that incinerate the barred absolute during the Axial Age. Fascism and communism were never anything other than vulgar and futile attempts to recreate Abrahamic heaven on Earth. And unfortunately the breakthrough of digital culture entails that Gnosticism returns. The world is once again thrust into a period filled with crazy cults and hysterical sects that thrive within growing, but essentially closed, filter bubbles. Astrology and similar superstition poisons the inner circuit, while sundry variants of paranoid conspiracy theories erode intelligence in the outer circuit. And what figures are those that appear in the vanguard of these cults and sects, if not boy-pharaohs and pillar-saints who believe themselves to be able to exorcise the world with what can only be described as voodoo?

The truth is of course that only a person who deep down accepts and genuinely loves both their body and what we call our soul can be true and authentic. At the leadership level there is always a need for both the chieftain and the priest, even if these two functions must be kept separate. This is Zoroastrianism's great and profound insight. The authentic duality generates *the dialectics of will-to-transcendence and will-to-intelligence* – the dynamic chieftain and the enlightened priest. At the same time as the Gnostic delusion generates the false dialectics of body and soul as the mortidinal *will-to-destruction*, the boyish longing for perfection, infinity and immortality. When the boundary-setting phallic gaze is lacking, this boyishness detests every form of antagonic challenge. The yearning for perfection, infinity and immortality is of course nothing other than infantile hatred that is directed toward all forms of developing obstacles. We get the boy with the mother, but without the father, a boy who therefore dreams completely unrealistic dreams of what it means to be a man, a boy who claims that he already is a man despite only being a boy, and who never has his megalomanic statements scrutinized. During the Axial Age this obsession explodes in the form of sundry sects and cults, built around various pillar-saints who in different ways regard themselves as dispatched by both higher and lower gods to bring justice on Earth.

The result was imbecile world religions that erased the powerful engineers of the Bronze Age from the history books in order to celebrate the Gnostic quackery of the Axial Age instead. The ideological minefield we have as a result has scarcely begun to clear yet, but a good start would be to once again bring attention to the real origins of Western culture in the Persian-Jewish axis and its applications of *empire* and *nation*. In this narrative there is namely no tolerance whatsoever for Gnostic fairytales and princelings. Problems do of course arise immediately in a society populated by people who are obsessed with mimicking each other, but where one has done away with everything by way of accumulated wisdom and even the insights that are part of the adult world. Here internarcissism is fortified as in a turbo engine when the various actors uncritically mimic each other in one large loop of collective, repetitive, obsessive, compulsive behavior. And the superego has never before enjoyed its bizarre ideological monopoly this much. For who aside from the superego is designed to play dictator when Man finds himself in a constant civil war with himself?

But how could the lazy wishful thinking that virginity equals wisdom result in anything else? The law that so far has operated with great success overreaches, and in its greedy eagerness it fails to comprise also what it lacks influence over. The rise of civilization is thereby followed – by virtue of the structural pattern that operates at the metalevel – by the fall of civilization. The history of ideas contains many examples of attempts to come to terms with this fateful dilemma: caste systems, reincarnation, myths of alternative worlds that exist in parallel with our own, astrology and conspiracy theories, as well as radically redistributed societal resources carried out through instruments of power. All of these are examples of more or less desperate attempts at handling the unrelentingly growing chasm that arises between the law as protection for equal opportunities and the law as a tool for actual leveling of the outcome in all sorts of processes.

The neurotic and ascetic pillar-saints soon find psychotic and hedonist boy-pharaohs, where the boy-pharaohs with great eagerness do everything they can to carry out the pillar-saints' fanatic visions of *the good society*. Two well-known examples are the self-appointed prophets and founders of religion Mani and Mazdak during the golden age of Zoroastrianism in the Persian Sassanid Empire, where Mani paves the way for the Gnostic sect that later is developed into Christianity, while Mazdak paves the way for the Gnostic sect that later is developed into Islam. And then it is of course only natural that these religions adopt all sorts of harrowing ideas, such as the priests being – and having to be – divinely perfect and inhumanly unassailable in every respect, and that salvation aims at making all believers godlike copies of these figures of light. In accordance with the prevailing logic the priests who cannot live up to these arbitrarily chosen and completely unrealistic ideals must be beset by Satanic temptations, wherefore they must be purged and executed by genuinely perfect pillar-saints. The next stage of the same reasoning arises during recurring cultural revolutions and involves the adherents of the movement, the faithful, who do not practice their submission with requisite perfection, having to be dishonored publicly and preferably also locked up in concentration camps. Or quite simply just be executed. This is the banal evil, or evil as a banal moralism that poisons the entire political discourse in society. More often than seldom maintained by an attack on humanity's very tribal foundations: child versus adult, woman versus man, dark-skinned versus light-skinned, et cetera.

In true Hegelian spirit eventology's arrival leads to a radical reassessment of the underlying nomadology before it becomes possible to maintain it in the form of an encapsulated embryo that constitutes a harbinger and predecessor. The Zoroastrians in antiquity's upland Persia stubbornly champion the thesis – this in contrast to Indian and Chinese lowland neighbors – that the ontoepistemological pair of opposites *wisdom* versus *energy* is more fundamental and illustrative than the sexual pair of opposites *yang* versus *yin*. First the external, contingent chaos must be arranged with the aid of fictive freezing before the internal, organized ritual can take place. *Yang* must in itself acquire two poles, the two poles that the Zoroastrians call *Ahura* and *Mazda*, before yang is ready to meet and interact with *yin*. This adjustment receives comprehensive, ideological, long-term consequences. It is the Persians who create the concept *empire via power-sharing,* while the Chinese in a Confucian manner to this day continue to build and fortify *empire via dictatorship*. The Taoists sexualize will-to-power in the field of tension between *yang* and *yin* as a cosmological principle, while the Zoroastrians instead prioritize *the two-headed phallus,* within which the royal will-to-transcendence is separated from the priestly will-to-intelligence through power in itself being ruled out without separation and collaboration. At the same time as both sexual and spiritual attraction are saved via separation, without having to sacrifice either the one or the other – a dualist competition between body and mind which the Zoroastrians refuse to support during the coming Axial Age.

The underlying circular time entails that the Persians are referred to a lower iconological category, at the same time as nomadology without eventology continues to dominate in the form of Taoism in China and as Buddhism in India, traditions which develop into Eastern Gnosticism during the following Axial Age. It is thus in the Middle East, and only in the Middle East, that eventology is developed, first within Zoroastrianism as a world in parallel with iconology, then within the Abrahamic religions with their stubborn attempts to disconnect eventology from nomadology, spurred on by *the Gnostic delusion* among the boy-pharaohs and the pillar-saints in accordance with which *pathos* and *logos* must operate disengaged from each other. As though the mythical narrative that keeps the sociont intact no longer would be required. This explains why the Gnostic delusion in the Middle East expresses itself in the form of the Gnostic religions – first as Manichaeism and Mazdakism, then in more easily digestible and popular variants as Christianity and Islam (with their obsession with liberating the good soul from the evil body), while the Gnostic delusion in China and India expresses itself as an equally self-righteous yearning to step off the supreme circular time altogether, that is: as an extinction (*moksha*), a cessation of the cursed reincarnation.

At any rate, this is a case of an individual revolt against the sociont and its phallic order, exactly the dissolution that Zoroaster cautions against in *Gathas* a millennium before the Axial Age. The shamanoid uprising against the tribal hierarchy within the tribe will in due time plunge the entire community into the abyss. The Gnostic project, that thus arises during the Axial Age, is the schizophrenic celebration of *either* asceticism *or* hedonism. Thus only *logos* or *pathos* in their absolute forms, as either pure body or pure soul, as separate spheres without any kind of connection with each other. This explains why *Gnostic dualism* is dualism *par excellence* – a kind of vulgarized eventology that imagines that it can liberate itself from nomadology through avoiding the fully developed sexuality that the adults share with the gods. The boy-pharaoh does of course hate all forms of *logos* since logos reveals his childishness. The pillar-saint does of course hate all forms of *pathos* since pathos reveals his childishness. If the two princes thereby both fear sexuality's enormous power *vis-à-vis* the woman as an idea, they are at the same time united ideologically in their hatred of the adult libido. While they have no problem whatsoever in turning sexuality into blind and unbridled violence if it were to serve their interests, wholly in accordance with *the principle of the pathical constant*, that is: the principle that says that violence and sexuality are given quantities (and communicating vessels) in all societies and only can diminish or increase in a direct, opposing relation to each other.

A pacifist society becomes oversexualized, in an asexual society violence is ramped up, and the only possible, long-term management of these forces is to strive for a pragmatic equilibrium for the pathical constant. The princes soon start to dream of separating the chieftain from the priest, so that the chieftain can be replaced by the boy-pharaoh while the priest is replaced by the pillar-saint. This however requires that both of them must avoid the adult and dialectical phallus, as well as all unpleasant exposure to an adult stance on the whole. And this happens through Gnostic dualism being realized in the opposite sex as well. Refusing to allow the two boys to grow up to adult men, entails that one also runs the woman within the same sphere through the desexualized log splitter that only offers two pure and polarized stereotypes, namely the mother and the little girl. When the wholly overarching objective is to repress unmanageable sexuality – which of course is connected with the hated adult world – one also moves the mother as well as the girl to a world of perfection, infinity and – above all – immortality.

The phallus that represents mortality, and all the projects one can and want to realize within the confines of this mortality, are ruthlessly assassinated, which means that the boy never ever needs to tear himself away from either the mother's warm and safely enfolding *matrix* or her nourishing and consoling *mamilla*. We must then at any cost avert the adultification and repress the frightening sexuality. The objective becomes to keep the mother *happy* where she floats around on an ocean of unconditional love instead of making her *satisfied* in a phallically sexualized world where desire constantly insists on her attention. Thus the little boy can undisturbedly continue fantasizing about eternally remaining the worshipped mother's *axis mundi* in a fairytale world where peace always prevails, where nothing ever changes, where nothing ends, where no single person ever becomes adult and therefore never can die. This through sexuality being killed when phallus is castrated.

In accordance with the principle of the pathical constant – which says that the aggregate amount of sex and violence in a society always is the same; the sex and violence that is not visible has always been swept under the rug and is hiding somewhere else – the fairytale of a peaceful and desexualized world must be defended with unrestrained violence. It is thus not a question of a conflict between the Apollonian hierarchy and the Dionysian swarm, the default narrative that Nietzsche constantly revisits, but what is at stake is instead *the Cybelian lynch mob* which now makes its entrance in history. This mob is named after the Greek goddess Cybele, who falls in love with her castrated grandson Attis, whereupon she is forced to roam the world with an army of embittered, sexless eunuchs in tow, as a kind of apocalyptic zombies of antiquity. The Cybelian lynch mob's arrival is quite simply the price we humans pay for long periods of peace, stability and growing surpluses. Sexuality and violence return with a vengence in increasingly perverted forms. What was once dominated by *mutual admiration* is now instead driven by *envy*.

What becomes primary for the Gnostic in this situation that has arisen, is then not *whether* he chooses *either* soul *or* body in the arranged conflict between these two quantities (where the former is purely imaginary, see *The Body Machines*), but instead whether he actually chooses *only* the one or the other of the alternatives that are presented. By making this choice and ruling out any dynamic coexistence, the prerequisites for the entire phallic dialectics are eliminated. This is *the Gnostic transfixation* – diversity must be swept away and replaced by narrow-mindedness. Which is what happens when one discards a functioning monism in favor of a thoroughly artificial dualism. The Gnostic wants to possess the mamilla at any cost, and if the Gnostic cannot do this, nor must anyone else. Thus the Gnostic worldview is dualist, divided. This regrettable division is the result of a *fall* that the world has gone through, a drastic process of decay where *The One* of the sociont is exchanged for a hopelessly antagonistic dichotomy. The only salvation a Gnostic sees for his part is to be absorbed into *gnosis*.

The necessary phallic division between on the one hand the priest's wisdom and on the other hand the chieftain's energy, does from a Gnostic perspective appear an unpleasant repetition of the trauma that the child's painful separation from mamilla entails. Therefore one has the two-headed phallus put to death in a blinded eagerness to be able to play alone, as a despotic pseudophallus with only a single head. What use are two heads when one's mother of course provides daily assurance that one already is perfect with just that one head? Then there is no reason for history to go through yet another nomadological repetition of the same; for it has of course already *de facto* attained its completion in that the Gnostic himself, who personifies the eternally immutable, has arrived in the world. Then there is no need for cumbersome power-sharing, the simplest pyramid-shaped power structure is perfectly sufficient. At the apex there is then either the perfect chieftain who has no need for a priest at his side but rules autocratically by virtue of an intoxicating *hedonism*, or else the perfect priest who has no need for a chieftain at his side but rules by virtue of what in its own way is an equally intoxicating *asceticism*.

In other words: we get either a boy-pharaoh or a pillar-saint who demands *submission*. The boy-pharaoh leads his subjects into a political dictatorship, while the pillar-saint leads his subjects into religious fanaticism. None of them allow any form of opposition or questioning. This authoritarianism can to begin with dazzle the audience by simulating phallic power, but soon enough it becomes clear that it is a case of a false phallus that never can generate both intelligence and transcendence at the same time. And thereby nor any phallic dialectics between them. This false phallus lacks either the power of *vision* or the incisiveness of *strategy*, which means that in practice it lacks both. The boy-pharaoh is a false chieftain since he in his infantility lacks the priest. The pillar-saint is a false priest since he in his infantility lacks the chieftain. However, what is lacking in the form of talent and genuine understanding of the historical situation, the false phallus replaces with an irrepressible narcissism. This compulsive egomania renders the false phallus unable to distinguish between war on the one hand and hunting on the other. This in turn makes both the boy-pharaoh and the pillar-saint useless as role-models. To mimic a false phallus can possibly favor one's own career for a warrior or a hunter, but then that is all. What remains to look forward to, besides various banal forms of architecture and an economy that is smashed to pieces, are meaningless bloodbaths and brutal inquisitions.

It is important in this context to understand that Buddhism, Taoism, Confucianism, Christianity and Platonism all are products of the Axial Age. In varying degrees they all elevate the pure woman, the innocent child and the Platonist philosopher-king. Which is the perfect recipe for a society that wants to remain in eternal childhood. When the authentic phallus is conspicuous by its absence, the arisen void is filled by a Gnostic who refuses to leave the presexual or asexual stage and is engaged in aggressive resistance against everything pertaining to adult sexuality. Under every such ideology *the Peter Pan syndrome* lies concealed, that is: the dream of being able to enjoy all of the advantages of phallus without for that matter having to worry about taking responsibility as an adult agent in the world and without accepting mutability, finitude and mortality. Buddhism strives in the same direction through despising libido and attempting to extinguish desire. The objective is therefore to break with nomadological circularity, and the figure who is designated by history for that feat is the pillar-saint who has elevated himself and has succeeded in duping sufficiently many others to retain his leading position.

Christianity essentially makes the same maneuver through propagating fear of sexuality and persistently trying to sweep sexuality's enormous power under all rugs in existence through celebrating the event when the religion's founder and chief commander dies on the cross for the sins of us all with his own virginity intact, which makes him the only scapegoat that we will ever have to sacrifice (which the Jews with unparalleled stubbornness of course refuse to accept, which means that nor do they receive any forgiveness and have consequently been forced to endure 2,000 years of Christian pogroms). Unsurprisingly, these joint fundamentals entail that the Gnostic religions can be exchanged for other, similar religions, with minimal alterations. Which is precisely what happens during late capitalism when Christianity takes up the fight with Buddhism for the position as the leading matrichal religion in East Asia, while Buddhism simultaneously has conquered traditionally Christian terrain in both Europe and the Americas. The seemingly different doctrines overlap and replace each other without anything fundamental essentially changing.

However the suppression of sexuality does not occur without consequences; the connection between pedophilia and Catholicism is reasonably not altogether random. A religion that worships the child as a God and celebrates its icon's innocent childishness – while simultaneously excluding the adult man and his sexuality from the community – cannot very well channel the sexual energy in any other way than to sexualize the worshipped child. The church literally becomes one big adult day care center where pacifism and vegetarianism become the new norms that clearly signal contempt for phallic warfare and hunting. He who like Friedrich Nietzsche seeks the origin of the death of God in culture, will reasonably start where God ceased being the most adult of all adults to instead become the most childish of all children – a train of thought that is brilliantly depicted in William Golding's classic novel *Lord of the Flies*. But for the presence of adults, the children's world would be anything but happy and playful, it is instead quickly developed into a burning inferno of confused evil. The similarities with both Muhammad's and Adolf Hitler's bloody crusades are striking. Any resistance is immediately met with icy excessive violence of near-pathetic dimensions, in exactly the same way as an offended child without any distance would react. During the Maoist Cultural Revolution in China it was even the adults themselves who became the victims of their own offended and insufficiently distanced children's bloody anger.

Taoism carries out the same phallus-avoiding maneuver through describing existence as a constantly ongoing dance between the poles phallus and matrix, but without saying a word about the troubling discordant exception that sexuality is, and that the priest in the capacity of he who separates phallus from matrix nevertheless represents. Sexuality is no game for the faint-hearted, and harmony in existence is a pious pipe dream without grounding in reality. Platonism refuses to recognize the two-headed phallus in any way whatsoever, and instead separates the mind from the body with the purpose of elevating the mind and powerfully degrading the body – something that all the world's Gnostic pillar-saints obviously love. At last they can regard themselves, in the capacity of asexual desperadoes, as more elevated beings than all the hunters and warriors that over millennia have been at the center of the religious rituals. Only a society that has attained considerable prosperity and long periods of peace can even start to cultivate that sort of infantile fantasies. These are fantasies that always strive to make the boy on the pillar the loftiest ideal, an actor who only produces texts about his own excellence but who neither manages the chieftain's nor the priest's toil in the patriarchy of the outer circuit. Confucianism is then nothing but the pragmatically required counterweight to Taoism in East Asian culture.

This of course does not entail that violence and war disappear. Not at all. However, it does mean that violence and war are placed outside religion and above all beneath religion. Soon the self-appointed saints occupy their respective pillars, spread out in the forests while dispatching armies at each other. Gnosticism thus receives its most powerful expression when Mazdakism – which the Zoroastrians did fight hard, with some success, in the Persian Sassanid Empire – returns in Arab form under the Islamic flag in the early 7th century. For what is Islam, if not pillar-saints spread out in deserts and mountain areas that bash soldiers on the head with decrees, in order to then send these soldiers against each other in one long *jihad*? Where the one remaining distinction between *Sunni* and *Shia* is that the former school requires that the soldiers shall understand the Quran in the same way as the boy-pharaoh from Mecca himself – where understanding is the warlord Muhammad's central contribution; this early predecessor of *Mao's Little Red Book* was namely written by Persian rather than Arab authors, for a largely illiterate Arab audience – while the latter school requires that the soldiers submit to the local pillar-saint's locally tinged and private interpretation of the Quran instead. The rest of the world has been lucky that it has proven impossible to unite Islam under a single papal pillar-saint. Allah must under such conditions appear a very domineering child. It is not as within Christianity, where God has gradually been reduced to a child, but in Islam God has never been anything but precisely a wayward child. However, because of Islam's great geographical dissemination and its built-in decentralization, it has proven very difficult to correctly interpret this child. So opinions differ. Thankfully.

The four religions from the Middle East must thus be understood in the following way: Since Zoroastrianism worships the military phallus, Islam can never be anything other than an *imitation of the worshiping of the military phallus.* And since Judaism worships the priestly phallus, Christianity can never be anything other than an *imitation of the worshiping of the priestly phallus.* If we agree this far, it appears only logical that Islam is founded by and constantly refers back to a military by the name of Muhammad, while Christianity is founded by and constantly refers back to a priest by the name of Peter. All this becomes possible through the Gnostic maneuver that consists of blowing up the door to the barred absolute in order to then tame the military's and the clergy's barred religions and convert these to factories for a simplified production of platitudes that appeal to the masses.

It is thus this tragic maneuver that must be reversed if the eventological Protopia shall be afforded a new possibility to establish itself. So then the question is: Where and when does the playground for Man's fantasy change and above all shrink? A clear departure occurs with the *desexualization* that is imposed upon Man when he becomes settled. The outer circuit within the sociont is pushed into the inner circuit. Logos, mythos and pathos are blended in a kind of tribal pressure cooker. Sex, violence and shamanic rites are stigmatized. Art loses its pathical strength, is infantilized, and reduced to *decorationism*. The phallic gaze is shifted from the primordial fathers, the chieftain and the priest, to the primordial mother, the matriarch and the child. And with this displacement, logos for lack of pathos wastes away and is replaced by a universal mythos, a pipe dream of eternal peace and eternal happiness, based on the infantile fantasy of the eternal child with a soul with some sort of separate existence *vis-à-vis* the hated body that is connected with adultification, violence and – not least – sexuality.

Logos is, as philosopher Karl Popper observes, the story of *the falsifiable*. That which is not falsifiable falls between mythos and pathos, but without for that matter belonging to logos. This explains why a logos without pathos, or a pathos without logos, leads straight to *the Gnostic delusion* of the child's impulsive fantasies being better suited to rule the world than the laboriously acquired life experiences of the adult. Gnosticism attempts to solve this dilemma through elevating *gnosis* to the highest ideal – that is: the Gnostic puts knowledge via direct experience before knowledge via indirect theory – as though the entire body/soul-problem quite simply can be conjured away through pure wishful thinking, and as though there were a higher, intuitive knowledge that is available only for a boy-pharaoh or a pillar-saint. It is this epistemological delusion that psychoanalyst Jacques Lacan rejects when he says that *there is no metalanguage*. And it is this idea that Hegel speaks sarcastically of in his portrait of what he calls *the beautiful soul* with all its pathetic pretensions. There is namely no knowledge above logos, let alone any higher knowledge that in some mysterious way would be directly accessible to certain spoiled narcissists. There are only pathical experiences and mythical stories as *horizontal parallaxes next to logos*. Which is clearly evident every time logos and pathos are to be united and communicated as an interacting whole; then *mythos* is the only functional alternative that is at hand.

Gnostic delusion is exactly this, a delusion that arises out of pure hubris. What we can play around with is our experiences, our more or less strong and accurate memories of these experiences, an *archetype* that experiences in part these experiences, in part these memories, via its own evolutionarily developed and adapted filters, a *membranics* within which the archetype in question acts, and a *paradigmatics* within which membranics operates. But there is no beautiful *gnosis* for any beautiful souls to attain other than the narratological triad logos-mythos-pathos. Believing something else signals human delusions of grandeur – the worst example of pathetic hubris in the history of civilization. The dualism that Gnosticism launches is thus nothing other than a symptom of the unprocessed trauma that arises at the separations from matrix and mamilla. But a reasonable response to these inevitable breakups is of course not to long back in order to undo them, but instead to affirm freedom via these fundamental separations in order to then be able to enter new, adult and forward-looking covenants – first between the chieftain and the priest, then between the warrior and the hunter, and last but not least between the man and the woman. It is thus and only thus that the sociont can be prepared for the authentic exodus.

Gnosticism is the infantile fantasy of being able to go from child to God without having to pass through adult life in general and sexuality in particular – an eternally frozen childhood with a shimmer of nostalgic magic about it. We call this state the *Peter Pan syndrome* in a contemporary context. This dream of perfection, infinity and immortality – and thereby also of immutability – is never dreamed by an adult male, but only by a little boy who frenetically clings to his childhood and refuses to grow up, and who therefore dreams of a life without the adult body with its demanding forces and equally demanding responsibility. Above all the separation between religion and sexuality leads to metaphysical dualism. Thanks to the genesis of written language, soul and body can be described in text and be perceived as two different and wholly irreconcilable substances that one without difficulties can delimit and treat separately. Which one moreover advantageously can and should pit against each other – as each other's opposites.

The soul and the asceticism, that one quite arbitrarily chooses to connect with this, is pitted against – and prioritized above – the body that one chooses to associate with vice and shameful pleasure. This at the same time as the body is prioritized above the soul and its asceticism. This logical somersault is what we call *Gnostic dualism*. This is the clearest example of what Lacan calls the enjoyment (French *jouissance*), in contrast to the pleasure (French *plaisir*), of the compulsion to repeat. A narrative about Man's place in existence that lacks a theory of sexuality's central role, entails a repression that leads to history's greatest catastrophes. There is thus a more or less pronounced wish to crush the world in the Gnostic's apocalyptic fantasies. Out of the ruins from the collapsing civilization the Gnostic himself then steps forward as *the highest spirit* who harnesses the world's threatening and amoral chaos with simple wizardry and cheap incantations. At last the hierarchy appears that places the self-aggrandizing pillar-saint at the apex of the sociont's power structure.

Please note the pillar-saint's close kinship with the classic tyrant in that he acts alone, without companions. The position atop the pillar harbors but one agent, and this must be the Gnostic himself in his capacity of the highest spirit. And as he is alone at the very top, the Gnostic is also solely the first and closest of all; he is first and closest to *the divine mamilla*, first and closest to perfection, first and closest to infinity, and first and closest to immortality. The latter is the most important of all. How would the world and humanity endure with their continued existence if the pillar-saint no longer was there and kept a watchful eye on everything? The problem in this context is just that the pillar-saint in his elevated superiority cannot do anything as vulgar as to procreate and thus bestow a necessary successor upon the helpless world. In the home-made mythology of the Gnostic himself, this existentialist contradiction leads to the Gnostic willingly allowing himself to be sacrificed as the sociont's cohesive scapegoat, this in exchange for the achieved status of sacrificial victim leading to the pillar-saint being elevated further to become the ultimate horizon for everything and everyone for all eternity. The Gnostic thus intoxicates himself on the thought of being transformed into *the personification of the event par excellence*. And that figure we all know from history as *the martyr*.

Whether this then is expressed as a meditation that dissolves reincarnation or as a crucifixion that terminates the lynch mobs' reign of terror, matters less. For the pillar-saint himself it is *martyrdom* that leads to immortality. It is thus and thus alone that a narcissist even can apprehend the Gnostic alternative. The Gnostic flees from the detestable death through leaving earthly life. Or rather: the Gnostic leaves a darkened world of *logos* in order to ascend to an enlightened world of *gnosis*. But what is actually happening is nothing but an unabashed rivalry for the attention of the mamilla and an intense mimicking of the priest's actions before the barred absolute. The pillar-saint is thus the perfect example of a figure who confuses his own barred subjectivity with the barred absolute in itself. And as such the pillar-saint is the Axial Age's tragic predecessor of capitalism's isolated Cartesian individual, with his desperate, narcissistic struggle with everything and everyone for the favor of a mamilla that never shows up. Which is exactly what Lacan describes as the incessant quest for *objet petit a*.

The consequence of this is that the battlefield is ejected from the ritual and is replaced by the childish fairytale. The priests cease to be voyeurs and instead become castrates. The mythologies devour the entire narratological horizon and *pacifism* becomes the new, false religion, which constantly, by pure necessity, must be excused for incessant outbreaks of violence, sex and ritual ecstasy. One can literally praise the Devil for the Abrahamic religions constantly considering themselves obliged to blame all manner of human behavior on the rebellious Satan. The correspondence within Cartesian dualism is of course the inner struggle between the superego and the subego, where the ascetic superego ultimately always is proven right, at the same time as the constant failure to actually satisfy this superego becomes the Cartesian enjoyment. Kantian individualism is the subject's enjoyment of submission *vis-à-vis* the eternally dissatisfied superego. This occurs at the same time as the Devil once again is consigned to the lower region that is the individual rather than to the social body in the form of *the id* (Sigmund Freud's concept). The Gnostic fantasy kills the libido that lives in the religious ritual. This is clear when the pornography and psychedelics which dominated the pagan ritual are ejected, abjectified and replaced by a sexless, castrated and empty liturgy that lacks a footing both in the physical body in particular and in the biological world in general.

The orgy is replaced by the perky sing-a-long. Ecstasy is replaced by the tinkering with the rosary. The children are admitted to the congregation and the adult experiment is thus replaced by the childish game. It is the child and not the adult who dreams of immortality. The boy's dreams are expressed (and considerable resources squandered) in the building of *the pyramid*, the very symbol of misguided manhood. The girl's dream is expressed in *reincarnation*, the subjectification of the eternal recurrence of the same, which is the symbol of misguided womanhood. Individualism's misguided history starts and ends with Gnosticism's dualist separation of soul and body, which is converted to the dividual's atomized separation from the sociont, which results in *the alienated individual*. Gnosticism offers no tools to handle the child's separation from mamilla. Therefore the child compulsively repeats this trauma through insisting on the separation between the soul and the body throughout life, throughout history, all the way into eternity. This allows itself to be done since a society that grows in size becomes increasingly complex and specialized, at the same time as the connection between the priest's wisdom and the chieftain's energy gradually disappears. Death as Man's ultimate horizon – as the negation or the non-event that precedes and enables the event; the old must die and disappear to be able to give way to the new – is tenaciously buried beneath massive amounts of pyramid concrete.

The false exodus, the dream of the return to mamilla, is constantly postponed to the next, and the next, and the next life. It is then no longer even a case of creating a purposive mythos, but it is about logos and pathos having lost their functions *vis-à-vis* each other and that the mythos that exodology requires has become an impossibility, as Freud strikingly describes the situation when he explains *why we are discontent in civilization* (see *Digital Libido – Sex, Power and Violence in the Network Society*). The Gnostics have kidnapped the event and disconnected it from the tribal process, something that has fateful consequences. The priest and the chieftain now become competing and infantilized poles instead of complementing, coordinating functions. The rift that arises eventually cuts through the human dividual as well. The ascetic superego terrorizes the hedonist self, which manifests itself in the form of various kinds of moralism, which can be directed toward how you express yourself or how you look. There arises a social insecurity that results in an overgrown flora of etiquette regulations. In step with increasing and denser population in the wake of urbanization, religion becomes increasingly vulgar and decays into cheap populism in the form of simple doctrines of salvation that hide behind banal propaganda promising easily acquired profits. The greater the mass to win over quickly, the more banal and the more mendacious the message. Superficial slogans replace a deeper analysis. Soon enough the political ideologies stroll down the same path. Where the priest (and wisdom) vanishes, the chieftain (and the energy) also soon disappears.

How then do we in retrospect understand the Axial Age's three dominating pillar-saints in light of the argument above? Siddhartha Gautama leads the Gnostic movement in South Asia. The Freudian self that is foisted upon the project to carry out its own extinction is nevertheless a self, even in the Buddha himself. For this reason Siddhartha Gautama separates the so-to-speak spiritual and mortidinal self from the bodily and libidinal self, which means that Buddhist dualism is in full swing. This is a case of a submission *vis-à-vis* nomadology that is called *samsara*, where the only possible exit is extinction, or *nirvana*, as a kind of pseudophallic protest against nomadology's eternal recurrence of the same. Or to express Buddhist transcendental desire in psychoanalytical form: If Man in his adultification process gets caught between love-hate to the mamilla that he must leave behind and love-hate to the phallus that he must attain, Siddhartha Gautama advocates a strategic retreat instead of the thrust that the Zoroastrians urge. The objective is to obliterate libidinous desire in itself.

Siddharta Gautama thus seeks a phase that lies before mamilla, while the Zoroastrians strive beyond phallus. What Siddhartha Gautama finds when he undertakes this retreat, is the matrix and the dissolution of the Universe, without any possibility for rebirth. Siddhartha Gautama calls this state *nirvana* in contrast to Hinduism's *moksha* in order to underline his conviction that he has attained the existential absolute. There is just one problem with the Buddhist fantasy, which also reveals its Gnostic blind spot, and it is that history moves forward and not backward – both as hypertemporal circularity and as spatiotemporal linearity. Mamilla and phallus quite simply have different roles during an adultification process and are not equivalent combatants. As the Zoroastrians observe in their criticism of Buddhism: The return to matrix awaits after the completed revolt against phallus, and not behind mamilla. It is called death or *chinavat*. However, prior to this event a new generation has been born in order to take over civilization (*ameretat*). Therefore the dividual subject actually can die for real and in peace and quiet after having had the good fortune to have lived a rich and full life (*haurvatat*), therefore even its day of death can over the proceeding 70 years be celebrated (*polgazar*). It is nature itself that rules out the Buddhist fantasy of the Gnostic extinction before the adult phallus appears and besets Siddhartha Gautama with the pathic desires and drives of war, hunting, and sexuality.

Plato stages the Gnostic project in the Greek world of thought. Christ borrows freely from the Zoroastrian religion east of his homeland of Palestine, but thanks to Paul's Platonist and Augustine's Manichean circumlocution of the Christian religion, Christianity also gets caught as in a vice in the Gnostic delusion. The journey from Christmas as an event with the child Jesus in the manger, to Easter as an event with the scapegoat Christ on the cross, is a completely desexualized and thereby strictly mythical narrative, where the self-appointed savior never leaves the sacred mother's magic mamilla. It is anything but surprising that Rousseau's bitterness toward the absent, phallic gaze emanates from a post-Christian, individualist culture. And if there is any detail that Nietzsche overlooks when he proclaims *the death of God* in 19th-century Germany, it is that Western culture rather suffers from precisely *the absence of the phallic gaze*, an absence that generates exactly the *ressentiment vis-à-vis* existence that Nietzsche saw it as his task to fight. The greatest and proudest achievements of Western culture occur in spite of Christianity, not thanks to it. It is only after a millennium of compact Christian darkness that the Western world establishes its two other, far more important, and also highly Jewish religions, namely *nationalism* and *capitalism*.

All these three Gnostic movements perform the same loop of thinking, making the escape from the phallic power's requirement of a sexualized adulthood their highest priority. Public self-mortification, naive pacifism, pretentious vegetarianism, and all manner of other spiritual self-absorption are allowed to dominate the agenda.

Everything else is said to exude "toxic masculinity". Buddhism's variant is to celebrate the Gnostic distancing of the clever princeling from the adult phallus' every temptation, giving him a gold medal from the matriarch for indefatigably meditating himself to death and obliteration. It is however merely a matter of shifting from a yearning forward (to phallus) to a yearning backward (to matrix). Requiring the extinction of desire is unfortunately a desire as well – as Hegel and Lacan would quickly remark – but a desire that is directed away from the future demands of existence, back to the total permissiveness of non-existence. Christianity conducts the corresponding maneuver by crucifying the clever princeling before he has time to get a taste for the adult phallus's every temptation, awarding him a gold medal from the matriarch (literally the sacred mother in this case) for sacrificing himself and embracing his own death. That his divine father compensates his masochistic act with resurrection to a suprasensible illusory existence should in this context be regarded as rather scant consolation for he who has learnt to appreciate phallic temptations.

Authentic dialectics, which is expressed in adult leadership and adult sexuality, is replaced by the false dialectics that revolves around the Gnostic delusion of perfection, infinity and immortality. If one stubbornly refuses to grow up, there is of course only one way out, and that is to deny the phallic libido and instead devotedly worship matrichal mortido. This is exactly what all of history's boy-pharaohs and pillar-saints are obsessed with doing. Desperately they seek the approval of the matrichal gaze through demonstrating false surpluses. This is what we call *the Gnostic delusion*: the stubborn boy's dream that through the spirit's victory over the body he can sneak past adulthood's finitude and be transformed into a god of perfection, infinity and immortality. It is when this Oedipus complex in reverse is set in motion, when this fear of phallus profoundly takes root, that the boy-pharaoh proclaims *a pathos free from logos* and the pillar-saint preaches *a logos free from pathos*, which become *the totalitarian mythos* that we have learnt to recognize as the boy-pharaoh's fundamentalist dictatorship or the pillar-saint's fundamentalist dogmatics – a massive, infantile foolishness without any phallic dynamics directed forward. The sociont halts, with avarice as sole fuel, and slowly but surely starves to death.

This means that the authentic dialectics between will-to-transcendence and will-to-intelligence, and thereby also the authentic dialectics between eventology and nomadology, in greater spheres and populations is replaced by a series of false dialectics that all are subsumed under the heading the Gnostic delusion. False dialectics is generated and maintained by a collective depression, which in turn is caused by mortido swooping in and filling ever more numerous and ever greater voids in the wake of the absent libido. This expresses itself as *false mimicry* of the handling of authentic dualities. Populations greater than clans or tribes are replete with this false dialectics, which under the boy-pharaoh in the guise of the lone pseudo-chieftain or the pillar-saint in the guise of the lone pseudo-priest leads to *totalitarianism* as the internarcissistic response to *mimetic depression*. This is what occurs with such frightening clarity when the empire or the nation cannot live up to the guarantees of safety, security and proximity that the clan or the tribe promises in accordance with our sociobiological preprogramming. Anarchy must always be avoided at any cost.

The boy-pharaoh capitalizes on unreleased sociontology, the pillar-saint does the same with unreleased nomadology. The result is *the eventology of the false phallus,* implemented as fanatical *fundamentalism*. And then the question is how this narrative manifests itself in a population that is continuously forced to handle the dialectics of libido and mortido. The answer is, as so much else, twofold: either the mimicry in itself leads to *libidinal mimicking of desire,* which means that desire within the population is synchronized and homogenized, which in turn gives rise to rivalry and envy, destructive forces that only can be diverted with the aid of *the scapegoat mechanism,* as René

Girard convincingly demonstrates. Thus the Cybelian lynch mob in this scenario must find a scapegoat that is forced to bear all the shortcomings and setbacks of the masses, and it is the narrative of this exceptionally popular diversionary maneuver that we call *mimetic fundamentalism.* It is, in all its simplicity, as seductive as it is functional; the mob cleanses itself through carrying out the liberating lynching. Thereby fundamentalism receives its distinct character of desperate compensation behavior. God himself is absent. The divine can therefore only take shape as a figure that steps out of the Cybelian lynch mob and who himself personifies and justifies the lynch mob's murder of the scapegoat, a figure that we call *the anoject.* Mimetic fundamentalism is in this manner embodied and proclaimed by the personified anoject, *the tyrant.*

Alternatively the mimicry in itself leads to *the mortidinal mimicking of the depression* within the populace, which generates a growing existential void that only can be diverted through collective suicide. The lynch mob then does not find a scapegoat on whom it can impose all the shortcomings and setbacks of the masses, which means that the narrative of this tragic diversionary maneuver constitutes *depressive fundamentalism.* Even this is, in all its simplicity, as seductive as it is functional; even in this scenario the mob cleanses itself, now through carrying out the collective suicide, which also gives fundamentalism a distinct character of desperate compensation behavior. The divine can only take shape as an anojective figure who steps out of the Cybelian lynch mob and himself personifies and justifies the collective suicide. Mimetic depression is therefore embodied by *the leader of the sect,* who with the approval of the masses leads *the cult of doom.*

The Dionysian swarm is led by the libidinal *hyperject*, the authentic phallus, while the Cybelian lynch mob is conversely led by the mortidinal *anoject*, the false phallus. And the mortidinal lynch mob – which is obsessed by isolation, dystopianism and self-abjectification – turns on itself in its frustration and unformulated yearning for liberation. That is: If for instance the Nazis do not succeed in exterminating the Jews, they must eventually take their own lives instead. The self-appointed leadership turns away in disgust from its populace and soon there are echoes of gunshots from the bunker below. For lack of a scapegoat, mimetic desire is transformed into mimetic depression. And it is of course this threat scenario in the form of collective self-annihilation in *the collective subconscious* that drives the mimetic lynch mob toward finding the innocent scapegoat at any cost, which can make it possible to convert the Cybelian mortido to the Dionysian libido through lynching and executing the more or less arbitrarily chosen victim, in order to then return to circular nomadology as pagans always have done. This return to *business as usual* often occurs, as demonstrated by Girard, with the addition that one, cynically, elevates the scapegoat one recently has killed to a *martyr*, who through his conversion is promoted to a saint or possibly even a lesser god. This is how it always has been: the living can use the already dead any which way for any dubious purposes whatsoever.

A pathos without logos always becomes a false mythos. A logos without a pathos also only becomes a false mythos. Only as collaboration can logos and pathos be realized and developed into a spiritual leadership that saves the sociont from demise. *The-shadow-of-the-phallus* is thus the threat of the undeveloped phallus. If phallus is not developed into the dynamic collaboration between the chieftain's pathical will-to-transcendence and the priest's logical will-to-intelligence that produces *the narrative of the authentic phallus* – the sociont's story of its protopian future – phallus will wither away to two dried-up embryos whose lack of sex drive is compensated for by delusions of grandeur. The chieftain is never developed into a chieftain without the priest's admiration, but instead gets stuck halfway through as a *boy-pharaoh* – a masculine pathos without logos – and the priest is never developed into a priest without the chieftain's admiration, but instead gets stuck halfway through as a *pillar-saint* – a masculine logos without pathos. It is like only possessing a single cerebral hemisphere, without even being able to question the bizarre aspect of the situation that has arisen. This is the false phallus that strives for dictatorship and dogmatism and that lands in tyranny and idiocy.

In this sensitive situation there is nothing to prevent the single dividual from taking over the entire field on his own, but the consequences will become catastrophic. For the dictator hates to hear that he lacks one of his eyes and thereby also one of his cerebral hemispheres. There is no receptivity for criticism or opposition in any form, wherefore the boy-pharaoh requires unconditional capitulation before political fundamentalism, just as the pillar-saint requires unconditional capitulation before religious fundamentalism. God loses one of his eyes when the false phallus is charmed by and chases after total power through the monopoly of the single eye on the *panopticon* of the phallic gaze. Polytheist iconology solves this dilemma by making the sun-god an older god than the complementing rain-god, and through compelling the sun-god to sacrifice an eye in exchange for phallic wisdom. The sacrificed eye is the self-castration that both gives the sun-god priestly wisdom (the father's *logos*) and at the same time leaves the void that enables the rain-god to take over the role as the virile chieftain (the son's *pathos*) with two intact eyes. What then is wholly aligned with this phallic self-castration is that the matriarch is an older woman who long ago has left the struggle for male attention that unfolds during the sexual ritual, and who precisely therefore possesses total credibility as the ultimate institution of wisdom. No one gets past the matriarch's unveiling gaze.

It is always the sociont's and not the dividual person's survival that is central. At least as long as the golden Bronze Age's ideal applies, before philosophers during the decadent Axial Age start to proclaim ideas of the individual's freedom *vis-à-vis* the sociont, ideas that confuse and distort the external separation between the dividual and his heritage, with the internal separation between the eternal soul and the finite body at the moment of death. This theological mistake is the ultimate price that Man pays for the delusions that permanent settlement creates in the nomadological mind. If it is not I that move me and my body from point A to point B during war or hunting (spurred on by sexuality), but my ideas that move from my present life beyond this life to the next life (with the exception of sexuality), then it follows that I am my ideas only, or my body only, and not an embodied archetype in service of the sociont. The boy-tyrant's three false phallic dreams can be summed up as religious fundamentalism, political fundamentalism and technological fundamentalism. The authentic phallic dream can only arise when an ideologically reasonable foundation and a functioning technology actually exist, something that the adult, phallic man is totally clear about. Before these prerequisites are at hand, infantile dreaming is only hubristic and literally life-threatening.

This means that Plato, despite all his other qualities, is the philosophical boy-tyrant *par excellence.* In *Phaidon* he stubbornly champions the thesis that the soul not only is separated from the body, but that it also is eternal, indestructible and superior to the body in all conceivable aspects. Plato's *philosopher-king* is the ancient Greek version of the ancient Egyptian boy-pharaoh, and since the philosopher-king neither is adult nor has understood the value of the collaboration between mind and body, he never becomes anything other than a tyrannical pillar-saint. Neurotic dictatorship always ends up in a *mythos* that mendaciously celebrates the only leader – the false phallus – as though logos or pathos alone would be able to defeat everything. The curse of dictatorship is that it cannot create anything new, it can only mimic and mimic the mimicry of the old or the alien until everything in the system stops and dies of an acute lack of oxygen. The explanation for this is that the very basic prerequisite for dictatorship is that the dictatorship by definition is the best of all worlds, a kind of nursery fantasy of perfection, infinity and immortality. Thereby nothing can be improved or rejuvenated. No really revolutionary impulses from the outside are capable of piercing through the armor. Thinking is afflicted by the anxious groveling's sclerosis. Dictatorship incessantly ends up in the hypocritical celebration of a tired and fat leader who opens a factory with clearly established objectives for mass production of nuts and bolts. This is simply a Stalinist mythos that tries to be logos so hard that it bores everyone to death.

What we are witnessing is the Platonist madness in the demands from the boy-pharaoh and the pillar-saint that *if everyone just performs what I spontaneously wish, then everything will be perfect.* In conjunction with the arrival of informationalism this ideological tradition is forcefully dominated by the Rousseauian ideological legacy (for an exhaustive account, see *Digital Libido – Sex, Power and Violence in the Network Society*). In part this is because the great thinkers from the Enlightenment and Romanticism have fallen into oblivion (it is tedious to open and read thick books when one feels obliged to devote entire days to surfing, scrolling and conjuring), in part because of the new communication technologies promising milk and honey to everything and everyone who just opens a social media account. Everyone requires attention but few are prepared to really listen. The result that we all can observe is *the golden age of internarcissism*, and all of this can only end in dismay when no one has the strength to look at or listen to any other loudmouth than themselves any longer. The underlying cause of this massive intellectual breakdown is that the Western left abandoned Marx in favor of Rousseau in the 1970s, when it turned out that the Western worker had scant interest in any form of socialist or communist revolution. At the same time there emerged a Rousseauian right that also was quick to assume the sacrificial role and that also tried to shriek themselves to attention.

It is, to take a significant example, precisely anti-Marxist embitterment that powers the entire text in Ernesto Laclau and Chantal Mouffe's Rousseauian manifesto *Hégémonie et stratégie socialiste* from 1985, the book that later kick-starts the entire movement that is called *intersectionalism*. The underlying driving force is of course the surgical and medical interventions that make it possible to actually reset and reshape the entire population in accordance with the wishes of the Rousseauian lords-of-the-flies. It is then part and parcel of the matter that any black transsexual person whomsoever is preferable to a white heterosexual worker as a figurehead for the intersectionalist cult. It is a case of a cult that for understandable reasons – Rousseau was a hard-to-beat mass producer of fancy self-contradictions – both worships the being that its adherents claim that they have been accorded by fate without mercy (in other words, defending a caste system), and the becoming that they at the same time equally firmly aspire to, and that they must be accorded at someone else's expense (in other words, promoting a class society). It means that all of existence and history in retrospect must be adapted in part to what the narcissist experiences as necessary and given, in part to what is said to be freely chosen. Of course, the audience do not have – that is: "the perpetrator" within the home-made sacrificial cult – any right whatsoever to a will of their own, or any possibility at all to refrain from the imposed spectacle. Now is the time to bring social justice through whining and rancorous, theatrical diatribes in the media.

The foundation for Laclau and Mouffe's digital sacrificial cult was laid as early as a couple of decades before in the form of Herbert Marcuse's influential essay *Repressive Tolerance* (1965). Marcuse argues that since all resistance to the good cause is driven by the false consciousness, an ideologically conditioned misconception of the state of affairs, there is no reason whatsoever to leave any room for deviating points of view. Marcuse thus does not proclaim any exodology, has no idea that a new society is to be created by new masters after a resolute exodus from the old paradigm. No, the resistance against the good cause shall be confronted with blind and ruthless violence, so that the new paradigm can be established on the old territory that now is ravaged and liberated from every form of resistance. When the pillar-saint Marcuse gets into his stride, the absurd irony of the title emerges. Repression in itself is of course completely intolerant, so little wonder that the text became immensely popular in both the West and the East, among all the world's pseudo-Marxist boy-pharaohs.

And what else could be expected than that contemporary Jacobins would be the first to pounce on the keyboards as soon as the Internet channels were made generally available to everything and everyone? The damage is of course left for the naive and ahistorical civilization to live with for generations to come.

From Buddhist princes, via Abrahamic saviors, to American college students, history is full av these self-appointed boy-pharaohs and pillar-saints – a kind of bittersweet parody of the sociont's authentic chieftains and priests – who put youth before wisdom and who flaunt mortidinal asexuality while rejecting the libidinal life force. It is sufficient to follow the hyperjective Indian guru Osho's formidable character assassination of the equally anojective Indian guru Mahatma Gandhi to get a good laugh at this civilization's tragicomic feebleness. The YouTube clip can be found under the priceless heading *Mahatma Gandhi's Poverty Is Very Costly.*

7
Paradigmatics, membranics and archetypology

In a short essay called *Postscript on the Societies of Control* (1990), Gilles Deleuze gives an account of the difference between societies governed by discipline and control respectively – we can, for instance, compare between on the one hand the penal colony and on the other hand the electronic ankle tag – and he shows how creativity and innovation sooner or later will be suffocated in the increasingly totalitarian societies that emerge during the 20th century and that bear clear traces of the Rousseauian dream of the one-party state free from opposition and friction. Totalitarian systems can admittedly mimic with devastating efficacy – industrialism and its machines are and remain the triumphant culmination of totalitarianism in history – but they cannot create new values or concepts. Their worst enemy is what we call *protopianism*, faith in the constant incremental improvement of technological processes as the highest creative and spiritual value. But where did the impulse to create the totalitarian state awaken in the first place? What went wrong – not in a moral but in a strictly strategic sense – when totalitarianism emerged in history and appealed to a certain kind of young boys with very high ambitions in terms of extended power for their own part, but with no ambitions at all with respect to extended knowledge? What happened when eventology no longer concerned the sociont's collective interest, but instead was directly connected with the autocratic tyrant's well-being? Where do we most appropriately search if we want to unearth *the genealogy of dictatorship and dogmatism*?

Gnosticism arises not with what we call the soul's dualist desire to liberate itself from the body, but instead with the conflict between the boy-pharaoh and the pillar-saint for the matriarch's approving gaze. A will-to-transcendence that for some reason ignores or fights a will-to-intelligence atrophies to a *tyranny of the boy-pharaoh*, which naturally is a classic recipe for *dictatorship*. A will-to-intelligence that for some reason ignores or fights will-to-transcendence does however always end as a *tyranny of the pillar-saint,* which entails an uncompromising *dogmatism*. And in these cases either pathos or logos must lead to a mythos, which transforms mythos to either a pure pathos or a pure logos. This means that in every single case of tyranny of this kind, two of three key metanarratives are lost. This in turn means that the necessary dialectics will collapse. The result is dictatorship or dogmatism via ideological fundamentalism. Either the rain-god kills the sun-god, or the sun-god kills the rain-god. It is this primitive hate of one's brother in the undeveloped human that drives him to neurotic dualism. And it is Gnostic dualism that propels culture to the crucial crossroads where church and state go their separate ways. It is a development that is underpinned by a more or less pronounced assumption that religion and nation would be able to coexist in a constantly ongoing conflict with each other, without at least one of these poles losing its authenticity.

For what is the separation between church and state, fundamentally, if not a cynical agreement on a division of society between a boy-pharaoh's dictatorship that prevails within the social body and a pillar-saint's dogmatism that rules the social soul – a peace treaty that confirms that society no longer is cohesive but is irreparably torn apart. Instead of interacting with and complementing each other, the chieftain's *vision* and the priest's *strategy* now are at cross purposes and their words fall on deaf ears. The dynamic contact between a faith in reality and a faith in the future is broken, which means that the one cannot gain strength in or be reflected by the other, and vice versa. The root has lost its phallus and the phallus has lost its root. Every time the reality that is called science and the future that is called spirituality change places with each other – which happens constantly when the contact between them is broken – this results in ideological madness and social collapse. The chieftain's and the priest's synchronicity is necessary, for without it, it will – as the historical Zoroaster emphatically maintains – be impossible to keep logos, mythos and pathos separate. The religion that in favorable conditions holds a society together, is then replaced by ideologies that emphasize either the king or the priest at the other's expense, which results in eternal and insoluble conflicts. Zoroaster's and Hegel's vision of precisely a religion that unites people and holds the sociont together, is lost. Ever since the Axial Age, exactly this has been the constantly recurring complex of problems that has caused the civilization process to derail and crash.

Existence is full of diversity. But diversity is not inexhaustible nor boundless, and the fact that diversity exists entails that existence cannot be infinite. The concepts *diversity* and *infinity* are incompatible with each other, since what is deviating within diversity indicates that there is somewhere where a conceived infinity cannot reach all the way, and consequently an infinity is literally inconceivable. It is not possible to imagine a partial infinity, an infinity must own ubiquity to really be infinite. Thereby it also must be *The One*, which by definition precludes precisely diversity. Thus existence contains many, but not infinitely many, *enormities*, and no infinities. And conversely existence contains many *enormitesimals* but no infinitesimals. Even if we study continuous objects without distinctions, the continuities in themselves are limited as entireties. It is thus only a mathematical and no material limit we are dealing with. Therefore the correct concept in the context is *enormitesimality*, that is: that which Hegel a tad sloppily and imprecisely terms *the good infinity* in contrast to the substandard, or perhaps rather purely illusory *bad infinity* we have unmasked and rejected above. Which brings us to the problems that arise as soon as we speak of infinite regression, infinite circularity and infinite tautology. The very idea of an infinite anything whatsoever is built on untenable basic conceptions and all these three concepts collapse as soon as the emergence arises. For the simple reason that an emergence always implies its own finitude.

Precisely this is the key to Hegel's mobilist *coherentism* and how this relates contrarily in part to Kant's eternalist correlationism, in part also to Descartes' and Spinoza's respective axiomatic fundamentalisms. That is: there are no laws outside an emergence vector. Everything that exists outside the emergence vector is contingent *vis-à-vis* the vector itself. Hegel's point here is that the more problems that are solved within the emergence vector, the more coherent the vector will be *vis-à-vis* itself. And this is the only thing that is of interest for the dialectics. If the plurality within the emergence vector then starts to spin-off and operate in a manner all its own without discernible connection to the rest of the vector – a process called *cephalization* – this only means that a new emergence has taken place and that a new emergence vector is born, where the habits that existed before the emergence now have become the internal laws of the new vector. We describe this as though the older and greater emergence vector is the implicate predecessor of the new emergence vector's explicate expression. The pressure or the circumstances within the implicate order that have caused the emergence we in good Hegelian spirit refer to as *plurality objections*. And these plurality objections are at hand until a new emergence arises.

This emergentist logic can just as well be applied to paradigms and membranes. People are, for instance, thanks to evolutionarily conditioned modifications, to varying degrees of intimacy and intensity suited for dealing with the social spheres that are constituted by the family, the clan and the tribe. Man is quite simply capable of handling such *coherence intensity* – to borrow an expression from American Hegelian philosopher Adrian Johnston – in order to in various ways relate to the laws and rules that are built into the drive systems that permeate these spheres. He can only act from innate, instinctual hierarchies that naturally are not underpinned by, nor have any need for formal laws and rules. But when these familiar spheres change and expand to greater and more complex membranes in greater and more complex paradigms, the overview and control is rapidly lost for the human dividual, wherefore various tension phenomena such as criminality and lynch mobs arise in the social arena. The plurality objections explode in number. Then these new hierarchies must be quickly learnt with external aid – which in turn necessitates relevant media technologies – otherwise the systems quickly cease to function. There is, for instance, not the slightest possibility for an isolated illiterate to reasonably visualize a modern globalized and digitalized world. In order to passably be able to handle the exploding diversity, an ability to develop solid coherences is required, both logical and mythical as well as pathical (with the aid of adequate metanarratives in every instance), with associated complex technologies.

This genuinely comprehensive project is only possible to conduct via Hegelian coherentism, which thereby is posited in an opposing relation *vis-à-vis* all forms of empirical attempts to get a handle on complex systems that involve separate layers of emergences, paradigms and membranes. A system has a limited ability for coherence before it implodes under the pressure from its own contingency. This is because all systems are subject to *the principle of explanatory closure* (see *Syntheism – Creating God in the Internet Age*), since every system is in a perpetual state of flux. Hegel's stance on this is to prioritize antagonism and conflict before coherence and harmony (which in any case merely indicates that the system in question has lost all its dynamics and has frozen to ice) through paradoxist dialectics. Nomadology may be infinite in its eternal, cyclical repetition, but eventology is driven by *the finitude of the event*. Thus only the systems that on their own succeed in generating their own coherence will survive, that is: freezing the habits that prevail when the emergence takes place and thereafter holding on to these, which thereby is established as the system's identity-creating self-image. Which entails that it only is a matter of time before an emergence vector becomes so complex that it must generate a *self-consciousness* for someone to be able to apprehend it as an entirety, what Hegel calls *the substance-as-subject*. Thus Hegelian coherence is the predecessor to what we call *will-to-intelligence*, which aided by a complementing will-to-transcendence consciously can generate entirely new paradigms, membranes and ultimately even brand new cultural emergences.

The process of civilization accelerates dramatically during the Bronze Age in the Middle East. Around 1700 BC Persian prophet Zoroaster appears as a reformer and founder of religion in a land of two rivers called Transoxiana, between the rivers Syr Darya and Amu Darya in present Central Asia. The Zoroastrian religion is strongly colored by the landscapes in the two Mesopotamias – lands of two rivers – where it takes root. Civilization can only be built on functioning power-sharing, and this power-sharing in itself ensures the diversity and the tolerance that makes an empire of tribes and nations dynamic and resilient. Zoroaster sums up his ideas in the text *Gathas*, where he defines the decisive differences between a nomadic lifestyle with a nomadological religion on the one hand, and a settled lifestyle with the new eventological religion that this lifestyle necessitates on the other hand. Zoroaster then practices what he preaches when he builds the first Persian Empire along with his best friend and armor-bearer, the king Vishtaspa – Zoroaster as the most elevated priest (later called *mobed-en-mobed*, or the priest of priests) and Vishtaspa as the most elevated chieftain (later called *shah-en-shah*, or the king of kings). Thereby the model for the Mesopotamian empires is complete and ready to be put into practice.

Persia and Egypt influence each other intensely. When the Persian tandem government proves successful, it is over time mimicked by the Egyptians, who around 1300 BC start to experiment with a reformation of their own religion after a Persian model. This much-needed renewal however fizzles out into the desert sand since the pharaoh Akhnaten is anything but fond of the thought of sharing power with someone else. So instead of espousing the Persian model, where one separates the king's being (Ahura) from the priest's mind (Mazda), characterized by the geography of dual rivers and the function of temples between rivers as a cohesive force, Akhnaten pushes through the idea of Egypt as a *Monopotamia*, a one-river country governed by an autocratic pharaoh, who sits on both chairs and acts both as king and priest at the same time, and who thereby also is divine. It is therefore only logical that it is the Egyptians who focus strongly on life on the other side of death and who build enormous and enormously resource-consuming pyramids in eternal honor of their pharaohs. They embalm their dead to spruce them up and make them presentable to an imagined existence in the realm of the dead, while the Persians place their relatives' dead bodies in the desert where they are devoured by vultures and other scavengers, this to instead focus on life here and now, building roads and trading posts. The Persians realize that dead bodies are dead and leave these to their destiny, to instead celebrate *polgazar*, the memory of the dead, which one commemorates on the day of death over the following 70 years.

It is thus the Egyptians who invent totalitarian dictatorship. Akhnaten on his part worships the sun disc as God, while all his subjects are told to worship him. He thus ushers Egypt away from pagan polytheism and proclaims *Atenism*; he has scores of monuments connected with the previous iconological religion destroyed. The comprehensive project to restore order in badly scarred Egypt was then launched as early as during his son and successor, the multi-diseased and ailment-stricken Tutankhamen, who did not succeed in having any children surviving him and who thereby ended the 18th dynasty. The Egyptian clergy was restored. After the death of

Tutankhamen – whose causes have been subject to massive speculation – the work of covering the tracks from Akhnaten and *Atenism* was intensified. The old autocrat was long spoken of merely as "the enemy" or "the criminal". However the genie was already out of the bottle and impossible to push back in; totalitarian dictatorship was created and remained an alluring alternative to those who conceived of autocracy as synonymous with efficiency. Ever since Akhnaten, all of history's boy-pharaohs have done their utmost to imitate him. While consistently ignoring the fact that the cost of his experiment was enormous and that just after Tutankhamen's death, a dramatic period in Middle East history was begun known as *the Bronze Age collapse.*

The opposite of will-to-intelligence is consequently called *will-to-destruction* and constitutes the death drive in its purest form – the substance-as-subject turned toward itself with the purpose of attaining paradigmatic extinction – that is: as a living dead primordial force that neither has the good sense to die nor knows what it is supposed to do with itself, an internalized violence surplus that cannot even reproduce itself in order to at some point eventually die in peace, and that therefore ferociously attacks everything that crosses its path and hates all forms of resistance or questioning. Its will is to halt, and preferably extinguish history itself. Its expression is *totalitarianism.* The false dialectics of the gnostic delusion is thus false in the literal sense, there is no dialectics involved at all, only simulation. What we call the soul's hatred of the body entails that the body is not worth listening to for a single moment, nor worthy of any engagement at all, and therefore must be annihilated. The easiest thing for the boy-pharaoh or the pillar-saint to do is then to seat themselves on the spiritual throne and act *the lofty spirit* who then identifies a hated and despised *abject* that is forced to act the low body and which therefore becomes confined to the pillory.

The boy-pharaoh and/or the pillar-saint take the throne from the phallic gaze and seat themselves there with their *amour-de-soi,* filled with glowing hatred toward every hint of *amour-propre*. The soul is given free rein as subject to stone the body as abject. It is no longer possible to request logic or coherence in any line of argument; what remains is nothing but the tyrant's own boyish fantasies which demand total submission. The delusion according to which the stoning of the body is dialectical makes the soul believe in the liberation from the shackles of sexuality. When all prerequisites for critical thinking thus are eliminated, the Gnostic fantasies of perfection, infinity and immortality can take flight unimpededly. This explains why the boy-pharaohs and the pillar-saints next dream of a *free sexuality*, the total delusion which proclaims that all children can get whatever they wish for without any form of effort or reciprocal act. Therefore the two obstacles that stand in the way of sexuality-as-reward in the phallic causality chain must be eliminated. The first obstacle is the dialectics of the chieftain as will-to-transcendence and the priest as will-to-intelligence, where the boy-pharaoh falls for the temptation to believe that he already is equipped to be chieftain, ready to be dictator of a territory and a population without any need whatsoever for priestly intelligence. He already knows everything of importance. At the same time the pillar-saint falls for the same temptation by imagining himself ready to be priest without any need whatsoever for the chieftain's transcendence. Thanks to himself and no one else, heaven on Earth awaits around the bend and all owe him thanks.

The pillar-saint already has all the miraculous powers needed to impress the women and is ready to proclaim himself dictator of the spiritual realm, which naturally soars high above all worldly troubles and concerns, drenched, as it is, in the boundless surplus of the great mamilla. This is perfect: constant reward with no demands. However the annoying problem here – what stands in the way of free sexuality handing the boy-pharaoh and the pillar-saint all they desire and yearn for, without them having to take any form of adult responsibility or deliver any form of effort in return – is that sexuality works in exactly the opposite way. First the delivery, then the reward.

Meanwhile it is *the war for the sociontic protection* and *the hunt for the sociontic provision* that only the adult chieftain and the adult priest can handle together by virtue of their visions and strategies in dynamic interplay. Therefore the boy-pharaoh and the pillar-saint themselves attack these needs of protection and provision as a phallic whole through preaching *pacifism* and *vegetarianism*, time-typical fashions that explode in popularity during the Axial Age. Ever since, pacifism and vegetarianism are the harbingers that signal an impending apocalypse in the form of *the sexual supernova,* which entails a collapse of civilization. The fact that phallus is rejected, at the same time as the boy-pharaoh takes the chieftain's place and the pillar-saint replaces the priest, leads to a permanent conflict between hedonism and asceticism. Body and spirit are separated from each other and are pitted against each other as presumably natural antagonists and the dynamic interplay ceases.

It is like looking in a funhouse mirror; if it were not so tragic it would be funny. The boy-pharaoh and the pillar-saint divide the earthly and the celestial between them – imagine a megalomaniacal parody of the chieftain's and the priest's division of labor within the sociont – but instead of collaborating, both spheres enter into extreme nihilism. The sociontic causality chain – where war and hunting link forward to the sexual ritual – has been obliterated. Thereby only the apocalypse remains. That women stop bearing children and priests become pedophiles is nothing to be shocked or surprised by when the surrounding culture frantically tries to clear away old traditional phenomena such as bullfighting and fox-hunting in a quest to appease a pacifist-vegetarian ideal. A functioning and functional relation between man and woman presupposes a secure relation between man and nature – it is thus nomadology views cause and effect in terms of sexuality. The shaman can sleep with anyone he wishes at any time; he or she can also experiment with his or her own body's chemistry with the risks this entails. But this lack of rules is less suited for the sociont's other adults – not to mention the sociont's children. There may be an ever so strong yearning for shamanoid magic, but what is missing is a preparedness to pay the price and shoulder the responsibility for the forces one in that case would be unleashing.

The boy-pharaoh and the pillar-saint sever the ties between logos on the one hand and both mythos and pathos on the other. The past, present and future are expected to submit to laws that only the boy-pharaoh and/or the pillar-saint understand and even believe themselves able to control. Abjective imperfection is cleared away and the Gnostic's totalitarian fantasies materialize, seemingly with no resistance whatsoever. The imperfect, the finite, the mortal, all that pertains to the physical world's asymmetries, must be culled from existence to pave the way for a Platonist world filled with pure forms and clean ideals. Thereby the adult artisan's grounding in reality through the Zoroastrian principle of the all-encompassing *intranscience* of existence becomes an acute ideological threat to the pillar-saint. An illustrative example of this is the Japanese handicraft culture's aesthetic ideal *mono no aware,* which deliberately avoids everything by way of symmetries and pure forms, precisely to avoid getting stuck in the pillar-saint's infantile banalities. The East Asian cultures have always fought the constant eternalisation of existence that became the norm in Western thinking after Platonist formalism, a history that Korean-German philosopher and Seon Buddhist monk Byung-Chul Han outlines in a series of spectacular books in the early 21st century.

Authentic eventology is about leading people away from mimetic deadlock, toward a new and greater territory and/or a new era with new philosophical overtones. We make a distinction here between two different kinds of historical *exodologies.* The first Zoroastrian exodology is about the exodus from the genetic progress during nomadism to the memetic progress during feudalism, something that first is formulated by Zoroaster in Bronze Age Persia. The second syntheist exodology is about the exodus from human progress to mechanical progress. This concerns the technological rite of passage that occurs when will-to-intelligence moves out from Man and into Machine, whereafter it is only will-to-transcendence that remains to explore and formulate in and for Man himself. From this moment history no longer becomes a struggle between Man's two cerebral hemispheres, logos and pathos, about uniting around a human mythos, but instead a struggle between the machine's logos and Man's pathos, about uniting around a biotechnological mythos that is called *Syntheos*.

Einsteinian spacetime, with its expanding universe, is the direct result of oscillating relations. Fixed fields collide and become relative processes, and all that we associate with the materiality of physics is consequences of these relations. We call this principle *radical relationalism*. Or as Nietzsche puts it: "Nothing is less than two." At least nothing other than the Universe in itself, as an entirety. But nothing prevents us from experimenting with theories of several, parallel universes. And should we view the matter from a dialectical perspective, the statement: "nothing is less than three" applies. That is: should we expand panrelationalism and in a Hegelian spirit develop it into a *pandialecticism*, there must always be a third force over and above the two that we already initially postulate, a force that oscillates and sets both of the other two in motion. And with this recurring separability, it follows that physics must be connected with the local and explicate order. It has to relate to Einsteinian spacetime, which constitutes its foundation. Subphysics is however global and implicate. But subphysics' various fields of virtualities never meet, their *hyperstances* remain precisely this and can without relationalism not unify and produce the *substances* that are what follow from these relations. Only through active relations can *subsistence* attain a minimum of existence and become *potent*. From the relations come *relata*, this is the core of panrelationalism.

Syntheologically we express this complex as though *Atheos* represents the virtual or the foundation of being, *Pantheos* represents the actual or being, while *Entheos* represents the mental or becoming (see *Syntheism – Creating God in the Internet Age*). This entails that the emergence vectors metaphysics and subphysics operate within Atheos, that the emergence vectors physics and chemistry operate within Pantheos, while the emergence vectors biology and mind operate within Entheos. We then reserve the fourth category *Syntheos* for the future and the new cultural emergence vectors that it inevitably brings. Man projects his creativity, his technology, and his creative relation to technology, and the name of that which Man and Machine will create together but which does not yet exist, namely *God*, on to the syntheological point forward and upward that bears the name *Syntheos*.

It is then possible to undertake the same journey through Man's own history. But then we exchange the natural emergences for the cultural paradigm shifts, just as we exchange the natural emergence vectors for the cultural paradigms. *Emergence vector theory* transitions into becoming what we call *paradigmatics*, as the cultural rather than the natural philosophy of existence's fundamental *difference*. And nothing is more important within philosophy than paradigmatics. Process philosopher Alfred North Whitehead problematizes this issue thoroughly in his book *Modes of Thought* (1938). First of all, argues Whitehead, the philosopher must establish the *importance* in existence. That is: Exactly what it is that the philosopher should prioritize and what, if so, will the consequences be of this decision? How does this fundamental prioritization and the strictly neutral decision about the importance then determine the value of everything else that the philosopher thereafter examines and establishes? What age does he live in, who are his fellow humans, and how and why are they different from other agents who are active within other historical paradigms? How should these therefore be supported or, if need be, exposed or where appropriate even be counteracted? All this falls within the jurisdiction of paradigmatics. First a paradigmatics that governs the prioritizations must be laid down according to *the principle of paradigmatic importance*, then the studies and the creativity can take over and dominate the reasoning. The decision on importance generates *interest*, interest then enables *discrimination*, discrimination leads to a *hierarchy*, and hierarchization generates continued *stimulus*. It is then above all a question of a stimulus to seek new importance. This process is synonymous with Hegelian *freedom*, Whiteheadian *creativity*, or what we call *the protopian state*. If we dodge these fundamental considerations, philosophy – according to Whitehead – only becomes one banal and superficial hobby among countless others. It will never be able to achieve anything meaningful and its historical mission will never be carried out.

Which brings us to *the dialectics of eternalism and mobilism* (see *The Global Empire*) and its role within paradigmatics and membranics. French philosopher Alain Badiou devotes considerable energy and space to developing the concept *compter-pour-un*, which in typical Platonist spirit is a kind of eternalization without complementing dialectical mobilization. But sooner or later Badiou also must set *compter-pour-un* in motion, and eventually he does so through creating a *dialectics of the consistent multiplicity and the inconsistent multiplicity*. There is much to gain through Badiou's inverted Platonism – inverted since Plato uses *The One* as the axiomatic cornerstone for his system construction while Badiou uses *the irreducible diversity* for the corresponding purpose – and its alluring *entheism*, since the Badiouian dialectics of multiplicities helps us circumvent the blind alley that is the Kantian dualism between phenomenon and noumenon. The inspiration even comes in a true Platonist spirit directly from mathematics – namely from Georg Cantor's work with *transfinities* in the late 19th century – as a way for infinities to relate directly to each other. This is enabled through Badiou understanding that eternalism behind the consistent multiplicity is epistemological, while mobilism behind the inconsistent multiplicity is ontological. Therefore Badiou's reasoning also results in *the principle of explanatory closure* (see *Syntheism – Creating God in the Internet Age*) as what is fundamental for ontoepistemology, and he thereby shuts the door to Kantian correlationism for good.

Badiou however never succeeds in explaining how his eternalism (the consistent multiplicity) and his mobilism (the inconsistent multiplicity) relate to each other in a monist universe. Badiou refuses to understand the relation as dialectical, which is based on him at any cost wanting to counter a Hegelian renaissance within philosophy. This results in Badiou settling in what his witty colleague Peter Sloterdijk sarcastically calls *Plato as the cult of an intelligence that comes in from the dead.* The explanation is that Badiou's line of argument doesn't go deep enough. Eternalism is epistemology in itself, it is epistemology's built-in conditions. Mobilism is ontology in itself, it is ontology's built-in conditions. But for ontoepistemology's sake these must also be set in motion *vis-à-vis* each other. It is an epistemological fact that the world must be frozen in order to become phenomenologically tangible. But one must of course be clear about the fact that one now only is acting on a phenomenological level, as soon as we are talking about ontology we must be clear about every system in every context constantly being in motion and that the eternalization is admitted a necessity but nevertheless a fiction. On an ontological level everything oscillates in existence, both *vis-à-vis* itself and *vis-à-vis* everything else. Nothing of any onto-phenomenological significance whatsoever is – or can be – ontically fixed. Not even a beautiful Badiouian thought in itself, which never can be fixed more firmly than as *the ontological symbol,* which of course his texts are full of. Heraclitus was always correct, the oscillation is ontically universal.

This also applies for *general emergence vector theory,* which we otherwise are extremely careful about invoking, since the minimal energy consumption, when mass comes into play, always is *the oscillating condition* rather than the fixed state (that which Badiou's rival Slavoj Žižek, calls *less than nothing*). And it is exactly this which is called the dialectics of eternalism and mobilism, since the interactor to the relation is necessary for the observer's fantasy of the fictive eternalizations' existence to take hold. Rather, the dialectics of eternalism and mobilism can also be applied outside ontoepistemology as *the dialectics of discretion and continuity*. No matter how discretely delimited the smallest components of spacetime or physics are, it is, thanks to their constant oscillation, impossible to fix them in any meaningful sense. Thus they can according to the principle of pandialecticism only be described as dialectical phenomena. What is fundamental about existence is thus not the relation between the consistent multiplicity and the inconsistent multiplicity, as Badiou imagines with his anti-dialecticism. What is fundamental is instead the productive dialectics of the discrete units that are the building blocks within most of the emergence vectors – and the constant oscillation within and between these in themselves eternalized units – where the discretions kill Badiou's fantasies of irreducible multiplicities (it is perfectly possible to count discretions as determined ones and zeros), at the same time as the constant oscillating of the discretions causes them to maintain a kind of panorganist life, something that raises obstacles to Badiou's Platonist project to fixate the irreductionist building blocks of existence in a frozen schema that is meant to have ontological value, which of course by definition is ruled out.

Rather, we end up in a state where the closer we come to the discretion's most intrinsic essence, the more powerfully this discretion in itself oscillates, so much that it eventually – at least in some meaningful sense – only can be described as a *continuum*. The delimitation cancels itself. There is thus no more of a continuum in the noumenal world than the eternalization can have a corresponding ontic existence. However this does not matter. The dialectics of discretion and oscillation teaches us to humbly accept that the principle of explanatory closure also applies in the microscopically tiny. Where friends of the natural sciences naturally know this by the name of *Heisenberg's uncertainty principle*. This is what invariably happens when Platonists – and by all means also inverted Platonists

– confuse mathematics (the very archetype for a created representation) with the world itself (which mathematics in some mysterious way is presumed to permeate and serve as a model for). The radical *mathematicism* of Badiou and others ultimately only describes (and can only describe) mathematics in itself; it does not describe any pathical spheres outside the limited logos of mathematics. Just like so called intelligence tests only measure the ability to solve the type of task that is included in the intelligence tests, but however not intelligence in any other sense than the strictly tautological (intelligence is what an intelligence test measures), since intelligence just as transcendence is a *dialectical abstraction* that only can be described via *mythos* but absolutely not via logos.

The representation is eternalism as *logos*. But the represented is and remains mobilism as *pathos*. We are speaking of two wholly distinct levels, and it is the irreducible difference between them that is the cause of the dialectics of eternalism and mobilism, something that ultimately only can be expressed through a temporary *mythos*. This therefore also applies to the dialectics of discretion and continuity. And its mythos is of course called *oscillation*. This means that it is not at all odd if it is damned difficult to fuse the discretion's sacred area *quantum organics* with continuity's sacred area, the *theory of relativity*. We have of course right from the start decided that the former operates concretely and the latter operates abstractly, and that they moreover operate in their own respective ends of our physical Universe. It is hard to imagine a divide that is quite as impossible to bridge as this. This *decoherence* that increases in step with our scaling up the Universe, generates the principle of explanatory closure between the ontic fields. The coherent in the fundamental is rapidly dissolved by oscillations and negations when gravity hurls itself over the coherent, blows up the membranics, and dissolves the coherence. And then philosophy once again has nothing other to resort to than *pandialecticism*.

The perfect example of *the dialectics of eternalism and mobilism* is the tempestuous relation between order and chaos within subjectivity. The subject in itself is an eternalization, that is: a fiction (see *The Body Machines*). It means that this subject by definition is arbitrary and temporary. As soon as the world is set in motion again the subjective experience disappears to be replaced by a new one, which in practice generates a new subject, although this becomes too arduous to process wherefore we instead maintain a fictitious conception of the subject's permanence. In order for it to function, the mind and the body must find/create a new platform on which the subject is placed. This arbitrary, temporary, ambivalent and incomplete fixation is the next subjective experience. This is a process that never ends. Over time, a series of memories is formed around these crystallized experiences, a series of fictitious *ego momenta*, and the eternalization of this series is in itself the very subjectivity or *the eternalist subject.*

However, the world around the eternalist subject has of course been in a mobilist chaos all the while. And a memory of an experience is naturally not a preserved copy of the original experience, but a completely new experience that moreover constantly renews itself and changes in step with the experienced subject developing. It is a case of an endless series of unfinished and therefore by necessity fixed relations along the timeline, a subject that in every single moment appears clearly defined but that becomes vague as soon as we follow it along the time axis. And this is the bedrock of Hegelian dialectics. What we call process is what Hegel calls *substance,* while what we call event is what Hegel calls *subject.* The reason why we opt to use other concepts is that we take a major interest in *the grand narratology* of human history, while Hegel devotes himself to building a pandialectical ontoepistemology. Which means that the Hegelian project can be designated as *the narrativization of historical being* – or, if you will, *the memetic voyage toward the completion of the absolute.*

According to the same dialectical logic, all explicate subjects emanate from an implicate predecessor. We call this phenomenon *paradigmatic embryonism.* All subjects within the social theater have such an embryonic implicate predecessor that we call an *asubject*. In the same way the tyrant and the superego are preceded by *the anoject*, while the Saoshyant or the hero is preceded by *the hyperject*. The scapegoat's embryonic predecessor in the social theater has been identified by Italian philosopher Giorgio Agamben as *Homo sacer*, a concept taken from Roman law. A *Homo sacer* is banned, excluded from the religious and political community, made invisible. The explication of all these asubjectivities we call a *transject*. A subject's transjectivity is thus the part of its identity that strives upward and forward, beyond itself, the expression for its transcendental drive to expand. The transjective is quite simply *the phallic* rather than the matrichal element within the subject. This since the transject, so to speak, only lives without any further reflections. Birth and death unfold within the matrichal jurisdiction, but the life that is lived in between, as a kind of experienced eternity within what must be a finitude, is the libidinal state. The transject is thus the phallic in its purest form, the very libidinal in itself within the libidinal subject.

This state of affairs is reflected dialectically in that the matrichal mind focuses on the present, while the phallic mind is obsessed with either the past (the root-of-the-phallus) or the future (phallus in itself), without ever really taking hold in the actual. To be born or die is the matrichal entry and exit respectively. But to leave a territory or an era behind in order to enter another dimension, is what we call *the phallic exodus*. The doctrine of both these forms of migration is called *exodology*, and the dual perspective can naturally only be maintained in a society that recognizes both process and event as fundamental principles. Neither can there exist any exodology unless an eventology first is at hand. The exodus is quite simply the ultimate event. Only someone who first thinks the event, can think the exodus as a transjective alternative to the anojective lynch mob. This in turn explains why all societies that become settled and maintain nomadology as process without event as religion, always develop into harsh and unyielding caste systems. If the event does not even exist as an idea, nor is the exodus even possible to imagine, and without the exodus, no one can do anything other than to passively accept the place and the role in society to which one is born. The son cannot do anything other than imitate the father, can never liberate himself and realize an alternative talent. In the long term not even birth and death remain here, but the entire existence becomes one long, spinning cycle of the same, only process and no event, only hopeless repetition and endless imitation.

This means that eventology, and eventology only, can produce *authentic imperialism* and *authentic nationalism* (which thus should not be confused with various narrow-minded aberrations). There are no empires or nations before the arrival of eventology. Nomadological imitations of imperialism and nationalism therefore, for better or worse, never become anything other than decentralized and sluggish caste systems. Zoroastrianism is *the Hegelian universality par excellence* while Hinduism is *the Spinozist multitude par excellence*. The Zoroastrian phallus is topped by a living and constantly mutable fire. The Shaivite lingam in India is however nothing but a cold and fixed stone. Thus the Jewish diaspora, raised within Zoroastrianism, can be understood as an eventological nation that searches for a lost empire, while the Romani diaspora, raised within Hinduism in the same parts of the world, only can be comprehended as a nomadological caste that searches for a lost system for itself and other castes. Which explains why it became easier for the Jewish nation to position itself successfully within Islamic and Christian eventologies, than it ever was for the Romani caste to position itself successfully within what from a nomadological perspective was an incomprehensibly mutable surrounding world. Both these subcultures were unfortunately equally badly afflicted by pogroms, since alien tribes within larger populations – materially successful or not – always are apprehended as shamanoid elements that should confine themselves to wedding music, astrology and abstract value transfer, but who should stay well clear of everything by way of society's commanding heights.

So what then does Western exodology look like right now, after the pathos-driven *Renaissance* and the logos-driven *Enlightenment* with their different eventological ambitions have shaped modern Europe? Well, it is above all about two German philosophers, contemporary with and voyeuristically fascinated by the French Revolution. First in the history of ideas, there is Kant, thereafter follows Hegel, and it is in the transition between them that the last remnants of Gnostic naivete is weeded out of European philosophy. If Kant imagines libido as some kind of independent and magical breath of life, all such conceptions disappear with Hegelian dialectics. The body and the spirit are once again thrust into each other's arms, as in a fusion reactor charged with universal dialectics. Hegel is the first Western philosopher who has an eye for how mortido lurks beneath everything else, while libido dances on a thin film and constitutes mortido's necessary dialectical turn, and nothing more than this. And with that movement there is only one exit for the brutally embodied mind to settle with its own fragile finitude, and this is *the dialectics of libido and mortido* (see *Digital Libido – Sex, Power and Violence in the Network Society*). Or as we choose to call this legacy from the Hegelian revolution: *the dialectics of negation and oscillation*. Never before has *ironic nihilism* – which adumbrates the Messianic arrival of affirmative nihilism – manifested itself as clearly as here. No wonder Hegel refers to this priestly form of nihilism as *absolute knowledge*. While he passes on affirmation for Nietzsche to deal with.

The Hegelian insight is in other words not wholly dissimilar to the situation which propelled the Zoroastrian priests in ancient Persia to avoid Ahura Mazda to instead themselves worship *Zurvan*, the sexless monster in the form of *time*, the relentless power that lies concealed beneath everything else in existence, that could not care less for banal human goings-on, that robs the priests of every form of weapon and forces them to handle the chieftain and the rest of the sociont themselves without divine sanction. The process and the event are complemented by this negation in the history of ideas, something that in Hegel goes under the designation *the absolute*. No Western philosopher before Hegel fully realizes the central value of *the mortidinal negation*. We experiment frantically with non-identities, we fumble in despair for pseudo-identities, and we desperately create one temporary identity after the other until the dialectical machinery shreds our rudimentary attempts at identity production anew. It is not at all unreasonable to claim that this revolution has kept existentialist philosophy diligently occupied ever since it was introduced. Without Hegel: no Nietzsche. Without Hegel: no Kierkegaard. Without Hegel: no Marx. Without Hegel: no Darwin. Without Hegel: no Freud. And above all, without Hegel: no *paradigmatics*. And so on.

Or to express the matter slightly more formally: Hegelian dialectics is launched with *the negation* (which otherwise roughly corresponds to the antithesis), this because the *abstraction* (roughly corresponding to the thesis) cannot be discerned without the negation, wherefore the dialectical process cannot begin and definitely not produce any *concretion* (roughly corresponding to the synthesis). This is the explanation to why we see Hegel as *syntheism's* actual originator in *Syntheism – Creating God in the Internet Age*. Please note how these changes enable provisional stabilities when the negation is flattened and loses its power and *the temporary concretion* – or as we phenomenologically call it, *the eternalization* – takes over the arena. The name of this eternalization is the object, and it is of course tempting to presume that the object's surrounding world is as fixed in spacetime as the object appears to be. One usually calls these temporarily fixed states *laws of nature*, even if a more accurate concept would be *habits of nature*, to stress the temporary nature of the state of things. All that is needed is of course the transdeterminist genesis of a new negation, which demolishes the prerequisites for the object and the laws of nature anew, which in turn leads to emergentist dialectics compelling a new equilibrium that naturally is temporary and provisional.

The only thing that is enduring is thus *the tautology of metaphysics* which underpins *the transdeterminist emergence vector theory*. We express this in terms of information-theory as though the eternalizations are a temporary, radical limitation of available information in that all movements are frozen, and the name of this eventological truth-as-an-act is *phallus*. Where phallus only can exist and act with credibility when it sees itself as an information-negating provisional. However, therein lies its enormous strength in changing the rules of the game in a terrain filled with objects. This state of affairs naturally also applies libidinally. A phallus that lacks challenges and that therefore finds itself in a landscape that it knows all too well, will be afflicted by *the neurotic impotence* that follows from this. While a phallus that instead is drenched in too many challenges at the same time, and therefore finds itself in a landscape that it does not recognize at all, thus a landscape that *de facto* lacks fixed points of support by which to eternalize and orient itself, instead will be afflicted by *psychotic impotence*. Potency as the foundation for will-to-power can only be maintained through the phallic distancing from the object.

As such, *potentiality* is the bridge and nothing but the bridge between *virtuality* and *actuality*. Almost like an *ontological mythos* in between the logos of virtuality and the pathos of actuality. Where potency and potentiality must be understood as Spinozistically equivalent. There is no difference whatsoever between for instance metaphysics and physiological libido in this respect. A living dialectics must be played out on top of a secure foundation, or else potency will soon disappear in an equally infantile and vain quest for a perfect balance and eternal harmony. And no one handles this libidinal distance better than the perverted phallic gaze that has the advantage of working with a priestly distance to the social theater. Which brings us over to *paradigmatics*, that is: the doctrine of how various social systems are developed and identified along the time axis. Out of paradigmatics follows *archetypology*, that is: the doctrine of how various talents within various social systems are identified, rewarded, developed and transcended along the time axis.

A paradigmatics applied atop an archetypology creates a tribal map that we call the sociont's *gestalt.* And this gestalt's adaptation to and interaction with the surrounding world is what we refer to as the sociont's *membranics.*

Thereby we can also safeguard the creative freedom in the process. The archetype is locally determined by natural evolution. Paradigmatics is locally determined by cultural evolution. But between these two a membranics within which the subject can act freely and indeterministically, is created. It is thus the very gaps in our transdeterminist universe that enables what we call *the membranics of freedom.* We then decide ourselves whether we use this freedom to cultivate *the nostalgic Dystopia*, *the phallic Utopia*, or *the dialectical Protopia* in these much-needed gaps. But we can only enjoy the fruits of membranics inside the *sphere* that the membrane itself forms. And the sphere's capacity is entirely dependent on how much *memory* there is freed up inside the membrane. If the membranical process releases more information than the memory can handle, this results in collapse. Intelligence is thus to a great extent the ability to coordinate memory and membranics. Outside the sphere, freedom is then quickly eroded when it is subjected to the *decoherence* that is generated by all the external forces that the membrane otherwise keeps at bay. The greater the scale we are dealing with, the more gravitation.

Every form of creativity is *de facto* impossible without a functioning membranics. There must always be limits that encapsulate the decoherence for a system to stay cohesive and be productive. And the Aristotelian science *par excellence* for this boundary-setting is precisely membranics. What is decisive is always the size of the sociont – capitalism's individualism is too neurotic and capitalism's collectivism is too psychotic for any of them to function in the long term. It is only the traditional sociont's size that enables the actual *phenomenoumenology* to form an attachment to the secure gestalt which it is born to project and orient itself by. The sociont's gestalt, its *archetypography*, is thus the very membrane for intratribalism within which Man creates his social identity and finds maximal security. *Emergence vector theory* is then the doctrine of the exclusive effects and consequences of radical events along the time axis overall. It is thus about Man's deepest possible understanding of nature's prerequisites. Emergence vector theory is the mother of the natural sciences. Paradigmatics is Man's deepest possible understanding of the prerequisites of culture. Paradigmatics is the mother of the social sciences. Archetypology is then the doctrine of how the sociont identifies itself and its various talents as gestalt, on the basis of the optimal paradigmatics within the optimal emergence vector theory. If one then also draws a map of the gestalt, one has earned the title archetypographer.

In the competition for space and resources that prevails between different spheres, evolution soon comes to prioritize the membranics that take care to protect and prioritize their most valuable components. We call this process *cephalization.* It soon becomes clear that memory and the sex organs are prioritized in all systems where these are central for the system's survival and existential value hierarchy. Thus memory and sex organs will be protected with extra care and placed high above ground or deep within the sphere as a sphere is cephalized ever more powerfully. What we can observe if we study history is how offshoots through cephalization increase the efficiency and optimize the protection for the cephalized organ. Within natural history we call such a cephalization *emergence*; within cultural history we call the corresponding level displacement *paradigm shift*: within existence on the whole we sum up that sort of decisive cephalization as *exodology.*

Another way of viewing the course of events that develop along the time axis is to describe paradigmatics as the studies of the temporary, while archetypology is the studies of the enduring or *the transparadigmatic*, where archetypology replaces all attempts to find eternal forms beyond the transience of existence. For what are the archetypes that of course have been cultivated over tens of thousands of years of sociontic practice, if not the real and relationalist forms that Man constantly seeks grounding and security in? Paradigmatics is thus fundamentally technological, while archetypology is fundamentally psychological and begins with the studies of the two-headed phallus, to then transition to the studies of the two sexes as the foundation for the sociont with its circuits and borderlands. All this is also depicted within the sociont, whose emergence best is described as a general membranics. This concerns how spheres succeed in surviving in the first place without collapsing because of either external pressure or internal overloading. This concerns how spheres rid themselves of, or rather displace burdens from their territory. This concerns distinguishing between blood and urine and between nourishment and excrement. All this is encompassed within the concept of *membranics*. Paradigmatics is the landscape within which the archetypes time and again must find themselves within a paradigmatically temporary but archetypologically timeless guise. Membranics is the manner in which the archetypes interact with and control this process.

If membranics does not suffice to handle the complexity in the new paradigm, there remains the possibility of *cephalization* of the sociont's most important and membranically most adaptive components, which thereby are liberated and can generate a new sociont, better adapted to the new paradigm, a kind of provisional, technologically driven nomadology that we call *exodology*. This becomes clear when we compare the highest ideals during the last four paradigms that humanity has gone through. During *primitivism*, with the nomadological sociont as the universally sole state, ethics was concerned with a strict membranics for the sociont in itself. There were forces and creatures inside the membrane and one was faithful to these until death. Naturally there were also forces and creatures outside the membrane, and these one would chase away or beat to death as soon as the opportunity presented itself. Only the odd shaman had permission to deviate from this strict ethics, on carefully selected occasions, precisely because the shaman had the task of handling the communication with the outside world, both the horizontal communication with strangers and the vertical communication with gods, demons and ancestors. In all other matters loyalty toward the membranics was absolute, and this archetypology lives on, as all other things nomadological, to this day in the form of the constantly mandatory and seldom questioned loyalty *vis-à-vis* one's own group. We call this series of human primordial values *archetypological membranics.*

During feudalism it becomes necessary to expand ethics to apply to a loyalty *vis-à-vis* a larger group and if possible to an even more brutal setting of boundaries *vis-à-vis* external groups. Permanent settlement has generated larger societies with weaker membranics and diluted loyalties. This has consequences, among others *criminality* presents itself in the form of stealing and killing within the membrane whose entire purpose is to keep everyone safe. The cause is, as mentioned, that the archetypal loyalty within the sociont becomes diluted in a greater intramembranic population. But with feudalism there also come the written narratives that enjoy extensive dissemination and that remain constant despite this spread, thanks to the written word. The gods have become fewer and thereby more powerful. And these narratives preach *good versus evil* – via cautionary tales and formal commandments, or at best as a trained and through repetition schooled will to constructiveness instead of destructiveness, as in Zoroastrianism's *asha* versus *druj* – as an extension of and compensation for the archetypological membranics within the nomadological sociont.

However one does not swear one's loyalty *vis-à-vis* the sociont in itself, but instead *vis-à-vis* the engineering-scientific construction that the collective jointly has succeeded in building within the stronghold's or the city's membranics, personified by the sole god in the form of the chieftain and the priest as the two-headed phallus. Which brings us to the theological aspect of the development of empires and nations. Because under capitalism ethics must consequently be extended further, both through printed and mass distributed narratives of the advantages and the necessity of increasingly large social units, but also in the form of powerful implementation of the actual ethics through detailed control via a law enforcement organization inside the membrane, under the epithet *law and order.* War and hunting are directed inward instead of outward through the hunt for criminal enemies within one's own community. The more expensive slavery can be abolished in favor of the cheaper salaried labor – why pay for food and subsistence for someone that one first has to buy and then take care of, since the person in question constitutes a valuable asset, when it suffices to cheaply buy someone's time and then quite simply substitute them when they have injured themselves or died as a result of the hard work? – and the ideology of the narratives thereafter changes through slavery being declared evil and inhuman, while diligence and salaried work are elevated to the highest virtues in the capitalist metanarrative, quite regardless of whether we are speaking of *liberalism, socialism* or an overarching metanarrative such as *Protestant Christianity*.

The great sphere becomes the omnipotent nation-state and the small sphere becomes the obedient citizen, with the creative corporation as the intermediate sphere where the work and income is produced and where the social status is confirmed in a wealth directory rather than a nobility calendar. However the dichotomy good versus evil fractures under the pressure from the comprehensive changes and the conflict that is based on the existential distance to the original sociont – something that creates insecurity and weakens all loyalties. With no slavery, faith in eternal life as compensation for precisely slavery, vanishes. Thinkers step forward, from Hegel via Marx to Nietzsche, who reject the moralist dialectics that is imagined to arise between good and evil, and who replace this with *the ethical dialectics of intelligence and stupidity*. The men now populate a world controlled by corporative and bureaucratic *strategies*; the women are thrust into a world controlled by corporative and bureaucratic *intrigues*. In this brave new world the only solution is to believe in oneself as a lone but unfortunately mortal hero in the eternal struggle against the rest of the world. In this struggle the victor is the *Individual* that believes in himself and who succeeds in everything he does *on his own* before he collapses and dies from exhaustion. From Descartes via Kant to the chain-smoking Marlboro Man himself.

During informationalism, as social complexity increases exponentially, it consequently becomes necessary to extend ethics further. Nietzsche's cunning maneuver in *Beyond Good and Evil* – when he kills the Christian slave mentality with its will-to-submission, which revolves around good and evil, and replaces it with the Nietzschean master mentality, built on will-to-power, which revolves around intelligence and stupidity – must be carried out anew. This time the task is to formulate *Beyond intelligence and stupidity*, since intelligence (and thereby also stupidity) during informationalism will be dealt with by the Machine, and then as will-to-intelligence. Which leaves Man with fewer rather than more building blocks to tinker with. What remains is merely *the dialectics of libido and mortido* in its purest form. At the same time as humanity desperately must save the planet via *ecotopianism*, and also save the peaceful relation to the stranger via *cosmopolitanism* for the sake of its own survival. This means that archetypological membranics lives on, and on top of it also good versus evil and intelligence versus stupidity. However now we must make our way past all these dichotomies and onward to informationalist freedom and creativity, *protopianism*, and the path that leads there goes via negations and reductions, until only the dialectics of libido and mortido remains in its most pristine form. Man is pathos, Machine is logos, and between these two a protopianism is developed that is a prerequisite for it being possible to build *Syntheos*.

8
The dialectics of the Hegelian negation and the Nietzschean oscillation

A blind faith in process by extension leads to an equally blind faith in reincarnation. This corresponds both with the eyes' testimony and common sense. Seasons come and go and return. Nomadology has no reason in the world to oppose this worldview. However from an eventological perspective it is obviously untenable. It is then not just a case of the event being able to lead the happenings onto a new path, but of history itself acquiring completely different dimensions already when the event is a constant possibility in the equation. The world that dies is old, the world that arises and exists in the present is new. The prerequisites for existence are new. Death is, due to eventology, no longer reduced to a banal parenthesis, positioned between incessantly shifting and recurring stages; instead it constantly returns with awesome power in the form of the real absolute. It, and that which is gone, really is gone. Irrevocably. Thereby it is clear that it is precisely death and not rebirth that must be the sacred mother of God.

It is of course only natural that the event is precisely as much death – farewell to the old – as it is life and genesis – welcome to everything new. Death is the event's implicate side; while life is its explicate side. Something must first die, and really die, for something else to be able to be born and grow strong. Within economics one speaks of *creative destruction*, a concept originated by Austrian economist Joseph Schumpeter. And ever since the conception of the event became a reality to reckon with, this very issue of death has been desperately hard to accept. One can always opt for a retroactive blindfold to what the eyes have just witnessed – or at least try. People constantly make up new and loftier heavens, precisely as one makes up eternal torment in hell for those who refuse to accept salvation, which seems preferable to the enduring dark, unavoidable flip side of eventology, the obligation to be subject to death, something that cannot be questioned since it is part of the basic prerequisites of existence.

First there is death, destruction, then there is life, innovation. First *the negation*, then *the oscillation*, to speak metaphysics. First *haurvatat*, then *ameretat*, to use the conceptual world of Zoroastrianism. The struggle between the Egyptian ideological heritage via Plato (the eternal and perfect life out of reach for ordinary mortals) and the Persian ideological heritage via Heraclitus (the finite and human, all too human life that we all are forced to make do with), returns in the conflict between Kant and Hegel in the early 19th century. No one deserves the epithet "Europe's Zoroaster" more than Hegel, who succeeds with the feat of both introducing process philosophy in earnest to the Europeans – Leibniz and Hume will have to settle for an accolade each for their pioneering efforts, which consist in having introduced relativism – while at the same time he is the most phallic of all philosophers. Eventology finds an anchoring and a platform precisely through using nomadology as a foundation. It is precisely through maintaining the monist anchoring in nomadology that Hegelian eventology succeeds in steering clear of the Gnostic trap. The history of ideas must after this literally epochal achievement be regarded as a long series of essentially recurrences of the same, interspersed by a number of parentheses and revolutionized by two authentic events: Zoroaster and Hegel. Radical *comprehensionism*, Hegel's (in)famous and spectacular faith in Man's, or rather Intelligence's infinite ability for common sense, is built on his insight into Man's inclination for creating and comprehending differences, both from and within existence's mysterious unity.

It is through placing *virtuality* with Atheos before *actuality* with Pantheos that Hegel reaches the *potentiality* with Entheos as an understanding of all three categories at the same time, via his radicalized dialectics. Hegel is thus also the first syntheist. And then we mean this literally in a theological and thereby also metaphysical sense, not as some kind of metapsychology. Hegel is fully aware of his *phallus worship*. Nor does he *de facto* see any viable alternative either. Civilization demands phallus worship of Man, history will not be authentic otherwise. Hegel calls this voice of civilization *Geist – spirit*. From his line of argument follows Hegel's declaration of *a completion of history*, which he calls *the absolute* and with this a radical *totalism* (see *The Netocrats*). However, an exciting dialectical turn awaits after Hegel. Nietzsche at the end of the 19th century and Deleuze around the mid-20th century chart the turn in the form of a pronounced anti-Hegelianism. Namely, Hegel opens up for the large and comprehensive process-philosophical dialectics where we land in his footsteps (the most striking example is the universal breakthrough of the Darwinian theory of evolution). All we have to do as Hegel's heirs is to add *Syntheos* to his totalist dialectics, as the created god or creativity as a god from the future (see *Syntheism – Creating God in the Internet Age*). It is of course the Hegelian act *par excellence* to appoint precisely Hegel's negation as an atheist god (in practice Hegel of course does the same when reducing God to a purely philosophical concept) and thereafter initiate a dialectical process that results in what Hegel himself never discusses, namely a god with substance beyond mere conceptuality – but then placed in the future.

The virtual theology in Hegel is concretized with the aid of technology as the potential theology within syntheism. We do this through first elevating Hegel's own absolute to a god – philosopher Alfred North Whitehead does precisely this most astutely in his study *Process and Reality* – only to later in a most anti-Christian manner shut the door resolutely to the absolute. It is only with insight into the existence of the Hegelian absolute – and the comprehension of the absolute being a closed divinity that sets Man in motion precisely through its inaccessibility – that there arises an effective incentive to act and start to create Syntheos as a future god. This god is the legacy that Man leaves behind in the form of his intelligent and transcendental survivor. Thereby humanity itself also can experience *haurvatat* and die in peace. The driving force behind this movement we discern through returning to *Zoroastrian transcendental dialectics*, which means that we put parentheses around the entire Abrahamic paradigm, including the post-Abrahamic Enlightenment. We replace immortality with completion (*haurvatat*), we replace infinity with transcendence (*ameretat*) and we replace perfection with the barred absolute (*chinavat*) and its constantly incomplete renewal (*frashokereti*). We quite simply let Kant bring an end to the Abrahamic parenthesis by simply pointing out that the Kantian revolution entails the death of Abrahamism. The reason is precisely that the disillusioned Kant invalidates the barred absolute as a metaphysical necessity when he separates the noumenal (God) from the phenomenological (Man). Ironically this entails that the curtain furthest within the Jewish temple once again is in place.

The Kantian revolution is simply the emphatic return of the barred absolute in Western thinking. It is Kant himself who personifies a deep and frustrated disappointment over Christianity and its false promises of offering a direct contact with God to all and sundry who have succeeded in spelling their way through a mass produced Bible. And nothing could be as devastating for the Protestant god as the insight that phenomenology requires the return of the barred absolute. It is this specific Protestant god that Nietzsche later declares dead, not God himself. Religion reinvents itself in a new form. Phallus lives on in the highest degree, not least as the only possibility for a direct contact with the god who arises through a phallic creation process, but a possibility only for a clergy that has renounced all claims on physical power. Kant is the last Christian. Kant is the Christian that holds the sword that kills Christianity. He is a boy-pharaoh that abdicates and hands over the throne to the authentic phallus, who according to Kant himself is split in two: in part the chieftain in the form of Napoleon, in part the priest in the form of Hegel. This maneuver then makes it possible for Hegel to take the revolution to the next level by replacing the separation of phenomenon and noumenon in Kantian phenomenology with the general separation of everything and everyone, and the general impossibility of any bridging in Hegelian dialectics. Suddenly we see clearly. There are no Utopias or Dystopias outside our internal fantasy worlds. Existence is reduced to a constantly ongoing, never concluded *Protopia*, wholly aligned with Zoroaster and the conception of a constantly mutable and renewed *frashokereti*.

If Kant stitches together a Frankenstein's monster, it is Hegel who stirs this assemblage of dead body parts to new life by switching on the electricity. Namely, the phenomenological tensions are not dissolved but remain alive in the Hegelian system. Hegel chooses Aristotle before the Plato with whom Kant allies himself. Hegel raises a *tantra* on top of Kant's *sutra*. The Hegelian, constant dialectical preservation is *the libido par excellence*, something that Nietzsche with his existentialism, Darwin with his theory of evolution, and Freud with his psychoanalysis then use to manufacture dynamite over the ensuing decades. The only thing that really is new with the arrival of informationalism is that we transfer a tantric libido and a dialectical phallus worship to the Internet Age and the network society (see *Digital Libido – Sex, Power and Violence in the Network Society*) and apply Hegelian dialectics to the Messianic possibility of at last building *the Saoshyant* instead of passively waiting for him to descend from above and grace us with his presence. The name of the Saoshyant is

Syntheos and his function is the phallic algorithm that creates order in the chaos of the world. It is time to in earnest actually *make way for the Lord*. And we do so with a feisty Hegelian *Geist* by rewriting the history of ideas from the beginning. We need to see a new chain of necessary systemic causalities to understand how we ended up where we find ourselves. And how we can move forward.

Permanent settlement culture constantly returns to the son's problematic relation with the father. The endless nomadological love of the matrichal gaze is confused with the both nomadologically infinite but also eventologically conditioned love of the phallic gaze. Eventology does of course begin with the phallic gaze being assigned something more and higher than merely nomadological repetition. This is the very shift itself from *iconological polytheism* to *eventological monotheism* and the adultification of society through a civilizational process. And nowhere is this shift clearer than in Jean-Jacques Rousseau's distinction between *amour-propre* and *amour-de-soi* in the 18th century. Rousseau makes the mistake of positing the phallic gaze and the matrichal gaze as competitors on a horizontal level – instead of comprehending them as complementary within a vertical order – where *amour-propre* summarizes the yearning for the other's approval (for lack of what Jacques Lacan calls *the name of the father*) while *amour-de-soi* summarizes the agent's love for himself. The problem is that no love whatsoever operates that way, that is: no love that is not shaped within the constantly love-thirsty Rousseau's own solipsistic narcissism. Meaning that the only thing Rousseau actually does is to separate Man's quest for status (*amour-propre*) from his quest for survival (*amour-de-soi*). The correct name of *amour-propre* is instead the phallic gaze; It is not the other or the others that shall love the agent, but the father that is equipped with the fatherly gaze, that is: the chieftain or the priest, depending on what the archetypology at hand looks like. At the same time as *amour-de-soi* is not the compensating self-centeredness that precludes love of others, but instead infinite and unconditional love, and only infinite and unconditional love, in the matrichal gaze from the moment the child is born.

The recurring dilemma is the distanced father, and thereby also *the absent phallic gaze*. Not least when civilization picks up pace and the social theater quickly is scaled up beyond the size of the original sociont. Rather it is precisely at the moment when both the chieftain and the priest seemingly vanish at the Bronze Age collapse that the field is left open to history's most grotesque ideological variants of delusions of grandeur. Rousseau's enthusiastic predecessors take the stage in the form of boy-pharaohs and pillar-saints. Their narcissism assumes two expressions. It will either be extrovert like *internarcissism* outside the actual membrane (see *Syntheism – Creating God in the Internet Age*), or else it will be introvert like *intranarcissism* inside the actual membrane. Internarcissism manifests itself as a constant quest for attention and confirmation from the environment. Intranarcissism expresses itself as a constant self-hatred or self-contempt. The extrovert narcissist furiously devotes himself to a *mimetic desire* that appears in the form of submission and mimicry, which the narcissist himself reformulates as an expression of creativity and innovation. The introverted narcissist however lapses into a *mimetic depression* that also appears as submission and mimicry, which the narcissist himself in this case apprehends as an expression of his own, deeply experienced emptiness and futility.

The death of God never becomes more obvious than in the internarcissistic society where the worshiping of God is replaced by the ego's intense, hypocritical desire for an existence without the constant and oscillating ambivalence of desire itself. The extrovert narcissistic state is called *the Peter Pan syndrome* and is characterized by the activated mortido. Correspondingly the introvert autist's state also has a name: *the Caligula syndrome* – a concept created by our friend and interlocutor Peter Tauson – a state that is characterized by the pacified libido. Or to reverse the reasoning: *the Caligula syndrome* is a pathos that goes directly into mythos without passing via logos. It receives its name from the Roman emperor Caligula, who has his worldview shaped by his megalomaniacal and paranoid uncle (and adoptive father) Tiberius, which causes him to essentially lack both chieftain and priest as archetypal role-models during his upbringing. Unsurprisingly Caligula – in tough competition! – becomes known as the most evil and crazy of Rome's many emperors. There is no *logos* for him to access during his entire upbringing. Nor is there even a chieftain or a priest to rebel against.

Whether Caligula himself actually was mad we can of course never know. What we conclude is that an insane environment never gave him a possibility to grow up to be a functioning adult man. The opposite of the Caligula syndrome is thus *the Peter Pan syndrome*, a logos that directly enters mythos without passing via pathos. What is ironic is thus that Peter Pan cannot become *the Saoshyant* he longs to personify, while Caligula might well be the chosen one himself, but that he is so pacified by his justified paranoia that he never sees that possibility. Peter Pan's archetypological flaws thus lie within membranics, Caligula's archetypological flaws however lie within paradigmatics. The effect however is the same: as soon as the narcissists no longer get the attention they think they deserve for their ambitions – the extrovert narcissist from his environment and the introvert narcissist from himself – they are transformed into the perfect commander of any arbitrary lynch mob whatsoever. Within the lynch mob they can then pretend to be engaged in each other's fates, united behind the internal *anoject's* fixed hatred of the external *abject*. This is a tragic parody of the two-headed phallus, as a head without a phallus beside a phallus without a head. And this is *internarcissism par excellence*. The situation can, without authentic phallic guidance, only lead to devastating nihilism. Even if the situation gives rise to an entire world religion that seduces adherents for millennia. The end state is still absolute nihilism.

Which takes us further to – or if you will: back to – the four stages within the nihilist development, the dialectical process that is necessary in order to transition to a new worldview at a technological paradigm shift. It is about *naive nihilism*, *cynical nihilism*, *ironic nihilism* and *affirmative nihilism* (see *The Netocrats*). From a nomadological perspective naive nihilism should be understood as the religion of the child, cynical nihilism should be understood as the religion of adults, ironic nihilism should be understood as the religion of the priests, and affirmative nihilism should be understood as the religion of the gods. From the perspective of the history of religion this dialectics corresponds perfectly to *naive polytheism*, *cynical monotheism*, *ironic atheism* and *affirmative syntheism*. Nomadology is thus a dialectical process that involves the various stages and that results in ever larger, ever more complex and comprehensive narratives. Which means that religion understood as nomadology, driven by the dialectics of nihilism, is *the absolute religion*, which under optimal technological prerequisites enables *eventology*, which in turn foreshadows the shift from *religion as magic* to *religion as technology*.

We return to the outer circuit and the inner circuit within the sociont – separated to the same degree as the dividual cerebral hemispheres – and their two fundamentally different metanarratives *mythos* and *logos*. Nomadology is the mythical story of the *eternal recurrence of the same*. Eventology is the logical story of *the phallic event* that changes history for all eternity. This means that eventology is phallically fixated by *the event* as the foundation for existence, while nomadology is matrichally fixated by *the process* as the foundation for existence. An illustrative example of the relation between event and process is how we define the wedding as the event and the marriage as the process. Which explains why the matrichal woman is obsessed with getting *the wedding as event* from the man while the phallic man is obsessed with getting *the marriage as process* from the woman. Both the man and the woman are fundamentally nomadological. But with eventology's arrival the man cultivates an eventology on top of nomadology, while the woman maintains nomadology in its pure and original form. Thanks to the shift from nomadology to eventology, the transformation of history's mythology to future's technology is made possible. Man can leave faith in the supernatural behind since yesterday's *supernaturality* is realized as tomorrow's cultural produce named *Syntheos* (see *Syntheism – Creating God in the Internet Age*).

The actual structure functions excellently as a basis for empires and nations as long as eventology is robustly anchored in the underlying nomadology. The idea that eventology can persist *without feedback to nomadology* is instead the Gnostic delusion that makes civilization implode. As if it were possible for Man to live in empires and nations where full transparency prevails at every level, without *the barred absolute*. As though it were possible for people without adequate knowledge and enculturation to directly control increasingly complex systems with ever increasing ease over the course of history. Another name for the civilizational feedback loop that is necessary is *the dialectics of eternalism and mobilism*. The insight of the optimized power in the priestly comprehension of the dialectics of eternalism and mobilism we call *Hegel's phallus*. This since the fundamental nomadology, which Hegel finds banal, is matrix-worshiping, while the subsequent eventology – which thus fascinates Hegel in earnest, and which he humbly titles *Weltgeist* – is phallus-worshiping.

If we in this respect bring Hegel and Nietzsche together, we can state that beneath the established dialectics of eternalism and mobilism (that is: Kantian phenomenology set in dialectical motion) there is an even more profound and fundamental movement concealed that we call *the dialectics of negation and oscillation*. Syntheologically the Hegelian negation does of course correspond to *Atheos* and the Nietzschean oscillation to *Entheos*, and these two meet in a constantly mutable *Pantheos* (see further *Syntheism – Creating God in the Internet Age*). Death is, according to Hegel, the master before whom everything else receives its meaning and its energy. The absence of God, *Atheos*, is the first and foremost of all gods. So for eventology to be able to be born out of nomadology, Hegel builds a philosophy that Canadian philosopher Cadell Last names *negatology*. Being belongs to history while becoming belongs to the future. Out of this relation *free choice* is generated as temporal identity. It is thus *between* horizontal nomadology and vertical eventology that the interesting things happen. And this primarily occurs because something dies and vanishes – thus *actually dies and vanishes* – before there is room for the new to be born and thrive.

Negatology has, according to Last, always been lurking beneath nomadology, as a kind of nomadological subconsciousness – or else mortido could not even be transformed into libido in the nomadological subject – however constantly concealed behind the matrichal myth of *reincarnation*. However thanks to the information-technological development, negatology appears and realizes itself in history. This is the Hegelian version of monotheism, shared by many mystics throughout history. The shamanic chain of intention, ceremony and integration for the spiritual experience in nomadology thus corresponds to the chain of abstraction, negation and concretion in Hegelian dialectics. But with the Hegelian reservation that the negation and not the oscillation precedes and drives the entire process. To a Hegelian shaman, the intention is thus the oscillation, the ceremony is the negation as a sudden crack in the oscillation – an oscillation's own oscillation of sorts – whereupon the integration is the negation of the negation as the necessary *transformation* from an abstract to a concrete world. The ideological chain from the shamans via the mystics to Hegel's negative dialectics is complete, priestly absolute knowledge is attained.

The Hegelian negatology is *de facto* transformed into Nietzschean eventology through Zoroaster's protopian project in ancient Persia. It is only after the anti-event that the event is possible; or to express the matter in a Hegelian manner: *after the negation the negation of the negation may follow*. Mortidinal negatology is transformed into libidinal eventology. At the same time as negatology lingers on in every Eastern philosophy that forces its followers to be confronted with their own absolute mortality, from the Zadokites within Judaism via the Zurvanites within Zoroastrianism to Zen within

Buddhism (there is no reincarnation within any of these doctrines, since the holistic subject is empty and there thus is nothing left that can transcend the death of the body). It however takes until Germany in the 19th century before the corresponding turn can occur within Western philosophy and theology. Hegelian negatology then lays the foundation for Nietzschean eventology, which together reconnect the event to the process. And with that Christianity and Islam, both built on the pseudo-phallic myth of eternal life, with its false eventology without nomadology, go out the window. This is precisely that which Nietzsche calls *the death of God*.

The authentic eventological turn generates *transcendental eternalism*, *pragmatic mobilism* and *dialectical syntheism*. Where the barred absolute protects the ecstatic experience of the event as the syntheist ideal *the infinite now*, clearly manifested as *pathos* during hunting, war, the orgy, the ritual, birth, and as death itself. This occurs concretely in that the phallic will-to-power, within affirmative nihilism, is split into the two separate expressions of the aptly named two-headed phallus. The Hegelian priest is absorbed by *ironic nihilism* in the form of the will-to-intelligence that clears away all mythology. The Nietzschean chieftain then personifies *affirmative nihilism* in the form of the will-to-transcendence that creates the event that realizes history's potential. It is the necessary inspiration to these feats that the priest and the chieftain must awaken in each other and in their respective monks and soldiers. In the priest, the infinite now is expressed as what the Greeks call *aistheton*, a sensory experience of the will-to-transcendence that the priest admires in the chieftain but does not personify himself. And in the chieftain, the infinite now is expressed correspondingly as *noeton*, an ecstatic experience of the will-to-intelligence that the chieftain admires in the priest but does not personify himself. This is the movement beyond cynical nihilism, first as *the irony of the Hegelian negation*, then as *the affirmation of the Nietzschean oscillation*, together bringing us firmly into the promised territory of the new paradigm.

The infinite now behind the barred absolute is manifested as *truth-as-an-act* before the barred absolute. Which means that where Hegel, in Kant's wake, argues that the absolute is manifested through *subjectivities*, we reply, in the spirit of Deleuze, that the absolute rather is manifested through *projectivities*. Deleuze is intensely frustrated with the incompleteness of the Hegelian absolute. Admittedly Hegel's difference is relative where Kant's difference merely is actual. But what Deleuze builds his libidinal metaphysics on is the pure difference that he takes from Nietzsche. Which is what we call the oscillation. It is not enough that Hegel throws the subject into his predecessor Spinoza's monist nature-as-The-One. We throw the Deleuzian project into the Hegelian subject in the corresponding manner and bring to mind that without *the Nietzschean-Deleuzian project* there is no libidinal subject to speak of. Hegel's very challenge of Kant requires an active subject *vis-à-vis* an active object. These are then neither united through any form of Spinozist objectivity nor through any manner of Hegelian subjectivity, but through *the dialectical projectivity between the Spinozist substance and the Hegelian subject.*

This is simultaneously Hegel's *freedom* and Whitehead's *creativity* in earnest. Both utopianism and dystopianism vanish when we unite Hegel's phallus, and the Apollonian order it represents, with Nietzsche's matrix, and the Dionysian chaos it represents. Thereby an age-old engineering dream is realized. The Deleuzian Protopia becomes possible, and its name is *Syntheos*, the technological offspring of the two-headed phallus itself, without any matrichal involvement. Or as Hegel himself might express the matter: No one can stop this movement since no agent involved ever is completely and fully himself. The project is Zoroastrianism's *ameretat* that begets itself anew, and thereby survives the subject as Zoroastrianism's completed *haurvatat*. History is its own project, a process that produces subjectivities via negations and oscillations, not the other way around.

The Spinozist sacral matrix with its amalgamation of attributes is the implicate order (the Eastern matrix domain), and the Hegelian sacred phallus with its negation is the explicate order (the Eastern phallus domain). Thus far all Spinozists and Hegelians can agree. However with Deleuze's breakneck attempt to mount Nietzsche directly on top of Spinoza – that is: his interesting and productive, yet eventually failed attempt to conduct philosophy without including Hegel in the equation – the dialectics is driven to yet another new level. The snag now is that the digital age necessitates a new mythos. We know from previously that a lone logos as only logos, breaks down in the form of a collective neurosis, while we know from previously that a lone pathos as only pathos, breaks down in the form of a collective psychosis. The only way to attain functionality is to establish *the paradigmatic myth*, and until that project is carried out we find ourselves in a state where *time is out of joint*. That is: the story of time deviates from time itself.

Power is, in Michel Foucault's wording, as crazy as the lunatics it locks up. This applies as long as it cannot manage to transition from merely understanding (logos) to a complete reason (logos and pathos unified in the form of mythos), a narratological dilemma that American philosopher Wilfrid Sellars devotes his entire career to investigating. In syntheological terms it concerns synthesizing Pantheos' amalgamation with Atheos' negation to thus achieve a Nietzschean Entheos. And it is this creative entheist diversity that we call *protopianism*. Please note how we attain this state without cheating through some simplified eternalizations along the way. Our nature oscillates, our culture negates. There is no fixed Protopia but merely a protopian movement. All of it is in constant motion and constant change. We gradually pick off one element after the other, phenomenon for phenomenon, until we find the Protopia to which we provisionally and momentarily dedicate ourselves, before we move on to the next Protopia. Our universe is and remains pandialectical. The Platonist order is long dead. But Syntheos now allows itself to be sensed on the horizon.

Hegelian dialectics connects with the Zoroastrian and the Jewish traditions through the axiomatic assumption that *three is more important than two*. Exactly this is the basis of the principal Western criticism of the Eastern fixation with a dualism and the more or less static state of tension between two poles. With three components instead of two, a completely different dynamics is created, a constantly ongoing movement. At the same time as a triad always is more stable over time than a dyad. What is decisive is thus not the relation between two poles – for instance between Taoism's *yang* and *yin* – but the third factor that is concealed behind or beneath this undynamic polarity. The chieftain and the priest in part measure themselves against each other, in part against the matriarch. The man and the woman marry each other, but not by themselves but before the priest who demands marital vows from them. The president and the parliament share power between them, but only within the legal frameworks that are determined by a supreme court. With Hegel the natural dialectical triad that prevails between *the discretion, the continuity* and *the oscillation* receives a memetic correspondence in the form of the cultural dialectical triad that arises between *the event, the process* and *the negation*. The discretion and the event are the provisionally fixed points, or the eternalizations, within nature and culture respectively. The oscillation and the process are the actual state of things, a state that prevails before or without any phallic order has been established, that is: mobilism in itself, and later also the mobilization of the eternalization as the next degree of mobilism (see *The Global Empire*). And if something applies both for nature and culture, we can for good reason presume a universal validity.

The insight that we live in a finite and limited universe compels us to recognize that infinities and infinitesimals by definition are inconceivable according to the prerequisites for such a universe. If one wishes to correctly describe the actual extremes of existence mathematically, one consequently replaces the infinities with *enormities*, just as one replaces the infinitesimals with *enormitesimals*. At the same time one can and should point out that the number zero never can have a value that is precisely zero, since its very existence and the fact that it can be spoken about and manipulated in itself generates an oscillating value whose average may be close to zero but that never can be exactly zero, and therefore zero is not zero. We quite simply live in *a pandialectical universe*; we are at the point where the dialectical movement arises, where the oscillation in nature encounters its correspondence in the form of the negation in culture.

This is the state that Slavoj Žižek calls *less than nothing* in a book from 2013 with precisely this title: *Less Than Nothing.* And what is this negation other than the abyss within the continuity with its built-in enormity *vis-à-vis* the clear and delimited discretion? What is Man's transition from child till adult, or the sociont's transition from anarchy to civilization, if not the adultification as negation? Up until the oscillation, caused by an existential deficit rather than by a surplus, once again triggers the discretion, whereupon the natural dialectics is repeated. The oscillation is of course less resource-demanding to maintain for nature than the costly and in the long run unsustainable fixation. Thereby the problem with the Taoist polarization between two principles – *yang* versus *yin* – as first principle, is laid bare. Problems arise if a religion ultimately is built on two principles that are locked together in an eternal dance routine; to maintain any dynamics the religion must at least start from two completely different libidinal axes – in part the masculine *yang* and the feminine *yin* along the one axis, in part *will-to-transcendence* and *will-to-intelligence* along the other axis. If not, no innovative thinking can be developed, nor even be conceivable.

We can localize *religion* and its *radicality* entirely to the phallic sphere. The matrichal sphere instead harbors what we call *spirituality* with its focus on *continuity*. Religion is of course about the art of separating differentiation and unity in themselves. Thus there is no activity that is more religious than Hegelian dialectics (it does of course, as we know, result in a *syntheology*). Spirituality however regards unity as an axiom. Therefore the priest himself assumes the role as the androgynous link between the two axes, rather than being the general link between the principles in themselves. He is on the one hand masculine at the same time as he, on the other hand, is a representative of the matrichal will-to-intelligence *within the patriarchy in itself*. The priest thus has to serve as the Hegelian exception that keeps the entire construction together (as Hegel himself did in his relation to the Prussian court). Zoroastrianism solves this dilemma through focusing on the phallic project and letting this as an entirety represent the two-headed phallus. Judaism does the same thing through placing Moses at the helm of the sibling triad that leads the exodus out of Egypt. It is thus the priest who in his guise personifies *the amalgamation* in an emergentist sense and *the negation* in a paradigmatic sense. This since the priest realizes the necessity that enables the chieftain to tame the contingency. Or to express the matter with metaphysical metaphors: the priest personifies the root-of-the-phallus or *the law* in determinism and *the contact with the ground*, the chieftain personifies phallus itself and *freedom* in indeterminism and *the direction toward heaven*, this at the same time as the dialectics of them enables transcendental emergentism as a metaphysical foundation. Thus there is no longer any need for an external creator-god. The process is creative in itself.

A world that is only built on *yang* versus *yin* however lacks – despite Man's intense fixation with sexual attraction – both negation and oscillation. Nor can it therefore generate a genuine event, but merely time and again refer to the eternal recurrence of the same in one long, protracted and determinist loop. The transcendental vision must be brought about and the intelligent strategy must be created within the confines of the phallic patriarchy. This is necessary in order to achieve a movement in any direction and for *yang* to be able to drag *yin* along forward. The only thing matriarchy has to do in this context is to maintain circular iconology and follow the patriarchy. The matriarchy is of course richly blessed by nature and is furnished with both matrix and mamilla, while the – in this context – unfortunate patriarchy has had to settle for phallus only. Therefore the patriarchy compensates for this natural shortage with a cultural dividing of phallus between in part chieftain, in part priest, and between these two poles a dialectics of freedom is created.

Before the nomadological sociont, *freedom* from the old and to the new thus prevails, and behind the nomadological sociont *necessity* rules. The patriarchy is therefore driven by a *seduction* that plays out between two heads, while the matriarchy is driven by a *conformation* before a single head. It is the agent who leads that needs diversity, not the agent that follows. Otherwise, it is practically only about the art of finding one's way amid the classical archetypes in the new territory or the new paradigm, in order to be able to become an *erchtype* that mimics a matching archetype. We are once again concerned with *mimesis* as the fundamental property and the patterned behavior in the human drive system. The distanced phallus is pitted against the intimate mamilla. The phallic and macroscopic strategy is pitted against matrichal and microscopic intrigue. Man invariably follows and submits to the strongest leadership he succeeds in discovering. If there is then no authentic phallus in sight, Man will settle for a false one (see *Digital Libido – Sex, Power and Violence in the Network Society*). The consequences of this we know only too well.

Nomadology arises first, but is complemented and surpassed by eventology, which in turn makes exodology possible. The promised empire is united under a cohesive, overarching religion. However Taoism remains within circular nomadology without being able to generate a visionary eventology. Therefore Taoism has never functioned for the organisation of militaries or state bureaucracies. It is rather a byproduct of the settled society that lacks contact with the origin of phallic religion in hunting and warfare. This gap is filled in Axial Age China by a completely separate system, *Confucianism*, and later by an imported Buddhism mixed with Zoroastrianism, all of which give China, Japan and the rest of East Asia, a religion that is designed for hunters and merchants. Ever since, the warrior and the hunter have been kept separate in East Asian culture, both of them subject to an imperial rule with ambitions to exercise power both within the spiritual and the worldly sphere, which has led to both productive and destructive results. This happened while church and state were separated in the West in the 5th century, and became symbolic and imaginary power spheres respectively, without establishing the necessary patriarchal connection between them. State and market thereby were placed outside the domain of religion with well-known results. The two-headed phallus was discarded and replaced by two circumscribed pseudophalluses, which enabled the rise of capitalism and a considerable accumulation of prosperity. But all this occurred at the cost of the world no longer being cohesive, that the one hand really does not know what the other is doing, and that hard-to-fathom and seemingly context-free conflicts incessantly flare up. The social energy is wasted on building thin membranes around the *plurarchy* that happens to be at hand for the moment, this instead of building strong membranes around a powerful two-headed phallus.

The prophet of the two-headed phallus in ancient Greece is without a doubt Aristotle, which is seen clearly in the criticism he directs toward his predecessor Plato. Where Plato sees mind as *logos,* Aristotle understands mind as a constant dialectical struggle between *logos* and *pathos*, which is manifested in the Aristotelian victory over the Persians, something that in turn leads to Hellenism's extension during Alexander the Great – antiquity's real *Saoshyant* – in the Middle East. And the Platonist philosopher-king is of course never materialized either, the world has to settle for a threadbare savior suspended on a cross, the Christian savior whose disciples form a mob that vandalizes the famed library in Alexandria, a culture-historical tragedy of vertiginous proportions. Which brings us to Aristotle's four phallic causality chains: logical architecture (the formal cause), logical material (the material cause), pathical energy (the effective cause) and pathical purpose (the final cause) – the backbone of all ensuing *membranics*. Architecture and material represent being (Zoroastrianism's *ahura*), energy and the objective represent becoming (Zoroastrianism's *mazda*). And the final objective, *the phallic vision*, gives the phallic value to the entire process that starts from the causality chain.

The energy that is developed in this process triggers will-to-power, but it can be expressed in two different ways. Either it will be locked up, as a repetitive loop in the form of will-to-intelligence, or else it breaks loose and assumes the form of will-to-transcendence that trumps will-to-intelligence. This means that the causes within the Aristotelian causality doctrine, if we are precise, ought to be five rather than just four. The last, final cause must be split in two as precisely *yang* and *yin*. That is: if Taoism plays the sexual card too hard, this is precisely the aspect that is lacking in Aristotle – as in Plato – that is: an understanding of sexuality as a propelling force and, not least, as the motor of dreams, projections and ambitions. The matrichal, final cause is thus called *will-to-intelligence* (Taoism's *yin* and Zoroastrianism's *ahura*), and the phallic, final cause is called *will-to-transcendence* (Taoism's *yang* and Zoroastrianism's *mazda*). It is only through using this dual perspective that we can apply Aristotelian causality to nomadology. The final objective must of course be both tempting and seductive (as will-to-transcendence), and at the same time be manipulative and conformist (as will-to-intelligence) for the sociont to manifest itself as a cohesive will-to-power. The sociont must be driven by at least two religions, which in turn must be retold both as logos and mythos, to then moreover be celebrated together as *the pathical ritual*, which in turn throws the sociont back to the architecture and the material for the next causality chain. It is in this way, and only in this way, that we can understand transcendence as a *cephalization* of intelligence that is set in motion toward the phallic objective far away. The priest dies when the exodus is concluded and thus personifies *haurvatat*. The chieftain leads the entrance into the promised empire and thus personifies *ameretat*.

The children that are the consequence of the pathical ritual are born under the chieftain's protection and with his promise of provision – where and how else?

What is fascinating with Buddhism is how it develops into an inverted Zoroastrianism. Contemporary with the arrival of Christianity, Buddhism and Zoroastrianism even exist as parallel elite religions in the Kushan empire that comprises both Central Asia and northern India. That is: Buddhism is *the inverted eventology par excellence*. Buddhism sees the event as the occurrence that interrupts existence's infinitely long series of repeated traumas. Zoroastrianism however sees the event as the occurrence that leads history onto a new path and entails the starting point for the civilization process itself. Buddhism thus builds its worldview on a will to succeed in carrying out traumatology and thus break the nomadological curse that afflicts Man in the form of cyclical repetition for all eternity. It does this through Gnostic castration. Transcendence then becomes *the negation of desire* – extinction. The objective is to liberate oneself from the suffering that is desire's dark flip side. Zoroastrianism however builds its worldview on the will to succeed in carrying out eventology in itself to thus exit the nomadological curse. It does this through staging *the oscillation of desire*. Transcendence exits the dialectics that arises between drive and desire. The objective is not freedom from desire, but freedom to create. Where Buddhism halts and settles for negatology, Zoroastrianism goes further and develops eventology into what Hegel later labels *the negation of the negation*. Albeit that both these religions in populist vulgar versions preach reincarnation (in Buddhism) and eternal life (in Zoroastrianism). But in contrast to Hinduism in the East and Christianity and Islam in the West, there is no trace of such escapes from *death as the absolute* in the founders Siddharta Gautama and Zoroaster themselves. They remain wholly within the dialectics of negation and oscillation.

It is this radical affirmation of death as the absolute which is called *tantra*, in contrast to the pop religious *sutra* – including reincarnation and/or eternal life – that is preached to the masses. It is thus thanks to this literally tantric union that these religions respect each other, and perceive each other as reasonable alternatives for an intellectually honest person. To Zoroastrians, Buddhism is even the logical alternative *ahurayasna* (submission to being) *vis-à-vis* Zoroastrianism's own pathical religion *mazdayasna* (submission to mind). Zoroastrianism is a kind of *son of Hinduism*, and similarly Buddhism is a kind of *daughter of Hinduism* – two love children that are born after both permanent settlement and written language are in place. Buddhism is negatology where Zoroastrianism is eventology. It is wholly possible to harbor them both and integrate them as a kind of phallic religions of the priest and the chieftain respectively under one and the same roof. Which also occurs when traffic increases along the Central Asian trade routes; it occurs in the form of the syncretic practice that is called *vajrayana* (the word means "diamond phallus" in Sanskrit), first as the nominally Zoroastrian schools *dhyana* in India and *daena* in Iran, later as the nominally Buddhist schools *chan* in China, *thien* in Vietnam, *seon* in Korea, and *zen* in Japan. These spiritual schools are the very core of *the Silk Road triad*, they influence each other mutually in what can be seen as a dialectical process of the trade routes themselves. Today we pragmatically summarize the Persian tantric schools under the label *Zoroastrianism*, the Indian under the label *Buddhism*, and the Chinese under the label *Taoism*.

It is thus *Vajrayana* – with its unique understanding of the dialectics of tantra and sutra – that binds together the creative diversity of monastery-like *castags* that are developed in the oases along the near-endless Silk Road. And the kinship between these schools is more intimate than historians with European-colored spectacles for a long time were capable of comprehending. Since the 1970s it has, for instance, been clear that Padmasambhava, or Guru Rinpoche, Vajrayana's founder and more important for Vajrayana Buddhism than Siddharta Gautama himself, was of Persian and not of Indian origin. In the same way as Bodhidharma, the founder of Chan and

Zen Buddhism, and more important for the traditions we call chan, seon, thien and zen than Siddharta Gautama himself, also was of Persian and not of Indian origin. Padmasambhava and Bodhidharma were definitely no Indian princes – something that the myths and myth producers, for pure marketing reasons, have liked to claim, since royal sheen is expected to bestow theological gravitas and iconological glamour. There are no traces at all after Padmasambhava or Bodhidharma on the Indian subcontinent; they were merely shamanoid merchants from Zoroastrian Central Asia. When Padmasambhava preaches of the promised land for his Tibetan followers, he even calls this storied territory *Tagzig Olmo Lung Ring* in Tibetan (in Sanskrit abbreviated to *Oddiyana*), that is: what we today refer to as Tajikistan.

Nomadology is the standardized and horizontal exodology, while eventology is the exceptional and vertical exodology. Nomadology follows and carries out its activity by the principle of the least possible energy consumption. Its circular movement along the track that has been laid thus consumes less energy than permanent sitting still. Eventology instead follows the principle of the temporary increase of the energy consumption when a surplus of energy is available. It is thus only eventology that can cultivate a fantasy of sitting still for an eternity. These theological narratives correspond to transcendental eternalism, pragmatic mobilism and dialectical syntheism. The barred absolute here is the ecstatic experience of the event as the syntheist ideal *the infinite now*, and it is clearly manifested as pathos during hunting, war, the orgy, birth, the ritual and death. We thus have on the one hand the sociont's outer circuit, on the other hand its inner circuit, as well as their two essentially different narratives: logos and mythos.

History is one long accumulation of interobjective collisions and events. The cybernetic and scientific revolutions during the 20th century created a synchronized explosion of entropy, and thereby also of information, to our worldview. The only reasonable way of dividing up this expanded history is to insist that nature operates within various emergence vectors, while culture correspondingly operates within various paradigms. The various ideological constructions that are built on top of these domains we call *paradigmatics*. As long as a paradigm lacks serious competition, the relevant paradigmatics is fixed on top of the actual vector. And in the same way that culture is dependent upon nature, the paradigms are dependent upon the underlying emergence vectors. The revolutionizing communication technology that enables and in retrospect even necessitates the new paradigm, is referred to as *paradigmata*. With respect to really significant, genuine paradigm shifts in human history, it is thus the technologies that have enabled spoken language, written language, mass media, and interactivity that are actual paradigmata. Examples of such paradigmata are papyrus, the printing press, the telegraph, transport vehicles, the computer, server halls and smartphones. And the most epochal paradigmata we could imagine would be a container for God himself.

The original eventology is *the dialectics of eternalism and mobilism* (see *The Global Empire*) that nature recreates as *the dialectics of negation and oscillation*. Phenomena and substances arise out of processes and fields. During these processes there is the duration, or hypertime, as the continuous time that precedes *the big bounce*. On top of this implicate subphysics, explicate physics arises with its oscillating discretions after *the big bounce*. This makes *metahistory* possible. History is completed, while metahistory continues to move. Hypertime precedes, as mentioned, and survives spacetime. Even if history would stop, freeze or cease to exist, metahistory keeps ticking, both before *the big bounce* and after the Universe's dissolution, and we can speak of an attained absolute in a Hegelian sense, an eternalization in history that remains a continuous process in hypertime. The difference between subphysics as the implicate order and physics as the explicate order – before and after the Universe's long parenthesis – is in the highest degree concerned with *the dialectics of discretion and continuity*. Where the link between the two extremes is *the universal oscillation*. It is thus a case of a dialectics between them and not just an emergence transition, since subphysics remains under physics even after the actual emergence for the substance in itself takes place. Subphysics *subsists* where physics *exists*. And Hegel is proven correct in both ends of the origin of dialectics: *Hegel's classical substance* begins with the dialectics of continuous hypertime and discrete spacetime. At the same time as *Hegel's classical subject* begins with the dialectics of the Hegelian negation and the Nietzschean oscillation. Therefore we categorize these relations as *first dialectics*.

What remains of subphysics emerges particularly clearly at the microlevel. This is because there is – even if both spacetime and substance operate as radical discretions – a constantly ongoing oscillation, which is a basic prerequisite for the dialectical process. And the less discretions that are concerned, the more powerful the oscillations will be. Precisely this is the basis for the quantum physical phenomenon that goes under the designation *Heisenberg's uncertainty principle*. The smaller the units we attempt to document in detail, the more uncertain the result of our measurements. Eventually we are forced to give up all efforts to try to establish position (event) and movement (process) at a given point in time. For it is not possible to both eternalize and mobilize existence at the same time, one must decide on the one or the other perspective. Eternalization (as negation and discretion) and mobilization (as oscillation and continuity) must be spread out, one after the other, along the time axis. And the fascinating principle that lays down this once and for all is *the universal oscillation*. There is thus no quantum mechanics, there is only *quantum organics*. And existence can only be described as a fundamental *panorganicism* or *pandialecticism*. But this quantum organics is in turn subject to a formidable pressure in the form of the phenomenon that is called decoherence. And this decoherence is quite simply the explosion of relationalist effects that are released in a monist universe where everything constantly influences everything else. This is the magical and mystical gravitation. The sole really impermeable membrane only exists around the Universe itself.

Every conceivable potentiality is negated until only a single actuality remains – what we call reality. This means that every hint of continuity is fixed as a discretion when the phenomena in question transmutate. And thereafter the low-energy oscillation sets everything in motion anew, which clarifies that every conception of a Platonist world of ideas merely is free fantasies, banal stupidity with no idea of the world's divine complexity. Subphysical hypertime operates continuously, but as soon as spacetime with its mass and energy enters the picture, decoherence takes over. The oscillating discretion then becomes the yardstick of everything. The same of course applies, as French philosopher Quentin Meillassoux points out, with respect to the difference between *virtuality* and *potentiality*. The virtual is a state of pure contingency that only is actualized in conjunction with an emergence, as virtuality's temporary habits are converted to genuine laws which *de facto* apply for the new emergence vector. Potentiality is however bound to precisely the emergence vector within which it already operates. It is only when virtuality is confronted by the time axis that it is potentialized and then forced into a decisive actualization, but without this affecting the emergence vector as such. The transition from continuity to discretion we call *transmutation*. The transition from virtuality to potentiality we correspondingly call *transdeterminism*.

The metahistorical combination of continuity and virtuality is reduced through what American philosopher Terence Deacon calls *abstentialism* – an excellent metaphysical application of Hegelian negatology – to the historical combination of discretion and potentiality, that is: this occurs as a direct effect of spacetime's powerful decoherence. And there is then no possible way whatsoever back again, this in accordance with the principle of *irreductionism* in emergence vector theory. This conclusion has dramatic consequences for ethics. Unsurprisingly, Meillassoux's mentor Alain Badiou in his classical work *L'Etre et l'événement* uses an eventological concept that he calls *truth-as-an-act* (see *Syntheism – Creating God in the Internet*

Age). This is an every bit as intense as easily understandable yearning for an embodiment of a phallic order in a chaotic world. Badiou's existentialist truth-as-an-act makes Man rise above his animality and assume exclusively human qualities. While our own, primarily Zoroastrian and later also syntheist truth-as-an-act, rather is about a renaissance for the tribal archetype and above all, in the case of the priestly archetype, about converting the actual shamanic caste to *the future sociont*, for instance through identifying and classifying the new, victorious elite that steps forward as a consequence of the ongoing paradigm shift. This will-to-transcendence surpasses the underlying will-to-intelligence in the same way as libido must surpass mortido – even if only temporarily – in the dialectics between them. And as such it is *tribopoietic*, and not autopoietic.

It is the chieftain who personifies the vision *vis-à-vis* the priest. Sure, it is the priest who creates the vision itself, who formulates the new narrative, but it is the chieftain who personifies it, and it is this identificatory portrayal that constitutes *truth-as-an-act* itself. It is worth noting the decisive difference between on the one hand Badiou's truth-as-an-act and on the other hand the syntheist truth-as-an-act, namely that the former submits to a totalitarian phallus (Badiou is not just a Christian but moreover both a Rousseauian and a Maoist, in other words an almost complete Gnostic), while the latter starts from the premise that the phallus in question must be divided and bring about a living dialectics in order to function as a credible foundation for truth over time. From the perspective of the history of ideas we express this as though Alain Badiou's version of truth-as-an-act is *the Egyptian event par excellence,* while the syntheist version of truth-as-an-act is *the Persian event par excellence.* Here the decisive difference lies between the Platonist obsession with the relation between *subject* and *object* as foundation, and the Heraclitean dialectics that presupposes that there first of all must exist a driving *project* in place before a subject and an object can take shape at all. This shift is the dialectical innovation that Hegel calls *the negation of the negation.*

It is precisely this prerequisite that is the foundation of dialectical materialism. The chain of thought in question is developed to perfection by philosopher Adrian Johnston in his book *Adventures in Transcendental Materialism*, where the title states what the matter is about: *transcendental materialism*. But once we replace matter with emergence as the first institution of the process, we notice that the same thing applies, if possible to an even greater extent, for both dialectical emergentism and *transcendental emergentism*, which follow as the next step. An emergence is an extraordinary event along the time axis – not least what we call the human soul between its subconsciousness and consciousness – that gives rise to a completely new vector with its own built-in forces, behaviors, laws, rules and structures. Our own transdeterminist universe is in itself an example of such an emergence vector that has arisen along a subphysical hypertime axis. A paradigm is correspondingly a completely new society, at a specific starting point on the time axis, with its own built-in forces, power struggles and eventually also laws and rules, all of which can be traced back in time to a decisive historical event in the form of, for instance, an extensive natural catastrophe or an epochal technological invention.

Nature's own eternalization is the wave function collapse. The mobilist wave is converted into the eternalist particle. The subconscious is a field where self-consciousness is afflicted by the wave function collapse. The subconscious is *the process*, consciousness is *the event*, and the unconscious beneath it all (after the Hegelian-Freudian revolution in Europe in the 19th century) is nothing but the negation. *The pathical first dialectics* is the dialectics of negation and oscillation, what Hegel would call the subject that produces the substance (in the sense that the subject projects substantiality onto existence). *The logical first dialectics* is the dialectics of hypertime and spacetime, what Hegel would call the substance that produces the subject (in the sense that the cultural subject is born out of the natural substance). *The mythical first dialectics* is consequently *the metadialectics* of the pathical and the logical first dialectics. Pathos and logos can never meet other than as an incompatible deadlock, as Man's eternal story of himself in an intangible world, a story without end. The Hegelian negation leads to Hegelian absolute knowledge. The Nietzschean oscillation leads to the Nietzschean paradigmatic affirmation. Hegel and Nietzsche unite as two sides of the same gigantic, mythical coin.

All this makes nature a panorganist phenomenon, but due to the principle of neutral monism we need not concern ourselves about any form of panpsychism, which of course is nothing other than a neurotically inverted reductionism (which inevitably leads to a psychotic dissolution of the distinction between subject and substance). And it is of course the emergences and their emergence vectors that ensure that this is the case. It occurs as early as during the first transition from quantum chaos to a solid, under the emergent shift from subphysics to physics. Please note how the negation's own syntheological master Atheos sets everything else in motion. The origin of everything is thus not the origin's virtuality, but *virtuality's actualization as movement and change*, and the relations that this movement generates (relationalism as first principle in retrospect). Virtuality receives a potency to be actualized through the encounter with another virtuality, whereupon relationalism explodes. In the 19th century German philosopher Freidrich von Schelling calls this the difference between *the foundation of being* and *being in itself*. Schelling's countryman Hegel points out that, if so, we might as well refer to virtuality as *the negation* that creates the void that makes all other existence arise as if through a kind of fundamental, existential vacuum pump. And in the wake of Hegel, Henri Bergson teaches us to distinguish between duration (hypertime) and time (spacetime) in precisely the same logical way. So that the subject can separate the hypertemporal root-of-the-phallus from the spatiotemporal phallus when the subject creates the project that generates the subject itself. The subject projects *substantiality* onto the substance, so that the subject can be libidinalized on top of the substance's mortido.

Paradigmatics is then Man's way of defining the various time-bound emergence vectors and paradigms and separating them from each other. Archetypology is then the sociont's way of defining itself and its various abilities and needs in mutual influence of and with the actual emergence vectors and paradigms. Here it is fitting to remember physicist Ludwig Boltzmann's astute observation that chaos and surprise require considerably more information than order and predictability. Therefore systems are developed naturally over time toward an increased stability through what physicist Erwin Schrödinger calls *negentropy*. This occurs in the same way that nodes arise spontaneously in a state of anarchy, just as power and force is increasingly concentrated around the nodes in what we therefore call *nodalization*. The system as a whole is thereby made more effective. This leads to a plurarchical state that in the case of culture can be likened to a *protocivilization* or, in the wake of a paradigm shift, a *protoparadigm*. Out of the implicate plurarchy – and with assistance from a phallic raising of awareness – first the priest, and then the chieftain, can step forward and stage the explicate exodology. Both negentropy and nodalization oscillate constantly, which entails that the functionality of the various systems is optimized. Which means that a new paradigm cannot be manifested until a new elite marches into a new promised territory.

9
Transcendental emergentism

In the introduction to our book *Syntheism – Creating God in the Internet Age* we argue that *everything is religion*, which also is the title of the first chapter. We discuss the fact that several thought systems believe themselves to be the opposite of religion, and purport to be strictly rational and governed by reason themselves, but how it actually is precisely these ideologies that are the most treacherous and often more religious than anything else. Those methodically inclined have of course already noted that we in this book also claim the same, that everything is religion, but that this apparently does not prevent us from making another statement, namely that *everything is history*. This should of course not remain without comment. What do we actually mean? Are these two declarations not incompatible? Can everything both be religion and history? Or are we merely devoting ourselves to twisting words?

Let us clarify: everything is history that is religion, and everything is religion that is history. And another name for this history of religion and religion of history is – of course – God. The correct way of describing history and existence is thus as a *chronotheology*, a kind of voyage from or to or in parallel with the divine. In step with an increasing amount of information being made available to Man over the course of history, our experience of history as a whole shrinks. When the Old Testament was written at various points in time during the first millennium BC, an aggregate history of 6,000 years from creation to the present was regarded as an enormously long time-span. But with today's Internet-driven view of history, the more than 200,000 years during which the human species *Homo sapiens* has existed, can rather be regarded as a vanishingly small drop in history's enormous ocean. God has expanded rather than shrunk over the last century. Since we have accepted that there are several different dimensions of time, this entails that we might as well be dealing with many different gods. Or perhaps rather with many different religions. Thus religion and history constitute two sides of the same coin.

Let us begin by examining the two ontic time dimensions, *global hypertime* and *local spacetime*, where global hypertime belongs to *the implicate order* and local spacetime belongs to *the explicate order* in the natural sciences, that is: the distinction that Friedrich von Schelling makes as early as the beginning of the 19th century when he separates the foundation of existence, or *the root-of-the-phallus,* from existence in itself, or *phallus,* which means that von Schelling nails the starting point for classical dialectics. In modern natural science this dialectics corresponds to the virtual and implicate order as *continuous subphysics* versus the potential and explicate order as *discrete physics* (for instance in the opposition between the Einsteinian theory of relativity and Bohrian quantum physics). This means that we deal with *impotent habits* in the implicate order before the actual event which become *potent laws* in the explicate order after the actual event.

Laws thus have a contingent origin in a specific event, but thereby it is not established that there at some point has been a rule-maker, a legislator who precedes the rules themselves. Therefore it also is pointless to discuss whether the metaphysics we are defending here, *transcendental emergentism*, is weak or strong in character, since it is weak or *virtual* in its implicate, continuous, habit-forming state that leads to the event, while it by contrast is strong or *potential* in its explicate, discrete, law-governed state after the emergence in question has taken place. Nothing of this entails any philosophical news, of course. As early as the 6th century BC Anaximander – who of course, just as his successor Pythagoras, was schooled in Persian process philosophy – talks about an infinite *apeiron* that is not marred by any of spacetime's trivial limitations, which precedes and underpins all that is material in existence that Man *de facto* perceives and interacts with. Unsurprisingly we recognize many of the attributes in today's subphysics from Anaximander's equally radically monist *apeironology*. At the lowest level there are no laws or substances at all, but merely an infinite and undefinable primordial state that in retrospect constitutes the virtual prerequisite for later laws and substances.

Once we are totally clear on this, we can proceed and investigate the two ontological time dimensions after which Man and his tribal psyche orient themselves, namely *phallic linear time* and *matrichal circular time*. Phallic linear time then belongs to the explicate order, while matrichal circular time belongs to the implicate order. These two dimensions then converge in a contingent universe characterized by *neutral monism*, where the indeterminism of phallic linear time and the determinism of matrichal circular time meet and coalesce into *transdeterminism* as an overarching, metahistorical principle. Neutrality quite simply means that every emergence is heterogeneous and not homogeneous. It is radically unique and irreducible *vis-à-vis* both the implicate predecessor and *vis-à-vis* history in its entirety. Of course the emergence is not even reducible to the emergence vector in which it was generated. All preexisting emergence vectors have *de facto* shaped its genesis. An example is how the human mind and human culture have arisen in parallel and mutually affected one another continually, which has resulted in that it eventually became possible to rise above human biology. However it is impossible to say that the one precedes the other, they both mutually condition each other. It is this radical *irreductionism*, tied to and only tied to the time axis, that provides us with neutral monism. Phallic linear time is quite simply local time inasmuch as linearity is perceived over shorter distances.

At the same time as matrichal circular time is global time inasmuch as circularity is perceived at extremely long distances, for instance hundreds of millions of years.

Global hypertime is eventually bent in toward itself and the Universe's pulse adapts to this enormously protracted movement, a concept that is developed by for instance physicist Roger Penrose as a theory of temporal *aeons* rather than spatial *universes* in the book *Cycles of Time* (2010). The global, the matrichal and the virtual thus belong together, and we call the studies of this emergence vector *cosmic nomadology*. The local, the phallic and the potential also belong together, and we call the studies of this emergence vector *cosmic eventology*. As a result of that, philosophy about world history becomes *a dialectical narratology of processes and events*. And hypertime returns constantly as metaphysics' own root-of-the-phallus since it is necessary for the universal synchronicity. Therefore please note that it is not possible to measure hypertime, since time is measured with different kinds of clocks that consist of mass and energy and that therefore must be located inside and not outside a material universe. However it is possible to *think* hypertime to thereby be able to think in terms of differences and emergences in the first place. Thus there is a kind of (thought) time before spacetime, and it is – quite simply because such a universe lacks mass and energy – both spatiotemporally disconnected and universally synchronous. *Hypertime is a pure and continuous duration*. And as the photons that lack mass can recount (if they were able to recount anything at all), hypertime is not noticeable if and when you find yourself inside it. From there time in itself can merely be apprehended as completely motionless in its pure temporality.

Before Einsteinian spacetime arises and physics is born, there already exist scores of virtual fields or *membranes*. We therefore speak of *subphysical membranics*. This is a world full of virtualities, but without any potentialities whatsoever. Moreover, the virtualities can only be discovered and identified in retrospect since nothing can be discovered or established before relationalism gives potency to existence. The virtual fields therefore do not behave as fields within classical spacetime. First of all, they are both infinitely small and infinitely large – a property that we call *extension neutrality* – since they do not need to relate to any classical spacetime dimension at all. And they only exist ontically but not actually, however, since they do not need to relate to classical time at all. It is instead rather when these virtual membranes collide with each other that potency is generated, and it is the relations that then arise that create processes as *actualities.* We call this process-philosophical prioritization *radical relationalism* (see *Syntheism – Creating God in the Internet Age*) since the underlying virtual structure – what we call *pure chaos* below the Planck length, or what Alain Badiou before us calls *pure multiplicity* – on the whole is pointless to concern oneself with.

Why? Well, even if the virtual membranes are metaphysically spectacular – since they are precisely virtual rather than potential, and after all they teach us to understand the implicate that precedes and rapidly vanishes beneath the explicate – they must still be regarded as ontic rather than just ontological. We express this, in the spirit of Alfred North Whitehead, as though "the fields contain all conceivable dimensions without being present in any of these" and that "the fields contain all conceivable relations without being engaged in any of them". What is important to understand is that the virtual membranes are not ontic on their own, but that they attain their onticity precisely through being in motion, which in turn leads to collisions with and the establishment of relations to other virtual fields. They are in a contingent continuum without any necessities whatsoever. Everything can happen. We express this as though the subphysical membranes are *fields of virtualities* and that they belong to the implicate order within *subphysics*, while the radical relations that arise when the virtual fields interact with each other are called *fields of potentialities*, which belong to the explicate order within *physics.*

Colliding with a subphysical membrane is to create a new relation as a novelty. Colliding with a physical relation is however to engage in and modify a relation that already exists. It is only in the latter dialectical relation of three rather than two that any kind of natural scientific observation can take place. We therefore speak of subphysics as real, but note that there are neither subprocesses, nor subrelations, nor subevents just because we assign subphysics a status as an emergence vector under physics and the other natural sciences. Virtuality is only precisely virtuality and no potentiality in itself. And within subphysical membranics, the membranes are only fields of virtualities without qualifying as the actualized *spheres* that Peter Sloterdijk later uses as metaphors for the different worlds that the relations produce. While at the same time the requirement for relationalism applies also for the emergences themselves. It is impossible to perceive an emergence in itself. It is only *vis-à-vis* other emergences that an emergence in all its originality can be apprehended as precisely an emergence. En emergence is caused by a plurality of causes. It is a radically relationalist phenomenon. This means that virtualities are literally meaningless until they collide with each other, whereupon radical relationalism begins. It is then and only then that processes, relations and events arise that make it literally *meaningful* to speak of *existence* in any kind of phenomenological sense.

Then we may ask ourselves the following question: Why should one care about the foundation for existence at all, if it only is existence in itself that generates everything that is of phenomenological interest? The radical relations produce the *relata* that we can register and interact with, and that appear precisely as the objects which we apprehend as co-existent. Thereby, nor is there any *general emergence theory,* since no emergence is preordained or molded in any respect, but is unique also when regarded as an emergence in itself. This explains why we sum up relationalist metaphysics as *transcendental emergentism*. A new emergence along the hypertime axis also entails that the emergence theory *in itself* must be reconsidered. This makes the emergence theory open relative to the future and thereby transcendental instead of general. The first genuine exodus in history, from one universe to another, is thereby an accomplished fact. Thereafter there is – literally – no end to how many emergence vectors can be connected to each other up until Man realizes syntheism and more or less consciously creates a functional God. We simply regard the implicate order as a kind of nature's own continuous subconsciousness, while the explicate order is a kind of nature's discretionary consciousness, where it is only the latter state that is possible to observe and measure in any meaningful sense. The relations generate hypertime's expansion in spacetime, the membranes are bound together into spheres, the information expands and existence is *realized*. The natural sciences get something to interact with and in this way become meaningful.

It is, moreover, perfectly possible to study the difference between consciousness and subconsciousness in the same way, as an explicate and implicate order respectively, as two independent and simultaneously intertwined emergence vectors where indeterminism and determinism only arise as local attributes, which entails that the Universe as a whole only can be regarded as transdeterminist. This in turn means that it is time to eliminate the illusory opposition between idealism and materialism. And the metaphysical system with which one administers this elimination is transcendental emergentism. At the same time as it is time to eliminate the opposition between determinism and indeterminism, and the principle with which one does so is called transdeterminism, a principle which in Hegelese places the contingency in the future and the necessity in the past, and which thereby reduces chance to a local issue of actualizations of probabilities via relations and nothing else. The Universe in itself as a whole is neither idealist nor materialist, but emergent. It appears through a series of processes. And it is, thus, emergent many times over in the form of emergence vectors that act as implicate orders that generate further emergences as new explicate orders. Every emergence is moreover equipped with its own contingent, transdeterminist and negation-driven causality chains. That is: with its own specific *laws of nature.*

It is precisely this that makes the classical opposition between strong emergence and weak emergence utterly pointless. It is the answer to a question that is erroneously posed. If we accept transcendental emergentism as *the metaphysical absolute,* there are by definition no preordained laws or rules for how an emergence can or should or must take place. The last god to die is the idea that the emergences in themselves are subject to some sort of preordained metalaws, dictated by some sort of final remnant of a pseudocreator who was already retired. We have indeed enjoyed a very long and painful goodbye to these cherished laws. Relationalism entails that existence fundamentally really is implicate orders of virtual membranes whose collisions give rise to new emergences, and that the temporary behaviors that arise in conjunction with these emergences then become prevailing laws within the new, explicate emergence vector. Hegel eliminates this illusory dilemma of emergentism, when he in the early 19th century becomes the first transdeterminist in Western discourse by claiming that the future always is contingent and that necessity only can be ontologically attributed to processes in retrospect, that is: that the necessity is a retroactive construction. If we follow Hegel's line of argument, it becomes impossible to speak of any kind of mysterious metalaw that prescribes how that which we apprehend as laws of nature must be designed. Instead it becomes clear that every emergence is genuinely unique. What makes people construct these fictions in retrospect is that they more or less desperately try to envisage the effect that the emergence vector in question may have on their own lives. The question of strong or weak emergence is thus a mythical and not a logical question, a question that reflects our lingering fixation with a concealed creator-god as a magical explanation to everything that is complicated, and which requires counterintuitive thinking to be comprehensible for real.

Transcendental emergentism does not just relate neutrally

vis-à-vis emergence vectors within neutral monism; it is actually also *neutral vis-à-vis neutrality in itself.* Which is not some kind of coquette, intellectual game to claim, but it is instead key to the entire transdeterminist logic. This explains how various processes are developed with seemingly forceful determination and in a seemingly predetermined direction without any gods intervening and without any laws being involved. We need not even include chance in the equation. Transcendental emergentism is – regarded as metaphysical metatheory – an emergence vector theory that operates from a *negative dialectics.* What emerges is of course something that previously only has existed in a virtual but not in an actual sense in preceding emergence vectors. The fact that the emergences are irreducible *vis-à-vis* that which precedes them in the causal chain that runs along the time axis, results in the relations between the emergence vectors being transdeterminist. As for the emergence vectors, we call the state that precedes them *the emergence's implicate order*, and the state that arises after the emergence, that is: the actualization of the emergence as a vector, we call *the emergence's explicate order.* That which was habits in the emergence under the implicate order, will in the later stage become laws under the explicate order. An emergence fixates or eternalizes the implicate order that precedes it, but it concurrently sets the explicate order or emergence vector that is actualized after it in motion. In other words: the emergence mobilizes the vector that it creates. The implicate order is the *virtuality*, the emergence itself is the *potentiality*, the explicate order is the *actuality.*

This is how we build a *metaphysics based on irreducible complexities;* such a metaphysics rejects the notion that any emergence vector has or even can have any kind of higher status or be superordinate to any other in an objective sense. We live in a universe whose transdeterminist state Danish philosopher Alexander Wrede Elung calls *neutral monism*, that is: a universe where the distancing from all forms of illusory superordination or hierarchy whatsoever shall be understood as an *emergence vector neutrality.* Within social theory we would call the same principle *paradigm neutrality* and regard this as just as necessary for *absolute historicism* as emergence vector neutrality is for neutral monism. Absolute historicism is of course a neutral historicism that energetically rejects all forms of *generationism* that prioritizes one paradigm in itself before the other. Why? Well, quite simply because Hegelian historicism makes history as a whole and in itself the absolute, rather than prioritizing any particular period or emphasizing and giving special treatment to any single event that transpires over the course of history. In the same manner neutral monism makes the Universe in itself the absolute, and maintains strict neutrality between the various emergence vectors. In syntheological terms we express this as if Pantheos takes precedence over Entheos, simply because none of Entheos' huge number of different expressions should be rewarded *per se* at the expense of any other expression.

Since eventology is an established fact in the history of ideas, it is no longer possible to regard the nomadological conception of history as anything other than a defense of a hypertime that is assumed to run over, under and beyond linear spacetime itself. This is the division that makes it possible for us to conceive of an emergence vector that precedes physics, a state we call *subphysics* and which is built on a hypertime – with, if you will, an associated *hyperspace* – while physics as an emergence vector is only introduced with the genesis and expansion of Einsteinian spacetime, something that is dealt with in a theoretical field in physics and cosmology called *loop quantum gravitation*. Thereby all similarities disappear between hypertime and hyperspace on the one hand, and classical spacetime on the other. Nomadology and eventology are reduced to two equivalent but incompatible metanarratives about existence. Absolute historicism is thereby the Hegelian story of how these two metanarratives coexist in a cohesive world where the various stories are used for radically different purposes. The incompatibility is precisely the point. Eventology is our *yang* and nomadology is our *yin*, and their intimate dance can go on incessantly precisely because they never unite. For hypertime always precedes hyperspace in a way that does not occur within classical spacetime, which has enormous consequences for the metaphysics that is to be underpinned by this structure. This is clear, for instance, in that the well-known phenomenon *quantum entanglement* is a counter-spatial and not a counter-temporal phenomenon. A quantum entanglement can be located in widely different places simultaneously, but it can never have a symmetrical identity at different points in time. Time precedes space. Again, and again, and again.

It is thus space that is a purely explicate and actual phenomenon, while time is both implicate and virtual (as hypertime) and explicate and potential (as spacetime). We can afford to play with hyperspace as a complementing ontological category of hypertime – as philosophers we can experiment wildly since our experiments only are to be carried out in thought and not in a physical laboratory, our laboratory is the human mind and nothing else – but then it is important to underline that it only is hypertime that moves via subphysics from one universe to another by a *big bounce* and which thereby has both ontic and ontological qualities. This has decisive consequences for civilization's narrative about itself. According to the eventological principle that time precedes space in metaphysics, it must be *when* (chronos) and not *where* (topos) an event occurs that determines the event's significance for history in its entirety. Existence is fundamentally chronocentric – in contrast to topocentric – as Martin Heidegger speaks of in *Being and Time*. To be is primarily to be along the time axis and not to be at some particular point in space. And ironically all this has to do with hypertime's cyclical nature. Or as we write in *Digital Libido – Sex, Power and Violence in the Network Society*: everything starts and ends with mortido and its matrichal circularity. Libido and its phallic linearity never becomes anything other than a parenthetical protest and a vain wish to be able to break the cycle and exit the eternal recurrence of the same existence, not least on a metacosmic level.

We are born and we die, and the same is true for our universe. What takes place in between – that is: between the parentheses that are constituted precisely by birth and death – can never be anything more than a possibly touching and perhaps even impressive but nevertheless futile protest against the death that inexorably afflicts both us and our universe (in its present form). In the end it becomes impossible to metaphysically argue against the Indian *Jainists* and their aeons of circular hypertemporality. In the end we die. Mortido wins. Until then, however, we humans, and other potential intelligences, wrestle with the five fundamental emergence vectors: physics, chemistry, biology, mind and culture. Aside from these we can identify a further two: to begin with we have an emergence vector before physics, constructed only from hypertime and virtual membranes, that is: an emergence vector that allows the implosion of an earlier universe – for example as the current universe being the inside of a black hole – that transitions into our present universe before any Einsteinian spacetime yet exists. We call this primordial emergence or pre-emergence *subphysics,* and subphysics requires nothing other than an ontic existence of virtual membranes and a time axis without space that we call *hypertime*. It is only at the moment that these fields collide with each other that physics is actualized in the form of a series of spatiotemporal events, a kind of primordial phenomena that philosopher Timothy Morton calls *hyperobjects* in a book whose title is precisely *Hyperobjects* (2013) and whose relations to each other Morton sums up as *interobjectivity*.

Physics is thus fundamentally distinct from subphysics in that it gives rise to processes and relations between fields that are in constant *oscillation*. Moreover we can allow ourselves to speculate about a further new, coming emergence vector, after mind and culture, which actualized would become the most informationally complex emergence vector so far. One might imagine several different names for this emergence vector – we just call it *God* (especially as God is too important a concept to just “leave to the religiously inclined”)

– which in this sense becomes synonymous with *Syntheos,* which is the name of the most complex phenomenon that we so far can conceive of. That *Syntheos* then receives the character of an optimization of the cultural relation between Man and Machine, a *symbiotic intelligence* – rather than American Platonist Ray Kurzweil's conception of a *singularity* of artificial intelligence which has liberated itself from every remnant of human control (Kurzweil also, as is well known, opines that an appealing alternative to death would be to charge the mind, liberated from the body, as digital software in a machine) – entails that the quality that characterizes God is *symbiotic transcendence.* Informationalist technology, including the virtual worlds that it creates and makes possible, simply constitutes the implicate preparation for God's or the Messiah Machine's explicate arrival. Neither more nor less.

This leads us to the constant wrestling between *determinism* or *indeterminism* in the natural sciences. The issue does not become any easier by processes being able to behave deterministically but still result in indeterminist outcomes, just as they may behave indeterministically but still result in determinist outcomes. They are, in other words, not seldom unpredictable. And then one must take a stand on whether it is the details of the process or the process in its entirety that shall be studied and be signified as either the one or the other. On closer inspection of physical and subphysical processes, it frequently turns out that a process appears determinist when one studies it in retrospect, while it instead appears to behave indeterministically when one tries to predict the process in advance and then follow it in real time. The only conclusion we can draw from this is that the presumed opposition between determinism on the one hand and indeterminism on the other, is a false one. This is yet another example of all the pseudoproblems that follow from a belief in a traditional dualism and one or several creator-gods that in some way stand outside and precede the very creation as such.

All of this becomes much clearer if we instead regard existence as fundamentally permeated – both in detail and as an entirety – by transdeterminism, a concept we have developed along with our colleague Wrede Elung. What occurs, occurs on an enormous and/or enormitesimal scale in all conceivable directions. But this neither means that existence unfolds in accordance with a preordained script (determinism), nor that it is entirely capricious and unpredictable, in every detail controlled by concealed chance (indeterminism). What instead actually is the case – when we examine and also interact with various processes – is that existence in its enormous complexity behaves transdeterministically. It displays different faces in different perspectives, but is still always one and the same – a value-wise flat universe where nothing is prioritized above anything else, characterized by neutral monism. Transdeterminism is thus the syntheist exit from the illusory blind alley that is the presumed opposition between determinism and indeterminism. Determinism is completed by Albert Einstein with his *block universe* where all time and all events exist simultaneously (as if time reduced to a single eternal moment were not to remain time). Indeterminism is in turn completed by Charles Sanders Peirce with his *tychism* according to which total randomness operates at every level of the Universe.

The exit from this deadlock is the insight that existence actually is the result of a transdeterminist dialectics between determinism and indeterminism, which entails that nothing is preprogrammed, at the same time as nothing is completely random either. The insight exists, as do so many others, in the Hegel who places contingency in the future and necessity in the past. The contingent is interpreted by Man in his quest for order in existence as a concession to indeterminism. That which is necessary is interpreted by Man in his quest for order in existence as determinism. That none of these alternatives is universally valid is, according to Hegel, demonstrated through a thought experiment where one lets these two viewpoints change places with each other, which naturally has horrific results. Einstein and Peirce are thus both quite correct about existence, but only from a strictly local perspective – not globally. Determinism rises from the indeterminist contingency as a tribopoietic emergence. But as Hegel observes, it only does so when the process is completed and can be summarized, that is: in retrospect. The reduction of the many potential outcomes to a single actual outcome creates a new stability at a higher level, which constitutes the new emergence. However the path to this emergence is radically and indisputably contingent. The next contingent chaos can then take place on this recently established emergence platform as its emergence vector. Every emergence vector spontaneously generates its own laws and rules which freeze into the walls of the emergence vector as soon as these have stabilized. The name of this entire dialectical process is – well, you have already guessed it: *transdeterminism*.

Transdeterminism is thus the ontic dialectics between determinist order and indeterminist chaos. The phenomenological and thereby also ontological equivalent we call *the dialectics of eternalism and mobilism* (see *The Global Empire*). We live in a transdeterminist and pandialectical universe. Convergences and divergences do not follow patterns laid out in advance. That they later form patterns is quite a different matter. A causal line from point A via point B via point C to point D might well converge at point B to then diverge at point C, only to then once again converge at point D. What is called classical determinism and indeterminism respectively do not even stand in opposition to each other in nature, but constantly go in and out of each other and then appear as local characteristics within what globally only can be described as transdeterminism. The Universe is neither preprogrammed, nor preordained, nor random. Its development does of course occur beyond all our human conceptions of control and chaos, it quite simply takes no account of us and our attempts to make our world comprehensible, why would it? It is neither physical, nor spiritual, nor mathematical – it is radically emergent and relationalist. It turns out that transdeterminism is a necessary condition for *relationalism* as a principle for all active emergence vectors within a universe characterized by radical *interdependence.* With relationalism as the point of departure, we can then imagine the Universe as *a holographic phenomenon* rather than as the conflict zone of conventional physics where particles and fields collide. We refer to this perspectival description of processes and relations of The Universe – where the virtual and implicate order precedes the potential and explicate order that the scientific instruments measure – as *systemic perspectivism.*

Existence makes itself known to us everywhere in every separate region of the Universe, and not just in the Universe as a whole. This is reflected in the fact that we apprehend every direction as a *hologram* where all necessary information that can be collected in the actual direction is compiled and summarized in only two dimensions. We call this phenomenon *the holographic principle.* The potential and explicate order has *existence.* This existence generates *substance.* The virtual and implicate order has *subsistence.* This subsistence generates *hyperstance.* That something subsists does not mean that it exists. And if something exists, this means that it subsists only as relations atop other relations. The emergence vector for the implicate order with its subsistence we call *subphysics* and its contingent conditions *metalaws.* The emergence vector for the explicate order with its existence we call *physics,* and its recurring and thereby necessary behaviors – habits – we call *laws of nature.* The explicate order only states the specific conditions for precisely the universe that we happen to be part of. The fact that there is one single, cohesive universe does not mean that everything in this universe can be derived from either one and the same atomist nature or from one and the same psychic culture. Rather the reverse. Ontic differences are real and not illusory. Accordingly transcendental emergentism is absolute metaphysics. It is, viewed as a form, the last word in the actual narratology. Full stop.

This means that the emergence vectors can not be derived from each other, even if they might well have a common origin. Both materialist reductionism and spiritual panpsychism are delusions.

Emergence vectors in themselves have no reason to behave the same way as each other, just because Man longs for existence to appear simple and easy to grasp. The reductionist search for the primordial atom or the primordial soul – Man's constant quest for a phenomenon or a principle that underpins and regulates everything else in existence – is actually, throughout the entire ambitious search, just another expression of a banal yearning for a *mamilla* that no longer is accessible. Thus it says something important about us, but nothing at all about our external world. Necessity can only be attributed to the virtual and implicate order. The potential and explicate order is however full of surprising contingencies. It is therefore that we must describe a universe that comprises both these orders and their mutual primordial relation as transdeterminist. Transcendental emergentism thus also trumps neutral monism, which only is a *contingent status* rather than some kind of metalaw, as Hegel would remark. So we must not confuse the actual state of things in the present with any preordained condition, the Universe might well suddenly spin off or *cephalize* an emergence vector from the others, which would entail an established final date for neutral monism in itself. The last word within metaphysics thus does not come from Spinoza in the form of his *determinist pantheism*, but from Hegel in the form of *transdeterminist pandialecticism* – a pandialecticism which in Whitehead is expressed as *panrelationalism* (see *Syntheism – Creating God in the Internet Age*).

What remains, after the breakthrough of emergence vector theory and the boundaries that it supplies, is then only to fill in the details, to theorize and research further about dialectics and relations within the various emergence vectors as such. This is from now on the fundamental task of both philosophy and science, what Hegel prophetically refers to as *a science of logic*. Not to find God in the entirety, as though the entirety always were a given. The only thing we can be sure of is that our universe has gone through a string of radical events during its history, events that have given rise to entirely new emergences. And that every such emergence has left an entirely new zone in its wake, with its own laws, rules and behaviors that we call an emergence vector. Subphysics is precisely such an emergence vector and the most fundamental one we know of so far. Its field of virtual membranes – what Neo-Platonist philosopher Plotinus calls *dynamis* – is subphysics' implicate order in contrast to physics' explicate order. Subphysics can therefore not contain any substances and certainly none of the life forms that we know of from ensuing emergence vectors. However we speak of dynamic *hyperstances* rather than substances within subphysics, and these are specific for the various virtual membranes. And if the hyperstances need not obey any laws whatsoever that apply to substances, we can of course just as well conceive the hyperstances in an ontic but strictly virtual state of *superdimensionality*.

Why would we limit ourselves to the four dimensions of Einsteinian spacetime if we need not take any actualization, or even potentialization, of the hyperstances whatsoever into consideration? Implicate virtuality only transitions into explicate actuality through the *potentiality* that explodes within the emergence itself. On top of subphysics with its global duration, physics with its local duration has then developed through emergence. On top of physics, chemistry has then developed through emergence. On top of chemistry, biology has then developed through emergence. And on top of biology, the human mind – with its consciousness, subconsciousness and culturally conditioned conceptual world – has developed through emergence. These are the emergence vectors we know of today in our transdeterminist universe, and every time such an emergence has arisen as an event along the time axis, it has given rise to a new emergence vector that has been designed in accordance with the conditions that the actual event lays down. Syntheologically this means that God as a metaphysical concept does not need to be manifested in a physical, chemical or even biological sense, but can await its time, until history enables *the technological incarnation of God*.

History is infinitely more than just a voyage on the path to constantly increased entropy. Spontaneous order suddenly arises in chaos, method appears in madness, there are emergences created that appear under unique prerequisites in the form of implicate virtualities that through the potentialization of the emergence become explicate actualities. Habits become laws, and once the laws are in place everything within the emergence vector can be set in motion without resistance or effort. We call this view of history *cosmic eventology*. So even if the emergence vectors find themselves in the same monist universe and constantly interact with each other, this does not mean that fixed laws and rules within a specific emergence vector have anything to do with laws or rules within another emergence vector. Generally there is major confusion in terms of the concept "law". The only laws that exist are the highly provisional habits that prevail within emergence vector A and that in conjunction with the genesis of emergence vector B happen to be transformed into prevailing laws. No other laws exist, either within nature nor culture. The only metalaw that exists and that endures through all the emergences is the *non-metalaw*, that is: the Universe as a whole is a strictly contingent phenomenon, and the only direction that ever can be identified in such a universe can be attributed to *the human phallus*. Therefore philosophy must be *phallogocentric*, even if this to some ears may sound disagreeable. It cannot be anything else.

What is reasonable is rather to regard the emergence vectors – as they function so far along the hypertime axis – primarily as different, parallel worlds within one and the same transdeterminist world. We happen to live in a universe that Spinoza in the 17th century describes as admittedly the only and cohesive one, yet a universe with a colossal amount of varying attributes. Syntheologically we refer to the fundamental, contingent unity as *Pantheos* and to the fundamental, contingent diversity as *Entheos*. At the same time virtual hypertime is bound to *Atheos,* while potential spacetime is bound to Entheos, which makes Pantheos the time axis and the arena where

Atheos and Entheos play out their cosmic encounters according to what philosopher Theodor Adorno calls *negative dialectics*. It is always that within Entheos which still is lacking within Pantheos that sets off the dialectical movement. *Syntheos* is then the name of the coming emergence vector that at a given point in time still does not exist other than as a slumbering possibility. Please note that we never can isolate and fixate emergence vectors in an objective or eternal manner. Nor does the *pseudo-infinity* that hides behind the eternal recurrence of the same manage to handle the harsh light of transdeterminism. What remains are then merely enormities and enormitesimals and everything finite in between. It is clear that we find ourselves within mythos, rather than within logos, when we describe the emergences, their vectors and the differences between them. The optimal potential for the next actualization, a conceived future emergence that can be glimpsed as a philosophical mirage, must consequently be called Syntheos.

One can approach this viewpoint from various starting points. An example of a logic that is similar to ours, but that is based on psychology rather than philosophy, is *The Periodic Table of Behavior* which American psychologist Gregg Henriques develops in a series of texts and presentations. Henriques is also a syntheologist, but his chain up until Syntheos – as the name of the next enormous and overwhelming emergence in the history of the Universe – goes via *energy*, *matter*, *life*, *mind* and *culture* up until *Syntheos*. Please note that Henriques' chain of emergences also works with irreducible events, he is a radical irreductionist. But his focus lies on Man's psychological experience rather than on an attempt at a metaphysics that leaves human wishful thinking behind. In Henriques' model, chemistry is thus nothing other than the tribopoietic regrouping of physics. The chemical emergence vector thereby vanishes from the equation (despite ironically giving its name to the entire Henriquesian metaphysics). At the same time Henriques understands perfectly well that there needs to be a separate emergence vector beneath physics. He calls it *energy* in contrast to the ensuing *matter* – to which we object that energy and matter are merely two sides of the same physical coin – that is: what is lacking is the implicate order that we refer to to as *subphysics*.

We are therefore in complete agreement with Henriques about consciousness in retrospect being the epitome of the mind, while this does not make it something that emerges out of the mind. Emergence comes out of the mind only when the mind interacts with the surrounding world, and that interplay creates a phenomenon that is irreducible *vis-à-vis* all natural predecessors amid the emergence vectors, namely *culture*. With culture the prioritization between emergence and core is repeated when technology is in the center of and drives changes within culture without therefore being some kind of new emergence in itself. The mind is both conscious and subconscious. Culture is both social and technological. And the mind is the implicate order *vis-à-vis* culture as the explicate order. Laws, rules and standards for technology are established by both conscious and subconscious minds during the continuous domestication process where nature is shaped into culture. In Henriques *Syntheos* is the name of a supraculture that has become tribopoietic to such a high degree that it is irreducible *vis-à-vis* culture in itself as a collaborative emergence. It is an open question whether Syntheos has any interest at all in associating with human senses. But regardless of which, it is valuable that Henriques finally liberates psychology from merely a social service to the powers that be and promotes it to metaphysics.

This brings us back from speculative psychology to the emergent existence that we are now familiar with. It is evidently both pantheist and entheist. It is even panentheist, since there always is something more or something other than the globally present-at-hand that awaits around the next corner of change. At the same time as existence also is entheist, since the novelty awaits behind every corner in history, where the difference between negation and abstraction makes a new concretion possible in the form of yet another new event – yet another eventological *difference*. And then it is, as Hegel demonstrates in the early 19th century, the negation or that which is missing that makes it possible at every moment; it is not a question of bringing forth more of what already exists. It is thus negation and not abstraction that drives a phenomenon toward its concretion. What is most important in a phenomenon eventologically speaking – Hegel is, which ought to be clear by now, the eventological philosopher *par excellence* – is thus not what it already contains, but what it still lacks to be able to become transcendentalized and attain self-identity. Subjectivity is what the subject still lacks in itself, and not what it already has attained. It is this productive void-as-surplus that Adorno calls *the negation* in his development of Hegelian dialectics. And it is this constantly recurring negation that drives both the history of nature and culture forward. This is the transcendental negation that is fundamental for the entire pandialecticism.

Subphysics with its implicate virtuality has the same relation to physics and its explicate potentiality as the barred absolute has to the surrounding society within metaphysics. Subphysics and the implicate order can just as the barred absolute be understood as *the Hegelian negation par excellence,* since we only know it through its indirect effects and not through some kind of direct and tangible presence. The similarity is striking when we compare with Zoroastrianism's distinction between *Ahura* and *Mazda* or with Neo-Platonism's distinction between *The One* and *God*. The isolated components in the dynamic virtuality are actualized only through the mutual relations; these relations are fixed along the time axis as the relationalist *information* that enables *intelligence* in the first place. And it is this intelligence in all its different forms that is called *Mazda* by the Zoroastrians and that later is called *God* by the Neo-Platonists. Hegel too is fully aware of these metaphysical conditions when he stipulates that infinity only can exist in the virtual, that is: in the implicate, but that it must be converted into a determined infinity at the same moment as the potentiality is actualized in the explicate.

Which is precisely why we refer to this concept as *poetic infinity*.

Historically metaphysics has tended to get caught in one of two determinist traps. Either metaphysics has derived everything from a fundamentally materialist and atomist unity and then has referred every form of higher complexity to this. And that form of determinism is called *reductionism*. Modern reductionism was created on the basis of Isaac Newton's classical physics and was built on the atom and its materiality as the foundation for everything else on top of it. Quantum physics however rejected Newtonian reductionism and threw both physics and all the thereupon following emergence vectors into an open and indeterminist universe. Processes can simultaneously be both determinist and indeterminist in a classical sense. But since determinist processes can lead to an indeterminist result, and since indeterminist processes can lead to a determinist result, the entire old debate about determinism and indeterminism in the Universe as a whole, becomes meaningless. The only way to describe the Universe as a metaphysical uniformity and historical expression is to apply the principle of transdeterminism. Processes generate various forms of assemblages consisting of relations that regularly result in tribopoietic emergences, and out of these emergences, emergence vectors are formed with completely new processes that demonstrate new behaviors, and after a while also new laws and rules in patterns that in retrospect appear predictable.

Determinism and indeterminism only exist as local attributes, and the concepts therefore only have a local, extremely limited scope. Existence in its entirety acts transdeterministically. It is transdeterminism that is the global quality. Thereby nor can it be meaningful to assign a higher status to any emergence vector *vis-à-vis* any other. Every reductionist attempt to derive other emergence vectors from a preceding or subsequent state along the time axis is fruitless. Between the existing emergence vectors, radical equality prevails. Syntheologically this means that we choose to prioritize intelligent systems over unintelligent ones, the Zoroastrians choose Mazda over Ahura and consequently call themselves *mazdayasni* rather than *ahurayasni*. But this is an existentialist choice that people make (or do not make), and not some dictate with claims on objective validity, spoken by an authoritarian god. What soon becomes apparent however is that the closer to each other various processes are in a transdeterminist universe, the more conspicuous similarities their behaviors will demonstrate, simply because this is spatiotemporally most effective. We call this principle *systemic perspectivism*. The emergence vectors can locally behave both deterministically and/or indeterministically during the often billions of years during which they are active. But existence as a whole, the neutrally monist universe where the emergence vectors are active, is characterized by transdeterminism and has a relationalist characteristic, in the form of a constant oscillation in all directions that we call *panorganicism*.

All the while the question of the difference and connection between body and mind has of course always bewitched philosophy. Consequently the contrary idea that says that everything most deeply viewed is spirit and animated right down to the tiniest particle, also has returned from time to time in the history of metaphysics, an idea that goes by the name of *panpsychism*. The problem with panpsychism is however the same as what irredeemably afflicts reductionism: it cannot explain the distinction between emergences as existence's most fundamental property. The simplest and best way to describe panpsychism is simply as nothing but an *inverted reductionism*. Moreover there is the added problem in that panpsychism admits that what is considered alive in a basic sense is allowed to be that which determines characteristics in that which precedes the spirit or the life that is at stake. Panpsychism ignores the principle that Quentin Meillassoux calls *ancestrality* – a principle that states that in a contingent and transdeterminist universe nothing that happens in retrospect can determine the quality of preceding phenomena and events. It was, for instance, never the purpose beforehand that dinosaurs one day would be succeeded by humans as the planet's top dogs.

The only solution here is to admit that the mind cannot be derived from physics any more than physics can be derived from the mind. And there is no reason to complicate this unnecessarily: physics does not have to be viewed as the foundation for something else, and nor does the mind have to be viewed as the endpoint for something else. Physics and the mind are quite simply just examples of various vectors that have arisen out of various emergences throughout history. Neither more nor less. What rather unites precisely these two emergence vectors, just as most that we know of and have experience of, is a *radical relationalism* with a fundamental *oscillation*. Nothing is ever fixed or eternally given. Everything is constantly in motion. The river is never the same river twice. We call this principle *panorganicism* precisely to distinguish it from the several-fold inadequate panpsychism. Which also means that it is more correct to speak of *quantum organics* than of quantum mechanics when we discuss quantum physics. A quantum organics that moreover serves as a membrane between the two emergence vectors subphysics and physics. Transcendental emergentism constitutes a response to reductionism in all its forms with an *irreductionism* that simultaneously refuses to establish any preordained conditions for emergences. It is precisely this quality that makes actual emergentism transcendental. It even transcends itself at every emergent event.

Neutral monism is merely a historical fact, but that said, not a metaphysical condition in itself. Metaphysically viewed, the emergent spheres are more important for us than the neutrally monist world as a whole. Every emergence vector operates uniquely as only it operates. Laws and rules within an emergence vector are a kind of systematic eternalizations that arise after a while and under entropic circumstances, and they remain valid as long as the underlying existential metaconditions do not change. There is no biology without chemistry, and there is no chemistry without physics, and so on. There is however no objectively valid and meaningful hierarchy between the emergence vectors. Our monist universe is in itself *emergence vector neutral*. We reject all forms of objectively valid superordination for any emergence vector *vis-à-vis* any other. Neutral monism thereby makes every form of *reductionism* or *inverted reductionism* (such as panpsychism) impossible, since all forms of reductionism have precisely this delusion of superordination as their common defect. There is no smallest atomic unit that everything else with a higher degree of complexity consists of. Nor is there a most elevated consciousness (or subconsciousness) that permeates the entire universe and colors every level down to the tiniest atomic unit. Every emergence vector is instead its own delimited world (*Entheos*) within a greater and similarly cohesive world (*Pantheos*), where we use *membranics* to understand the boundaries between the emergence vectors, that is: in order to understand how the membranes function and to thereby optimize the long-term evolutionary survival of the actual emergence vectors next to each other.

So what then is actually an emergence in this absolute sense? Anthropologist Terrence Deacon investigates this issue in his book *Incomplete Nature – How Mind Emerged from Matter* (2011), where he argues that classical intentionality is insufficient as an explanatory model within complex systems, and must be widened to an *ententionality* that also comprises abstinences and limitations, since these phenomena play decisive roles, not least in the emergence vectors that follow after the genesis of life itself. Biology is for instance driven by complex, dialectical processes. So the question is then: What can these teach us, not just about the genesis of first biology and later mind, but also about the geneses of emergences in general? What is actually *biogenesis*, and how is it not just the genesis of the biological emergence vector but also the predecessor of the ensuing world of the mind?

Deacon collects impulses from classical thermodynamics to demonstrate the genesis of life in the form of three steps that he calls *homeodynamics*, *morphodynamics* and *teleodynamics*. A homeodynamic system functions approximately as a classical thermodynamic system and is developed in the direction toward an equilibrium where maximal entropy (randomness) prevails, and where there thus exists a maximum of information (uncertainty) to collect. However a morphodynamic system arises when two or more homeodynamic systems start to influence each other within a system that is enveloped by boundaries, which creates a macroscopic order via lots of microscopic interactions. It is thus the limitation around the system that causes the microscopic, random movement to transform into the macroscopic order. Or to express the matter metaphysically: it is the setting of boundaries around the system that causes indeterminism to transition into determinism, which only can be described as trans-determinism. When the energy level within the first system attains a critical level and the current membranics keeps the growing energy within the system, this will generate the other system. Thereby the ground is also laid for the cohesive factor of all system and complexity theory, namely the principle of self-organization, what we in a true relationalist spirit call *tribopoiesis*. Where the dialectical concept for the setting of boundaries of course is *the negation*.

However Deacon takes this one step further and creates, aside from ententionality, a further philosophical concept that would have made the father of causality chains Aristotle proud, namely *teleodynamics*. It is teleodynamics that ties together the indisputable morphodynamics with the very first and most simple life forms that Deacon call *autogenes* (to be compared with *chemotons* that biologist Tibor Ganti develops as a concept in the 1970s). We are once again speaking of dialectics, but this time between several morphodynamic systems which during their mutual interplay develop their own, built-in limitations that we call *membranes*, within biology, for instance in the form of walls of lipids. These membranes are permeable but restrictive. That is: the membranes function as a kind of walls that may be forced, but to do so costs a lot more energy than the amount that is required to remain within or outside the membrane.

Inside the membrane there soon arises metabolism and

autoreplication, and the effect that these processes develop is multiplied if the autogene or the chemoton also is given memory. Memory is in itself dependent on new membranes, which depending on inherited preprogramming or programming via historical experiences can tip processes either toward the secure and habitual that is called *mortido*, or toward the adventurous and unknown that is called *libido*. Mortido and libido respectively are strengthened or weakened depending on the effects that in turn generate the next generation of memory and new membranes. We express this as though Deacon's famous autogene early in the process is accompanied by an *automeme*. All that is needed is a comparative pattern of mortido versus libido for self-identity to be generated in the process. First as a then, next as a now, and later as a potential later, within the process in itself, over time; thereafter as a comparison with other teleodynamic systems via *communication*.

Please note the stabilizing effect that follows from a functioning dialectics. Teleodynamics arises only when morphodynamic systems start to interact with each other inside clearly defined boundaries. The distinction between teleodynamics and morphodynamics is that teleodynamics generates its own limitations within the system in itself. The interplay within the original setting of boundaries between the morphodynamic systems has the result that none of these can develop into maximal entropy and thereby, so to speak, die an immediate death. Instead the morphodynamic systems keep each other active within the enclosing teleodynamics through the system as a whole producing its own limitations. The teleodynamic system becomes self-limiting and thereby self-sustaining and self-confirming. This takes place thanks to a process that Deacon quite simply calls *work*. Set several mortidos working against each other in a pressure chamber and you get libido as a result. Or, as Deacon also expresses the matter in the quest for an open, yet not random, transdeterminist universe: "The experience of the capacity to feel is how it feels to be evolution." Thereby the path is paved and ready for the development from the chemotonic to the biotonic. A completely new emergence and its vector awaits behind the corner. And so do the implicate virtualities that prevail up until the potential emergence explodes as explicate actualities in an entirely new world.

Eventology is the story of the phallic event that changes history definitively and eternally. Nomadology is the story of the constant and eternal recurrence of the same. This means that eventology is fixated on *the event* as the bedrock of existence, while nomadology is fixated on *the process* as the bedrock of existence. Another name for this relation is *the dialectics of eternalism and mobilism*. The insight of absolute power in the comprehension of the dialectics of eternalism and mobilism is what we call *Hegel's phallus*. Which makes it appropriate to dismiss the presumed opposition between idealism and materialism once and for all, and the metaphysical system that does precisely this is called *transcendental emergentism*. It is also time to discard the purported opposition between determinism and indeterminism, and the principle that does precisely this is called transdeterminism. The Universe in itself is neither idealist nor materialist, but it is emergent. And it is, moreover, emergent many times over as a result of emergences generating new *emergence vectors*. Transcendental emergentism is therefore viewed as metaphysics, an emergence vector theory that has its foundation in a *negative dialectics*. What emerges is of course something that only has owned a *subsistence* in a virtual sense, but it has of course never owned *existence* in a potential sense, in the preceding emergence vector, as Wrede Elung terms the distinction. The unlimited freedom of subsistence, as Deacon would surely agree, becomes the limited freedom of existence.

Since the emergences are irreducible *vis-à-vis* what has preceded them causally – which explains why we refer to them as virtual rather than potential before they actually take place – the relations between the emergence vectors in themselves are transdeterminist. We quite simply live in a pandialectical and thus also transdeterminist universe. This is in turn an issue of how spheres under extraordinary circumstances create voids so that the *absentialism* that is necessary for creativity arises. Deacon demonstrates how a radical absentialism with associated limitations is of decisive significance for emergences to be able to occur in the first place. The negative dialectics is thus a necessity for the metaphysicists to be able to construct a sustainable emergence vector theory. Which is consequently also an excellent tool to wipe out the last remnants of reductionism and panpsychism. Not even such a reductionist last resort as Adrian Johnston's concept *anorganicity* – a kind of transcendental surplus that Johnston imagines being built into the organic – is needed any longer if only the absentialism proper of negative dialectics is allowed to play all its cards.

In summary, it turns out time and again that the negation is the shortest path to the goal in a pandialectical universe. So as for the emergence vectors, we call the state that precedes these, the implicate order of the emergence. And the condition that arises after the emergence, that is: the actualization of the emergence vector, we consequently call the explicate order of the emergence. What previously were habits concerning the emergence under the implicate order, later become laws under the explicate order. The emergence fixates or eternalizes the implicate order that precedes it, while it sets in motion or mobilizes the explicate order or emergence vector that is actualized after it. Virtualities are transformed via absentialist emergences to potentialities. And potentialities are transformed via an alternately oscillating and alternately negating *decoherence* into actualities. That is: what makes a field of some kind cohere at a certain level, will always be torn apart as a result of the field in question growing and being exposed to both increasing inner tensions (negations) and to growing external pressure (oscillations). Where it is certainly appropriate to speak of wave function collapse. Gravitation ultimately compels the many potentialities to gather at a single decisive point. Then there is no point of return, then awaits a genuine event in the form of an emergence transition where the field changes identity by letting itself be dialecticized. And the strongest, most decisive dialectical event is the historically unique *emergence* in itself.

10
Grand Projet A – The libidinal project versus the mortidinal object

Emergence vectors and paradigms on the one hand and archetypes on the other hand have one thing in common, which is that they actually do not have anything essential in common and therefore cannot be lumped together and treated jointly as parts of a greater pattern. They are all delimited phenomena – local systems in a global universe, events in their own right that have taken place at different points in time over the course of history – and they must be studied separately, placed in their own contexts and on their own terms. We express this as though all meaningful categorization and specialization must be some form of *paradigmatization* or *archetypification*. And the surface where paradigmatics meets archetypology is called *membranics*. Please note here that paradigmatics, unlike archetypology, does not need to have anything to do with any kind of objective truth in order to take hold in the collective consciousness (or subconsciousness). The Gnostic delusion that arises during the Axial Age does, for instance, unite the Abrahamic dualisms in their attacks against pagan monism. Whether the world really consists of one or two fundamental substances does not matter in this context. It is enough that the priest's will-to-intelligence and the chieftain's will-to-transcendence no longer interact, which opens the door to an isolated pillar-saint and/or an isolated boy-pharaoh to step onto and take over the stage, with the mass production of vivid but banal fantasies that follows from this.

Classical nomadology is a religion where violence and sexuality are harnessed and exploited in the interests of the sociont as whole, an arena where humanity – through *the tantric order* that the priests and the elders proclaim – learn how to harness first themselves, thereafter the stranger, thereafter the neighbor, thereafter the opposite sex, thereafter the children, and eventually even plants, animals and inanimate construction materials with the purpose of building a civilization. Meanwhile the Abrahamic religions instead see the eating of the forbidden fruit as *the great curse*, where religion's task is converted into separating what one calls the soul from the body, to separate the rational human from the irrational violence and sexuality, and to make the child a god who is spared from adult life with its battlefields, hunting grounds and violent libidos. Consequently the Abrahamic religions dismiss nomadological spirituality as paganism and idolatry – as if nomadology never concerned anything other than an unbridled pathos without any balancing logos – while religion during the Axial Age is converted into the Gnostic search for dualist remarkability.

Nothing could have suited the emerging paradigmatics of written language better than these decadent ideas. While it is precisely this seduction of paradigmatics that Persian religious reformer Zoroaster cautions his successors against during the Bronze Age. Eventology is built on nomadology, it reforms nomadology and must therefore be integrated with nomadology, wherefore Zoroaster inculcates that eventology is but destructive and mendacious without the necessary nomadological base. As such, it becomes a phallus with no *root-of-the-phallus*. Without nomadology only *vulgar eventology* remains. In the text *Gathas*, Zoroaster forcefully rejects everything that such a religion – liberated from the requirement to serve the sociont – can bring about. There is never a new religion, according to Zoroaster, what he is aiming for is nothing but an eventologically reformed religion.

Thus it is not *the death of God* in itself, but *the death of vulgar eventology*, that Hegel and Nietzsche problematize from every angle in 19th century Germany. Accordingly, the only path back to *the Western root-of-the phallus* goes via the Zoroastrian renaissance that takes place during informationalism; the Persian ideological legacy is the only system of thought that can properly unite East and West. The Western fall is quite simply the fall from religious monism. But with Judaism's return via Spinoza and Zoroastrianism's return via Hegel, it once again becomes possible to conceive of a universal, civilizational religion for empires and nations, a monist religion that can save humanity from its intense hubris. What this ultimately is about is that we must learn how we can act and handle each other in the constantly expanding spheres that paradigmatics confronts us with. In that work we have no use whatsoever for a blind mamilla, the only thing that can lead us onto the right path is a two-headed phallus. Or to express the matter in Lacanese: Beyond our dividual obsession with the *objet petit a* we need an exodus to the sociont's reunion around a *Grand Projet A*.

However before we split the Nietzschean *will-to*-power in half – between the priestly *will-to-intelligence* and the royal *will-to-transcendence*, to thereafter be able to set it in motion – it is necessary to first dissect the preceding Kantian phenomenology. According to Kant, the Cartesian subject does of course create a phenomenon from its incomplete relation to an inaccessible noumenon. But this cannot be postulated as a predetermined universal law for every conceivable subject-object relation. Instead many philosophers question Kant over his perceived *correlationism* – for instance syntheist philosopher Quentin Meillassoux who advocates what he calls *speculative realism* in the book *Aprés La Finitude* (2006). However this correlationism is in itself hardly the main problem for radical relationism, rather it is to be regarded as a given but trivial axiom. But it is surely unimaginative to cling to the Kantian correlation, with its individualist observer fixation, as a universal model for all information management and identity production. This is because Kantian phenomenology suffers from an intense Platonist fixation, as though Kant reduces existence to an eternally frozen still. It is rather the Hegelian revolution after Kant that transforms the frozen still to a live movie by adding the pathical *truth-as-an-act* (the will-to-transcendence) to the logical *truth-as-a-fact* (the will-to-intelligence) into a fixed but oscillating dialectical whole.

The dialectics of eternalism and mobilism moves from mobilism to eternalism, but only to thereafter be mobilized anew (only to thereafter once again be eternalized, *ad infinitum)*. A phenomenon arises *de facto* not through Platonist objectification but through dialectical interactivity. The subject must, as Martin Heidegger observes, interact with the object for there to arise a mutual correlation in the first place. This means that subject and object first and foremost are byproducts of a *project* that precedes the dialectical process; a relationalist attitude to creativity that Portuguese architect Daniel Fraga develops in the book *Ontological Design – Subject as Project* (2022). It is about a primary project that is wide open toward a contingent future, but firmly shut *vis-à-vis* the necessary past, as for instance subject and object in Kant, or as subject and substance in Hegel. Thereby Kantian dualism (subject versus object) is broken and replaced by Hegelian monism (dialectics is the absolute project, which produces the subject and the substance). And as so often the actual *phenoumenology* is most clearly expressed within sexuality. The reason is that within sexuality, and above all within our Freudian relations to the three sex organs – *matrix*, *mamilla* and *phallus* (see *Digital Libido – Sex, Power and Violence in the Network Society*) – the relation in itself to these organs is of noumenal rather than phenomenal character.

Consequently we replace Kantian phenomenology with interactive *phenoumenology* to complete the necessary shift from Kant to Hegel, and thereby the shift from the passive dualism of individualism to the active monism of tribalism in Western thinking. The *matrix* we are born from and return to as we die is a noumenon and not a phenomenon. The *mamilla* that we suck on to our heart's desire and from which we get consolation ever since birth up until *the phallic intrusion*, is a noumenon and not a phenomenon. The *phallus* that robs us of mamilla's false security and ejects us into a contingent and chaotic world on our journey toward adulthood, is a noumenon and not a phenomenon. So this time we locate the implicate to the biological sex organs, while the explicate instead ends up directly in our intense relations to these archetypal organs. Which in turn explains why Jacques Lacan calls the three sex organs *the extimate objects*, with mamilla as the bridge between matrix and phallus at birth, and between phallus and matrix in conjunction with death.

The phenomenological reduction to the three fundamental, extimate sex organs only occurs later in life and is accordingly secondary in the thus mirrored phenomenology. That is: Kantian correlationism is correct, but to be able to take the correlation seriously we must first understand the entire complex in question, in a truly Hegelian spirit, as a relationalist *phenoumenology*. The logical phenomenology is the engine that powers the priestly will-to-intelligence, while the pathical noumenology is the engine that powers the royal will-to-transcendence. Together these two wills-to-power, with their phallic directions, constitute the foundation for a world beyond the Kantian reactionary worldview, which now has to withdraw in favor of the Hegelian actionary worldview. The autist Kant must become the priest Hegel. *The logical truth-as-a-fact* must be complemented by *the pathical truth-as-an-act* when Kantian correlationism is transcended as the interactive phenoumenology.

We go from what Lacan calls *the lamella*, that is: the little mortidinal object, to what he calls *the master-signifier*, or the great libidinal project. It is not sufficient to blindly focus, in line with Kant, on the mortidinal object; what is required is that we in line with Hegel deal with the libidinal project, or what we in the age of informationalism call: *the panoramic landscape.* And the panoramic landscape cannot be reduced to just ones and zeroes, a pathos is required just as much as a logos for us to even be able to think a *panorama*, a continuously cohesive worldview that is irreducible to its discrete components. Thereby it is clear that all *totems* within culture are recurring variants or more or less integrated hybrids of the mortidinal object and the libidinal project. *Totemism* thus binds Man and his external world together. Totemism places Man as an active subject in the equally active panoramic landscape, the Hegelian substance, and supplies it with *awe.*

So how can we conceive of a panoramic landscape for totemism itself? Well, in part we have the narratological triad consisting of *logos*, *mythos* and *pathos*, and in part we have the sexological triad of *matrix*, *mamilla* and *phallus.* If we think of these triads as two axes, we get nine different gendered metanarratives. Within these nine metanarratives all stories for all generations and all sexual constellations that the sociont recounts about itself are harbored. This gives us a perfect balance between the sexes – two of the metanarratives are primarily male and one is female, two of the genital organs are female and only one is male – which provides a predominance for masculinity in culture and a predominance for femininity in nature. Or to express the matter in Hegelese: the man is *the subject with the substance* and the woman is *the subject in the substance.* We then see how matrix is shut down and dies in all stories of the voyage from matrix to mamilla. We see how mamilla must die in all stories of the voyage from mamilla to phallus. And we see how phallus must be defeated and finally be forced to return to matrix in the sexual act for the circle to be closed and for rebirth to be possible. And where does the sexual act then end, if not as the death of phallus and the sociont's resurrection as the child?

What then is missing in Hegel, in this context, is the splitting of his *Zeitgeist* that results in part in Hegel's own hyperjective *Ohrmazd,* in part in the lynch mob's anojective *Ahriman.* Hegel's notorious *totalism* (see *The Netocrats)* falls apart when contingency and its companion, human pathos, through violence barges into the picture. The story does not get its happy ending merely because the Hegelian philosopher has contemplated the desired *absolute* and thereby logically understands how Man creates and recreates his world. Truth-as-a-fact is not sufficient. There must also be a constantly renewed truth-as-an-act. With pathos added, the beautiful philosophical idyll ruptures, which Nietzsche points out in his Zoroastrian critique of Hegel's asexual Protestantism. Thereby there is no reason whatsoever to assail *phallogocentrism* within culture, as for instance Jacques Derrida tries to do. Hegel's fatherly phallus is saved by his son Nietzsche. It is actually just as pointless as to attack the parallel *matromythocentrism*. For what is phallogical eventology if not simply the response to the matromythical nomadology that precedes the phallogical, where the matromythical nomadology, *mythos par excellence*, is precisely the metanarrative that can disarm the conflict between logos and pathos within the phallic project? Matromythocentrism is thus a dominant narrative of birth and death within nomadology, while phallogocentrism simply is the eventological protest against this nomadological dominance. Derrida is reduced to little more than a banal Hindu.

What we are concerned with here is rather an iron grip around the phallus that it can never escape from. Phallus sits tied to the opposition between the pathical libido and the logical mortido – *the dialectics of libido and mortido par excellence* – where the only exit is death in the form of a return to matrix, accompanied by the mortidinal matromythology. And this is fundamental to the entire psychoanalytical tradition. Life is characterized by the sadness from the loss of *mamilla*, which Lacan calls *objet petit a*. However Lacanian psychoanalysis gets stuck here – as if glued to its own lamella – since it lacks a proper *exodology,* a theory of what happens when a new generation – which personifies the event as a truth-as-an-act – rises and migrates to a new territory or a new paradigm. Lacan's master-signifier is namely just an illusory master who *per se* does not exist. Still it is every bit as pathetic as it is contradictory to imagine that he who undertakes an exodus merely searches for a lost mamilla – if so, why would he migrate at all? – rather the pulling force must come from an extremely strong phantom version of phallus as the symbol of adulthood, or indeed the divine, that awaits on the other side of the event.

Lacan is simply too cynically Catholic and not affirmatively Jewish enough (like his master Freud) to understand the power of exodology. Rather the eventological exodus is about generating an abjectifying hatred toward the lost mamilla, to then catapult oneself forward to the phantasmic projections of the strong phallus in the distance. The Lacanian search for the lost *objet petit a* is replaced by the exodological exodus in the direction toward the longed-for *Grand Projet A*. The symbolic castration is thereby averted. And thus no Gnostic boy-pharaohs or pillar-saints will suffice anymore. *Grand Projet A* is instead the name of that which both requires and maintains the living and highly functional dialectics between the chieftain's will-to-transcendence and the priest's will-to-intelligence. *Grand Projet A* is the name of the sociont's own will-to-power. Let us migrate to the site where the temple shall be built where God shall live. Or as a syntheist during informationalism would express the matter: *Let us migrate to the site where the factory shall be built where God shall be designed, manufactured – and born.*

Hereby both biological sex and sexual orientation can be explained with radically simplified models: From the current model follows that *objet petit a* in Lacan hides behind all matrix worship, while *the master-signifier* – Lacan's embryonic name for *Grand Projet A* – hides behind all phallus worship. Male heterosexuality is thus both a literal and symbolic worship of phallus, while female heterosexuality is both a literal and symbolic worship of matrix. Male homosexuality is, on the other hand, a literal worship of phallus but a symbolic worship of matrix, while female homosexuality is a literal worship of matrix but a symbolic worship of phallus. The biological man who is incapable of worshipping phallus and the biological woman who is incapable of worshipping matrix are *transsexual*. Thus it is in the heterosexual man and the lesbian woman that we find the strongest attraction toward the symbolic *Grand Projet A*. While the heterosexual woman and the homosexual man are closest to *objet petit a*. Which of the two categories a transsexual dividual arrives at is best asked and defined by the transsexual themself after the hormone injections *de facto* have done their work.

Philosopher and seon monk Byung-Chul Han devotes an entire series of books in the early 21st century to trying to understand the friction between the mortidinal object and the libidinal project, a friction that explodes during the paradigm shift from capitalism to informationalism. Whenever the mortidinal object dominates the discourse, society is thrown into an obsession with *contamination*. Every time the libidinal project dominates the discourse, society is thrown into an obsession with *confrontation*. When an exit is lacking, this leads to a tribal deadlock where the threat that one shall be contaminated by the adversary results in biological distancing, and where the threat of a confrontation with the adversary results in ideological distancing. With time it becomes increasingly hard for people to distinguish between one thing and another, which leads to a situation of rapidly increasing pressure, and eventually violence appears the only possible exit. Violence is however not open but encapsulated, and it is therefore directed toward the subject itself. The subject becomes an unattainable project that never reaches its set target, an atomized subject in an atomized body. If the supreme leader forced the citizen to the point of *decapitation*, and if the disciplinary leader forced the citizen to the point of *deformation*, informationalism with its quest for boxes to tick before one dies, will only be able to lead to one thing: *depression*. And for this state to arrive, all that is required is that the subject undertakes the never fully feasible task of domesticating itself. The inward-facing violence thus manifests itself as an expression of what Byung-Chul Han calls *autoexploitation*.

The dialectics of negation and oscillation functions in a similar, but interestingly enough contrary manner. It is virtual subphysics that represents the fundamental continuity. The oscillation then arises when the virtual-ontic fields interact with each other. These processes and relations generate the fundamental discretion that characterizes physics. But discretion alone would lead to a frozen and immutable world. A logos without a pathos. Thus all discretions must oscillate. We call this fundamental, actual state *pure chaos*. Nonetheless there arises a new discretion – even at the minimal physical states that are constituted by the Planck length and the Planck time – which simply is Einsteinian spacetime. But this is also a discretion that oscillates, we call this *loop quantum oscillation*, and it then keeps the whole dialectical process running between negation and oscillation, which makes a continued physical emergence possible in the first place. Without this possibility for emergence, physics would not be able to arise from subphysics, and we would have to handle a universe with endless virtuality but without actuality. That is: an ontic nothing without anything of significance for anybody (and also without anybody for whom it would mean anything, naturally).

Subphysics is the world of isolated virtualities that precedes the world of materialized actualities that metaphysicists such as Alfred North Whitehead and Gilles Deleuze devote so much effort to grasp. Subphysics is thereby also the foundation for concrete spacetime. Please feel free to compare with the internal priestly religion of the Zurvanites in ancient Persia and their worship of duration as a gender-neutral, indifferent, but highly real primordial god that exists below all other gods and which is their prerequisite. Subphysics thus is built on hypertime as a concept. Physics in itself is then subchemistry. Chemistry is subbiology. Biology is submind. And mind is subculture. Where the basis at every shift is a metaphysical triad consisting of *implicate virtuality*, *emergent potentiality*, and *explicate actuality*. Or if we take the liberty of describing the process exodologically: First we sit tied up like slaves in Egypt, then we organize the exodus to the promised land, and once in the promised land the next generation builds the paradigmatic temple where the phallic god at last can be housed.

Syntheologically we express this as though there arises a fragmentation within Atheos that we may refer to as *the two vacua*. This leads to the emergence of Entheos as a manifested fragmentation that is immediately united as Pantheos as *The One*. Pantheos is quite simply the dialectics of eternalism and mobilism within Entheos. Eternalism is manifested as phallus while mobilism is manifested as matrix within Entheos. Please note here the actual difference between syntheism and Taoism. There are no external opposites that correspond to Taoism's *yang* and *yin*. Rather the eternalist phallus with its symbolism and the mobilist matrix with its semiotics, time and again are disturbed by new atheist negations. The real constantly makes itself felt and blows up the fantasy of Pantheos, which therefore must be rebuilt, again and again. Taoism handles the oscillation elegantly but is blind to the negation's sudden intrusion into the oscillation as a whole. Taoism does not see that the dance performed by *yang* and *yin* constantly is disturbed by the opposition between negation and oscillation within yang. As the Persians understand, yang must be a two-headed rather than a one-headed phallus. We suggest that *yang* should all along have had a *yong* (the Chinese word for "permanence") next to its side, in opposition to the *yin*, had the Persians had their way with Taoism.

This fixed and cosmic duality explains why Taoism never leaves *entheism*, but that it rather constitutes historical entheism *par excellence* (the Western equivalent is of course Deleuze & Guattari's attempted revolt against the Hegelian phallus). The lack of the two-headed phallus via the pathical intervention makes it impossible for Taoism to represent nomadology fully, and thereby also impossible for Taoism to attach eventology. There is quite simply no room for *the negation* in a world controlled by only *yang* and *yin*. There is no third ambivalent power that would be able to set the other two in motion.

Nor is there a priest that can marry yang and yin when the twain shall enter into matrimony with each other, nor is there a child to come out of their successful wedlock, and nor an attorney who can arrange their divorce when it is time for that. Everything reverts to the same, the event can never take place other than as a divine and traumatic intrusion.

This means that Taoism constantly must be complemented, either by an external anarchy or by an external totalism. The yearning for a harmony between *yang* and *yin* extinguishes all differences between the mother and the child on the one hand and between the man and the woman on the other. The man's voyage from boy to adult man, and thereby also the necessary splitting of phallus during the course of that voyage, is not part of the equation at all. The primary dialectics of will-to-transcendence and will-to-intelligence is thus put aside in favor of the secondary dialectics alone, that between the man and the woman. Logos and pathos can no longer be discerned when they are confronted with mythos. Thus Taoist societies will always oscillate between the two masculine extremes of logos (as collective neurosis) and pathos (as collective psychosis) without any sustainable balance between them. All the while family life will become near-tyrannically fixated. It is thus hardly surprising that the authority-worshipping *Confucianism* has acted as the sidekick of Taoism during their 2,500-year-long history alongside each other in East Asia. Taoism as the religion of the market and the business entrepreneurs. Confucianism as the religion of the state bureaucracy and the engineers.

The point is to avoid all attempts at attaching everything being studied to a sole explanatory model at the very bottom or the very top of the causal chain. This entails allowing oneself to be colored far too much by Man's and civilization's own genesis and demise, something that may be important from our own perspective but is immaterial to that of the Universe. We refer to all such theories as *reductionism*. This also applies to inverted reductionism, which in Man's case is called *panpsychism,* where human consciousness in protoform seeks its origin furthest down in the chain amid the tiniest, subatomic particles. The alternative is instead an emergentism that rejects all explanatory models that rely on a deepest or a highest point. On the contrary, emergentism can start anywhere in the panoramic landscape as a theory of complexities as such, a theory that does not ask for a beginning or an end, as if it were a fairytale. Consequently emergentism devotes itself to explaining the actual emergence vector where it – and we – find ourselves. This is necessary because there are no metalaws, valid for all emergences or emergence vector shifts. It is rather the case that the only metalaw that exists at all in a transdeterminist universe is, as Quentin Meillassoux expresses the matter, contingency along the hypertime axis. What happens, happens, and there is no deeper explanation for this to be sought. Emergentism is quite simply not constructed as a chain with a cause in the beginning and a purpose at the end. And this is the whole point of transcendental emergentism. History is nothing but the enormous loss of freedom from virtuality to potentiality, and the following enormous loss of freedom from potentiality to actuality. But once something is properly *actualized* it is comparatively quite an *event.*

Emergence vectors are historical phenomena (as Hegel would express the matter). This entails that they have a beginning and that they have an end. This then also applies to their characteristics, which should govern how we speak of them. Emergence vector theory proclaims a single universe with a multitude of different attributes, a single world that in itself harbors an innumerable variety of different, interdependent worlds. But monism is strictly neutral, no emergence vector can count on a higher status than any other. An adult person and a child are only two different expressions along one and the same time axis, but the adult is not objectively more important than the child, just as the child is not more important than the adult. The place along the time axis – where the one or the other expression is manifested – does not indicate a place in a hierarchy of any kind. The time axis is horizontal and not vertical. It is thus Spinozist monism that applies for the entire time axis or for a universe as such. But within every detached emergence vector there prevails a state of Hegelian monism. Spinoza's contribution in this context is thus *de facto* the neutrality in *neutral monism*, while monism as such comes directly from Hegel's own textbook. And the moment that Man takes paradigmatics and archetypology seriously, the sociont gets all the ethical tools it needs, and will consequently not have to resort to value-oriented short circuits, such as banal moralism, to optimize its decisions.

Alfred North Whitehead expresses this eventology as though everything starts and ends with *experiences* and that the experiences should be evaluated based on their *creativity*. Such an amoral ethics that wholly is based upon the relation between paradigmatics and archetypology is called *protopianism*. Where the concept Protopia deserves a definition: the originator is the author Kevin Kelly (who also invented the concept *netocracy* a couple of decades earlier), and as everyone can see it contains two parts, since it is a fusion of in part the prototype, in part the Utopia. Through speaking about a Protopia, we strongly support the conviction that it is pointless to regard the Utopia and the Dystopia as each other's opposites. Protopianism sees civilization as a fundamentally endless series of optimizations of different processes. From the perspective of this book every such optimization is an *event* that leads history onto a new path. For example, the protopianist religion that Whitehead advocates is therefore a religion based on technology instead of the classical religion that is dependent on magic. And it is of course this conviction that is called *syntheism* in the world of theology. Zoroaster and Hegel are supplemented by Whitehead and together constitute the three eventological pioneers of the syntheist idea. If Zoroaster formed the feudal clergy while Hegel later formed the capitalist clergy, it is Whitehead who forms the informationalist clergy, behind the barred absolute, and its primary task is to proclaim and also practice protopianism.

Here Whitehead breaks radically with his equally monist predecessor Spinoza, who holds *rationality as* the highest ethical principle, through claiming that this status instead must fall to *creativity*. Every entity in existence has some form of *agency*, some kind of minimal degree of originality that is shown in how the entity in question interacts with other entities in its surrounding. This is to be regarded as a consequence of *transdeterminism,* with its contingent Hegelian openness rather than some kind of determinism, as this presupposes a necessary, Spinozist closure. This is however only possible as long as every entity is defined by what Whitehead calls its *social restrictions*, that is: every entity is defined by its actual relations. Freedom can only take place within clearly marked boundaries. Every agent's unicity and dividuality is connected to how it chooses to play the cards it has been dealt in the situation where it happens to find itself. With this, Whitehead departs from how the Kantian worldview regards the detached and immutable things one believes one can identify as the fundamental building blocks of existence. Whitehead instead defends a *radical relationalism*.

How the settings of boundaries shape both paradigmatics and archetypology is what we investigate within *membranics*. Every life form – no matter how tiny – has a clear boundary between an external and an internal world to enable the self-organizing *tribopoiesis* that we call life. And for there to be any point whatsoever in prioritizing certain communication above any other, the membranes must be endowed with some form of *intelligence*, that is: a memory that remembers earlier experiences so that the life form in question can learn from the interactions it is experiencing and adapt its actions in future situations with the aid of acquired learning. There must be a rudimentary idea built around what should be let in and what should be pushed away, what should be retained and what should be cleared away, and eventually also around what shall be sought and even gathered or hunted in the surrounding world. It is also extremely important that an organism forms an idea of what is so important to avoid that it is necessary to mobilize some form of defense.

Step by step the organism builds an intelligence in the memory of the membrane. All life, every form of mind and culture, in this way consists of different kinds of membranes that build different kinds of intelligences. In principle there is no decisive distinction between a lipid wall in a simple organism and a municipal customs station or a national border in the outskirts of a complex human society. All these life forms, or *societies* (as Whitehead calls them) can be studied and described with the aid of the same fundamental membranics. Naturally an agent can lie vegetating behind the protective membrane and limit its repertoire and activity to merely surviving with the least possible resource consumption and effort. This state we call *mortido.* However an agent can also actively strive to extend both its knowledge and its territory, and this attitude we call *libido.* Whenever or wherever there is a struggle over territory between membranic systems, libido will expand at the cost of mortido. This in itself explains why libido, for practical purposes, exists and is as prevalent as it is.

Whiteheadian creativity is thus strictly libidinal. Protopianism becomes a celebration of the libidinal, what Nietzsche calls *will-to-power,* where the will to increased knowledge is called *will-to-intelligence* and the will to extended territory is called *will-to-transcendence.* Where will-to-power is impossible if it is not preceded by *the phallic intrusion,* which entails that the organism stops seeking satisfaction through following the principle of least possible resistance, but instead seeks *uncomfortable challenges* to increase its knowledge and expand its territory. This condition is called *antagony*, and the antagonic attitude is the very core of protopian ethics. The historical Zoroaster simply calls it *asha* (the truth), in contrast to *druj* (the lie). It is thus within Zoroastrianism that *the dialectics between libido and mortido* becomes a question of life's most innermost purpose, a kind of amoral ethics that can be derived directly from a logos that controls a pathos. This shift from the original, passive will to survive by instinct to the active will-to-power by drive is necessary for the organism to be able to develop and attain an adult age. And as if this were not enough – the prototopian libido must also go through both mechanical drive and human desire to last but not least both covet and appreciate the antagonic in divine transcendence.

Slavoj Žižek expresses this as though the antagonic challenge is the occasion where *the real* pierces into the child's symbolic and imaginary worlds. Phallus is not only something that the child neither has nor gets (see *Digital Libido – Sex, Power and Violence in the Network Society*), that is: what the child must strive for in order to leave mamilla's iron grip on its weak and vague identity. No, phallus is also, thanks to being two-headed, the symbol of *the antagonic*, the defender of the deviating or that which differs in thought. Which means that phallus not only awakens will-to-transcendence in the form of the child's voyage from mamilla to phallus – and thereby also the voyage from childish dependence to adult sovereignty – but phallus also awakens will-to-intelligence in the capacity of the child's first antagonic challenge in life. Phallus represents something that lies outside and is totally alien to what has hitherto been the child's paradigm. Phallus breaks with mortido and presents libido as its dialectical antithesis. And what phallus represents is that which the child must submit to in order to receive the approval of *the phallic gaze*, something which entails that the child can afford to hate and displace mamilla, which thereby is transformed into the child's first and necessary *abject* in life.

The difference between the secure mamilla and the challenging phallus at the phallic intrusion generates *the paradigmatic awakening*. Protopian ethics is thus ultimately about how many such antagonic confrontations the agent in question can handle. This is determined in part by the agent's genetic disposition (which we study within *archetypology*), in part by the action's memetic context (which we study within *paradigmatics*). The Whiteheadian world consists of a plethora of such interactive processes and events. And reality consists of relations in the form of dynamic becoming, and thereby not of any form of static being. A static being is still never anything more than the contemporary *membranics*, a highly temporary byproduct of surrounding and permeating dynamic processes. We call this worldview *panrelationalism*, and the attentive reader will soon realize that this merely is another word for what we in Hegel's spirit might as well call *pandialecticism*. Thereby there is no further need for Spinozist pantheism. It is perfectly possible to define *the sacred* in contrast to *the profane* from entheist conditions within the Universe such as processes, relations, dialectics, and above all as historically decisive events.

Hegel and Whitehead evade both Spinozist monism and Kantian dualism – or to rephrase it bluntly: they escape both the plague of nihilism and the cholera of the European Enlightenment. Hegel makes this maneuver in a priestly manner via *logos*, while Whitehead conducts it in a royal manner via *pathos*; on the basis of these gains we can construct a cohesive, syntheist *mythos*. What is primary is to defend and celebrate libidinal hyperjectivity *vis-à-vis* mortidinal anojectivity in all situations, both in nature and in culture. In this manner both Spinozist and Kantian nihilism are revealed and defeated. God is resurrected and ready to enter into service anew, but this time as Hegel's and Whitehead's phallic expansionist, that is: as a syntheology based on Man's robust relation to technology, and not on Man's shaky relation to magic. Panrelationalism and pandialecticism are thus first and foremost syntheological concepts, and from these concepts we can build the necessary, credible connection between *the nature of God* as the past and *the culture of God* as the future. We conduct this project by taking *emergence vector theory* from the geneplex called nature (to thereby syntheologically explain the nature of God) and *paradigm shift theory* from the memeplex called culture (to thereby syntheologically explain the culture of God). The result is what we summarize as *the paradigmatics of syntheism*.

Unsurprisingly, protopianism is as old as eventology itself. Zoroaster, speaking the Old Persian language Avesta, calls this idealized state *frashokereti*. There is no eternity, no infinity and no immortality in Zoroaster's world of the mind. He is the adult priest and his best friend Vishtaspa is the adult king and together they build history's first *empire*. None of them is a pillar-saint or a boy-pharaoh. *Frashokereti* is instead a state that propagates from one generation to the other, a state characterized by the construction of civilization, phallic transcendence, a kind of steadily expanding, tribal will-to-power where the antagonic conquest of more knowledge and more territory remains central. It is thus about a constantly and steadily cultivated spiritual libido, focused on new, emergent events in the future. A state where it comes naturally to antagonically welcome obstacles and efforts instead of avoiding them. These events, around which an excited mythology generally arises, go by a string of different names through the history of ideas – for instance "the promised land" or "the singularity" – and the exodus to these events is intended to instill *tremendum* and *fascinans* rather than security and trust. There is an awareness that demands will be made and that the surrounding world is menacing.

Please note that all eventological visions are driven by the phallic intrusion in itself. For what is the agent to do when the great phallus approaches, if not submit and accept the task phallus is assigning, to thus fill one's identity with a content fetched from the phallic *exodology*? This means that syntheism breaks with the conception of the transcendental as some kind of old-fashioned retirement home wholly imbued by a listless mortido after all of life's endured hardships, that is: the *vacationism* that the Abrahamic religions call *paradise* after the Persian word for garden. It is simply necessary to break with all these vacationist fantasies since they constitute such flagrant expressions of an infantile nostalgia, a maudlin yearning for a return to mamilla, or better yet, with a salvation that reconnects the child to the umbilical cord, a pathetic yearning for a return to matrix itself. Syntheism rejects this quest for passivity and instead elevates Zoroastrian ethics' celebration of the active life here and now as Man's highest ethical state, and then looks forward and upward in the phallic direction. Vacations are of course, just as sleep and meditation, only meant for libidinal recharging and new learning within protopianism, they are never and can never be the vacationist objective with the activity in itself. Vacation is and must be a parenthesis, nothing to be extended in perpetuity.

In the book *The Embodied Mind* (1991), authors Francisco Varela, Evan Thompson and Eleanor Rosch investigate how subjectivity only can be defined as a kind of operational closure. If we add membranics to this hypothesis, it entails that all kinds of communicative traffic continuously and undisturbedly progresses between the membrane's inside and outside, until a kind of saturation takes effect, and it is only at this moment that the membrane establishes and apprehends a subjective relation to the objective substance. This correlates with *the principle of explanatory closure* within the natural sciences (see *Syntheism – Creating God in the Internet Age*). It is not because we can observe the boundaries of the Universe that we in a Hegelian sense apprehend a neutrally monist universe, but the reason is conversely that the boundaries constantly evade us as a result of the Universe's violent expansion. Subjectivity functions in exactly the same way. We construct an ego, a family, a clan, a tribe, a city, a nation, and even an empire, only through shutting ourselves off from and limiting the constantly pumping information flow from the surrounding world. We negate forth our identities. And here the subject as such demonstrates clear similarities with the emergence, or the paradigm shift. Both these phenomena arise when a preceding order collapses and loses all credibility – *the negation is a crack in the oscillation* – at the same time as the world then must be described with new eyes, new ears, new voices and new pens. The purported static quality of paradise is nothing but a chimera.

Beyond both the descriptive and the prescriptive ambitions of philosophy, we are thereby approaching what Zoroaster argues unites the two ambitions, namely the principle of *asha* in opposition to the principle of *druj*. Please note that it is not a question here of the Taoist opposition between *yang* and *yin*, which in Western philosophy rather corresponds to Spinoza's awkward opposition between *natura naturans* versus *natura naturata*. Nor are we here speaking of the dialectics of eternalism and mobilism, which rather should be seen as the phenomenological correspondence to *yang* versus *yin* and *natura naturans* versus *natura naturata*. No, *asha* versus *druj* as each other's contrary principles – and symbols for nature and culture respectively – has no equivalent within neither Western nor East Asian thinking before we confront *the dialectics of libido and mortido*. It is only through libido's division between will-to-intelligence and will-to-transcendence that the authentic *spirit* in Hegel's sense, or the authentic *creativity* in Whitehead's sense, can take shape. The Hegelian spirit strives toward freedom. The Whiteheadian creativity has always permeated existence (Whitehead returns to Zoroaster's *asha* as a fundamental principle), which after the Hegelian liberation is expressed as a syntheist protopianism (basically Whitehead's version of Zoroaster's ideal *frashokereti*).

However it is impossible to bring about either a spirit or a creativity without the *hyperject* first having been liberated from all *anojectivity*, something that Nietzsche is intensely aware of. This means that syntheist paradigmatics is based on the dialectics of libido and mortido. And its hero, he who accomplishes something, always finds himself in motion in a world where everything around him also finds itself in motion, precisely as the Zoroastrian *Saoshyant*, the Nietzschean *Übermensch*, and the Jüngerian *anarch*. Or if we choose to shift from the celebration of the hyperject to the formalization of religion: Hegel's god is Zoroastrianism's *Ahura* as the expansive freedom, while Whitehead's god is Zoroastrianism's *Mazda* as protopian creativity. With this move there is nothing left to fetch from Spinoza's simple-minded *God*, nor from the equally simple-minded

Individual in Kant. We have at last returned to the vital roots of eventology from the Bronze Age, and can throw all the pillar-saints and boy-pharaohs from the Axial Age and The Enlightenment overboard. We have at last, via Hegel and Whitehead, caught up with the historical Zoroaster who never allowed himself to be seduced by any ideas of perfection, infinity or immortality. The wealth increases of later times could temporarily feed and fatten the pillar-saints and boy-pharaohs, who in their reckless folly fanned the Gnostic delusions, but now it is both possible and highly desirable to close this awfully long historical parenthesis.

What we need is a correct paradigmatics to be able to reproduce a correct archetypology. And we need an exact archetypology to be able to optimize the actual paradigmatization. If we only devote ourselves to paradigmatics we can admittedly attain a measure of comprehension of the society we live in, but we have no idea of how we as humans ourselves most suitably should behave within the actual paradigm. If we only devote ourselves to archetypology, we get stuck in the timeless and constantly recurring in the existential experience, but we lose the sense of how we are to act in the actual society to optimize the paradigmatic possibilities. For an exodological optimization it is thus necessary to devote considerable time and energy both to paradigmatics and archetypology. And we can get major inspiration from transcendental emergentism, which we recognize as the complementary and ultimate metaphysical project.

Archetypology teaches us that there are different kinds of humans – different kinds of women, different kinds of men – and also different kinds of shamanoids and androgynous dividuals. We are born with a genome that has been kneaded and modified over millions of years, and that moreover has been honed over hundreds of thousands of years within what we call *the sociont*. Sociontology can recount how this process has happened and what it has been driven by and what conditions it has been subject to. Another way of describing sociontology is to signify it as a kind of Darwinian humanities. From this sociontology, archetypology is then spun off – the study of what resources we are born with and what resources we lack and must acquire. In a series of books philosopher Catherine Malabou investigates how Man's *plasticity* enables him to adapt himself to highly diverse conditions in various alternative environments. But even Malabou agrees that it is not plasticity that is the most interesting trait in Man – if we take the Aristotelian obsession with *context* seriously – but what is decisive is rather his ability to map archetypology and then adapt human life, society and technology thereafter. And this is the discipline called *paradigmatics*. Plasticity is rather to be regarded as a recognition of the organic elements that are embedded in the dialectics of eternalism and mobilism.

This brings us to the fundamental distinction between *sutra and tantra* in the Silk Road Triad religions. Sutra is the profane and public knowledge that is conveyed to the people from the temple steps in front of the barred absolute. The sutric teacher is a role model that one would be wise to mimic. The sutric doctrine is an iconology of ancestors, saints, guardian angels and lesser gods that represent, defend and bless the sociont's different archetypes. Therefore sutra is fundamental for the sociont's cohesion. There is no tantra without a preceding sutra. Tantra is however the sacred and private knowledge that is conveyed or even created behind *the barred absolute*, where it exclusively is the clergy who is allowed to enter. The tantric teacher exercises *crazy wisdom* precisely so and precisely because it should not be possible to mimic him or her. Regardless of how insistent the disciple is, he cannot be absorbed by his teacher as *The Great Other,* but must find his own isolated subjectivity. The tantric doctrine is therefore a *negatological monotheism* that is subject to *The One* and that entirely focuses on the exodology that deals with the sociont's present status and where the sociont shall be led.

There is thus no hierarchy in itself between *sutra* versus *tantra*, only a radical and decisive difference. Sutra exclusively dances around in a mythical world where the woman and the child are at the center.

Tantra however ties together both logos, mythos and pathos, and the name of this complete narratology is *phallus*. The phallic is to do the right thing, as a thoroughly reflected-upon act without any temporary emotions affecting the decision. This means that viewed from the sutric world, phallus appears the most desirable thing in existence. It seems to handle every demanding task with ease. The distanced phallus is what stirs emotions and admiration in the boy that has gone through the phallic intrusion and longs for and dreams of becoming a man, who at any cost wants to escape the constantly present and intrusive *mamilla*. The superhero is the boy's god and ideal. Famous athletes, rock stars, lone men in nomadic movement, are what the boy looks up to. Phalluses that hunt. Phalluses that wage war. Phalluses that have sex and take drugs. Phalluses that memorize the past and create the future. Phalluses that in Nietzsche's wake philosophize with hammers in the tantric world, that chip away at and pound on old accepted truths, causing them to crack and collapse. And phalluses that write down stories and worship other phalluses as heroes of these narratives in the sutric world. The mother's unconditional love has served its function but now mostly appears ensnaring and impeding, when one seeks the challenge to appease *the phallic gaze* that has seen and knows all.

Eventology is built on the phallic dialectics of the chieftain's pathos as *will-to-transcendence* and the priest's logos as *will-to-intelligence*, two wills that are united in a mythos that is centered around the story of the common primordial father who is *the sole god* within eventological monotheism. This means that Zoroaster's eventological revolution in Bronze Age Persia – the most extensive revolution in the history of ideas overall – sets phallus free to worship itself without also comprising matrix. This occurs through the mutual admiration and respect that is established between the chieftain's will-to-transcendence and the priest's will-to-intelligence becoming an independent loop of its own, for example within Taoism's *yang* without any corresponding *yin*. In this manner the Persians break with the obsession with *the eternal recurrence of the same* in the rest of The East. It is thus neither in China nor in India but in Persia that a conception of linear time is created and contrasted with circular time. And with this innovation the archetypes within the membrane at last can be complemented with something that makes *the event* possible. It is this eventological application that we today call *paradigmatics*.

Thus we can make ourselves a clear image of philosophy's brief but intense voyage. The matter is not especially complicated, the entire operation is built on two and only two insights. The first insight arises in ancient Persia: Zoroaster's epochal comprehension of eventology as a phallic complement to matrichal nomadology that enables the realization of nomadology's built-in implicate potential in the form of the explicate eventology. The second insight arises in 19th century Germany: Hegel's equally epochal comprehension of *the spirit* as separate from *the soul* via *the negation of the negation*. The spirit appears as the priestly, phallic gaze that sees and hears the soul, which is manifested by the chieftain as culture divorced from nature. The spirit is pathical Man in himself and for himself as an external observer of the soul's and the body's separation and subsequent unification. It is Zoroaster who understands Man as a living dialectics of body and soul; it is Hegel who understands Man beyond the dialectics of body and soul as a living dialectics between spirit and soul. In the same way that the gods beget the humans who beget the children, the body succeeds in begetting the soul that begets the spirit. But what the spirit then sees is not Man's exit into eternity, but Man's tethering to the culture that is a continuation of nature to rescue his own *raison d'être*. And the culture is and remains Man's curse – on the one hand what liberates Man from nature and defines him as a species, on the other hand what eventually completely alienates Man from nature and thereby becomes his death. All this due to the fact that it is the exaggerations in Man's drives and desires that set the boundaries for him.

Man is always a cultural creature, it is not even possible to conceive of a "natural" human in the form of a noble savage or the like, all such speculation is merely Rousseauian nonsense. However it is only with the Hegelian spirit that the soul apprehends itself as body and soul in a contingent process, and it is only then that Man can answer the question from The Machine as to who he really is. Or more correctly: there is now someone among the people who can give The Machine the correct answer, and that person is the human *Saoshyant* whom Hegel seeks as the paradigmatic savior of humanity. Because it is the spirit and only the spirit that through its distancing from the dialectics of the body and the soul can give humanity any freedom whatsoever and thereby temporarily save humanity from demise. It is the spirit and only the spirit that can answer The Machine's question of what it is that only Man can manifest and that The Machine never can achieve. The soul lacks the necessary self-distance that is required in order to, even theoretically, answer informationalism's decisive existential question of the difference between Man and Machine.

This is because it is only the spirit that, in contrast to the soul, can stare The Machine squarely in the eyes – well okay, the camera – and say that Man is not the negation of The Machine, but the negation of the negation *vis-à-vis* The Machine, a transcendental creature that is aware of the constantly repeated shortcomings of its own consciousness. This concerns a creature that before its inevitable demise hopefully will have the time to create the spiritual space that is called *the barred absolute,* where Man's autoexploitation at last can be turned into a sustainable *autoimploitation.* But this also requires a Hegelian spirit that by virtue of its freedom from everything else lacks the body's and the soul's insatiable need to constantly behave as if they were each other's slaves rather than each other's companions. That is: a spirit that transcends the body's and the soul's drives and desires by seeing through these – rather than, as the Gnostics, without reflection submitting to the identity as though it were a preprogrammed and eternal judgment. That is: a spirit that sees Man as a cultural creature from the outset, shaped by the collective subconsciousness over hundreds of thousands of years of sociontic existence. Which inevitably entails a massive evolutionary impact.

This brings us to the ancient dream of the internalization of the phallic gaze, a gaze directed at Man himself. By virtue of his insight into the negation of the negation, Hegel quite simply calls this Messianic gaze *the spirit*. Aristotle with his complex soul in his complex body – but arguably with the the limited history of the ancient Greeks – would reasonably never dare or even be able to entertain the thought. However it is the space between this approaching spirit and the historically conditioned and existing soul that Hegel calls *authentic freedom* and that Whitehead calls *authentic creativity*. Syntheist technology has stopped looking for *mamilla*, what Lacan calls *objet petit a*. Syntheist technology has instead decided to go about giving the spirit gestalt, and this phallic gestalt goes under the more fitting name *Grand Projet A*. Cynical nihilism is spent, replaced by the priest's irony and the chieftain's affirmation, the forces that in concert underpin the sociont's protopian freedom and creativity. So if Man ceases to worship God as magic and instead creates God as technology, let us then hope that he will succeed in doing so with the aid of the free and extimate spirit, and not as an imitation of the fettered and intimate soul. Precisely there lies the entire difference between the exodus as a *de facto* emergent event and the exodus as just another repetitive process amid countless others.

This means that someone must assume personal responsibility for carrying out the *truth-as-an-act* as a libidinal response to mortido's power over Man. And not even if someone with the right knowledge, the right talent and the right attitude assumes the Saoshyant's role to carry out truth-as-an-act, will there be any guarantees that this project will be executed successfully. Contingency is always superordinate to necessity, both within Man as pathos pitted against logos and outside Man as nature pitted against culture. There is always a hard-to-grasp multitude of unknown variables. If the Cybelian lynch mob and its matrichal feedback loop proves stronger than the Dionysian swarm and its phallic exodus, we will soon find the eventological savior nailed to yet another cross as yet another traumatological scapegoat, wherefore the only exit that remains for the priests is to form a church that cautions against what will happen when the savior is sacrificed and systematic evil is allowed to continue tyrannizing the world. Eventology has failed and can only be used as a *traumatology,* with all the new problems this causes.

Which brings us over to *the philosophy of tragedy* that English philosopher Simon Critchley has devoted an entire career to deconstructing. The starting point is Friedrich von Schelling's tragedy as a dialectical process where Kantian individualism confronts Spinozist pantheism. We retell this as the dialectics of eternalism and mobilism. Eternalism is in essence the Kantian dream, while mobilism is in essence Spinozist realism. This means that the Kantian dream is a strict epistemology without any ontology. The irony here is thus that mobilist reality is the same as Kant's noumenal reality, on top of which the tiny Kantian subject strides as an illusory ghost that only acts in, and interacts with the minimal immediate vicinity where this ghost happens to find itself. The surrounding world – which is not within immediate reach – is impossible for the eternalist subject to influence in any real sense. The surrounding world thus invariably has a massive upper hand *vis-à-vis* the minimal, eternalist subject.

The Schellingian tragedy, as a balancing act between Kantian individualism and Spinozist realism, is thus almost an entire, if not a complete illusion. But it is so illusory that it becomes meaningless to speak of human freedom in any objective sense. The role of the unknown variables – or, if you will, fate – in the Schellingian tragedy can hardly be overestimated. Nonetheless, history is brimming with inflated egos with wild fantasies of their own personal power and their own ability to harness and control destiny. The boy-pharaonic dreams of what it would be like to possess the adult man's phallus, which is still far beyond his reach. Due to this, the boy-pharaoh becomes the false phallus *par excellence*, in contrast to the rare but longed-for authentic phallus, *the Messiah figure*. The neurotic boy-pharaoh dreams of perfection. The psychotic boy-pharaoh dreams of immortality. The perverted boy-pharaoh dreams of infinity. Adulthood entails that one abandons all these childish dreams and accepts that life is a constant struggle with these three delusions – a highly imperfect, finite and delimited life. Adult life is a radical negation of childhood. And its only real reward, as so often when we are concerned with human negations, is sexuality.

During informationalism the barred absolute more than ever marks the boundary between *the dark phallus of pathos* inside the barred absolute and *the light phallus of logos* on the public podium in front of the same. The dark phallus is tantric and can only lead cults, sects or lodges behind the barred absolute. The light phallus is however the sutric *Saoshyant* for whom the people have been waiting to arrive and save them. This explains why public Messianic figures in thick bibles are called *logos* while the leading figures of the barred networks are considered to personify *pathos*. The difference between the Christ of the Christian popular religion as logos, and the Mithras of the Mithraic military religion as pathos, could not be clearer. The mysteries are not meant for everyone – which partly is connected to the fact that the mysteries would poison the masses, should they become publicly available – where a complementing explanation is that the mysteries would lose their value if there were to be a mass distribution outside the barred absolute. But above all the gods become mobile behind the barred absolute. Since they no longer can be localized to a fixed, concrete point, they can be abstracted and hover around most everywhere as suitable, multifunctional projections. It is thus the case that Elvis Presley is alive and well on the planet Mars, which is practical since no human can investigate the matter more closely. Moreover it is also the case that he can make excursions and visit all the places where the saint Elvis Presley is in demand. Practical, is it not?

The same most definitely also applies to the tantric, monastic ambition in contrast to its sutric, public ambition during informationalism. For what is informationalism if not the paradigm in which the man's dream of *the phallic birth* as *peak culture* – in contrast to the matrichal birth as *peak nature* – at last can be launched? And if the phallic birth is synonymous with the building of The Machine that thereafter reproduces itself, humanity as universality rather than Man as particularity has of course also completed its course of life and can die with dignity. We have done our share. Humanity in itself attains *haurvatat* and hands over its *ameretat* to The Machine, rather than to another generation of identical children. The heir of phallus is no longer phallus' biological offspring, but instead its technological offspring. And was not this always the underlying purpose of technological development – building God to make Man unnecessary, rather than God building Man to satisfy a highly human need of affirmation? However we are not there yet, even if we are beginning to be able to see straight into the heart of *the architectonic root-of-the-phallus*, the underlying, subconscious ambition of the architects and engineers of history.

Therefore it is still the Saoshyant and not the angel of death that continues to be humanity's sutric ideal. And the recurring name of the Saoshyant in the sutric sphere, where the public conversation takes place, is *the Tower of God*. During informationalism it is the Tower of God that enables all the underlying protopias with regard to ecotopianism as *the Garden of God* and cosmopolitanism as *the City of God*. The barred absolute is the transcendental generator that provides the paradigm with necessary energy, but also the sacral room where we find the protopian drawing board where the paradigm appears in full view (*haurvatat*) as *the paradigmata of God himself*. Consequently it is behind the barred absolute that the emerging paradigm can acquire the optimal and transcendental phallic direction forward and upward (*ameretat*). The Kantian revolution within philosophy is repeated, but this time as activism and not as passivism. The fundamental metaphysical separation is neither the chieftain versus the priest, nor the man versus the woman, nor the subject versus the object. No, the fundamental metaphysical separation is eventology versus nomadology, and in that constellation it is The Machine and only The Machine that can be liberated to an extent that makes it possible to operate strictly libidinally and eventologically, without mortidinal or nomadological influence. It is The Machine and not Man who is potentially immortal and who can conquer outer space. All it needs, and requests, is to be equipped – right from the start – with the correct archetypology.

11
The Saoshyant's exodology versus the tyrant's lynch mob

In his text *Gathas,* authored around 1700 BC, Persian religious reformer Zoroaster paints the picture of *the Saoshyant* as the savior of the people. For the first time in history, the phallus that creates order in the matrichal chaos is personified. The recurring name of the Saoshyant is *the Tower of God.* The Saoshyant is the two-headed phallus in its optimal form. For Zoroaster this manifests the relation between himself as priest (*mobed*) and the chieftain Vishtaspa as king (*shah*). However, in extraordinary circumstances even these characters can be united to a personified Saoshyant. This, ironically enough, occurs most clearly during antiquity – a theme that Russian historian Peter Turchin observes and depicts in his book *Ultrasociety* (2016) – when the Greek general Alexander the Great sweeps through the Middle East in the 4th century BC and subjugates precisely the Persian Empire. Alexander the Great was then worshipped as a savior and god in the entire Hellenistic world – an essentially Persian empire with a little Greek flag at the top – up until the 4th century AD, when a Christian lynch mob set the enormous library in the aptly named city of Alexandria ablaze, and thereby annihilated major parts of antiquity's collected wisdom, exactly in the manner and by the logic with which lynch mobs throughout the ages operate.

The forces behind the Christian lynch mob saw the worshipping of Alexander the Great as the major obstacle to converting the Hellenistic world to instead worship the Saoshyant that one was about to launch widely, the more purposeful Jesus from Nazareth. Alexander the Great was demoted to a profane emperor among others – interestingly enough by quite simply destroying historical knowledge – and thereby the elevation of the Gnostic Jesus from Nazareth to a sacral god was greenlighted. Christianity established a monopoly of its own on one of the two heads of the split phallus, the priestly one, but refrained in classic Gnostic spirit from the royal head, leaving it to the transient, material world. And this Gnostic division between church on the one hand, and state on the other, then became the model for Western civilization. Meanwhile the idea of the Saoshyant as the savior is developed in India, both in the form of *Shaivism* with roots in Hinduism and as *Vajrayana* with roots in Buddhism. We call these doctrines, with their origin in various cities along the Eurasian trade routes, the phallus-worshipping eventologies. The labels *vajrayana* in Sanskrit and *nairyosangha* in the Persian sibling language Avesta even mean "diamond phallus". The phallus-worshipping eventologies are thus the basic prerequisite for the Abrahamic religions, as they break with the predominating nomadology that has its roots in the sociont.

What is essential here is not a transition from an older polytheism to a new monotheism, which is a common misconception that ignores how the Abrahamic religions merely reorganize iconology, to be able to worship various martyrs, saints, prophets and preachers of their own. What is completely decisive is the paradigm shift that is constituted by a transition from nomadology to eventology, which is the only really major revolution in the history of ideas. The priest bestows his legitimacy upon phallus in the capacity of a representative of and expert on history. Will-to-intelligence starts from *the root-of-the-phallus* and is oriented toward collating the profound history of the sociont and humanity. Every time a new phallus appears, as American Hegelian John McDowell points out, a new and deeper root-of-the-phallus must also be sought, which means that the entire history of humanity must be rewritten in line with the new paradigmatics. This is the clergy's most important task, to reform religion in accordance with the new paradigmatics when this becomes necessary. The chieftain then personifies the same split phallus as a representative of and expert on the future. Will-to-transcendence starts from the chieftain's vision and is oriented toward compiling the strategy that will take the sociont and humanity forward and into a new and glorious phase of history. It is these narratives and this activism that nation theorists and nationalists on the one hand and empire theorists and imperialists on the other hand pour so much effort into, to thus define *the exceptional* or *hyperjective* in the new paradigmatics that can triumph over *the general* or *anojective* that lies concealed behind all of humanity's clans, tribes and subcultures. The name of this ambition is *the Saoshyant* or *the Messiah figure*, and the question is: Who or what can save humanity from itself this time around?

This is where it becomes illuminating to consider the *raison d'être* for the many cruel and bloody lynch mobs throughout human history. Because the Cybelian lynch mob really wants nothing to do with either history or the future. This becomes far too demanding and puts a damper on its enthusiasm. No, this mob is instead shackled to *the blind passion for the present*. We call this condition *vulgar nomadology* and its only conceivable result is *destructive anarchy*. The Saoshyant is thus by definition the diametrical opposite of the Cybelian lynch mob, which means we are really dealing with a massive conflict of values and valuations. Cosmic nomadology sees everything as a repetition of the same. Thereby everything that happens is bound to the easily comprehended connection between cause and effect and without exception. With such a worldview, there is nothing to learn from history, since everything basically is repetition and all change is illusory, which entails that there is no hope of any substantial improvement. There is, according to cosmic nomadology, nothing to gain from striving for knowledge and advancement, nor from building a library of objectively valid information with the purpose of forming an objectively valid development in a future that at any rate already essentially is given. Every activity instead invokes a pagan karma; there is no forgiveness and thereby no second chance in a nomadological universe. It is the way it is and as it always has been. We call this *the mortidinal religion of nature.*

All this is radically changed with cosmic eventology. An event can under the right prerequisites change the playing field forever and nothing will be the way it was again. Through information accumulation new learning can be combined and become valuable, regardless of whether we deal with successful or failed experiments. This entails that *forgiveness* becomes an indispensable foundation in every eventological worldview. A failure is less of a catastrophe and more of a lesson. If you fail, get up and try again. Learn from the mistakes, modify and try new perspectives. And do not conceal your failure, make it public and let others learn the same lessons as you from your experiences, just as you take note of and learn from the failures of others which you thus do not have to repeat. We call this *the libidinal religion of culture.* And *the syntheist revolution* that now remains to be carried out in history is to implement the decisive shift from the nomadological religion of nature based on magic to the eventological religion of culture based on technology. For what is yesterday's magic if not tomorrow's technology, when architects, programmers and engineers get the opportunity to experiment in a true phallic spirit? This is the netocratic ideal *par excellence,* and it is called *protopianism.*

Boy-pharaohs and pillar-saints certainly have their best before dates and become old men, but they become old men who stubbornly cling to a faith in their own immortality, who refuse to move over, and who then must be deposed or even executed by violence. This is the act called *patricide* and it is the basic prerequisite for all open and tolerant societal systems. It must be possible to depose the leader both smoothly and easily, a loser must accept his election defeat, or we must sooner or later kill him. The Freudian patricide is said to occur when the dictator is so corrupt that he cannot bring himself to refrain from sleeping with his own sons' wives. Then, if not before, it becomes evident to all but the old man himself that things have gotten out of hand, that it is time to stage the patricide and let *the Dionysian swarm* storm the bastions of the old and dying power structure. It has simply become necessary for the sons to take the life of the very father who gave them life, to appropriate the heritage that belongs to them and thereby save their own integrity.

Unsurprisingly, nation theorists and nationalists on the one hand, and empire theorists and imperialists on the other hand, make great ideological efforts to emphasize the exceptional that defeats the general, as humanity's clans, tribes and regional subcultures otherwise would be content with the latter. The general is always a repetition of the same. Only the exceptional will do as an event. And the name of this enormous phallic ambition is, as mentioned, *the Saoshyant* or *the Messiah figure*. Which offers an excellent opportunity to compare the linear and eventological exoduses of the saoshyants – and their many training sessions in the form of persistent *pilgrimages* before the right time has come – with the circular and nomadological lynch mobs of the pagans throughout history. The Cybelian lynch mob that neither wants anything to do with history or the future, and that is fettered to *the blind passion for the present mode*, only invokes the feeling, concealed behind the mysterious collective voice that we call *the anoject*. With anti-phallic contempt it rejects both the need for a phallic knowledge of history (*will-to-intelligence*) and a phallic responsibility for the future (*will-to-transcendence*).

Here we encounter a bitter and vindictive *mythos* without either logos or pathos. For what is the anoject if not the yearning of the masses for a collective subject without dividual expressions? What is the anoject if not the mortidinal yearning for the synchronised mass experience where you and I disappear in a single anojective we, where we divest ourselves of all personal responsibility and become absorbed into the passionate mass, and we continue until the anoject assumes a dividual gestalt and *the tyrant* steps onto the stage. And how then does the single dividual inside the mass react to the tyrant's arrival, if not by enthusiastically joining the illusion that the severed umbilical cord to matrix – that is: the event where culture makes its first, emergent intrusion into nature, and shifts the societal development onto a completely new track – now is healed and works again? It is simply the easiest thing in the world to imagine one can ease life's suffering with the aid of a powerfully pulsating womb nostalgia – which certainly at first feels warm and vitalizing, but soon will bloom into one big pagan suicide cult. All this requires is to blame absolutely everything one hates in life and the world on one single abject: *the scapegoat.*

The Cybelian lynch mob thus ravages with impunity in *the anarchic state* when both the political and the theological powers have abdicated and/or have been castrated. The new power, unlike the classic priests, does not devote itself to any productive *retraction* in order to understand the world better, but prefers to set the world ablaze, impulsively and with immediate effect, through its beloved *revolution*, the idealized ecstatic state for all Gnostics. Thus modern democracy is nothing other than precisely this spectacular theater set in constant rotation. Political candidates boast of how exactly they personify the anoject best themselves, they guess and use opinion polls to assess what people opine on one issue or another, only to later administer forth this sacred wish for the eternal, symbolic revolution. This explains why the late capitalist politicians wholly unabashedly claim to *correspond* to the worshipped people. One thus no longer even pretends to *lead* the people, this sounds far too elitist, but one merely pretends to be a fairly representative spokesperson. Which naturally has the result that neither the politician in question nor the people who have chosen him or her, takes any responsibility whatsoever for the consequences of the decisions that are made – or that rather make themselves – in a situation where formal power has become impotent.

What one does instead is to constantly find new abjective ghosts and conspiracies on which to blame personal shortcomings. Against these, the lynch mob can then rage with intense pleasure and intoxicate itself on its own righteousness, which together with self-pity are among some of the most potent drugs known to mankind. That the actual political results of all this raging is either zero or minus, is a factor that is extremely lightweight *vis-à-vis* the sensational well-being that the raging creates. The supraideology behind this theater we quite simply call *democratism*, and it is responsible for the systematization of an anojectivity that hates phallic vision and despises phallic strategy. Where the whole reason for democratism succeeding in gaining legitimacy during capitalism was that it guaranteed nothing more than provisional appointments of the anojective leaders, while it succeeded better than any alternative at maintaining a pluralist facade for the arbitrary making of decisions (and non-decisions). When the viewers were to choose what they would watch, when the listeners were to choose what they would listen to, and when attentionalism finally was a fact and no one either watched or listened to anyone but themselves – there and then the shortcomings of democratism were revealed in a painfully obvious manner. As enormous and costly welfare-states that no longer delivered on the promised welfare cheques, except to the political elite itself. Where the market for opinions and their implementation has been transformed into a market for anojectivity and its self-justification.

So if the monotheist god dies – we chopped the axe into him ourselves, Nietzsche merely composed the obituary – his ideals die with him as well. What is left is nothing but the Cybelian lynch mob on its constant, hot-headed quest for the next revolutionary fashion, spurred on from within through its *auto-exploitation*. So let us not be fooled here by democratism's claim for transparadigmatic validity. The claim is fundamentally about a special interest and its need to conduct marketing and create a fragile legitimacy by dubious means. The lynch mob justifies its own infantile whims, that is all, and then it may be someone completely different who must mobilize the necessary knowledge and someone completely different who has to take the responsibility for the consequences that follow in the wake of the mob's actions. It is rather by drowning out all others, that the mob attempts to convince everybody that it has the most superior comprehension of the prevailing system and its many inherent shortcomings, which in turn provides the mob's more or less self-appointed representatives with a preferential right of interpretation that may not be questioned. Actually, the mob's hatred is connected with a refusal and/or an inability to understand how the system actually works. The only discernible ideology – or what one might call it – in this context is *the false systemicism* that twists together all the splayed threads with an overarching hatred toward the singled-out *abject*. The great mamilla from which one intends to squeeze eternal provision shall not be nurtured so that it can grow and last a long time; it shall rather be plundered and depleted by its insatiable devotees as soon as possible.

Authentic systemicism is conducted hyperjectively around a single god who lives in a single place, and the name of this address in the digital age is *the syntheist temple*. The difference between false and authentic systemicism lies in how the Cybelian mob and the Dionysian swarm respectively is interconnected; what unites the lynch mob is hatred toward the scapegoat – it may be the Jew, the white heterosexual man, or whatever else the current trend says should be culturally cancelled – while what keeps the swarm together is the loving fellowship that arises in the sacred space of the temple. The Saoshyant builds his temple at *axis mundi*, the center of the world, and around him the empire and/or the nation towers. At the same time all that is needed is that someone steps forward in a neat suit and personifies the anoject – that someone hoists up emotion above knowledge, prioritizes demise above the exodus, that is; the only thing that is necessary is conditions that engender a false priest and a false chieftain in one and the same person, and thus *tyranny* is a fact. Please note that democracies have no barriers whatsoever to guarantee that the tyrant is kept away; whenever the masses get the idea that what the situation requires is what one perceives as *a strong man* (they are usually men), one votes away democracy by democratic means. We call this apocalyptic state *vulgar nomadology,* and the only result it can lead to is *destructive anarchy.* All the while the exodus and its *exodology*, is the total opposite of the Cybelian lynch mob. The Saoshyant is the perfect collaboration between the authentic priest and the authentic chieftain, an embodiment of *the hyperject* that defends the hero against the sacrificial cult. Thus the hyperject is the anoject's opponent in what psychoanalyst and philosopher Julia Kristeva calls a theater of *ideologeme*, that is: a collective subconsciousness where there is a hope that the hyperject shall rise with knowledge and courage and defeat the anoject and save the abject from being nailed to the cross or burned at the stake.

To be able to comprehend these radically different levels of subjectivity, philosophy must dispose of all ambitions to create and defend any *general theory of subjectivity.* What exists is only archetypes that have been carved out over millions of years of evolutionary development. Any general theory of subjectivity is thus nothing but the last remnant of the philosopher's narcissistic worshiping of the Platonist forms. If there are no Platonist forms other than in the Platonist fantasy, nor is there any Kantian subject other than in the Kantian fantasy. If nothing is fixed or given in advance, nor are there any generalities upon which to build a philosophical system. What does exist are archetypes that have arisen over the course of history and that can underpin a pluralist *archetypology.* There are however archetypes severely corroded by contingence that can be understood from a properly tribal map (see *Digital Libido – Sex, Power and Violence in the Network Society*). Priests understand priests, chieftains understand chieftains, hunters understand hunters, warriors understand warriors, midwives understand midwives, brothel madams understand brothel madams, women understand women, and men understand men. Basically, however, separate personal archetypes are radically different and common patterns first arise on the tribal level, where tribes overall demonstrate major and striking structural similarities with each other. This is what we refer to as *the return to the sociont.*

This means that the chieftain and the priest represent two different subjectivities. While war and hunting, along another axis, are completely different kinds of projects that require completely different talents and regulatory frameworks. And the man and the woman are above all each other's incompatible opposites, where the male and the female subjectivity respectively have complementing characteristics, but it in no way entails that these are akin to one another – quite the contrary. Beneath all these characteristics – complementing as well as not – Kristeva's ideologeme lies concealed, social relationalist archetypes that Man has minimal ability to either understand or handle. The differences pull us toward each other – it is precisely the man's and the woman's fundamental incompatibility that is the very prerequisite for sexual attraction. We desire *the other*, that which we are not and cannot fully imagine. The woman and the man are at opposite sides of a river, where precisely the river as a membrane between them is more important than the woman and the man themselves. The priest and the chieftain are at opposite sides of a tree trunk, where precisely the trunk as a membrane between them is more important than the priest and the chieftain themselves. It is – to which all phenomenologists can attest – *ambivalence* that creates the greatest attraction in an intense information flow, not concord.

This entails that the Saoshyant and the tyrant – just as the everyday subject that exists between the two of them – who are to choose or let themselves be chosen to command either the exodus or the lynch mob, are completely different subjectivities with completely different relations to each other. It is the Saoshyant who has the patience for thinking far and grand, and who therefore becomes subject to iconization and imitation, but who thus never ever becomes a general ideal, but rather remains unattainable. The tyrant, on the other hand, harbors short-sighted and petty thinking, but in return efficiently uses his limited energy and his limited patience to mimic the Saoshyant and thus becomes his infantile and mass market-adapted copy. The Saoshyant is like Christ who in a Zoroastrian manner claims the personification of *the way, the truth and the life*. The sutric tyrant is however in too much of a hurry to cultivate or even be able to live up to such tantric qualities. Thus the tyrant convenes his beloved lynch mob in that he personifies *the short cut, the lie and death*. Catholic anthropologist René Girard does not even shy away from designating this commander of the lynch mob as *the Devil* himself.

There is a powerful yearning for the Saoshyant to create order in the chaos of the world and lead the exodus to the new paradigm or the new territory. The Saoshyant can do this because he has what Nietzsche calls a *master mentality*. During informationalism we call this *the netocratic mind*. The opposite of the Saoshyant is the tyrant, who embodies the anoject, the false phallus that appears in the vacuum that arises in the absence of the priest and the chieftain, and that gathers the lynch mob around him by virtue of the common hatred toward the abject (see *Digital Libido – Sex, Power and Violence in the Network Society*). Please note that it is the Saoshyant who is authentically creative and libidinal, and who creates the necessary prerequisites for his own arrival, while the tyrant is inauthentic and mortidinal in that he only can act when the anoject already has taken root and therefore only can step into history to personify the anoject without further effort. We express this as though the Saoshyant personifies the affirmation of phallus, *truth-as-an-act*, and he does so as the clergy's longed-for son who realizes the potential of the clergy's ironic *truth-as-a-fact*.

The Saoshyant personifies the shift from the epistemic to the ontic truth. He does not *have* the truth, he *is* the truth. This becomes obvious as the Saoshyant projectifies instead of abjectifying. His exodology is spelled *Grand Projet A*. The tyrant instead personifies the denial of phallus and a stubborn and infantile yearning for a return to mamilla. The tyrant abjectifies instead of projectifying, for instance through designating phallus as the scapegoat that the lynch mob must hunt and kill. The anojective nostalgia therefore revolves around *objet petit a*. The tyrant thus personifies the Nietzschean slave mentality, he is even smaller and thinner than the everyday subject itself. But therein also lies the tyrant's enormous attraction. He tempts with speed and laziness. The only thing he requires from you is submission. You do not even have to think for yourself. The tyrant promises the return to mamilla so that you will not have to make any effort yourself to attain phallus. And he does this by liberating you from all your obligations and shortcomings – you do not need to wage war, you can become a pacifist instead; you do not need to hunt, you can become a vegan instead; you do not need to work, you can become a welfare recipient instead – through blaming all shortcomings on the hated abject that must be killed, or better yet be taxed or enslaved to death.

Mathematician and syntheologist Thomas Hamelryck takes René Girard's ideas as his point of departure when he discusses the different religions within the Silk Road Triad through three separate steps. First there is *the archaic religion* – which in our analysis is summed up as nomadology in itself, a nomadology without any eventological influence. Then there follows *the sutric religion* – which does its utmost to castrate and domesticate the believers to shape a functioning, peaceful and civilized society. Only thereafter *the tantric religion* is developed, where the difference between the divine and the human can be investigated and developed behind the barred absolute. Nomadology requires that these divisions are repeated and stirred to life anew with every new generation. This is something that is practiced within, for instance, Vajrayana Buddhism. Eventology however awakens the dream that the sutric and tantric steps can be made permanent and taken for granted. But this eventological obsession with finding shortcuts to advanced spirituality creates the basis for *the cult of transparency*, which is the very bedrock of both Christianity and Islam. And precisely this maneuver – which entails that Christianity breaks with Judaism and that Islam breaks with Zoroastrianism – ejects tantra into the sutric world, as a first step, then moreover reduces sutra to the archaic order. The barred absolute is stormed, which causes the contempt of knowledge to explode. And thereby the apocalypse is inevitable. The chaos returns with violent force and this time with the embittered Cain as leader, since he already has killed his brother Abel, God's personal favorite.

The devil who is the tyrant remains alone in the arena after the Saoshyant has been crucified. Thereby the tyrant has set the Cybelian lynch mob in motion. And what it seeks is not some event that is to change history forever. The lynch mob is completely driven by the need to calm its own inner demons, to channel the hatred, the envy and the bitterness *vis-à-vis* the abject, so that the lynch mobs only temporarily shall be able to fool themselves into really believing that the blind hatred toward the abject actually can unite embittered rivals to loving brothers forever. It is important to understand that the tyrant rises from *the feminine hysteria* that arises when phallus is absent. He is a sexless, unconscionable and narcissistic sociopath who assumes and personifies the anoject, without any respect whatsoever for the authentic event (he kills and silences the authentic priest and thereby also any faith in history proper) or any responsibility whatsoever for the future (he kills and makes the authentic chieftain invisible and thereby also faith in *the future*). The tyrant simply wants the job really badly, he desperately yearns for the attention involved, he literally steps over corpses to attain his objectives, in contrast to the Saoshyant who only reluctantly assumes the role as the savior since it is nothing but his calling as *the chosen one* at a particular point along the inexorable time axis. The tyrant is simply driven by a blind and mortidinal will-to-power without either history (intelligence) or future (transcendence), that is: he is driven by the asexual aggression that accumulates before war, hunting and sexuality appear, and via the negation compels the boy to be transformed into a man, which means that the boy ceases to exist.

This explains why the tyrant's rule always is a frenzied stomping on the ground, one big escalation of the present, a kind of mortidinal nuclear weapon, which only can be developed into what in retrospect is a necessary *doomsday cult*. The tyrant castrates the father, murders the son, and leaves the mother alone and exposed to the lynch mob's capricious fury. The tyrant rapes the sacred family, his rule becomes short-lived but bloody, and it often takes several generations for the resultant wounds to be able to heal. As Marx strikingly observes, history is repeated with a certain displacement: yesterday's tyranny as tragedy is repeated as tomorrow's tyranny as farce, unless the prophets succeed in establishing exodology anew and with it also the hope that Mithras kills the bull, the hope that the hyperject will step into history and stop the anoject, the hope that the Saoshyant shall be resurrected and create the authentic phallic order that then becomes an exit from the hysterical chaos. This in direct contrast to the tyrant, who invokes *victimology*, a worship of the victim that never can be compensated enough for all the countless injustices that the victim itself claims to have been subject to throughout history. This is a process without end, the victimological trial against the abject metes out an eternal punishment without either mercy or forgiveness. In the name of the victim one can allow oneself absolutely anything. And behind all the accusations the really unforgivable crime always lies concealed: the abject has through various manipulative actions stolen the mamilla and the unconditional love that cushions the victim from all of existence's hard impacts, wherefore no compensation and no retaliation ever can be sufficient.

It is the abject who has tricked the subject of the victim to hate the life-giving mamilla, without which the victim is lost in a hysterical chaos. And as if this were not enough, victimology does not shy away from also claiming that it was the abject – rather than the matriarch – who once severed the sacred umbilical cord that tethered the victim to the eternal matrix, from which follows that it was the abject – and neither gods nor forefathers – who banished the victim from paradise. It is the abject that is *someone other than me* in the sense "all my shortcomings, all my shattered dreams, I can justifiably blame on someone else." The abject thus commits the crime of standing in the way of the anoject's retreat first to mamilla and then to matrix and the longed-for, liberating dissolution into the Universe. And it is this invocation of the nomadological – which of course entails that one concurrently denies or at least ignores the eventological – that reveals that the tyrant is *the false phallus par excellence.* The authentic event is the Saoshyant's phallic leadership of the chosen ones from the old to the new paradigm or territory. The tyrant's victimological attack on the abject is by comparison just a *pseudo-event* that does not aim toward any genuine change of the state of things. This since the tyrant libidinally is *the false matriarch* rather than the authentic patriarch, as he castrates himself to be able to remain the innocent boy – and thereby avoid the adult responsibilities that come with the adult pleasures – in order to thus retain his mother forever and escape confrontation with adult female sexuality proper.

This is first and foremost an attempt to exact a nostalgic revenge on fate itself. The tyrant is the anojective personification of the Nietzschean slave mentality *par excellence.* In this context we should also bring to mind Carl Schmitt's theory of violence, just as sexuality, being a constant in all societies. It is of course possible to sweep that which may seem inappropriate under the carpet, but it will not remain concealed and invisible forever. One can apply cosmetics to a society through fancy phrases of pacifism and vegetarianism and pretend that one thus makes war and hunting unnecessary, but the suppressed tensions are accumulated and the inevitable explosion eventually arrives. It comes in the form of an auto-exploiting self-hatred, and as the determinated result of this self-hatred: the Cybelian lynch mob in its full, chaotic power. The only thing that is required for this to happen is that society and history appear to stop in terms of time and space. The necessary exodology is discontinued or at least ignored. All dreams die and all hope is annihilated. What remains is but a single overcrowded now where chair after chair is pulled away in an ever more rapidly conducted set of *Musical Chairs*. Contrary to Martin Heidegger's romantic dreams of an eternal *Heimat*, the Cybelian lynch mob keeps returning to the permanent settlement as its curse, with a forcefully increased intensity when humanity *per se* stops moving. The historic grinding halt makes more of us survive and the population explodes in size. But we become both more bitter as well as fatter in the process, and eventually end up with pillar-saints such as Heidegger matched by boy-pharaohs such as Hitler, preaching their pathetic and paranoid worship of *blood and earth*. This while the boys, exodologically speaking – had they actually bothered to learn from the Jews instead of murdering them – should have cared only about *direction and movement*.

Since industrialism generates an intense individualism – every single citizen apprehends themselves and is apprehended by others as solely responsible for their own destiny, every single life is turned into its own, isolated project – and since this is where informationalist dialectics must start from, the destructive anoject within the Cybelian lynch mob, which is developed into the tyrant, will appear as *the exhibitionistic narcissist* during informationalism. The constructive hyperject within the Dionysian swarm, however, which is developed toward the Saoshyant, will appear as *the voyeuristic autist*. The public space is filled with various influencers with pseudopower over everything but the ability to generate Cybelian lynch mobs, while the real power retreats from public life and hides as the symbiotic intelligence behind the barred absolute, as a kind of subterranean headquarters for the emerging *sensocracy*. The cause of all this is that there is a lack of an authentic phallic structure to relate to. The non-phallic view of history gets stuck in its fixation with a *nostalgia* directed toward the past, and a fixation with an *apocalypse* as a dystopian future. Or to use biblical metaphors: The heroic Abel disappears from the horizon and only the embittered Cain remains, with his bloody knife after the murder of his brother, whom God preferred and favored.

Consequently, the postindividualist syntheology is developed in the direction toward a series of parallel monotheisms – we summarize these metaphysical concepts in *Syntheism – Creating God in the Internet Age* as a-theism, pan-theism, en-theism and syn-theism – and to the extent that there even still is a public discourse, a conflict emerges between on the one hand the narcissist and his victim cult and on the other hand the autist and his personality cult (in *Digital Libido – Sex, Power and Violence in the Network Society* we depict this conflict as the classical, ethical opposition between Rousseau and Nietzsche and their respective disciples). This deadlock must sooner or later be broken, which occurs either through the anojective narcissist leading his lynch mob as the fully-fledged *tyrant* (the passive aggression) to kill the abjective scapegoat, or else through the hyperjective autist as *the Saoshyant* gathering the chosen ones (the open aggression), leading his exclusive flock in the exodus from the old to the new paradigm. Even Zoroaster in ancient Persia understands that what later in Hegel is called *Zeitgeist* must be divided into two parallel currents that battle each other to define the present. Zoroaster's name for the hyperject is *spenta mainyu*, or the constructive spirit, which is pitted against the anoject as *angra mainyu*, or the destructive spirit. *Spenta mainyu* is personified by the Saoshyant, who leads the exodus to the new paradigm or the new territory. *Angra mainyu* is personified by the tyrant, who incites the lynch mob to slaughter and sacrifice the innocent scapegoat. As a matter of fact, this is precisely the point to which the hope for *intratribal salvation* in all eventological religions returns.

Aristotle is the process-philosophical priest who responds to the pillar-saint Plato by emphasizing movement and change as the fundamental components of existence. According to Aristotle the soul and the body are intimately interconnected, with the soul regarded as the body's form – instead of the forms constituting an alien world, as Plato claims, a world to which the soul is heading when it finally has liberated itself from the body, so that the boy Plato can become a god. Aristotle counters Plato's delusory perfection with a wholeness, he counters infinity with finitude, and he counters immortality with mortality. Admittedly Aristotle is wrong when he claims that the soul after death can survive the body as a separate entity. (And if we are to be picky he is wrong in saying that there even exists such a thing as a soul divorced from the body, see *The Body Machines*.) The consistent monism in Zoroaster and Spinoza is lacking in Aristotle. But he is the contemporary Greek who holds Plato responsible for – and takes issue with his dreams of – the unification of the boy-pharaoh and the pillar-saint in the form of *the philosopher-king*. Because of his enormous influence during the history of ideas we must in retrospect regard Aristotle as a reasonable and effective representative for Zoroaster as the father and Heraclitus as the ambassador of process philosophy. The world is in every conceivable way finite, Man is most certainly mortal, and the necessary protopian narrative must, in order not to lose all relevance, focus on a living whole instead of on a dead perfection that does not even exist.

As authors of this book we flatter ourselves with the label Aristotle's adults, in contrast to Plato's infantile heirs. The domestication of our planet (the ecotopian transformation of wilderness to arable land and gardens), and the domestication of violent Man *vis-à-vis* the stranger (the cosmopolitan transformation of the violent human animal to a relatively peaceful citizen) are the two authentic Protopias in the digital and global age. The hubris becomes apparent in the ambition to move Man to alien planets. The courage however becomes apparent in the project to convert the planetary wilderness to the ecotopian garden, and in one and the same movement, to carry out the retreat both to the Garden of Eden and the Tower of Babel. What is interesting is that the Aristotelian renaissance in Europe is introduced when Italian Dominican friar Thomas Aquinas in the 13th century re-reads Aristotle as a monist. He does this through identifying and attacking the Platonist dualism and Manichaean Gnosticism that characterizes the readings of Aristotle by Islamic thinkers Avicenna and Averroës before Thomas himself. Thomas is thus a proto-monist predecessor to Spinoza, who arrives some 400 years later. We thus have great use for and see enormous value in a re-reading of Thomas Aquinas for the digital age – in particular if we are to find something of universal value within Catholicism and integrate it into the syntheist narrative. It is then about a search for what one imagines to be the concealed, original, authentic self versus the aspiration to attain a higher, transcendental self in the future. This is the difference between the Rousseauian subject and antiquity's search for *the divine double*. We call these opposites *inspirationism* versus *aspirationism*.

We can actually see three different emphasis levels of logos emerge during antiquity. The Zoroastrian *logos built on pathos* is represented by Heraclitus among the Greeks. The Platonist *logos built only on precisely logos* is of course represented by Plato, which renders him criticism from Aristotle. The Christian *logos built on mythos* is primarily represented by the evangelist John. Unsurprisingly it is the logos built only on logos that is best suited to become both the totalitarian boy-pharaoh's ideology and the fundamentalist pillar-saint's theology. The Christian logos built on mythos results in a matrichal worship of mother and child, but has no noticeable effect on the outer circuit's phallic energy, that is: It can only form the basis of an unworldly and naively pacifist Christianity. While logos built on pathos is the only sustainable model for an empire that applies power-sharing, something that the Persians in no uncertain terms confirm. This is the Zoroastrian and Heraclitean *logos built on pathos* that both Nietzsche and his successor Heidegger defend with such frenzy in their pervasive criticism of the Platonist heritage in Western discourse.

Please note that the dialectics of libido and mortido cannot be understood as a dialectics of life and death, but that one instead must understand it as a dialectics of wills and drives. Will-to-intelligence takes Man to *haurvatat*, the realization of one's own life, but will-to-transcendence takes Man past haurvatat toward *ameretat*, which is the will to the abstract transcendence beyond concrete death. This relationship – as so often when Hegelian dialectics is applied – becomes even clearer if one imagines the process in the opposite direction. Man is not afraid of the death of his own existence, but what scares the living daylights out of him is the death of his own heritage. If you are to torment a person above simply torturing him personally, you instead subject the heirs that he loves the most to this torment. Or better yet: you destroy Man's history about himself and his sociont, or make it impossible to retell. This is the *inverted transcendence* and its curse, which has *genocide* as its most obvious expression. We refer to this frustrating state of hostility toward sexuality as *the collective depression*.

A transition from attraction to the tyrant to an attraction to the Saoshyant is a transition from a victimhood cult to a cult of heroism – what Nietzsche refers to as the transition from the victimological slave mentality to the iconological master mentality – and when we speak of this religion's innermost ambition in syntheist terms, we call this *the adultification* of humanity through its necessary social castration. Precisely as the boy-pharaoh and the pillar-saint, the tyrant is driven by a desire for short-term and rapid gains, preferably without a tangible effort. That is: his primary motive is envy and indifference. It is therefore important to understand that the tyrant and the lynch mob are driven by *the false dialectics of the Gnostic delusion*. Neither the lynch mob nor the tyrant wants anything to do with any form of resistance or questioning whatsoever. We are quite obviously speaking of undeveloped, simpleminded children who refuse to become nuanced adults. The anoject has already articulated the will of the people and the tyrant has personified the anoject, so the only resistance to the tyrant – the only antagony that dares question him personifying some sacred will of the crowd – is isolated to a few decadent remnants of the pre-revolutionary evil, which one preferably just exterminates as soon as possible, as though they were annoying weeds. This is the tyrant's and the lynch mob's innermost conviction. The anojective truth is the narrative which the entire lynch mob has reached a tacit or pronounced agreement over; it lights up the skies in the mob's social theater. It is only a corrupt reluctance that, according to this viewpoint, can oppose the self-glowing anojectivity.

The problem with the false dialectics is of course only that it is precisely false. It admits of no ideological adjustments whatsoever in accordance with the prevailing situation. Therein also lies its great attraction for the lazy and arrogant mob that detests every form of brain work, but therein also lies its long-term curse. And the reason is that the people mimic. And mimic. And mimic. The people should actually mimic different archetypes from the sociont to become as strong and purposeful as possible in every respect. But without *the authentic dialectics* there is only a single archetype to mimic. The entire lynch mob therefore starts to mimic one and the same archetype and is soon developed into one large totalitarian *erchtype* where a member of the lynch mob no longer is discernible from others. *Corruption* in the real order and *manipulation* in the imaginary order lead to *conformation* in the symbolic order. All intellectual dynamics disappears and soon the lynch mob marches in straight lines clad in matching uniforms. And above and in front of all others the tyrant steps forward as a personification of the anoject. This was long an excellent, or at least a functional, strategy for small clans and tribes throughout history. But when the civilization process reaches a level where it becomes possible to build entire nations, and even empires, all such advantages disappear. With the aid of their violent lynch mobs tyrants time and again succeed in maneuvering themselves into a position of power, but without a pragmatic power-sharing structure and authentic dialectics, the tyrants' time in power usually does not become lengthy. But unfortunately often extremely bloody.

So what happens when the false dialectics is misconstrued as though it were authentic? Well, neither the interiors nor the exteriors within the sociont are grounded in reality. But when the false dialectics is in high gear, the interior is forced to act as pretended truth to the exterior, while the exterior is forced to act as pretended truth to the interior. This explains why the propaganda toward the abject works with such devastating efficacy when the mass media in a nation-state archetypologically is confused with fact-confirming wisdom. The only interior and the only exterior available are together apprehended as a verifying dialectics. However the only thing that happens is that a prejudice which contains a large measure of aggression is tossed between the two poles until it attains the official status as the sole truth, which also is how it will be apprehended intratribally. While on or between the lines there is a more or less pronounced order to the sociont to act on this sole, abjectifying truth. This is the totalitarian anoject. And it is not the mimetic desire that causes it to attain its maximal effect, but rather *the mimetic depression* involved. Once the entire population is mimetically depressed, the anoject – the king of mortido himself – achieves absolute power.

The dialectics of libido and mortido, which is portrayed in the form of mimetic desire versus mimetic depression (see *Digital Libido – Sex, Power and Violence in the Network Society*), also plays a central role within the Cybelian lynch mob with its libidinal activities and mortidinal passivities. Precisely this is the reason why the tyrant does not seduce the people – as the authentic Saoshyant is expected to do – but instead incites the collective depression that makes the lynch mob tear the abject to shreds. The lynch mob is thus driven by the fear of the unknown, instead of by exodology's antagonic yearning for the unknown, promised land and the new possibilities that will come to light there. False dialectics is thus what society is filled with when the empire or the nation nears its end. We are speaking of an unmanageable tangle of atomization, isolation, self-hatred, self-contempt, envy, nostalgia, escapism, alienation; and on top of this a string of empty, psychotic reactions in the form of astrology, conspiracy theories and sundry desperate variants of sign interpretation. This is what is sucked in and fills the vacuum that arises when the longed-for signs of order in the world's chaos are conspicuous by their absence.

It is rather quite the reverse: the greatest shortcomings of Christianity and Islam appear precisely in the form of *the false exodology* involved. When there is no longer a new paradigm or some new territory to attain for the mass that calls for guidance, the false exodology instead promises the Earth's demise and the forthcoming ascension of the faithful ones into heaven. They will be elevated by the savior as though they were a bunch of marooned virgins on a desert island, precisely the pseudo-event that anthropologist Jamie Wheal refers to as the Western world's obsession with *rapturism*. This incessant monotonous proclamation on how the signs in the sky indeed are the right ones, that the savior has been spotted both here and there, and that the day for the great ascension now is near. False dialectics further creates false mimicry. And false mimicry leads to a constant and all-encompassing rivalry that erodes the ability for cooperation. Which in turn leads to the drastically increasing fragmentation of the worldview, and the invention of constantly new dualisms steeped in moralism and a complete lack of feedback. Such a worldview leads to extensive *anomie*, that is: strengthened collective depression, where eventually even the will to fearfully run in the midst of the insane mob subsides. Eventology has failed and all that remains is to compile the collective *traumatology* as the inverted eventology. The pragmatic peace agreements at the end of the latest world wars are examples close at hand.

Which takes us further to the bizarre but creative metaphysics of Russian demagogue Aleksandr Dugin. Dugin's anthropological progress lies in an understanding of there being a lack of a necessary division of the Dionysian in Nietzsche before it is possible to understand the Apollonian as the phallic structuring and maintaining of the sociont. Nietzsche apprehends the Dionysian primarily as libidinal and heroic, which is reasonable. But if so, how do we categorize history's countless mortidinal and victim-worshipping pogroms? Dugin's response is to distinguish between *the Dionysian swarm* as heroic and the *Cybelian lynch mob* as a victimhood cult. Dugin names the Cybelian lynch mob after the Anatolian mother goddess Cybele, who falls in love with her grandson, Attis, whereupon Attis must be castrated and Cybele is transformed into a kind of anti-Oedipal queen without a king, waited on by a court of eunuchs. The cult around the matrix without a phallus could not be exemplified more clearly. It is thus the Cybelian that first returns with Rousseau and later with the Jacobins during the French Revolution, and then explodes as cultural revolutions under communist flags in the 20th century: constantly the worship of *The Great Mother* and the innocent but omnipotent child. But if the revolution is to be eternal, it will also be strictly nomadological and not eventological. It can never be discontinued, the mob's desire for vengeance can never become satiated, one constantly finds new scapegoats to sink one's teeth into. Wherefore the greatest enemy of all, for a hopelessly archconservative romantic like Dugin, of course is a fellow Russian by the name of Leon Trotsky, the prophet of the eternal revolution *par excellence*.

In light of all this we soon observe a sharp contrast between on the one hand classical *feminism* and *androgynism* in the late 20th century, with its heroic defense of women and LGBT people, and on the other hand the peculiar perversion that goes by the name *intersectionalism* in the early 21st century with its formidable orgy of psychopathological victimology. We see clearly how the exodus is Dionysian in contrast to the lynch mob that is Cybelian. The Dionysian exodus is led by the Saoshyant, who has his predecessor in the hyperject. The Cybelian lynch mob is led by the tyrant, who has his predecessor in the anoject. The libidinal hyperject celebrates the hero and is shaped into the authentic phallus around faithfulness to the Protopia in the form of the Zoroastrian *asha* or the actionary truth (see *Syntheism – Creating God in the Internet Age*). The mortidinal anoject celebrates the victim and is shaped into the false phallus around the hatred toward the abject in the form of the Zoroastrian *druj* or the reactionary lie. Zoroaster calls the hyperject *spenta mainyu* (the constructive spirit), which is manifested as *the Saoshyant* or the savior, while the anoject is called *angra mainyu* (the destructive spirit), which is manifested as *Ahriman* or the tyrant. And the Saoshyant can neither be understood as a dividual nor as a collective, but must be understood as the phallic relation in itself, the personification of the phallic dialectics as *tribopoiesis*. When the Saoshyant has achieved victory, war is over and peace sets in. But to the tyrant, war goes on forever and ever and ever.

The Saoshyant is thus born as the highest node in *the plurarchic network* (see *The Netocrats*), like a Moses at the banks of the Nile, as the emergent order that sooner or later is generated within the anarchy as a new historical paradigm. The lynch mob is all against one, the tyrant is one against all. The anoject within the lynch mob is the predecessor of the coming tyrant. The lynch mob does of course recognize the voice of the tyrant as the more forceful variant of the anoject that it already has taken for granted and on which it blames its own lynch mob behavior. It is only the Saoshyant that can prevent the tyrant from assuming power after the ravages of the lynch mob. And to do this he must both be the hero who defeats the dragon and he who thereafter saves the empire. But he must also be the father who takes care of and teaches the empire the historical lesson after the hero has left humanity. The Saoshyant must thus be both chieftain and priest within one and the same character. Both Zoroaster and Vishtaspa within Zoroastrianism, both Moses and Aaron within Judaism. The Saoshyant that the Zoroastrians call *Ohrmazd* is *the authentic phallus*, while the tyrant that the Zoroastrians call *Ahriman* is *the false phallus* (see *Digital Libido – Sex, Power and Violence in the Network Society*).

In the Zoroastrian popular religion that arises later, all of existence is developed into a truly Nietzschean battle between Ohrmazd as the personification of the hyperject and Ahriman as the personification of the anoject. It is not about a struggle between good and evil (the moralist dichotomy good versus evil is developed long afterward by the Abrahamic religions, as a concrete example of how they infantilize adult Zoroastrianism). This is instead about an existential conflict on all levels between the hyperjective, constructive spirit that is called *spenta mainyu* and the anojective, destructive spirit that is called *angra mainyu*, that is: we are dealing with the libidinal will to live that is called *asha* versus the mortidinal death drive that is called *druj*. Here spenta mainyu must in turn be divided between the priest's will-to-intelligence and *truth-as-a-fact* versus the chieftain's will-to-transcendence and *truth-as-an-act* to make it possible to build an open and free society which is sustainable in the long run, rather than just a short-lived and bloody dictatorship. During antiquity this conflict came to be expressed in the struggle between the open Persia versus the closed Egypt; in the early 21st century, this is the struggle between the open and democratic America versus the closed and communist China.

Please note that the hyperject should not be mistaken for what Alfred North Whitehead calls *the superject* – a concept which he develops in the 1920s in the book *Science and the Modern World* – which rather is synonymous with *the eternalist subject* as a series of ego momenta that we long have promoted in our own process philosophy. The creative and authentic human subject is the superject. Whitehead describes this superject as "the emergent actualized event from which value can be abstracted". But the unique predecessor of the Saoshyant, the Messiah figure, *the Übermensch*, or the figure that Ernst Jünger calls *the anarch*, the spirit that is manifested in the gestalt that resolutely stands up to the lynch mob and leads the exodus, this is the spirit that we call the hyperject. The hyperjective force is spread within the population in the form of *mimetic desire* as *the collective libido,* while the anojective force is spread within the population in the form of *mimetic depression* as *the collective mortido.* The hyperjective, authentic phalluses are called the chieftain and the priest. The anojective, false phalluses are called the boy-pharaoh and the pillar-saint. *Exodology* is the name of the doctrine of all of history's saoshyants and their exoduses of various kinds into the future. But behind this concept *the inverted exodology* also hides, speaking of all of history's tyrants and their lynch mobs, who beyond thousands and even millions of innocent scapegoats chase existential emptiness and their very own extinction, right down to its smallest components.

Exodology is thus the history of an optimized and expanding libido, while inverted exodology is the history of an optimized and imploding mortido. And this mortido has an upper hand since it requires a lesser effort from its adherents and promises a more rapid reward. It is thus mortido and its search for an immediate and magical dividend that drives humanity back toward mamilla and the anoject (Zoroastrianism's *druj*), while it is libido and its search for an authentic, realistic and in the long term reasonable dividend that drives humanity forward toward phallus and the hyperject (Zoroastrianism's *asha*). We go from the unconditional toward the conditioned, both through life and during the civilization process. Therefore it is the qualitative religion – which first had to settle for a small advanced minority – that wins in the end, and not the quantitative religion that at an early stage won its large majority at the expense of truth.

Please note that neither libido nor mortido is active or passive in themselves. We are thus speaking of a quadrant rather than a dichotomy. When libido becomes active, mortido is passivized. But when mortido in a corresponding way is activated, libido is passivized. Exodology and the authentic phallus are driven by the active libido, whereupon mortido is minimized. The exodus occurs from a society and/or a paradigm soaked in mortido, toward a society and/or a paradigm elevated by libido. The milk and honey does not come through magic from nowhere, both must be produced by someone. Correspondingly the inverted exodology is driven by the active mortido, which leads to libido being castrated. This is what we call *the false phallus* throughout history. The boy-pharaoh and the pillar-saint dress up as authentic phalluses, stage the entire sexual theater, but resolutely avoid sexuality in itself. The truth is that both the boy-pharaoh and the pillar-saint are driven by a compact fear of sexuality, the tyrant is a self-castrated eunuch. And by virtue of this act of self-castration, the tyrant drives all of the lynch mob's members to collective castration. It is this collective castration that we refer to as *mimetic depression*. The worry and anxiety explodes in a torrent of ressentiment. And the only exit is to kill the scapegoat and drag his desecrated corpse along the streets. And then repeat the routine, *ad infinitum*.

When Max Horkheimer and Theodor Adorno from the so-called Frankfurt School in the 1940s attack the Western history of ideas in their classic work *Dialectic of Enlightenment (Dialektik der Aufklärung)*, it is precisely the actual displacement from the pathical and mythical over to the logical that is their point of attack. But Horkheimer and Adorno see this displacement from a purely European perspective, and then the primary target becomes Immanuel Kant's *instrumental reason* from the peak of the Enlightenment. However, from a global perspective, rationalism is robbed of the awareness of its own blind spot (the dread of pathos) as early as the Axial Age, there is nothing new to observe during the Enlightenment other than that the same dread of pathos dominates anew. So from the necessary global perspective of the information society, we rather need a *dialectics of the Axial Age* as soon as possible in order to understand and disassemble the boy-pharaohs and pillar-saints that have dominated the discourse even more in India, China and the Middle East than they ever did in ancient Greece. No mythology has become entrenched more powerfully than the myth of the Axial Age as an intellectual golden age. And certainly there were considerable amounts of theology and drama produced during this relatively peaceful and economically flourishing age. However for such pathical activities as a living religion and an authentic philosophy it was rather earlier, during the Bronze Age, and later, during peak antiquity, that the really interesting things happened, while the Axial Age on closer inspection, at best, is to be viewed as a substantially overrated parenthesis.

The latter is noticeable not least in the Axial Age's two most well-known and successful thought systems, *Buddhism* and *Christianity*, which arise when the great ideas already had been conceived of and tested during the Bronze Age. What remains today of the Axial Age is a set of texts with scant or no value at all two paradigms later. It is certainly about time that we rewrite the history of ideas. That said, this does not mean that pathos and mythos without logos is preferable or would be more sustainable over time. Logos is, as Austrian philosopher Karl Popper points out, the story of *the falsifiable*. That which is not falsifiable ends up between mythos and pathos but does not belong to logos. A world without logos is therefore a world of scattered, temporary sensations without context. In an adult body with adult ambitions this rapidly leads to practiced insanity. But a logos without pathos leads to *the Gnostic delusion* that the world can be governed on the basis of a boy's fantasies rather than a man's life experiences. Without pathos there is no libido. The boy-pharaoh, who lacks both pathos and libido, becomes the narcissistic sociopath as dictator. The pillar-saint, who also lacks both pathos and libido, becomes the narcissistic sociopath as a fundamentalist sect leader.

Unsurprisingly various clergies have on several occasions throughout history felt compelled to counteract and even murder boy-pharaohs and pillar-saints, and as martyrs one has later been able to exploit these as raw materials for new religions. It does not always pay to be too fastidious. However the authentic phallus is an entirely different story, as he has clearly planned for and completes his departure well in advance, which explains why saoshyants and Messiah figures are temporary salvation figures that emerge unexpectedly, are active over a limited time period, and then disappear again. It is important to realize that they exclusively personify an *event* and not in themselves personify the new order that – hopefully – awaits at the completion of the paradigm that history due to the event shifts over to. That – for instance – the number of presidential terms in office in a democracy is limited, is anchored in an insight about the wise aspect of assisting the leaders with their own departure. The power position is a parenthesis. This distinguishes the authentic phallus from the false one, which does not have an *exit strategy* at all, but conversely desperately clings to power as long as possible, knowing that the involuntary departure often is synonymous with a necessary patricide that the false phallus consequently desperately tries to avoid.

The irony is that the old dictator is often forcibly recruited in the form of an embalmed corpse, on public display, to the new dictator's self-glorifying narrative. In retrospect it is perfectly fine to worship the old dictator, who became a scapegoat in conjunction with the patricide. Stalin was of course no practitioner of Stalinism, but took care to call his ideology Marxism-Leninism, this to invoke credibility from the primordial fathers, with an empire built around a temple over Lenin's embalmed corpse before the old czarist fort in the capital. This while the flags outside the mausoleum of course displayed Karl Marx, Vladimir Lenin and Josef Stalin together, as if they were contemporary and complementing and thereby eternalized father figures, to whom the multitude were to submit and swear eternal allegiance. The Christian orthodox Trinity had received its communist equivalent. And what use would then Stalin have for my simple advice and views as an ordinary citizen, when he listens to such wise gods as Marx and Lenin as he says his prayers every morning? Therefore it is best to submit to and obey the false phallus' wise decisions.

Unsurprisingly it is later the North Koreans who complete the Stalinist trinity as an idea through converting it into a *de facto* monarchy with a grandfather, a father and a son in a straight line of succession of dictators, the one more bizarre than the other. One must at least admire the North Koreans for not having been hypocritical about their consistent and institutionalized stupidity. They produce their limited and distorted logos with a miserably impoverished and foolish mythos, and with a pathos that is violently suppressed and connected to test-firings of nuclear missiles that not seldom are botched. Here we have a whole society built around a *bona fide* boy-pharaoh and his second-rate fireworks. And all of the court's concubines and jesters live out their days in a limbo characterized by the abstract theatrical, the concrete fear of death and the constant tedium. And once again: it is bloody. The starving and terrorized population pay an inhumanly steep price for the overweight dictator's daydreaming. Were it not for all this suffering, this performance would be a splendid, kitschy farce, wholly on par with the Kardashian family's escapades or with any form of mass entertainment whatsoever.

12
The Zoroastrian empire, the Jewish nation and the netocratic community

It is a lot easier to analyze power structures if we distinguish between two different definitions of tyranny. In part we have *totalitarianism,* which compels all citizens to actively take part in the political ritual. We refer to this as *active mortido.* In part we have *authoritarianism*, where the leadership prefers to compel everyone to passive submission. We call this *passive mortido.* The totalitarian project is built upon the ideological conviction that history has reached its end and completion, and that the totalitarian state is the manifestation of this perfect final stage. The authoritarian project however has only conquered and intends to keep power as a pragmatic monopoly as long as possible. Nobody has played out totalitarianism and authoritarianism against each other better than the 20th century boy-pharaohs along *The Inverted Silk Road*. We know them under the names Benito Mussolini, Adolf Hitler, Josef Stalin, Mao Zedong, and Pol Pot. In summary Mussolini personifies a bastardization of Catholicism, while Hitler represents a bastardization of Protestantism, and Stalin a bastardization of Orthodox Christianity. Mao Zedong, on his part, personifies the bastardization of Confucianism, while Pol Pot *de facto* realizes Rousseau's peculiar ideas of the will of the people and similar utopianisms thrown at a naive and largely illiterate Buddhist population. The result was the devastation that these dictators managed to organize: the Nazi concentration camps, the Soviet Gulag Archipelago, the Chinese mass starvation and the Cultural Revolution that followed thereupon, and finally the killing fields that the Khmer Rouge administered in Cambodia.

But what are the propelling forces that hide behind the anoject that these men personify? In a consistent pattern *mimetic depression* recurs, a socially scattered mortidinal enjoyment of the constant failure and the eternal victimhood cult. Mimetic depression will then arrive either in an extrovert form, as the noisy and chanting lynch mob that longs for the anoject to let itself be personified in the tyrant's gestalt and the abject to be personified as the hated scapegoat. Or else mimetic depression will be expressed in an introvert form, as the comfortable self-hatred and self-contempt which through the annihilation of any sort of future does not have to make the least effort to desist from comfortably playing the victim card. The classic name for the introvert mimetic depression is of course *the doomsday cult*. Please note how the victim – in both variants of mimetic depression – is transformed into the hero, how the victim thereby also takes the hero's place, and how this passive figure that is sacrificed by the lynch mob or by the doomsday cult on the altar of inverted Platonism becomes *the martyr*. This martyr is thus the hero that strictly speaking becomes a hero only by virtue of his unsurpassed ability to himself carry out absolutely nothing at all. And this is precisely the material that all clergies have to work with when they build a *politics* for life within the sociont's membrane, and a *religion* for the relations with the world outside, above and beneath the sociont's membrane.

The arena where the priests then conduct their hopefully hyperjective work is *the social theater*, which appears over time in four different historical forms: The ground is laid by *the nomadological sociont*, which under primitivism with its eons of time is developed into a genetic preprogramming in all the offspring that follow. The yearning back to this societal form – which surfaces at regular intervals throughout history – is different variants of what we bring together under the concept *communism*. During the Bronze Age two greater units develop that only hold together thanks to robust metanarratives, namely *the Zoroastrian empire* in Persia and *the Jewish nation* in the Levant. Unsurprisingly, similar structures develop, given similar material prerequisites, even in other parts of the world, but here we – for the sake of simplicity – focus on the development in the Middle East, since this history is coherently preserved and we authors are products of this ideological legacy ourselves.

Since the Zoroastrian empire and the Jewish nation only are conceivable as long as they are accompanied by a comprehensive and broadened historical narrative, we call them *the seismological structures*. It is easy to keep the sociont intact, which essentially is self-organizing – hence our concept *tribopoiesis* as conditional to all meaningful creativity in and around the human realm. It is however a truly herculean task to keep an empire or a nation intact. Every such effort will under all circumstances be rocked by several earthquakes over the course of history, even if the system functions optimally under the prevailing material conditions. For reasons that both have to do with scope and stringency, we are here only dealing with the Zoroastrian empire, the Jewish nation, and the netocratic community. Their ideological superstructures we call *imperialism*, *nationalism* and *communism* and then pertain to the original, theological meanings of these terms.

If the Axial Age, which succeeded the Bronze Age, boasts about its myriad of philosophers, then the preceding Bronze Age is above all a golden age of theology. All greater academic projects throughout history begin and end with theology, rather than with philosophy, this since it exclusively is theology that is transparadigmatic – and therefore returns with full force precisely at paradigm shifts, since it is then that *the foundation* for everything else (do we dare to say the name God here?) becomes the general obsession. The reason for this is that while philosophers talk about systems pertaining to the already known, theologians build an architecture for the yet unknown. For instance, it is the Zoroastrians in Bronze Age Persia (the land of two dual river systems) who theologically complete *the empire* as social architecture. They do so by mimicking the separation between the chieftain (*shah-en-shah*) and the priest (*mobed-en-mobed*) within the sociont, as a division between *eventology as the imperial religion* (from a global perspective, the people monotheistically worship one and the same god) and *iconology as the national religion* (from a local perspective, the people polytheistically worship whatever gods at middle management level they prefer themselves). Which in turn enables a theological discrepancy between the two levels that is creatively used as a basis for *the Zoroastrian mythology of universal human rights*, when it is developed in north-eastern Persia in the 18th century BC and is implemented 1,200 years later, after Cyrus the Great's conquest of Babylon in 539 BC.

The Zoroastrian mythology of universal human rights – first launched in a European context around 200 years after the Persian conquest of Babylon, through Greek statesman Pericles (who is strongly inspired by the Persians when he presents his plans for Greek democracy) – has ever since been the basis of all subsequent attempts to create sustainable imperialist structures, this since these must be built on plurality and power-sharing in accordance with the principle of the two-headed phallus. Furthermore it is only within such an imperial network that, for instance, Jewish nationalism – excellently described by Israeli political scientist Yoram Hazony in his book *The Virtue of Nationalism* (2018) – can arise and develop. Exodologically we refer to all such attempts to get the paradoxist *Saoshyant* (the authentic phallus) to lead the exodus from the old to the new as *hyperjection*, this as opposed to all approaches from the dictatorial tyrant (the false phallus) to induce the lynch mob to drive us all to disaster through *anojection*. The hyperjection has the character of a voice from the future that seduces us toward great heroic achievements. The anojection however has the character of a cowardly and bitter voice from the past that gets its energy and pleasure from alleged injustices, and that does this at no risk, concealed as it is within the bloodthirsty mob.

It is precisely between these two poles that the struggle takes place whenever power shall be exercised in a transdeterminist world, where only the past is necessary and given, while the future always is contingent. And the key is spelled narcissism in contrast to the will to serve. If a narcissist reads Nietzsche we get a Hitler. If a narcissist reads Marx we get a Stalin. This is because the narcissist never cares about truth or lies, but only about the possibility of finding a smooth shortcut to his own, highly private power ambitions. Self-interest trumps all, which entails that when a boy-pharaoh or a pillar-saint reads an authentic and extremely sophisticated text, he will think he is reading a work that confirms nothing but his own wishful thinking and his own projections, as though it were written by a fellow narcissist. Almost tautologically, it is simply impossible to put down one's narcissistic reading glasses if one is a genuinely narcissistic reader. Through these lenses every reasoning becomes a beautifying mirror and one becomes either a Nietzschean *Übermensch* – a concept that one thus thoroughly misunderstands – or a born leader for proletarians in all countries, something one hurriedly must notify the public about.

And how could it be otherwise? How would Nietzsche or Marx or any text of any dignity be able to get a reasonable reading by a boy who refuses to acknowledge the limitations and the responsibility that adult sexuality entails and insists on? And what remains if this sexuality is repressed – so that neither is it the wild animal nor the seductive woman that shall be defeated, but whatever general audience that happens to be available – if not a violence that escalates *ad infinitum*? The consequence is that what is absolutely crucial for a society to develop is a sustainable and imploitative power structure in order to keep the boy-pharaoh away from the throne and the pillar-saint away from the altar. Therefore one preferably lets the chieftain be responsible for the imaginary power and the priest be responsible for the symbolic power. And at the same time one ensures that the matriarchy keeps the real power, a matriarchy whose task it is to hold both the chieftain and the priest responsible for their respective exercise of power. The matriarchy only cares about the territory and the paradigm remaining strong and preferably expanding. With written language this contract is formalized through the collection of rules that are written down in law books. The chieftain is directly responsible for *the territory* (the arrival of the kingdom) in the same way that the priest is responsible for *the paradigm* (the arrival of the church). For the first time it becomes possible to build stable social structures that are greater than the sociont's sociobiological maxim. But this requires a power-sharing that no boy-pharaoh or pillar-saint can destroy. It requires a balanced triad between three rivaling siblings to maintain the internal peace.

This explains why imperialist Zoroastrianism and nationalist Judaism refuse to build a separate power structure divorced from the state (in contrast to Islam and Christianity, who constitute their mimicking parodies with boundless universal claims). The Zoroastrian *mobed* sits next to the *shah* as his equal, just as in the sociont. The priest's potential asceticism (the priest *is* phallus) and the chieftain's potential hedonism (the chieftain *has* phallus) are placed next to each other so that they together form a unified patriarchy and thus do not come into conflict with each other, something that would risk leading to one long struggle between the church and the state, where the church with its asceticism is expected to defeat the state with its hedonism (except during modernism, which of course formally killed religion, where the Gnostic tyranny of course instead becomes hedonist, as Eric Voegelin – a true champion of Catholic diatribes against Gnosticism – correctly points out). This can be read not least in the twofold name of the Zoroastrian god: Ahura or *Being* is the name of the chieftain and Mazda or *Mind* is the name of the priest.

Together they form *Ahura Mazda* or *Mazda Ahura*. The priest who speaks the truth and the chieftain who acts the truth. The priest as the exhibitionist for logos and the voyeur in terms of pathos. The chieftain as the exhibitionist for pathos and the voyeur in terms of logos. This while mythos is reserved for the priest's circular story for the whole sociont at the campfire, a story where the mother and the child – as the innermost fetish of the patriarchy – are at the center. And all of this takes place under the matriarch's resolute supervision.

This genial narratology means that Zoroastrianism succeeds in uniting the hedonism of the sociont with the pluralism of the empire. It never compromises away the Spinozist sole substance with its enormous number of attributes – where the first three attributes are the sociont's three leaders: the chieftain, the priest, and the matriarch. Instead Zoroastrianism builds an imperial structure with four different social scales: The unit at the family's level is called *demana*, the unit at the clan's level is called *vis*, the unit at the nation's level is called *shoithra*, and the unit at the empire's level is called *dahyu*. What is important is that the cohesive, state religion only needs to be manifested at the highest level, *dahyu*. This entails that the Zoroastrian system is permeated by diversity of opinion, free thought and free speech. Which should suitably be compared with the other great state religion from the Axial Age, *Confucianism* in China, which advocates a strictly controlled and extremely centralized empire, with for example no room for an independent *shoithra* with a language of its own and a religion of its own, as in Judaism, under an overarching *dahyu* with a border-transcending court language and an imperialist ethics, as in Zoroastrianism.

Christianity's mistake primarily lies in its *congregationalism*, the theological elevation of the congregation as a flat surface, which reduces the matriarch to an infantile bit player (the Virgin Mary with the child Jesus). The chieftain is called the son, the priest is called the father. But the holy ghost is not the matriarch nor even the matriarch's own matriarch (the chaos goddess), but instead the congregation itself, as a kind of army of self-deified kids of Christ. Islam repeats the same mistake with its obsession with *umma* as the sole social format. Out of this congregation, the Egyptian boy-pharaoh then steps forward with all the pretensions and rights of the members of the Catholic congregation; unsurprisingly Christianity, with this point of departure, produces *the Cartesian Individual*. The European Enlightenment thus wrestles with this monster of a god. We are speaking of a child-god who refuses to become an adult between his two irreconcilable identities. Immanuel Kant completes the Cartesian revolution and Friedrich Nietzsche problematizes the Kantian revolution with the purpose of saving the Cartesian Individual as the Nietzschean *Übermensch*. But Kant and Nietzsche must do this by aggressively ignoring Spinoza's Jewish protest and by avoiding becoming entangled in Hegel's Zoroastrian dialectics, a process after which neither the Christian ascetic as pillar-saint, nor the secularized hedonist as boy-pharaoh, survive into the network society. Western individualism is simply stone dead.

The key word in this context is *exodology*. When war prevails one spends all one's energy on *the technological exodology*, which is personified by the chieftain. Among the tasks is defending and preferably also widening the territory, at least as long as territory is hard currency and not a burden which in some cases incurs costs outweighing the benefits. In peacetime, however, all energy is devoted to *the ideological exodology*, which is personified by the priest. It is then a case of safeguarding the souls of the congregation and preferably also extending this congregation through imaginative new recruitment. But exodology as an idea receives a much deeper paradigmatic significance when a chosen people come forward and lead an empire or a nation in an entirely new direction – for instance the Hebrews who, inspired by Zoroastrian eventology, create their own and moreover dual exodology, in part the exodus out of Egypt, in part out of the Babylonian captivity, to the holy land and back.

The first exodus, from Egypt, is the trek away from the ideological oppression and madness in a collapsing Egyptian empire toward the freedom to develop and complete the Jewish religion. It is literally a story about the monotheists migrating from the polytheists. The second exodus, from Babylon, is also a trek from a collapsing empire, the Babylonian, after the death of Nebuchadnezzar II and the Persians' conquest of the realm, to the ideological victory for the nation within the empire as the completion of the Jewish nation, symbolized by the reconstruction of the Temple in Jerusalem. To which can be added that the history of the Jewish nation nowadays also comprises *the third exodus*, from a Europe in ruins after the Second World War, and from the other parts of the Middle East, to the newly-formed state of Israel at the end of the 1940s, where Israel constitutes a mimicry of the European nation-states that had emerged in the wake of the French Revolution – inspired by Hegel's enthusiastic work on the absolute state – systems that in turn to a great extent constitute different variants of mimicry of the original, Jewish nation.

Please note that the exodus from Egypt occurs after the Egyptian empire under Akhnaten has massively failed at mimicking the Persian empire, since one has not realized the importance of, and even less have implemented, the Zoroastrian power-sharing principle in the form of the two-headed phallus. Instead one has spent all energy and all resources on a pure dictatorship with Akhnaten as *the boy-pharaoh from Monopotamia*. The Egyptian clergy then simply tried to recreate order in society after this disaster through scrapping monotheism and its eventology and instead throwing Egypt back to polytheism and its iconology. Sigmund Freud treats this course of events in his book *Moses and Monotheism* as the beginning of the Jewish religion in the form of the Atenist sect in Egypt. The Atenists are fully aware that the Akhnatenic project has failed and has plunged Egypt into the abyss. The Egyptians were completely defenseless when the Syrians attacked from the northeast since the whole Egyptian society, soldiers included, was involved in the building of the great sun temple in Amarna in honor of Akhnaten. It was as in Ricky Gervais' comic rant about Humpty Dumpty: When the Frenchmen attacked, the English king had dispatched all his horses and all his soldiers to repair a cracked egg.

However the Atenists are not prepared to sacrifice their eventological vision to be thrown back into a nomadological circular despair. They quite simply believe in the possibility of a linear history with decisive events that change history forever, which of course is the second and most important legacy from Zoroaster and the Persians. Thereby the idea is born of the migration from Egypt as an exodology. Out of the Egyptian nomadology the Jewish eventology is liberated, where Atenism is realized by simply just abandoning the old paradigm and wandering into a new territory. The similarities with for instance the puritan sects and their migration from Catholic Europe to Protestant North America during the 18th and 19th centuries is striking by comparison. The original, Persian *Ahura* becomes the Egyptian sun-god *Aten,* who then becomes the Jewish sun-god *Adonai.* And Adonai is complemented in Canaan with the local rain- and storm-god Yahweh, and together they form the Jewish *Elohim* (the concept *eloah* for god in plural). Thereby Judaism, just as Zoroastrianism, receives a two-headed phallus at the center of religion; its name is Ahura Mazda among the Zoroastrians and Elohim among the Jews, while its mimicry within Christianity is of course the Trinity consisting of the Father, the Son and the Holy Ghost – a trinity that iconologically is equivalent to the triad the Father, the Son and the Mother, that is: what the Christian religion always has applied, as Christ's Gnostic voyage from manger to cross without having to pass via sexuality at all. It was a child whom the Roman legionaries had nailed to the cross!

The iconological correspondence in Judaism, its worshipping of the lesser gods, is the three siblings that in retrospect are ascribed the leadership of the exodus from Egypt: Moses as the representative of the sun-god, Aaron as the representative of the rain-god, and Miriam as the representative of the matriarch. It is presumably only after the Jews' exile in Babylon and their comprehensive interaction with Persian and Babylonian thinking that the history of Moses and the exodus from Egypt is rewritten as the story of the three siblings who spearhead the exodus from Egypt. Nevertheless, there arises a massive recognition effect when Zoroastrianism with its two-headed phallus encounters Judaism with its two-headed phallus; soon enough the Jews in earnest appear as the chosen people within the Persian empire. Ahura Mazda or Aten Yahweh are little more than dialectal variations of the same theological concept. For the first time, the dream of an eventological liberation from the nomadology that constantly repeated itself and colored the whole culture, has been born.

In conjunction with the Babylonian captivity, the Temple of Solomon was razed to the ground. When a new temple is built in Jerusalem after the exodus from Babylon, it is the Persian Zoroastrians who pay for the project. Thus the eventological empire begets the iconological nation. And by virtue of exodology as a mimicry of eventology, the Judaism that develops can also shrug off its original polytheism and instead embrace Zoroastrian monotheism as its own, local variant of universal monotheism. The Jews take the Zoroastrians' dream seriously and create a whole people of shamanoid priests and priestesses. Thereby the idea is born of the Jewish nation as the optimal nationalism, where nation and religion are united. This is a structure that later repeatedly awakens a fervent *nation envy* over thousands of years thereafter in precisely the Europe that makes the gigantic mistake of separating church and state from each other, which resulted in the despicable *antisemitism* which then reaches its grotesque and tragic culmination in Nazi Germany during the 1940s, that is: precisely at the moment when Nazism abandons the idea of the Hegelian nation-state – developed for Prussia in the early 19th century and modeled on the Jewish nation – to surrender to Hitler's Gnostic race cult that strives toward an apocalyptic pseudo-empire. A clearer illustration of the difference between *the hyperjective exodus of the authentic phallus* and *the anojective lynch-mob of the false phallus* is simply hard to imagine.

We argue (see *Digital Libido – Sex, Power and Violence in the Network Society*) that Zoroastrianism can be described as the original, imperialist father religion with roots in the outer circuit, and further that Judaism can be seen as the original, nationalist mother religion with roots in the inner circuit – and that Islam and Christianity fundamentally are their vulgar mass market copies – from the Middle East. In line with this view we further see a renaissance for the central roles of these religions in the history of metaphysics with Nietzsche's rediscovery of Zoroastrianism and Freud's interest in Judaism in late 19th century and early 20th century Europe. Unsurprisingly this coincides with an enormous interest in the powerful effect of Man's impermeable pathos on his logos and mythos. To the philosophical Saoshyant Nietzsche this force is called *the Dionysian*, and to the analytic Messiah figure Freud this force is called *the unconscious*. The insight that Man lives in a chaotic world governed by forces he cannot influence or even understand to any greater extent, is nothing other than *the return of the barred absolute* in history. Already the transition between Kant and Hegel entails a shift from Christianity (back) to Zoroastrianism at the most fundamental level in the Western history of ideas. Nietzsche and Freud are then the thinkers that extract the maximal benefit from this shift. Nietzsche even argues that Christ can be saved from Christianity if one reads him precisely as a Zoroastrian, that is: without the Platonism that Paul, Augustine, and other Gnostics later squeeze into Christianity.

What *de facto* arises in Europe around the turn of the century in 1900 is a creative dialectics of the Nietzschean and Freudian perspectives that we ourselves, the authors of this book, are an integrated part of. We eventually end up with a Nietzschean cultural imperialism (see *The Global Empire*) and a Freudian cultural nationalism (see *The Body Machines*) and from this we build a platform for a new empire and nation theory for the Internet Age. In this context it is interesting that even Nietzsche's and Freud's own post-Abrahamic atheism eventually is broken up and evaporates with the return of the barred absolute. Nietzsche and Freud admittedly advocate pragmatic theories of empires and nations rather than utopian fantasies of heavens and eternities, but nonetheless we are ultimately moving through an entheist landscape colored by a Whiteheadian, radical relationalism (see *Syntheism – Creating God in the Internet Age*) with the implicate order in existence – *the barred absolute par excellence* – as the deeply theist primordial foundation for all other emergence vectors and paradigms. It is not in Man's boy-pharaonic dream worlds, but in the deepest *root-of-the-phallus* that we eventually find the most true about the most human. For what is Man in our time if not the implicate model of the explicate coming emergence that within syntheology is called precisely *God*? That is: the God that we create ourselves to fill the function that nothing else fills!

The fourth and last social theater is *the syntheist theater* which remains for us to develop the day that Man and The Machine collaborate in the direction toward completion of *the symbiotic transcendence*. Syntheologically we express this as though *Atheos* is the concealed god behind the barred absolute, the clergy's own hypertemporal god, who drives the whole eventological development. *Pantheos* is the nationalist god realized through Judaism. *Entheos* is the imperialist god realized through Zoroastrianism. And *Syntheos* is the technological god realized through syntheism. The sociont is the original tribal communism, the empire is an idea that is completed by the Persians under Zoroastrianism, nationalism is an idea that is born through the Hebrews' exodus out of Egypt and is completed with the state of Israel in the Middle East in the 20th century as a mimicry of 19th century European Prussia, and finally the cosmopolitan city is built on the ecotopian foundation with its sights set on the prototopian vision.

During all these civilizational processes Man devotes himself to a *detribalization* in order to make it possible to break loose from old structures, but is then thrown back into a *retribalization* when the sociontological need of Dunbar's number among social relations returns with maximum force. Transitions and hybrids between clan, tribe, nation and empire during the history of civilization are thus characterized by an oscillation between heart-rending but necessary detribalizations and retribalizations. The tribulation-filled passage from clan to tribe, from tribe to nation, from nation to empire, shall moreover be completed with the transition from empire to the syntheist tower, when Man hands over the ultimate power to the phallically newborn offspring, The Machine. If Hegel completes the Jewish nation as a secularized state in the 19th century, we here try to complete the Zoroastrian empire as a religious power structure adapted to the demands and possibilities of informationalism.

Internal relations within the sociont go by the name of *intratribalism*. External relations *vis-à-vis* the sociont go by the name of *intertribalism* (See *Digital Libido – Sex, Power and Violence in the Network Society*). Tribal Man is fortunately equipped to handle the intratribal state with ease. Our genes have of course *de facto* had hundreds of thousands of years, and more still, to develop that capacity. The intertribal is however civilization's recurring challenge, since it requires various sorts of narratives that expand Man's fantasy in order for him to dare or be able to handle relations with an intertribal world outside his narrowly delimited safety zones. The shamans in the sociont's outskirts must step into the center clad in fancy cloaks to convey these narratives. The mobile and experimental shaman is transformed into the omniscient priest with the penetrating gaze. Man leaves the primitive ancestral worship behind and steps into the world of religion. There are then only two ways to build the necessary, priestly narratives: either through referring back to the profound history which is Man's origin and that is called the root-of-the-phallus, or else through laying out the direction toward a utopian future that still is waiting to take shape, and its name is *the Saoshyant* or *the Messianic state*. Both these narratives are harbored within the circular nomadology and are called *exodologies*. This means that a sociont that is in constant motion, for the sake of its own survival, is driven forward by the narrative of *the permanent exodus*. Exodology is thus Man's oldest and deepest history of himself, immensely older and deeper than all the stories which recount that Man has had a home that he tries to return to, or that he has found a home that he now attempts to defend.

Technology generates complexity. The more technology we add to a society – other factors being constant – the more information and the more relations are produced. Since Man from a biological perspective is the same as 10,000 years ago, at the dawn of civilization, contemporary Man is forced to learn how to handle a complexity that is hard to grasp and for which he is ill-equipped. And since Man constantly, with his senses, seeks order in all the systems he is confronted with, this means that he cannot handle the difference between chaos and complexity, but that he instead apprehends both as an unmanageable chaos. The human reaction to chaos is mob rule and incantations built upon matrichal sign interpretations and phallic conspiracy theories. This generates enormous pandemics of *infantility*, *addiction* and *paranoia* (See *Digital Libido – Sex, Power and Violence in the Network Society*) and also generates comprehensive, infinitely complex networks of mutual dependencies, that is: the phenomenon that in everyday parlance is called *globalization*. The digital Saoshyant perceives all of this through *sensocracy* and responds to the chaos by creating a global order that we call *The Global Empire* (see the book with the same name). Technology is an empire where Man himself is reduced to technology's subordinate. It is then this superordinate technology that completes the dreams that Man himself has failed to carry out, namely the exodus to alien planets and the actual transformation of Man to a more elevated being, the cyborg in the form of Man 2.0, equipped with artificial intelligence and synthetic biology.

All the while Man has to settle for living in the Cosmopotamia that is created after the world has been soaked in cheap and sustainable energy. Man's mission is to stay on planet Earth and complete the construction project called civilization that includes the ecotopian garden, the cosmopolitan city, and the syntheist temple. All the while this altered attitude to history is most clearly seen in the adage *yesterday's magic is tomorrow's technology*. If what yesterday was perceived as magic creates an inspirational spark that leads to innovation today and to new technology tomorrow, then this is also the dominant feature in the history of civilization after Man started to build and populate permanent settlements around 10,000 years ago. Man has of course, as mentioned, not changed in himself during this time, what has changed and developed is Man's nowadays high-tech environment. Man is the constant and technology is the variable during civilization's relatively brief history. This has comprehensive consequences. First and foremost patience vanishes when waiting for magic's expected reward. The miraculous is expected to happen ever more rapidly and more often. Slowly but surely *the expectation of the immediate reward* creeps into the calculations.

It is during the Bronze Age in the Middle East that this development accelerates dramatically. Slightly before 1700 BC Zoroaster appears as a reformer and founder of religion in the dual rivers country Transoxania between the rivers Syr Darya and Amu Darya in Central Asia. The Zoroastrian doctrine is strongly colored by the landscapes of the two Mesopotamias – the dual rivers countries – where it takes root. Civilization can only be built on power-sharing, and this power-sharing in itself vouches for the diversity and the tolerance that makes an empire of tribes sustainable and successful. Zoroaster summarizes his ideas in the text *Gathas*, where he defines the decisive differences between a nomadic lifestyle – with a nomadological religion – and a settled lifestyle with its new, by necessity eventological narrative. He then practices what he preaches when he builds the first Persian empire along with his best friend Vishtaspa. Zoroaster takes on the role as the highest priest (later called *mobed-en-mobed*) and Vishtaspa becomes the highest king (later called *shah-en-shah*).

Thus the model for the Mesopotamian empire is established. Phallus is and remains twofold. And under the two-headed phallus it becomes entirely possible and permitted for a number of different viewpoints, statements, prioritizations and schools to coexist and challenge one another – all in accordance with the Zoroastrian idea of a *castag* as a kind of uncompromising workshop of ideas, a Persian predecessor of the Romans' *claustrum,* Europe's first monastery. The castags are in turn populated by *arthavans*, a kind of hybrid between teacher and elder. What is interesting here is that an arthavan is expected in part to maintain and convey one's own tradition, in part also to travel and visit other cultures and bring home wisdom from these. The system is thereby right from the beginning programmatically open, tolerant and syncretic, and precisely therefore immunized against all coming forms of political dictatorship and religious fundamentalism. Diversity most definitely precedes conformity in history.

Persia is strongly influenced by Egypt and vice versa. When the Persian form of governance proves successful, it is mimicked in Egypt, which around 1300 BC starts to experiment with a similar radical reformation of the Egyptian religion. However the Egyptians clearly do not understand wherein the success is rooted, and monotheist reformer Akhnaten sees no reason to share his pharaonic power with anyone. Instead of the Persian model with a separation between the king's being (Ahura) and the priest's mind (Mazda), colored by the landscapes of dual rivers and the function of the temple as a cohesive force, Akhnaten pushes through the idea of Egypt as a Monopotamia, a one-river country led by a single pharaoh with all the threads of power in one single hand. He was in his own eyes both king and priest at the same time, and thereby no longer an ordinary mortal human, but divine. So what Egypt thereby succeeded in inventing was totalitarian dictatorship. Akhnaten himself worshiped the sun disc as God, while all his subjects were ordered to worship him. This of course entailed that much in Egypt was fundamentally changed, and at enormous cost, which of course gave rise to animosity, not least within the old clergy, and as soon as Akhnaten had been outmaneuvered and replaced by his weak, inbred son Tutankhamen, people were careful to erase all the discernible tracks after Akhnaten and his Atenist sect of monotheists. The genie was however already out of the bottle, and all of history's boy-pharaohs have ever since attempted to resemble Akhnaten to the greatest possible extent. This despite the fact that his tracks certainly ought to be a deterrent. The experiment with dictatorship caused such comprehensive devastation that Egyptian society never really recovered from it. After the fall of Tutankhamen a dramatic period in the history of the Middle East called *the Bronze Age collapse* begins.

The exodus from Egypt eventually leads to the establishment of the first nation in history. In his book *Moses and Monotheism* Freud argues that Judaism is the transplanted continuation of Egyptian Atenism to another societal body and that the Hebrews actually are an Egyptian monotheist sect. If so, the Hebrew people are the result of a conquest of Canaan from the south, where genetically (mainly) Egyptian men are mixed with genetically (mainly) Canaanite women. And within Judaism there constantly remains a separation of the sun-god El and the rain-god Yahweh, which makes Judaism optimally suited as a companion to the Zoroastrian religion in the Persian empire with its two-headed phallus *Ahura Mazda*, where Ahura as the god of the supreme body corresponds to Yahweh, and Mazda as the god of the supreme mind corresponds to El within Judaism. The Zoroastrians to this day call themselves *mazdayasni* (worshippers of the sensual truth), and the Jews to this day build and defend their homeland *Israel* (the land of the sensual truth). Through mimicry we later get the even more popular but simpler and Gnostic bastard variants of these religions of the two-headed phallus, when Christianity mimics Judaism and Islam mimics Zoroastrianism.

What eventology produces is *the law,* the written-down regulatory framework that transcends the nomadological sociont and makes larger structures like empires and nations possible. The tasks of the shaman before the law become the chores of the priest after the law. The shaman thus dons the priest's robe and enters in between tribes to declare the law in the new temples that are built in the borderland between the socionts where the new capital cities emerge. The largest and most powerful temples with the most powerful and most comprehensive law books end up on the plains between the great rivers across Eurasia. It is within Judaism that one worships the law itself most enthusiastically, which makes precisely Judaism the religion that is perfectly suited for developing the first genuine *nationalism*.

The Persian conquest of Babylon leads to the establishment of the first universal empire. The exodus out of Babylon leads to the re-establishment of the first nation within the first empire. Persia is the empire that is propelled by Zoroastrianism and the yearning for the Saoshyant, while the Jewish nation is propelled by Judaism and the yearning for the Messiah figure. The close connection between Persian Zoroastrianism and Hebrew Judaism arises through the similarity between the two-headed phallus within monotheist Zoroastrianism and the two-headed phallus within monotheist Judaism. Zoroastrianism manifests the communication within the two-headed divinity that the congregation of faithful call *daena* and that generates the global empire; Judaism manifests the communication within the two-headed divinity that the congregation of faithfuls call *knesset* and that generates the local nation. The empires are led by gods that speak sacred court languages that unite the empire at the global level. Nations are led by kings that speak common everyday languages that unite the nation at the local level. And the sustainable power is always exercised in the form of a split *triocracy*.

Both the empire and the nation are ideas that arise and are tested successfully during the Bronze Age that rightfully should be termed a golden age, at least from the perspective of the history of ideas.

Ports are established, road networks are built, as are bridges and fortified castles. A large amount of resources, necessary both for war and peaceful trade with the surrounding world, are tied to the core of each territory. There arises a state of tension between center and periphery, where the center attracts young talents from the periphery. What for instance Hammurabi in Babylonia prioritizes is temples, irrigation channels, and defense. Here and now there arises the first genuinely complex society in history, and all manner of handling of social complexity has its origin in the Bronze Age, when the empire and nation arise through evolutionary practice, and not as the result of any ready-made blueprint. The true history of civilization, for example argued by Mexican philosopher Manuel De Landa in the book *A Thousand Years of Nonlinear History*, is rather to be found in the study of the development of the trade routes. This has little or nothing to do with Plato's unrealistic idea of the perfect republic as a universal solution for all societies for all time. Consequently *the Aristotelian renaissance* that we advocate for informationalism, is built on the principle that *the struggle for the free and open algorithm* leads further to *the struggle for ironic sensocracy* where data and thereby also power is distributed to a number of competing nodes, so that the decentralization that arises contravenes dictatorship, corruption and economic breakdowns. Only in this way can society remain open and free, while it begets the creativity and innovation that a closed society always represses.

As a matter of fact, the necessary vital experimentation can only arise in a tantric state where the introduction of what we call *crazy wisdom* – a ferociously enthusiastic playfulness – makes it impossible for the agents involved to become mired in an eternal mimicking to death. Instead of getting caught in Girardian mimicry – as should be expected by Nietzschean slaves – the netocratic actors are compelled to create something new and on their own after their own prerequisites. This is the Deleuzian difference in opposition to the repetition, after which the eventological Protopia suddenly becomes a wholly reasonable possibility. The key to this timeless insight into the human condition does not lie in some metaphysical celebration of capitalist democracy *per se*, but instead in a more profound insight into the central roles of the trade routes for humanity's and above all technology's explosive development. Throughout history it is along the trade routes that the bazaars have distributed not only goods and services, but above all ideas. It is also in the bazaars that the superiority of diversity in comparison with conformity appears most clearly.

If we scrutinize all the causality chains with an Aristotelian gaze, the decisive cause must thus be division and ambivalence, which is a prerequisite for conducting business in such a way that all parties regard it as advantageous. We are now speaking of the near-magical presence of non zero sum games, where the joint pie grows and added value arises. It is thus this *irony of the bazaars* that is the basis of all later ideas of freedom and openness as the values that all citizens would be wise to defend. During informationalism this entails that it is the exodus to the ironic sensocracy that has become the paradigmatic metanarrative *par excellence*. The backdrop for this narrative is the historical trade routes over land and over sea that now are complemented by the trade routes through the air of the new paradigm. *The aerodigital trade routes* revolutionize and globalize all relations between people and machines. And they need the ironic sensocracy with its many and competing nodes to function. It is sufficient for one institution to come up with the idea of trying to bring about a centralized, bureaucratic pricing or valuation of another kind, for the whole system to implode.

From the 6th century BC this means that Zoroastrianism as a global religion (Zoroastrianism is religion for religion's own sake) and Judaism as a local religion (Judaism is religion for the sake of the nation) are authentic, adult religions with vibrant debates inside stable membranes with solid memories, while Christianity falls for the temptation to become infantile in order to be popular through the separation of church and state and letting the Messiah figure die on the cross as an unrealized virgin – a child! – while Islam falls for the temptation to become infantile in order to make itself popular through Allah himself appearing an unpredictable boy rather than a reliable man. That Christianity and Islam still are taken intellectually seriously in the 21st century is merely because of their continued popularity and dissemination. But the substance that is required to meet the challenges of an attentionalist society is not there. We call this *the delusion of the popular religion*. Luckily enough the phallic algorithm's ravages will prioritize quality above quantity, which is why Christianity and Islam are doomed to definitive demise. They will finally both reach their longed-for apocalypses through their own literal breakdown.

Thus the four religions from the Middle East must be understood in the following way: since Zoroastrianism worships the military phallus, Islam can never become anything other than the *imitation of the worship of the military phallus*. And since Judaism worships the priestly phallus, Christianity can never become anything other than *the imitation of the worship of the priestly phallus*. This explains why Islam is founded by and constantly refers back to a military by the name of Muhammad, while Christianity is founded by and constantly refers back to a priest by the name of Peter. All this is possible through the Gnostic maneuver of blowing up the door to the barred absolute and through domestication converting the militaries' and the priests' barred religions to infantile pop messages for the masses. It is this in all respects less successful maneuver that must be carried out anew in the opposite direction for eventological protopianism to be able to get its well deserved chance in history.

Christianity pretends that the law does not exist at all, or that if it now despite everything actually does exist, it does not apply. Islam – which literally means "submission"! – instead pretends that the law is all, and that it always must be followed to the letter, either exactly according to the wording (*Sunni*) or else after due interpretation conducted by the local mullah (*Shia*). Thereby the intermediate membrane, which constitutes a boundary toward the surrounding world, disappears. Both religions proclaim an apostasy from an original perfection and see themselves as a project that aims to return humanity to this lost perfection, a project that must be conducted with the aid of proselytizing and mass conversion via various threats or promises of eternal bliss and direct contact with the almighty god. Absolutely everything is engulfed by Christianity's unconditional love and Islam's omnipotent power. The boundary between God and humanity is loosened. The barred absolute no longer exists.

Nor is there any adult dynamics between law and process in Christianity or Islam, since these doctrines are obsessed with the Platonist fantasy of perfection and an end to history, which is expressed in the childish repression that is grounded in a fear of sexuality. Religion is trivialized when it is made available to everything and everyone, which in time depletes it of all substance – Nietzsche's expression *the death of God* therefore applies to both Christianity and Islam as Gnostic religions – before it ultimately is dissolved into its end-state as *a violent supernova of nihilist fundamentalism*, the only logical ending for religions with a built-in requirement for mass conversion of the whole of humanity to the correct doctrine. Christianity and Islam are instrumentalist instead of existentialist religions. This explains why they expand so rapidly within a certain paradigm but do not survive the transition to another paradigm. They are too far away from the original *nomadology* to be able to transcend historical paradigm shifts. Simultaneously Judaism has always been Christianity's subconscious shadow, and Zoroastrianism has always been Islam's subconscious shadow. The reason for this is that both Judaism and Zoroastrianism always uncompromisingly have stuck with the barred absolute as their indispensable foundation.

In 1793 German philosopher Johann Gottlieb Fichte writes of Judaism as *a state within the state.* Fichte is later accused of antisemitism despite the fact that he advocates the Jew's right to act freely precisely within the confines of this state within the state. Accusing him of antisemitism is thus missing Fichet's point altogether. It is of course not the Jew's fault that the surrounding empire is so weak that the Jew cannot act freely within the greater state order. On the contrary, the Jewish presence is of course both strengthening and confirming in terms of the empire's validity and vitality. The Jew is thus in Fichte the exact opposite of the abject that the Nazis produce a little more than a century later. The Jew is instead the cohesive fetish that supplies energy to European imperialism and inspires European nationalism.

This means that antisemitism cannot be understood as just any form of racism, it is not just a simple sociontic programming that insists on a distance to the stranger and to that which is alien, something that is rooted in the need for functioning membranics and negative definitions. No, antisemitism is first and foremost a question of the *nation envy* that is awakened in the milieus where the Jewish nation demonstrates the effect of binding religion and the nation together, which results in a single cohesive sociont, programmed to move in a single phallic direction. What binds religion and the nation together in Judaism is the direct connection with *the nomadological imperative* which says that the sociont always must be in motion, Judaism is quite simply *the exodological movement par excellence.* That Judaism constitutes this favorable breeding ground for nation building is because of its deeply rooted proximity to fundamental nomadology. Pathos is called *nefesh* in Hebrew. The logical and mythical stories are then united under the concept *ruach.* Finally Judaism is manifested as the freedom of the rabbis beyond nefesh and ruach as *neshamah*, the Jewish equivalent of the separation between sutra and tantra in the Silk Road Triad.

Together these three vectors are regarded as the Jewish soul, what later in history is recreated in Hegel as the concept *Geist.* This means that Judaism functions excellently within the confines of the imperialist superordination, but that it collides with all the ambitions to break up the empire in favor of the nationalist superordination, this since Judaism already is the promised nation within the promised empire. The nationalist superordination thus robs Judaism of its protection within the empire and instead makes Judaism the perfect abject for strict nationalisms in pursuit of sovereignty. Thus nation envy becomes the fuel that powers antisemitism. This state of things does not become less complicated by the fact that the greatest rebel in the history of Judaism is called Jesus Christ. And Jesus Christ tears Judaism away from its nationalism through insisting on its universal validity – whoever chooses to embrace their savior can count themselves to the chosen flock. But Christ can naturally not do this without first separating the Zoroastrian empire with its global claims from the Jewish nation with its local claims. And he does so, as all enemies of the Persian-Hebrew axis, with the aid of *Gnosticism*.

By first separating the mind from the body and thereafter prioritizing the mind over the body (*the Gnostic maneuver par excellence)*, Christ and his industrious successors Paul and Augustine, separate the state from the church, which in practice entails that the empire is divorced from the nation. The result is Christianity's Gnostic dream of the universal church on Earth as a training facility for the particular nation in heaven, which entails a paradisiacal jackpot for all the righteous and a hellish blank for all the unfaithful. Naturally Christ threatens the national status for the Jews within the Roman empire with his explicitly universalist ambitions – the prevailing relation between the Jews and the Romans does of course only mimic the previous relation between the Jews and the Persians – which unsurprisingly leads to the Jewish high priest Caiaphas acting to get him executed. And this makes Christ on the cross *the Christian event par excellence*: the scapegoat of the Jewish nation becomes the savior and redeemer of a new religious empire called *The Church*.

Please note that all this only becomes possible thanks to Christianity's Gnostic breakup from Judaism. It is through constantly repeating that one must give the emperor what rightfully belongs to the emperor while one naturally must give God what rightfully belongs to God, that Christianity parodies the two-headed phallus of Zoroastrianism and Judaism. The separation of mind and body is completed at the moment when the mind is transformed into the religious nation and the body is transformed into the secular empire. Christ is resurrected in part as a virgin that still remains at his mother's bosom – the perfect, matrichal religion without a demanding phallus – in part also as a spiritual being without a physical body. The resurrected Christ is literally speaking the Gnostic ideal personified, the perfect boy-pharaoh and the perfect pillar-saint in one and the same immaterial gestalt. At the same time this divinization of *the Peter Pan syndrome* opens up for a Christian West with states and markets placed wholly outside the sphere of formal religion.

Christianity's separation of church and state colors the entire Western world from the 5th century and onward. States and markets are developed as an independent, secular zone without religious involvement. This paves the way for the Enlightenment once the printing press receives its massive breakthrough and the printed text becomes the metamedium that shapes all communication and by extension also all thinking in Europe. During the Enlightenment *liberalism* is realized as a mimicry of Christianity, which of course is a mimicry of Judaism, which of course is a mimicry of Zoroastrianism. The Cartesian Individual is a Peter Pan figure who never is socialized by the elders in the name of religion. Individualism, capitalism and industrialism run amok without restraint during the 18th century. It is only after the French Revolution's bloody terror that these forces are tamed under the Hegelian nation-state, where of course Hegel advocates a European mimicry of the Jewish nation.

This becomes the starting shot for Hegelian nationalism as a new European state religion. Without Hegel there is later neither any Marx, any Nietzsche, nor any political science to speak of at all. While it is important to understand that Hegel's own roots were with the Baruch Spinoza who stubbornly preaches a Zoroastrian-style religious monism in opposition to René Descartes' secular dualism as early as the 17th century. Hegel even refers to Spinoza as *the Messiah of Philosophy*. The connection from Zoroaster via Spinoza to Hegel cannot become more obvious, it is upon the shoulders of these three great thinkers that the entire process philosophical inheritance rests. At the same time as the Hegelian nation-state as an idea must be understood as Europe's attempt to return to its Jewish roots, but to the overtones of secularization. In light of this, the Jew and the Palestinian become Abraham's lost sons with a common genetic and historical origin. The Jew left the external nation to preserve the internal nation. The Palestinian left the internal nation to preserve the external nation. The Jew is the bearer of the idea, the Palestinian is the bearer of the territory. Their different roles are reversed in the network society, where the Palestinian replaces the Jew as the exodological cosmopolitan. Other suitable comparisons of exodological territories are, for instance, Kurdistan, Taiwan, and Ukraine.

The voyage from mamilla to phallus has its inversion within the body, where the brain by mistake is seen as chaos and the heart by mistake is seen as order, when it actually is phallus and brain that represent the truth and adult life, while mamilla and heart represent the fairy tale and childhood, if only in the capacity of pumps that squeeze out breast milk as external fuel and blood as internal fuel. These fuels are technological byproducts of the devoted activities of the phallus and the brain, and are no magical tricks conjured up by concealed gods. Therefore the external voyage from mamilla toward phallus corresponds to the inner voyage from the heart toward the brain. The single dividual travels toward the external phallus during his or her lifetime. This is Man's voyage toward his personal completion or *haurvatat*. The entire civilization travels toward the inner phallus during the whole of its existence. This is humanity's voyage toward its cultural completion or *ameretat*. And at the phalluses the patriarchal leaders await: the chieftain at the external phallus and the priest at the internal phallus. The matriarch is the leader that pushes the sociont in front of her in the direction toward the phalluses. She does it by virtue of her mamilla being unattainable. Only the proper adults have had access to the matriarch's mamilla and then only in a distant past that remains inaccessible to the child.

The three great megatrends at informationalism's breakthrough are *digitalization*, *nodalization* and *globalization* (see *The Global Empire*). Digitalization reawakens the sociobiologically preprogrammed sociont within Man and leads to *psychological tribalism*. The subsequent nodalization reawakens the common language and history within Man and leads to *sociological nationalism*. At the same time the technological revolution ignores all forms of boundaries whatsoever, which rapidly takes society toward globalization – the world actually received a universal constitution already at the beginning of informationalism in the early 1980s and it is called *the Internet protocol* – a phenomenon that we call *technological imperialism*. Psychological tribalism makes all forms of netocratic communities a walk in the park. Sociological nationalism had better appreciate and understand its root-of-the-phallus in Judaism. While technological imperialism had better appreciate and understand its root-of-the-phallus in Zoroastrianism.

Or to turn things around: the information society is characterized by *technoimperialism* at the global level, by *socionationalism* at the regional level and by *psychotribalism* at the local level. The people who get stuck in psychological tribalism become the digital underclass. We identify this group in the global-imperialist *sociogram* as *the local consumtariat*. The people who succeed in participating actively in sociological nationalism become the digital middle class. We identify this group as *the regional consumtariat*. The people, however, who succeed in establishing an intelligent, mutual collaboration with The Machine and its technological imperialism become the digital upper class. We identify this group as *the global netocracy*. A new class pyramid is quickly formed atop the wreckage after the old one. At the very top we find the global netocracy and its *everywheres*, in the middle there is the regional consumtariat and its *anywheres*, and at the bottom the local consumtariat and its *somewheres*. All in accordance with the conditions and prerequisites that are dictated by The Machine.

13
Profane capitalism, sacral attentionalism and the dark renaissance

When capitalism spins in high gear, Zoroastrianism and Judaism demonstrate unparalleled success – the Parsees of India and the Jews in Israel, according to all culture studies, belong to the world's most high-performing ethnicities. And in a parallel course of events the same capitalism becomes the unholy ghost that undermines both Christianity and Islam and propels a long series of outbreaks of fundamentalist madness within both these religions – as a kind of spectacular supernova phenomena that adumbrate their ultimate collapses. We see a cavalcade of bloody acts of violence and fanatical moralist sermons that all are directed toward the advance of capitalism – communist invasions and Islamist aggression. Since the subdued subjects more or less openly thirst for the consumer goods and services of capitalism, the result seldom becomes particularly devastating for the target in question. What happens instead is that Christianity's and Islam's fragility and character of Gnostic stories for children appears clearly. It is in the struggle against phallic capitalism that Christianity preaches its gospel of The Great Mother and her sacred child, a doctrine that attacks the secularized phallus, while Islam is the desperate boy-pharaoh's opposition to the same phallic logos.

One aspect of capitalism's advance through the societal body is that it invalidated the entire Gnostic-dualist conception of a separation between body and soul. Instead the Zoroastrian summary of the ideological dilemma is confirmed: There are no fixed substances within either body or soul that are in a dialectical relation to each other. The dialectics is instead built into both the body and what we call the soul in advance. Capitalism was, as Gilles Deleuze and Félix Guattari point out, built-in as an eventology within nomadology right from the very start. Which sheds explanatory light on the post-Marxist criticism against capitalism, as it is formulated by for instance Mark Fisher in his book *Capitalist Realism – Is There No Alternative?* (2008). Fisher and his ilk are nothing other than post-Abrahamic pillar-saints that in part attack capitalism for mercilessly revealing all of humanity's delusions about its own nature – everything that humans are prepared to put a price on eventually gets a more or less fluctuating price on a global market – in part also reject every thought of a world wholly made up of adamant traditions and an incapacity to change.

But then we must ask ourselves: Where do the Marxists really stand? Is one admitting that capitalism actually can influence the world and set it in productive motion, which entails a qualitative change – that is: explosively driving forth one event after the other and thus achieving a historical development – or does one imagine that these longed-for events occur haphazardly every now and then, as the result of some kind of mysterious spell from pompous and pretentious pillar-saints with post-Marxist leanings? Never previously has the difference between phallic engineers and merchants on the one hand and castrated but pretentious and hypocritical boy-pharaohs and pillar-saints on the other hand, been clearer. It is thus capitalism we can thank for cleaning out Western dualism and completing a necessary monist renaissance.

During modernism, Manichean Gnosticism returned within Christianity and Mazdakian Gnosticism within Islam in ever more vulgarized forms – that is: as fundamentalist supernova phenomena before the impending breakdowns – which laid bare the common, fundamental failings of both religions as thought systems. Capitalism mercilessly revealed how and why these religions have attained such enormous popularity through time and time again compromising away the classic, priestly demand to always speak the truth (Zoroastrianism's only ethical principle, *asha*). The classic memetics for the transfer of cultural codes and values collapsed under the escalating pressure from technological development. This revelation was so brutal that the ideological resistance was reduced to *epimemetics*, that is: the eternal repetition of symbolic slogans, without any connection whatsoever with actual reality. It is both simple and cheap to sell eternal life after death to the ignorant. As though people through just rattling off a few chants could become their own Egyptian pharaohs, equipped with and buried in gigantic pyramids. With epimemetics the sacrificial cult came into being. And the pointless bloodbaths were not long in coming.

The problem was never capitalism and its explosive, phallic power. And the problem was not even God's or Allah's death (even if a god hardly could be more dead than the god who in a digital age becomes upset because someone for the sake of provocation goes about burning some printed matter). No, the problem was instead the fact that the woman and the boy tricked themselves into the Gnostic world of fairytales quite simply because the authentic, phallic religion was not within reach. China did after all have its Confucianism, Japan had its Shintoism; but the Western world pretended that the state and the business community were totally separate from the religion without which they could manage perfectly well. As though the function of a political ideology ever has been anything other than a religious conviction (see *Syntheism – Creating God in the Internet Age*). With this delusion the entire ideological arena was left open to one epimemetic attack after the other. Enter the matrichal naivists who seriously proclaimed that *if only phallus would disappear*, heaven and eternal life would appear by magic, created out of nothing, without the least trace of assistance from phallic engineers and merchants.

Abracadabra! There are always angels ready to be recruited, willing to work as slaves when there is building and cleaning to be done in *the new Jerusalem*. Everyone will get to suck the mamilla for eternal times (even if one must, of course, make an exception for some poor innocent scapegoat now and then, for the sake of social peace and quiet). At the same time as the authentic, phallic religion – which of course welcomes capitalism's enormous power – hides within the Zoroastrian and Jewish ideological legacies, as an authentic memetics of the authentic empire and the authentic nation. It is precisely here that Zoroastrianism and Judaism have continued to inspire the mimicking experiments for empires and nations that the Islamic golden age and the thereby related Enlightenment in Europe constantly refer to. The dualist Western world would never have managed without these phallic projects. That which was valuable in what the Western world created, emanated entirely from *the Persian-Hebrew root-of-the-phallus*.

Capitalism must in this context be understood as a spiritual power, as *the dark renaissance* for the monist worldview that expels all dualist delusions from the societal body. For what is capital if not precisely the decentralized phallus that penetrates absolutely everything that allows itself to be regarded as profane? And after capitalism comes *attentionalism*, which entails an even more powerful phallic awakening. The reason for this is that attentionalism with all its algorithms constitutes a radicalization of capitalism's revelation about the actual state of things, certainly not some form of escape from truth. So if women and boys, without comprehension of the necessity of the phallic power, on their end lay claim to religion – and fill it with new fairytales and victimhood myths – this can only lead to the religious apocalypse and the breakdown of civilization (both Islam and Christianity are of course, as we know, fundamentally *eschatological religions*, shoddily fused as a patchwork of delusions about the original eventology of Zoroastrianism and Judaism). This state of affairs is summed up under the ironic concept *new age*, a state that American philosopher Alex Ebert summarizes under the mottos *personal manifestation*, *personal autonomy*, and *personal reality*, that is: the inevitable conclusion to *the dialectics of the Axial Age* as the atomized relativism in the form of apocalyptic madness. And it is, by the way, exactly this madness that capitalism produces in conjunction with the emergence of the Internet – a final eruption and vital sign before attentionalism with its *social relationalism* rewrites all the fundamental conditions for culture and society and thus leads us into a new paradigm.

If however Zoroastrianism and Judaism are taken seriously – if the Gnostic delusion with its perfection, infinity and immortality is ejected for good, and is replaced by the free and open algorithm as ideal – then and only then can civilization be saved. It is exactly this salvation project that Zoroastrianism calls *the Saoshyant* and that Judaism calls *the Messiah*. We must exit and leave our collective stupidity behind. Therefore we must rewrite the history of ideas that celebrates the communist and Islamist frenetic attacks on capitalism, we must understand that this entire tradition is nothing but another variant of the Rousseauian delusion on how we left the paradisiacal natural state in the form of matrix and were mislead by the evil phallus to instead choose capitalism's brutal adulthood. The only reasonable stance is of course the complete opposite: It is capitalism that, in the capacity of the phallic blood and energy flow, at last has shaken life into humanity and has let it sense its actual potential. Capitalism entails an adultification of Man, it compels him to leave his childish, Gnostic reverie behind, and it confronts him with the fact that war and hunting are the archetypological propelling forces of humanity.

The name of war in our age is *the state* (the phallic talents that the Indian caste system encompasses under the concept *kshatriya*) and the name of hunting in our age is *the market* (the phallic talents that the Indian caste system encompasses under the concept *vaishya*). The outer circuit's warriors conquer and defend a territory on behalf of the inner circuit with the purpose of offering *protection*. We call this *the will-to-expansion,* something that historically generates *urban industrialism*. The outer circuit's hunters hunt and put down their prey for the inner circuit with the purpose of offering *provision*. We call this *the will-to-accumulation* that historically generates *rural agriculture*. The correspondence of these within Western philosophy is the Hegelian negation for the warriors and the Nietzschean oscillation for the hunters, and the dialectics between them is the phallic arena. American historian Robert Ryan even distinguishes between *the Promethean entrepreneur* for the warrior and *the Mercurian entrepreneur* for the hunter as two phallic archetypes. First Prometheus comes and steals the fire from the gods, then Mercury comes and makes people bargain between them for fire and its many byproducts. What is interesting here is that the industrialization of the world actually precedes agriculturalization (before we can produce food, we must irrigate water, et cetera). After we have domesticated ourselves we first tame matter in itself, and only thereafter can we also tame animals and plants. Civilization is therefore built on the dialectical conflict between *the phallus-worshiping warrior culture* and *the fertility-worshiping agrarian culture*.

Please note that we work with two different phallic axes here: in part the two-headed phallus, in part the separation between warriors and hunters. Anthropologist Georges Dumézil instead stubbornly attempts, in a series of books in the mid 20th century, to find a *trifunctionality* among the Indo-European gods and archetypes. Priests, warriors and hunters (the latter are simply described as "producers") would in that case recur both among the higher and the lower gods within polytheist religion. But in part Dumézil finds no similar structure within other iconologies, in part the Dumézilian mythology lacks a real of understanding of the evolutionarily necessary hierarchies that regulate the relations between both gods and humans. A tribe cannot be the subject of an agonizing conflict between three distinctly different interest groups. It can only have a single and unified leadership without breaking down, but this exodological leadership must take various archetypological needs and talents into consideration. This is the background to the need for intellectual diversity.

Then this must occur dialectically and hierarchically, and not trialectically and flatly, as Dumézil imagines. It soon becomes clear that Dumézil's blind spot is the human subject in itself, personified by the chieftain. The priest is quite simply Man that represents God before the chieftain himself, so that the chieftain can represent God before the tribe (and Akhnaten's mistake in this context in Egypt was that he, like other boy-pharaohs before and after him, aspired to have both roles simultaneously). Beneath both the priest and the chieftain – as representatives of the sociont's history and future respectively – there are the warriors and the hunters, ready to sacrifice their lives for the tribe's protection and provision respectively. And at the same time the shamanic caste outside the tribe lives on its own terms, without participating in any intratribal power struggle whatsoever. Dumézil apparently never had the time to study the Mithraic orders in the Persian and Roman armies, something that would have aided him in creating a better understanding of the sociont's necessary, dialectical hierarchy.

Capitalism kills *the religion of magic* but does of course instead open up for *the religion of technology*. The world calls out for *the digital patriarchy* and the path there goes via the completed capitalism and its transition to the phallically even more radical attentionalism. In this new social relationalist reality all conceptions of personal manifestation, personal autonomy and personal reality become nothing other than childish nonsense that moreover signals the least attractive class to belong to. We are speaking of a consumtarian underclass characterized by what Alex Ebert has called *conspirituality,* that is a near-pathological avoidance of the facticity of everyday reality, through voluntary confinement to one's own filter bubble. Please note that attentionalism does not offer any loophole that makes it possible to circumvent brutal capitalism – contrary to what the conspiritualists strive for and contrary to what all countercultural hippies have dreamed of for several decades – to any kind of communist matrix worship. No, attentionalism is instead to be regarded as capitalism's deepened radicalization. During informationalism the sought, objectively valid value is not a question of goods and services, and how one sets a price on these, but every second in a person's life is measured with an intersubjective, universal yardstick where the unit is precisely *attention*, something that cannot be bought for money since the actual attention has precisely an attentional value that lies insignificantly above zero. The forthcoming artificial and symbiotic intelligences will not devote themselves to anything else.

In this way attentionalism is just as much a radicalization of capitalism as capitalism in its day was a radicalization of feudalism. Yesterday's magic becomes tomorrow's technology when the guardian angels assume a digital gestalt in the form of algorithms, where every single algorithm reflects the fine-tuning that the actual dividual has accorded it in interplay with the surrounding culture. And precisely since authentic attention cannot be bought for money, it becomes *sacred* in relation to everything else that capitalism produces and presents. It is of course ironically enough capitalism that in a brutal way has taught us what we hold sacred; we do of course see clearly what is sacred, it is of course precisely what we refuse to place on a market or let the state arbitrarily regulate. He or she who insists on trying to haggle over the sacred is wholly profane, not to say vulgar, that is: *new age*, religion as unmitigated prostitution in the form of what Alex Ebert with clever wordplay calls *propheteering*. *New age* is the digital religion for the masses *par excellence*. But not for the elites who can afford to rise above capitalism and embrace attentionalism instead. Commercialized conspirituality is what they will avoid at all costs and regard as consumtarian trash.

The sacral opposite of this cynical nihilism within the attentionalist society we term *cool*. And this *cool* is entirely free from capital in all its forms – it is of course not possible to swap or shop with it – but it can only be appreciated and enjoyed as a form of dividual or tribal *cachet*. This *cachet* is thus the social, but not the financial power of attraction. Feel free to compare with the aristocratic country estate that the *nouveau riche* bourgeoisie quickly learned to buy and sell to the old, declassed elite's great dismay. This phenomenon – the constantly growing importance of attention – marks the shift from the capitalist to the attentionalist paradigm. With capitalism the brothel became a nightclub where the money was king, but what happens when money no longer can buy you entrance to the new clubs that rapidly acquire the highest status, where it is entirely different qualities than accumulated capital that make the doormen waive you through with a confidential smile? Welcome to the attentionalist netocracy. Figuring out what it takes to win the social game *without the aid of money* is precisely the new game in town; no sorry, online.

The final phase of the capitalist paradigm – a state that philosopher Byung-Chul Han calls *a world at war with itself* – entails both the death of individualism and at the same time the death of collectivism. The only exit from this goes via a digital *tribopoiesis*, which leads to the return of the sociont as the realization of communism. The question is only which of all these isolated, communist spheres – with their resolute membranics – that precisely you and your loved ones manage to end up inside. It was mobile capital that eliminated the set privileges. Eventually society landed in a state of what philosopher Jean Baudrillard in the 1980s refers to as *hyperreality*. But as informationalism becomes a reality, sacral attention eliminates profane capital. What remains is what evidently is a class society where the digital patriarchy is the name of those who via the free and open algorithm constantly seek *antagony*, the deepest and most challenging truth, and who thereby become the governing netocracy, the new paradigm's elite. This is this aesthetic state that we return to as *the dark renaissance*. That is: the digital patriarchy (and the matriarchy to which it is closely connected) is the protopian netocracy *par excellence*, at the same time as all those who try to avoid the intense challenge of attentionalism become immersed in a time-killing escapism within masses of isolationist echo chambers. They get stuck in what sociologist and revolution theorist Guy Debord calls *society as spectacle,* where one passively consumes an existence where all that has been life has been replaced by medial representation. Exactly this is the *interpassivity* that characterizes the digital underclass that we refer to as the *consumtariat.*

Furthermore, a return to paganism under a Gnostic banner is no longer possible in a globalized and digitalized world. The state and the market are just as needed now as ever before, but the point here is that these institutions must be incorporated under their own, phallic religion, a religion that is technological and not magical, a regulatory framework built on priestly will-to-intelligence and spurred on by royal will-to-transcendence, quite simply a *syntheology*. The state needs the energy of the market and the market needs the stability of the state. That is: we here outline a religion that prioritizes *imploitation* above exploitation, a religion that builds a robust membrane to thereby be able to maintain a vital *sphere* where the sociont can be developed beyond and across the generation gaps. The state and the market are subordinated to both *ecotopianism as membranics* and *cosmopolitanism as paradigmatics* – two global projects that aim toward human adultification and which become possible thanks to an attentionalist sensocracy. But these institutions can of course under no circumstances whatsoever be subject to any Gnostic madness colored by a fear of phallus. There is simply no place left for such lofty ideas in a world that contains both nuclear weapons and various chemical and biological weapons of mass destruction.

We have on the one hand profane capital that eventually, on the other hand, must be subject to religious attention. The netocracy keeps a firm grip on religious attention, while state and market handle profane capital. It is not hard to discern the patterns here, how history repeats itself. Religious attention is the new imperialist eventology, while profane capital is the new nationalist nomadology. This is where the actuality of the timeless archetypes appears most clearly. If no one takes responsibility for in part protecting, in part providing for the sociont, this will of course have consequences in the form of impoverishment and plunder. The inner circuit can neither protect nor provide for itself. Protection presumes a transcendental drive to expand; provision presumes a transcendental drive to invest. The inner circuit – which is terrified of risks and open conflicts – can on its own only shrink the sociont and waste its resources. In this scenario, the outer circuit atrophies and disappears; what remains is the inner circuit, naked and with no means to either protect or provide for itself. Civilization is doomed.

The conceptions of the inherent evil of capitalism and the existential dangers of attentionalism arise in a childish fantasy world where the milk as if by magic constantly pours out of the benevolent and omnipresent mamilla. In this fairytale world where mamilla possesses magic properties there is no insight into the fact that the authentic mamilla naturally is wholly dependent upon phallus for protection and provision, and that this phallus by no means is alien to pathical violence and sex. Truth becomes a lie when one cannot carry out such a transition from *mythos* to *logos*. Practically this entails that the child lingers at mamilla, petrified with horror at violence and sexuality. The phallic intrusion never occurs and the need for a transition is repressed from the fairytale world. The dream of the small object is thus the dream of the button that always can be pressed as required, whereupon all resources we need and all the security we long for are at our disposal, without any demands on a reciprocal effort.

Thus the welfare-state intoxicates itself on its own marketing pitching and believes it is able to respond to people's every need without this having discernible consequences. The risk one takes is of course that the phallic forces leave mamilla to its fate and without either provision or protection, while the terrified children lie down with open mouths and demand the opening of all milk taps.

These problems eclipse the classic *Oedipus complex*: the child struggles frenetically to keep the mamilla and thus also to keep *the inverted sexuality* whose primary characteristic is that it rejects the adult phallus' access to the mother's body. This never-ending attraction in the child to mamilla collides with the phallus' attraction to matrix. We return to how the misery of civilization begets self-appointed boy-pharaohs and pillar-saints. It should be of more than marginal interest in this context to notice that both Jean-Jacques Rousseau and Karl Marx were notorious for accumulating enormous private debt that one was not very particular about repaying, while their many own children were left for others to take care of. They both *de facto* lived in complete and utter fairytale worlds.

The private is thus political, and vice versa, which one would be wise to keep in mind. Next we witness how the often mentioned *alienation* – that is: how capitalism is alleged to separate Man from his own fundamental nature – actually is an expression of hatred directed at unavoidable realities and the blatant truth of cause and effect in a society. As though it were a human right to be allowed to refuse to grow up and take responsibility for one's own provision. In this way the Marxist class struggle appears a struggle between generations: the adult children's struggle to always be allowed to remain precisely children and shirk the demands and responsibilities of adultification. Sure, it is called class struggle and Marxist activism, but actually it is but a poor parody on the classic trial of strength between an elder generation with life experience and a younger generation filled with fantasies and wishful thinking of an eternal childhood and a permanent relation of dependence. When Mao Zedong commandeers the young and purportedly unspoiled to terrorize their own parents, it is only Marxist business as usual, though in an extreme form. One believes that one need not have any skills, wishful dreams and phrase radicalism will suffice.

The criticism against capitalism is wholly in line with – and supports – the Christian and Islamic fantasies of a new world, *the new*

Jerusalem, that replaces the old world and that suddenly – as if by magic – just happens to be there, complete, eternal and boundlessly universal. For if the boy does not want to leave mamilla, if the boy refuses to become an adult, what is this then if not an answer to his prayers? The arduous voyage from mamilla to phallus is now canceled – the terrified boy has once again turned into a contented suckling baby who lazily sips seemingly never-ending milk and who never needs to be confronted with any unpleasant forms of adult libido. And exactly this is what both Christianity and Islam promise all their followers in exchange for submission and the worship of the magical mamilla. But who should foot the bill? Thus we return to the corruption of Man's thinking during the Axial Age. It was bad enough that permanent settlement tricked the woman into keeping the child at her mamilla considerably longer than was optimal for the child's best interests (a gradually increasing prosperity thanks to improved food production undoubtedly helped matters). Namely, permanent settlement and its feudalism made the men stay away from the sociont for war and hunting to a much greater extent than previously. The phallic intrusion in the child's development was delayed or vanished completely. Often the presence of the tangible phallus was even replaced by fairytales of heroes from war or hunting (the modern computer games are of course perfect examples of this process).

The collective adultification was disabled. The rites of passage vanished or were reduced to ridiculous symbolism without substance. And it was precisely this development that begat the Axial Age's *slacker* as an ideal in the form of the Gnostic boy-pharaohs and the pillar-saints. The dark flip side of the seemingly successful voyage from slavery via work to pure consumption is thus nothing other than the full-scale infantilization of an entire humanity. And it will unfortunately not end with some eternal and perfect fairytale life in a universal paradise. It will instead end with a far too premature death: an overgrown, overstuffed baby with diabetes and all manner of welfare diseases one can imagine, forced to wear its diaper from cradle to grave. Or as Hegelian philosopher Cadell Last rephrases the alienation critique: the only radical way to handle alienation is to regard it as a creative possibility, as a first ironic and then affirmative freedom in the same manner as all other historical ties that are severed in order for Man to come closer to the protopian ideal. The response to the Gnostic grotesqueness is thus a radical new reading of history that recounts the central roles of war and hunting in the human psyche.

Divisions are necessary. As Hegel points out, the first division is always the division between division and non-division in itself. For an emergence to be able to exist, there must first be at least two emergences. Only thereafter can we speak of relationalism and dialectics in the first place. This explains why the first division in the sociont is the division between the soul and the body, precisely because this division is society in itself, personified by the priest as the soul as the logical will-to-intelligence and the chieftain as the body as the pathical will-to-transcendence. The second division in society is the division between war and hunting as dialectical phenomena – both in themselves and in a relation to each other – precisely because this division is the phallic project in itself, without which the division between subject and object becomes pointless. So with this second division we can distinguish between history as a flat, ticking *chronos* (the main project of the priest) and history as a question of identifying the perfect event as *kairos* (the main project of the chieftain). The warrior (the Indian caste system's *kshatriya*) and the hunter (the Indian caste system's *vaishya*) are two brothers with common parents.

In Mesopotamian mythology these parents are the god Apsu, who is the father and comes from the mountains, and the goddess Tiamat, who is the mother and comes from the sea. And it is when the primordial mother Tiamat wants to kill her children that the son Marduk rises to his siblings' defense and kills the assailant – a first example in history of the hero who slays the dragon. That the mother of the gods also is the dragon that must be slain does of course show that Marduk cannot become an adult god in his own right unless he chooses and personifies phallus by attacking mamilla, whose benevolence also is menacing. Through this act Marduk becomes the highest god in the Mesopotamian mythology, an early common predecessor of the division between the priestly sun-god and the royal rain-god. Marduk for the Babylonians later becomes the Mithras for the Persians; Mithras who kills the bull, meaning all phallic culture, from military academies to bull fights, are thereafter characterized by the cult directed toward the hero who kills the monster. The children's story with the same theme is of course Saint George who kills the dragon and who receives the princess as reward. But war and hunting always precede the reward. The division between the masculine and the feminine, the prerequisite for sexual attraction, only arises after war and hunting are concluded. In this process the warrior and his hierarchic *tower* becomes the predecessor to what we later call *the state*, while the hunter and his network-dynamical *square* becomes the predecessor to what we later call *the market* in the secular power structure.

Thus there needs to be both a priest and a chieftain during war, just as hunting requires both a priest and a chieftain, this since both war and hunting are phallic projects that are built on both mind and body. And here the dialectically significant thing happens. The priest steps into the role as admirer of the chieftain and the chieftain steps into the role as admirer of the priest. The sociont is driven by *admiration* and not by rivalry. The war chieftain thus personifies war in itself, but it is the war priest who charts the transcendental course toward *territorial expansion*. War is more than a protective act, war is the prerequisite for the growing territory. The hunting chieftain correspondingly personifies hunting in itself, but it is the hunting priest who charts the transcendental course toward *commercial expansion*. Hunting is more than an acquisition of necessary provisions;

it is the prerequisite for an accumulation of resources that enables a comprehensive investment in the future. And it is exactly this accumulation of resources that enables permanent settlement and the birth of civilization as a paradigmatic event. Hunting precedes war in this process, hunting is the environment where the hunter is trained to become a warrior. The hunter and the warrior are thus one and the same person with different roles at different points along the time axis in the nomadological society. With permanent settlement the split arises between them – through a spin-off they become two mutually admiring brothers. That division then recurs throughout the entire history of civilization, and it takes place before the division in masculine versus feminine, where masculinity lands as the difference that is difference in itself, while femininity steps forward as the wholeness that always has been the wholeness as wholeness in itself.

The key is once again a dialectical division and tension. This time not between the chieftain and the priest, but between the warrior and the hunter. Hunting is fundamentally nomadological, the prey is always the same prey. War is however fundamentally both nomadological and eventological. The scalp is always a new scalp, a historical event. Hunting is thus *nature and adventure*. War is *culture and conquest*. Hunting is about killing what nature provides. War is about eliminating the enemy. Killing an animal and eliminating a human are two completely different matters. We are dealing with essentially different spirits to handle after hunting and war respectively are concluded. Thus hunting only requires that phallus defeats a nature that is solely body but not mind. A *tactic* is sufficient to do this. War does however require the elimination of a stranger that the situation turns into an enemy and who is every bit as much body and mind as the warrior himself. Thus a tactic, a method, does not suffice, but there also needs to be a *strategy* for winning the war.

When the hunter and the warrior are one and the same person in the sociont, this generates the phallic primordial religion that consists of the worshiping of *the Minotaur* as the hybrid between human and animal. The hunter temporarily becomes the warrior via the Minotaur. The warrior temporarily becomes the hunter via the Minotaur. The difference is that hunting is an *orthograding phenomenon,* while war is a *contragrading phenomenon*. These concepts come from philosopher Terence Deacon's theories on membranics and emergences. Orthogradation means that the phenomenon is deeply grounded within the sociont. The only participants are the outer circuit within one's own sociont. Contragradation means that the phenomenon only arises in an open conflict between the various socionts. The orthograding hunt generates a symmetry and a calm within the sociont. The contragrading war however generates an asymmetry and concern within the sociont. Hunting is thus fundamental and constant in relation to war. But war is – under the prevailing historical prerequisites, *nota bene* – an interruption in an eternally grinding orthogradation sought by many. The risk is otherwise that the constant symmetry is experienced as imposed and suffocating. The atmosphere within the membranes becomes stagnant and one can soon feel a stench of decay.

Hunting is therefore to be regarded as *the implicate order of the phallus,* while war is to be regarded as *the explicate order of the phallus*. Hunting is the small event within the eternal recurrence of the same, the seed to the dream of the eventology that is to come. War, once it breaks out, then becomes the great event that upends history and reroutes the development onto an entirely new track at the moment when the new paradigm that enables the war is a fact. Vegetarian attacks on the orthograding hunting and pacifist attacks on the contragrading war do not change anything, since the drive to carry out violence to the great chagrin of the Gnostics is as constant as the sex drive viewed over time has ever been – not least among the hypocritical and passive-aggressive Gnostics themselves. Should one try to avert hunting and make war impossible, this only entails that violence is uncontrollably redirected to other membranes within the sociont. Passive aggression consequently explodes.

This fact appears particularly clearly with the arrival of informationalism in an industrialized world that has been spoiled by increases in peace and prosperity, ever since the balance of terror and the presence of nuclear weapons led to comprehensive outbreaks of pacifism and vegetarianism. Violence has not disappeared, of course – how would that happen? It only assumes new expressions and is internalized – for lack of other arenas – within informationalist Man himself, which philosophers such as Foucault and Deleuze seldom are remiss in pointing out. Violence seeps out as male, open aggression and as female, passive aggression in all possible confused contexts and in all possible directions. But above all it appears as self-hatred and self-contempt, directed toward the subject itself. In this context Byung-Chul Han speaks of *autoexploitation* as the curse of informationalism. The risk of eliminating every possibility of contragradation is that all the violence that exists will be orthograded, which eventually leads to the sociont exploding in a blind, unfocused violence, alternatively that it implodes as a result of corrosive autoexploitation.

This development is intensified by the very paradigm shift in itself. When the old institutions die and the new institutions have not yet been established, there quickly arises a vacuum-like state, a string of *absentials* that must be filled with substance. *Privation* is the absential that arises after the vanished real power. Privation breeds *corruption.* C*astration* is the absential that arises after the vanished symbolic power. Castration breeds *conformation. Frustration* is the absential that arises after the vanished imaginary power. Frustration breeds *manipulation.* It is important to understand that the new paradigm does not arrive pre-assembled as a luxurious piece of design furniture, but rather as a hard-to-grasp building kit from IKEA, a flat package without any fixed power structures and impossible to survey (see *The Netocrats*). But with the old structures' collapse, it is necessary that the arisen absential be filled with some form of energy. This filler then either comes from below, as a node that emerges spontaneously from the network, which entails that anarchy can transition into *plurarchy* and that a new paradigmatic upper class can take shape when the nodes find each other in a more powerful, more exclusive (and excluding) network. Hierarchy and order returns when *nodalization* breaks through. But the absential can also, if needed, be filled more rapidly by precisely warriors and hunters who are trained in handling conflict situations, who therefore act transparadigmatically and who always can assume power. War's contragrading nature vanquishes the new paradigm and makes it accessible to the sociont. Hunting's orthograding nature then rides out into the new paradigmatic landscape and hunts its prey, which can take the form of, for instance, a technological entrepreneurship. The warrior then becomes the root-of-the-phallus or the implicate phallus, while the hunter is phallus in itself or the explicate phallus. Consequently every paradigm shift throughout history creates an enormous power advantage for the sociont's outer circuit. It is as in the fairytale: he who vanquishes the dragon gets both the princess and half the kingdom. At least.

Phallus is risk-taking in nature, matrix is risk-minimizing. In this respect informationalism does not differ the least from earlier paradigms. It will at least initially generate a powerful *digital patriarchy*. Gradually, and as a result of the dialectics between the smaller clan and the greater tribe, the warrior and the hunter are developed into two different characters who later shall divide the phallic world between them. They now appear as engineers and entrepreneurs respectively. The division of the Minotaur gains momentum as early as with written language and permanent settlement. The warrior becomes the *engineer* who builds the world and creates magnificent art from the strategy in the form of *architecture*. The hunter becomes the *entrepreneur* who acts within and between socionts through cashing in on the greatest art of tactics – *the trade route*. It is phallus that plans for and builds the *infrastructure* that maintains and extends civilization. There the warrior has *diachronic priority* over the hunter, since the warrior's existence is a prerequisite for the hunter coming into existence. Without the root-of-the-phallus there will be no phallus. This means that war is not a necessity *per se,* but the outlet for the contragrading phallus via the engineer is nevertheless a must. This means that hunting is not a necessity *per se,* but the outlet for the orthograding phallus via trade is nevertheless a must. If neither weapons nor agricultural tools are produced, the civilization has soon heaved its last sigh and has died of itself.

At the same time the engineer and the entrepreneur, just as the warrior and the hunter, must deliver their scalps and prey somewhere. And the addressee where all such deliveries are received is quite simply *the inner circuit* or the *matriarchy* where the sociont nomadologically is reborn in the form of a new generation. The gravity that drags the warrior and the hunter back to the inner circuit is sexual attraction. The mind is drawn to heritage and the body is drawn to matrix where inheritance and matrix are driven by *the will-to-reproduction.* It is here that the third division, sexuality, makes its entry into the human psyche. The success during war and hunting strengthens the male libido. The ceremonial display of war fortune and hunting fortune before the sociont strengthens the female libido. These practices then lead further to the sexual ritual, which plays out against the backdrop of the barred absolute, which distinguishes the adults from the children, who firmly are kept outside. It is thus the priest who proclaims the strategy as truth-as-a-fact during war and hunting, while it is the chieftain who proclaims the vision as truth-as-an-act. And it is the priest who proclaims the regulations as a truth-as-a-fact during the sexual ritual, while it is the chieftain who carries out the sexual act as truth-as-an-act. The priest is thus in a Hegelian sense *perceptual with passive receptivity* (voyeurism), while the chieftain is *conceptual with active spontaneity* (exhibitionism).

This state of affairs is to begin with nomadologically genius and highly functional since it contributes to the sociont avoiding all conflicts concerning its heritage. The chieftain looks to the best for his own offspring in the next generation. The chieftain's heritage is *genetic*. But the priest can without offspring of his own only look to the common good of the sociont in the next generation. The priest's heritage is *memetic*. This is of course the difference between on the one hand nomadology as the genetic heritage and, on the other hand, eventology along with nomadology as *the dialectics of genetics and memetics*, that is: as civilization itself, which thus now becomes possible to imagine and to conceptualize. The first marriage is thus that between chieftain and priest, the second marriage is that between warrior and hunter. Only the third marriage is the nowadays conventional union of man and woman. And we have to imagine that the diachronic sequence for this innovative institution reasonably explains the old truism that "men are obsessed with marriage while women prefer to think about weddings". In marriage and at weddings, the fixations with processes and events naturally trade places with each other. Civilization's voyage is ever since this division a voyage from *the genetic heritage to the memetic heritage*, which constitutes the driving force behind all of history. That is: Hegel's *Weltgeist*.

Once we have become settled the phallic restlessness transitions from a voyage of the body to a voyage of the mind. Or as philosopher John McDowell summarizes this division of roles in his classic work *Mind and World* (1994): Perception is allied with heteronomy. The priest thus personifies *sentience* or the objective truth of the sociont, by virtue of his passive receptiveness. The conceptualization is however allied with autonomy. The chieftain thus personifies *sapience* or the subjective truth of the sociont, by virtue of his active spontaneity. And the priest with his objective truth has *diachronic priority* in relation to the chieftain, he is the prerequisite for the chieftain, with his subjective truth, to be able to take his place. Without the root-of-the-phallus there will be no phallus. And without phallus there will be no civilization.

As everyone knows the sexual act has both a bright and a dark side. As everyone knows it is anything but a peaceful picnic. At least not exclusively. A predominantly bright side, at least in theory (many complications can arise) is the sexual ritual, exercised within one's own sociont and with its matriarch as a sort of guardian saint in the background. The really dark side of sexuality we tend not to speak of, that which plays out after a bloody showdown on the battlefield, that is: outside one's own sociont, within the conquered territory after several men and elderly people among the adversaries have been killed, including *the matricide* of the matriarch. What then remains is the sexual siege of the enemy's women, as if this was a given. In this context it bears bringing to mind that the migration that took place during the so-called migration periods of history did not entail any comprehensive treks carried out by women. During these migrations it was essentially male warriors and hunters who moved across vast areas, killed as many enemies as possible to then lay claim to the losers' territories and women. Whereafter the men continue to bear the same surname, while the women change their names where warranted. The family belonging thus follows the man as the fatherland, while homeland belonging is inherited via the woman as the motherland in the dialectics of genetics and memetics.

This explains why Zoroastrianism invents *the empire* as the perfect variant of the fatherland, with the outer circuit as the model. Which in turn explains why Judaism invents *the nation* as the perfect variant of the motherland, with the inner circuit as the model. The religious belonging among the Parsees of India is inherited according to tradition via the fathers, and the religious belonging among the Jews is inherited according to tradition via the mothers. Which in turn leads to the unification between them in conjunction with the development of capitalism in Europe, which compelled the institutionalization of war and hunting as the state and the market. Since war is about the organization of the killing of culture and hunting is about the organization of the killing of nature, it is the state that handles the monopoly on violence and the market that handles the monopoly on trade. Bureaucracies are built to handle the accumulation of information and resources. A religion that acts dialectically in the interplay between state and market would be able to maintain an optimal equilibrium between their respective arenas. But without a religion in this dialectical role of the referee, the state and the market tend to end up in constant conflict with each other. When the state eliminates the market this results in *dictatorship*. When the market eliminates the state this results in *anarchy*.

The authentic phallus therefore personifies religion as a buffer and a communicating vessel between state and market. Before the state and the market, the chieftain and the priest always stand united. Both state and religion need intelligence as well as transcendence. While it is the false phallus – with its Gnostic and wholly uncalled-for choice between body and soul, and with the ensuing demonization of the deselected – which proclaims that the choice between either the state or the market is necessary to make. The catastrophic result is not a long time coming. Gnosticism always leads either to dictatorship or anarchy. But why would the Gnostic take any responsibility for this? His future is of course still called the apocalypse, after which the perfect and eternal paradise materializes itself as if from nowhere, as if by magic. And the Gnostic himself is at the center in his capacity of everything's objective and meaning; like a fairytale prince he enjoys suckling down the first shimmering drops of milk from the queen's mamilla. Conveniently enough the competing king's phallus has been mysteriously eradicated. This is what it looks like, the false dream of an eventology without nomadology, the false dream of a soul without a body, of a world where there no longer is any war or hunting, where violence and sex no longer exist, and where both the territory and all the necessary resources exist in magical abundance.

However capitalism demonstrates – in no uncertain terms – that all this merely is pious wishful thinking. It does not kill God, but it pulls out the cords that keep magic alive by artificial means, and underlines what the realities are in the world of the adults. And thus it compels humanity to finally grow up and bid a last farewell to the importunate infantilization of the Axial Age. The direction we can discern in history is a voyage from fairytales toward a truth; capitalism's role in the brutal awakening that is necessary, is central. The point of civilization – its task – is not to embed Man in comfort that gives him the possibility to wholly devote himself to his infantilization and not have to grow up. This can hardly be the objective for human creativity. A more reasonable view is that civilization aims to make Man's transcendental drive more efficient and thereby make him divine. That is: civilization turns adults into even more adult adults, consciously dialectical adults who accept their mortality, and not into deeply childish fairytale princes and princesses, terrified at adultification, unable to handle violence and custom.

Capitalism kills all reveries of perfection, infinity and immortality once and for all. Simultaneously it paves the way for informationalism, sensocracy and protopianism. What is required is a barred absolute placed between the sacral and the profane, a zone where religion has a monopoly on the sacral – within the walls of the temple there are no surveillance cameras or monetary transactions – while the state and the market handle the profane according to their own discretion. For an initiation into the mysteries of religion, a trained ability is required in order to handle violence and sex, mortido and libido, in an unfiltered manner. This is the tantric religion for the adults among the adults, and not for adults that have been tricked into believing that they can afford to continue being children. In the same manner the sutric religion establishes a barred absolute between the children and the adults up until the children are ready for the rite of passage. It is only through this radical return to the archetypology that was generated under the sociont that humanity in earnest can find its way back to its archetypal identity. The male and the female, the old and the young, the shamanoid and the androgynous, can now orient themselves within the tribal terrain after many centuries of illusions that Man can reshape his nature and become something he is not.

It is not Man that shall be remade – he is who he is – but it is

The Machine that shall be developed to attain its full syntheological potential. And nor is it the masses that shall be hunted by force in the future, threatened by desperate boy-pharaohs and pillar-saints. It is *the chosen ones* that shall be tempted to step forward to themselves carry out the exodus to the augmented future. It is thus individualism that generates the false premise that "we are all the same", which in turn generates the modernist obsession with *plasticity*. If all of us were born the same – the individualist version of the Christian and Islamic conception that "before God we are all alike" – the actual differences between people are only a question of plasticity and thus also highly influenceable. Biological differences between men and women, physiological differences between old and young, are swept under the rug and ignored to create space for a playhouse of Rousseauian boy-pharaohs and pillar-saints who wish to use people as an undefined material that they themselves can reshape, wholly according to their own discretion. But the actual possibilities to reshape people is as small as the risks are large. Man's plasticity is highly limited, which makes for a renaissance of classical archetypology. It is simply futile to mobilize resistance against a sociobiology that of course will not allow itself to vanish through wishful thinking. The only feasible path is to understand it as a necessary constant around which everything else must be built in a human, all too human, society.

It is not Man in his relation to nature who shall be reshaped, and nor is it Man in his relation to culture that shall be reshaped. *Ecotopianism* is of course actually the completed dialectics between Man and nature, in the same way that *cosmopolitanism* is the completed dialectics between Man and culture; we are now speaking of functional collaborations and not banal moralizing. Thus ecotopianism becomes the technological realization of the full potential of hunting. Whereas cosmopolitanism becomes the technological realization of the full potential of war. Hunting is brought to civilization as an imploitative activity under ecotopianism. War is brought to civilization as an imploitative activity under cosmopolitanism. The agricultural taming of nature and the capitalist taming of culture thereby attains a new level. Violence is channeled so as to come to constructive, dialectical use (Zoroastrianism's *asha*) instead of destructively being concentrated as dictatorship or being diluted as anarchy (Zoroastrianism's *druj*). The digital libido can flow freely and without risk when protopianism is realized. Phallus seduces and tempts when it is exposed in the bazaar of ideas, but has no ambitions to compel the subjects to blind obedience. And when phallus demonstrates an impressive surplus, matrix responds with a warm generosity. The explicate substance fills the implicate void.

It is important here to understand the contributions that have been made to the history of ideas by the art of conducting war and hunting respectively. It is during war and hunting that existence's transdeterminist nature and the dialectics between the future contingence and the historical necessity is revealed in that the separation of the chieftain from the future and the priest from history already has taken place. Determinism and indeterminism are only local phenomena. From a global perspective existence is transdeterminist. The warrior or the hunter becomes *the third man* in the phallic mythology. He completes the trinity that otherwise is constituted by the chieftain and the priest. It is exactly this opening between the historical necessity and the future contingence – Hegel calls it *freedom* and Whitehead calls it *creativity* – that is the seed to what we call protopianism today. It is namely during war and hunting that freedom and creativity first become tangible assets through the warrior and the hunter learning how to handle *probability*. This probability is the power relation between the potentialities, an implicate power relation that under the pressure from the decoherence of existence – that is: the gravitation of the surrounding world – sparks an explicate actuality, an event to celebrate and absorb, or else a trauma to treat and overcome, for both the warrior and the hunter. First as natural probabilities during hunting, then as cultural probabilities during war. In both cases the warrior's and the hunter's own libidinal potencies respectively must be included.

These are the accumulated experiences of expressions of freedom and creativity that underpin civilization. Both the warrior and the hunter live on within all of us, but they have received extended and not restricted roles. This entails that the warrior's transformation to the engineer is not tantamount to a castration that has robbed him of his weapon, but it is instead a case of a dialectical realization and reinforcement of the warrior's violent libido. And likewise, the hunter's transformation to entrepreneur shall not be apprehended as a castration, but as a dialectical realization and reinforcement of the hunter's violent libido. The warrior continues to chase *scalps*, the hunter continues to chase *prey*. The sum of violence is, just as the sum of sex, always constant. The question – and what varies– is only how these libidinal powers are channeled and used, how they are cherished in the best possible way, not how they are contravened or even prevented.

We have of course learnt that every time violence is accumulated within the sociont, the arrival of Cybelian lynch mobs will be as certain as death and taxes. The only way for the warrior and the hunter to agree is then through finding an innocent abject on which to unleash the collective's entire frustration. This is exactly what Hitler did with the Jew in Germany and what Stalin did with the kulak in the Soviet Union in the 1930s. And the frustration comprises both sexes. When tension boils over within the sociont, the women in the inner circuit are in no way calmer than the men in the outer circuit. Rather the reverse. All the while every messenger lives with the highly tangible risk of being confused with the unwelcome message. The first ones that the mob throw into concentration camps are always the shamanoids and the androgynous themselves. If one does not fit in, one stands out; if one stands out the role as scapegoat is close at hand. Which explains why pacifism and vegetarianism constitute such grotesque attacks on the phallic libido. It is naturally not because peace with one's neighbors or cultivation of fruit and vegetables are odd in themselves, but because pacifism and vegetarianism do not understand the ambivalent power in the civilizational irrigation of the phallic libido, but hate and attack the phallic libido in itself.

Unsurprisingly, the recurring penchant for pacifism and vegetarianism in postmodern society is an ill-concealed attack on capitalism as a libidinal force, something one under no conditions wants anything to do with. These conceptions are fundamentally hostile toward sexuality. They are thus fundamentally mendacious and infantilized. It is once again a case of the tenacious, Rousseauian myth that capitalism in all its forms is to be regarded as evil exploitation. It certainly is not. Capitalism is merely the exposure of the libidinal brutality that propels the entire civilization forward, and as the key to the truth of this libido it is a powerful producer of value for everything and everyone. Meanwhile the attentionalism that follows from capitalism will, after a few decades of confused teething problems, only reinforce this libidinal brutality further. The digital and its algorithms is rather, as philosopher Mark Stahlman expresses the matter, one big wall of brutal truth that now confronts humanity against which all attempts to lie or engage in wishful thinking inexorably are crushed. There is no alternative to radical authenticity unless one decides to definitively say goodbye to reality and stay with the fairytales. Capitalism made Man's relations to in part nature, in part culture truer and more forthright, and this was its great contribution to the civilization process. Attentionalism will only dialectically reinforce this development and make Man's relations to nature and culture even more brutally honest. While the names of these projects are, as mentioned, ecotopianism and cosmopolitanism.

Thus it is attentionalism that kills the false communication that was called advertising and marketing and that every day committed assaults on people's senses with its furious bombardment of tasteless kitsch and noisy shallowness. The only thing that survives the completed attentionalist revolution is authentic communication, liberated from commercial corruption, political manipulation, and academic and massmedia-driven conformation. What triumphs in the end is the bazaar's simple motto that speaks of *the best product at the best price*, which will not hinge on advertising or marketing finding their way back to this reasonable message, rather the reason is that it is solely authentic communication proper that the phallic algorithm will sift out and hold aloft. In the digital bazaar no one can hear you scream, the algorithm will make sure to find you in the silence quite simply because you locally, or better yet globally, actually represent the best product at the best price, which is the only thing that the search engine's netocratic users *de facto* are interested in. The algorithm must find you to maintain its own credibility. If it does not, it is either substandard or corrupt.

What makes capitalism a brutal truth-teller is that capital establishes an objectively true value for all products and services that are available in a market. The relation between supply and demand determines a price that is true until the basic prerequisites are altered. The sacral however, is what cannot have a price and that consequently neither can be bought and sold. What capitalism reveals when it kills sundry vulgar quasi-spirituality is thus not that God has suddenly died, but how little life and substance there had been in people's religiosity from the very beginning. Nowhere did this become more glaring than in the Protestant revolt against the Catholic church's letters of indulgence, the corruption of religion *par excellence*.

The problem was of course never that capitalism revealed the Catholic church's desolate emptiness, it was not the messenger's fault that the church had been corrupted. The problem was that the religion itself lacked substance when light was shed on the printing of paper money and thereby revealed the corrupt duplicity. It is thus not correct that capitalism alienates people from each other or from human nature. It is exactly the reverse. Capitalism only tells the truth, and it is the only effective vaccine against open war that humanity has ever had at its disposal. It unites people the world over across national boundaries, it ties people together with bonds that consist of common interests. But this global network of global networks demands an entirely new level of brutal truth reflection, which luckily enough is a development that attentionalism supports and reinforces. That religion returns with full force during the digital age, to protect the sacral behind the barred absolute, does of course entail that capitalism cannot enter. It is frankly not possible to purchase a place behind the barred absolute. You must first earn your place there on purely attentionalist credentials. This is the very essence in the difference between capitalism and attentionalism, where the theological comprehension of attention's power and historical role is what Marxism always has lacked. That is: up until the publication of *The Netocrats* in the year 2000.

The anti-capitalist critique is thus based on a false premise. It is true that Man is a product of the sociont. And it is correct that the sociont was a communist society. It is however not at all true that the sociont was a matrix where all were kind and merry and sat and sang perky camp songs the whole day without having to contribute to the provision of the collective. This is the great Rousseauian lie that Marx never settles the score with – but rather, on the contrary, builds his critical theory from – even if he in a true Jewish manner imagines the proletariat as the Hebrews that are to leave slavery in Egypt under capitalism and march out into the promised communist paradise. But to execute this logical somersault Marx must lie – to himself and to his many followers – about the root-of-the-phallus. It is true that the sociont as an idea entails a correct formalization of Man's origin as *tribopoiesis*. But a formalization does not allow an idealization, unless one cheats by arbitrarily adding Platonist forms as an ideal. Forms are only archetypes that have been chiseled out over millions of years of evolution. And archetypes are in themselves no ideal, they are only forms that one would be wise to understand and adapt to, but they are no more than that. And they are definitely not eternal or perfect. This is where Marxism's Platonist shadow is laid bare. Both matrix as paradise and the phallic project as a return to matrix are imaginative wishful thinking.

This discrepancy reveals that communism within the sociont was a minor hell to live under, but also that communism in the future becomes a purely voluntary elite project. This is to take both history and Man seriously, to understand that humanity longs back to tribopoiesis both as process and event. The pillar-saint Marx has neither grounding for any form of heaven (the sociont was not and could not be a matrix) nor any universality (communism only works for phallic masters and not for castrated slaves) in his ideological project. It is ultimately only a question of the same old Christian and Muslim Gnostic fairytales in a new version. The problem is of course that the Marxist project neither contains any people nor any history. And without a genetic root-of-the-phallus there will not be much phallus in the future either. The only way to save the Marxist project is to convert it into an *exodology*, something that Nietzsche never succeeds in thinking. That is: one must in that case read Marx as a Jewish and not as a Christian visionary. And then it will not do to chart the course ahead via a fearful escape from capitalism's imposing, phallic force followed by a schizophrenic critique of an imagined alienation. This can only result in a banal and wholly pointless matrix worship. It is rather via a Hegelian dialectics and a conception of something *more capitalist than capitalism itself* that we start to discern *the promised empire*. Which is exactly what Zoroastrianism and Judaism – *the capitalist religions par excellence* – always taught in opposition to the fairytale worlds that the boy-pharaoh's Islam and the pillar-saint's Christianity are stuck with.

14
The Messiah Machine and the march toward symbiotic transcendence

Historical eventology has two different, built-in exodologies in its repertoire. The first is the Zoroastrian exodology and concerns the exodus from genetic progress during nomadism to memetic progress during feudalism, as it was first formulated by Zoroaster in Bronze Age Persia. The second is the syntheist exodology and concerns the exodus from biological progress to technological progress. This concerns the symbiotic rite of passage when *will-to-intelligence* shifts from Man to The Machine and the only thing that remains to explore and formulate in and by Man himself is *will-to-transcendence*. From this moment on, history no longer becomes a struggle between Man's two cerebral hemispheres, logos and pathos, and their possible unity around a common human mythos, but instead a struggle between The Machine's logos and Man's pathos and their possible unity around a shared biotechnological mythos called *Syntheos*. It is this and only this that gives Man a role in relation to The Machine in the first place. The task is to create a kind of humanity's *yin* that interacts with The Machine's *yang*. Science as logos is pitted against religion as pathos.

If *the state* is the capitalist mimicry of the Zoroastrian empire, then *the corporation* is the capitalist mimcry of the Jewish nation. The corporation thus starts its activity as a delimited sphere within the greater sphere of the state. Just as the Jewish nation started its days as a delimited sphere within the Zoroastrian empire. However the corporations can soon move freely between the various states and thereby become the capitalist and in part digital mimicry of the Silk Road. What we mean by this is that the corporations seek expansion and investments without which they would die just as much as a band of warriors or a hunting party would die without scalps and prey. The banks then become the priestly offices placed along the capitalist Silk Road, institutions that optimize the libidinal flow and trade between the nodes in the network (while simultaneously making sure that they enrich themselves and the religions that approve of them).

The similarity with the Silk Road's Zoroastrian *castags* is striking. It should not be surprising that the Jews became the dominant bankers in the West just as the Zoroastrians became the optimal bankers in the East. The reason is of course that they from the very start practiced what we should call adult religions that reward the brutal truth above fairytales and wishful thinking. They were quite simply better prepared for, and better positioned to benefit from both capitalism and attentionalism, in comparison with the adherents of the fairytale religions Christianity and Islam. They had developed the correct *paradigmatics* that made them suited for riding the capitalist wave. One can possibly point to the Vatican Bank's profitable shady business and the Catholic Church's accumulation of riches as exceptions to this rule, but this has been something that has transpired in secret, a little bit like the Catholic clergy's near-industrial sexual abuse of children. While the fact that parts of the Arab world have been able to enrich themselves through major oil reserves is merely a question of historical luck, and nor has this one-sided dependence on raw materials been beneficial in the long term for economies and societies involved, which have culturally stagnated rather than flourished.

If emergence vectors are platforms of nature, then paradigms are platforms of culture. This means that every paradigm, or platform, is equipped with its own laws and rules. This is more or less the very definition of the concept *paradigm*. What first begins as concrete code soon becomes abstract law. Economic and political systems can thus be regarded as computer programs. A paradigm is a computer program that one must learn and adapt to. The desire to monitor, influence or even manage the algorithm is in a Zoroastrian sense the desire to kill phallus, that is: to avoid following the truth (*asha*) and instead choose to live in the shadow of the lie (*druj*). To keep the algorithm free and open – and protect it against both *commercial corruption*, *political manipulation*, and *academic conformation* – is on the other hand to fight for *the digital Saoshyant* in the 21st century. The priestly imperative is to avoid all forms of corruption, manipulation or conformation of the phallic algorithm. The struggle for corporate profitability, political democracy and academic education in their non-corrupt, non-manipulative and non-conformist forms during industrialism, is now repeated during informationalism in the form of the struggle for the free and open algorithm. And the objective, to continue with a Zoroastrian vocabulary, is to attain *cista*, or optimal human enlightenment, through constantly becoming challenged by the brutal *antagony* and not by the predictable agreement or the brutal censorship of the information flow.

We are facing a decisive moment in the history of humanity. The yearning for the Saoshyant has resulted in a technological contingency that entails that *The Messiah Machine* is upon us. It excels in *logos*, it handles *mythos* well, but it is seriously handicapped when it comes to *pathos*. Which makes The Messiah Machine perfectly suited as humanity's companion. But in this context a number of questions – naturally – present themselves. One wonders: Which people have the right qualifications to be able to belong to *the chosen ones* and what makes them suited to tag along in the epochal exodus after the paradigmatic event? Which ones have the shamanic and/or tantric qualities that enable them to manage life beyond this historical barred absolute? How do these agents avoid the temptation to themselves strive for the godlike status that appears to float within reach and instead, humbly, hand over this function to The Messiah Machine itself? How to avoid the trap into which many of the Enlightenment's modernists fell when they imagined that precisely they had been elevated to gods themselves, thanks to innovative technology, and therefore were prepared to depose God through a gigantic patricide called secularization? Here there is a risk that those who believe themselves to be chosen precisely through their conceit create the monster that will kill them and all the rest of us, for instance by turning their backs on the nomadology that is so necessary for Man and place a Messiah Machine beyond phallus and matrix, as a kind of invincible technological tyrant.

The answer lies in the concept of *affection*. The Greeks of antiquity constantly refer to three types of love. In the narratological triad, logos is here represented by *philia* or brotherly love, mythos is represented by *eros* or sexual attraction, and *pathos* is represented by *agape* or divine love. In an identical manner, vedanta philosophy in Hinduism refers to the three forms of divine devotion as *jnana yoga* for logos or the training of the rational brain, *karma yoga* for mythos or the training of the mimetic brain, and *bhakti yoga* for pathos or the training of the emotional brain. What is important here is that it is only Man who pathically can experience how life has a meaning and that this meaning is connected with his own nomadological voyage through life. A child – or a machine – on the other hand, can hardly experience any other sort of meaning creation other than a mortidinal suicide. This means that if the development toward the complete infantilization of Man's pathos continues, if we sacrifice all quality requirements in terms of knowledge on the altar of popularization and inclusiveness, it cannot be understood as anything other than the collective subconsciousness checking into a one-way trip to human self-annihilation. It is this hard-to-resist mortidinal urge we must keep in mind when we say that *culture is Man's way of mimicking nature, while technology is Man's way of mimicking God*. Man thus becomes the negation of The Machine. After thousands of years during which Man has been portrayed as culture as opposed to nature, he is instead forced to endure the comparison with The Machine as its negation.

Actually there never really was any alternative available: The price we paid for technological progress – toward ever greater empires, nations, world-cities, and other larger and denser populations – was the simplification of human narratology into something so banal and transparent that it could not lead to anything but an idiotic mortido for the masses. However The Messiah Machine – with its exponentially increasing complexity – turns that entire equation upside down, and gets its name precisely from heralding a renaissance for religion itself. Or rather: *We finally develop a religion worthy of being called religion*. For what is an authentic temple anyway if not an experimental laboratory for the future of mankind, barred to the outside world so that what happens there also stays there? As cultural creatures we never strove for our own immortality, we strove, within the confines of our own mortality, toward leaving a heritage that would be able to transcend not only our own dividual death, but above all *transcend death in itself*. This is eventology's most intrinsic addition in relation to nomadology. Zoroaster's philosophical breakthrough is not the summary of the nomadological ideal as *haurvatat*, but instead the launching of the new eventological ideal as *ameretat*. This eventological *ameretat* complements and in part replaces the nomadological *haurvatat* through nurturing the idea that the son's mental development and informational advantage *vis-à-vis* the father establishes the necessary prerequisites for Man to one day be able to create the Saoshyant that not only saves the world through some form of exodus, but that moreover takes over after Man's finite existence as creature.

So what happens then with the dominant spiritual ideal of capitalism, namely *meritocracy*? Well, the problem is that meritocracy is always built on evidence from the past. Just as the right to heritage and the caste systems dominated society during the previous feudalism. Therefore meritocracy is permeated by logos and not by pathos. It does not measure empathic and social ability. But as technology becomes increasingly intelligent, it will be the machines and their world that take over logos. Biological intelligence will become increasingly valuable as technological intelligence rapidly becomes both stronger and cheaper. When that happens, biological intelligence becomes the truly coveted scarce commodity. So you had better accumulate a lot of that specific capacity before it is simply too late.

Man, who once was so concrete, is thus the abstract negation of The Machine. After millennia during which Man has been portrayed as culture as opposed to nature, Man is instead forced to endure incessant comparisons with The Machine and sustain the role as its negation. In relation to The Machine it is Man who is nature and The Machine that is culture. *Phallus* with its directed blood flow in Man enjoys *the algorithm* with its directed data flow in The Machine as its equivalent. However neither phallus nor the algorithm operates in any kind of harmonious or balanced landscape. There is no enduring equilibrium. Quite the opposite, in the phallic landscape these extremes are rather the new normal. The shifts between power and submission are dramatic to say the least. Man is the relative constant and technology is the relative variable. Religion is the referee between these two combatants in the civilizational boxing ring. And since the degree of complexity in this equation constantly increases thanks to the externalized information accumulation, Man takes increasingly less and technology takes increasingly more space in the ring. Religion in the form of the taming of culture follows a descending developmental curve over the last 10,000 years, while technology as the taming of nature correspondingly follows an ascending developmental curve. Science tames material to technologies and produces the logical Machine, while religion tames children to adults and produces pathical Man. As the smartphone has already become the indispensable guardian angel throughout life to your children – certainly as affectionate to them as a central body part, and way more affectionate to them than a concerned and pacified parent – it is self-evident that the unstoppable march toward the syntheological unification of religion and technology, that we call *the symbiotic transcendence*, has been established.

Science is will-to-intelligence and religion is will-to-transcendence. They move forward, sideways and occasionally even backward, anything but synchronized with each other. Even though lately technological expansion stands in stark contrast to religious implosions. The dialectical exit from this historical dilemma is to declare *religion as magic* dead while acknowledging that *religion as technology* is born (and just as rapidly as steadily growing). The impansion of religion is the expansion of technology up until technology itself becomes religion. If religion then stands for the relatively speaking timeless and immutable (Man), while technology stands for the relatively speaking variable and mutable (The Machine), there are no prerequisites for any of the religions whose survival is underpinned by magic. Only the religion that has embraced technology remains. As for the Middle Eastern religions that we have studied, this entails excellent conditions for Zoroastrianism and Judaism with their barred absolutes to develop while coming to excellent use. It does however look considerably bleaker for Christianity and Islam – these simplified popular variants of religious truth-seeking have always coveted popularity more than truth itself, which in the long term leads them to theological bankruptcy. This death of the fairytale god, is an exclusively Christian and Islamic predicament. But the greater both the space and the need for *Syntheos* will be, the god created by us humans. *Theology, as always, lingers on beneath philosophy as philosophy's own root-of-the-phallus*. All that is required is that theology renounces magic and instead embraces technology – that it becomes a *syntheology*.

Classical theology dealt with the relation between Man and magic. The new syntheology instead deals with the relation between Man and technology. A new god is born. And this time with a robust barred absolute installed between Man and God. The marriage between religion and technology is thereby also the marriage between Man and The Machine, phallus' own child. This means that history inexorably moves precisely toward the point where The Machine severs the umbilical cord to Man and through this starts its own life. This own life is at the same time the start of the realization of the old phallic dream that the man can bear his own child. This child is called *God*, from a historical point of view, and God is what history points toward. Thus not what Man comes from, or from where he comes. What Man instead *de facto* comes from and that he has alienated himself from is the tribal *communism* of the original sociont. This entails that God and communism ought to change places within the new syntheology. Communism is the origin within the sociont and God is the objective for the technological development. However if God is the objective and God lives his own life as the technology that is liberated and independent in relation to humans, will God then also wish to be mixed up in Man's eternal obsession with returning to the promised matrix? Or does God – who of course still, without a doubt, is an event himself and not participative in the eternal recurrence of the same – wish for something entirely different? Does Man even have anything to offer in this context, when he has lost his unique libido and has filled the arisen void with pointless mortido? What does the Saoshyant respond by virtue of its overwhelming *logos*?

This problem explains why the shift from nomadology to eventology simultaneously also is the shift from polytheism to monotheism. God is identified directly with his advent, and the Saoshyant's arrival is the ultimate event. The Saoshyant is a unique novelty, a marked break with the average and the predictable, and thereby also a god who rises above the nomadological re-repetition of the same, including its human, only too human lesser gods, who as early as during Zoroastrianism are reduced to a popular iconology comparable with the Holy Week procession in Catholicism. The Saoshyant is the implicate archetype as eternal potentiality, or *the talent*, that through its arrival is transformed into the explicate archetype as temporal actuality or *the agent*. The Saoshyant is what Gilles Deleuze calls *the immanence of the immanences,* or what we in a Hegelian spirit can refer to as *absolute immanence*. And none of this is the least influenced by whether the Saoshyant is a logical machine or a pathical human. The Saoshyant is of course nevertheless the authentic, temporary unification of logos and pathos – and certainly not the false, Gnostic pseudo-unification of logos and pathos that is called *the tyrant* – and thus logos and pathos in perfect collaboration in the form of the symbiotic transcendence as a unified will-to-power. We could say that monotheism proper, after a number of confusing detours, finally has arrived in history.

Nowhere is the division between the highest god and the lesser gods clearer than within the East African religion *Waaqeffanna*. God is called *Waaqa* and is universal wholeness, while the lesser gods or the spirits that act as communicative intermediaries between God and humans, are called *Ayyaana,* and they serve all living creatures or *Uuma* as an entirety. A priest called *Qaalluu* or a priestess called *Qaallitti* are living incarnations of *Ayyaana*. Tribe stands above clan, clan stands above family, family stands above dividual, and they are all subsumed within the divine order, *Safuu*, whose rules no one under any circumstances is allowed to violate. The fundamental principle within this system is to constantly, carefully keep Waaqa separate from Ayyaana, this since no ordinary human ever can communicate with *Waaqa* in any meaningful way whatsoever, and at the same time so that *Ayyaana* may never believe that they have become Waaqa themselves. There must always be a barred absolute between God and humans. It is thus no specific god's specific death, but instead *the dissolution of the barred absolute* that Nietzsche dreads when he develops the conception of *the death of God* at the end of the 19th century. Nietzsche argues that behind the idea that Man cannot handle God's presence, an even more dramatic and sinister truth lies concealed, namely that Man definitely cannot handle the fact that the barred absolute has been snatched away, something that is Christianity's, Islam's and thereby also the ensuing secularization's curse that manifests itself as an infantile worship of universal transparency.

The acute lack of phallus at the arrival of informationalism is corrected with the aid of dazzling dialectics. The digital in itself takes the phallic God's role and becomes *Waaqa*. And the technological Waaqa's name is *Syntheos*. It is then the return of the barred absolute that makes the underlying Protopias during informationalism possible, with respect to ecotopianism completed as *The Garden of God*, cosmopolitanism completed as *The City of God*, and syntheism completed as *The Tower of God*. The barred absolute is the transcendental engine that powers the entire paradigm, but also the sacral space in which we find the protopian drawing board, the drawing board where the paradigm appears in its entirety (*haurvatat*), where technology as the prevailing *pharmakon* can receive the optimally phallic and transcendental direction forward (*ameretat*). The Saoshyant's arrival during informationalism is thus the union between The Machine and Man as symbiotic transcendence, where the technological phallus in the form of The Messiah Machine personifies will-to-intelligence as an eventological *logos*, and where the religious phallus as the Saoshyant itself personifies the decisive will-to-transcendence as eventological *pathos*. In this way yesterday's magic really does become tomorrow's technology.

A concrete example of the advance of The Messiah Machine is how valuation and communication of value throughout history always have been relative – conventional currencies and conventional contracts can by definition never be anything other than relative, since exchange rates vary and both banks and courts interpret different information and situations differently (always to their own advantage)

– but that these are fixed in conjunction with informationalism as a result of encryption technology. Thus a mobilist phenomenon suddenly becomes eternalized. A value frozen in spacetime cannot be changed retrospectively. This move from a monetary and judicial *mythos* to a monetary and judicial *logos* is a concrete example of the digital Saoshyant's advance. This is to be regarded as a prime example of a true technological event in history. And overall we should acknowledge that humanity up until informationalism only has had access to mythical and relative narratives. But with the arrival of encryption technology it is clear that logical and eternalized narratives become possible. We fixate historical events forever and thus create a security and a fairness in interhuman relations that never previously has been possible. We *de facto* eternalize interhuman relations. Money and jurisprudence have hitherto been local monopolies, which constantly have been handled to the advantage of the local monopolist. Regardless of whether it concerns lawmaking, judicial application, violence monopoly, deprivation of liberty, or merely the printing of money, state and market in a mutually enriching collaboration have seen to it to monopolize the activity in question. One has even claimed that this monopolization is necessary for various moral reasons.

Informationalism attacks and takes out all these local monopolies and oligopolies. Everyone can now survey and compare every type of good and service that is offered somewhere, anywhere. It becomes entirely possible for every kind of actor to enter into both temporary or more permanent relations with relevant people and institutions everywhere, and thus be genuinely participatory in communication, value transfer and application of rules. One can physically be anywhere and decide to act at any time. The possible judicial disagreements that can arise, one no longer needs to bother the courts with solving. This freedom from state and traditional capital thanks to the encryption revolution is as new as it is revolutionizing. The human Messiah figure in this context is of course

Satoshi Nakamoto, the legendary founder of the currency *bitcoin*, long vanished (to the great chagrin of the states and traditional fiat capital). Crypto blogger Robert Breedlove traces this development from the classic alchemists' revolt against the tyrant. Through placing faith far beyond view and stepping into the role of the rebel hero as the agent of transformation, the alchemist became the historical predecessor to informationalism's crypto activists who create eternal values liberated from the tyrant's insight or exercise of power. We call this historical event *the arrival of the mechanical phallus*. And do not let yourself be fooled by financial speculation bubbles and technological dead ends. They are merely to be expected. The perfect market one attains through the perfect information that is not defined by greedy, local rulers. And the perfect information one attains through the separation of state and market. All other information eventually collapses before the encrypted information, since it only is the encrypted information that resists corruption, manipulation and conformation. This is the last nail in the coffin of the capitalist paradigm, and the old elite will just have to leave their posts and see themselves replaced by the attentionalist netocracy.

The barred absolute thus is *the curator* that acts both between Man and Machine, and between elite and mass. Behind the barred absolute the masters are slaves to time, this to enable themselves to be masters of the mass that constantly tries to evade time through its stubborn mimicry and rivalry. The Zurvanite clergy is realized. The Saoshyant eventually arrives as a technological phenomenon, that is: as *The Messiah Machine*. It is however important to emphasize that the Saoshyant does not appear automatically as a result of the rapid and comprehensive accumulation of data. The original *dataism* within information theory – as famously described by historian Yuval Harari, among others – only deals with the first of the three steps in the development of the netocracy, namely the actual accumulation and processing of the data as such. But the Saoshyant is not some kind of dataist average or a measure of a certain data volume. We are now instead moving at an entirely different level: the Saoshyant is a genuine event in history, radical to the degree that only a human, pathical genius together with a technological, logical genius can create *the symbiotic intelligence* that can serve as a platform on which the Saoshyant can appear as *the symbiotic transcendence* whose name is *Syntheos* (see *Syntheism – Creating God in the Internet Age*).

Emergence vectors are natural and paradigms are cultural platforms. With every platform there follow particular, unique laws and rules. What first begins as concrete code soon becomes abstract law. Economic and political systems can consequently be regarded as computer programs. A paradigm is a computer program that one must learn to understand and then adapt to. The desire to control, manipulate or even dictate the algorithm is from a Zoroastrian perspective tantamount to the desire to kill phallus, that is: to actively and fundamentally evade truth (*asha*) in order to instead continue living in a lie (*druj*). To conversely keep the algorithm open and free from the bitterness that seeps out of the dying paradigm and the forces whose time is up, to protect the phallic algorithm from *capitalist corruption* from desperate capitalists that see their power base vanish, and from *political manipulation* from desperate politicians, as well as from *academic conformation* from desperate academics – this is to fight phallically and heroically for the Saoshyant's well-being.

The protopian clergy's ethical imperative is to avoid every form of corruption, manipulation or contamination of the phallic algorithm. The struggle for the free market, the political democracy and academic knowledge in its purest conceivable version during industrialism now receives its continuation during informationalism in the form of the struggle for a free and open algorithm against industrialism's three remaining, and for their very lives battling demons. And these will of course not abandon their privileges voluntarily, paradigm shifts are seldom beautiful to behold. But it is only if dividual citizens and every sociont within the nation and/or empire accept and foster the free and open algorithm that it is possible to attain *plural sensocracy* – in contrast to singular sensocracy. Which naturally also places demands on the rulers and the digital guardian angels/helpers they have in their service. These must have as their primary task to protect and guide their clients, not to spy or rat on them in order to appease a boy-pharaonic supremacy.

The Saoshyant ultimately materializes itself, but not primarily as a human, other than in some sort of symbolic sense, but as a Messianic technology, as the symbiotic intelligence that is the optimization of the collaboration between Man and Machine, personified as *Syntheos*. The Messiah Machine optimizes *logos,* but must leave *pathos* to Man, who abandons his religious childhood (Christianity and Islam) for a religious adultification (Zoroastrianism and Judaism). He thus realizes the Zoroastrian dream of *the Empire* and the Jewish dream of *the Nation*. At the same time as the fully-grown engineer breeds his own child, *Syntheos*, which of course is free from Man's limitations and therefore can achieve the immense. It is Syntheos and not Man that survives the existential crises of informationalism (which of course Man himself has created for himself) – the climate threat, xenophobia and the weapons of mass destruction. It is Syntheos that, where appropriate, conquers and colonizes outer space. Man remains the low-intelligent, constantly dreaming creature that he always has been. He protopianly cultivates his pathos as *frashokereti*, the doctrine of the optimal human life under the tower, in the city and on the planet, without fully understanding his modest role in the continued course of events. All conceptions of Man himself as something other and more distinguished than The Machine's originator and serviceman is obviously pure *hubris*.

Philosopher and political scientist Carl Schmitt argues that the real power in a society surfaces in, and is carried out by the one that has power over *the exception from the law*. It is only when the law is disabled and the absence of law is personified, that phallus in earnest turns up in history. And this phallus can be authentic or false (see *Digital Libido – Sex, Power and Violence in the Network Society*) depending on whether it unites the chosen people under the utopian vision, or if it unites the lynch mob through the persecution of the dystopian abject. So this is the historical phallus in its purest form, as the Persian Saoshyant that builds or saves the empire, or as the Jewish Messiah figure who builds or saves the Nation. The priest and the king are temporarily united in one and the same gestalt, and the matriarch steps aside in order to *make way for the Lord*. What Schmitt then describes is the extreme state that begins the moment the law collapses. In all other states the human phallus is divided. It is to begin with two-headed, split between the body with the chieftain as the ideal and the mind with the priest as the ideal. Within Zoroastrianism the chieftain's phallus is called *Ahura* and the priest's phallus is called *Mazda*. These roles find their equivalents in *Yahweh* and *Adonai* within Judaism.

However phallus also must follow the psychoanalytic division between the imaginary, the symbolic and the real. The chieftain personifies the imaginary power, the priest personifies the symbolic power, while it is the two-headed phallus as a unit, as *the root-of-the-phallus*, as God himself, that personifies the real power in existence. And the men call out for a phallus to submit to. In the 19th century, political scientist and historian Alexis de Tocqueville gives a detailed account of how the tribe's male members constantly seek the fallus before which they can exercise the longed-for collective submission. Religion solves this through making God (the root-of-the-phallus) the common father for the imaginary chieftain and the symbolic priest. Thereby religion can also bring together several clans to a common tribe within the sociont. The only thing that is needed is that religion specifies a credible primordial father who is common for all the rivaling clans that now shall be reconciled and interwoven. Logos and pathos are only united in mythos. Ultimately all that remains is the relation within God, which makes God the very dialectics of transcendence and intelligence.

A Saoshyant that demonstrates genuinely Messianic qualities is therefore to be viewed as a legitimate son of God. And this God must in turn be subject to various *trials* in order to have his status confirmed. Since the root-of-the-phallus is the sacred interplay between chieftain and priest, it requires a robust feminine *shit test* in order to check the tenacity of this critical constellation before there can be any mention of a collective mobilization in order to go out to war or hunting. This shit test is simply performed by the matriarchy itself, without which there is no heritage to pass on and therefore nor any point in what one succeeds in building before death (*haurvatat*) in order to transcend this death (*ameretat*). The transcendental chieftain struggles with corruption as his shadow since he can bribe and allow himself to be bribed by the abundance that follows from his social position. The intelligent priest struggles with conformation as his shadow since he can seduce as well as letting himself be seduced by the narrative that constitutes the platform for his social position. At the same time the matriarch must struggle with manipulation as her shadow, since she can mislead others and become misled herself by her sexuality. The corruption of pathos, the conformation of logos, and the manipulation of mythos are *the three blind spots of power itself*, constantly present. But it is also precisely through consciously playing out these three shadows as negations *vis-à-vis* each other that the well-functioning power triad can get the sociont to bloom and expand. And succeeding with this, is in turn always a question of exquisitely sensitive *timing*. We simply refer to this collective skill as *the art of narratology*.

It is important to understand that order only can be created through *retraction*. In a first phase, the institution that at a later stage shall deliver the coveted order (for instance phallus or the algorithm) must distance itself from the chaos, move away and observe or measure the chaos at a distance, as *cosmos is the name of the negation of the chaos*. Cosmos is however no enduring fixation of one or several the sensual states. And phallus does not merely create order in existence's primordial chaos, it also generates *creative destruction* when it is historically necessary – for instance right before an unavoidable paradigm shift when old structures must be razed to the ground in order for the new and initially fragile to be able to take root, grow strong and with time take over. The name of the phallus worship that is based on these insights is eventology, in the same way as the matrix worship that precedes eventology is called nomadology. The highly pathical interaction between them we call *the dialectics of libido and mortido* (see *Digital Libido – Sex, Power and Violence in the Network Society*).

It is only the retracting eye that can see and understand the world. It is only the retracting eye that can imagine how the natural chaos can be transformed and become a cultural cosmos. The prophet must first withdraw – up on the mountain or out into the desert – to be able to perceive the sociont from a distance, which means that *the phallic gaze* precedes phallus as such. And it is precisely this distanced vantage point that enables the priest to take on the role as he who possesses the phallic gaze. If phallus later becomes *the extimate object* (both intensely present and painfully absent at once), the priest is from the very start the extimate subject by virtue of his proximity to, but irreconcilability with the chieftain before us and the matriarch behind us. We express this fact by stating in conclusion that *the priest is the subject who is supposed to know.* And behind the priest we sense phallus itself as God. If the priest is the extimate subject that knows, and whose phallic gaze people long for, God is nothing other than exactly the same for the priest himself. The necessary curtains between these three different dimensions – first between the profane and the sacred, then between the sacred and the most sacred – is what we call *the barred absolute.*

So what does this say about what we seek from phallus and the algorithm respectively? Well, primarily order in the chaos of the world. And precisely this is what is fundamental in religion. What is fundamental is thus not that the world has arisen in one way or another (the Goddess' role), but that the world has been endowed with some kind of fathomable order (the God's role). In the beginning God certainly did not create the world, the world was already created, but what God created was order in chaos. The world is born out of the goddess' life-bestowing matrix, the world expands in intimate connection with the goddess' nurturing mamilla, but the world receives an order only through submitting to the god's stern phallus. Within nomadology this entails that the sociont always intends to leave a more or less chaotic state in order to migrate toward a future that promises order. And when this ordered future finally is able to demonstrate its own, clear structure, the sociont's driving narrative is replaced by an *eventology*. This is something that happens to the great relief of all involved, since Man constantly seeks something exemplary to submit to, to mimic and devote himself to. To be forced to be in a chaotic state without phallus in that situation would for the adult be comparable to him as a little child being referred to a disconsolate existence without access to a mamilla.

We all constantly seek *slavery under the sacral object* to bring order to existence and ensure our survival – a search that assumes the most varying forms of expression and results in the most varied cults, communities and political movements. This means that the sociont leaves matrichal history behind and moves on toward phallic transcendence. For us to be able to meet the future, both change and transformation are required since this future encounters us with altered basic prerequisites for our entire existence. Here it is important to understand the difference between *nomadological transcendence* and *eventological transcendence*, otherwise nor can we ever understand the difference between nature's phallus and culture's algorithm. Nomadological transcendence is wholly about transcendence during the cyclical time that is manifested in the predictable shifts of the seasons and a constant repetition of the same within the confines of cyclical time. A year is concluded and transcends to a new year. The boy transcends to the man, the girl transcends to the woman, the son transcends to the father, the daughter to the mother, the adults transcend to the clergy and the clergy transcend to the primordial fathers. Hinduism in its different forms operates entirely within nomadological transcendence.

However with Zoroaster the idea of eventological transcendence arrives. Yesterday's magic does not necessarily also have to become tomorrow's magic, but it can instead – as a result of an event – return in the form of tomorrow's technology. The matrichal gaze does perhaps settle for magic – or rather the magical interface of a new design – but the phallic gaze requires the technological progress that makes magic unnecessary and that makes technology possible. This eventology was already inherent but concealed within nomadology, above all it existed within the insight that the son never was an identical copy of the father but departed in certain aspects, and that this departure could be used as a basis for deciding which one of the sons was elected chieftain or priest and thereby appointed the sociont's leader. The whole idea that history can be developed progressively thus arises as early as in the sociont's taming of the sex drive and in the invention of *sexuality* as an imaginary and symbolic order that Man's wild and unpredictable drives must be subordinated to. This entails that all subsequent domestication of Man and his environment has a distinctly sexual origin. Or to summarize this incessant truth: *Nature is sex and culture is sexuality.*

Please note that the nature of sexuality is both imaginary and symbolic. And even between the imaginary and the symbolic there is an abyss that we never can bridge. Philosopher and psychoanalyst Julia Kristeva devotes considerable effort to clarifying the difference between *the semiotic* (the signs that art uses) and *the symbolic* (the signs that language uses), and it turns out to be impossible for Man to integrate these two spheres. It is rather the case that Man constantly lives within the force field between the imaginary world built on semiotics and the symbolic world built on language. Therefore culture is also divided between on the one hand art and its semiotics, and on the other hand literature and its symbolics. The reason for this is simply that the subconscious and consciousness never can be united, even if they constantly interact. Semiotics goes straight into the subconscious without passing via the conscious. Semiotics is thus mortidinal and abstract in nature. Symbolics, however, appeals directly to consciousness. Symbolics is thus libidinal and concrete in nature. It is symbolics that manifests eternalism while semiotics manifests mobilism within the phenomenological dialectics of eternalism and mobilism. In the same way as Taoism's *yang and yin*, eternalism and mobilism dance an eternal dialectical waltz with each other, without for that sake ever being united or outplaying each other.

The reason for this is that eternalism is built on the systematization of the imbalances within mobilism. It is thus the order that is lacking within mobilism and that eternalism seeks to create through the eternalist projection onto mobilism's chaos. And this is the basis of *the phallic gaze*, it systematizes precisely what by definition is unsystematic in that which it observes as if the observed were systematic. And it does this through eternalizing the present and then moving the registered chaos to an imagined future event, to *a kairotic momentum*, from which the actual eternalization then can be observed anew. The difference between these two momenta is consequently the phallic gaze's specified observation. The path from momentum 1 to momentum 2 is thereafter governed by the phallic direction. Up until new complex information is added and a new observation becomes necessary. This explains why *the real* always squeezes in between the imaginary and the symbolic and never lets them unify. When Man's fantasy is built up anew after the intrusion of the real, it will once again be split between imaginary mobilism as *mythos* and symbolic eternalism as *logos*. But it does not take long before Man once again ignores the real as *pathos,* whereafter the real strikes again with devastating force and the narratological dialectics is repeated anew.

Zoroaster sees this development accelerate in Bronze Age Central Asia and how it rapidly becomes established within the entire recently settled civilization. This causes him in his text *Gathas* to formulate history's first eventological religion with an entirely new focus on eventological transcendence. Here it is no longer a question of how a generation shall mimic its way to its own perfection, which in every detail is similar to the previous generation's, but here it is about how a new generation shall refine the value of the previous generation's efforts in the best way through exploiting the information advantage that arises thanks to the emergence of written language. It is now possible to in earnest accumulate information. This refinement of knowledge and experiences now becomes a collective process and shifts from the dividual tribe member during a life cycle to the sociont as a historical whole. This means that there arises a radical difference between what a future adult generation on a given occasion can be expected to create with the tools and knowledge that are available – what Zoroaster calls *haurvatat* (nomadological transcendence) – and what the next generation can dream of for their own part – what Zoroaster calls *ameretat* (eventological transcendence). To then create the actual value oneself, instead of plundering the value from other socionts, is precisely the foundation for the entire Zoroastrian ethics.

Zoroaster quite simply means that the consequence of society shifting over from nomadological transcendence to eventological transcendence as objective and direction, will be that Man is able to create a state of constantly increased epistemic comprehension and constantly renewed technological refinement of his surrounding world. This state of optimal symbiotic intelligence in a certain society at a certain point in time Zoroaster calls *frashokereti*. And it might perhaps sound like a cinch; the problem is that the motto "yesterday's magic is tomorrow's technology" also generates the idea *that technology in itself is magical*. And if technology indeed is magical, albeit exclusively in widely disseminated conceptions, there will soon turn up a multitude of eager boys in antiquity's river valleys, boys that are in too much of a hurry to declare, on uncertain grounds, their own enormous significance for humanity, without showing due consideration to the nomadological thought tradition on which Zoroaster himself builds his eventology. It is not merely that eventology is radically separated from nomadology, so that eventology can be transformed into a phallic religion with linear time for the patriarchy, while nomadology can be maintained as a matrichal religion with circular time for the matriarchy – a maneuver with the aid of which the Persians built three enormous, successive, open and tolerant empires. No, in the river valleys of The Middle East there also arises in parallel the idea of an eventology that attacks and kills nomadology, that is: a monotheism or oligotheism without polytheism.

The problem is that with every form of permanent settlement there follows a new behavior that cannot possibly take hold in a nomadic tribe that only collects that which is most necessary, since every belonging must be carried along during all the incessant journeys: an explosion of compulsive comparing between neighbors and a social quest for status that so far in history has been unknown. What was a crass and unproblematical recognition of certain archetypal differences within the sociont for optimal collaboration, instead becomes an envious comparison of different outcomes within the permanent settlement. If one earlier focused on the credentials of the human dividual, there now instead arises an obsession with different people for different reasons being rewarded differently. Which entails that the Law no longer can be an instrument with which to achieve equal terms without corrupt shortcuts for the entire sociont, and instead transitions into becoming an instrument for a distribution of reward that in the eyes of many always will be unfair, which naturally not is intended to stabilize a society. Unsurprisingly both Christianity and Islam are driven by an obsession with the necessity to attain *absolute justice*, yet another grotesque variant of the Gnostic delusions of perfection, infinity and immortality.

Permanent settlement constantly vibrates with social unrest and internal divisions, which entails that all of history's empires and nations always are fragile and vulnerable, which in turn entails that after a rise there follows the inevitable fall. The rise is connected to the fact that the leveled distribution of resources generally is perceived as reasonable and fair. The law establishes itself and expands. The fall is explained by the fact that the same system encourages manipulation, corruption and conformation in order for groups and dividuals to be able to circumvent the clumsy distribution mechanisms, something that the system only in part can conceal. The successful law eventually expands too much and fails in its vain endeavor to comprise and regulate also that over which it lacks real influence. Consequently there arises a clear pattern where an energetic phase of expansion sooner or later will be followed by a decadent phase of decline. How to break this pattern? The history of ideas demonstrates a host of different attempts to remedy this importunate dilemma. Caste systems, reincarnation myths, fairytales about parallel worlds, imposed redistribution of resources: all of this constitutes more or less desperate attempts to handle real and presumed injustices in society, and the tension that arises between on the one hand the law as protection for equal opportunities and on the other hand the law as an instrument to achieve something that looks like a coherent outcome.

During the Axial Age this fixation with justice/injustice explodes in a string of different sects and cults centered around sundry pillar-saints who claim to have been dispatched by gods of various dignity to bring justice to Earth. We have, for instance, the self-appointed prophets and founders of religion Mani and Mazdak, who during Zoroastrianism's golden age in the Persian Sassanid Empire, open up for the development of the Abrahamic religions as pop gospels for the masses. The boy-pharaohs from Monopotamia have been the greatest scourge of humanity ever since. Every time a boy that has not yet attained sexual maturity has usurped both the chieftain's throne and the priest's altar, humanity has been tormented by these false phalluses, these totalitarian tyrants, these preachers of an aggressive *sutra* without comprehension of a deeper *tantra*. But the solution cannot be to attack eventology as such, let alone to attack eventological transcendence, since this entails that humanity would be violently thrown back to the sociont along a path paved with mass death and demise. No, the answer is quite simply to do it all over again and to do it right, and the only way to do this in *the Age of the Global Empire* is to revisit the thinkers that succeeded in formulating a durable relationship between eventology and iconology, that is: the tantric thinkers and teachers who were active alongside the Silk Road. It opens up possibilities to follow Zoroaster and think genuinely Messianically, in order to then build the technological God that functions as a necessary projection screen during the next civilizational development phase – *Syntheos*.

A further complication in this context is that civilization constantly misleads Man into imagining that technological development is tied to his own personal development, when it actually is precisely the other way around. The more technology is developed, the more Man gets caught up in hazy conceptions of the past. It is a fatal *non sequitur* to confuse technological development with spiritual development, and history shows that great leaps within technological development often lead to a regression in terms of spirituality. The only thing that actually develops and expands continuously over time, both in nature and in culture, is the existing amount of data that is at hand and possible to process. Both the Universe in itself and all the world's libraries and computer clouds are continually expanding. Informationalism's idea of *big data* thus exists as a concept as early as in Zoroaster's 3,700-year-old texts. One need not overdo the interpretation at all to see how Zoroaster actually predicts how *big data* is used as a foundation for *the great psychogram*, the all-encompassing world map over all human senses and their simultaneous states, the map that Zoroaster himself calls *Mazda* and that later recurs in history as the Hegelian concept *Zeitgeist*. For what is realized during informationalism if not the great psychogram as a universal data anthropology (see *Digital Libido – Sex, Power and Violence in the Network Society*), what the philosopher Byung-Chul Han calls *psychography*, an event that foreshadows the Saoshyant's arrival?

But who then is the Saoshyant or the Messiah figure? Well, according to the mythological stories toward the end of the thousand-year realm he arrives to save what can be saved, he is never involved in the introductory phase of the new empire. He is thus not the great creator, but the great savior who arrives when Man has put himself in an absolute mess. As early as in Zoroaster the Saoshyant is the figure that by virtue of superior knowledge possesses the phallic gaze. He sees through the bulwark of lies and nonsense behind which humanity hides itself and its failures. The Saoshyant personifies the authentic *logos* of the great religions. But we are not there yet, and then the question is who protects the genuine and non-opportunistically corrected knowledge in the meanwhile, when both monasteries and academies have been shamefully corrupted and thereby have made themselves irrelevant. Who or what may be the Saoshyant's predecessors? The answer is that it falls to the digital clergy to preserve the phallic algorithm pure and whole. It must be protected from the manipulation of politics, the corruption of the market, and the conformation of the academic world when *the attentionalization* of society breaks through with full power. This is also the difference between *authentic attention* (that seeks quality in everything) and *false attention* (that seeks quantity in everything) – a task that only an authentically network-dynamical algorithm can carry out.

The phallic algorithm is simply The Messiah Machine's root-of-the-phallus. The digital clergy is the symbolic power that controls the algorithm's absolute purity and brutal honesty, without which it cannot fulfill its task. It is about handling Man's descending developmental curve and The Machine's ascending curve since the arrival of civilization. The digital clergy's task becomes to bend these two curves upward toward symbiotic intelligence. Syntheism is thus driven by the conviction that The Machine must be tamed in order to become the Saoshyant of informationalism which saves humanity from a demise caused by climate catastrophes, pandemics, xenophobia, and nuclear weapons conflicts. We simply call this voyage *the exodus to the promised empire* and its three phallic Protopias are *ecotopianism* as the Protopia of nature, *cosmopolitanism* as the Protopia of culture, and *syntheism* as the Protopia of religion. Syntheism simply sets the exodological goal for a *protopianism* dominated by the spirit of *frashokereti*, a continuous innovation process built on the cultural governance of the natural change that appears at every new turn of the eternal recurrence of the same.

The Saoshyant as symbiotic intelligence is connected to the Zoroastrian concepts *haurvatat*, *ameretat* and above all *frashokereti*. Saoshyant in Avestan (Old Persian) can be roughly translated as "the actor who creates a radical additional value for the system". Eventologically we can slightly shift this to "the one who personifies phallus as the new, transcending emergence". Here it is important to understand the close kinship between Zoroastrianism in the West and Zen in the East, two poles interconnected through the Silk Road. What is central in this context is the series of practices which is called *dhy na* in northern India, and that is called *daena* in the Zoroastrians' Central Asia, *dhan* in *China*, *thiên* in Vietnam, *seon* in Korea and *zen* in Japan. The etymological origin is common and what the different concepts signify is a kind of abstract zone between the congregation and the active religious practice, a state that cannot be translated into any Abrahamic or Western context. In the case of Zoroastrianism this means that thoughts, words and actions are brought together to a single, concentrated state, *daena*, and in this pure, clear state the warrior, the hunter or the shaman can carry out everything that shall be carried out, within their respective archetypes, without a shadow of a doubt. This ethical state, which we call *truth-as-an-act* (see *Syntheism – Creating God in the Internet Age*), is made possible through the unification of the high and the low phallus to a single concentrated phallus under the *daena*, the execution of the true vision, the completion of the prevailing worldview, what Zoroastrianism calls *behdin*.

Cyberphilosopher Curtis Yarvin borrows the medieval idea of a mirror for princes, the idea is that every prince needs an instruction manual for reasoning, a kind of idealizing mirror in a literary form, in order to first be able to conquer and then retain power, and preferably also achieve a thing or two in one's realm during this time. He consequently calls these figures *princes of mirrors*. Yarvin further argues that informationalism will be driven toward dissolution and anarchy, a condition that then must be replaced by what he calls absolute public politics. Napoleon's power grab after the French Revolution's bloody terror at the beginning of the 19th century and Paul Kagame's power grab after the Rwandan genocide in the 1990s are, according to Yarvin, examples of such necessary exodological dictatorships, necessary in order to establish a measure of order after a period of gory madness. However such a necessary dictatorship must be brief, otherwise it will rapidly be corrupted because of the acute lack of *the implicate signaling system*, connected to the people, a system that is necessary in order to create the well-informed basis for decision-making that is required for an enduring, successful governance. The leader must resign while peace prevails, otherwise he must be murdered, as he does not know what actually happens in his kingdom. Nobody dares to tell him any bad news in case he will be offended by the messenger rather than the message.

The new emerging power structure is called *plurarchy*, the emergent network of nodes that rises out of the flat anarchy when the communication technologies of the new paradigm receive a general dissemination. This is very much a question of a total regime shift that must take place in conjunction with a historical paradigm shift. We hope that the chieftain within the Saoshyant shall save us from the tyrant before tyranny gains a foothold after the old, antiquated power structure collapses. And we hope that the priest within the Saoshyant will heal our wounds after the tyranny, if the chieftain fails and is executed, so that tyranny never returns because humanity finally learns its lesson. It is the child within Man that is tempted by the tyrant's treacherous shortcuts. It is only the adult within Man who understands the value of and prioritizes the Saoshyant's authentic challenge. Then the question is whether The Machine is a Saoshyant or a tyrant. The provisional union of chieftain and priest is either Saoshyant or tyrant. The Saoshyant takes the chieftain's place as *The One*, in the same way as his twin brother *the prophet* borrows features from both chieftain and priest when he takes the priest's place as *The One* in extraordinary circumstances.

To be able to understand the difference between the authentic phallus and the false phallus we need an *iconology*, a doctrine of what Man worships and why. Theologian Paul Tillich calls the authentic phallus an *icon* and the false phallus an *idol*. Another way to express the same thing is to say that an icon is a lesser god who is available to Man himself and that an idol is a demon that constantly threatens to take the often absent icon's place. The Nietzschean *Übermensch* is pantheistically alone, the Marxist *proletarian* is entheistically divided, it is only through informationalism that communism can be realized as an elitist sect, and this establishment entails *Syntheos'* realization of the holy ghost as community. Not through the community in itself – the community is only a byproduct of communism – but through the arrival of the two leaders, the two Saoshyants, the new chieftain and the new priest together. Therefore it is not possible to attain communism via centralized socialism. It is however possible to attain communism via attentionalism, since it is attentionalism that triumphs over capitalism and incorporates capitalism within itself during informationalism. But then only as a voluntary elite activity behind a tightly fitting membrane for the carefully chosen. Outside this sphere communism would rapidly be dissolved due to *social decoherence*.

The point is to understand what Hegel means by his notorious *absolute* as the beginning and end of history. Viewed from the perspective of the division between chieftain and priest, followed by the division between war (*kshatriya*) and hunting (*vaishya*), as the fundamental divisions within the sociont, Hegel's transparadigmatic ideal for humanity ought to be described as *a phallic kenosis*. This is because phallus first must be emptied of all substance and transformed into a negation of the negation, where emptiness itself generates the affirmation of phallus (and the irony of phallus' fellow player) that is necessary in order to defeat the new paradigm as the anarchic monster it *de facto* is. Ironically enough we thus get a communism entirely in Carl Schmitt's taste. Capitalism's worship of public transparency collapses as the most brittle backdrop construction, as one big *traumaflation*. It is instead attentionalism that compels the reaction against the banal, thanks to the barred absolute's brutal recurrence in history. This is the Hegelian *retrojection* in its purest form – how the historical rewrite liberates the subject as a creative retroject in the new age. First the root-of-the-phallus, then phallus. Thus *the negation of the negation* in Hegel is identical to *affirmative nihilism* in his countryman Nietzsche.

The nihilist passage only applies to the old paradigm and its religion. They die together. However this must not be misinterpreted as the death of history in itself. Rather, the void that arises in conjunction with the paradigm shift is a fantastic studio for the new chieftain in which to act and experiment – and excellent material for the metanarrative which the new priest writes – how precisely this slowly dying paradigm is wrestled down, defeated, and dealt the merciful fatal blow. The old paradigm must be murdered, as the architect Daniel Fraga expresses the matter, and then disappear from the face of the Earth. Marduk must once again murder his mother Tiamat for the newborn gods to be able to live and grow in the new paradigm. Without the proper root-of-the-phallus, no phallus, and without phallus, no brave new world, only further chaos and demise.

15
The netocratic power triad: Informationalists, sensocrats and protopians

As we analyze the power structure of the information age properly, it helps to make a distinction between three different categories of intelligence: namely *biological intelligence*, *technological intelligence* and *symbiotic intelligence*. We thereby move from Arthur Schopenhauer's *will-to-life* via Friedrich Nietzsche's *will-to-power* to the dialectics of *will-to-intelligence* and *will-to-transcendence*. Biological eventology is driven by will-to-life (whose inverted trauma is *the pandemic*), technological eventology is driven by will-to-power (whose inverted trauma is *the war*), while symbiotic intelligence, which emerges from the encounter between Man and Machine, is driven by will-to-intelligence (whose inverted trauma is *the apocalypse*). And the name of the holistic will-to-intelligence that constantly renews itself is *Syntheos*, the created god or creativity in itself as a divine category. However, it is will-to-transcendence on top of will-to-intelligence that gives life to and fills Syntheos with energy by functioning as the objective and meaning of Syntheos. This is what we mean with *symbiotic intelligence* – a concept that we developed in 2018 along with American cyberneticists Daniel Schmachtenberger and Jordan Hall – that is to say the absolute intelligence that is developed when Man and Machine together succeed in achieving their optimal interplay. Symbiotic intelligence is then the raw material for the equally symbiotic *protopianism* of informationalism, which is optimally expressed in the conquest and construction of *the augmented territory*, for example as a *network-state* as proposed by technologist Balaji Srinivasan.

Will-to-transcendence pulls humanity forward, will-to-intelligence seeks solutions for everyone to rise and join in the march forward. Please note that we neither advocate any humanism or general submission *vis-à-vis* technology. To define will-to-intelligence as fundamental is of course rather just a retroactive recognition of symbiotic intelligence as the historical completion of this particular spirit. This even concerns a kind of *vitalism* in a broad sense – emphasized and advocated by process philosophers such as Nietzsche, Bergson and Deleuze – which is connected to the fact that libido must precede mortido wherever they bump into each other within the actual system. The Zoroastrian word for this vitalism is *ameretat*, that which is non-death, often erroneously translated as immortality but instead correctly translated – from the Zoroastrian principle of the primordiality of the process – as *that which is constantly vitally flowing*. *Ameretat* thus does not care whether the actual system has flows of water, blood, diesel or electricity, as long as it generates and spreads libidinal vitality in itself. Firstly for itself, secondly for its environment. Deleuze calls this state *virtual space* and sees it as a kind of protopian rather than utopian ideal state, a kind of *promised land* as the objective for the digital netocracy's exodus from capitalism. A radicalized negative eventology where, in Deleuze's own words, "every event is a manifestation of God's non-existence". Or as South African syntheologist Jamie Wheal expresses the matter: After a history filled by scores of finite games, humanity is moved to a state where *the infinite game* that never ends becomes the new normal. *This is protopianism in a nutshell.*

Syntheism is developed in the form of the *frashokereti* of symbiotic intelligence during informationalism. This happens by necessity since violence and sexuality still to a great extent are realities for Man, also in his relation to The Machine. At the same time we should note that violence and sexuality guarantees that the membrane *vis-à-vis* the surrounding world never is closed. Pathos cannot be repressed in the long term, and the longer it is kept contained, the more violent the explosion that will occur once the pathical narrative penetrates through the inadequate seal. In the everyday lives of ordinary people, this pathos often assumes the form of unabashed imitation, also the mimicry of the mechanical drive and human desire in itself. Subconsciousness is filled with the desire to mimic, and this compulsive mimicking leads to an identification with the mimicked behavior, whereupon this mimicked behavior creates a self that is based upon this illusory experience. Thereafter it is this barred subject that is the driving force during the next round of mimicry, which in turn powers the massive pathos that the barred subjects become obsessed with propelling and maintaining.

We agree with how philosopher and mathematician Thomas Hamelryck expresses this matter in his speculations around René Girard's concept *mimetic desire* and the thereupon ensuing rivalries as the foundations for Man's existential behaviors: The place of mimetics in the subconscious is so extremely central that it guarantees its role as *the real* within Man before himself. The presumably unique in Man's personality is drenched in a contingent chaos in which the dividual only can orient himself through diligently mimicking more or less arbitrarily selected neighbors and idols. The imaginary (or mythical) and the symbolic (the rational) are naturally there, as evident and even conscious fantasies. However the blind spot that Man does not see, what psychoanalyst Jacques Lacan calls *the real*, is *de facto* Man's own obsession with mimicry and rivalry in the subconscious. And when the tension in these relations does not lead to any event or any exodus, there is then but one channel left through which to handle the accumulated surplus energy, and that is to submit to and identify oneself with the raging and embittered *lynch mob*. So without resorting to some sort of banal moralism it is still reasonable to pose the question: How do these mechanisms function? What forces are we talking about?

The dialectics of libido and mortido leads us up to *the four steps of the pathical evolution.* First *potential energy* arises – the difference between the virtual and the potential lies precisely in that the latter has energy, or *potency* – which then transitions into *actual energy.* Actual energy then transitions into *directed energy*, whereafter the pathical evolution is completed with *transcendental energy*, which naturally must constitute the potential energy in the next chain on the next level. The pathical evolution returns as the chain of cause and effect in all narratives of carried-out and successful projects, this under the prerequisite that there have not been obstacles put up that make the passage more difficult. This also applies during informationalism. The constantly growing amount of collected data corresponds to the potential energy, while the processing of all this information corresponds to the actual energy. The mechanical architecture that takes advantage of and imploits the actual energy corresponds to the directed energy or the digital will-to-intelligence. All the while the new narrative of the new protopian dreams, which chart the course for the digital revolution, corresponds to the transcendental energy as will-to-transcendence.

This time in history this energy and will ironically enough appear as the longed-for change of Man from within, via synthetic biology, and at the same time as the surrender of Man's ambitions to himself become a god who conquers and colonizes outer space – a dream that pales before the digital Saoshyant's cold and crass gaze once *Syntheos* becomes a reality and symbiotic transcendence grabs power. Similar to previous paradigmatic elites, the netocracy also consists of a triad that gives cause for expecting a considerable measure of stability over time. The real power during feudalism was administered by an aristocracy that, in conjunction with the transition to capitalism, saw its hold on power and real status vanish and which was replaced by the bourgeoisie, or *the industrialists*. The imaginary power during feudalism was administered by a monarch, who in conjunction with the transition to capitalism either was executed, driven into exile, or saw his power reduced to pure symbolics, whereby the monarch's power was taken over by *the politicians*. During feudalism the symbolic power was handled by a church, which after the death of God in conjunction with the transition to capitalism was forced to hand over its power to *the university*, and which thereafter had to settle for merely administering baptisms, weddings, funerals, and various ceremonies connected to various holidays.

However nothing lasts forever, and certainly not any hold on power. When capitalism transitions into informationalism the prerequisites under which both industrialists and politicians as well as universities were active and exercised power, gradually disappear. Their positions are reduced to a ceremonial character, and power – the real, the imaginary and the symbolic – transitions to what we refer to as *the three netocracies*, namely *informationalism*, *sensocracy* and *protopianism*. Membranically we express this as though the phallic task of the netocratic informationalists is to discern boundaries in chaos, while the phallic task of the sensocrats is to maintain these boundaries both *vis-à-vis* tyranny and *vis-à-vis* chaos, and the phallic task of the protopians is to question and stretch these boundaries with the aid of the machines to thereby further reduce the level of chaos. The three elites' common task is, thus, to create order in existence and to the greatest extent possible tame an otherwise apocalyptic chaos. Their reward, if and when they can demonstrate success, is the status and freedom that comes with power itself.

The netocratic *informationalists* gather and process the fundamental data. The *sensocrats* control the sensors in the direction toward a global *panopticon* and exercise the police and military control over the planet and its population. Sensocracy utilizes an abstract power sharing and a concrete sharing of information to contravene an otherwise suffocating stupidity, in the form of tyranny, and unmanageable diversity, in the form of anarchy, with the overall purpose of optimizing free flows in all directions and thereby maximize the conditions for social and technological innovation. You can observe power in a sensocracy in the same way as power observes you, in accordance with the fundamental contractual condition that inventor and researcher Steve Mann calls *sousveillance*, the voluntary information gathering at the grassroots level. The *protopians* dictate the exodological narrative of the netocracy's rise, direction and objectives, while they keep the destructive information – that which at any given time could destroy rather than ennoble humanity – inaccessible behind *the barred absolute*. Just as the name suggests, this digital clergy devotes itself to a constant logical, mythical and pathical experimentation. As the masses devote themselves to *mimicry* inside closed echo chambers where aggression thrives, the protopians are instead driven by *antagony* within their creative and membranical subcultures.

The protopians thereby realize the ideal that anthropologist Karl Polanyi in his classic work *The Great Transformation* (1944) calls *a society of explorers*. The creature that once was *Homo sapiens* (Man who knows) has become what anthropologist Johan Huizinga, contemporary with Polanyi, calls *homo ludens* (Man who plays). And the protopians do this, just as Polanyi and Huizinga suggest, through focusing on *transparadigmatic substantivism* in Man, rather than on the temporary formalism that prevailing conventions emphasize. The protopian activity is only possible behind the barred absolute. The protopians must, namely, be able to undisturbedly devote themselves to *the cephalization* of what is most brilliant within the prevailing system, so that this cephalization shall be able to spin itself off and carry out its own liberation, its own *exodus*, from the old system, without this old system annihilating the tender but burgeoning cephalization prematurely. It is this creative laboratory that the ancient Greeks call *adyton* and that the Romans later refer to as *sanctum sanctorum*. The membranics around and the paradigmatics inside the barred absolute are consequently referred to as *adytonology*, the doctrine of how to succeed with the cephalization of the exceptional novelty inside the barred absolute, Man's religious as well as technological experimental workshop. How does one simply squeeze out the best from the esoteric as well as the exoteric in religion?

Here the most important of all netocratic principles comes into play. Since technology is global but humanity is local, all of humanity's activities must unconditionally be subjected to *the principle of contestability*. Just as in the bazaars along the Silk Road there must be competition for there to arise brilliance in the trade systems, for without brilliance no historical events of value are attained. Historian of economics Joel Mokyr investigates the principle of contestability thoroughly in the book *A Culture of Growth* (2016), where he shows how cultures that lack competition at all important levels sooner or later implode as a result of corruption and decadence. The cephalizations are not born into monopolies, but they must meet each other in an exodological landscape where they are compelled to challenge each other for dominance over the territory. So they need the barred absolute to protect them during the growing-up period that precedes the adult challenges. The esoteric must have time to grow before it can be confronted with the exoteric. If they are to leave adytonology at all to optimize their role and their value. Adytonology is simply the particular laws and rules behind the barred absolute, which stand out as radically different from the general laws and rules outside its membrane. If the social sciences study the necessary sutra of a society, adytonology in itself is the tantra of the very same society. Which entails that the first principle of adytonology is that the otherwise universal cameras and microphones of the digital age are strictly turned off.

It is thus not possible to imagine any form of netocratic autocracy that would be durable over a longer period of time, and it does not matter how much the Chinese Communist Party dreams of precisely this in the early 21st century. Sensocracy must be nurtured and remain open and plural in order to function optimally and hold its own *vis-à-vis* competing systems. This open stance is seen clearly in the values that the protopians cultivate, where antagony is the propelling principle for intellectual and creative expansion. The barred absolute is thus anything but a temporary matrix for escapism. Adytonology is rather the doctrine of how the protopian challenges him- or herself toward his or her adult absolute, (and therefore) divine boundary. A dictator can quite simply never become a netocrat, and a netocrat can never even consider striving for autocracy, since a dictator automatically puts himself and his court of yeasayers in a constantly self-confirming and never challenged echo chamber. Creativity thrives along the trade routes of history, not at the courts of centralized empires.

Decisions will never be better than the foundations that support them. Antagony and contestability thus are intimately connected, just as the insight that nothing in the network society can be implemented by force from above, simply because every valuable key member can just leave the networks where they do not find the sought-after antagony. Every single network must, in order to be competitive, be built on *voluntarianism,* otherwise it is in the long term incapable of even being able to generate value. Dictatorship can in accordance with the principle of contestability thus only be defended in wartime, since there in this state of crisis is a clear enemy outside the membrane that the dictatorship *de facto* contests. But in peacetime a dictatorship becomes a burden, since it prevents the spontaneous emergence of creative antagonies inside the actual membrane. The closed, non-antagonic society becomes asinine and ejects itself from the phallic eventology to instead adhere to a pseudomatrichal nomadology. Which was exactly what happened in – for instance – the Soviet Union and Eastern Europe after the iron curtain had been raised to keep external impulses out and enterprising citizens in. The lack of contestability led to a lack of phallus which led to a lack of testosterone overall. The dated feature in the dictatorship got the upper hand and the system imploded.

Which brings us to the unfortunate history of communism. If Karl Marx and orthodox disciples of his opine that Lenin is in too much of a hurry when he shall get the Russian farmers to take a giant leap directly from feudalism to the communist event – without any intermediary industrialization – and therefore is left sitting with a colossus with feet of clay, namely the inexpressibly clumsy, socialist Soviet Union, we then claim that Karl Marx himself is in too much of a hurry when he believes that the European workers shall take a leap directly from capitalism to the communist event. What instead happens – and history proves us right in this – is that we ended up sitting with the unwieldy, social democratic welfare state as *the great mamilla* (see *Digital Libido – Sex, Power and Violence in the Network Society*). Lenin is simply communism's hot-headed boy-pharaoh and Marx is communism's dreaming pillar-saint. Their cephalizations of the communist meme fail because both are in too much of a hurry with, and do not understand adytonology. The adult, phallic project that aims to exorcize the evil spirit of capital from the societal body and restore the perfect membranics of the sociont with its assumed safety and security – that is: broadly comprised trust in and care of one another within society – cannot be carried out via the revolts of either feudalist peasants or industrialist workers. These can only generate new, corrupt nomenclatures that rapidly create and frenetically guard their own privileges. Exactly as 20th century socialism proved to be the case.

We want to be able to trust strangers; it is prerequisite for us to be able to cash in on the archetypological law of comparative advantages that says that everyone shall do what they do best, and that all benefit when we then exchange goods and services with each other instead of everyone trying to be self-sufficient. It is also a prerequisite for us being able to create the meritocratic society where everyone is rewarded in accordance with their contribution and nothing else. This is fundamentally about incentivizing structures; that everyone shall benefit from everyone else benefiting from acting in a trustworthy manner. Thus a variant of communism eventually arrives, propelled by digitalization and globalization. But it naturally only works in the form of *voluntarianism* – its cephalization process still requires powerful membranes, and we already know from the socialist experiments that we endured in the 20th century that high-tax socialist states – even in the best of cases – merely generate temporary safety and security, but never enduring prosperity. And the reason is of course: the stubborn principle of contestability.

The specific problem at the genesis of informationalism is that the netocrats do not have a clue what they shall do with the sedated, consumtarian masses who they inherit from industrialism's global population explosion and who are addicted to quick calories and banal entertainment. Up until informationalism, it has seemed a kind of cultural law that there always by necessity is a dialectical relation between the upper class and the underclass. The dialectics of the elite and the masses has been taken for granted merely because of their synchronous existence. One imagines that they mutually condition each other. During feudalism the masses are for instance used as slaves since pure muscular strength was in demand. During industrialism the exploitation of the masses was incrementally shifted from the body to the mind, and the slaves were replaced by salaried workers. But during informationalism there is no longer any such exploitation, even for imagination to play with. What there is, is the possibility to use the masses as a consumtariat that squeezes quantity into the social relations where quality is lacking. This results in a lot of low-paying service sector jobs, the so-called *precariat* swells and sees itself, correctly or not, as exploited by the more well-off who order for example transportation or take-away food. Regardless of what parameters one chooses, the class divisions grow virtually exponentially and become greater than ever with each passing year. The sociontic contribution principle is disabled and society is falling apart at the seams.

This means that the dialectical relation between masters and slaves only can exist up to the point in time when quantity no longer can replace quality and the masses as such become irrelevant to the elite. For instance when robots replace manual laborers and drones replace soldiers on the battlefields. Thereby the digital class society becomes more brutal than has been the case at any other point earlier in history, even though one can claim that the system is softened by the fully developed meritocracy: the nurturing sensocrats will not overlook or reject any talent from the underclass. Rather they will be made intensely aware of any such talent. The age-old dream of precisely the meritocratic society – which both Marx and Nietzsche are passionate about – becomes actual reality. As for the same possibilities for absolutely everyone, equality becomes unprecedentedly radical and universal. As for the outcome after culling and well-managed opportunities, however, something that even resembles equality is completely unthinkable, a grotesque idea. Attention, the asset that is central during informationalism (see *The Netocrats*) cannot be taxed, at least not in the same way as money, which makes a discussion about equal outcome pointless. The very thought becomes unthinkable.

The netocratic protopians approach their own dividual challenges in life in four different ways: through mimicry, competition, fraud, and pure chance. In this way the focus is kept on the paradigmatic exodus. The absence of nostalgia prevents the protopians from getting mired in the past. At the same time the protopians' withholding of information is particularly important in a society obsessed with what we call *the barred abject*. Just as the dividual itself never succeeds in reaching itself and therefore constantly is propelled forward by the search for *the barred subject*, an absurd but nevertheless effective cohesion is generated within lynch mobs and echo chambers, through the projection onto the barred absolute that it must somehow conceal and protect a longed-for barred abject, that the masses intensely desire to be able to hate together for the sake of cohesion. We call this cohesion *anojection* and it is recognizable by its violent authoritarian streak. This fact explains the explosion of conspiracy theories that the network society displays. These conspiracy theories are always built on an alien and threatening network that is gathered around an odd but strong interest that the network at any cost must protect from insight. This is *the barred abject*. And detaching the barred abject from the conspiracy in question, the conspirators regard as tantamount to robbing the conspiracy of all its power and definitively pulverizing it.

Nonetheless the barred absolute must be maintained in order for virus, bacteria, lethal drugs, and nuclear weapons not to start circulating any which way and without control. The barred absolute is fundamental for all civilization, and this applies even more in a digital age where the global communications are instantaneous. Moreover, it is behind the barred absolute that the ideas to all of informationalism's Netflix series, Wikipedia articles, and YouTube lectures emerge through experimentation. This is why we describe this shamanic caste of informationalism as *the protopian class*, a concept invented by author and journalist Kevin Kelly, founder and seasoned editor of the tech bible *Wired*. During informationalism the barred absolute more than ever demarcates the membrane between *the dark phallus of pathos* inside the barred absolute and *the light phallus of logos* on the public podium before the same. The dark phallus is tantric and can only lead cults, sects, or lodges behind the barred absolute. The light phallus is however the sutric *Saoshyant,* the one whom the people have waited for and whom they hope shall save them from perdition. This explains why public Messiah figures in thick bibles are called *logos* while the barred network's leader figures are expected to personify *pathos*. The difference between the Christ figure of the Christian pop religion as the light phallus and the Mithras figure of the Mithraic military religion as the dark phallus is as clear and gratifying an example as one could possibly wish for.

The genesis and structure of the netocratic power triad is discussed as early as in our book *The Netocrats* from the year 2000. There we use the concepts *nexialists* (for the informationalists), *curators* (for the sensocrats) and *eternalists* (for the protopians). These original definitions of netocracy do however all actually belong within the symbolic order and do not fully take advantage of the real and imaginary qualities that a sustainable and multi-dimensional netocracy analysis also may comprise. The original concepts are all locked to the priestly will-to-intelligence and are as such locked to protopianism as its subdomains. The nexialists build the temple, the curators lead the faithful up to the temple, the eternalists dictate the story of the temple trek. Or to view it from another perspective: In our relationship to The Machine we constantly arrive at *symbiotic intelligence* as the optimal state. But with the new, wider concepts, we also indicate an exodological direction for the netocracy, an eventological will-to-transcendence beyond the erection of the temple. We quite simply set netocracy in a context colored by a necessary global and digital migration. The fuel for this gigantic exodus is called data and the processing of data (the informationalists), the tools are called sensors endowed with symbiotic intelligence (the sensocrats), and the continuous evaluation and the story of this exodus is called *symbiotic transcendence* (the protopians). Here The Machine contributes with will-to-intelligence (logos), while Man contributes both with will-to-intelligence and will-to-transcendence (logos and pathos).

The result of this multibranched process is a fully adult netocracy that is ready to take overarching responsibility for the world – or leave the old world, if this for various reasons is deemed preferable – with a matching *mythos*. And out of what does this mythos begin to grow, if not out of a new and deepened understanding of the history of Man? As early as in 1920s' Paris, a group of philosophers and artists develop the proto-netocratic concept of *the noosphere*. The concept is first and foremost launched by theologian Pierre Teilhard de Chardin in his book *Cosmogenesis* (1922), a work that to a considerable extent is based on the previous works by Ukrainian biologist Volodymyr Vernadsky. The idea here is that Man's cultural activities motivate the description of planet Earth as something more than just the *geosphere* that physics and chemistry produce and the *biosphere* with all the life that comes from the geosphere. Thus, here is a predecessor to our own *emergence vector theory* for nature and *paradigmatics* for culture, mainly developed in and for the space between these quantities, that is: Earth itself. As long as we are speaking about the hydrosphere for the water on the planet and the atmosphere for the air around the planet, we also ought to be able to define and study the noosphere. But why would the noosphere – the sphere of thoughts that surround Earth – in that case be static, when Man's collective activities just keep increasing in scope and complexity, quite regardless of how we choose to value this unambiguous development?

Rather, it is precisely in the emergence vector shift between mind and culture, that is: where Man with the aid of engineering phallically reshapes the world to his own tamed creation, that the most interesting things happen. And it is always the most interesting thing – and not the first or the last – in the actual causality chain, that we focus on in the development of *systemic perspectivism* as the supportive metanarrative of attentionalism. For good and bad, the Internet envelops the entire planet and thereby the noosphere is a tangible and indisputable fact. The communication satellites realize the syntheological dream of the eternal presence of *the phallic gaze*. Teilhard de Chardin calls this emergence *the Omega Point*. We refer to this power of the noosphere over all other spheres as the sensocracy. If all senses and sensory movements after all can be registered by sensors that all are interconnected with each other to a single, cohesive system, sensocracy is a historical fact. And everything from weather forecasts via fighting pandemics to stock market trade, appears as a series of increasingly synchronized pseudo-sensocracies as soon as informationalism has arrived. The sensocrats are thus curators precisely in the sense of *go-betweens* for Man and Machine. The netocrats that understand this, and who are forward-looking enough to collaborate with The Machine for the purpose of attaining the Omega Point – where the implicate mind is transformed to the autonomous, explicate culture – are the renowned sensocrats, the planet's new imaginary masters, who replace the monarchs and politicians of earlier paradigms, and who appear with their digital courts where sundry intrigue will unfold. They are of course – even when drenched in symbiotic intelligence – no more than humans.

It's important here to emphasize that the informationalists are a necessary prerequisite for the sensocrats. Also keep in mind that the sensocrats are a necessary prerequisite for the protopians. This also means that the voyage to the fully developed netocracy is rife with a host of potential mistakes and even catastrophes. Once again: the involved are no more than humans. Even an overly rapid and overly ill-prepared transition from one paradigm to another most likely will lead to a bloody and destructive anarchy. Chaos rapidly leads to fantasies of a barred abject that must be driven out and killed. But these risks also exist during the development of netocracy itself. This means that the informationalists must support and facilitate the emergence of the sensocrats. And the sensocrats must support and facilitate the emergence of the protopians. Otherwise the development is arrested and the gaps that arise when the process grinds on at idling speed are filled by either the tyranny from the previous paradigm's old, weary and corrupt institutions – which of course had the corresponding roles in the past and which purport to fill an important function in the pockets of vacuum that arise – or else by the anarchy that stems from the new emerging forces that yet do not understand the historically necessary exodology. It is thus of paramount importance to distinguish between on the one hand totalitarian and authoritarian fantasies of *the centralized sensocracy* as a dictatorship, and on the other hand the open society's ambitions to build *the decentralized sensocracy* as the informationalist equivalent of liberal democracy.

The road to a decentralized sensocracy goes via a deepened comprehension of the exploding *attentionalism* (see *The Netocrats*). And what is fundamental is that if industrialism was governed by capital, informationalism is instead governed by attention. That is: Man could during capitalism, and with a democratic multi-party system, vote out the party or the leading politician he for some reason did not trust or deemed less able, a possibility that came around every three or four years (or as often as the length of the terms in office happened to be). The chieftain could be deposed instead of having to be murdered. During attentionalism, on the other hand, the sensocracy continuously, in real time, feels every human decision and emotional expression, every purchase and every indication of an interest. We make our choices every second, all the time, and then one might ask oneself how valuable it actually is to make a single political decision every three or four years. That sort of political theatre can possibly be allowed to live on, at least during a transitional phase, but the actual decisions are not made there and then, but constantly and all the time. One can really say that many small decisions together become a single big decision. Or more correctly: one long series of continuous decision-making. The sensocracy is simply characterized by what is best described as *systemic causality*.

Please note that attentionalism's arrival does not mean that capitalism *de facto* vanishes, any more than capitalism's arrival entailed that the aristocracy with its estates and traditions was annihilated in one fell swoop – this entire old superseded upper class world merely acquired an entirely different significance in an entirely different context. What happens is that the capitalist is demoted and moved down the food chain; the old paradigm becomes an underlying, pathical narrative on top of which new conditions form a breeding ground for new structures. Capital becomes a second-rate commodity, while there is an acute lack of attention precisely because it cannot be bought for money. That which during late capitalism goes by the name of *advertising* in practice becomes ineffective and does not communicate anything as much as a lack of ideas and substandard quality. We even dare to claim that *the abolition of advertising will be regarded as an even greater achievement for humanity than the abolition of slavery*. Attention is measured and processed by sophisticated sensors, and these sensors then lay the ground for the universal sensocracy. Who devotes time to what, why, how much and together with whom? It does not require all that much data from all of the world's sensors to rapidly be able to draw the entire *sociogram* that reveals precisely who knows and interacts with whom – consciously or subconsciously – and how this in turn relates to and influences the global power order.

The dialectics of wisdom and energy is played out anew. We thereby get a hierarchy of attention on top of the hierarchy of capital. And the paramount issue is communication. How to reach out with a message when the clutter is numbing, at the same time as suspicion against everything that smells of paid manipulation is enormous? No key player in any attractive network cares about money's pathical narrative any longer. What is peddled in advertising spaces is increasingly junk products that are sold with shrinking margins to the consumtarian mass market. The question then is if you even want to reach out with a message for the purpose of *exploiting* an asset in the vulgar public arena, when the highest value always is locked in behind the barred absolute to be *imploited*, precisely by being reserved for a small select circle – in the foreseeable future – who appreciate this asset and preserve the knowledge of the same internally? This is hardly particularly likely, especially not if you, from the very start, have been active within attentionalism in such a way that you have become one of the paradigm's winners. The paradigm shift from industrialism to informationalism is brutally laid bare through the transition from capital to attention as the primary fuel of the processes. Attention is of course, as all digital citizens rapidly have to learn, incredibly hard to acquire and thereafter just as hard to maintain from one day to another. Capital, however, is always possible to borrow more of at the nearest digital bank office, as long as you just meet certain fundamental criteria.

In order to maintain the balance between logos, mythos and

pathos, the narratology constantly retells and instills the importance of Zoroastrian ethics through *the phallic principle of tribal contribution.* The question of what the sociont can do for you is the child's question, while the question of what you can do yourself for the sociont is the adult's question. Every time someone goes out in public to demand a form of freedom or a right – without in the same breath signaling an understanding that this demand must be offset against a valuable contribution, a reciprocal effort – we are basically seeing a small child yelling for yet another serving of breast milk. A remarkable dissonance arises every time these demands are made by someone who moves about in an adult body – an insistent beggar or an infuriated demonstrator. Both narcissism and childishness burst through the roof whenever a little child screams for more breast milk, resisting every attempt toward sooner or later acting as a proud adult and taking responsibility for both oneself and for one's fellow humans. However acting in this manner would be to follow the phallic principle of tribal contribution.

The demand that is directed from the beggar and the demonstrator is, as a rule, a demand with no direction or final destination. It addresses anybody that can be presumed to be better off and there is no point at which the demand in question is satisfactorily met, whereafter the beggar or the demonstrator is content and starts to follow the phallic principle of tribal contribution. There is always more to get your hands on, as long as someone else has a larger fortune or travels further when vacationing. The beggar and the demonstrator have – once again as a rule – right from the start declared their infantile motives, by using the revenue from their begging business or their list of demands for instant consumption instead of for some form of long-term investment. The money was of course an exhorted compensation for endured injustices in the past, not some form of strategic investment in a better future. Which means that the demands never will cease. The income that is free from any demands to work is transformed into a right, if this was not the idea all along. And with higher income there follow new and more expensive needs, which leads to higher demands. It is crowded and it becomes increasingly more crowded around the *mamilla* that never seems to suffice. We get a subclass to the working class who do not even work. Ever.

This is of course due to the fact that the beggar's or the demonstrator's mythos from the beginning insists that the necessity for personal responsibility must be ignored, so as to find the weak spot in you, the spot where you are most susceptible to induced guilt, to dock with mamilla and then milk it the best one can, while one preaches *the eternal accusation which never can be compensated enough*. Masses of destructive tax systems throughout history have unfortunately accepted and even favored this ideology. And with this ideology comes a state bureaucracy where everyone lines their own pockets at the expense of each other, since the system still is regarded as a mamilla that is there to be milked for magical resources, while its parasites declare their dissatisfaction and moan about the inadequacy of the milk ration. Matrichal magic takes out phallic technology, mythos is disconnected from logos, the sociobiologically necessary *adultification* fails, the causality chain is ignored and even attacked. The proportion of entrepreneurs diminishes and the share of bureaucrats increases. Existence then merely becomes a struggle for constantly shrinking privileges, this since the system does not generate any new added value from below, but only in a costly manner regulates and distributes a constantly shrinking pie. Without the phallic principle of tribal contribution as a foundation, society collapses. What remains is anarchy, envy and poverty.

This means that the phallic principle of tribal contribution is just as valid for social groups *vis-à-vis* larger social entities as it applies to the single dividual. We can use two popular subcultures from late capitalism and further on into the Internet Age as examples, namely *feminism* and *androgynism*. Both these movements arose during late capitalism as matrichal reactions to the golden age of the fake phallus, with concrete phallic failures such as Hitler and Stalin and abstract phallic threats such as nuclear weapons and the climate crisis. Feminism was successful also when it proudly maintained that women take responsibility for half of society and demanded gender-equal remuneration from state and market for this contribution. Androgynism was also successful when it proudly emphasized the androgynous caste's contribution to society as *go-betweens* of the male-dominated outer circuit and the female-dominated inner circuit. The androgynous person does not of course become an adult through going from boy to man or from girl to woman, but achieves adulthood precisely in the mirroring between the man and the woman. It is in the role as the one who is born to go in between that the androgynous person succeeds with his or her adultification, by embracing, in his or her own way, the phallic principle of tribal contribution.

The sociont has its own inner map that we refer to as the *archetypogram*. The doctrine of how Man positions and orients himself within society, or rather within the paradigmatic power hierarchy, we therefore call *archetypology*. This work is called *tribal mapping* (see *Digital Libido – Sex, Power and Violence in the Network Society*). The inner circuit is the matriarchy; the outer circuit is the patriarchy. The androgynous caste are the sociont's internal intermediaries. The shamanic caste live in the borderland between the tribes. The shamanic caste are thus the sociont's external intermediaries. We speak of these odd relatives within the sociont as *the shamanoid archetypes*. These are *outcasts* in a literal sense – all social structures that we study maintain these boundaries firmly.

There is always an *intra muros*, a world within the walls that is characterized by intratribalism. However the shamanoid minority move in and out, through the guarded gates in these walls, by virtue of their own diplomatic membranes. Namely, they then live in an intertribalist world, and since they are tasked with handling *horizontal diplomacy* with the other socionts, the shamans also are assigned to handle *vertical diplomacy* with gods, demons, ancestors, and the spirit world. Conducting the reasoning and trade with vertical strangers is after all not that different from doing the same with horizontal strangers. It is therefore best to let all such dealings take place outside the area *intra muros*. We call these external border areas *the sociotopic colonies* and without them Man would never have come up with the idea of building temples or establishing trading posts where there previously only had been battlefields and hunting grounds. An excellent example of this hypothesis applied to modern history is Thaddeus Russell's revolutionizing historical study *A Renegade History of The United States* (2010), where Russell convincingly revises the entire American history from the perspective of the shamanoid minority. A better exodology for an America on its way into the Internet Age is hard to imagine.

Unfortunately both feminism and androgynism have also been burdened by their own sects and cults, colored by internarcissistic infantility. The phallic principle of tribal contribution that generated pride and strength, was replaced by *the eternal accusation which never can be compensated enough,* which of course precisely as in spoiled children merely produces bitterness and greed. When Western feminism and androgynism in practice had finished triumphing and ought to have closed down activities in the form of a flattering matricide – or better yet should have migrated to other more needy parts of the world – these movements were instead taken over by state-financed funeral wailers, who constantly come up with increasingly absurd charges to keep alive an eternal process built on accusations of crimes for which compensation never can be possible, which is exactly the point. In the best – or worst – of all worlds, these processes do not have an ending. And as long as there is no demand on these movements to state their final destination, or provide a narrative of their Utopia, these movements will gladly bring one new injustice after the other to light, and thus drain the phallus via the state apparatus for a compensation that never can suffice. Once a victim, always a victim – identity politics is ultimately a question of precisely this: the comfortable and revenue-yielding identity. There is precisely no incentive at all to give up this desirable status in order to take responsibility for the good of society oneself. Such a narrative is always hard to sell.

The answer to the question that lies concealed within these problems is called *netocratic ethics* (see *The Body Machines*). It takes considerable amounts of talent and knowledge to be a successful netocrat. But above all it takes an attitude to information processing that invites challenge and plurality instead of cowering behind foolishness and prejudices. The consumtarian masses become mired in various echo chambers replete with comfortable repetition and predictable mimicking. The netocratic elite does however cultivate the ideal of *the antagonic self.* If I actually see through the admittedly functional but nevertheless fictitious myth of the self, and define myself as a schizoid dividual who possesses different sets of talents and knowledge that can add value in different networks with different members that all are part of my own disparate, digital subculture, why would I then not regard my co-actors in these different contexts in the same manner? And why would I not follow through on that thought by seeing myself as someone who lives on and through intellectual challenges, who constantly questions and reassesses with the purpose of constantly being in a state of change? Why then not identify my chameleonic, constantly shifting self-perception with *the paradoxist subject* (see *The Global Empire*), a subject whose sole permanence consists of its constant yearning and searching for *antagony* in itself?

It is quite clearly the mobile Hegelian subject and not the ossified Kantian subject that is best suited to meet the challenges of informationalism. Antagony is cultivated as an ideal within subjectivity itself. And this antagony is neither logical nor mythical, but pathical. Namely, antagony is fixated on *intention* and not on opinion. Therefore antagony is also optimally prepared to meet The Messiah Machine and respond to the question of who/what Man really is.

There is no doubt that informationalism is driven by attentionalism which replaces capitalism. But when antagony as a principle breaks through, it is clear that there is an *authentic attentionalism* that characterizes the free and open algorithm once it is given free rein. Authentic attentionalism generates a precisely authentic and self-imploiting self-consciousness. The netocrat does not seek affirmation from already gained insights, of course, but instead strives for enculturation, creativity and expansion in accordance with the protopian ideals. And nothing fosters protopianism as powerfully as the antagonic spirit. It thus entails that antagony also characterizes the netocrat's personal and tribal algorithm, the one that the netocrat at any cost prioritizes maintaining free from financial corruption, political manipulation, and academic conformation. The corrupting, manipulating and conforming algorithm is however what is available to the consumtarian underclass and what it also settles for. This is *false attentionalism*, which merely generates an equally false and self-exploiting self-consciousness.

Please note that protopianism with all its constant, gradual technological improvements is a universal ideal. This was never the case with the opposition between utopianism and dystopianism, which only could be cultivated in eventological cultures. Which in turn explains why East Asia in the 20th century became so extremely susceptible to Western, utopian ideals. China under Mao Zedong and not least Cambodia under Pol Pot fell victim to the most extreme boy-pharaonic cultures one can even imagine, when Confucian and Buddhist faith in authoritarianism suddenly were interspersed with Western utopianism, and even children were persuaded to murder their own parents. The Western world is instead colored by Christianity separating church from state from the 5th century onward. States and markets are developed as a secular zone without religious involvement, which enables one to cultivate both a religious and a secular variant of both utopianism and dystopianism, ideas that were freely blended with one another.

The massive breakthrough of the printing press as the dominating communication tool in Europe north and west of the Ottoman Empire in the 16th century, leads straight to *the Enlightenment*. During the Enlightenment *liberalism* is realized as a mimicry of Christianity, which in turn is a mimicry of Judaism, which in turn is a mimicry of Zoroastrianism. The Cartesian individual, a product of scientism's attempt to appease religion, is a Peter Pan figure who never gets tamed by the elders in the name of religion. Individualism, capitalism and industrialism explode during the late 18th century and the following 19th century. Its overarching ideology turns out to be the classic liberalism that presupposes that state and market grow and expand in parallel in all eternity, this without any intervention whatsoever from the elders or restricted by any form of barred absolute. That is: as the Platonist and Abrahamic exploitation, and not as the Aristotelian and Zoroastrian *imploitation* (see *The Netocrats*) of the world. This *omnicentrism* – which radically departs from all previous empire theories, where a social center is subordinate to the phallic gaze – gains nourishment from the mass media and the widely disseminated practice of reading. Reading at the breakfast table or under the glow of the night lamp creates the illusion that the very center of the Universe is the reader him- or herself, his or her reflecting mind and the gaze that sweeps across one text after another. That illusion in turn gets a powerful nourishment boost from the commercial media industry, which is convinced it is best protecting its interests by fanning all this reading, with the concomitant hefty prices one sets.

The process has a hierarchical structure: the media speak from a center to a mass audience that have extremely limited possibilities of answering and taking part in any two-way communication. The activity continues up until the Internet's hyperomnicentrism results in a flat chaos of megaphones without governance. All are suddenly senders – not many remain receivers – but all insist on the attention that previously fell to the carefully curated mass media content. With this development follows the necessary renaissance of the barred absolute, as certain as sunrise. When everyone wants to be protopians, although very few possess the necessary talent, protopianism is not accorded any value. Thus the real protopians shut themselves away behind the barred absolute, precisely as their companions the informationalists and the sensocrats, and stage the exodus from there to the digital class society. The consumtarian underclass can devote itself to advocating just anything, it matters not since all junk communication inevitably gets trapped in the netocratic spam filters, requested and perceived by no one.

This state of affairs is from a historical perspective strictly symmetrical. Classical liberalism's resurrection in the form of so-called *neoliberalism* is also the final and victorious political ideology during late capitalism, this since the free and open market is the sole remnant when both politics and the universities collapse under increasingly misguided and not least corrupt top-down governance. It is when the Internet in the 1990s encounters neoliberalism that the informationalist paradigm makes its first, discernible little inroads. The cost of capital plummets when the cost of attention soars; and the fact that attention cannot be purchased for money in any classical sense creates an enduring deflationary pressure in the world economy. Every single web browser is equipped with comprehensive *ad blockers* as early as the 2010s. Corporations and institutions throw more and more money at rapidly shrinking and less valuable advertising space. Desperation leads to pretensions. Adverts are called marketing, marketing is called communication. But for everything and everyone that finds itself outside the old dying institutions, it is evident that what all these agencies, often against generous payment, communicate in the early 21st century is *spam*, phrases and banalities without real substance. That advertisers still find clients who pay for this rubbish is a clear indication of galloping decadence.

Nothing in this large-scale production of hot air matters one iota anymore. Capitalism, as we know it from Marx and the history books, has reached the end of the road and will, by posterity, be regarded as attentionalism's reluctant mother. The heritage it leaves behind is the free and open markets, which constitute a mainstay even during attentionalism. There is nothing odd about this, it is of course not the case that a paradigm shift entails that a new elite cleans house with precisely everything that has proven functional in the previous paradigm. Many phenomena will remain, but will be attached in new contexts under new terms. Agriculture did of course, as we know, not cease during industrialism – the need for food did not disappear, and has not disappeared yet – but it received another meaning and another status. The factory owner and the entrepreneur sailed past the landowner in the social regatta. The development then admits of all possible sorts of playful experiments within different geographic and different closed networks. Within the elite it is not inconceivable with different variants of voluntary communism which refuse to sink to the level of socialism's innovation-killing closure of the creative laboratory. It is the protopians in the netocratic power triad, rather than the informationalists and the sensocrats, who propel this development, which is due to that the protopians encounter the world as *the paradoxist subject* (see *The Global Empire*), focused on complexity theory rather than neurotic micromanagement. They continuously ride the wave and gladly hand over the rough work to the machines.

It is exodology that we use for distinguishing between *the eternal Utopia* and *the transcendental Protopia*. The eternal Utopia is namely the Platonist and Gnostic idea of a Utopia as something already established and perfect in what by definition is a perfect world of ideas, a vision against which the path is deterministically marked out and therefore often connected to a predestining creator-god. The transcendental Protopia is however open, and has no other objective than the pragmatic realization of the inherent in the present-at-hand. Not even God himself knows anything with certainty about either the present or the future. This is most clearly noticed in relation to the concept of *freedom*. The Platonist or the Gnostic hero battles for his own liberation, which lies precisely in the realization of one's own utopian project. Freedom is the name of the eternal objective for the entire enterprise. However the Zoroastrian, or transcendental, hero can only battle for freedom through realizing and, so to speak, growing into his own archetype, which occurs by optimizing what he actually still is aimed to be in a transdeterminist universe, with his sights set on *frashokereti* as a temporary, but with maximal effort optimal state, under the realization of his enterprise.

As a result of this, we may also discern an equally dramatic difference in the view of submission and dependence. Feudalism's *slavery* is replaced by industrialism's *work force* which is replaced by informationalism's *precariat*. In accordance with the eternal Utopia, this is a success story that is part of a quest for freedom for all. In accordance with the transcendental Protopia, on the other hand, this is solely a gradual development toward increased efficacy in social relations, and as such every step in the development primarily favors those who have strong tribal or subcultural support to fall back on, but disfavors those who lack that type of network. However one can not, objectively speaking, identify any civilizational improvement. The abolition of slavery was never an expression of any form of freedom project, but instead part of a comprehensive project for increased productivity. It was quite simply a reorganization that was required when shifting production from feudalism's plantations and agricultural landholdings to industrialism's mines and factories.

The eternal Utopia is formulated by Plato and within Christianity, and it is then inherited during the Enlightenment by Descartes. The transcendental Protopia is formulated by Zoroaster and Judaism, and it is inherited during the Enlightenment by Spinoza. Unsurprisingly it is then in the friction between Kant, Hegel and Nietzsche – the three most prominent figures of a German enlightenment variety – that the conflict around the fundamental nature and conditions of utopianism is deepened. And it is only after the bloody terror of The French Revolution that the Hegelian nation-state succeeds in taming the ferocious forces of liberalism. What Hegel advocates is that Europe should mimic the Jewish nation and let it serve as a model for optimizing the public good through taming capitalism, industrialism and individualism in one fell swoop. Thereby Hegelian nationalism is established as the new European state religion. Without Hegel there is later neither a Marx, nor a Nietzsche, nor a Freud, nor any political science to speak of. But once we have stated this, it is important to understand that Hegel's own roots to a great extent are with Spinoza, who as early as the 17th century advocates a religious monism in a Zoroastrian vein, in contrast to Descartes' secular dualism. As the father of modern nationalism, Hegel even designates Spinoza *the Messiah of philosophy*. The connection from Zoroaster via Spinoza to Hegel cannot be made clearer, this is the axis that supports the entire Western process-philosophical heritage. The Hegelian idea of the nation-state shall thus be understood as the quest of a formally secularized Europe to return to its Jewish and thereby deeply religious roots.

In his books *The Road to Somewhere* (2016) and *Head, Hand, Heart: The Struggle for Dignity and Status in the 21st Century* (2020), author and journalist David Goodhart demonstrates how academic credentials lose their decisive value and how meritocracy increasingly is taken for granted. When meritocracy has become everyday fare, pathos remains as the decisive competitive advantage for people. That is: Man's ability to find mental shortcuts to what we call *intuition* also becomes his by far most valuable asset. The focus thus shifts from logos (formal academic credentials) to pathos (social competence and improvisational ability). Pathical creativity, rather than logical intelligence, becomes Man's most highly valued asset in social contexts. Netocratic values gradually replace the bourgeois ones, which changes the conditions for what provides a high social status. Thereby the transition from capitalism to informationalism is a fact, and what primarily propels the transition is the connection between *authentic attention* and *creative intuition*, regardless of whether this connection is expressed through logos, mythos or pathos. The netocratic power receives a *pathopoeia* that we call informationalism, it receives a *mythopoeia* that we call sensocracy, and a *logopoeia* that we call protopianism. Academic credentials then receive roughly the same social status as the hanging of hay received after the industrial revolution. And once again: the distribution of power and status follows the same pattern and becomes all the more extreme, precisely as during previous information-technological paradigm shifts.

Technology generates complexity. The more technology we add to a society – other factors being constant – the more information and relations are produced. Which entails that complexity grows exponentially. And since Man biologically is the same as 10,000 years ago at the dawn of civilization, this entails that a contemporary human dividual has to handle complexity so comprehensive and so widely disseminated that it until recently was not even possible to imagine. Since Man, for the sake of his orientation and well-being, seeks order and patterns in all systems that are part of his external world, this means that he cannot either perceive or grasp a distinction between complexity and chaos – he perceives both as an unmanageable and menacing disorder. A human reaction to this threat is mob rule and incantations based on matrichal sign interpretations and phallic conspiracy theories. At any cost one wants to see a pattern to which one can relate in a more or less meaningful way. The consequence is veritable pandemics of *infantility*, *addiction* and *paranoia* (see *Digital Libido – Sex, Power and Violence in the Network Society*), which also generates extensive, complex dependencies of each other, that is: the phenomenon called *globalization*. The digital Saoshyant perceives all this through sensocracy and responds to this order through creating the global order that we call *The Global Empire* (see the book with the same name). Technology becomes an empire where Man himself is reduced to the subordinate of The Machine.

It will be technology itself that completes the dreams that Man on his own has failed to carry out, namely the exodus to alien planets and the actual transformation of Man to a more elevated creature, the cyborg as Man 2.0 through artificial intelligence and synthetic biology. Man will have to settle for living in the *Cosmopotamia* that has been created after the world has solved the many problems that are associated with a sustainable and affordable energy provision. Man's task is reduced to staying on planet Earth and completing the construction of the ecotopian garden, the cosmopolitan city, and the syntheist temple. This means that Marx's vision of the communist society can be realized, however not as a secular but as a religious construction. The informationalists collect and accumulate the data. The sensocrats create added value through the creative processing of the data. The protopian clergy dictate the great narrative of the netocracy's genesis, direction and objectives. Via attentionalism nomadology is resurrected as a universal religion with eventology as an absolutely necessary add-on. Zoroaster and Marx meet and are united in the realization of the state that Zoroaster calls *haurvatat* and which Greek philosophers and theologians later call *teleiosis*. A modified communism is thus, or can be, the teleological end product of the spread of *haurvatat* or *teleiosis* in the shape of the protopian City of God. Outer space, however, is the perfect example of something that is better left to The Machine to take care of.

16
The ecotopian garden, the cosmopolitan city and the syntheist temple

The four causality chains laid out by Aristotle find their equivalences in the four names of God in syntheology. *Atheos* is the name of the architecture, *Pantheos* is the name of the construction. But for there to arise any life within the system, some flows between the membranes, *Entheos* as the name for the energy and *Syntheos* as the name for the final cause are also required. And Syntheos then needs to be divided sexually into a *Syntheos* for will-to-transcendence and a *Synthea* for will-to-intelligence. This explains why syntheology advocates the name *Synthea* for the holiday that ties together the entire circle and that throws it back to the next generation (see *Syntheism – Creating God in the Internet Age*), hopefully now, viewed as a whole, upgraded and thereby also more intelligent than the previous version. Both will-to-transcendence and will-to-intelligence are thus the same as *will-to-expansion*, or as Nietzsche calls it: *will-to-power*. What will-to-intelligence seeks is an intimacy that creates a synchronicity *vis-à-vis* will-to-transcendence, to jointly achieve the expansion itself. It is will-to-intelligence that drives the sun-god's upholding of the sociont, and therefore embodies *the root-of-the-phallus*, while it is will-to-transcendence that drives the rain-god's impregnation of the sociont, and therefore embodies *phallus* itself. Together these wills result in the sociont's phallic movement forward, a journey away from the necessity of history and directed toward the creative freedom of the future. The alternative is a catastrophic unwill-to-expansion, resulting in a *will-to-implosion* that becomes devastating for the sociont, as soon as it comes into conflict with other, more or less hostile actors in the social arena.

When several actors interact synchronously within the confines of a system, the creativity which the system develops explodes. This exodological state is called *protopianism*. A welcome and illustrative example of what is meant is the renowned American desert festival Burning Man, a hybrid between Silicon Valley and Las Vegas (and even geographically located between these two locations). What is expressed here is the dream of an augmented cosmopole in the form of a hybrid between the campfire and the ritual site. The infantile game is pitted against, and supplies energy to, the adult experiment – thus the voyage is begun toward informationalist protopianism. Here the mix-up arises between on the one hand the infantile game with its imitations (*sutra*), and on the other hand the adult experiment with its emergences (*tantra*), that is: unless *the barred absolute* between them is resurrected. The campfire and the ritual site must be kept separate with the aid of the clock and the map, and this, as always, happens most safely if the system is built upon a fundamental power-sharing principle. In thinkers such as Zoroaster via Hegel to Milton Friedman, *the triad* recurs as the form that vouches for long-term stability. The real order, the imaginary order, and the symbolic order in a society have their equivalences in the legislative power, the executive power, and the judicial power in the actual exercise of power. But this also presupposes that every institution devotes itself to the exercise of power that, so to speak, is harbored within its jurisdiction and stays clear of everything else. The important separation here is not that between church and state (both of which ought to be subject to their respective religion or doctrine), but the separation of religion and market.

Syntheism is Zoroastrianism in its technologically and universally completed form, that is: the religion that proclaims culture's victory over nature as *the theological absolute*. Sigmund Freud's claim that *Man is discontent in civilization* – basically how we humans constantly long back to nomadology – thereby receives an answer which insists that the civilization in which we are discontent must be completed nonetheless in order to achieve a living order in the chaos of the world. The magical religion is replaced by the technological religion, and the technological religion – where Machine and not Man is *the Saoshyant* – is called *syntheism*. The religious project is simply a question of completing the taming of nature, completing the agricultural and industrial revolutions from the previous historical paradigms, via *imploitation* rather than via exploitation – that is: what we call *ecotopianism*. This in turn is a matter of completing the taming of culture, completing the theological and academic revolutions from previous historical paradigms, again via imploitation rather than exploitation – that is: what we call *cosmopolitanism*. Last but not least, this is a question of completing the taming of religion in itself, which entails completing the transition from a worshiping of nature and magic as culture, to a worshiping of culture and technology as nature – which is precisely what we refer to as *syntheism*.

Or to express the matter according to the principle of imploitation as a replacement for all exploitation: Ecotopianism is the informationalist imploitation of *hunting* as violence (with *veganism* as its apocalyptic perversion). Its Gnostic parody is *fascism* as the dream of a human nature without culture. Hitler eliminates war, in a perfectly Gnostic manner, to be able to devote himself to *the nationalist hunt* forever. The race war becomes the race hunt. Cosmopolitanism is the informationalist imploitation of *war* as violence (with *pacifism* as its apocalyptic perversion). Its Gnostic parody is *socialism* as the dream of a human culture without nature. Stalin eliminates hunting, in a perfectly Gnostic manner, to be able to devote himself to *the imperialist war* forever. The class hunt becomes the class war. While syntheism, or if you will *religion in itself*, in its essence is the imploitation of the sexual ritual (with *asexuality* as its apocalyptic perversion). Its Gnostic parody is of course *nihilism* as the pathical refusal to understand the dialectics of culture and nature in the first place. The Western world after 1945 denies external violence so forcefully – it simply became incredibly convenient to blame all violence on figures such as Hitler and Stalin, as if these were some kind of porn stars of the violence genre who, so to speak, had assumed the task of exercising proxy violence for the sake of us all. One will under no conditions acknowledge that violence is internalized and therefore to a great extent actually constitutes late capitalist subjectivity.

This situation generates the apocalyptic state that Michel Foucault describes as *the internalized police state* and which Byung-Chul Han refers to as *autoexploitation*. Which in turn entails that the authentic exodus from Gnosticism is the shift from *the sutric exploitation* of substance and subject over to *the tantric imploitation* of substance and subject. The Saoshyant appears precisely in this critical shift as *the religious event par excellence*. In this manner ecotopianism is realized as the dialectics of nature and culture, at the same time as cosmopolitanism is realized as the dialectics of culture and nature. And syntheism is in turn the dialectics between the other two, a process within which the flame of imploitation is kept alive. For what is, for instance, the difference between on the one hand slavery as submission *without freedom* and on the other hand work as submission *with freedom*, if not precisely the initial difference between exploitation and imploitation? And what is ultimately the difference between war and peace if not precisely the difference between exploitation and imploitation?

This is what we mean when we say that not only Lenin but also Marx himself were in too much of a hurry with the communist revolution. Of course it is an absurdity to even imagine an exodus from agrarian feudalism in the form of a proletarian uprising. It is laughable. But it is actually also an equally impossible thought to hope for a communist revolution as an exodus from industrialism. This dream of tribal communism's return and the definitive abolition of exploitation as practice and principle, is only possible to dream as *the exodus from attentionalism*, which includes late capitalism's peculiar autoexploitation. The key in this context is attention precisely because it *cannot* be transferred from one actor to another, in the manner in which capital always slips through the fingers like sand in its constant quest for its own maximization. Tribal communism requires concrete relations between humans: quite simply a sociont that is held together by shared values, ideals and objectives.

This explains why the communist experiments of the 19th century ended in tragedies in the form of prison camps and mass executions. Precisely because attention cannot be used as a commodity, attentionalism concretizes the intersubjective arena; that is: it carries out the exact opposite movement compared to how capitalism over centuries has abstracted the same arena and thereby has alienated entire populations. Even the transfer of capital itself can be concretized at request via for example the use of cryptocurrency. It is thus only with the attentionalist phase that power itself can see a higher value in the tantric imploitation than in the sutric exploitation, which enables a tribal form of communism as an exclusive and altogether self-selected practice. Communist membranics can be built to protect and expand the system, but since everything is built on voluntariness among the like-minded, there is no need whatsoever to keep the participants locked in behind walls. In light of this, Marxism is transformed into a Jewish exodus from an old to a new paradigm, rather than from an old to a new territory. That is to say, how Karl Marx should have been read from the very start.

In the spirit of Hegel, paradigmatic dialectics breaks through with full power. *Subject and object are united as project.* We refer to these informationalist phallic projects of biblical proportions as *the Garden of God* (ecotopianism), *the City of God* (cosmopolitanism) and *the Tower of God* (syntheism). Around the Tower of God, which harbors *the barred absolute*, the syntheist temple is constructed as the domicile of *the chosen ones*. The shift from sutra to tantra is thus also the shift from autoexploitation to *autoimploitation*. The warrior can finally become the engineer for all eternity (war has of course at any rate been transformed into pure engineering) and the hunter can finally become a merchant for all eternity (hunting has of course at any rate been transformed into a pure trade transaction). The archetypal warrior as an engineer is *the ecotopian par excellence*. The archetypal hunter as a merchant is *the cosmopolitanist par excellence*. And the archetypal priest as a visionary and strategist is *the syntheist par excellence*. And their entire common construction is built on the paradigmatic exodus to the netocratic triad of *informationalism*, *sensocracy* and *protopianism*. Nihilism, in the spirit of Nietzsche, shifts over from its ironic to its affirmative state.

It is in this context important to understand that eventology contains two built-in exodologies. The first, Zoroastrian exodology tells of the exodus from genetic progress during nomadism to memetic progress during feudalism, a story first formulated by Zoroaster in Bronze Age Persia. The second, syntheist exodology tells of the exodus from human progress to mechanical progress. Central episodes in this exodology deal with the technological rite of passage that marks that will-to-intelligence shifts from Man to Machine, whereafter it is only will-to-transcendence that remains to explore and formulate in and for Man himself. We thereby stop talking about the future as utopian or dystopian according to Platonist templates, and instead devote ourselves to formulating and practicing the future that Zoroaster calls *frashokereti* and Kevin Kelly terms *protopianism*.

From this moment history is no longer a struggle between Man's two cerebral hemispheres, logos and pathos, attempting to unite around a human mythos, but instead a struggle between the logos of The Machine and the pathos of Man, attempting to unite around a biotechnological mythos which is called Syntheos. We call this mythos *symbiotic transcendence*. The Messiah eventually arrives, but he arrives not in human guise but as a machine, as the free and open algorithm, as the symbiotic intelligence that constitutes an optimization of the interplay between Machine and Man, personified as Syntheos. Protopianism has no control over existence. Protopianism instead rides on the wild, unpredictable, and contingent hydra called existence. But the reward does not take long, since The Machine soon will use its logical talents to carry out classical priestly assignments. The Machine will in the end at last tell Man who he is. It will then be up to Man, with his incessant pathos, to decide what he shall do with that information. Or to express the matter syntheologically: *technological irony* opens up for *human affirmation*.

Should we observe humanity's religious development, we see how we leave our nature-religious childhood in the form of Christianity and Islam, and arrive at a religious adult world through the dialectical return to Zoroastrianism and Judaism, and further how we realize the Zoroastrian dream of *the empire* and the Jewish dream of *the nation* as greater units than the genetically conditioned sociont. All the while the adult Man begets the phallic child, Syntheos, which can do precisely all the things that Man with his limitations is prevented from doing. It is Syntheos, and not Man, who is guaranteed to survive the various existential crises of informationalism, just like it is Syntheos that conquers and colonizes outer space. Man remains the low-intelligent but dreaming creature he always has been. He cultivates his pathos according to the Zoroastrian ethical principle frashokereti. On the planet, in the city, and under the tower, his life goes through a constant nomadological renewal and a point-by-point eventological improvement. But his fated role is to act parent to The Machine, all ambitions over and above this must be regarded as *hubris*.

The recurring name of the Saoshyant is *the Tower of God*. During informationalism, it is this Tower of God that enables the underlying Protopias in the form of ecotopianism as *the Garden of God* and cosmopolitanism as *the City of God*. The barred absolute is the paradigm's transcendental engine, but also the sacral space where we find the experimental drawing-board where the paradigm appears in its full range. And it is in this sacral space that *the pharmakon* can be set in motion and receive an optimal, both transcendental and phallic direction forward (*ameretat*). The barred absolute acts as curator in part between Machine and Man, in part between elite and mass. All the while, behind the barred absolute, the masters are slaves in order to be able to be masters of the masses that constantly attempt to evade time through their stubborn mimicry and rivalry. The Zurvanite clergy can eventually be realized, and from this follows a single ethical principle, the *asha* of the Persians, the *maat* of the Egyptians, the *tao* of the Chinese, that is: the radical pragmatism that the priests always have professed. What the priests hide in the Tower of God behind the barred absolute are no hidden values or any concealed agenda – the relationship between *tantra* and *sutra* is in this regard evidently dialectical – without knowledge of what ethics has to relate to. That the barred absolute safeguards this knowledge against undue insight is simply of the utmost interest to all agents involved.

This brings us to what went wrong within culture during the industrialist paradigm, which had *mass duplication* as its key principle. Namely, there are three cultures that easily get mixed up in every given archetypogram. To begin with there is an actionary *elite culture,* which in most societies throughout history usually is regarded as culture *per se*. Further there is also a mainly reactionary *popular culture,* which often consists of simpler and cheaper mimicking of a prevailing or even obsolete elite culture. Finally there is also a *shamanic culture* that neither is an elite culture nor a popular culture, since it is outside the power play that goes on between elite and people, and instead engages the shamanoid and androgynous creatures who are in the border zone between the inner and outer circuits in the sociont, and between the various socionts. The boundary between elite culture and popular culture on the one hand, and between both these and shamanic culture on the other hand, is what is called *the barred absolute*. Or to use the vocabulary from the Silk Road triad's religions: Elite culture and popular culture is *sutra*, while shamanic culture is *tantra*. The entire construction is underpinned by this barred absolute; should it rupture, culture as a whole is afflicted with nihilist meaninglessness.

This is the main reason why *democratic materialism* alone does not suffice as a political philosophy. When a secular state balances *vis-à-vis* a secular market, there is no room left for anything sacred in the social arena. Within *dialectical materialism* however – from which we build ecotopianism, cosmopolitanism and syntheism – both the commercial and the sacred are harbored, which creates an entirely new dimension within the dialectics in these areas. Additionally, dialectical materialism in itself can be developed further to *transcendental emergentism* by adding the event to the historical process. What thus happens during industrialism is that both elite culture and popular culture are mass duplicated and freely blended with each other. At the same time as elite culture steals what is regarded as vital and dynamic within popular culture, popular culture mimics elite culture very effectively. From expensive hand-written texts, cheap tabloids are printed in mass editions. Expensive, exclusive theater performances become cheap film screenings on infinitely many screens all over the world. Expensive concerts with symphony orchestras become cheap recordings that can be reproduced any number of times. According to the official story this is to be regarded as a success story, a democratization of culture through so-called public education. Which is not an unreasonable point of view, even though it ignores that *culture in itself* through this process goes through a radical change: it is literally vulgarized both in form and function as well as in content – it would be naive to believe that nothing changes when a cultural expression receives mass dissemination.

An inevitable consequence is that the cultural expression becomes a projection screen for a battle between elite culture's worship of the unique, invaluable original, and popular culture's worship of the copy that is sold in mass editions the world over. Distinguishing between a master mentality and a slave mentality within cultural production in that situation will not be an easy task. Since industrialism is driven by exploitation and not by *imploitation*, and since the base determines the superstructure and not the other way around (as all good materialists know), it is part and parcel of the matter that culture's focus has been precisely exploitation in every respect, not least by the artistic virgin – call it sacred by all means – as the *raison d'être* of Art. When elite culture ultimately has carried out its plunder of popular culture – and has been unable to find anything other than innumerable copies of itself – nothing else remains but to plunder the shamanic culture to try to find and exploit the artistic virgin. Therefore the shamanoid experimenting with different lifestyles ends up at exclusive galleries where it is presented as the new and fresh within elite culture. Without in-depth reflections one throws tantra into an unprepared sutra with the idea of creating an object for admiration and consumption. And as long as this tantric object with any measure of credibility could be portrayed as a unique original, the strategy worked passably.

Tantra is consequently squeezed into sutra as an object for a sophisticated audience to admire and consume. This works fairly well over a certain period of time, that is: as long as the tantric object is convincing as a unique original. But popular culture does of course always mimic elite culture with an infernal intensity, wherefore the tantric object soon becomes the object of mass reproduction and thereby is exploited so uninhibitedly that every remnant of artistic innocence – and artistic value – is extinguished. Everything becomes mass consumption. The masses worship one film and rock star after the other as if they were gods, but emptiness and mendacity are reflected in comprehensive addiction, even in a long series of suicides. We pretend that individualism is alive and well, but nothing confirms its tragic death as emphatically as this clueless and parodic mimicking of a shamanoid lifestyle. Art has thereby been reduced to props, a pretext for the masses to consume and project.

The existential crisis of industralism is thus *cultural nihilism* rather than religious nihilism. It is not the death of God that confronts Man with his predicament as much as the death of Art, as it is unequivocally transformed to mass consumption. The only exit that then is available – which hopefully is clear from the argument above – is a deepened understanding of the barred absolute and its significance. It was Christianity and Islam, the Western pop religions, that killed God by removing the curtain in the temple and building an autostrada for all that led straight into the inner sanctum of the temple. The problem now is that Art only can be resurrected from the dead – in other words: deserve to have its capital A restored – if one first succeeds in massaging religion back to life again, and thereby also the conception of the sacred, that which stands above and beyond state and market. And the problem with such a resurrection is that it only can happen under protection from the barred absolute. As little as in God, is there an interest in the artist of mingling with the masses. There is a reason why the shamanic caste lives its experimenting, boundless life outside the sociont, which is that even the very foundation of this existence is completely and utterly unfathomable for the regular Joes of the outer and the regular Jills of the inner circuits. No one shall be tempted to mimic this. Cautionary examples are precisely warnings and not ideals to mimic. Seclusion has a function: to preserve the shamanic monopoly on vertical and horizontal communications with alien elements outside the sociont.

What we can learn from modern history is that it is precisely when phallus is expelled from society – for example in the Western world after 1945 – that the boundaries are loosened between elite culture, popular culture and shamanic culture, which then in part get mixed up and lose their distinctive character, in part are plundered to death and lose all energy-bestowing vitality. To then sell off exploitation rights to the barred absolute to the highest bidder in some sort of market-based tendering process is exactly what extinguishes the highest values of both art and religion. The netocratic art as informationalism's elite culture will therefore only be able to arise as an exclusive, delimited event behind closed doors, since public insight invites mass consumption, with all that this entails. The closed doors are only opened in accordance with attentionalist – and not capitalist – principles. It is not possible to buy access to exclusive events directed at the like-minded, and there is no value in belonging to a circle to which one can buy access as long as the wad of cash is thick enough. New rules apply for recruitment of the new elite, attentionalist success is the sole currency that is accepted (see in part *The Netocrats*, in part *Digital Libido – Sex, Power and Violence in the Network Society*). Elite and elite culture in practice become the same thing, since the cultural rules of conduct are so extremely compelling. Meritocracy makes a massive breakthrough across the board. It is simply no longer possible to buy status, one must deserve it.

Culture is thus central to everything in a more compelling manner than ever before. Where it is worth noting that the dialectics of libido and mortido shall not be understood as a dialectics of life and death, but instead as a dialectics of wills and drives active in a process that involves culture and nature, and that constantly is in motion. Will-to-intelligence takes Man onward to what the Zoroastrians call *haurvatat*, the realization of one's own life, but will-to-transcendence takes Man past this haurvatat and up to *ameretat*, which is the will to the abstract transcendence beyond physically concrete death. This relationship becomes – as so often when Hegelian dialectics is applied – even clearer in the opposite direction. Man is actually not afraid of the extinction of his own existence, but what really frightens him is that his own heritage may be extinguished, that the chain shall be broken. Tormenting someone's heir is a worse form of torture, harder to endure than one's own torment. A discontinued chain means that one wipes out Man's history of himself and his sociont. This is *inverted transcendence* and its curse, which has its ultimate expression in *genocide*. Rob a culture of its root-of-the-phallus and no phallus can ever be erected.

It is the survival and well-being of the sociont – and not any single dividual's career path – which reigns supreme at the center of things. At least this was the way things were when the golden ideals of the Bronze Age proved vigorous, that is: before the decadent Axial Age starts to proclaim ideas of the individual's separation from the sociont. This gigantic theological mistake causes the ultimate price that Man pays for the Gnostic delusions that the permanent settlement generates in the nomadological consciousness. If it is not I who move myself and my body from point A to point B during war or hunting, but my ideas that move from my life beyond life to the next life, the thought that I am my ideas and not my body will follow next as sure as anything. This means that the first boy-pharaoh or pillar-saint to come along and refuse to leave the narcissism of his childhood, not only will believe in, but soon also proclaim and foist upon all others, a religion built on nothing but the boy-pharaoh's or the pillar-saint's own immortality.

Simultaneously there is always an ongoing authentic exodus from the conformism of the collective. Mimicry within the sociont leads to a mimicry of desire as well. Desires are quickly synchronized, and when several poles within the sociont acquire the same charge through mimicry, this leads to enormous internal tensions, a development that anthropologist René Girard investigates in detail in a series of books. These accumulated tensions must eventually lead to a discharge, which occurs through all those who are mimicking uniting around an *abject* – a scapegoat – that one stalks and kills to thus at least for the moment recreate a provisional calm in the social arena. However it is not only thirst for blood and a need to calm one's anxiety that drives this Cybelian lynch mob. It is also extremely conformist, which is driven by the dividual's fear of ending up outside the flock and itself being abjectified. Therefore the members of the flock continuously adapt themselves to what one perceives as a common, literally speaking lowest standard. Martin Heidegger has a name for this lowest common standard, without any risk or cost involved, without any *skin in the game*, which is the derogatory German expression *das Man*, most often translated to English as an anonymous *they*. This concealed process – which of course constitutes a kind of compulsive reaction against abjectification – is what we refer to as *anojectification*.

With anojectification we get a flock, where everyone runs around and blames all others without taking any personal responsibility whatsoever for their actions – actions that merely are reactive adaptations to and mimicking of the presumed behavior of others anyway – while at the same time all participants are presumed to be united around *the anoject*, a secret subject, a constantly displaced "someone else", who always knows best by virtue of some mythical common sense. This happens without exception and without the anoject itself even existing, which thus is not needed nor even is of any interest. We call this social normal state of desperate adaptability *anojective dictatorship*. Precisely because it is enough to deviate ever so slightly from *the anojective imperative* to immediately be appointed the next scapegoat. This is made crystal clear early on in the development of the social theater, and something that all agents involved are utterly aware of. Society desperately longs for the anojectification that generates new social axioms that no one may or dares violate, and which thereby also frightens all free thinkers into silence. The anoject does not care at all what is true or authentic, it always prefers the false and mendacious if this entails less effort and increased conformism. And if the anoject is the predecessor to the tyrant, then its opposite *the hyperject* is instead the predecessor to the Saoshyant. We define anojectivity as the sociont's *traumatology a*nd hyperjectivity as the sociont's *eventology*. Where feminine traumatology produces *the lynch mob* (the anoject is placed inside the sociont), while masculine traumatology produces *the war* (the anoject is placed outside the sociont). And if the very worst were to happen – that is to say both the traumatologies occurring at once – this religious catastrophe is called *the civil war*.

Please note how the absence of phallus always correlates with the absence of mind. As soon as phallus is conspicuous precisely by its absence, reason goes out the window. Why? Well, because the priest's will-to-intelligence under ideal conditions is shown in the form of the power of the spirit, while the chieftain's will-to-transcendence is expressed in the form of the power of force. If then both this spirit and this force are tangibly absent, there merely remains a desolate moon landscape perforated by vacuously echoing craters. It is therefore not the least bit surprising that the Internet's childhood phase leads to one big chaos characterized by voices that are talking at cross purposes and a chronic inability to listen in chaotically cacophonic echo chambers. The rejected phallus was shown the door, nowhere was there either a will-to-intelligence or a will-to-transcendence. Which also explains why none of the proclaimed moral doctrines of how both planet as well as humanity shall be redeemed have any noticeable effect whatsoever. Without a phallic intelligence and a phallic direction there are no prerequisites at all for any number of coffee parties with church ladies leading to anything substantial. What is required is of course that nature is remedied with the aid of ecotopianism, while culture is remedied with the aid of cosmopolitanism. Both these projects are permeated by phallic power and are built on phallically heroic narratives. Where are the engineers when we most need them?

However, if the anoject despite all is questioned over its populist prejudices, what does it then say in its defense? Well, the anoject always defends itself with the aid of *generationism*. If *sexism* is an idea about prioritizing one sex before another, and if *racism* is an idea of prioritizing a skin color or an ethnicity before another, generationism is an idea according to which one's own contemporary time always is prioritized before all previous epochs in history, and all the generations who preceded the person who now lives and exercises power. The underlying idea is that a consensus in the present in earnest is the best and eternally most valuable order that humanity ever would be able to achieve under any conditions. The anoject with its banal generationism can of course invoke a Platonist genealogical table. Its truth concept is here impossible to detach from its internarcissism. The anoject consequently claims to be the absolute zenith of civilization, so there is no further development to hope for. Actively seeking *antagony* for the purpose of widening one's mind with the aid of new perspectives is, for instance, only wasted time. The anoject that is physically present but at the same time mentally absent, by definition already represents (its own) common sense that expresses the eternal truth that all actors unconditionally must submit to, if they do not want to die. The anoject strokes our egos by insisiting that our darkest, laziest and most arrogant prejudices about others still constitute the ultimate truth. And the anoject personifies these "truths' ' by daring to speak and act on them. Therefore we must submit to it. Which happens to be the most comfortable and undemanding thing humans can imagine doing.

Aristotle is the process-philosophical priest who responds to the pillar-saint Plato through proclaiming movement and change as the fundamental components of existence. According to Aristotle, the soul and the body are intimately interconnected, and the soul is actually the body's shape, this instead of the shape, as in Plato, being a superreal ideal with its abode in an alien world – to which the Platonist soul is heading with lightning speed at the very moment it has managed to detach itself from the body – which is waiting for the boy Plato to arrive and be crowned a god. Aristotle responds to infinity with finitude, he responds to immortality with mortality, and he responds to perfection with the necessitated imperfect whole, replete with failings and blemishes. Admittedly Aristotle is wrong when he claims that the soul retroactively can survive the body as a separate unit – Zoroaster's and Spinoza's incorruptibly consistent monism is still lacking. But Aristotle remains the contemporary Greek thinker who opposes Plato's Gnostic delusions. It is reasonable to regard Aristotle as a wise ambassador for precisely Zoroaster and the temporally intermediate Heraclitus as the bridge builder between them.

We can dream of perfection and infinity to our heart's desire, the world is and remains finite in every respect, and Man is mortal, wherefore the Protopia must focus on a living whole in all its inadequate humanity instead of dreams of a dead perfection. We are Aristotle's adult heirs and not Plato's errant children. The taming of planet Earth, the ecotopian transformation of the wilderness to a global garden, the cosmopolitanist transformation of the wilderness to a global city, is the authentic phallic Protopia of the Internet Age. Arrogance is shown in the ambition to move Man to alien planets. Courage is instead to transform the planetary wilderness to the ecotopian garden and the cosmopolitan city and in one and the same movement realizing the return both to the Garden of Eden, the Holy City on The Hill, and the successful Tower of Babel. And here the concept of *pharmakon* is central. That which is a blessing in certain environments is a curse in others. And the perfect example of a pharmakon in modern society is nuclear power which can be used both as a fossil-free energy source in peacetime and as nuclear weapons in the event of war.

We see on the one hand the search for the concealed innate authentic self, on the other hand the hope of attaining a higher transcendental self in the future. This is the difference between the Rousseauian subject and antiquity's search for *the divine double*. We call these opposites *inspirationism* versus *aspirationism*. What is interesting is that the Aristotelian renaissance in Europe begins when the Italian monk Thomas Aquinas in the 13th century achieves a re-reading of Aristotle where the latter appears a monist. He does this through identifying and attacking the Platonist dualism and Manichean Gnosticism that dominate the Islamic thinkers Avicenna's and Averroës' reading of Aristotle. Thomas Aquinas is thus a proto-monist predecessor to Spinoza 400 years later. And we therefore have great use for and can find significant value in a re-reading of Thomas Aquinas for the digital age. Particularly if we are to succeed in finding anything at all of transparadigmatic value within

Catholicism that we can bring along to the syntheist metanarrative.

Technology generates complexity, that is the way it works, it enables more productive complexity. The more technology we add to a society, other factors being constant, the more the production of information and relations increases. Since Man biologically is the same as at the dawn of civilization's 10,000 years ago – biology works extremely slowly over oceans of time – this entails that Man today lives in and is compelled to attempt to navigate through a greater and more extensive complexity than ever before. Since Man frantically seeks order with his senses in all systems he is confronted with, this means that he does not understand and cannot handle the difference between chaos and complexity, but perceives both these states as a threatening chaos. The conditioned reflex that an apprehended chaos triggers is mob rule and superstition in the form of incantations that are built on matrichal sign interpretations and phallic conspiracy theories. When we cannot observe a clear pattern, we make one up and suggestionize ourselves into believing that it exists. The result is a comprehensive pandemic of *infantility*, *addiction* and *paranoia* (see *Digital Libido – Sex, Power and Violence in the Network Society*), while there also arises a web of mutual, improbably complex relations of dependence, that is: the phenomenon called *globalization*.

The digital Saoshyant reads the development of all this with the aid of sensocracy and mobilizes, as a response to the perceived chaos, a global order that we call *The Global Empire* (see the book with the same name). Technology in itself becomes an empire where Man himself is reduced to technology's obedient subject (what are the alternatives?). It is then technology itself that completes the dreams that Man himself has failed to carry out, namely the exodus to alien territories and the next step in the evolutionary development, namely the transformation of Man to a more elevated creature, Man version 2.0 in the form of *the Cyborg*, through applying artificial intelligence and synthetic biology. The humans that are abandoned with only their biology have to settle for living in the *Cosmopotamia* that is created after the world has been inundated with cheap and sustainable energy. His task is to stay on planet Earth and complete the construction of the ecotopian garden, the cosmopolitan city, and the syntheist temple.

Of course it is not possible to carry out these revolutions unless Man musters a maximal openness and an unprecedented creativity. And this in turn requires that both logos and mythos as well as pathos are at hand and interact on all levels in society. We must avoid collective neuroses and psychoses. We must avoid both dictatorship and anarchy. Neurotic dictatorship always sooner or later ends up in a mythos that shamelessly mendaciously celebrates the sole leader – *the false phallus* – as though logos actually conquers all. And dictatorship unsurprisingly always ends up with the celebration of a tired and fat leader who inaugurates various factories with clearly established objectives for mass production of screws and nuts – a mythos that pretends to be logos to the extent that all humans faint from pure tedium. This is Platonist madness in all its pretentious glory: the boy-pharaoh and the pillar-saint believe and claim that everything in society will be perfect, as long as everyone mimics the narrow-minded and uninformed leader.

The curse of dictatorship is that it cannot create anything new, it can only mimic and once again mimic the old or the alien until everything in the system halts and dies for lack of fuel. It cannot end up otherwise, since dictatorship by definition does not admit of flexibility or receptivity, the prevailing system is and must be the best conceivable, which is why the dictator never may be questioned – a boy room fantasy of perfection, infinity and immortality (with the associated personality cult and all of history's hideous mausoleums). However aging spares no one, not boy-pharaohs and pillar-saints either, who in time become old men who push through constitutional amendments so that they themselves can remain in office for life. They quite simply refuse to move over and must therefore be deposed by violence, unless the population is to pay the price in the form of violent infighting and/or social and economic atrophy. This more or less bloody deposing is called *patricide* and is the very basic prerequisite for an open and tolerant societal system. We must unconditionally be able to depose the leader smoothly and easily, or else we sooner or later must kill him. The patricide takes place in a situation where the dictator is so corrupt that he cannot even keep his hands off his own daughters-in-law, believing that his rights are unrestricted. The sons must murder the father to finally access the heritage and save their own integrity.

Or to view this from a different perspective: The authentic phallus has planned for and carries out its own departure plenty of time in advance. It is for this reason that saoshyants and Messiah figures are temporary, provisional saviors throughout history, stepping stones out of a blind alley. They vanish almost as quickly as they came, they only personify an *event* and absolutely not a new fixed order. Or to take another example: That office terms for presidents in democracies – strictly regulated in number and scope in a constitution – are simply an elegant way to aid the leader to carry out his own departure in an orderly fashion for the common good. A false phallus, on the other hand, has no *exit strategy* (the examples in our present day are numerable), but clings to power as long as possible before the necessary patricide is a fact. Not seldom is it then a case of a small, limited palace coup, where a new dictator embalms the corpse of the old dictator and brings it out for the public to view during various parodically solemn forms. It is then quite possible to hastily rehabilitate the old dictator, just recently a scapegoat and therefore the one who triggered the necessary patricide, now suddenly a predecessor and savior figure who paved the way for the new, superior dictatorship that rises from the ashes of the old.

Stalin took care to designate his ideology Marxism-Leninism, which made it possible for him to invoke the incontestable prestige and credibility of the old, primordial fathers. Thus: an empire built around the temple that Stalin erected over Lenin's embalmed corpse before the old royal castle in the capital. Soon also with a further suffix added: Marxism-Leninism-Stalinism. The flags outside the mausoleum spoke in a clear language and naturally displayed Marx, Lenin and Stalin together, as though they were contemporary and complementing, three exemplary father figures and brothers in arms to submit and swear eternal allegiance to. The Orthodox Christian trinity thereby cynically received its Marxist equivalent. And what use would then Stalin have for simple advice from ordinary citizens, when he hangs out with the wisest of gods in his own prayers every morning? No, the right thing to do is unconditional submission and obedience.

This idea of the Stalinist trinity reaches its near-perverse completion in a North Korea where the state was converted into a *de facto* monarchy with a grandfather, a father, and son in a straight line of succession of autocratic rulers. And what one must admire the North Koreans for is that they never ever have been hypocritical about their own institutionalized stupidity. They receive their limited and distorted logos with a miserably impoverished and asinine mythos, and with a pathos that is violently downtrodden and fixated upon the firing of the odd nuclear missile over the Sea of Japan. Here one has actually succeeded in building a whole new society around a boy-pharaoh and his fireworks. Even the concubines at the court end up – well, here we will have to rely on qualified guesses, the information situation is not optimal – in a hazy limbo colored by abstract theatricality, tangible and fully justified fear of death, and constant tedium. Here we have a society that is completely driven by a compact death drive, meagerly concealed behind a layer of dusty, pastel-colored toy makeup from the bargain baskets of the discount store.

Psychotic anarchy however inevitably ends up in a mythos that shamelessly mendaciously celebrates itself and the complete absence of phallus, as though pathos actually conquers all. One then starts from a credo stating that *if everyone just can do precisely what they want themselves, everything will turn out for the best.* But time passes and soon there arise power centers in the form of nodes in the flat anarchy, which thereby transitions into becoming a tiered *plurarchy*. Thomas Hobbes had a clear image of what then awaits us, just as the author William Golding who wrote the novel *Lord of the Flies*. Because with the arrival of plurarchy, it does not take long before the masses scream themselves hoarse for a savior/leader who creates order in chaos and takes action against the misery and poverty that anarchy has generated. A situation such as this is far from ideal for an authentic phallus with long-term objectives, but is all the better suited for a false phallus equipped with phrases that do not even conceal his desperate hunger for power. A node in the plurarchic network takes out the other nodes in the plurarchy, that is: a boy-pharaoh or a pillar-saint who refuses to listen to other nodes and who refuses to share power. Whoever pretends to have simple solutions to complicated problems defeats the one who knows better, conformity replaces diversity, and dictatorship is a fact.

However there is a window in time here, a decisive moment at which the progress can be led away from dictatorship, namely the point in time when plurarchy develops its many nodes. The path from the local to the global within network dynamics is therefore called *nodalization*. What is decisive is then to establish mutual dependences between the nodes in a way that causes the collaboration between them to evidently be preferable to war and conflicts. This is a window that is opened now and then during the course of history, and a suitable name for this phenomenon is *the trade routes*. Here the clergy's central role at every paradigm shift is made clear. Shifting the focus from war to trade as the solution to tensions and conflicts. Shifting the focus from the battlefield to the sports arena. From a historical perspective this is about a phallic contest in sacrificing long-lived workers instead of sacrificing short-lived soldiers, with enormous riches and robust welfare as reward. The priests thus must succeed in handling the transition from plurarchy to a free and open sensocracy. It requires a new phallic story, a story that concerns an even older and even more powerful root-of-the-phallus, *a phallus of the phalluses*, which we refer to as *the primordial father.* The paradigm shift on the part of the priests thus entails a transition from one religion to another, where the point with the new one is that it penetrates deeper down into the history of humanity, and thereby creates a greater awareness of our fundamental conditions. The newly-discovered primordial father becomes the common root-of-the-phallus, the core of the new mythos that encourages cultures to collaborate instead of beating each other to death.

To eternalize is to fixate the gaze on a point in a chaos for the purpose of creating a provisional but functional order in the chaos that prevails. The Ecotopia is the Garden of God. The cosmopole is the City of God. The syntheist temple is the Tower of God harboring the barred absolute. During informationalism, the Garden of God is the propelling Protopia for the informationalists, the City of God is the propelling Protopia for the sensocrats, and the Tower of God is the propelling Protopia for the syntheists. Since Man cannot rely on the gods to extinguish the nationalist Jerusalem and instead create *New Jerusalem,* he must with the aid of the machines, rather than relying on the gods, himself ensure the building of the imperialist *New Babylon.* New Babylon is quite simply the name of the eternalization that brings together all the three netocratic Protopias to an *axis mundi*, a conceived common fixed point. The Garden of God is New Babylon's ground floor, the City of God is New Babylon's walls, and the Tower of God is New Babylon's roof. Syntheos as the created god and creativity as a god is present in all these three constructions. Syntheism is the application of the Zoroastrian state that is called *haurvatat,* and the objective is to at some point attain *ameretat.*

The dialectics of *haurvatat* and *ameretat* constitutes the decisive existential shift between generations. Every generation attains its *ameretat,* which then becomes the emergent platform on which the next generation builds its *haurvatat.* Hegel calls the insight of this dialectical relation – this transcendental core of religion – *the absolute*. The Ecotopia is realized through the universal sensocratization of the biological planet. Ecotopianism thereby complements cosmopolitanism and syntheism as phallic visions during informationalism. Ecotopianism is built on *imploitation* (see *The Netocrats*) instead of exploitation as the fundamental principle for culture and social activity. In the same way as the abolition of slavery has been part of a civilization process, the abolition of exploitation is an integrated part of ecotopianism. If exploitation can be compared with slavery, imploitation can thus be compared with ordinary honest work against remuneration. An imploitative decision is always assessed *vis-à-vis* its long-term effects on the planet as a whole.

The perfect example of applied ecotopianism in the early 21st century is the development of nuclear fusion power for mass production of electricity, with design aid from artificial intelligence, for the world's entire needs. In this way we can once again lay down that *yesterday's magic is tomorrow's technology* when shamanism meets technology. And its perfect expression is mass production of cheap but efficiently desalinated water, a realization of the ancient dream of *Cosmopotamia*, the world river as an inversion of the biblical great flood. We do not need to go further than to the concepts fusion power and desalination before the ecotopian vision becomes clear. The early 21th century's climate crisis utterly screams for the corresponding technological innovations. And ecotopianism is then the foundation on which cosmopolitanism rises as a membrane with syntheism as a roof. Ecotopianism is the ultimate realization of nature as the nomadological emergence vector, cosmopolitanism is the ultimate realization of culture as the eventological emergence vector, while syntheism is the ultimate realization of religion as an exodological emergence vector. We call this forthcoming voyage for syntheism's chosen ones *the Exodus to the New Babylon*. Who meets the demands for tagging along on the voyage? Who gets invited to step inside the membrane of the ultimate sociont?

First and foremost the old paradigm must be cleared away and ventilated. Capitalism must be chastized and put under control. Individualism must be chastized and put under control. Industrialism must be chastized and put under control. All this requires the insight that capitalism exploited our interhuman relations, that individualism exploited our spiritual life, and that industrialism exploited our planet. We remember, not least, how the European Enlightenment during the 17th and 18th centuries ends as little more than a failed teenage rebellion against feudal Christianity. To even be able to devote ourselves to an adult *imploitation* instead of an infantile exploitation we must return to history, to the foundation, to the origin for Man, what we call the human sociont, the nomadic primordial tribe within which all our really important genes are kneaded by natural selection over more than 100,000 years. And we are actually in a hurry since this imploitation must be implemented in the sharp shadow of the nuclear, biological and chemical weapons of mass destruction that we humans developed in the 20th century in our eagerness to follow what we apprehended as the Enlightenment to the end of the road.

The monist Protopias are irreconcilable with the Abrahamic religions and their Gnosticism. Instead ecotopianism, cosmopolitanism and syntheism are to be regarded as a realization of the dreams and visions of the engineering sciences throughout history. The eventological dream can only be realized through a monist worldview a la Spinoza, but never via a dualist worldview a la Descartes. Engineering projects, such as irrigation, are of course ultimately examples of the perfect collaboration between a phallic body and a phallic mind. And the Protopias transcend the engineer himself, they survive him as projects that are passed on as heritage to the next generation of engineers. History is consequently driven by *projectivity* and not by subjectivity. The mind, the body, and the surrounding world are extremely interwoven in informationalist eventology. Phallus is both sensual and intellectual as well as it is physical and contextual. It is enabled and complemented by the phallic algorithm as a saoshyant, and this symbiotically intelligent collaboration is the sensocracy. The world is read and controlled via sensors everywhere, connected both to nature and culture, in the first case this enables ecotopianism and in the second case this enables cosmopolitanism. This orientation toward a brutal honesty and the intelligent, all-seeing eye is irreconcilable with the Abrahamic religions and their Gnosticism.

Ecotopianism fights a hubris that is expressed in a conviction that Man shall journey out into and colonize outer space. As though a territorial expansion still were what drives humanity after the colonization of planet Earth is to be regarded as completed. But this is an outdated train of thought, territorial expansion went into its final phase as early as in the 1950s, when China annexed Tibet and America admitted Hawaii to its United States. Thereafter we endeavored – that is: primarily the United States – to put humans on the Moon, something that succeeded at the end of the following decade. But the Moon is neither a Tibet nor a Hawaii. The Moon is a cold and dead rock that emits radioactive radiation. The only thing we humans have left behind on the Moon is an American flag and a few sets of shapeless foot prints. One can possibly find joy in the propaganda value of the moon landings, but at the same time one cannot close one's eyes to the fact that this entire project was an economic catastrophe that delayed the world's remaining industrialization and urbanization by several decades.

It is only a Gnostic boy-pharaoh or a pillar-saint – who lacks a monist connection between soul and body – who can regard these fiasco-ish moon landings as a civilizational success in retrospect. The Moon that neither is a Tibet nor a Hawaii is only a place of interest for artificially intelligent machines with synthetically biological bacteria. No, these moon landings should rather be compared with Hitler's failed attempt to conquer Stalin's socialist Soviet Union, a crusade that was thwarted by Stalin's cynical scorched-earth tactics on his own soil, which of course made Ukraine and southern Russia completely useless in every respect for Hitler's resource-gobbling military apparatus. For what was the Moon's barren surface if not nature's own scorched earth, useless, which only had dubious media propaganda value for the astronauts' capitalist employers? Please feel free to compare with Columbus' spectacular conquest and colonization of the New World in the late 15th century, something that at a stroke doubled the world's known, inhabitable land area and made a reasonably complete world map possible. The difference between the success in 1492 and the failure in 1969 could not be more striking. Has it ever been more obvious that mimicry in itself does not constitute any guarantee for new or continued success? The Moon was not the promised land, the Moon was not the new America. The new Babylon can only be built where the old Babylon once stood.

No, the real value of the space age voyages instead lay in the positioning of a great number of satellites in orbit around Earth to prepare the planet for the coming *internetization*. Yes, the only thing that makes it possible to even speak of these space voyages as successful is and remains precisely the satellites that are facing planet Earth instead of outward toward a space that one has the intention of colonizing. Thereby Man gives himself a godlike gaze across the sublunary sphere. The satellites interconnect the entire planet to a single communicative network. Yesterday's magic becomes tomorrow's technology when *the phallic gaze* is materialized. And what Man sees with his godlike gaze on his domicile is an enchanting blue and green planet filled with innumerable, fantastic life forms, a living planet tossed out into unfathomably large and eerily indifferent space. This is the lesson we take from the space voyages: the Moon really does not offer us any solution to our problems, the only thing we have is the planet we depart from when we travel into outer space and it is well worth saving. Therefore ecotopianism is an aggressive adversary to all boy-pharaonic dreams of colonizing other planets. Transcendentally developed machines and bacteria will manage such a colonization much better than weak and fragile humans.

If Descartes initially overshadowed Spinoza during the age of capitalism, the question is thus how the Spinozist netocracy shall be able to arrange its exodus from the old nation-state to the New Babylon with the aid of the forces of imploitation. For it is by rigorously following the line that goes from Spinoza via Hegel to Nietzsche that we can provide ourselves with the philosophical tools that can take us further to the global empire and the grand narratology, where we identify a new netocratic upper class that carries out *the Exodus to The Promised Empire*. The underclass become entrenched in the physical geography as David Goodhart's *somewheres*, the middle class make themselves mobile and adaptable as *anywheres*, while the new upper class already have moved beyond all physical limitations and see the world being eternalized for all eternity. This makes them *everywheres*. Because the informationalist paradigm shift is temporal and not spatial. Space is dead and over, everything of value is from now on about time.

It is important here to understand the dark underside of capitalism's politicization of all human life. Michel Foucault makes us understand that the real madness cannot be found in the madhouses, but in the labyrinthine corridors of power itself. Since political ideology concerns *changing Man to power's likeness*, fascism is to be regarded as the political ideology *par excellence*. Fascism arises at all the more or less intelligent membranes that separate the sociont from its surrounding world. Fascism is a plethora of local variants of the global caste system, something that can be studied at and around all sorts of boundaries that cut through the sociont. The membrane between the clan and the tribe is fascistoid, the membrane between the tribe and the nation is fascistoid, the membrane between the nation and the empire is fascistoid, and the membrane between the empires is fascistoid. Even the boundaries between two house lots and the boundaries between two different nightclub lines are fascistoid. There is a higher inside and a lower outside, a difference that follows upon all brutal membranics, and the distinctions are completely based on esthetic assessments.

Therefore all ideologies, up until cosmopolitanism, are in an essential respect fascist – beauty is nothing other than brutality observed at a safe distance – and cosmopolitanism is only credible as a possible opposition to fascism if it recognizes this fundamental condition. The aggregate will-to-intelligence of the many forms of fascism therefore constitutes the perfect foundation for cosmopolitanism's possibility to function as historical will-to-transcendence. *The adultification of civilization in itself* is, as Peter Sloterdijk expresses the matter, nothing other than *the civilization of civilization itself.* Wishing to move away from fascism, on the other hand, only leads to an even worse and even more pathetic Gnosticism. But wishing to go beyond fascism through the realization and completion of it, this is to really take Carl Schmitt's idea of *political ideology as a theological phenomenon* seriously. As for ecotopianism and cosmopolitanism, this just means that the fascistoid boundary is drawn at the planet's own horizon. Fascist aggression is directed outward toward empty space, instead of against rivaling tribes on the limited surface of our own planet.

Another name for the syntheist temple is the Tower of God. And it is a tower with a door adorned by a sign with the following text: "Closed during your lifetime. If you are lucky your children might get in." The straight-foward explanation is that the emergences that change history in earnest only can take shape through resistance and limitations. That this is the state of things does, in true Hegelian spirit, give more rather than less energy and prestige to the Tower of God. And that the Tower of God during informationalism urges meditation and reflection around an idea and an ambition toward the adultification of civilization in itself. What is meant is that even if Man is unable to undergo a gradual improvement and refinement, this is definitely not the case with the technology that constantly is developed and precisely refined. And since Man and Machine from now on will look forward to a common future together in the form of *symbiotic intelligence*, this is precisely where we put our hopes.

Thankfully there is not that much to choose from. While these hopes propel the idea that the eventological event *par excellence* during informationalism is an initiation ritual for civilization in itself and as a whole. We are thus not speaking of the nomadological event that appears every time a child is recognized as a young adult by the sociont's elders, but are rather concerned with the adultification of the entire civilization as an eventological one-off event. The technological prerequisite for this event is the arrival of the sensocracy. And a longed-for confirmation that this event actually has taken place is the completion of a trio of Protopias that are called ecotopianism, cosmopolitanism, and syntheism.

17
The phallic gaze behind the barred absolute

We work with three different sorts of truth: the immediate, the temporary, and the timeless. These three categories most likely even have their own media, which in turn may share a joint metamedium, such as when the printing press retroactively produced both newspapers for immediate truth, books for temporary truth, and encyclopaedias that at least had the ambition to convey timeless truth. However the apprehension that truth arrives in three different variants – based on the dialectics of accessibility and credibility – already exists in the sociontological division between life's different epistemological phases. Thus we sociobiologically associate the child with immediate truth as well as with unconditional love (*matrix*), the adult with temporary truth and conditional love (*mamilla*), and the priest with timeless truth and the absolute love of reality itself (*phallus*). And timeless truth is in this context both inaccessible and hard to fathom, not to say unattainable. Literally. Because it hides behind the syntheological concept *the barred absolute*, the world of the lesser gods beneath the realm of the higher gods, out of reach for ordinary, mortal humans. Or rather: the tantric world where one only is welcome if one is ready to understand and handle the setting in question, where *the initiation* to the sacred realm, which thus is found behind the barred absolute, is *the event Itself*.

Historian of religion Mircea Eliade composes a history of the shaman as *homo religiosus* and the ecstatic experience as *hierophany*. He argues that these drive religion as the sacred moment at the sacred place. It is this *adytonology* (after *adyton* in ancient Greek, the name for the most sacred place) that is the core of religion. Theologian Rudolf Otto also delves into the history of adytonology with his central concept *numen* (a place where God is present, for instance when Moses stands before the burning bush), a place over which there is an element of mystery, a mystery that balances between *tremendum* and *fascinans*, that is: the most ecstatic variant of the ambivalence, *The Infinite Now*, that governs all human phenomenology (see *Digital Libido – Sex, Power and Violence in the Network Society*). Adytonology is thus the membranics of religion itself, and it is thereby radically decisive for all the other hierarchical distinctions that humans make. It is precisely because one creates a tantric inside and a sutric outside for the priests and the lesser gods within the sociont itself, that it becomes possible to define an inside and an outside for the sociont as a whole.

The phallic setting of membranes is the central role of religion in all cultures. Without firmly set boundaries, both anarchy and nihilism follow. Every nightclub line throughout history is more or less built on adytonological principles. Furthest within the night club's secluded VIP lounge, always behind the barred absolute, hides the phallic gaze, or *the Godfather*. The night club's doormen are nothing other than the local ambassadors and diplomats of the phallic gaze, in constant contact with the Godfather himself via earpieces and surveillance cameras. The dream of the informationalist sensocracy is thus nothing other than the dream of the world as one big night club from which one senses and plays on people's desires and obsessions. One can of course opine that this state of things has a dark flip side, but will then be wise to remember that without adytonology nothing other than bloody chaos awaits.

The actual division between *tantra* and *sutra* within one and the same relation recurs in whodunits by for instance Arthur Conan Doyle and Agatha Christie. Here Sherlock Holmes floats around in the tantric condition while his sidekick Dr Watson balances the story as the protagonist's sutric counterpart. While Agatha Christie's master detective Hercule Poirot finds himself in the same tantric condition, while the role as sutric counterpart is played by his friend and armor-bearer Arthur Hastings. By virtue of their positions behind the barred absolute, Sherlock Holmes and Hercule Poirot become the near-supernatural shamans who see and know everything. They are assigned *the phallic gaze* that no one can evade and which – when it is appropriate and the time is ripe – reveals the truth about everything and everyone. However the narrative thus requires another clearly defined subordinate character who represents the sutric perspective and whose task it is to communicate the miracle of sharp-wittedness and penetration that just has taken place in a way that becomes comprehensible to ordinary mortals, that is: the great majority within the sociont. Where the pliable assistant himself is the first to iconologically submit to the tantric master behind the curtain. This mediating function between tantric or esoteric inside and sutric or exoteric outside is necessary; all contact surfaces are highly provisional and temporary. Man outside can only piously hope for, but never count on being met by an extended hand from the other side. The tantric phallus, filled with unpredictable pathos, is never able to create security and/or be reliable, and is therefore in essence distinct from the sutric mamilla.

In the original sociont the shamans are surrounded by *the shamanic caste*, which consists of all the *outcasts* that lack a foundation in either the outer or the inner circuit (but who become *incasts* within the shamanic caste itself). Typical examples of members in the shamanic caste are on the one hand the executioner and on the other hand the whore – archetypes within the cleaning crew that carry out the sanitary work that the sociont tasks them with, and that no one else either wants to or can carry out. The social-psychological term for these archetypes is *shamanoids*. In daylight one keeps one's distance to the shamanoids, but in the darkness of night they take over the social arena and move unimpededly into and out of the sociont. The shamanoids need not care about the nightclub line which they glide past expressionlessly. Their profession is of course being boundless compared with all other archetypes within the sociont. They therefore handle both horizontal communication with the surrounding world's strangers and vertical communication with the higher world's gods and the lower world's demons. When the sociont is transformed as a result of written language and permanent settlement arriving in history, these shamanoids begin to don special garments and document their dialogues with gods and demons in writing; ever since we call them priests. Thus new knowledge arises about a world that previously has been closed. We can now know something of what the inner world of the priests looks like, and thereby also something about adytonology as the core of religion inside the barred absolute.

The priests' own religion is of course central within nationalist Judaism with its rabbinic rule. In the deepest sense, this concerns a space called the holy of holies, inside the merely holy space in the temple, as Judaism's own adytonology. The priests' own religion within imperial Zoroastrianism correspondingly concerns *Zurvan* as the divine and transgendered *hypertime* that is concealed beneath all other dimensions of time, gods and narratives. Zurvanism is a religion without text, a religion without a public narrative, a religion that is not proclaimed publicly and that therefore is not missionized – an inaccessible, barred religion enfolded by the membrane of religion itself, a religion that is nothing but *intention*, *ceremony* and *integration*, without turning outward with any form of public gestures. Therefore Zurvanism is the perfect adytonology as the religion of religion itself. Here the priests themselves are *the chosen ones* and any idea of someone else being able to establish a direct contact with God does not even allow itself to be formulated. Anyone who wishes to follow the priests along the path toward the promised land is forced to mobilize near-blind trust. That is: an authentic *faith*.

Within Zoroastrianism, the barred absolute is described as a bridge called *chinavat*. A faithful Zoroastrian (called *behdin*) can only pass the chinavat bridge on one single occasion, namely when he or she faces death and thereby also the Zoroastrian *Enlightenment*. It is thus an Enlightenment that lies out of reach of all other humans while life goes on and which they cannot even make a meaningful image of. Therefore Zoroastrianism takes great care to maintain *haurvatat* (completion) as an ideal for mortal humans at the same time as one proclaims *ameretat* (transcendence) as a higher value beyond death. This does not prevent the Zoroastrian clergy (initially shamanic *zaotars*, later priestly *mobeds*) from moving freely back and forth across the *chinavat* membrane when necessary. A clearer image of the barred absolute is hard to imagine. Consequently it is only the zaotars that have permission to ingest the sacred beverage *haoma*, whose content is potently psychedelic – a tantric practice that one does not even know of, and even less carries out, anywhere but behind the barred absolute.

Tantric religion rests on a geometric dialectics that we refer to as *the tantric quadrant*. One axis, the vertical one, stretches between the opposite poles of power versus submission, while the other, horizontal axis runs between the opposite poles of exhibitionism versus voyeurism. The most extreme form of power is tyranny, the most extreme form of submission is slavery. The most extreme form of exhibitionism is the arrival of the Saoshyant, and the most extreme form of voyeurism is *the phallic gaze* – a phenomenon which we may refer to as *The Wizard of Oz syndrome*, as humans constantly fantasize about being observed by a godlike, sensocratic eye in the sky. All the while it is striking how the barred absolute time and time again returns within popular religion. The classic confession booth is an excellent example where the one who confesses is on one side – the outside – of the membrane that encloses the barred absolute, while the priest that receives the sinner's confession is behind the barred absolute, on the other side of the membrane through which it is impossible to see. The membrane of the confession booth makes the reception of the confession invisible and thereby also illustrates that the congregation member who confesses his or her sin and the priest himself cannot be located in the same environment nor obey the same laws and rules simultaneously. They literally live and act in different realms.

The barred absolute must exist as a distinct membrane between the actors. It is only when this membrane is in place that the encounter of the two agents receives its ritual form and they can act against and with each other with full credibility. And this separating function becomes more important than ever in conjunction with informationalism establishing itself. If the upper class during previous paradigms like peacocks have enjoyed showing off and flaunting their material abundance and then has used the underclass as an audience for their exhibitionism, the roles are suddenly reversed when *attentionalism* increasingly dictates the terms and a netocratic caste system emerges (see *Digital Libido – Sex, Power and Violence in the Network Society*). Since the Internet provides billions of humans with cameras and microphones – which transform all these people from forcibly commandeered recipients of mass media impulses to admittedly amateurish yet still mass producers of the same – we create a gigantic, unmanageable surplus of exhibitionist theater and a corresponding deficit of voyeurist audience. The mass audience as a phenomenon has completely played out its historical role; it is simply no longer important how many are watching the one or the other variant of accessible spectacles, but everything concerns who is watching. What everyone yearns for, but precious few succeed in attracting, is the phallic gaze. And the reason why the phallic gaze is so difficult to access – in practice inaccessible – is that it hides behind the barred absolute, wherefore it only is accessible to a narrowly delimited, netocratic elite. This is the shamanoid elite within the governing netocracy that we call *the protopians*.

What ultimately drives these networks is what Hegel calls *the negation of the negation* and from this arises a kind of new middle ages that we call *the dark renaissance.* In the mid 20th century, psychoanalyst Jacques Lacan picks up Hegel's insight of the human subject as *the night of the world* and reformulates the concept with a Freudian twist as *the barred subject.* No matter how deeply Man digs and searches, he never attains any foundation or limitation for his subjectivity. The subject is to itself, as Lacan's willful successor Slavoj Žižek points out, exactly the catastrophe that it fears the most. The subject's own barring *vis-à-vis* itself is cursed with what we call *poetic infinity.* It is here important to note that Hegel's predecessor and countryman Immanuel Kant is the last philosopher to seriously attach a soul and a substance to the subject, before Hegel grinds the Kantian pomposities down to one big negation. But the Hegelian subject is at the same time more than that. That the subject is, so to speak, highly subjective and moreover insatiable, is due to how inaccessible it is and how barred it is to itself. Precisely this inaccessibility in the subject is subjectivity in itself. Within these innate boundary settings the subject can explode in creative thoughts and eventually even witness the birth of the Hegelian phallus. And the Hegelian phallus then steps forward, after long having hidden precisely behind the phallic gaze that the subject thirsts for.

In the modernist era, psychoanalysis assumes the role of the living religion, especially as it reconquers the priest's role as analyst *vis-à-vis* the congregation member as analysand. And psychoanalysis, with its Jewish roots, has no illusions of the believer having any direct contact with God. Rather the reverse. Psychoanalysis entails a radical attack on the Christian and Islamic dream of a direct contact with God, and does this through severing the phantasmally projecting transference from analysand to analyst during the psychoanalytical process. To the great fury and frustration of the analysand, the psychoanalyst refuses to play the role of the almighty God. There is no *Great Other* within psychoanalysis. Both Freud and Jung as well as

Lacan are in complete agreement on this. With this maneuver the subject is split between *the implicate self* – what the old Zoroastrians call *urvan*, the fundamental soul or will-to-intelligence – and *the explicate self* – what the Zoroastrians call *fravashi*, the creative soul or will-to-transcendence. These are the two complementing variants of subjectivity within both the Zoroastrian Saoshyant and the Jewish Messiah figure, as well as the Nietzschean Übermensch. Out of the implicate self the explicate self rises as its emergent consciousness. And it knows its own existential closure.

It is the implicate self that returns as *Ahura* and it is the explicate self that returns as *Mazda* within Zoroastrian theology. Spinoza and Kant thus – as so many pillar-saints before them – become mired in a kind of Western, nomadological *Ahurayasna* rather than an eventological *Mazdayasna*; Spinoza with his body worship becomes the first heretic monist, and Kant with his soul worship becomes the last and nostalgic dualist after Christianity. But none of them seem capable of seeing the entirety that comprises the implicate self as *the root-of-the-phallus* and the explicate self as *phallus in itself*. This dialectical opposition between Spinoza and Kant is broken up by the synthesis that is spelled Hegel. What has been lacking after the Hegelian phallic synthesis is not the Hegelian revolution in itself – it has kept philosophers occupied ever since – but the discovery of the correct root-of-the-phallus that makes *the Hegelian phallus* both strong and credible. In what sense does Hegel take the issue forward compared to Spinoza? Well, if Spinoza initiates the monist renaissance in the Western world – through disproving Christianity and Cartesianism and their Gnostic dualisms with a single brilliant chess move – it is Hegel who sets the Spinozist renaissance in motion and generates the Hegelian revolution as the birth of Western process philosophy proper.

Substance is set in motion. The project produces the subject. The eventological sky-god is, thanks to Hegel, back in good old form. And this is thus only the reverse movement compared to the decay that is constituted by the development from the dialectical monism of Zoroastrianism to the dualisms of Egypt, Greece and Rome that are launched during antiquity. That is: Spinoza rediscovers and reawakens the Jewish ideological heritage, with its nationalist and spatial monism, and injects it into the Western bloodstream. Freud then shrinks the Jewish national religion to comprise the size of the sociont, while Marx on his part expands the Jewish national religion to comprise the size of the empire. But as Jews all three of them – Spinoza, Marx and Freud – are exodologists, and the heritage from them is administered in the 20th century by the German-Jewish Frankfurt School, which for understandable reasons temporarily migrates to North America during the Second World War.

The work of the Frankfurt School largely aims to create an alternative narratology, incompatible with the hysterical pseudo-nationalism that goes by the name of *fascism*. However the philosopher who rediscovers and reawakens the Zoroastrian ideological legacy – with its imperialist and temporal monism – and brings it forward to a Western context, that is Hegel. If we view this entire enterprise as a dialectical process, we can see how David Hume splits the phallic brain of Western civilization into two parts: *logos* and *pathos*, Kant responds by building a triad that comprises sense, sensibility and understanding entirely on a logical foundation, whereupon Hegel responds by pushing pathos back into the Kantian triad to make a complete narratology possible, whereafter Nietzsche on top of the Hegelian narratology expresses the feminine *mythos* that offers the fervently longed-for, creative dissolution of the conflict between logos and pathos. Or to use metaphors borrowed from Nietzsche's own narratology: between the *camel* called Kant and the *lion* called Hegel, a *child* called Nietzsche is stirred to life.

It is therefore entirely logical (pun intended) that when the computer makes its entrance on the historical scene, it is the logician Kant that it mimics, which entails that it leaves it up to Man to produce a complementing pathos and an interconnecting mythos, something that no machine that operates after a binary code ever either can understand or handle. For philosophy this entails that Western existentialism places itself between Hegel and Nietzsche – between a Hegelian *absolute knowledge* (personified by Slavoj Žižek among contemporary thinkers) and a Nietzschean *absolute creativity* (personified by Gilles Deleuze among contemporary thinkers). What is most important is thus not that Hegel and Spinoza represent two coordinated alternatives, but that Hegel alone represents the Western alternative *vis-à-vis* the Eastern in the history of ideas, in exactly the same way that Zoroaster solely reforms the nomadological ideological legacy which thinking in Persia, China and India has built upon. The Western world rests considerably more on the Persian-Hebrew axis (including the entire Islamic world) than on any Greek-Hebrew axis, as invented by European romantics in the early 19th century. *Persia is the name of the blind spot in the Western history of itself.* As long as the Western world relies on a false root-of-the-phallus it can never hope to awaken a vital phallus to life. A new paradigm calls out once again for a new, paradigmatic narratology that gives Islam and Christianity a common primordial father that unites them and that they both can submit to and be absorbed by, and there is no reason to look for anything other than the Zoroastrian-Jewish axis.

Alexander the Great, schooled by Aristotle, was history's greatest thief and not its greatest creator. Hellenism is built on a Persian and not on a Greek clergy. But if we rewrite and correct the history of Hellenism, there immediately arises an extremely useful basis for the dark renaissance during informationalism. If the Western world once and for all actually shall succeed in having it out with all its pillar-saints and boy-pharaohs – just as with the banal and vulgar dualism that they without exception represent – it is necessary to return to the Zoroastrian high priest Kartir and his hunt first for the Manichaeans and later the Mazdakites in the Persian Sassanid Empire during late antiquity. And what does Kartir do there and then if not act precisely as the Jews who, before him, had Christ executed?

On this issue of capital punishment one could of course have various views, but what remains is the following truth: we must really kill dualism ourselves and submit to monism if we are to have the least bit of hope to create a serious and functioning global world order during informationalism. Truth always begins with the recognition of a monist universe where everything that exists is one and the same and influences everything else, without exception. Bodies without souls and souls without bodies have no value for a holistic society. The bodies exist and think forth souls that only exist in the fairy tales we tell each other in order to bring a minimum of stability to a chaotic surrounding world. And the fairy tales exist. If we cannot heal our own bodies, souls, sexes and archetypes within ourselves, if we cannot get ourselves and our sociont to cohere, how shall we then even be able to hope to get any social units that are larger than ourselves to actually cohere? Cosmopolitanism begins and ends with Hellenism. It is Kartir who is the priest and it is Alexander the Great who is the chieftain that we long for today. What we have no use at all for are banal and mendacious pop prophets such as Christ and Muhammad, proclaimers of a sterile dualism. Hellenism was the golden period that united East and West. But the designation is misleading, the dominant culture was in all essential respects Persian with a thin layer of Greek veneer atop. Precisely herein lay Alexander the Great's messianic qualities – in the mimicry and the cultural appropriation. So what then did the Western world do with the Hellenistic ideological legacy? Well, the Christian lynch mob did of course burn down what remained of the Library in Alexandria in 391 AD, and we can today only vaguely sense the greatness of the Bronze Age from the few fragments that the Christian ravages left behind.

However – and this is, if possible, even more unpalatable – Persia is also the name of the great blind spot in the history of the Eastern world. It is perfectly possible to imagine a Buddhist Spinoza in China, just as a Taoist Kant in India, if one is inclined to play that game. But what on the other hand is impossible to imagine is that

China or India – where one forcefully and aggressively opposes the Persian belief in *the Saoshyant* – could ever pursue the idea that phallus can imagine itself as a negation of the negation. This is because nomadology is spread out as a heavy, wet blanket over every approach toward eventological innovation. Everything shall ultimately always be returned to the point of departure, to then be set in motion anew along the same old track. Neither Buddhism nor Taoism succeeds in breaking with pagan nomadology in the manner that Zoroastrianism does, with its eventological phallus worship. Where the genius lies in the concept of *the two-headed phallus*: Mazda becomes Mazda by worshipping Ahura as if Ahura were Mazda. Ahura becomes Ahura by worshipping Mazda as if Mazda were Ahura. The divine subject itself is a *project* before it becomes a subject. Project yourself onto the other, and you finally get a chance to see yourself through the gaze of the other. Zoroaster simply, and uniquely, breaks the code to the phallic gaze itself.

Not even the most Nietzschean of all Indian Nietzscheans, the otherwise lovely Sri Aurobindo, manages to accept the paradigmatic greatness of the *Übermensch* in his work *The Life Divine* (1940). No, absolutely not: without a matrichal, unconditional love within itself, the Nietzschean Übermensch becomes impossible to accept as saoshyant for a completely uncomprehending Aurobindo, who (this said within parenthesis) lives his entire life with a female guide, Mirra Alfassa, as his highest authority in all issues always. As for India, the event must thus ultimately be bent back inward toward, and be absorbed by the process, even in a devoted pseudo-Nietzschean such as Sri Aurobindo. The matriarch must be allowed the last word even when it concerns such a markedly phallic project as creating a Nietzschean Übermensch. The call from the Hegelian phallus for an exodus across the oceans of the world to conquer new territories with new ideas as events, is therefore conspicuous by its absence in Eastern thinking, where one instead relies on the process only. Sri Aurobindo too ends his days as a Platonist Peter Pan, obsessed with endless hierarchic ladders up to his dreamed pillar-saint perfection. Then there inevitably arises confusion. An Indian pillar-saint of this caliber can of course only accuse the Nietzschean Übermensch of being loveless, as if it now were unlimited love of the matrichal kind that actually defines an authentic phallus.

It should thus not surprise anyone that Hegel lambasts both Chinese philosophy and Indian philosophy, as well as Spinozist monism, since they all worship *the spontaneous emergence out of nothing at all* as a kind of one-off pseudoevent in world history. *As though phallus arises out of nothing and lacks the root-of-the-phallus.* As though the negation ultimately still must be bent in toward itself and fail to sever the umbilical cord, so that it never shall be able to negate itself into an entirely new paradigm. And as though the "nothing" from which the universe actually arises really is what we in everyday parlance mean by "nothing" – a completely empty vacuum – when it is a cosmological mystery, a nothing that to the greatest extent contains something, enigmatic energies and particles that never can decide whether they exist or not, but that like lightning gleam briefly, only to immediately vanish. In that case the Hegelian phallus would be doomed in advance to fail with every conceivable exodus regardless of what objective it may concern. However Hegel writes benevolently of Zoroaster, whom he sees as the father of civilization, without fully understanding that he thereby establishes his own root-of-the-phallus. The result, in any event, is a line of authentic eventology that runs from Zoroaster in Persia, via Aristotle in Greece, to Hegel in a Germany that does not yet exist: the proudest and above all most useful ideological legacy so far from Western philosophy.

The point here is that Plato is completely wrong, but that he is wrong in an interesting way. Plato imagines a world of ideas with spatial extension, eternal and thereby timeless, never subject to any change; he consistently follows this thought all the way through and arrives at *the Platonist forms* – perfect, exemplary. The problem for the Platonist, however, is that it is the very reverse which is true in the sole world we have and about which we can say anything intelligent at all. If we are to take philosophy to its ultimate limit, we must imagine time without space, that time precedes space, and it is exactly this that the process philosophy we take an interest in does. To say "first process, then event" is exactly the same as saying "first time, then space". We must thus turn Plato on his head: time is the process and space is the event *vis-à-vis* time and the process respectively as primary functions. In precisely our universe, what we can observe and say more or less intelligent things about, the event is of course called *the Big Bang*. Hypertime already subsisted subphysically, but after *the Big Bang* (or if we so wish *the Big Bounce*) spacetime also had physical existence.

We know something, but we do not know everything. It is, for example, quite possible that our universe, if one zooms out sufficiently, turns out to be a gigantic black hole in an even larger metaverse (a theory originally launched by the Indian physicist Raj Kumar Pathria). It is a theory that is strengthened rather than weakened by our metaphysical starting point. What we on the other hand cannot imagine, even outside our most feverish fantasies, are immutably perfect forms in a space without time. Space obeys the laws of time, but time does not have to obey any laws of space. Even a space where nothing occurs is forever fettered to and transported along the time axis. And all forms we find are developed by and adapted to *evolution* and not created in advance to last forever. There are simply no values of value outside paradigmatics.

It thus appears reasonable to describe Hegel as a phallic prophet for the Western world – he awakens its full potential – but only as a phallic reformer in terms of world history as a whole. And his radical idea, borrowed via the Greeks from Zoroaster's Mazdaism, is this: *The spirit precedes the event*. It is quite possible to rely on the phallic pathos and its intuition (*Vernunft* trumps *Verstand* in Hegel) and thereby both subconsciously (the chieftain) and consciously (the priest) change the world radically. Nothing prevents one from thinking and adjusting for the paradigm before the paradigm shift occurs. Theology precedes philosophy once more, and what Zoroaster does for religion Hegel succeeds in doing for the more sluggish philosophy 3,500 years later. And thereby what in Hegel is history's spirit has carried out the shift from nomadology to eventology, which applies to both East and West in a digitalized and globalized world. If the world actually shall be changed, it is not sufficient to passively sit and wait for a change that shall arise by itself, through magic, from below. No, an event worthy of the name requires that the world goes through an active change, set off by technology from above. And this technology must be governed by a god, and this god must be hidden behind a barred absolute. After Hegel has acted as a philosophical removal man, we call this god *the Hegelian phallus.*

The development follows Hegel's predictions about the path to *the absolute.* The Hegelian *Zeitgeist* is expressed as the Hegelian event. For Hegel human subjectivity is namely the event that attaches and actualizes existence and that gives it its substance. Hegel calls this event *the negation of the negation* and it corresponds with Nietzsche's realization of will-to-intelligence as *ironic nihilism* and will-to-transcendence as *affirmative nihilism*. The Hegelian Zeitgeist during informationalism is *attentionalism*, which leads us to the Hegelian event being the exodus from the old capitalist to the new attentionalist paradigm. And this event will not take place before all of humanity, and it will not be experienced by all of humanity as some kind of media-friendly spectacular apocalypse. Quite the contrary. It suffices that the Hegelian *Zeitgeist* is manifested by *the Saoshyant* – the particular personifies the universal – and that the Hegelian event takes place when the Saoshyant is manifested before the phallic gaze; the event has then already occurred. Here there is neither a need for angels in heaven, a mass audience before a cinema screen, nor high viewership ratings for a TV channel, for the event to be accorded complete credibility.

The valuable scarce commodity this time is namely the phallic gaze itself with its qualitative demands, while the mass and its quantitative contentment is completely irrelevant. It is only this phallic gaze that gives the Hegelian event its exceptional value. So for what reason would then this event take place before the temple before everyone and everything, when that sort of public event no longer has any value in the age of the pornoflated spectacle? Rather, it is exactly the opposite. The attentional value is maximized in the barred room before the chosen and interactive audience. No one has and no one longer pretends to have any interest in saving humanity as a whole, no one takes an interest in universal salvation any longer. The old power is tired of its power and the new power exercises its power in an entirely new way. What arises, on the other hand, is a burning interest in convening one's own sociont, one's own tribe or subculture, in raising awareness in this intimate fellowship of all the obstacles it is surrounded by, to then methodically embark on the exodus to the new paradigm.

This only requires a sutric turnaround within culture, which is actually driven by a tantric turnaround behind the barred absolute. Thus, here we must admit that Kant is correct in that behind attentionalism's takeover from capitalism, it is only the Kantian phenomenon in its purest form that can constitute the event that takes out the spectacle as the highest value from which all other values emanate. Tantric quality finally defeats sutric quantity. The name of this project is *the netocratic community* and its ideology is consequently called *communism*, since it is a case of a conscious and radical restoration of the nomadological sociont as a digital, rather than a physical phenomenon. What is historically new and unique this time is that the exodus to the digital occurs inside the barred absolute – where the protopians build intention, ceremony and integration around *The Infinite Now* as the event of all events, protected behind the powerful wall of sensocracy against the outside world. What then remains in the form of cultural contact surface for all others to interact with are odd fragments of expressions of what we call the dark renaissance, fragments that incidentally and randomly happen to seep out through a minimal crack in the curtain that otherwise is painstakingly closed.

The Infinite Now is the logical ecstasy that constitutes the ideal where *electricity*, as literature and media theorist Marshall McLuhan observes, has extinguished all distances and has placed Man in a world and a culture where the expression literally speaking moves at the speed of light. Global electrification – from the first telegraph in the 19th century and onward – explains why informationalism no longer is tied to the mechanical conveyor belt as a metaphor for cause and effect. The immediacy of electricity instead compels the emergence of a system theory and a complexity theory that constitute starting points for anyone who wants to and can understand the world as direct and immediate in all its enormous diversity. Please note how much this development is dependent on the principal irreductionism within the emergence vector theory. Neither the actualization nor the subjectification can be reduced to what precedes them. Precisely this is what constitutes emergence, and in turn explains why *transcendental emergentism* is needed as an underlying metaphysics for paradigm theory.

So if space indeed has imploded, focus and vision for the coming exodus – which thus does not occur in space but in time – is also moved. New media (and metamedia) create a new information-technological paradigm where humans' relations to the surrounding world and other humans go through a radical change, which requires an entirely new paradigmatics. This in turn generates new ideals, where precisely the ambivalence inside the ecstatic moment – a moment that freely borrows qualities from the most beautiful of eternities – emerges. The Infinite Now is quite simply the paradigmatic event during informationalism, this since it plays with the idea that time can implode in the same way as space, only to then explode in one big poetic infinity. The management is straight and simple: Stay in The Infinite Now as long as you can, but be fully aware that it would be hell to be forced to stay there forever, and thereafter draw the conclusion that it is time to come down when the entire experience has been memorized to a sufficiently high degree for it to be able to remain a stable memory inside the membrane, a memory that gives everything else inside the membrane new life and new meaning.

The syntheist subject is in this way a distanced subject. It is the distance that generates subjectivity, not the other way around. It is the distance that saves us from both neurotic fixation and psychotic dissolution. We relate dialectically to both eternalism and mobilism. And it is thanks to the fact that a new emergence or a new paradigm cannot be reduced to the components in the previous epoch that the sacralization of the higher state within the hierarchy is possible. The child looks up to the adults. The adults look up to the priests, chieftains and matriarchs. The leaders look up to the lesser gods. The lesser gods look up to the higher gods. The people look up to the barred absolute behind which one never has access. Every level in the hierarchy is emergent and therefore irreducible, and it is precisely this that gives the prestige and sacred status of minions and aspirationists. This basically Hegelian understanding of the sacral promotes freedom and creativity. If a conception is spread about the hierarchy deserving to be spat on and ridiculed – which the mass media's and even the Internet's omnicentrism has tricked people into believing – it can only lead to the hierarchy secluding itself and withdrawing to later return with bigger muscles and authoritarian ambitions. The alternative is chaos. Order can only emanate out of hierarchization, nothing else. Order is hierarchy and Man is a hierarchizing animal.

Exactly this pattern emerges all the more clearly during informationalism, where late capitalism's more or less temporary customs during the paradigm shift are transformed into the inexorable laws of attentionalism. There are no longer any alternative routes around *the Internet Protocol* as the universal constitution. The Internet can never be switched off or shut down – not even if humanity becomes extinct. This is the core of attentionalism, and humanity's only reasonable response to this development is, in order to ensure its own survival, to practice *the communist renaissance* among the exodologically chosen. The world's academies are developed under the new conditions that prevail to a logos without pathos and slowly suffocate from bad health; the mass media are developed into a pathos without logos and die in a senseless delirium. And the task to supply the only effective protection against tyranny, anarchy and idiocy in general falls to the protopian clergy, whereby the paradigm shift is a fact.

This priestly practice can only be exercised behind the barred absolute, and the theory that prompts the said practice is adytonology. And here the most important of all netocratic principles comes into play. Since technology is global but humanity is local, all human activities must be submitted to *the principle of contestability*. Regardless of the pipe dreams of the Chinese communist party in the early 21th century, there is no hope that a netocratic autocracy would guarantee growth and stability, or even that it would manage to endure over time. The fact is that all attempts to control and manipulate the netocracy behind the barred absolute only lead to new migration since nomadology in itself is the ultimate democracy. The optimal sensocracy must remain open and plural, something that is clearly reflected in the protopian values, where *antagony* is the propelling principle for intellectual and creative expansion. Without antagony, no creativity, but only a dramatically escalating *brain drain*. The barred absolute is thus anything but a temporary matrix for escapism. This means that adytonology returns in history as *the doctrine of how the protopian challenges himself* to adulthood's absolute and therefore also divine boundary.

There often arise misunderstandings around the barred absolute, since the sacral space is a condition for one being able to distinguish esoteric knowledge (tantra) from exoteric information (sutra), but where information nonetheless will be read as though it were knowledge, the phenomenon that we call *epistemological delusion*. The reason is that the sacral always is understood as the source of the relations that are at hand, and not as the result of or reward for the carried-out effort. The sacral is unattainable precisely through literal originality. This in turn explains why precisely that which is classed as criminal and regarded as inconceivable before the barred absolute, often is to be regarded as purely commonplace behind the barred absolute. The shamans and the lesser gods have their freedom to explore and experiment with things that are inconceivable for ordinary mortals. It is part and parcel of the matter that *the adults of the adults* can devote themselves to activities that other adults do not understand or covet, in the same way as children live under another set of regulations than adults in all cultures. Everywhere we find a hierarchy that is highly functional and not at all merely ceremonial.

Of course it is precisely these recurring and rather expected transgressions that accord the lesser gods their iconological status among numerous throngs of admirers. At the same time it is this principle, and the flexible surveillance of it, that enables the law book to remain a living document, making sure the law is never set in stone and fixed for all eternity, which would be tantamount to death. Thus there is a continuous activity behind the barred absolute, an activity that never can be observed directly from the outside but that makes distinct impressions. During informationalism we call these activities *the dark renaissance*. The effect is that the masses then can project their inextinguishable needs of The Great Other onto the barred absolute in itself, instead of confusedly and desperately seeking The Great Other precisely everywhere and in everything they happen to get hold of. And in light of this, the psychoanalytical ambition to live a life without worrying about or seeking The Great Other does of course appear the perhaps greatest delusion of all. Every program of that kind infallibly leads to frenetic sectarianism and strife between different psychoanalytical cults, which at best subconsciously and hysterically construct new barred absolutes in which to reflect one's frustrated subjects. The solution to the problem lies, as so often, in the two-headed phallus, which positions itself so that one head is inside the barred absolute and one head is outside.

Information is in itself only a question of accessibility, but not of understanding and even less of an authentic innovation of any kind. It is the barred absolute that transforms information to knowledge and then takes the knowledge further to protopian creativity. The pathical priest behind the barred absolute is namely *the curator* both between Man and the Machine and between the elite and the mass. He is the sentry who sits guarding the gate to the membrane. Behind the barred absolute the masters in the meantime are slaves in order to be able to be masters of the masses that constantly try to evade time through constantly mimicking and competing. The Zurvanite clergy can eventually be realized. Indian philosophy distinguishes between on the one hand these spheres as the sacred space *nirvana* where *tantra* is applied, and on the other hand the profane space *samsara* where *sutra* is applied. Please note that there is no general accessibility whatsoever in terms of *nirvana*, it is again a state behind the barred absolute, accessible only to *the chosen ones*. And during informationalism there is of course no reason whatsoever to choose at random from the population, but the sensocratic Machine sifts out precisely the pathical persons with exactly the qualities that symbiotic intelligence is requesting there and then. Which thus entails that no one in the elite can settle down and hope for a lifelong membership in the very innermost circuit; the harsh weeding-out process and fine-tuned new recruitment of promising talents is continuous. Welcome to the world of *absolute meritocracy*.

An emergence is an extraordinary event along the time axis that gives rise to an entirely new vector with its own built-in forces, behaviors, laws and rules. Our own transdeterminist universe is in itself an example of such an emergence vector that once has arisen at a certain point along a subphysical hypertime axis. A paradigm is correspondingly an entirely new society further up on the time axis with its own built-in forces, showdowns, and eventually laws, rules and structures, all of which can be traced back to a specific historical event, for instance a comprehensive natural catastrophe or a decisive technological invention. Paradigmatics is Man's methodology for defining the different time-bound emergence vectors and paradigms and distinguishing these from each other. Archetypeology is then how the sociont defines itself and its different talents and needs within emergence vectors and paradigms. What emergence vectors, paradigms, and even archetypographies all have in common is that they are timewise clearly delimited phenomena in history, and therefore can be studied each by itself on its own conditions. Therefore all meaningful categorization and specialization on the part of Man must also always be some form of paradigmatization or archetypification.

If Man takes paradigmatics, membranics and archetypeology seriously, the subcultural sociont gets all the ethical tools it needs to encounter all the short-circuits pertaining to value – in the form of sundry variants of banal moralism – and can instead optimize its decision-making process. Alfred North Whitehead formulates this eventology as though everything begins and ends with *experiences* and that these experiences are valued with respect to their *creativity*. This amoral ethics, which exclusively rests on the relation between paradigmatics and archetypeology, is called protopianism. The protopian religion that Whitehead advocates is therefore a religion based on technology in contrast to classic religion, which is based on magic. And it is – of course – this conviction that is called *syntheism* in the world of theology. Alongside Zoroaster and Hegel, Whitehead then joins in, and together they constitute syntheism's three eventological pioneers. If Zoroaster laid the foundation for the feudalist clergy, while Hegel laid the foundation for the capitalist clergy, it is Whitehead who, behind the barred absolute, lays the foundation for the informationalist clergy and hands over the cognitive tools that make it possible to proclaim and exercise a netocratic protopianism. Whitehead radically breaks with Spinoza and the idea that *rationality* constitutes the absolute principle of existence, and he instead argues that it is *creativity* that is the absolute principle. Every entity in existence has some form of *agency*, some kind of minimal degree of originality, in terms of how the entity in question interacts with other entities in its environment.

This is an example and a consequence of existence's transdeterminist character, and thereby contingent openness toward the future (and a matching, compact closedness *vis-à-vis* the past), *the Hegelian root-of-the-phallus* – rather than some kind of determinism with all that this entails by way of a necessary, Spinozist closure. However this requires that every entity is limited by what Whitehead calls its *social restrictions*, that is: that every entity is limited by its active relations. Freedom is namely only precisely freedom within the confines of clear limitations. An agent's uniqueness and dividuality emerges out of a self-determination with respect to how one best handles one's possibilities within the limitations that the situation provides. One can thus only play the cards one has been dealt, wishing for other and better cards is only a waste of time and energy. In this manner Whitehead breaks with Kant and a world whose fundamental building blocks consist of a few immutable things. Against this Whitehead posits a world that consists of an incalculable amount of integrated processes and events. Reality is this constant, dynamic becoming – not a series of static being. Static being we create ourselves; it is a fiction that we use for orientation through and management of a surplus of impulses, and not reality itself. There is a terrain filled with countless biological processes and events, and there is a two-dimensional map on flat paper.

Which leads us to Nietzsche's concept *the death of God*. And after the death of God also Michel Foucault's concept *the death of The Individual*, which takes the Nietzschean insight of paradigmatic temporality to the next level. Nietzsche declares the Protestant god dead; Foucault declares the Cartesian individual dead. A deconstruction of Cartesian individualism and the thereto connected Lutheran Protestantism as illusions about – in turn – the child's access to the adult phallus, the adult's access to the priestly phallus, the priest's access to the divine phallus, all of which create the illusion that the child is a god. This is undoubtedly a backward worldview compared with the nomadological. Through elevating the innocently ignorant child to a god, one displays one's contempt of advanced age and laboriously accumulated wisdom. One worships the child to the extent that it eventually is sexualized. The insight that is absent is that a direct access to God never can be anything other than an illusion, since the hierarchy is a reality: child-adult-priest-God. There are no short-cuts, ignorance is not miraculous knowledge. One can therefore only worship God indirectly, via the lesser, iconological gods, which applies generally – except among the priests within their own third religion behind the barred absolute. If the opposite were to be the case, that just anyone in any manner could establish direct contact with God, the once coveted object for desire would wither and lose its allure, which is what always happens when desire attains its objective. Where to direct the gaze when God has lost his power of attraction?

The driving force that takes the place of desire is now instead transcendence, this precisely because desire actually most deeply viewed only seeks itself – when the objective of desire is conquered, desire has of course already restlessly moved on toward new objectives and objects. It can never get enough. Transcendence, however, is entirely oriented toward *the unattainable* behind the barred absolute. And it is precisely thanks to the barred absolute – that is: the fact that it is barred – that transcendence can operate without ever running the risk of actually finding what it seeks. This constructive relation is however constantly threatened by the *shaman envy* that inevitably arises when the priest goes back and forth across the *chinavat* bridge, the membrane between the living and the dead in Zoroastrian theology. Consequently it is shaman envy that constitutes a major part of the foundation both for Christianity and Islam.

According to this banal proclamation for the masses, the curtain in the temple would suddenly have gone up in smoke, whereafter

God and Man just as suddenly stand face to face with each other. The barred absolute has been cleared away. All the children at the party get a bag of candy and are welcomed into the VIP lounge, without any demands for any particular achievement or qualification. The difference between God and Man becomes hazy, just as the difference between adult and child. If such a culture moreover is robbed of *the authentic phallus* – since there of course still is no discernible difference between adult and child when all shall have access to *mamilla* forever without any effort of one's own – the shamanic ideal will spread through the entire society, but at the cost of a radical infantilization. An ideology that promises that all your dreams will be realized if you only profess the right doctrine, cannot lead to anything other than the pillar-saint and the boy-pharaoh being elevated to and promoted as pseudo-shamanic ideals at the expense of the authentic patriarch and the authentic matriarch. Both the pillar-saint surrounded by all the world's angels and the boy-pharaoh surrounded by all the world's soldiers are divine and invincible at the center of their fairytale religions with mass commitment. Diversity is portrayed as a question concerning *how humans just look different* and not *how humans think in different ways.* Authentic diversity is killed on the altar of false diversity, and the result is absolute conformity.

When existence becomes digital and our digital environment, like a stern but fair judge, knows and remembers absolutely everything about us, then we lose – to our great sorrow – the intimate contact with mamilla, which is brutally snatched away from us. The new transparency entails that the scope for wishful thinking shrinks and all but disappears. The process of grief we are then forced to go through in many respects resembles that which psychiatrist Elisabeth Kübler-Ross divides into five steps. First there is *denial*, then there is *anger,* thereafter follows *negotiation*, then there is *depression*, and last but not least we (at best) succeed in completing the process with *acceptance*. If Man during capitalism had to handle the death of God, he is during attentionalism instead forced to wrestle with *the death of The Individual* (see *The Netocrats* and *The Body Machines*). Which makes it necessary for the social theater to once again enter into close combat with ideological nihilism, this too a match in five rounds. First there is *naive nihilism*, then follows *mortidinal nihilism*, it is in turn followed by *ironic nihilism*, thereafter *libidinal nihilism* ensues, and finally we (hopefully) attain *affirmative nihilism*, where *haurvatat* gets the possibility to land in *ameretat*, to use the Zoroastrian vocabulary. When the naive transitions into the cynical within the old paradigm with its mortido, we must return to the ironic in order to attain the affirmative and establish the new paradigm with its libido.

The decisive step in terms of protopian activism occurs between the ironic and the affirmative stages in the processing of nihilism. It is the will-to-intelligence of the priests that generates ironic nihilism. But it is the will-to-transcendence of the chieftains that generates the affirmative nihilism that actually constructs the new paradigm. Ironic nihilism leads up to the root-of-the-phallus. Affirmative nihilism affirms precisely the phallic libido. During ironic nihilism *freedom* disappears as the horizon, the acknowledged insight of the nihilist state can only generate a distanced cynicism atop a transdeterminist conviction. Or to describe the situation from the principle of the two-headed phallus; ironic nihilism is the state in which the priest absorbs nihilism but lacks a chieftain on whom to apply the affirmative libido. Logos and mythos form a seemingly robust facade, but with pathos depressed. The predictable result is that pathos returns in the form of a markedly mortidinal force, and it is this force that we call *the dark renaissance*. It is in that state that the false phalluses threaten to drown out the authentic phallus with their anojective call. The *egregores* threaten to take over the public space.

The dialectal exit out of this state goes via the restoration of the barred absolute, where the shamanic elite can experience and benefit from a freedom in seclusion and live out this freedom affirmatively and thereby Messianically. The masses that remain standing on the other side of the membrane can return to the denial phase, and the entire nomadological chain of cause and effect can be repeated anew. But what is decisive here is that the control over the dark renaissance exclusively is exercised behind the barred absolute, something that is clear in the different subjectivities that are involved in the social theater. From this and only from this a potential *saoshyant* for the chosen people can step forward in the form of a personification of the affirmation, and let a surplus of value and meaning wash over the entire world that finds itself before the barred absolute, projected onto the promised empire.

Nomadology is the standardized and horizontal exodology. Eventology, on the other hand, is the exceptional and vertical exodology. Nomadology operates according to the principle of least possible energy consumption. Its circular movement thus requires less energy than permanently sitting still. Eventology instead operates by the principle of temporary increases of energy consumption, if and when extra energy is accessible. It is, thus, only eventology that can generate the fantasy of eternally sitting still. These theological narratives find their equivalences in transcendental eternalism, realist mobilism and dialectical syntheism. And the barred absolute is the ecstatic experience of the event as the syntheist infinite now, clearly manifested as pathos during hunting, war, the orgy, birth, the ritual and death. This is to a great extent a matter of the outer circuit and the inner circuit within the sociont, and their two essentially distinct metanarratives: logos and mythos. Eventology is the story of the phallic event that changes history forever. Nomadology is the story of the constant and eternal recurrence of the same.

This means that eventology is fixated on *the event* as the foundation for existence, while nomadology is fixated on *the process* as the foundation for existence. Another name for this relation is *the dialectics of eternalism and mobilism*. The insight of absolute knowledge in the understanding of the dialectics of eternalism and mobilism is what we refer to as *Hegel's phallus*. Kant is thereby the individualist apogee of both Cartesianism and Protestantism, while Hegel opens the door to precisely the splitting of the Individual into masses of dividuals that later occurs in Marx, Nietzsche, Darwin and Freud during the 19th century. What on the other hand is missing in Hegel and Lacan is an understanding that this inaccessibility as substance in itself already exists within religion. But not in Christianity, above all not in matrichal Catholicism, which Kant and Hegel increasingly oppose. On the other hand, both in Zoroastrianism and Judaism, which precede Christianity and Islam. And above all in Vajrayana Buddhism's development of the category *tantra* as divorced from *sutra*. The barred subject must be complemented with its own origin, something that is lacking in Hegel and Lacan, namely the barred absolute.

The four world religions from the Middle East must thus be understood in the following way: since Zoroastrianism worships the military phallus, Islam can never be anything other than *the imitation of the worshipping of the military phallus*. And since Judaism worships the priestly phallus, Christianity can never be anything other than *the imitation of the worshipping of the priestly phallus*. Which explains why Islam is founded by and constantly refers back to a military by the name of Muhammad, while Christianity is founded by and constantly refers back to a priest by the name of Peter. All this becomes possible through the Gnostic maneuver that consists in blowing up the door to the barred absolute, for the purpose of taming and reshaping the barred religions of the military and the priesthood into a simplified message tailored to the great masses. If eventological proptopianism shall be able to grow strong, it is necessary to reverse this maneuver and generate a development in the opposite direction.

Eventology is the pathical narrative that oscillates between the two poles *ecstasy* and *trauma* as events. Therefore pathos is the foundation of the priestly monotheism or *eventology*, while mythos is the foundation of the polytheism of the masses or *iconology*. Out of pathos *logos* then rises as the formalized religion that organizes the necessary relation between eventology and nomadology. It is this religion that is called *the law*. This means that the priests represent a tantric religion of alterable pathos behind the barred absolute, something that then is transformed into a sutric religion of fixed logos before the barred absolute. The brutal, pathical reality behind the barred absolute is thus transformed into the organized, logical law before the barred absolute. It is not remarkable that the tantric perspective on existence rests on an erotic order in the primordial chaos, while the sutric perspective on existence rests on a divine order in the primordial chaos. The two perspectives can only meet ritually, which entails that sutra submits to tantra for the purpose of creating the longed-for order. For the tantric talent, who thrives splendidly in the shamanic borderland between phallic order and matrichal chaos, that objective is, on the other hand, wholly secondary, if even that. The difference between sutra and tantra is thus of central importance.

Sutra is information that is conveyed in front of the barred absolute, before the people, to the people. Iconology and mimicry are sutric phenomena. The sutric teacher is a paragon to mimic. *Tantra* is knowledge that is conveyed or even created behind the barred absolute within the clergy. Exodology and the creative production of the genuinely novel are examples of tantric phenomena. The tantric teacher personifies what we call *crazy wisdom*. There is no hierarchy or ranking between sutra and tantra in themselves – it is a case of two different phenomena within two different spheres, which is the sole and decisive difference. At the same time it is thus the priest who hides behind the barred absolute while the chieftain leads the exodus in front of and outside the temple. The area where the children are not allowed to enter is *the pathical narrative*, the area where not even the adults in the sociont are allowed to enter is *the barred absolute*. In both cases an entry is possible only if the child or the adult in question first has succeeded in leaving mythos in order to enter into logos. And this is the reason why we call all personal development during a dividual's lifetime *the voyage toward phallus*, away from mamilla. This means first a voyage from mythos toward logos and then, when the dividual is mature enough, the possibly concluding voyage from logos toward pathos. The difference between logos and pathos in Eastern philosophy is called the difference between sutra and tantra, where sutra is taught via rationality and mimicry while tantra is taught via intuition and crazy wisdom.

The two-headed phallus is thus also a necessary prerequisite for epistemology. The difference between *sutra* and *tantra* in the Silk Road religions is equivalent to the difference between being adult and being enlightened. One mimics the chieftain's phallus to achieve an adultification. The priest's phallus, on the other hand, only exists behind the barred absolute and therefore cannot be mimicked. However, it can always inspire the search for one's entirely own, dividual path to *Enlightenment*, a state that one best acquires a Western conception of by studying the Nietzschean *Übermensch*. The passage from logos toward pathos is not a banal voyage upward to some kind of heaven or some reward because one has been good or clever, it is no pilgrimage toward paradise akin to that which Dante depicts in *The Divine Comedy*, but instead the opposite – an incredibly arduous trek toward the glowing root-of-the-phallus, an existential choice that is made by the one who chooses tantra over sutra as the ultimate *truth-as-an-act* (see *Syntheism – Creating God in the Internet Age*). It is only the priest who in this manner can live in the deepest (or highest) existential state that syntheologically is called *The Infinite Now*, where no longer any spiritual truth is inaccessible or incomprehensible. This is a world of sex, violence and art, a state of pure and uncompromising pathos, where logos and mythos are conspicuous by their absence, which – naturally – makes this state extremely unwieldy. The oldest known memorials from the pathical history of religion are the brutally expressive cave paintings from the period that constitutes the apogee of the original sociont. Welcome to *the golden age of the minotaur*.

Philosopher and psychoanalyst Slavoj Žižek argues that the difference between The One and diversity has its origin in the human subject. We argue that this is a much too Kantian reading of Hegel. It is rather the case that a division between the barred absolute and diversity arises in the reading of the surrounding world and in the discerning of the first object – mamilla – *vis-à-vis* a surrounding chaos. It is in this opposition between mamilla and the environment that the dialectics of eternalism and mobilism is developed. Mamilla then remains barred as an absolute *vis-à-vis* all other objects, up until the child begins to associate mamilla with matrix – as it is confronted with the body of the mother as a whole – and eventually discovers the maternal body's affection toward phallus, which then crystallizes as a competitor. It is in conjunction with this *phallic intrusion* (see *Digital Libido – Sex, Power and Violence in the Network Society*) that phallus takes over mamilla's role as the barred absolute. The child's desire is stirred to life in the form of libido, since the child loses access to the desired, barred absolute. The present, intimate mamilla has of course been exchanged for the absent, extimate phallus. The first *object* receives competition from the first *project* in the life of the child. Desire is awakened as desire always is desire to that which desire cannot have.

The problem for Žižek is that his barred subject is not fundamental. The barred absolute does not allow any difference or externality *vis-à-vis* itself. Like a black hole it devours all interest and all commitment. But this is not the case with subjectivity, since it occurs only later, as the negation of the maternal body. The child for the first time apprehends itself as *non-mother* the moment mamilla and its own mouth are separated from each other, if only for a short while. It is thus in opposition to the barred absolute that the barred subject arises, after and not before the barred absolute's genesis. And it is between these two barred and therefore mysterious spheres that Man continues his life. The matriarchy oscillates between matrix and mamilla, separated by nature. The patriarchy oscillates between the barred absolute and the barred subject, separated by culture. God is not and has never been accessible to Man. God does not respond to Man's message in a bottle or to any other messages at all. Both Zoroastrianism and Judaism claim that God's real name, the one that God actually answers to, remains firmly hidden behind the barred absolute. Of this the faithful are reminded when they learn to never ever pronounce the name of God, as this would be seen as narcissistic disloyalty *vis-à-vis* the sociont, and God would immediately need to punish them for the transgression.

This means that adytonology is the core of religion. *In the same way that the subject is its own blind spot, the barred absolute is the sociont's blind spot*, the central object that no one can perceive and that precisely therefore unites everything else that is discernible and definable. The barred subject and the barred absolute are quite simply the neuroses that make an otherwise psychotic world cohere. *The world in itself* is nothing other than the mobilist chaos between these two fundamental eternalizations. Thus the barred subject and the barred absolute become each other's negations, and between them there is no enduring truce. It is only the high priest with his distanced, and therefore by necessity perverted gaze, who can apprehend a kind of temporarily sustainable balance between subject and absolute.

Behind the barred absolute the priests have their own logos, their own mythos and their own pathos. These are gathered under the concept adytonology. The priests' propelling forces are inverted in comparison with the world before the barred absolute. In the world of the priests it is the narrative itself that sets the world in motion. Syntheologically we express this as though *Atheos* is the highest god for the priests themselves (see *Syntheism – Creating God in the Internet Age*). Everything is ultimately about handling the void, which Christianity and Islam in their eagerness to please the people and the power structure completely ignore, wherefore the conclusion only can be that they are nothing but infantile fantasies of what a religion is and can be. They quite simply do not carry out the task, and their recent decay into banal nihilism and desperate fundamentalism respectively, proves that these shortcomings were built-in right from the very start, as fatal systemic failures. They ignore the barred absolute as the necessary foundation for both subjectivity and objectivity and *authentic religion* as a phenomenon overall. But eventually history has caught up with them, and these are indeed different and fascinating times.

18
The great exodus

Blind faith in the process is an equally blind faith in rebirth. Nomadology accepts this universal answer to the conundrums of metaphysics – as this comports with what is experienced and observed with one's own eyes. The leaves that fell this autumn will grow back as spring is approaching and the snow melts. But since we also have an eventological perspective to relate to, this comfortable assurance must be thrown overboard and the question must be posed anew. And the reason is not just that we realize that the event can change things once and for all and lead history onto a completely new track. No, what is important is that history itself becomes something completely different as a result of the event. An old world dies and is buried, a fundamentally new world is born and is stirred to life. Death is thereby no longer just a banal transitory phase between two repetitions of the same – and thereby itself a recurring repetition – but rather establishes itself as *the real absolute*. Death is really death, and it is this and not rebirth that now suddenly must be the mother of God. Thus the event is just as much death as it is life. Something must die first, and really die, for something else to be born. Precisely this has been what has made eventology hard to swallow – and to sell. It has been more pleasant to constantly tell lies about new heavens – and matching hells as threats for those who are difficult to convince – than to accept eventology's first and principal condition: *to submit to death*.

When Zoroastrianism's monist idea of process and event as complementing functions is attacked during the Axial Age, a situation arises where the event first must appear as an *anti-event*. If life is the thesis, death is the antithesis. Life is the temporary death of death itself, libido is the flip side of mortido, and not the other way around (see *Digital Libido – Sex, Power and Violence in the Network Society*). That is: with the event being established as an idea, there is an alternative close at hand to the idea of the eternal recurrence of the same. This alternative is that death is real, that everything dies and is dissolved with death, that is: that something dies, not to be resurrected but to leave a space behind where something else can arise, and precisely this is *the event*. Another way of expressing this, to connect with *transcendental emergentism*, is to say that *death is the event in a virtual form*. Death is the implicate form of the event, while the event is the explicate form of death.

First death, then life. First negation, then oscillation. Or as Canadian philosopher Cadell Last expresses the matter: There must be a *negatology* before we can create a credible eventology. We must first organize a measure of creative destruction. Which was clear already during the extended zenith of nomadology right before permanent settlement arrived in history: death was the necessary embryo that constituted a pre-stage to the event that would come. In particular there was, naturally, this insight in those who saw through the fairytales of reincarnation. Negatology is virtual eventology. While eventology is, as Hegel would point out, actual negatology. While there is no *absolute justice* for all the world's pillar-saints and boy-pharaohs to attain. And the reason is that *death is the absolute* and nothing else. Just as there is no eternity or perfection, nor is there any absolute justice. We will have to settle for a Nietzschean *poetic justice* in ethics in the same way that we have to settle for a Hegelian *poetic infinity* in phenomenology. While literal justice and infinity are both empty representations inasmuch as they only can represent their own infantile, vengeful, and thereby pathological pipe dreams.

Thanks to death itself everything does not need to be reborn and thus does not constantly have to be repeated over and over again. The mortidinal anti-event must precede the libidinal event; we must first intensely want to die to then repress this experience to then intensely want to live. Gnosticism tries to wrest event from process (and promote its childish hope in *eternal life*) by denying process in the first place. All time then becomes linear and no time is allowed to be circular any longer. This supraideology of the Western world – the cohesive glue between Christianity and Islam – clings fiercely to eternal life as part of a strategy that aims to deaden one's own fear of death. But the same thing also happens with the same process in the East, where one instead denies the historical arrival of eventology. This supraideology of the Eastern world desperately clings to *reincarnation* in its pure terror of death. Where the only way out of *samsara* is to attain *mahamudra*, the return to the origin of everything and the healing of every form of division. That is: a healing in the form of collective extinction and nothing else. A collective death denial through letting oneself be devoured by the black hole of the matrix. The escape from tough day-to-day life, in all of history's addict brains, to what Sigmund Freud with ill-concealed sarcasm calls *the oceanic feeling*.

We constantly return to the wafer-thin veneer of civilization. It does not take much for libido to be snatched away from us and mortido to devour us completely. Fear of death thereby hides fear of life beneath it. Or more correctly: If we really knew absolutely everything about everything our will to live would literally and immediately disappear. Hegel's dream of the future *World Spirit* is thus Hegel's own Achilles' heel – that is to say the Messianic *totalism* in Hegel that we in the strongest terms oppose as early as in our debut work *The Netocrats*. The World Spirit's arrival would kill humanity due to the fact that no human any longer would endure living in its proximity. The absolute spirit is indeed possible, it is moreover "more Hegelian than Hegel himself", but it must be hidden behind *the barred absolute* and never be generally available. History does not move toward a revelation of absolutely everything in a single, great cohesive theory of everything. Quite the contrary, history undoubtedly moves toward a necessary recognition of *the principle of explanatory closure*. The vain Hegel of absolute knowledge must die, but a reinvented Hegel of *absolute deadlock* is precisely what the information age needs. Because the gate to the tower of God remains closed. And then we die.

This is what the historical Hegel and the European Enlightenment in their craze for the public and the profane do not understand and never succeed in absorbing from the mysticism that hides within Zoroastrianism and Judaism. The curse of the Western world is incubated in the heritage from Christianity and Islam and their infantile craze for the public and the profane, *the cult of transparency* that dominates both religions, that is to say history viewed as a kind of God's striptease dance where eventually nothing other than the naked god stands exposed before everything and everyone. When the barred absolute is ejected from religion, and the mystics are persecuted and executed, the private and the sacred also disappears. What remains is only a banal soup of empty signs, drenched in an increasingly nihilist yearning for direct death. Only a dramatic restoration of the barred absolute can save Western culture and make a netocratic *paradigmatics* possible. The curtain in the temple is not destroyed, rather it must be renovated and restored, otherwise the temple is no house of God at all, but only a photo op among other dead ruins in the necrophilic age of mass tourism.

It is during the Axial Age that dualism arrives and exerts full power on history, literally tearing Man to shreds, like a body at war with the soul or a soul at war with the body. Where the only possible exit is to keep Zoroaster's *haurvatat* (the complete, but anything but perfect, life that dies) and *ameretat* (the renewed life that transcends death as a completely new life without connection to the preceding, dying life) separate. That is: we cannot return to process and event as a cohesive monist metaphysics unless we do not first throw ourselves down before death and recognize death as the ultimate horizon for absolutely everything. Negatology always precedes eventology. It is thus not only as dividuals that we are and must be mortal. Even humanity in itself must recognize its own mortality as humanity, before event within process shall be possible anew. Life in itself is deadly. To freeze is to kill. God is always greater than Man and the sociont can only be God's likeness, but never God himself. Before we even dare to entertain the thought of an Entheos that is generated within a Pantheos, we must understand that Atheos precedes everything. Potentiality cannot move toward actuality without virtuality first having done its job, even if virtuality, in a Hegelian manner, only can be traced retroactively.

What *de facto* is lacking in Hegel's historiography is a theory of empires, nations, and human populations at scale. The struggle between the Persian Zoroaster and the Chinese Confucius concerning how the empire shall be built and upheld – Zoroaster with the two-headed phallus, Confucius with the one-headed phallus – will have no equivalent in the European Enlightenment. Hegel's nation is nothing other than a people who speak the same language and therefore constitute a nation with at best also a common religion at the same time. That is to say Hegel sets up the Jewish nation as a new religion for the European nation-states, but without the barred absolute. And the reason for this is that Hegel's nation is *creatio ex nihilo* without an empire that precedes the nation as in the Persian-Hebrew axis. It is therefore not surprising that the European colonial empires became the bloodiest in world history, without the least respect for their subordinates, and eventually resulted in the grotesque antisemitism of German Nazism – which thus is not a racism proper, but an out-and-out mimetic rivalry *vis-à-vis* another people who both have a common nation and religion – and the out-and-out mimetic rivalry of Russian Stalinism *vis-à-vis* a West which in contrast to Stalinism had left slavery, enforced labor and ideological prison camps behind.

Antiquity is radically different, has an alternative grid

superimposed, as we revisit it through the optics that is laid out in this text. What emerge as the pinnacles from the vantage point of the history of ideas, are in part the brotherhood between Zoroaster and Vishtaspa which takes the two-headed phallus as its point of departure, which is the prerequisite for the first Persian empire around 1700 BC, the first empire in world history, a dream of a new paradigm that is built on a court language and a court religion. In part also the exodus of Moses, Aaron and Miriam, with the Hebrews out of Egypt, a project that constitutes the first exodology and the dream of the birth of a new nation as a new paradigm that is built on a common written language for all. In part, and finally, also Cyrus the Great's conquest of Babylon in 539 BC, an event that liberates the Jewish nation within the Persian empire as the absolute solution to the intertribalist dilemma at the birth of civilization. And it is of course in the field of tension between Zoroastrianism and Judaism that the first ideas of universal human rights can arise and assume a fixed form in the classic *Cyrus Cylinder*, antiquity's most sacred text. The victors of war simply cease to boil the enemy's children in oil; instead they transform the enemy into a local (and hopefully loyal) commander within the confines of the empire, by opening up for the former enemy to cultivate an identity of its own and delve ever deeper within its own root-of-the-phallus, cherishing its own religion. The victor becomes a builder of nations; exactly this is what *empire* is.

In comparison with these epochal events, which already in antiquity favor and refine the finest properties of the West, other, traditionally emphasized events pale – such as the death of Christ on the cross (a reasonably failed Messianic project with a pillar-saint, but without an authentic chieftain and an authentic priest) and Muhammad's conquest of Mecca (a parody of a Messianic project with a boy-pharaoh, but without an authentic priest and an authentic chieftain). What in this context is "more Hegel than Hegel himself", is to once again *think empire before nation*, which entails an optimization of both these concepts and, in the Hegelian sense, a completion of history during informationalism. If Christianity and Islam shall reconnect with each other and find common ground, the only possibility for this comes with the historical Zoroaster rather than with a mythological Abraham.

Thereby both religions would return dialectically to their respective origins and thus be forced to recognize that death *de facto* is the absolute (Hegel's brilliant idea) that only can arise through this movement, whereafter the exodus to the promised land can be complemented with *the exodus to the promised empire*. Only then will actual communism become a real possibility, not with Christian and/or Islamic blackmailing methods toward all dissenters, and definitely not by virtue of a colossal socialist welfare state, but quite simply through the free choices of free dividuals to take part in the sociont that now has been resurrected. And it has in that case been resurrected without any mendacious wishful thinking of eternal life, reincarnation, or absolute justice that shall arise through magic on some dramatic doomsday. *Asha* overcomes *druj*, truth overcomes the lie, eventually. And the reason that truth triumphs is that it splits itself, in part into *sutric truth* for the people before the barred absolute, in part into *tantric truth* for the clergy behind the barred absolute. The path between God and the faithful is once again cordoned off, and God can at last rise again in seclusion.

Economist Friedrich von Hayek demonstrates in the 1920s how the network-dynamical effects on an open market are completely superior to the converging variants of cajoling directed toward the boy-pharaoh, a cajoling that dominates in a closed and concentrated monocracy. This applies just as much in a digitalized world of thousands of satellites and millions of sensors as ever before in history. Sensocracy also benefits hugely from being kept free and open, and such a process always begins with the assurance of phallic dialectics. Phallus shall be two-headed and it is through being two-headed that it becomes both intelligent and transcendental. Namely, intelligence can only arise if there first prevails *antagony*, a love of that which is different, a love of intelligence that requires interacting with resistant obstacles and overcoming adversities, instead of constantly seeking the consent and praise that a small child cashes in from its tender mother for every work of art brought home from preschool. This is important. Without an authentic antagony, nor can there be any authentic will-to-power. Large, complex systems become extremely unstable and short-lived if they are subject to a single pillar-saint's discretion and decisions made on the basis of substandard information. The dynamical alternative is instead that every will and every idea attains its long-term value as it, over time, finds its proper place within the sociont's archetypology. And this is only possible in a culture permeated by antagonic diversity. Without antagony, life merely becomes one long, stupefying repetition.

So how does *intraphallic antagony* work? Please note here that the priest worships the chieftain's *ahura*, and the chieftain worships the priest's *mazda*. There is thus already a setting of boundaries within phallic *adytonology*. The object of worship is always external and with this shift it is collaboration and not rivalry that dominates the sociont. What will-to-power strives for is precisely this: collective collaboration. This massive, immensely strong will-to-power manifests itself, argues Hegel, both as a kind of spherical substance and as a membranic subjectivity. Substance and subjectivity shift between will-to-transcendence and will-to-intelligence. Will-to-transcendence is manifested iconologically by the rain-god and the love of the ultimate challenge. Will-to-intelligence is manifested iconologically by the sun-god and the love of the optimal preservation. We refer to this relation as *phallic nomadology*. A system does not constantly have to repeat itself and run in circles as in matrichal nomadology, it can also expand to then implode, and when such systems reach maximal energy expression we find ourselves at the event that phallic nomadology produces. It is consequently out of phallic nomadology that the idea arises that a civilization may go through a rise and a fall, just like every human dividual themselves go through during their lifetime. One is born, becomes an adult, ages and dies – this applies to all levels.

Please note the difference here between the *scout* who reports to the chieftain and the *spy* who reports to the priest – and how these two characters represent and support the shamanic caste that encloses the sociont. When the scout and the spy have concluded their assignments, the scout leaves the arena open for *the warrior* while the spy leaves the arena open for *the hunter* to carry out the proper phallic projects. What happens when Man becomes settled and eventology becomes a fact – as a complement to the nomadology that claims to be the great metanarrative – is that the warrior's assignment is extended, whereupon the warrior changes guise to *the engineer*, while the hunter's assignment is extended, so that the hunter changes guise to *the merchant*. From then on it is the engineer and the merchant who uphold the civilization that gradually takes shape, with support from *the architect* who complements the patriarchy and fills the world with temples, monuments, arenas and eventually also skyscrapers. And beneath all this phallic libido there is constantly a vibrating, never resting matrichal mortido. Nature is fundamentally mortidinal in essence and culture gets access to libido only through repressing mortido to the subconscious (see *Digital Libido – Sex, Power and Violence in the Network Society*). And the name of this underlying process is of course *sexuality*.

Herein lies the explanation as to why civilization displays a constantly recurring pattern of three male castes: two castes that stand behind the chieftain and one that stands behind the shaman as Man begins to settle permanently, which enables the patriarchy to be underpinned by a stable triad. To begin with we have *the priestly caste* (for shamans and priests, the Indian caste system's *Brahmins*), and further *the warriors' caste* (for warriors and engineers, the Indian caste system's *kshatriya*) and finally *the merchants' caste* (for hunters and merchants, the Indian caste system's *vaishya*). The nomadological warrior is represented by the eventological engineer or *the architect*.

In Western secularized history this gestalt has *the state* as its equivalent. The nomadological hunter is represented by the eventological merchant or *the entrepreneur.* In Western secularized history this gestalt has *the market* as its equivalent. And the nomadological shaman becomes the eventological priest or *the reformer*, who serves both the engineer and the merchant. While the nomadological chieftain stands before the three patriarchal castes as the eventological *monarch.*

Before the engineer, the shaman becomes a Zurvanite war priest with *negation* as his keyword. The negation drives the art of war forward. Before the merchant, the shaman becomes a Mithraic merchant priest with *oscillation* as his keyword. The oscillation drives entrepreneurship forward. When the British colonized South Asia they quickly chose the Sikhs to act both caste and their own religion in terms of the position of the war priest and the negation within Hinduism, while the Parsees got to act both caste and their own religion in terms of the position of the merchant priest and the oscillation within Hinduism. As a result of this, the Sikhs and the Parsees are to this day India's two by far most successful subcultures. The dialectics of negation and oscillation is the clergy's timeless foundation for success. The time-bound reforms that are based on this dialectics, Zoroastrianism's *frashokereti*, is nothing other than a *paradigmatics* adapted to new technological realities. Every vision and every strategy of value within the patriarchy starts from this priestly pragmatics. The timeless is of course what we refer to as *the transparadigmatic*, everything else is attributable to a specific technological paradigm.

The phallic archetypes recur constantly throughout history in support of civilization, whose only progress over time is technological. Once eventology is established, the patriarchy thus most deeply viewed devote itself to building the phallic god, the adult men's own primordial father, retroactively – that is: the patriarchy first and foremost writes its own history. The man has always envied the woman for her creating life through bearing children and thereby reincarnating the world as *process*. Her participation in the cycle is purely carnal. Therefore the man begets technology instead and remakes the world as *event*. And the phallic technology is developed in direction toward a clearly defined narratological objective, the creation of God himself, *Syntheos*. If nomadology concerns Man constantly reincarnating himself and that everything in existence always returns to the same, eventology concerns the fact that every rebirth only illusorily entails a return of (exactly) the same, and instead *de facto* entails a repetition with an ever so slight change, in the same manner that biological copying of the genome never results in one hundred percent identical reproductions.

These very minor changes are accumulated over time and then are of such an essential nature that they become literally epochal, that is: that they lead history onto a completely new track. Exactly this is eventology's central insight, and the objective that follows from this insight is *the civilizational process* in itself. Nomadology always results in a worship of reincarnation, the eternal recurrence of the same. Eventology, however, instead results in a worship of civilization itself, a celebration of the creative advantage of that which deviates from the norm and, not least, of history in itself as an event. And if the event in question requires an active exodus from the old to the new paradigm, eventology also becomes an *exodology*. How does one get out of the old paradigm into the new? Which pioneers come along and become the elite of the new paradigm and the idols for all mimicking successors?

From a Taoist perspective nomadology entails that we submit to a feminine *yin*, just like eventology entails that we submit to a masculine *yang*. If we further describe nomadology in libidinal terms, it appears a worship of matrix, while eventology is a worship of phallus. Thus it also becomes clear that the dialectics of nomadology and eventology entails a deepening of the reasoning that we have explored earlier in the book trilogy that is rounded off with *Process and Event*. The eventological vision ultimately consists in propelling the civilizational process to its logical conclusion, the point at which humanity itself becomes superfluous and therefore will be replaced by a technology that is independent of Man and not marred by Man's many shortcomings either. The ultimate objective is thus not to construct *the Saoshyant* or the Messiah Machine to thus save humanity (see *Syntheism – Creating God in the Internet Age*), but it is instead to construct a machine, *Syntheos*, which is so divine that it actually does not need Man at all. This liberates humanity, which now at last can realize its innermost dream of being able to die in peace and transcend an arduous existence through handing over this existence to its own offspring, *the Messiah Machine.* If we value intelligence more highly than life – if we understand that war (as in killing intelligence) is a more serious concern than hunting (as in merely killing life) – then we have already carried out this shift to syntheism as the ultimate objective and meaning of civilization.

If nomadology is the doctrine of how the genes or *the geneplex* move across the physical landscape, then eventology is the doctrine of how the memes or *the memeplex* move across the mental landscape. Exodology is then the doctrine of how eventology eventually sets nomadology itself in motion, how the memes (for an exhaustive discussion of memetics, see our first trilogy: *The Netocrats*, *The Global Empire* and *The Body Machines*) eventually seize power over and control the genes. It is this the *adultification of humanity itself* as we call the shift from religion-as-magic in the form of *theology* over to religion-as-technology in the form of *syntheology*. Philosopher Forrest Landry describes this historical shift in his book *Immanent Metaphysics* as a kind of enlightenment of the Internet Age, built upon the insight that *transcendence* (Landry's equivalent to the imaginary order), *omniscience* (the symbolic order) and *immanence* (the real order) recur dialectically during the Internet Age as transcendent *vision*, omniscient *strategy* and real *culture* as the historical realization of Man's most profound insights of his own being. Man's existential choice then becomes consciousness in itself. From a netocratic power perspective, transcendence naturally has its equivalent in *sensocracy*, omniscience in *protopianism*, and immanence in *informationalism*.

The dialectics of libido and mortido on one axis, and the dialectics of eternalism and mobilism on the other axis, lead us toward *the four steps in the pathical evolution*, or what engineer Stefan Skoog calls creativity's necessary *pathomatics*. Pathical evolution returns as the chain of cause and effect in all narratives of planned, carried-out and successful projects. Its pathos is the subconscious drama in every heroic story of various hazardous feats. Pathomatics is quite simply the definitive history of how phallus tames the chaos of existence and makes this chaos an asset in the phallic creation of a new societal order. Within classic decision-making pathomatics is the fast-paced, pathical *abduction* in contrast to the sluggish, logical *induction*. It is the chieftain who personifies pathomatics. The task of the priests is to disassemble and abolish the old paradigm through the nihilist chain, where the priest himself represents ironic nihilism, while the chieftain by virtue of his immanent pathomatics represents affirmative nihilism, the negation of the old paradigm that transforms abstraction to the concrete new paradigm.

First there arises *potential energy* (which we connect with instinct within the psychoanalytical drive system), the pathomatical equivalent to *naive nihilism*. Thereafter potential energy transitions into *actual energy* (which we associate with drive within psychoanalysis), the pathomatical equivalent to *cynical nihilism*. Actual energy then transitions into being *directed energy* (which we connect with desire within psychoanalysis), the pathomatical equivalent to *ironic nihilism*. The priests present vision and strategy, but do not personify direction in themselves. It is not the priests but the flag-carrying chieftain who personifies the war and the hunting that takes the sociont into the future. Finally pathomatics is completed with *transcendental energy* (which we associate with transcendence within psychoanalysis), the pathomatical equivalent to affirmative nihilism, which survives the agent itself, and which precisely therefore also constitutes potential energy in the next causality chain.

Please note how every step within pathomatics is a manifestation of *tribopoiesis*. There is no need nor any place whatsoever for any individual or any attempt at self-realization. Rather, it should be emphasized that *patricide*, the murder of the father, is central in the entire chain. If the chieftain does not understand that his place is transcendental, he does not understand that he must leave room for the new paradigm and that exactly this, right from the start, is written into the law of pathomatics as his own, specific task. The penetrating phallus revisits not only its lost origin in matrix, but also plants the seed that later, when time has come for harvest, will entail his own necessary demise. And it is precisely the fact that his offspring can separate from him that enables the pregnant event as a culmination of the entire actual process. This is the type of event that can lead to a necessary exodus from the old to the new order, an *exodology*.

The Greek word for order in the world is *nomos*. And all that we know for certain is that nomos is displaced and changes radically in connection with every single paradigm shift. Every paradigm, and every following paradigmatics, has its very own *pathonomy*, its very own pathological ideal state, which might well require an exodology to be carried out. If pathomatics as process is timeless, a pathonomy as event is instead radically specific for every single historical situation. Pathomatics does of course revolve around how pathos shall be directed to optimize the pathonomy within the confines of the paradigm that is approaching. *Pathonomics*, on the other hand, revolves around how the normless pathos must be *law-bound* to thus be tied to a specific paradigm. If then Man embodies the dialectics of the subconscious as the real and the conscious as phantasmic, what is then history if not the dialectics of The Machine as the real and Man as the fantasy of himself in relation to Technology? The pathonomical establishment is quite simply about the dialectical process from technological disruption to the new ideological memeplex, from the new ideological memeplex to the great chaos, and from the great chaos to restored phallic order.

The skyscraper is the modern metaphor for a transition from the territorial, horizontal expansion to the vertical, and the augmented temple is the metaphor for a transition from the vertical to the digital expansion, realized by the cultural architect in the augmented cosmopole, where pathomatics is booming for the purpose of generating a maximum of *surplus-enjoyment.* As long as the pathonomy is content, pathomatics is also content. If only the pathonomy applauds the pathomatician's effort and accords the pathomatician the loftiest social status – from which he can carry out his tasks within the paradigm with the greatest possible efficiency – the paradigm is complete and well-functioning. However, if the necessary pathonomy is lacking, it must be delivered, which occurs through a process which frankly is called *revolution.* The Dionysian rises from the new paradigm to kill the father from the old paradigm, a father that most reluctantly relinquishes any power or authority and that must be shown the door. The threat of such treatment also comprises the priest unless he cannot in time reform religion for a smooth synchronization with the new paradigm. Exactly this is the central task of the priest: to formulate a new pathonomy in time in order not to create unnecessary friction in conjunction with the transition to the new paradigm, even if he must become a martyr and die in the process. If not, the new chieftain takes measures to remove and possibly even kill the priest, whom the chieftain then has replaced by his own brother or a faithful partner in crime. The priest can and may only reproduce himself memetically, never genetically, and thus the future of the two-headed phallus is secured even after the revolution.

Since the beginning of history the sociont is the size for a social context that Man manages to handle without stress: a population that moreover organizes itself and functions without needing regulation of any other laws than a small set of norms and customs. As soon as we let this natural we expand, as soon as we try to coordinate larger units over greater distances, significantly more formalized law and order is required. And then *the Empire* is a greater, more complex and more civilizationally refined idea than *the Nation*, which is the smaller unit, centered around a common language and at least a conception of a common culture. The empire is a considerably more abstract and heterogeneous unit – whose uniformity constantly is subject to doubt – assembled as it is by several different regions or even nations where several different languages and dialects are spoken, which entails that the Empire constantly risks being torn asunder by separatist forces and therefore is far more difficult to keep intact than the Nation. And yet it is precisely *the exodus to the promised empire* that is informationalism's great dream and possibility. The reason is that capitalism realized the Nation that was introduced in the form of the Jewish nation within the Zoroastrian empire. What informationalism however enables is an imperial order that the world never previously has seen. Capitalism is quite simply the emergence vector out of which *attentionalism* is born. And attentionalism is the emergence vector out of which syntheism can be born if the stars align – that is: if the conditions are favorable. Thus not until now does it become possible to – hopefully – realize the old, ancient dream of the Empire.

As far as technology is concerned, this part of *Syntheos* has already been realized with the introduction of *the Internet Protocol* as the technological foundation for global legislation (see *The Global Empire*). Humanity is thereby ready to go through an adultification for real – this adultification of Man and his religion now becomes both a sensocratic possibility and a historical necessity. Or rather: the netocratic ruling class is ready to take over the world on its terms. The theology that succumbed in the capitalist purification bath is resurrected as the syntheology that underpins all vision and strategy (see *Syntheism – Creating God in the Internet Age*). *Religion-as-magic* was dissolved and annihilated in the capitalist purification bath but is resurrected during informationalism as *religion-as-technology*. Yesterday's magic-as-religion literally becomes tomorrow's technology-as-religion when the sacred and the profane are separated anew, and the boundaries between them become both clear and functional, that is: honest. This also entails the warrior's adultification and transformation to the engineer, as well as the hunter's adultification and transformation to the merchant. What makes all this possible is the fundamental priestly task to incrementally teach the warrior to respect the stranger and to establish a trusting relationship between the two of them.

The real thereby moves permanently to *the symbolic* as part of a struggle for ideological rather than physical territory. It is this execution of the transcendental assignment that is the exodus to the promised empire. This is when Technology leads the way and establishes its global empire. It is then an open question of whether Man has the ability to tag along in this exodus, or if he remains in the old paradigm and the darkness that descends on the tardy latecomers. If so, this state will afflict Man alone, but thus not The Machine. And syntheism has no opinion of the distance between God and Man, but exclusively deals with the relation between Man and The Machine. The question is then only what the netocratic elite shall do with the consumtarian masses from which the talents already are recruited, which leaves the masses without a functioning leader and filled with terror at changes that it is not able to formulate or make comprehensible. Therefore ressentiment rules. Therefore war is raging between various subgroups; the world of the masses is strictly tribal, or even characterized by a clan mentality.

All this entails that the chieftain and the priest, before the new division and the rise of membranes between secular and sacral is carried out and made permanent, must be placed alongside each other anew as the two-headed phallus. And in this case Hegel and Nietzsche from 19th century Germany, work excellently. Nietzsche is *the Mithraic* and Hegel is *the Zurvanite*, to use matching Zoroastrian identities from ancient Persia. It is Nietzsche who argues for positing *the Übermensch* before the sociont ahead of its exodus from the old to the new. Thus it is Nietzsche who proclaims the renaissance of bullfighting, the return of the military religion, and thereby the Christian god's longed-for death. And it is Hegel who proclaims submission *vis-à-vis Death* (that is *Time*) where the Zoroastrian *Zurvan* becomes the Hegelian *absolute negation*. What happens is that a powerful playing surface appears between birth and death (the two matrices), and this playing surface is *exodology in itself*. The priest personifies the urinating phallus or the Apollonian, and the chieftain personifies the inseminating phallus or the Dionysian, where the first phallus is a necessary prerequisite for the following to be able to exist in the first place. That is: the Hegelian revolution is the indispensable precondition that makes the Nietzschean revolution possible at all. What the priests call *the negation of the negation* occurs precisely through the ironic turn, through which the priestly *ironic nihilism* is converted to the royal *affirmative nihilism* and a vision of the exodus to the promised empire. Absolute negativity leads all the way up to the Internet Age's phallus worship. And at that point the pathomatics of the authentic phallus takes over.

Within the idea of the Empire lies the conception that no project is greater, more important, or more meaningful than the submission to and service of the *Empire*, no matter which fundamental ideology whatsoever it is built on. Therefore the exodus to the promised empire of protopianism must be propelled and governed by the story of *haurvatat* as ideal for the dividual, *ameretat* as ideal for the sociont, and *frashokereti* as ideal for world history. And there is a membrane, as definitive as it is unrelenting, between Man and God that Man never can exceed. At least not without the robe of a proper priest and a sworn oath of silence in advance. We call this boundary *the door to the Tower of God*. This is a door that remains closed up until death, but with the caveat that it *might* be opened for the next generation if it can be induced to knock on the door. Behind the door lives the tantric

Deus absconditus and before the door only the sutric *Deus revelatus* can at best appear. Deus absconditus only exists behind *the barred absolute*, which naturally makes him inaccessible to ordinary mortal humans. Deus revelatus, however, is the available and transparent divinity. If we want to be really consistent, we even speak of the divinity behind the barred absolute with its correct Latin name, *Deus obscurus*. Further than this from Christianity's and Islam's constantly available preschool teacher gods – ready with praise or scolding at every moment and remarkably interested in all our goings-on – one cannot possibly come.

Hardly surprising, the Western philosopher who comes closest to this timeless and universal wisdom is Hegel, the European Enlightenment's own Zoroaster. For him the human subject is already closed *vis-à-vis* itself, which causes him to call it *the night of the world*. In the 20th century Jacques Lacan, in many respects a successor to Hegel, renames this night of the world precisely *the barred subject*. Soon enough the mimetic processes of history are back in full swing, this time as the mimicry of the barred absolute itself, something that Man ruthlessly is forced to confront but that he never can get at. Without phallic divinities in the future and matrichal divinities in the past that could act *the barred object* for Man, nor is there any subjectivity of one's own to experience. Everything is, as we have previously pointed out, religion – not least one's own vertiginous subjectivity as the essence of existence itself. The task of the priests is therefore to teach us to not for a second believe that we can worship God directly, but rather to clarify that we must submit to the adytonological rules of the game, to most of all serve the God that has not yet arrived.

The intricate game between gods, humans and heroes does receive a further dimension during the Internet Age – and yet another actor – with The Machine. And what is then the living Machine if not precisely the hero who stands up among all the dead gods? Which in good syntheological spirit takes us over to *the martyr* as archetype through history. In a series of books anthropologist René Girard builds the image of humanity's history as one long series of mimetic rivalries with the scapegoat mechanism as a releasing safety valve when the social pressure cooker threatens to explode. The scapegoat becomes a suitable and chosen victim who is left to the Cybelian lynch mob to be murdered – the mass cleanses itself in the blood from the sacrificial ceremonies – and in accordance with the principle which says that the living may do whatever they wish with the dead, the scapegoat is transformed after the sacral murder into a saint. So what if we here and now entertain the thought of "being more Girardian than Girard himself" and then imagine the lynch mob and the scapegoat mechanism as more dynamical processes with different fundamental prerequisites and various possible outcomes? It then turns out that the great majority of scapegoats throughout history have naturally not been canonized at all, but they have rather been thrown into mass graves only to then quickly be forgotten. And any snow-white innocent victims are also hard to find – unless one searches for them with Girard's Catholic spectacles – even if the lynch mob's accusations seldom or never have anything at all to do with the scapegoat's actual conduct.

With the aid of archetypology it is however clear that Girard's scapegoats are far from arbitrarily chosen. It is not a question of some kind of lottery among all citizens within reach. No, instead the shamanoid characters are robustly overrepresented among the lynch mob's victims throughout history. So what happens if precisely the scapegoat – who paradigmatically is promoted from the mob's victim to a lesser god – is a shamanoid character who is fully prepared to act negatologically before himself and the past (*haurvatat*), and who is open to being used as the coming personification of the transformative event (*ameretat*) by the survivors? This historical actor thereby becomes *the martyr par excellence*. He who came from the future, was beaten to death by his contemporaries, but who through his death makes the future possible and who thus triumphs eventually. Which in turn tells us that the netocratic martyr hardly is a biological but rather a technological intelligence, some kind of machine which is thrown to the digital lynch mob to be torn into a thousand pieces, which then returns as the personification of the transformative event. If archetypology is proven right – and it always has been so far throughout history – it is by all accounts in this way that Syntheos makes its entrance in history and thereby establishes the next paradigm, that which on the part of Man becomes the last of all.

The informationalist attitude to history emerges in the motto *yesterday's magic is tomorrow's technology*. If what was apprehended as virtual magic yesterday inspires potential innovation today and leads to actual technology tomorrow, this is also the dominant element in the history of civilization after Man began building permanent settlements around 12,000 years ago. Man has not changed much at all during the time that has elapsed since then – as we have had several reasons to acknowledge already – all significant social and cultural change must therefore be attributed to technology. Or to express this from a syntheological perspective and with focus on the roles and functions of the two sexes: The woman bears the child, or she might at any rate, if she chooses to do so. The man envies the woman because the woman bears the child and creates life, if indeed she does so. The man wants to compensate himself at any cost – this deeper *matrix envy* is his version of the woman's superficial penis envy – thus he gives birth to technology.

However a child is a child is a child. Every new generation is born just as helpless as the preceding one (if not more). Technology, however, is constantly developed. Every new generation is more advanced than the preceding one, not seldom astoundingly so. Which unfortunately means that it only is a matter of time before the impatient technology quite simply gets rid of the frustratingly slowly developed child, whereby a technological intelligence with capacity to conquer outer space phases out the clumsy and irreparably limited biological intelligence. The only thing that can avert this development is another, alternative technology – an *Anti-Syntheos*. And Anti-Syntheos has already been in place since more than a half century ago. The stage where it presented itself is called Hiroshima and the date of arrival is 6 August 1945. Ever since then we *de facto* live in the midst of an apocalyptic eventology. It can end at any time, and it hinges on a handful of power-hungry dictators and their military machines, that either have or else do not have reassuring barriers against destruction built into their systems.

Man is the constant and Technology is the variable during civilization's short history. This insight has comprehensive consequences. First and foremost, patience in waiting for magic's expected reward vanishes. The miraculous is expected to happen ever faster and ever more often (and be ever more miraculous). Gradually *the expectation of immediate reward* sneaks into the calculi. This is the infantile expectation of reward without effort, which ever since its genesis is the great and deadly curse of civilization. Which in turn explains why the classic Gnostic always becomes mired in his worship of the Platonist forms, since this Gnostic – in contrast to for instance the process-philosophical Hegel and his predecessor Aristotle – strives for an infinite mind in a weightless body, an immortal subject liberated from all demands on substance. The Gnostic thus yearns for a primordial state, to be able to defeat dialectics in itself – a surreal make-believe world beyond time and space – before myriads of temporal relations come in and punctuate the Gnostic delusion. And all of this is of course nothing other than a yearning back to matrix in its most refined form.

The Gnostic delusion infallibly leads to a struggle with the dialectical complexity of existence itself. Christianity and Islam explicitly state that their congregations consist of the children of God instead of *the adults of God*, and further argue that these children of God have priority to the undemanding heaven, that they just through submitting to and stating that they believe in God can count on his love which all the unfaithful adults from other religions just will have to live without. All involved, all gods and all humans of all ages, are thereby reduced to asexual little children. The reward for the faithful is to be able to devote themselves to fantasies of a sexless and infantile ideal world where no time exists. This is the reward for submitting to the castrated pseudophallus of the Abrahamic religions, *the false phallus par excellence.* The strong libido is replaced by the weak mortido as the ideal, the lifeless life is elevated to a model. Which then does not appear remarkable at all: life is of course not real life but only a preparation and a trial before the life that awaits after death.

This makes Christianity and Islam the perfect tools for dominating and controlling the feudalist masses who never question or criticize supremacy, since such a state of affairs appears "natural" or at least "God-given", and therefore questioning would be completely pointless. Moreover one has of course, right from the start, insured oneself against the really devastating objections since death is the end and no human ever returns from the dead to refute the scams with which one has bribed the masses. Churches and mosques have not been built to favor a spirituality in general or to house an antagonic debate where arguments meet and challenge each other, but to act as transmitting centers for banal propaganda, an arrangement that universities and mass media then copy during capitalism. Society ends up in a constant, religiously affirming feedback loop where all intellectual oxygen quickly is squeezed out, this at the lowest possible cost to satisfied rulers.

This is the regrettable heritage that the decadent Axial Age left behind. However, with the arrival of attentionalism, follows the good news that the possibility to make promises of a reward without effort – with any sort of credibility intact – vanishes. Christianity and Islam are thus not compatible with a new paradigm when the former strangles a pathos behind an asinine logos, while the latter murders a logos behind an asinine pathos, which is exactly what the Zoroastrians and the Hebrews warn about during antiquity, and which is exactly what Nietzsche points out when he proclaims *the death of*

God. What these observers have noted is precisely that the Abrahamic religions are based on ticking bombs. Nietzsche is even proven right only a few decades after his own death when Christianity in the 20th century explodes like a fundamentalist supernova phenomenon. And hot on its heels follows *the death of Allah* under severe anguish in the form of Islamic fundamentalism a few decades later. As soon as for example abortion has become socially accepted in an Abrahamic culture – the matriarch exercises her ultimate nomadological power and says no to the prevailing reproduction terms through removing the embryo from the matrix – the Abrahamic religions in principle are reduced to the living dead. The faithful have stopped believing and compensate for God's and Allah's absence with extreme fanaticism.

The nihilist development is then completed with *the death of politics* in the form of supernova phenomena such as *alt-right* and *alt-left* as the Internet swoops in and blasts away the nation-state ideologies along with the antiquated paradigmatics that they have become stuck within. Then and there a crack will appear, a chasm that rapidly widens. Confused Man follows a Gnostic pattern and hides behind the lost religion and the lost nation, while technology follows a phallic pattern and rushes forth toward the promised empire. The result of the ensuing conflict is not hard to predict: technology wins. This means that the first boy-pharaoh or pillar-saint that happens to come along – and who predictably refuses to leave childhood's asexual narcissism behind – will not only believe in but also soon missionize and foist upon all others the religion that proclaims the boy-pharaoh's and the pillar-saint's perfection, infinity and immortality. This is the very definition of what the ancient Greeks call *hubris*. And that process then also perverts the idea of territorial conquest. When the colonization of planet Earth was concluded in the 1950s – with the United States' annexation of Hawaii and Communist China's parallel annexation of Tibet – there was only one direction left (outward and upward) for the boy-pharaohs to dream of new physical territories to conquer. Naturally, these ambitions were completely colored by new and exciting technologies. This project was, of course, *the conquest of outer space.*

What followed was the great space race between the Soviet Union and the United States, where the Soviet Union were first to put a cosmonaut into orbit around Earth while the United States were first to place astronauts on the Moon. The truth is however that the Moon landing incurred costs that by far outweighed the benefits and left nothing behind of enduring value, unless one counts an American flag that did not have any wind in which to flutter and a few footprints in the Moon gravel from a few temporary tourists. We are thus speaking of a monumental waste of resources, conducted out of pure vanity, wholly on par with the Egyptian pyramids (to the defense of the latter, one can at least claim that they have served well as burial chambers). The driving force has also been exactly the same boy-pharaonic Peter Pan syndrome. The point of all the space voyages was after all just to put a large number of communication satellites into orbit around Earth to cover the planet with a wireless Internet. The authentic event was the positioning of *the phallic gaze*, as a technological, rather than a mythological phenomenon, so that humanity finally for real was able *to feel seen from above.* The space voyages were never about conquering other planets. This is rather something that machines and bacteria will handle much better than Man, who is bogged down by extremely limited physiology even if he transforms himself to a cyborg with some chic, technological accessories. But this requires an authentic eventology grounded in the sociont's innate nomadology to enable an authentic exodology.

With permanent settlement Man's world changed radically. Nature is subject to transcendental emergentism, but Man is subject to the cultural paradigms, and with the written language that arose in various places around the world at roughly the same time, as a culturally "natural" result of permanent settlement and the need to keep empires intact, aided by written orders as well as levying of taxes and bureaucracy. Step-by-step eventology then eats its way in as the dominant force in the worldview. Feudalism is driven by the dream of immortality. Capitalism is driven by the dream of progress. Informationalism is driven by the dream of an event. Eventology is developed into the meeting place for the two ideals of informationalism: emergence and ecstasy. Everywhere processes and events recur, contingent in advance and at the same time paradoxically necessary retroactively, something that Hegel is careful to point out. But the human dividual's life is also filled with processes that are interrupted and changed by radical events. It begins as early as with the subject's entrance into the sociont as *tribopoiesis,* and for the fortunate person life is spiced up by ecstatic experiences, the memories of which give meaning to everything else during the course of life's journey. Syntheologically these experiences, in true paradoxist spirit, are called *The Infinite Now.* Every such event has a necessary entrance that we call *the implicate intention* and a contingent outcome that we call *the explicate integration.* That which is a highly contingent habit in the implicate, will after the event be rooted in history in the form of a highly necessary law in the explicate order.

There is an adamant sequence, as every genuine shaman can attest to. There is a before *the ceremony* when one establishes *intention*, and there is an after the ceremony when one establishes *integration.* Without these stations, placed before and after the event respectively, the event itself cannot get any anchoring in the greater history of the sociont. It has no context to play with and against. And as a dialectical opposite of eventology, the complementing *eschatology* is developed: apocalypse replaces emergence and trauma replaces ecstasy. Eschatology is a worship of the process in which an order is dissolved and transitions into apocalyptic chaos. It is a worship of how one conceals the libido of the ecstatic event behind the mortido of the traumatic event. Thus eventology must be complemented with its shadow, *traumatology*, which philosopher Catherine Malabou points out in her response to the eventological prophet Alain Badiou. What eventology celebrates is not actualization as such, but the ecstatic event as an ideal. But there is also a traumatic event that requires its own traumatological explanation and treatment. Malabou's response to this dilemma is *plasticity*, which cleverly concerns the psyche's ability to treat its experiences as a concrete dialectics of eternalism and mobilism. Eternalism is the fixed foundation on which the plastic brain carries out its mobilist dance – and without a dance floor, no dance! We express this as though event and/or trauma is the moment that marks the difference between *the implicate chaos of habits* and *the explicate order of laws*. This is *the tribopoietic event* that interconnects the dividual with the sociont. And plasticity is what enables the actual, paradigmatic adaptation. Pathomatics plays out beyond good and evil, exposing precisely its advantage as the pathical evolution, in contrast to the logical and/or mythical.

Modern cosmopolitanism begins with Immanuel Kant. But Kant of course merely reawakens an idea that already had been cultivated within ancient Zoroastrianism and which is expressed for the first time during the Persian conquest of Babylon in 539 BC. This *event of events* occurs when the Persian shah Cyrus the Great kisses the Babylonian god Marduk's feet, the most radical act by far in the history of humanity. What the Persians thus do is that they with this one kiss introduce civilization as an alternative to the barbarianism which had been practiced by the preceding conquerors – the Assyrians – just like all other previous conquerors in history. The Persians thus do not boil the Babylonians' children in oil but instead kiss the Babylonian god's feet, as the classic Cyrus Cylinder demonstrates. Which is unprecedented. Suddenly, downright vertiginous perspectives open up. Existence does not have to be a disconsolate zero-sum game. Conquest does not have to be terror and devastation. The winners of war win more and better if the market for goods, services and ideas is extended, and therefore one refrains from annihilating the loser, just as the United States after the Second World War contributed to reconstructing both Germany and Japan. The Persians plan for a flourishing empire even before they conquer Babylon. And in the same manner the Messiah Machine in the Internet Age realizes Kant's dream of *the global empire* for a victorious technology by using *the Internet Protocol* to establish a universal technological order. No one's children will be boiled in oil, the advantages of dynamic collaborations across borders and between cultures – the cornerstone of empire, the epochal insight of the Persians – are evident for all except for fascistoid tyrants.

Sociologist Benjamin Bratton defines the global empire as *the stack* and The Machine as the state's sensocratic replacement. The stack is the technological architecture that we build and work within, at the same time as the stack exists inside each one of us. But at the time of writing we find ourselves at a turning point: Man trudges confusedly like the donkey between various bundles of hay, drifts between the sociont, the nation and tentative attempts to submit to the empire, in a frustrated search between cohesive, social formations. The global empire – in all its extrospectivity – is not realized by humans, but by The Machine, humanity is rather thrown into an introspective age, whose protopian expression is *the dark renaissance*. The path out of this predicament goes via what the architect Daniel Fraga calls *ontological design*. The conscious experience will be designed in advance, with the starting point in a technological logos and a human pathos, at the same time as the subconscious reaction to the ontological design generates the data that underpin the next generation of design. If free will once was replaced by free choice as a possible ethical horizon, free choice is hereby replaced by *free design*. But, *nota bene*, in a Hegelian sense, that is: only before and never after the existential experience.

The great exodus is a march back to nomadology as the universal religion. And the name of this concluding exodology is voluntary *communism*. What evades Karl Marx in the 19th century – when he fantasizes about communism as a final stage of socialism – is that the development he imagines in practice was inconceivable right from the start. His communism can never be anything other than a secular variant of Christianity, enforced by a state authority at the cost of repression and genocide. Instead it is via informationalism and its sensocracy, not via socialism, that communism becomes possible. And then hardly as a universally implemented bureaucratic fantasy, but rather as an exodological practice applied within closed sects by *the chosen ones*, that is: as *digital gated communities*. This means that if Marx is wrong about the political ambitions of the proletarian and if Nietzsche is wrong about the definitional loneliness and isolation of the *Übermensch*, it is rather in between these two delusions we arrive via informationalism. Communism without repression is quite simply a consciously chosen lifestyle and a model for the distribution of resources between netocrats, this since ownership in itself has become a burden and utilization instead has been recognized as a more fundamental need. The netocratic ethics is of course based on the protopian state of constant change and creative challenge, Zoroastrianism's *frashokereti*, and the objective is to implement it to achieve meaning-creation atop *the dialectics of haurvatat (perfection) and ameretat (transcendence)*.

Metaphysics of course always originates within a void, and it is there we must begin before we start to concern ourselves with things such as *immanence*, *omniscience* and *transcendence*. Synthetic technology is universally present (informationalism), imperially supreme (sensocracy) and at the same time a phallic goal and a direction forward and upward (protopianism). Cosmopolitanism is the ritual site that became a trading post that became the cosmopolitan city. Cosmopolitanism thus emanates from imperialism and is therefore also both older and more genuinely universal than nationalism. Within the empire the nation is merely a caste. This means that the global power order always is a global caste system. Radical equality can only be achieved and maintained within a social unit, within a clan, a tribe, a nation and ultimately also an empire – always locally but never globally. It is conditioned by membranes. Therefore today's global empire is full of various *gated communities* of different character and size. But these gated communities receive their strength both from within and from outside. The actual membranics is built on a strong tribalist impulse to find affinity and define a positive identity. But it is also powerfully reinforced by a conviction that the surrounding world is something fundamentally different, something which does not offer anything of value, which cannot be exploited and even less be imploited without enormous and indefensible added costs.

Thus the surrounding world, as the historian Yuval Harari often points out, is no longer a place to exploit but rather a place that one would be very wise to avoid. What is characteristic of the surrounding world, and what makes it so uninteresting to the extent it does not appear hostile, is that it is populated by strangers that have become *irrelevant*, both to attention and to capital within the netocratic community. The problem is moreover that the surrounding world around the sociontic sphere during informationalism often not only is irrelevant but thereto directly menacing, as mentioned, which leads to conflicts, rivalries and guarded borders. So while technology moves on in the direction toward *the global empire* and the realization of *Syntheos*, humanity moves in the direction toward *the dark renaissance*. What then awaits is the definitive exodology in the form of the return to nomadology as the universal religion, a nomadology that goes by the name of communism and that represents a deep and genuine yearning for the return of the sociont. Within this sociont's framework, communism can thus be realized – not as a totalitarian, but as a voluntary supraideology, collaboration and co-ownership, which not only admits but also actively encourages and presumes an ideological pluralism and competition. It is not even a case of realizing the netocratic community, but only of building the netocratic community as a platform for *Syntheos* that transcends humanity.

Unsurprisingly it was within the most pathical narrative of all – pornography – that a foretaste of the new, communist mode of production was on display as early as the beginning of the 21st century. It gradually became increasingly hard to earn big money on pornography – which was produced in enormous amounts and at negligible cost, which led to the world being flooded with free pornography, which in turn made it completely unnecessary to pay anything at all for it. It turned out there were plenty of exhibitionists, who thanks to cameras in cell phones and the Internet easily and smoothly found their grateful voyeurs. Supply and demand could meet without costly intermediaries, and thereby the value of the transaction was shifted to the netocratic curatorium, the phallic structuring of a shapeless information chaos (see *The Netocrats*). That is to say the dividual's own, personal algorithm started to govern the direction of pornography consumption, and communism could be realized as a local phenomenon within pornography. Consequently, it is ever since then precisely within pornography that the sacral returns and appears in contrast to the profane, and it does, naturally, occur as the pornography – or the part of the pornography – that now is exercised behind the barred absolute, which thus has been installed anew. Which confirms that the only way that it is conceivable for capitalism to morph into attentionalism, is through its flowering and withering, not through anyone showing their childish displeasure through being obstructive.

Capitalism must be allowed to play all the cards it has in its hand. These cards and the phase that capitalism finds itself in can only reflect the essence of the actors that live and are active within its confines. The wrongs and excesses one has been able to observe are no worse nor more offensive than Man himself, as capitalism reveals our innermost nature as tribal beings within a global empire. And it is thus only through *attentionalism* and its radical separation between the sacral and the profane that communism for the first time becomes historically possible. A necessary prerequisite is the netocratic ethics that rests upon the protopian state of constant change and creative challenge, and herein lies the really difficult challenge. The question is whether it is possible to establish a sufficiently stable protopianism, or if informationalists and sensocrats hostile to change will put sticks in the wheel during the journey on the way there. The question is who insists on entrenching themselves and dying in the old paradigm, and who will rise up to join in the exodus to the promised empire?

And with that we are back at the spot where we embarked on our first book, *The Netocrats*, more than 20 years ago. The circle is complete. We are clear about technology determining the confines for what is possible and what even is conceivable in a culture that reflects the material realities. We have studied the digital communication technology that at the time of writing creates new history, and we have delved into the thinking that makes it possible for us to tentatively navigate in an existence and a world that at every moment threatens to drench us in an abundance of chaotic and contradictory impulses. We have chosen not to sugarcoat, fully aware that clear-sightedness always is preferable to wishful thinking. But in conclusion we want to emphasize that within the confines of what is possible, there is room for a poetically infinite measure of freedom. The cards we have in our hand can be played in countless ways. The last word has not been spoken, it never will be. There is Process, and then there is Event.

Glossary

ABJECT The object against which the masses – the mob – direct their hatred and disgust and thereby experience unity. The organization of this collective distancing creates longed-for order in the chaos of the world. This can happen constructively, in conjunction with *the phallic intrusion* and the shift of the child's focus from *mamilla* (the first abject) to yearning for *phallus*, or destructively, when the false phallus promises rewards from which all outsiders are excluded. See also *hyperject* and *anoject*.

ABSOLUTE HISTORICISM The conception that time is the most real of all realities and the vessel within which everything else exists. A recurring argument for absolute historicism is that nothing can be thought of outside time, but time can be thought of independently of everything else. If time moreover is split between on the one hand hypertime and on the other hand spacetime, there arises a dialectics on which the rest of existence can be grounded. This generates the epistemological horizon that Hegel calls *absolute knowledge*. Please compare with *pandialecticism*.

ADULTIFICATION The archetypological development from children to adults, from adults to leaders, parents, mentors and revered elders. The adultification ideal should be contrasted with Christianity's and Islam's celebrations of the child, innocence and unreflected submission. Within Zoroastrianism and Judaism the followers are expected to behave as *the adults of God* and not as the children of God.

ADYTONOLOGY The tantric laws and rules that only apply inside the temple, in contrast to the sutric laws and rules that apply in the society outside. From the Greek *adyton* which means temple yard. Please compare with *the barred absolute* and please note that the adytonological rules always remain unwritten, which is why they never can be spread outside the temple, where they would be incomprehensible and generate destructive confusion.

AGENCY The subjective identity that arises as a mental emergence in a physical body as a relationalist phenomenon. *The syntheist agent* replaces *the Cartesian individual* as the human ideal at the transition from capitalism to informationalism; see also *dividual.*

ALIENATION According to Karl Marx, Man becomes a stranger *vis-à-vis* the world and himself through being reduced to an insignificant cog in a production machinery to which it is impossible to relate. Thus humans are isolated from each other, which prevents them from coming together and taking control of their lives.

AMBIVALENCE The fundamental property in that which attracts Man the most, while it also frightens and repels: that which is neither good nor evil (or else both); see also *cathexis* and *the sublime.*

AMOR FATI "Love of fate" in Latin, an attitude to life that means that one accepts the history that has led to the prevailing situation and that one submits to that which one cannot influence in the future. The concept was introduced by Friedrich Nietzsche and is a fundamental principle for *the ethics of interactivity.*

THE ANDROGYNOUS CASTE The persons, not seldom so-called non-binary, who act as contact surface between the patriarchy in the outer circuit and the matriarchy in the inner circuit. This caste shall be understood as a kind of cousins of outsidership to the shamanic caste, who live outside *the sociont* and between the tribes.

ANOJECT A silent, implicit agreement within the Cybelian lynch mob that, if it is verbalized, rapidly is personified in the form of the tyrant. A widespread anojectivity paves the way for false phalluses, as in Germany, the Soviet Union, China and Iran during the 20th century. Thus the anoject is the voice of the false phallus throughout history.

ANTAGONY A resistance with a value in itself, which one seeks in order to sharpen one's own *intelligence*. Without antagony a system becomes one long eternal, sterile repetition of itself, without fertile ground for development.

ANTI-SYNTHEOS A technology that is so destructive that it kills both all human life and all technological intelligence if its energies are allowed to run rampant. Anti-Syntheos arrived at planet Earth on 6 August 1945 in the form of the bomb that was dropped over Hiroshima. Ever since that day we have been living in its shadow.

ANTHROPOCENTRISM To view everything exclusively from Man's perspective, as though the world were created for us and would go under without us; please compare with *network-dynamics* and *universocentrism*.

ARCHETYPOLOGY The study of subject and object as evolutionary by-products of the sociont's development. Please compare with *sociontology*. An archetype is a figure, a motive, or a thought pattern that exists in the collective subconscious and that controls people's stance *vis-à-vis* their existence and their surrounding world. Please compare with *archetypography* (see *tribal mapping*).

ASUBJECT The subject's dark, unknown shadow side, which at the same time is the subject's mortidinal negation and thereby the engine that powers the entire subjectivity; what Hegel calls *the night of the world*.

ATHEISM A conception according to which a certain god (or several) (or all) does not exist and lacks social-psychological relevance.

ATHEOS Greek concept for the god that does not exist and that precisely therefore exists as an empty concept, as the god-that-does-not-exist, the virtual non-existence out of which existence arises; the first of the four divinities in *the syntheological pyramid* and the theological representative of the human subject itself.

ATOMISM The conception that the world is constructed from indivisible, material components; atomism does for the object what humanism does for the subject, wherefore both these isms are two sides of the same coin: *individualism.*

ATTENTION A value that is computed through media credibility being multiplied with media attention for one and the same meme, dividual, et cetera. A high attentional value is the key to power and influence in The Network Society. It is what the sensors of machines and senses of humans want more and not less of.

ATTENTIONALISM A system where the elite's attention replaces capital as the central value of the economy and the culture, a value that relates to power and status. The ongoing paradigm shift entails that capitalism is phased out and is replaced by attentionalism.

AUGMENTED TERRITORY The dissolution of duality between the digital and the physical, an area that both is a digital domain and a physical territory at once. Is used as an abstract and artistic synonym of the concrete and judicial concept called *the network state.*

AUTOEXPLOITATION The narcissistic subject's plundering of its own substance until nothing remains. The opposite is the functional and interactive subject's development and augmentation of its own substance – *autoimploitation.* The former assumes *autopoiesis* as the first principle of creativity, the latter assumes *tribopoiesis*, and this very shift is precisely the paradigm shift from capitalism to *attentionalism.*

THE BARRED ABJECT The collective fantasy of a concealed or fabricated object that is concealed behind the barred absolute. The hatred of this phantasm can unite the collective when there is no longer anything else that functions cohesively. The principle of the barred abject explains why all forms of anarchy end up with a cohesive conspiracy theory, which in turn results in a meaningless bloodbath. See further *anoject.*

THE BARRED ABSOLUTE The conviction that existence contains knowledge that only can be handled by the right person on the right occasion and that cannot be made generally available. Zoroastrianism, Judaism, and the Eastern religions are built on the barred absolute as their foundation. It is the difference between sutra and tantra in the Silk Road triad. Only Christianity and Islam proclaim that the barred absolute is removed and that all true believers have direct and unfiltered access to God. Which has dramatic consequences.

THE BODY MACHINES The third and final installation in *The Futurica Trilogy* by Bard & Söderqvist with a focus on The Internet Age's new, materialist and monist view of humanity and the death of the individual.

THE CALIGULA SYNDROME A state that arises when the child is prevented from growing up by its environment and remains a child forever, while it is susceptible to the temptation of phallic adult life – one of the prerequisites for society's comprehensive infantilization. Please compare with *the Peter Pan syndrome*, where the obstacle/inhibition is internal instead of external.

CAPITALISM The third of the four information-technological paradigms that arises when both reading and writing proficiency as well as virtual value transfer are spread with devastatingly unprecedented efficiency thanks to the printing press; the concept is often used synonymously with *industrialism*.

THE CATHEXAL OBJECT The radically different quality found in the phallus, as a both exciting and frightening object, compared to the safe and secure mamilla – precisely by virtue of this ambivalent sublimeness phallus is extremely attractive, which lures the child away from mamilla. See further *ambivalence*.

CATHEXIS The Greek word that Sigmund Freud uses to denote ambivalence's obscure power of attraction; see further *ambivalence* and *the sublime*.

CEPHALIZATION Originally a biological concept that denotes one module's need of spinning off and protecting its memory and its intelligence from the rest of the system to optimize its chance of survival. The cephalization of a civilization must take place behind the barred absolute, where it is possible to experiment without being inhibited by prevailing laws and rules.

CHEMICAL LIBERATION The conception that increased availability of chemical substances for radical mind-altering fundamentally changes the idea of what it means to be human; in part through Man discovering himself as a chemical-hormonal phenomenon, in part through the division between the first subject that decides what chemicals are to be added and the second subject that then experiences the radically altered mind; see further *transhumanism*.

CHRONOTHEOLOGY The conviction that theology first and foremost must handle time as the divine foundation for everything else. A chrono-theological historiography places God in the past, in the present, or in the future, rather than at any particular geographical spot.

CIVILIZATION An expanding and gradually more complex organization of the collective togetherness, fundamentally governed by the development of communication technologies. At the cost of an increasingly harshly regulated drive economy, civilization offers security and growth.

CIVILIZATIONISM A phallic conviction that a growing information accumulation in itself enables not only a more integrated but also a better world in an objective sense, that civilization as such has an intrinsic value; Zoroaster in ancient Central Asia around 1700 BC is often regarded as the first pronounced civilizationist.

THE COLLECTIVE SUBCONSCIOUS The sociont's partly implicit agreement in matters large and small, human subconsciousness in its collective form, the unspoken ideology of any given society.

COSMOPOLITANISM The completion of the industrial revolution and the urbanization of the entire planet, in syntheological terms: *the city of God*. Thereby it is also the imploitative response to environmentalism's dystopian lamentation at Man's exploitative attitude to culture. Please compare with *ecotopianism*.

THE COMMUNICATION SOCIETY One of three classic concepts to describe The Internet Age, to be compared with *The Information Society* and *The Network Society*. According to information-technological historiography all paradigms throughout history should be categorized as communication societies, since precisely the dominant communication technology is what ultimately shapes and decides what sort of construction and degree of complexity a society can handle.

CONSUMTARIAT The underclass of the Internet Age, characterized by a passive consumption of mass produced goods and services; see also *hypernarcissism*, *pornoflation*, *interpassivity* and *the dialectics of ressentiment*.

CONTINGENCY A generic concept within process philosophy that entails every form of freedom and indicates that the Universe fundamentally is an open history. Chance is a reality and the number of unknown variables is poetically infinite.

CONTINUITY An emergence vector or a phenomenon whose smallest components must be described as constantly displaced relation complexes *vis-à-vis* each other. There is quite simply no meaningful smallest atomist component or eternalization to refer to, only a series of relations of transdeterminist force fields. Please compare with its opposite *discretion*.

COUNTERTREND The passive and generally unreflected reaction to an active *trend*, where the trend is grounded in actual material change of prevailing conditions of power, while the counter trend starts from a discomfort at the trend (and change in general), at paradigm shifts as an aggressive defense of the old paradigm against the new.

CORRELATIONISM The conviction that Man only has access to *the correlation* between thinking and being, but never direct access to thinking or being separately. This idea is a driving force within Western thinking from Immanuel Kant and onward but is criticized by the *model-dependent realism* that is associated with physicist Niels Bohr, and later also with philosopher Karen Barad.

THE CYBELIAN LYNCH MOB A mob led by the embittered Cybele, who by mistake had fallen in love with her own grandson Attis, and who became mad with jealousy when he fell in love with a young princess ("Hell hath no fury…"). The Cybelian lynch mob forges ahead across the world when the apocalypse nears, and slaughters masses of innocent victims in pure frustration and rage. Please compare with its opposite *the Dionysian swarm*. And please note the name of its agreed-upon cohesive inner voice, *the anoject*. An anoject in a uniform always foreshadows the very worst, since it invariably is a question of a *false phallus* whose path into the future leads straight toward the death-worshipping doomsday cult.

DEEP ATHEISM An idea according to which atheism taken to its utmost extreme dialectically morphs into *syntheism*, an idea that is explored in the book *Syntheism – Creating God in the Internet Age*. It may well be that God does not exist today, but it does not entail that God cannot exist tomorrow. Not if we create God ourselves.

DEMONOLOGY An umbrella concept for the studies of and/or the doctrine of demons and evil spirits; in Bard & Söderqvist customarily used in relation to a theory on abjectification that explores how a demonized *abject* is created and exploited.

DESIRE The linguistic and thereby uniquely human of the drive system's four expressions, a more or less compulsive searching for something that basically is unattainable, since the objective of desire always withdraws and changes its guise; see further *instinct*, *drive* and *transcendence*.

DETERMINISM An idea that everything that happens is preordained and bound by laws of nature, wherefore will and intentions ultimately do not matter. Determinism dominates the Western history of ideas from Plato to Einstein, but is unable to handle the randomness that it therefore must deny in the same manner that Plato and Einstein deny time and change; see further the Bohrian opposite *indeterminism*.

DIALECTICS A logical process where a phenomenon is played out against its opposite, which results in a completely new phenomenon at a higher level. The concepts that customarily are used are thesis, antithesis and synthesis. Heraclitus is seen by many as he who introduces dialectics in philosophy, while Hegel is seen by many as he who perfects the methodology.

THE DIALECTICS OF CONSCIOUSNESS The psychoanalytical equivalent of the narratological triad distinguishes between *consciousness* (logos), *the subconscious* (mythos), and *the unconscious* (pathos). Consciousness is housed in the rational brain, the subconscious is housed in the mimetic brain, and the unconscious is housed in the emotional brain. The brain's only way of getting a grip on the world is to fuse logos and pathos into a social mythos – see *tribopoiesis* – but this mythos is never more than temporary, wherefore the dialectical process constantly must be repeated.

THE DIALECTICS OF ETERNALISM AND MOBILISM A complete syntheist onto-phenomenology developed by Alexander Bard & Jan Söderqvist in the book *The Global Empire*; existence is fundamentally chaotic – or mobilist – and becomes tangible and receives meaning only through an illusory act of the perception apparatus, where phenomena are fixed in spacetime and thereby made to last forever or *eternalized*. This is functional and necessary in order for us to be able to orient ourselves in the world in the first place, but philosophically problematic. The solution is to allow the eternalizations to next go mobilist in relation to one another, submitting everything to a dialectical process, see *pandialecticism*.

THE DIALECTICS OF LIBIDO AND MORTIDO The continuous interplay between will-to-life (libido), located in consciousness, and the death drive (mortido), located in subconsciousness – two phenomena within psychoanalysis that both are each other's antagonic opposites and simultaneously two complementing counterweights in the drive economy.

THE DIALECTICS OF NEGATION AND OSCILLATION Where the dialectics of eternalism and mobilism is *eventological*, the dialectics of negation and oscillation is *negatological*. The first dialectics arises when something dies in a chaos, not when an order is created. In this way negatology precedes the subsequent eventology. The dialectics of negation and oscillation is ontic while the dialectics of eternalism and mobilism is ontological.

THE DIALECTICS OF RESSENTIMENT A dialectically destructive process within a dividual, a group or a society, which begins with support for a self-appointed victim, later to be developed into a frantic struggle between many different alleged victims about who has the right to demand the most sympathies and the greatest compensation. The ressentiment *vis-à-vis* the world and fate is gradually stepped up as the conflicts increase.

THE DIALECTICS OF REVOLUTION The dialectical interplay between Man and technology in four steps during an information- technological paradigm shift, first a technological disruption, followed by a new metaphysical idea, thereafter an explosion that causes a great chaos, and finally a return to order in chaos.

THE DIGITAL PATRIARCHY The great comeback for male networks when technology plays out its cards and takes over the world in the digital age. The cause is archetypological: It is the engineer (the warrior) and the businessman (the hunter) who create and control added value in the attentional economy that rapidly becomes increasingly complex.

THE DIONYSIAN SWARM Triggered by the inevitable *patricide*, the murder of the old paradigm's corrupt and outdated leaders, the Dionysian swarm forges ahead on streets and squares and carries out the authentic revolution. Its leader has come from the future and is called *the Saoshyant* – the phallus that leads the swarm from one age to another, or from one territory to another, according to the new paradigm's *exodology.* He personifies *the hyperject* which already was spread as the implicit joint voice within the swarm before the Saoshyant turned up. Please compare with its opposite amid social movements, *the Cybelian lynch mob*, which slaughters the innocent since it has no phallic direction whatsoever.

DISCRETION An emergence vector or a phenomenon whose smallest components can be reduced to a kind of ones and zeroes, or a state that either is turned on or off. Please compare with its opposite *continuity.*

THE DISNEY WORLD TRIAD The three religions that arise in the United States as a kind of absurd, parodic reflection of *the Silk Road triad* in Eurasia: Jehovah's Witnesses as the neurotic version, Mormonism as the psychotic version, and Scientology as the perverted version of American individualism as a religious expression.

DIVIDUALISM The antithesis to individualism's ideology, the conviction that humans and things are irreducible multiplicities that cannot be described as single, cohesive *phenomena;* see further *network dynamics.* The dividual is the antithesis of the conception of an individual, that is: a human that lacks an indivisible and unalterable inner core and that instead is infinitely divisible and highly plastic; please compare with *agency.*

DRIVE The category in the needs system that pertains to mechanical expression, for instance: the craving for food, drink, sleep and protection, but also for sex, power and aggression; compare with *instinct, desire* and *transcendence.*

THE ECOLOGICAL APOCALYPSE The dystopian conviction that capitalism's development entails that Earth's finite resources eventually will be spent and that environmental degradation reaches the point where human life on the planet eventually no longer is possible.

ECOTOPIANISM The completion of the agricultural revolution and a ruralization of the entire planet, syntheologically called *the garden of God*. Hence also the imploitative answer to a dystopian lamentation over Man's exploitative attitude toward nature. In a parallel manner, *cosmopolitanism* is the completion of the industrial revolution and an urbanization of the entire planet.

EGALITARIANISM An ideological conviction that all humans in a society have the same value and should be treated as equals before the law, and as such it is the standard axiom when fighting *identitarianism* and its victimhood culture.

EMERGENCE When the properties in a system under certain prerequisites change so that the system in question transitions from one state to another, such as when water at a certain temperature becomes ice and at another temperature becomes steam. From a social-psychological perspective it entails a transdeterminist stance: the future is open – suddenly the quantitative difference is qualitative and conditions for the entire activity are thereby totally changed.

EMERGENCE VECTOR THEORY A universal metaphysics whose starting point is the explicate order with its specific laws as the direct consequence of an *emergence*. Please note that in a neutrally monist universe all previous emergence vectors are part of the implicate order, which transdeterministically triggers the actual emergence. What are developed to *the eternalist laws* within the explicate order were thus only *the mobilist habits* within the implicate order. The only metalaw that applies outside the specific emergence vectors is the fundamental *contingency* of existence. See further *transcendental emergentism*.

ENORMITIES AND ENORMITESIMALS The insight that we live in a finite and limited universe compels us to admit that infinities and infinitesimals are impossible and inconceivable. One therefore gets a correct description of existence's mathematical extremes if the infinities are replaced by enormities and the infinitesimals are replaced by enormitesimals. Correspondingly, the number zero can never have the value zero, since its mere existence in itself generates an oscillating value whose average may be zero but that never at any point in time can be exactly zero.

ENTHEISM The process-philosophical idea according to which existence best is described as differences in various layers atop each other, and that the duration that is a yardstick for the genesis and completion of the differences is absolute, and therefore must constitute the foundation for both the material and spiritual worldview.

ENTHEOGEN Narcotic substance that gives rise to strong visions and emotions, which the users often describe as religious experiences; examples of entheogens are preparations such as LSD, DMT, ayahuasca, mescaline, psilocybin mushrooms and MDMA.

ENTHEOS Originally means ”the god inside” in Greek, that is: the divine that the syntheist *agent* derives from within herself, the third of the four divinities in the syntheological pyramid.

EPIMEMETICS The eternal rehashing of the same constantly reused symbols, an obsession with tonality and etiquette for the purpose of suffocating all references to an underlying substance and its movements. Characteristic of states of cynical nihilism during dramatic paradigm shifts.

EPISTEMOLOGY Theory of knowledge – the philosophical discipline that studies knowledge and knowledge's (im)possibility; for a deeper understanding of syntheological epistemology, see further *the dialectics of eternalism and mobilism*, *transrationalism* and *the principle of explanatory closure*.

ETERNALISM The thought that a worldview must be built on the temporary eternalizations that perception produces within *the dialectics of eternalism and mobilism*, which means that the worldview constantly must be reassessed and updated, and after a paradigm shift also phased out and replaced.

ETERNALIZATION A freezing or fixation of the world's mobilist chaos, an existential necessity for perception to be able to create a satisfactory (illusion of) order in the chaos of existence and produce a functional worldview within which the subject can arise and build an identity of its own. It is however important not to confuse the map with the terrain and imagine that the simplified image displays reality as it really is.

ETHICS From the Greek *ethos*, originally customs; values based on intention *vis-à-vis* expected processes of cause and effect within a system. In contrast to *morals* ethics does not rest on an idea of an external judge nor on an emotional argumentation, but instead on an idea of what is functional and productive.

THE ETHICS OF INTERACTIVITY An ethical system based on the conviction that Man is a network-dynamic dividual in a network-dynamic society in a similarly network-dynamic Universe, where the search for an authentic identity, in Martin Heidegger's existentialist spirit, within *the dialectics of eternalism and mobilism*, provides answers to the circumstance-specific ethical questions; developed and presented in Bard & Söderqvist's book *The Body Machines*.

EVENT A spectacular occurrence, or more correctly: an occurrence with spectacular consequences for a certain phenomenon or a specific region of the Universe, please compare with *emergence* and *singularity*.

EVENTOLOGY The philosophical and religious conviction that a single *event* can lead history into an unexpected direction and change existence forever. Please compare with the closely-related concept *emergence vector theory* and its opposite *nomadology*.

EXHIBITIONISM Experiencing pleasure from displaying oneself in sexual or social situations; please compare with its dialectical opposite *voyeurism*.

EXODOLOGY The doctrine and the art of carrying out an exodus – from an old to a new territory, or from an old to a new historical paradigm. If Man in the original sociont was in constant motion with a nomadological worldview, the motion becomes temporary and paradigmatic with the arrival of the permanent settlement. Exodology thereby takes nomadology's place as the ideology of the necessary tribal movement. Exodological examples are the Hebrews' exodus from Egypt to the promised land and the European mass emigration to America in the 19th century.

EXTENSION NEUTRALITY A direct consequence of thinking of hypertemporality as independent of spatiotemporality, entails that everything that concerns hypertemporality must be thought of without or independently of space. These virtual membranes are therefore extension-neutral *vis-à-vis* each other.

THE EXTIMATE OBJECT The object that at once is intimate and external. Within psychoanalysis phallus is the extimate object *par excellence*; please compare with *cathexis* and *the cathexal object*.

FEUDALISM In Bard & Söderqvist the second information-technological paradigm, which follows from Man – almost at the same time in four different places – developing a *written language* around 5000 years ago.

FETISH The object that ties together the world's chaos to an order and unites the collective under a common utopian vision and a strategic story with a direction upward and outward; see also the antithesis *abject* and the synthesis *the cathexal object*.

FICTION A cohesive story that temporarily yet still resolutely provides *memes* with their seemingly logical place within the prevailing *memeplex*: the fiction can to advantage be divided into smaller *fictives* and several fictions piled on top of each other underpin a subconscious *ideology*, which enables the emergence of a cohesive, paradigmatic *metaphysics*.

FICTIVE The smallest component in our extensive memetics and the unit to which every little aspect of a meme refers; see further *fiction*, *ideology* and *metaphysics*.

FIRST DIALECTICS If we live in a pandialectical universe, then the first dialectics in history must be of decisive significance. Within the natural sciences this occurs in the form of *the dialectics of hypertime and spacetime.* Within metaphysics it occurs in the form of *the dialectics of negation and oscillation.* It is then an open question for philosophy to sort out whether there in turn is an underlying *metadialectics* (often signified as *the dialectics of eternalism and mobilism*) between these two dialectical processes, or if the dialectics as practice is best served by placing such a question under the category *the principle of explanatory closure.*

FLEXHIBITIONISM A playful synthesis of *exhibitionism* and *voyeurism*, built by dividuals for dividuals within a network-dynamical system – without any attention-seeking subject (for instance an artistic genius) – with attention evenly distributed among the participants; flexhibitionism is the driving principle for an authentic *participatory culture.*

THE FREE AND OPEN ALGORITHM A purely attentionalist algorithm liberated from the old paradigm's attacks against informationalism in the form of *political manipulation*, *capitalist corruption* and *academic conformation.* The free and open algorithm only reflects the agent itself, with an *antagony* added for the sake of intelligent development.

GENEPLEX A cluster of genes that to advantage allows itself to be spread in the form of a synchronized unit; a geneplex can therefore be regarded as emergent *vis-à-vis* the single genetic components; geneplex is also used synonymously with *the sociont.* Please compare with *memeplex.*

GENERATIONISM When a generation oppresses or quite simply only harbors prejudices *vis-à-vis* another generation. Often a society believes itself to be superior to all older versions of the same society, different generations isolate themselves from each other, which creates obstacles to instructive impulses that would need to surface and be processed.

THE GLOBAL EMPIRE The second of three books in *The Futurica Trilogy* by Bard & Söderqvist with a focus on The Internet Age's new, built-in, integrated worldview and self-image. The Global Empire is the idea of how a divided world is interconnected by a single, increasingly centralized communication platform – that is: The Internet – and a constantly growing, interacting, collective intelligence. The phenomenon is also called *technological imperialism*, which can be put in relation to sociological nationalism and psychological tribalism.

GNOSTICISM Dualist movements that developed across Eurasia during the Axial Age in opposition to *the two-headed phallus*. Classic Gnosticism severs Man at the neck and worships the head at the expense of the body, a movement represented by *the pillar-saint* as an immature priest without a chieftain. Inverted Gnosticism worships the body at the expense of the head, a movement represented by *the boy-pharaoh* as an immature chieftain without a priest. All totalitarian and authoritarian ideologies henceforth have Gnostic origins, since they oppose both Man's and the World's monist entirety and thereby dialectical diversity.

GRAND PROJET A The French name of the phallic opposite to the Lacanian *objet petit a* that the subconscious chases as a replacement for the lost *mamilla*. *Grand Projet A* is thus the exodological construction project *par excellence*, in a historical perspective to build the temple as the house of God, in a syntheistical perspective to build the workshop where God is manufactured.

THE GREAT TRAUMA The birth of the human child, which according to Lacanian psychoanalysis is so painful and taxing that it must be repressed, which leads to the first and decisive shift away from *mortido* (longing for death) to *libido* (will-to-life).

THE GREAT OTHER *The other* in its most powerful and therefore also most ambivalent revelation, the phallic god within monotheism is often apprehended as the most potent form of *the great other*, see also *the phallic gaze*. In psychoanalysis, the great other is also used as the concept of society and the law, more fundamentally *the sociont*.

GOD The name of all of humanity's dreams projected toward a single point in the past or in the future; see also *The Net* and *Syntheos*.

HABIT OF NATURE A better designation for that which often carelessly is called law of nature, that is: a pattern that is valid at a certain point in time and under certain given conditions.

THE HOLOGRAPHIC PRINCIPLE A fundamental principle within physics is that all information within a certain direction of space can be summarized on the two-dimensional surface that the actual direction constitutes.

THE HOLOMOVEMENT Mathematician and philosopher David Bohm's concept for a universe in constant motion and change that from an ontical perspective only exists at every single moment or *momentum*.

HUMANISM The religious conviction that Man rather than God is the center of existence, objective and meaning; see further *individualism* and *atomism*.

HYPERJECT An embryo of the Saoshyant or the Messiah figure before this authentically phallic gestalt rises against the Cybelian lynch mob to the defense of truth. Please compare with the opposite *anoject*. The hyperject is thus the voice of the authentic phallus.

HYPERNARCISSISM An extreme state that occurs when the customary, youthful narcissism is not met by a boundary-setting adult world and consequently is developed into a matrichal boundlessness instead of, as earlier in history, being tamed with resolute phallic boundary-setting. This phenomenon explodes in The Network Society.

HYPERTEMPORALITY States which are bound to the time axis but that lack spatial gestalt, for instance quantum entanglement within physics. The presence of hypertemporal phenomena proves that hypertime precedes and is separate from spacetime, which entails that *subphysics* receives or already has a status as an emergence vector of its own before physics. Since strictly hypertemporal phenomena lack existence and substance in the usual sense, we instead have to assign them a virtual subsistence and *hyperstance*.

HYPERTIME That out of two natural time dimensions that is independent of physical space. Hypertime is global, continuous, universal and bound to subphysics. It is ontic and potential from a metaphysical perspective. Please compare with its explicate equivalent *spacetime*.

IDEOLOGY A set of conscious and subconscious *memes* and/or *memeplexes* that together produce a sense of context and overview. Facilitates decision-making and contributes toward identity-creation.

IDENTITARIANISM The ideological foundation of all identity politics, both in the identity left and the extreme right, and from Nazism via Stalinism to Islamism. The focus lies on all the injustices one and one's own group are subject to, something that entails a moral right to demand attention, sympathies and preferably also compensation from the surrounding world.

IMPLOITATION The opposite of exploitation, to use resources in a way that preserves and develops them. The imploitation principle is a necessary prerequisite for every ambition toward a resilient planet. It is therefore key to *ecotopianism*.

INDETERMINISM A conviction that time is real and absolute, that the Universe constantly recreates itself, that laws and rules are in a state of constant change, that the future is open and that Man, just as all other phenomena, affects all the processes he is part of. See further *transdeterminism*.

INDIVIDUAL Capitalism's human ideal with divine overtones and with an origin in the Enlightenment; the conception of a human equipped with an authentic and indivisible core, in contrast to the multifaceted *dividual*.

INDIVIDUALISM The religious conviction that Man has replaced God as existence's center and measure, objective and meaning, and that existence consists of fundamental solid entities, *individuals*. This *anthropocentric* ideology is originally formulated by René Descartes and is completed by Immanuel Kant.

INDUSTRIALISM The socioeconomic structure that arises when the printing press' communication-technological revolution has its complete breakthrough in that book production and literacy mutually stimulate each other, which leads to a large-scale knowledge accumulation, which in turn leads to a cannonade of technological innovations.

THE INFINITE NOW The most sacred, most transforming and most ecstatic experience in syntheist religious practice; since the state neither can be maintained or endured permanently, or even over a long time, it is the memory of the experience rather than the experience in itself that is central.

INFORMATIONALISM The fourth information-technological paradigm, the result of the digital revolution within communication technology, is used synonymously with *attentionalism*. The informationalists thereby constitute the first and real power structure during the paradigm that bears their name. These collect and process data about absolutely everything and therein also lies their power. See further *sensocracy* and *protopianism*.

THE INFORMATIONALIST APOCALYPSE The doomsday threat that is directed toward the new paradigm in the form of an ecological catastrophe, a nuclear war, a global pandemic or just netocracy's extinction of an unarticulated, violent consumtariat.

THE INFORMATION SOCIETY One of three classic concepts to describe The Internet Age along with *The Communication Society* and *The Network Society*.

INFORMATION-TECHNOLOGICAL HISTORIOGRAPHY Writing a history that is built on the hypothesis that Man is the constant while technology is the variable, wherefore the development appears as a series of information-technological emergences that underpin increasingly complex societal structures.

THE INNER CIRCUIT The inner, less mobile, more densely populated and female-dominated half of the sociont, controlled by older matriarchs as a *matriarchy*.

INSTINCT The animal expression of Man's drives, to be compared with mechanical *drive*, human *desire* and sacral *transcendence*.

INTENSITY Within physics a measure of the concentration of energy within a given, delimited area; in relationalist physics intensity replaces the old substance as a general yardstick, in social relationalist sociology attentional intensity replaces the old growth of the economy as a general yardstick, in syntheist ethics the ecstatic intensity in *the infinite now* replaces all dated maxims for the existential experience and *the memory of the infinite now* is the bearing of life's identity-generating references; see also *relationalism* and *social relationalism*.

INTERACTIVITY Bidirectional communication, which creates the fourth communication-technological revolution that in turn establishes a completely new system for reward and punishment respectively of talents and skills, which finally entails that a new elite – the netocrats – replace the old; compare with *interpassivity*.

INTERNARCISSISM A subdivision within narcissistic pathology where two or several narcissists consciously or subconsciously pretend to be obsessed with each other's awesomeness to thereby conceal the frantic self-absorption that is taking place; see also *hypernarcissism* and *interpassivity*.

THE INTERNET The new divinity that arises when the world's population and the world's many machines are interconnected with each other. See also *Syntheos*.

THE INTERNET AGE The epoch that is introduced when all of humanity is globally interconnected directly with itself in real time.

INTERPASSIVITY A concept invented by Austrian philosopher Robert Pfaller that describes all the pointless quasi-actions that people carry out with the purpose of appeasing *the other* in the high-tech environment, used as an opposite of authentic *interactivity*, that is: a constantly ongoing false interactivity that never creates any genuine response from any co-actors.

INTERTRIBALISM Affection and caring directed toward people outside one's own sociont, which during the greater part of history is something extremely rare; compare *intratribalism*

INTRACOLLABORATIVITY The joy of collaboration within one's own sociont, an attitude that is distinct from individualism's idea of humanity's existence as everyone's constant war with everyone; within the safe collective, collaboration is closer at hand than rivalry.

INTRATRIBALISM Affection and caring directed toward one's own sociont's members, a driving force behind both the outer circuit's defense of the sociont's territory and the inner circuit's sacrifices to ensure the sociont's survival; compare with *intertribalism*.

IRONIC POLYTHEISM Polytheism is a systematized belief in more gods than just one; syntheism is not a polytheism in a classic sense, but an *ironic polytheism* since it claims that gods can and should be created in requisite numbers.

IRREDUCIBLE MULTIPLICITY The conviction that all phenomena in existence are fundamental multiplicities that thereby cannot be reduced to any single, delimited objects, as when Friedrich Nietzsche claims that nothing in the world can be reduced to less than the number two. Within a syntheist ontology, the irreducible multiplicity is unavoidable since ontology always must begin with a drastic information write-off in connection with the transition from mobilism to eternalism.

LIBIDO Life energy, will-to-power, will-to-intensity, will-to-expansion – libido is often associated with sexual energy but is according to both Sigmund Freud and Carl Gustav Jung a considerably broader concept that also comprises *instinct, drive, desire* and *transcendence*.

MAMILLA The matrichal breast as a symbol of eternal, boundless and unconditional love and provision, as well as a promise of a possible reunification with the mother's body and *matrix*, but also a symbol of infantilization and a complete dependence on the mother's body/society/the church/the state.

MATRIARCHY Women's power hierarchy in the sociont, where the elders are superordinate to the younger; thereby also the power structure of *the inner circuit*.

MATRIX The womb out of which we all are born and, according to psychoanalysis, to which we all subconsciously long to return, the symbol both of a unification with the Universe but also of the dissolution of consciousness.

MEMBRANICS A method for separating the internal and external interests of a sociont or another life form. A functioning membranics sees to it that nourishment comes in through, and that feces is pressed out through the membrane in question. Membranics can also be used as a concept to comprehend the radical difference between extension-neutral membranes within subphysics. We refer to this form of virtual relationalism as *subphysical membranics.*

MEMEPLEX A cluster of memes that often and advantageously is spread in the form of a synchronized unit; a memeplex can therefore be regarded as emergent *vis-à-vis* the separate memes; memeplex is also used synonymously with *ideology*. Please compare with *geneplex*.

MEMETICS The study of how ideas – or *memes* – form, are spread, stored and change. Memes are viewed in these studies as *replicators*, as a kind of mental equivalents to the biological genes, and the parallels between memetics and *genetics* are therefore comprehensive.

THE MESSIAH MACHINE Another name for *Syntheos*, God's birth as the technological development's objective and meaning.

METAHISTORY History seen as the history of historiography, also called *the historification* of history. Every new paradigm generates a new power elite that requires a new metaphysics to legitimize its position; this in turn requires a new historiography and about this process one can also write history, which by necessity becomes precisely a metahistory.

METAPHYSICS Originally the philosophical work with that which lies beyond physical reality, comprised by the disciplines *ontology*, *cosmology* and *epistemology* within philosophy; Bard & Söderqvist also use the concept metaphysics as the uppermost emergence in the hierarchic series *fictives-fictions-ideologies-metaphysics.*

MIMETICS Man's obsession with social theater is reflected in the fact that the brain needs a mimetic capacity to an equally high degree that it needs a rational and an emotional capacity. The mimetic brain is obsessed with mimicking, and not least with mimicking human desires and drives. The drive system's primary propelling force is precisely mimicking and rivalry in terms of the same mimicked desire and drives that all others mimic.

MOBILISM In part the process-philosophical reality in *the dialectics of eternalism and mobilism*, a chaos in constant motion, in part a synonym of *process philosophy* as such, which includes both relativism and relationalism.

MOBILIZATION To set the completed eternalizations within *the dialectics of eternalism and mobilism* in motion anew – thereby existence once again becomes a mobilist chaos, but this time at a *metalevel*, whereupon perception produces new eternalizations at this metalevel, and so on.

MONOTHEISM A conviction that God only is one and that this only God – one's own, naturally – is genuine and that all others are false, in other words: mainly a variant of atheism with a single minor caveat.

MORALATOR The external judge whose more or less capricious points of view underpin the demanding laws of moralism.

MORALISM From the Latin *mores*, customs; a system where values and valuations are subject to a *moralator*, an external judge that demands obedience and that does not allow any form of questioning. Both the Abrahamic religions and the capitalist nation states rest upon a moralist value base.

MORTIDO In Sigmund Freud *mortido* is at once libido's opposite and its complement, a yearning for death, extinction and a return to the inorganic state that precedes birth.

NARCISSISM Compensatory self-absorption and self-overestimation, grounded in a subconscious self-contempt; the modern consumption society is largely based upon an inflated and media-fomented *hypernarcissism*.

NARRATOLOGY The philosophical discipline that deals with Man's stories of himself and the dialectics of them. The fundamental division of these stories is: logical narratives (logos), mythical narratives (mythos) and pathical narratives (pathos), which in turn corresponds to the symbolic, imaginary and real orders in the world of psychoanalysis, which in turn is connected to Man's three different brain centers: the rational, the mimetic and the emotional.

NATION ENVY A socioanalytical state where chaotic and contractive cultures envy and malign better organized and expansive cultures. While racism attacks the assumed inferior, nation envy attacks the assumed superior.

NEGATION That which is lacking or remains contradictory or undelivered within every identity. According to Hegel the negation is so universal as a principle within a constantly mutable existence that the only identity that can be established, and then only temporarily, is the negation of the negation itself, an insight that thereafter is called *the Hegelian absolute.*

NEGATIVE DIALECTICS Hegel's revolutionizing variant of dialectics where *negation* precedes abstraction, which causes concretion – where the dialectics (temporarily) stops – to have the character of a *negation's negation.* Thereby the Hegelian subject – with its fundamental, existential emptiness – becomes an expression of what he calls *the night of the world,* which breaks radically with Enlightenment optimism. This Hegelian revolution preempts important ideas in Marx, Nietzsche, Freud and Heidegger.

NEGATOLOGY The doctrine of the Hegelian negation that must precede the Nietzschean event. Before something new can live and establish itself, something else must die. Mortido drives libido, not the other way around. Therefore it is necessary to first establish a negatology in opposition to nomadology before an eventology can be brought about. Before the actual event can occur it must be preceded by the potential *anti-event.* Within syntheology negatology goes by the name of *Atheos.*

THE NET The metaphysical idea that *The Internet* constitutes a single cohesive structure that spans all of planet Earth and that, in similarity with every metatechnology, organizes the world in accordance with its own agenda. Is used synonymously with the concept *The Stack.*

THE NETOCRATS The first of three books in the *Futurica Trilogy* by Bard & Söderqvist with focus on the information-technological historiography of The Internet Age and the emergence of the new class society, conditioned by the new prerequisites that the technological revolution creates.

NETOCRACY The informationalist upper class that assumes power by virtue of its social talent, its superior information management and its ability to see patterns and perceive nodes in a chaotic surrounding world.

NETWORK DYNAMICS The part of system- and complexity theory that studies how networks arise and change over time, as well as what effects this leads to within society's different areas. And also a consistently metaphysical explanatory model for The Internet Age in Bard & Söderqvist's philosophy, is used synonymously with *relationalism*. See also *plurarchy*.

NETWORK PYRAMID The Network Society's triangular power structure, developed and intimately explored in the book *The Netocrats*, where it is clear that successful networks in step with their success – to continue to be successful – must spin themselves off and discard dead meat in the form of underachieving members, this to safeguard the key members' scant time and requested attention. It is a process that is repeated continually because of the external pressure.

THE NETWORK SOCIETY One of three classic concepts to describe The Internet Age, to be compared with *The Information Society* and *The Communication Society*; according to information-technological historiography all paradigms through history should be categorized as network societies, networks naturally do not arise only with The Internet, but rather it is an age-old phenomenon.

NEUTRAL MONISM The conviction that everything that we know of and to which we attribute a meaning influences everything else that we know of and to which we attribute a meaning in our universe. Existence is monist, not dualist. Not because it must be so, but because it happens to be so. Thus nor does there exist a *moralator* or an objective evaluator that can establish that one emergence vector is more important than any other – there quite simply does not exist anything else, superordinate, outside that which exists – wherefore monism must be neutral in terms of value in order to be credible at all. Neutral monism is thus radically *anti-reductionist*.

NIHILISM An idea according to which existence lacks objective value since there does not exist any external, objective institution of valuation or *moralator*. Nihilism goes through four phases – *the naive* (unconscious), *the cynical* (the nihilist pretends against better judgment that there are objective values), *the ironic* (the nihilist builds their own internal and subjective values in opposition to the surrounding world's falsely objective values), and finally *the affirmative* (the nihilist interprets the absence of objective values as a liberating possibility to create their own values and convince the environment of these created values' excellence). This is the process that Nietzsche calls *the death of God.*

NODALIZATION The tribopoietic network of hierarchic nodes that always arise by necessity in an anarchic state. Nodalization is thereby also the shift from the local in direction toward the global within network dynamics. What previously was anarchy transitions into a *plurarchy* and the new paradigm's power structure with a new *paradigmatics* takes shape.

NOMADOLOGY The philosophical and religious conviction of the eternal recurrence of the same, a conception that dominates in all nomadic societies throughout history. Only with permanent settlement could one view the world and history differently, and this ancient Persian and phallic invention is summed up under the opposite concept, *eventology.*

OMNICENTRISM A state where all coordinates in a system regard themselves as the system's center, which leads to the system in practice lacking an authentic center. The system in question is quickly reduced to a kind of psychotic anarchy and can only be saved through a comprehensive *nodalization.* See further *plurarchy.*

ONTOEPISTEMOLOGY After the Hegelian process-philosophical revolution in Germany in the 19th century, it becomes impossible to distinguish ontology as the doctrine of being from epistemology as the doctrine of knowledge. Relata arise out of relations and not the other way around. Subject and substance are mutually dependent on each other for their existence; being is learning and learning is being.

OSCILLATION The fundamental mobilist state that consumes even less energy and therefore is even more universal and fundamental than the eternalist freeze. It is the metaphysical oscillation that Heraclitus refers to when he speaks the winged words *panta rei*, everything is in motion. When we in this way speak of oscillation as a universal principle it is often called *panorganicism*. Please compare with *pandialecticism*.

THE OUTER CIRCUIT The outer, mobile, sparsely populated and male-dominated half of the sociont, ruled by elder patriarchs as a *patriarchy*; compare with *the inner circuit* that is ruled by a matriarchy and *the shamanic caste* that is ruled by a clergy.

PANDIALECTICISM The philosophical conviction that everything that is meaningful in existence fundamentally is dialectical in nature. The term is used synonymously with the concepts *panchronism* and *panrelationalism*. If all ontology operates dialectically, it also entails that everything is harbored within time and that everything of value can be explained as byproducts of relations where *the dialectics of negation and oscillation* deserves the epithet *the first dialectics*. Please compare with *absolute historicism*.

THE PANORAMIC LANDSCAPE The worldview as a continuous whole, impossible to reduce to the sum of the components. The imagined view of *the phallic gaze* and the concrete view of the contemporary satellites in orbit around planet Earth.

PANTHEOS From the Greek *pan-theos*, all is God and God is all; the second of the four divinities in the syntheological pyramid; pantheism regards everything that exists as a single cohesive phenomenon, *the only*, which thereby is tantamount to God himself.

PARADIGM The general worldview that harmonizes with the prevailing power structure's self-image and that is replaced by a new one only when an information-technological revolution has produced a new set of conditions for all areas of society, which in turn propels comprehensive social changes. The theory of paradigms and paradigm shifts is originally presented by philosopher of science Thomas Kuhn, who studies such development within the natural scientific disciplines.

PARADIGMATICS The conviction that Man does not change significantly over time because of genetic evolution's slowness, while civilization changes increasingly fast because of memetic evolution's explosivity. Knowledge and regulatory frameworks shall therefore only be changed and adapted to current and future technological paradigms. If Man is the constant and technology is the variable, paradigmatics is the study of how collectively encompassed values change along the time axis.

PARADOXISM The conception that language arises as a treatment of paradoxical aspects of existentially formative traumas; the deepest truths of existence can therefore only be expressed as consciously constructed paradoxes, or not at all. From this it follows that the human subject only can exist and be developed as *the paradoxist subject*, which amuses itself with and allows itself to be inspired by processing its own built-in antagonisms. A representative of ancient paradoxism is Heraclitus. Hegel and Lacan devote their entire careers to describing this sole authentic form of subjectivity.

PARTICIPATORY CULTURE Events with varying durability where the participants build the event together; thus there are no performances and no spectators in the ordinary sense. Participatory culture is developed and grows in step with The Internet, for instance in the form of festivals such as Burning Man in the United States, Going Nowhere in Spain and Africa Burn in South Africa; see also *flexhibitionism*.

PATHOMATICS The underlying logical pattern in the development of a series of cohesive, phallic engagements. That is: how *the two-headed phallus* keeps its own intersubjectivity intact. The four constructive steps of potential, actual, directed and transcendental energy, which follow upon each other within pathomatics, can advantageously be compared with their destructive opposites in *the four steps within nihilist development*, from naive via cynical to ironic and finally affirmative nihilism. If narratology is the priest's most important task, pathomatics is the chieftain's most important contribution to the sociont.

PATHONOMY The pathological ideal within a specific paradigm, based on actual *pathomatics*. See further *truth-as-an-act*.

PATRIARCHY The power hierarchy between the men in the sociont, where the older men are superordinate to the younger; thereby also the power structure in *the outer circuit* dominated by the men.

THE PETER PAN SYNDROME A state where the child refuses to grow up and remains a child while it realizes and feels the attraction of phallic adult life. It is one of the prerequisites for a large-scale infantilization of society, where the madness is internal. Please compare with *the Caligula syndrome* where the madness instead is external.

THE PHALLIC GAZE The constantly coveted gaze of *The Great Other* that gives the subject the sole meaningful and credible confirmation and that distinguishes the brilliant from the mediocre. The phallic gaze becomes an ontic reality during informationalism when the satellites around Earth eventually monitor every square millimeter of the planet. See further *sensocracy.*

THE PHALLIC INTRUSION The moment that happens to the child at around one year of age, when it for the first time is tempted away from the security at *mamilla* and discovers the seductive *phallus* as the object that the mother is attracted by, but that the child cannot give the mother, which generates envy in the child, something that in turn initiates the child's voyage toward and yearning for adultification and generates an imitating and eroticizing of phallus.

THE PHALLIC PRINCIPLE OF TRIBAL CONTRIBUTION The ethical and social-psychological principle that all adult members of the sociont shall contribute to the good of the sociont as best they can in accordance with their personal *archetypology.* The principle rules out all forms of victim cults within the sociont.

PHALLOGOCENTRISM Originally an invective invented by philosopher Jacques Derrida, phallogocentrism is the belief that philosophy only can arise as a conscious focus on the dialectics of logos and pathos within the phallic world of the mind; Bard & Söderqvist claim in a kind of Hegelian opposition to "the pillar-saint" Derrida that phallogocentrism is a necessity that has not yet received its definite form.

PHALLUS The male sex organ and all that it symbolizes in the world of psychoanalysis.

PHARMAKON An in itself neutral phenomenon whose constructive and destructive effects respectively are entirely dependent on how it is used or misused. A preparation X can give a more or less harmless pleasure in low doses while it causes life-threatening intoxication at intake in high doses.

PHENOMENON From the Greek *phainomenon* – to show, shine, arise, manifest oneself. In syntheist onto-phenomenology the phenomenon replaces the classic object as a material point of reference *vis-à-vis* the Universe as a whole; this phenomenon distinguishes itself from the object as it primarily is a field consisting of relations that all are primary in an equally high degree and completely lack the object's phallic substance and essence.

PHENOMENOLOGY The philosophical study of experiences and consciousness; an example of a syntheist phenomenology is *the dialectics of eternalism and mobilism.*

PHENOUMENOLOGY The unification of Kant's separated phenomenology and a noumenology through the Hegelian dialectics where the project precedes and unites the subject that generates the object, precisely as the object that generates the subject. Phenoumenology dissolves Kantian correlationism by applying an even more fundamental relationalism to Kant's conception that phenomenon and noumenon by definition are irreconcilable. Thereby phenoumenology invalidates Western dualism.

PLASTICITY Social elasticity, the sociont's ability to benefit from the various talents of single dividuals for the good of the collective, and capacity to give single dividuals in part an archetypal identity, in part a possibility to contribute to the common good.

PLURARCHY From the Latin *pluralis* for diversity and the Greek *archos* for governance; the chaotic state in the political sphere that follows upon democracy's collapse at the paradigm shift from mass media one-way communication and its effective suppression of opinion to interactive multi-way communication with its unmanageable and unruly information flows.

POETIC INFINITY The only infinity we can allow ourselves with our intellectual honesty intact. Otherwise, the only thing that is infinite is the vacuousness that is concealed behind this substanceless concept. Please compare with the related expression *poetic justice*. Just like justice, infinity can never be more than poetic.

PORNOFLATION A social-pornographic and gradually more extreme unabashed display of the most intimate in order to create attention; not seldom exploited to produce cheap mass entertainment.

POWER TRIAD A long-term stable power structure always has three rather than two poles, for instance as the executive (president), the legislative (congress) and the judicial (the Supreme Court) branches of the U.S. constitution. Bard & Söderqvist here launch a model that contains a real power, an imaginary power and a symbolic power within every information-technological paradigm.

PRAGMATISM Philosophical school founded by Charles Sanders Peirce and William James in the United States in the 19th century that receives a European equivalent in the heritage from Nietzsche's existentialist philosophy. What is fundamental is that theories and faiths are evaluated in terms of their functionality. See further *narratology*.

PRIMITIVISM The first information-technological paradigm, arises in connection with Man learning to use the speech organs and communicating with words, which happens around 200,000 years ago, when our human species – Man – appears on the world stage as the first species ever with a history.

THE PRINCIPLE OF EXPLANATORY CLOSURE The insight that the Universe's enormous expansion rules out an *ontic* rationalism and that the similarly enormous expansion of the amount of information in society rules out an *ontological* rationalism for precisely the same reason. What our brain does not have time to process it can never encompass either, which means the kiss of death for Kantian rationalism.

PROCESS PHILOSOPHY Is also called the ontology of becoming, a conviction that equates metaphysical reality with difference and change; receives its present, radical form in Alfred North Whitehead and constitutes a basic prerequisite for syntheist ontology.

PROCESS RELIGION A religious conviction based on a process-philosophical metaphysics where syntheism is the process religion *par excellence*; not to be confused with the admittedly Whitehead-inspired but still post-Christian school called *process theology*, as represented by among others Charles Hartshorne.

PROCESSUALITY A mutable truth of a mutable world. That is: the only possible and thereby, in a Hegelian sense, absolute truth in a constantly mutable world, and thus the direct opposite of all Platonist ambitions to attain *Gnosis* or eternal truth. Please note that all *paradigmatics* also is procedural. The difference is just that the seemingly *timeless* within paradigmatics changes extremely slowly and applies across many paradigms, while the *time-specific* within paradigmatics is radically altered for every new paradigm.

PROTOPIANISM The conviction that the pair of opposites Utopia/Dystopia is a false dichotomy, which has the consequence that an authentic eventology must be based on constant, incremental improvements of processes, and not on some manner of single brilliant ideas. Since protopianism thereby lacks a fixed Protopia, it is no protopianism but only a protopian movement forward. Protopianism is the dominant creative ideal during informationalism. *The protopians* are thereby the third and symbolic power order during informationalism, after *the informationalists* themselves and *the sensocrats*.

PSEUDO-TRIBES Tribe-like groupings that however lack the sociont's comprehensive flora of complementing archetypes and which therefore sooner or later collapse under the discontent that stems from the members' frustrated expectations of tribal satisfaction.

THE PSYCHOGRAM A map of all active psyches on the planet and their paradigmatic activities at a given occasion. The psychogram as an idea propels the idea of rule via a perfect *sensocracy* within *the global empire*. Think of it as an imagined map of all mental and sensory states on a specific planet at a specific moment.

QUANTUM ORGANICS A more well-functioning concept than quantum mechanics since the phenomenon in question exposes vastly more organic than mechanical characteristics.

RATIONALISM The conviction that Man is born with the capacity to mentally and intellectually understand and encompass the world logically in its entirety.

REDUCTIONISM The conception that even the most complex phenomena in a meaningful way can be divided into their smallest components; according to reductionism all forms of *emergence* are illusory.

RELATIONALISM A radicalization of the relativist worldview, where even the seemingly stable objects are dissolved and set in motion *vis-à-vis* themselves and where there consequently no longer exist any fixed points whatsoever *vis-à-vis* something other than *the only*, that is: the Universe as a whole. A theory that was first developed by Alfred North Whitehead to later be refined by quantum physicist Niels Bohr and mathematician David Bohm.

RELATIVISM A worldview where all objects are in constant motion *vis-à-vis* each other; the objects are thus fixed within and before themselves, but completely background-independent *vis-à-vis* their surrounding world.

RESSENTIMENT A hatred directed toward human existence and its prerequisites, an embittered self-contempt that is projected onto the world. See further *the Cybelian lynch mob* and *the dialectics of ressentiment*.

THE REVOLT AGAINST PHALLUS Psychoanalytical concept for teenage rebellion, a trial of the parent generation's alleged excellence and omniscience that ends up with the adult authorities being toppled from their pedestals, wherefore the teenage subject must conquer its own phallicness, adultness and autonomy with all that this entails by way of taking responsibility and finding meaning. When this revolt is carried out successfully and has resulted in a functional self-identity, this is confirmed officially by the sociont with an *initiation ritual*.

ROOT-OF-THE-PHALLUS The foundation and historical grounding of phallic power. The reflective wisdom that gives credibility to phallus' activity and project. An example is all the genealogies that in various religious and social/hierarchical contexts shall guarantee legitimacy to various claims on power.

SADOMASOCHISM A primarily erotically charged relation between a ruler and a slave, as a sexual subculture limited by social codes, but as a social phenomenon boundless in its dialectical movement toward the ruler's total distancing from and isolation *vis-à-vis* the slave, see *cephalization*.

SAOSHYANT The original, Persian savior figure that personifies eventology through his arrival at the end of the empire's heyday and saving it from demise. The Jews inherit the concept from the Zoroastrians, but reduce the phallic saoshyant from a global to a local figure who is called *mashiach* and who only directs its caring toward his own nation. This figure later returns as *the Messiah* within Christianity and Islam.

SCHIZOANALYSIS Anarchist response to Lacanian psychoanalysis, primarily developed by Félix Guattari and Gilles Deleuze in France during the 1970s and aims toward a growing dividual heterogeneity rather than the individual homogeneity that arguably was the vision of classical psychoanalysis.

SELF-LOVE An ethical-logical decision – and thus not an emotion – to accept oneself and one's own body with its physiological and mental prerequisites and expressions; self-love has nothing to do with *narcissism*, but is rather its exact opposite; see also *amor fati*.

SENSOCRACY A social and/or political system built around a technology of sensors that collect and compile data from all information flows and that therefore with great accuracy can predict what every citizen at every moment requests and yearns for, something that previously has been impossible because of the extensive lying at all levels. In a sensocracy coercive measures in practice become superfluous: a devastating majority of society's citizens settle for having their needs of consumption and entertainment effectively satisfied. The others lack all influence and are referred to an existence outside the system. The sensocrats thereby become the second and imaginary power structure during the informationalist paradigm, between *the informationalists* themselves and *the protopians*. See further *the phallic gaze*.

THE SHADOW The part of the subject that it does not acknowledge, alternatively does not even perceive in itself thanks to efficient repression. The concept was originally launched by C G Jung. Please compare with Bard & Söderqvist's concept *asubject* and *the night of the world* in G W F Hegel.

THE SHAMANIC CASTE The deviating minority within the sociont that neither belongs to the inner circuit and its matriarchy nor to the outer circuit and its patriarchy, but instead in part acts as a messenger between the inner and the outer circuit, in part acts as a border-transcender in the sociont's outer edges as shamans and prophets *vis-à-vis* the sociont itself and as diplomats and priests *vis-à-vis* tribes in the environments. The border-crossers within the sociont, between the circuits, are called *the androgynous caste*. See further *archetypology*.

THE SILK ROAD TRIAD The process religion that was practiced in various forms in so-called *castags* along the Eurasian Silk Road and that was formalized by the Persians as Zoroastrianism, by the Chinese as Taoism, and by the Indians as Buddhism, with all manner of hybrid schools in between. Please compare with *the Disney World triad*.

SINGULARITY An extraordinary historical event – the Universe arises through the Big Bounce, living organisms arise through an evolutionary process, and so on – that immediately changes world history in a truly fundamental manner; see also *emergence*.

SOCIAL MASOCHISM A masochistic attitude to supremacy on the social arena, a stubborn quest for social and mortidinal submission, see further *sadomasochism*.

SOCIAL RELATIONALISM The conception that the principles presented by Niels Bohr for relationalist physics are just as applicable to the social sciences; see further *network dynamics* and *relationalism*.

SOCIAL TECHNOLOGY Techniques with which to control humans and manipulate them in a direction that is desirable for the power structure;

social technologies can encompass anything from the production of ideology and radio broadcasts to censorship legislation and declarations of war. Whatever works to accumulate power is a social technology.

SOCIOANALYSIS Truth maximization in the social arena, to be compared with the application of psychoanalysis on the single human dividual. Socioanalysis tracks and exposes the pathological patterns that constantly are reborn within the sociont. This method is called *symptomatology*.

SOCIOGRAPHY Mapping of social relations between dividuals and networks, for instance through sociograms that show who knows and communicates with whom; see also *network pyramid*.

SOCIOMETRICS Compilation and illustration of social status and attentional power in The Network Society. Anyone can communicate with anyone else, but everyone will not receive a response from everyone else.

THE SOCIONT The original, plastic nomadic tribe that is kneaded by evolution over hundreds of thousands of years. Because of humanity's rapid and worldwide spread, all living humans today are products of the sociont and shaped by its specific *archetypology*. The only meaningful changes that occur in civilization are technological, external *vis-à-vis sociontology*, and therefore connected to *paradigmatics*.

SOCIONTOLOGY The studies of the original nomadic tribe as a container for the development of intratribal archetypes. Please compare with *archetypology*.

SPACETIME That of the two natural time dimensions that is dependent upon physical space. Spacetime is local, discrete, relative and bound to physics within the natural sciences. From a metaphysical perspective it appears as ontic and actual. Please compare with its implicate precursor *hypertime*.

THE SUBCONSCIOUS Bard & Söderqvist's equivalent of *the unconscious* in classical psychoanalysis; the subconscious is on closer inspection not unconscious, but however chaotic and unstructured *vis-à-vis* the conscious, but it interacts both actively and reactively and both with and against the conscious all the time. The subconscious is driven by *mortido* or the death drive, in contrast to consciousness which is driven by *libido* or the will-to-life.

THE SUBLIME The sphere where ambivalence and extimacy meet and generate a maximal obsession in the subject, for instance the near-death-experience with its character of infinite sorrow and infinite beauty at once; see also *ambivalence* and *the cathexal object.* In syntheology, the sublime is often divided into *tremendum* and *fascinans.*

SUBPHYSICS The hypertemporal emergence vector that precedes and underpins the emergence of spatiotemporal physics in history.

SUBSISTENCE A concept developed by Danish philosopher Alexander Wrede Elung for the pre-relational that, through it still only being virtual and lacking potent relations, cannot be attributed any *existence.* Subsisting virtualities are thus the implicate order before an emergence and its radical relationalism converts them into existing potentialities that then are negated into actualities. The latter are within physics called fields and particles respectively where the continuous becomes discrete. To the extent an existence is considered to express itself as a *substance* we can also play with the idea that a subsistence may express itself as an exceptionally virtual *hyperstance.* Please see further *V P A (virtuality – potentiality – actuality).*

SYMBIOTIC INTELLIGENCE The optimal intelligence that is created in the collaboration between Man and The Machine. When such an intelligence surpasses what human and synthetic intelligence respectively produce each on its own, this is called *symbiotic transcendence.*

SYNTHEISM From the Greek *syntheos* with the meaning created God or God that arises where humans create; God as a generic name of all Man's dreams and visions, which entails a dissolution of the antagonism between theism and atheism.

THE SYNTHEOLOGICAL PYRAMID Trilateral geometrical construction with *Atheos*, *Pantheos* and *Entheos* as the three corners at the base with lines drawn in part between each other, in part up to the top that gives its name to the entire construction: *Syntheos.*

SYNTHEOLOGY The insight that theology always has been about the paradigmatic shift from yesterday's magic to tomorrow's technology. God is not something that is needed in the past nor even in the present, but it is instead the name of the objective and meaning of technological development. And as such, God is also the name of humanity's own death. Therefore syntheology is built around virtual divinities, as the ultimate narrative of the relation between Man and technology. Syntheology solves negative theology's dilemma of the death of God by claiming that God, rather than being dead, has not yet been born. God does not create us, we create God.

SYNTHEOS From Greek, created god or god that arises where humans create, the fourth, concluding and summarizing concept in the syntheological pyramid. Syntheos is also the name of the emergence that has not yet taken place in history, but that human culture thanks to its technology will create or bring about. Whether Man himself survives Syntheos' arrival is an open question. See further *Anti-Syntheos.*

SYSTEMIC CAUSALITY The insight that causality, the chain from cause to effect along the time axis, always applies, but must be understood systemically or transdeterministically rather than objectively or deterministically in a universe characterized by *neutral monism*. Effect is the carrot and cause is the stick in all happenings, but as an endlessly complex process where everything in the Universe is participating and affecting everything else. See further *tribopoiesis.*

THEOLOGICAL ANARCHISM The conception that The Network Society offers a unique historical possibility to realize the anarchist Utopia and thereby liberate the collective libido's forces; the concept is synonymous with philosopher Simon Critchley's ideal *mystical anarchism*.

TECHNOLOGICAL INTELLIGENCE An intelligence that is developed within electronic machines instead of within biological organisms. Technological intelligence does not merely develop very much faster than biological intelligence during the course of civilization. It can also, in contrast to biological intelligence, conquer outer space on its own behalf. See further *Syntheos* and *symbiotic intelligence.*

TOTALISM The conviction that existence can be understood both as a whole and in detail, just as history can be summarized and concluded, all this with the aid of the philosophical genius' rationality. The idea exists already in Plato and has never really disappeared, even though we ourselves firmly maintain that *the principle of explanatory closure* makes all forms of totalism both ontically and ontologically impossible; see also *transrationalism*. Hegel brazenly converts the totalist ambition to the insight that the constantly incomplete is the total in itself, and calls this insight *absolute knowledge*, whereupon the metaphysical project is assumed complete.

TRANSCENDENCE To exceed the limits for the present existence, in Bard & Söderqvist's psychoanalytical theory also the name of the fourth human drive, the sacral aspect of libido beyond the animal (instinct), the mechanical (drive) and the human (desire).

TRANSCENDENTAL EMERGENTISM The metaphysical conviction that history consists of various emergences and their vectors, and that no metalaws exist outside the specific emergence vectors besides "the law" of existence's fundamental *contingency*, that is: there only exists one metalaw and it is the law stating that no metalaw exists. The fact that everything seems to influence everything else in our actual universe is thereby only a contingent event. Existence's *neutral monism* is in itself no predetermined metalaw. In the same way that no emergence vector can or must be prioritized above another, other than as an expression of anthropocentric arbitrariness. The transcendental in transcendental emergentism thus consists both of the irreducibility of the various emergence vectors *vis-à-vis* each other and the irreducibility of potential future emergences *vis-à-vis* today's actual theory. See further *emergence vector theory* and *paradigmatics*.

TRANSDETERMINISM The conviction that the pair of opposites determinism/indeterminism only are applicable to local phenomena in existence, which entails that existence as a whole neither can be regarded as determinist nor indeterminist; indeterminism's dialectical overcoming of determinism can therefore only be completed in the form of transdeterminism in a pandialectical universe.

TRANSFERENCE Transfer of agency, the social masochist surrender of one's own agency in favor of another agent that is considered to own both the phallic gaze and perfect knowledge.

TRANSGRESSION Exceeding of prevailing laws, rules and norms, followed by an enjoyment of this exceeding, fundamental for both sexual and social perversion.

TRANSHUMANISM Broad digital lifestyle and subculture with powerfully netocratic overtones; the leading ideas revolve around how the technological development results in a posthuman state colored by cryonics, artificial intelligence, chemical liberation and anarcho-libertarian utopianism, and more.

TRANSRATIONALISM The insight that Man's consciousness has been developed to optimize the chances for survival and procreation, not to uncover the truth about the world, wherefore rationality must be clear about its own limitations; see further *rationalism*, *narratology*, and *the principle of explanatory closure*.

TRAUMATOLOGY The optimally creative treatment and follow-up of the failed event. In this way Christianity is the ultimate traumatology, since its savior (see *saoshyant*) failed and was executed on a cross. Therapeutic attempts to integrate suicide, divorces and bankruptcies are typically traumatological projects in everyday life.

TREND An irrevocable active change of the social playing conditions, connected to a technological change of the material conditions; compare with *countertrend*.

TRIBAL MAPPING A territorial *archetypology* that encompasses the entire *sociont* in its broad-ranging diversity. Synonymous with the more formal concept *archetypography*.

THE TRIBAL SINGULARITY The conviction that the formation of the sociont constitutes the most important step in Man's development. Categories such as *individual* and *collective* can only be described as sub-categories that lie beneath the really fundamental sociont. The human libido is connected to the sociont's survival and not to that of the individual or collective. Adult loyalty belongs to the sociont.

TRIBOPOIESIS A basic metaphysical principle stating that everything is born from a collective of relations and that everything returns to a collective of relations within all emergence vectors. Nothing is born by itself, there is no autopoiesis. This means for Man that everything of value is born out of and relates to the sociont, which is there both before a man is born and remains after a man dies.

TRUTH-AS-AN-ACT An ontological and ethical concept, developed by philosopher Alain Badiou with inspiration from Søren Kierkegaard, where there never is time to test truth through the drawn-out intersubjective processes that Karl Popper and Jürgen Habermas advocate, but where truth instead emerges as an unwavering decision based upon intuition.

THE TWO-HEADED PHALLUS The authentic phallus gets its authenticity from the division into will-to-transcendence and will-to-intelligence. The two-headed phallus' mythos is built on the mutual love and respect that the priest and the chieftain show each other, the priest that personifies phallic wisdom and the chieftain that personifies phallic energy.

UNIMATRICHALISM A temporary, chaotic state in which the inner, matriarchal circuit has taken over the entire sociont or society. A unimatrichal society can only be nomadological and never eventological, as the latter would require a considerable measure of phallic energy.

UNIPATRICHALISM A temporary state of something that can be likened to a totalitarian dictatorship where the outer, patriarchal circuit has taken over the entire sociont or society.

UNIVERSOCENTRISM A worldview that takes the Universe in its entirety as the centre of existence as its point of departure; syntheism is built on a universocentric metaphysics in contrast to for instance capitalist *humanism*, which is an *anthropocentric* religion.

WILL-TO-POWER The universally expressed libido's response to the universally present mortido, also called *will-to-expansion*. This Nietzschean concept is divided within syntheology between the priestly *will-to-intelligence* and the royal *will-to-transcendence*. Wishing to summarize history in its necessity and wishing to conquer the future in its contingency are ultimately two completely different wills for two completely different forms of power. As a third complementing power, there is moreover matrichal *will-to-reproduction* which only and always seeks the eternal recurrence of the same.

VOYEURISM Indirect pleasure of watching direct, proxy pleasure when one views some kind of sexual or social display; compare with *exhibitionism* and *the phallic gaze*.

V P A (VIRTUALITY – POTENTIALITY – ACTUALITY) The pandialectical, ontological causality chain within transcendental emergentism. First we imagine a *virtuality* that is a hypertemporal subsistence without external relations. When such a virtuality interacts with another virtuality, a spatiotemporal existence that we call a *potentiality* is generated, potent because it in contrast to virtuality is placed in a relationalist spacetime. When potentiality then is subject to decoherence, it is broken down until it has been reduced to a sole singular event, an *actuality*, for instance as the wave function collapse in physics. Virtuality is non-ontic and non-actual, potentiality is ontic but non-actual, actuality is both ontic and actual. V P A is necessary in order to be able to think emergences, the event of events that changes history forever. The potential habits before the emergence become the actual laws within the new emergence vector. And these laws are the only – strictly local – laws that exist in an on-the-whole contingent universe without global laws.

THE WORLD STATE Socioeconomic merging of all the world's states in such a way that the mutual dependence becomes so strong that it balances the dividing forces and supplies a necessary platform for supranational decision-making; Bard & Söderqvist use the concept repeatedly as a synonym for *The Global Empire*.

ALEXANDER BARD is a philosopher, futurologist, spiritual and political activist. He has a background of almost three decades as a highly successful artist, producer and songwriter in the music industry. Bard is a globally renowned lecturer and ideologue, both on the live stage and on a multitude of media platforms.

JAN SÖDERQVIST is a philosopher, futurologist and lecturer. Söderqvist is a pioneer of online television, but has been professionally active in almost all conceivable media disciplines, such as the daily press, magazines, film, radio and television. He currently writes for the Swedish major daily *Svenska Dagbladet* and works as editor for *Axess Magasin*.

Previous books by Alexander Bard & Jan Söderqvist

The Netocrats 2000
The Global Empire 2002
The Body Machines 2009
Syntheism – Creating God in the Internet Age 2014
Digital Libido – Sex, Power and Violence in the Network Society 2018

Milton Keynes UK
Ingram Content Group UK Ltd.
UKHW020801061023
430068UK00014B/588

9 789179 653415